W9-BNC-825

A HISTORY OF AUSTRALIA

By the same author:

MACQUARIE'S WORLD

AUSTRALIAN OUTLINE

SYDNEY: THE STORY OF A CITY

In collaboration with Flora Eldershaw:

PHILLIP OF AUSTRALIA

THE LIFE AND TIMES OF CAPTAIN JOHN PIPER

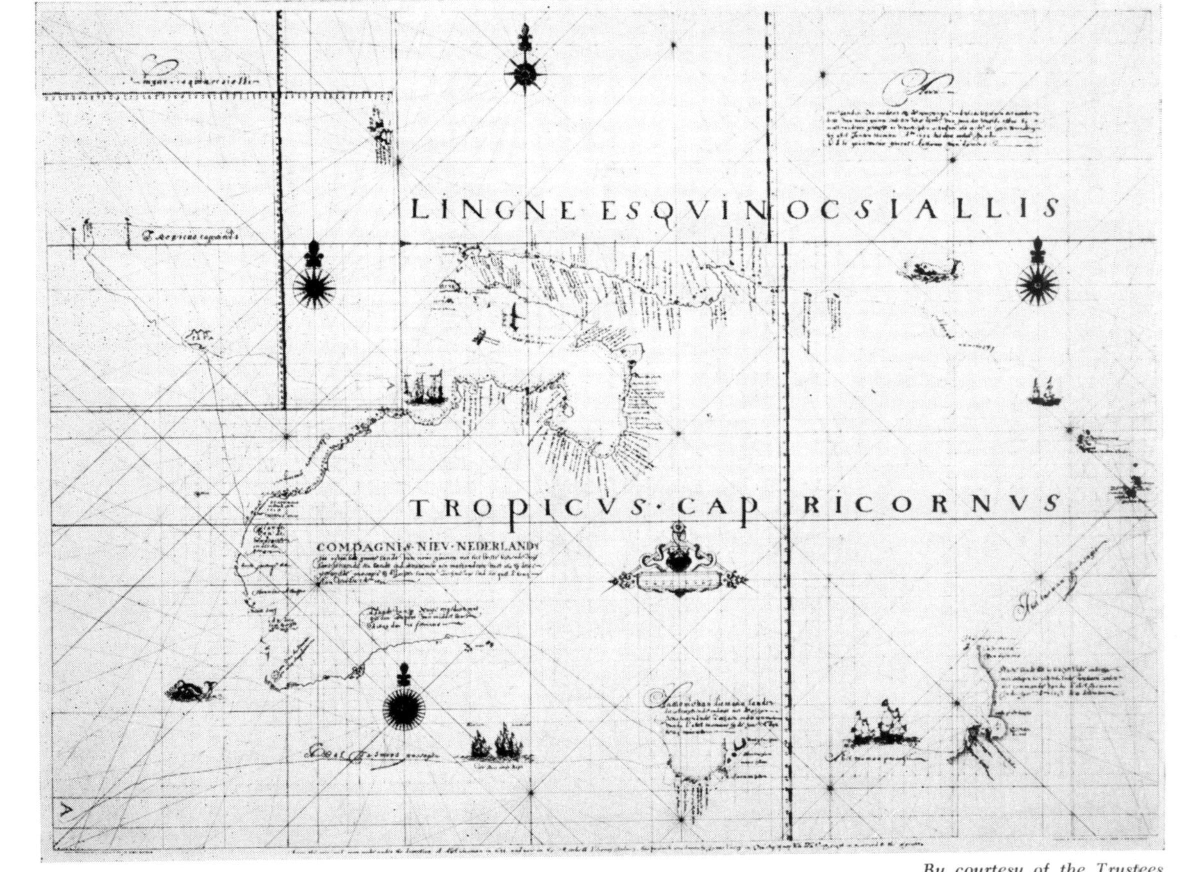

By courtesy of the Trustees

THE TASMAN MAP OF 1644

From the facsimile made by James Emery of the map in the possession of the Mitchell Library, Sydney

A HISTORY OF AUSTRALIA

By

MARJORIE BARNARD

FREDERICK A. PRAEGER, *Publishers*
NEW YORK • WASHINGTON

BOOKS THAT MATTER

Published in the United States of America in 1963 by
FREDERICK A. PRAEGER, INC., PUBLISHERS
111 Fourth Avenue, New York 3, N.Y.
Third printing, 1966

Library of Congress Catalog Card Number: 63-12493

PRINTED IN AUSTRALIA BY HALSTEAD PRESS, SYDNEY

ACKNOWLEDGMENTS

I wish most sincerely to thank:

The Librarian and staff of the Mitchell Library, and in particular Miss Margaret McDonald, for constant assistance over a period of four years.

Mr E. W. Steel, sometime Librarian of the Fisher Library in the University of Sydney, for access to and loans from that collection, and Miss Beatrice Wines of the same library for her practical kindness.

Miss Ida Leeson, without whose expert (and tolerant) advice I should not have dared to publish this book.

V.M., whose help and support on the home front have been invaluable.

MARJORIE BARNARD.

CONTENTS

LIST OF ILLUSTRATIONS

MAPS

CHAPTER I

BACKGROUND

If you would read history, and most particularly Australian history, study your atlas, for in the long run geography maketh man. It presents him with gifts and problems, and his history is the story of how he takes advantage of the one and grapples with the other; it moulds his way of life and in the end, if the crowds on the surfing beaches are any criterion, will alter the pigmentation of his skin.

Australia belongs in culture, outlook, and way of life with the European nations, more particularly with Great Britain. Yet, geographically, she is set between the Pacific and Indian Oceans and is in the Asian and Pacific sphere. The Pacific was the last of the ocean seas to be explored, the least known, the most romantic. It is a vast area of water dotted with islands, discovered, lost, rediscovered, named and renamed. The legend of the earthly paradise still lingers. There are strange patterns of migration that ethnologists are still unravelling. There is the puzzle of Easter Island with its colossal idols. There are desert islands and lonely coral atolls, cannibals and gentle lotus-eating men. The ocean is a patchwork, the scrap-bag of forgotten races. Now most of the archipelagos have come under the influence, by annexation, protectorate, or mandate, of one or other of the great powers bringing to them their old-world rivalries. War on a global scale came to the Pacific after the fall of Pearl Harbour in 1942. Civilization has moved in. Islands screened in the mystery of sea and distance can become naval or air bases, hostile stepping-stones; they are so many and so far flung.

Australia has no frontiers, but the Pacific has become a doubtful barrier against the world; it could be an ambush, an uncanalized danger. Its very weakness is a threat, for there is no people who could or would fight a delaying action. Of the Pacific Islanders themselves there are probably few who would even greatly care who came or went or brought gifts or threats. Australia is wide open to this unpredictable ocean. Australian defence policy calls for a screen of islands. The need for this was recognized from the very beginning of white settlement. Within a month of the arrival of the First Fleet at Sydney Cove a small colony had been planted on Norfolk Island, 930 miles east of Port Jackson, not only to remove some hungry mouths to a more fertile island but to protect the infant settlement from the French, who were at that time taking a keen interest in the Pacific, purely scientific or not, or, more practically, from pirates who could use the uninhabited island as a base. A scheme had indeed been mooted in England to establish a factory, or trading post, on Norfolk Island, a depot for the fur trade. This sounded so curious in official ears that the Imperial Government, suspecting piracy, disallowed it. No foreigner or pirate came to trouble Norfolk Island, and indeed the settlement there was considered as a preventive measure rather than as a cure, since it was never strong enough to rebut an attack, had it been made.

So began the "screen of islands" policy, and now, with the development of air power and long-range weapons, it is becoming obsolescent.

It is one-sided to think of defence or aggression as the only aspect of the Pacific relevant to Australia. It could be a sphere of influence and a source of trade. Trade has existed and does exist, but not in very great volume. The *Commonwealth Year Book* gives no figures. Again, it is brought home to Australians that they are a nation outside their geographical sphere. The Pacific Islands produce commodities we want only in a very limited degree; those that we have to sell are too expensive for them to buy because of the high standard of living and wage protection in Australia. Influence, except missionary endeavour, has little meaning, the difference in outlook and civilization is too great.

Looking north, the problem is the same but less nebulous. What for England is the Far East is for us the Near North. Asia, learning from the West, has become militant and nationalistic. Her teeming millions need more room to live. The Malays and probably the Chinese knew of Australia centuries before any European touched her shores. The Malays had a name for her: "The Land of the Dead". Except for fishing off the coast, the continent had nothing to offer them. We have now made a valuable asset of it. We have the space, they have the ever increasing population. We have bitterly offended them by our unfortunately named White Australia Policy. It is a dangerous equation. There is a cry constantly raised, "Populate for defence", but no rise in the birth-rate, no possible immigration scheme could compete with the increase of population in the countries of the Near North. We are cut off from them by ideological differences, by social habits, by religion. . . . In a word, we are Europeans and they are Asians. As men they are our brothers, but in practice much divides us and that division may be crucial. Australians at this day and hour are not ready to accept One World.

The danger of submersion is not only a hypothesis, as Japan showed in the Second World War. That danger should not have taken us by surprise. As long ago as 19th January 1911 the *Bulletin* published a cartoon by Norman Lindsay called "Sleeping at his Homework", in which the child, Australia, in his false security, sleeps over his essay on "A White Australia", whilst over him leans a Japanese soldier, sword in one hand, ink-bottle in the other, from which he spills a blot of black (or yellow) ink, shaped like Australia, on the child's copy book.

The threat from the Near North of infiltration, of conquest, of annihilation, is a fact. The atlas proclaims it. It is not so much a moral, political, or economic issue as a matter of geography. We are their Near South, we are at a different, but not necessarily superior, stage of development. We not unnaturally want to retain our own traditions. Our pride and our European outlook forbid a compromise or a sharing. This is not a moral judgment but a statement of fact.

Strong bonds of trade are lacking in the north as in the Pacific, and for the same reason: Australian goods are too expensive. Wool is one of the exceptions, for this Japan is a good customer. For example, in 1954, 96,900,000 bales of Australian wool went to her.[1]

To a foreboding proximity add another ingredient, distance. Australia has a long coastline, eight thousand miles of it, and much of it lonely and vulnerable. Experts, Lord Kitchener, General Edwards, Sir Ian Hamilton and Admiral Sir R. Henderson came, looked, and unanimously reported the continent to be indefensible. The coastline could not be held, the population was too scanty in proportion to area, the distance from the naval concentrations of any friendly power too great. A successful war for the preservation of Australia could only be fought outside her territory.

Distance is the continual theme and has been one of the main conditioning factors in Australian history. She was distant and dependent, a continent swinging on a long chain in antipodean darkness. Port Jackson, the small new star on the dark continent, was about sixteen thousand miles from London. In the early days the Suez Canal had not been cut and the voyage round the Cape of Good Hope, often *via* South America, and then far south to skirt Van Diemen's Land, was much longer and more dangerous than it is today. Now, by the most direct sea route, it is 11,509 miles. From Cape Town, until 1814 in possession of the Dutch, the new settlement was distant 6396 miles; from the nearest point on the South American coast some seven thousand miles; 6467 miles from San Francisco; from China more than four thousand miles; from Batavia, the not very friendly Dutch centre, 3800-odd miles. In the age of sailing ships these distances were apt to be greater and the time taken to cover them far longer than today. But they are still significant.

The First Fleet took eight months and a week to reach its destination, but that was not all sailing time. A week was spent in the Canary Islands, a month at Rio, and another month at Cape Town taking on necessary supplies. This was a fast voyage. The Second Fleet made faster time, under six months; but at terrible cost to the unfortunates aboard, for there was only one stop on the way. It was not unusual for ships to take longer than eight months. Hunter, sailing in *Sirius* to Cape Town for provisions, was forced by the season to circumnavigate the globe. This voyage took from 2nd October 1788 to 9th May 1789. The dangers of the sea were many, sickness was prevalent, the fear of mutiny was always present on such long journeys and shipwreck a very real risk. *Sirius,* the flagship of the First Fleet, was to be lost on the coast of Norfolk Island in March 1790, but already a more spectacular wreck had affected the colony deeply. In 1789 the Home Government had really bestirred itself and had fitted out H.M.S. *Guardian* with £70,000 worth of supplies for the colony, livestock including deer and rabbits as well as cattle, sixteen chests of medicines, gardens fitted up on deck under the supervision of Sir Joseph Banks to bring plants to Port Jackson since seeds spoiled on a long journey, seven superintendents of convicts, and twenty-five farmers and mechanics, as well as convicts of good character. *Guardian* should have arrived in January 1790 and would have rescued the settlement from its state of most miserable starvation. But unhappily on 23rd December, twelve days out from the Cape in fog and heavy seas, she met an iceberg. Lieutenant Riou, the brave but ill-advised commander, brought his ship up to the "floating island" in order to load lumps of ice because he was already short of water for the animals. Wind and current carried the ship onto the submerged shelf of the berg.

> . . . her rudder broke away, and all her works abaft were shivered. The ship in this situation became in a degree embayed under the terrific bulk of ice; the height was twice that of the mainmast of a ship of the line. The prominent head of the ice was every moment expected to break away and overwhelm the ship. At length after every practicable exertion she was got off the shoal, and the ice floated past her.

To lighten ship the animals with their fodder were "committed to the deep to perish". Water poured in, the pumps broke down, the lieutenant sat down in his cabin and wrote a report to the Admiralty. On Christmas Day the ship's boats were hoisted out and all but twenty volunteers abandoned ship. Except for the longboat, none of these was heard of again. The boatswain takes up the story:

> After the boats left us we had two chances—either to pump or sink. We could just get into the sailroom. We got up a new forecourse and stuck itt full of oakum and rags, and put itt under the ship's bottom; this called fothering the ship. We found some benefit by itt, for pumping and bailing we gained on hur; that gave us a little hopse of saving our lives. We was in this terable situation for nine weeks before we got to the Cape of Good Hope. Sometimes our upper-deck scuppers was under water outside, and the ship leying like a log on the water, and the sea breaking over her as if she was a rock in the sea. Sixteen foot of water was the common run for the nine weeks in the hold.

The ship would not steer, but she, being only four hundred leagues from the Cape, eventually fell in with a Dutch East Indiaman with whose help she crawled back into port. Of all the stores only seventy-five barrels of flour, some salt meat and a few oddments were salvaged, but Riou found himself a hero.[2]

The story of the wreck of the *Guardian* illustrates better than any other I know how long and dangerous a passage from England to Australia was, and that passage was the colony's lifeline. There was no other source of supply except the Cape of Good Hope, which, being a station solely for the use of the Dutch East India Company, was sometimes unable or unwilling to supply the British colony's needs and negotiate the treasury bills of a foreign power.

Today Australia is less than a month distant from England by fast passenger liner, two days by air, yet the distance remains. We can be cut off by war, our traffic can be diverted by a crisis such as that over the Suez Canal. In the nineteenth century we had the undoubted protection of the British Navy, now we must handle our problems ourselves and arrange for our own protection—just as the petty officer during life-boat drill on a liner remarked: "Your lifebelts will keep you afloat for twelve hours, after that you make your own arrangements."

Distance used to mean isolation. Australia had more than a hundred years to develop in safety, to maintain her racial integrity, and by the tolerance and generosity of the Imperial Government, so often and so wrong-headedly overlooked, to build and set her house in order according to her own ideas. Distance kept the Australians a small people, it was so much easier to emigrate to America where, to boot, "the streets were paved with gold". It was easier to return thence, too, if the new home proved disappointing. Perhaps the Australians will always be a small, wide-flung people. Competent authorities have set a limit to the carrying capacity of the country. Griffith Taylor, for instance, gave it as his opinion that the continent could not support at most more than sixty million people. But the advances of science may change all that.

Isolation became something of a cult in Australia before the advances of applied science, particularly the cable and the aeroplane, broke it down. The Australians, as they early came to call themselves, felt protected by it. They were alone to grow in their own way, to make their mistakes in private. The Pacific was as innocent as a garden. European powers might enter it and become a menace, the French, the Dutch, the Russians. . . . There were scares from time to time, but they passed over. Decade after decade Australia held the blue ribbon for the continent to which nothing happened, no wars, conquests, rebellions, no foreign policy even, no plagues.

Yet this isolation was always a figment. Distance was real, isolation was a wilful state of mind, for all it looked like a corollary of distance. Australia could not step outside geography. She could believe herself isolated, but the logic of position had her in a net.

Then, too, she has always been bound to the mother country and in a less degree to the other members of the Empire. To begin with, the settlers could not eat unless England fed them. Later, when the country was self-supporting as regards foodstuffs, her prosperity depended on the markets of the old world. It still does. A slump in London or on Wall Street is echoed in Australia, so is their prosperity and buoyancy. Wars begotten in the old world are Australia's wars. Less materially, so are policies, ideas, ideals, and fashions, whether in thinking or of clothes. To take examples, Chartism, which sprang up in England in 1836 and reached its full flower between 1840 and 1848, had a strong influence on Australia. Some of its tenets, such as universal suffrage, were not only adopted in Australia before they were in England but became and have remained essential parts of our social and political system. The Durham report (1839) by which a disaffected Canada was "settled" by the granting of responsible government, became a text for Australian patriots and progressives. Lord John Russell, hero in England of the Reform Bill of 1831-2, was Secretary of State for the Colonies from 1839 to 1841 and his liberal outlook and later that of Gladstone affected colonial relations and ensured the bloodless and natural evolution of a sovereign state out of the erstwhile penal settlement. On the whole, the Australian people have not shown themselves to be thinkers, philosophers, or innovators. Whilst too often exporting their brightest sons and daughters they have imported most of their political and economic doctrines. They have put them into practice, but they have rarely invented the basic idea. From its birth strong influences from Great Britain and later from the United States of America and Europe have worked upon Australia. We have much to learn and some of it we have learnt. The more we learn and adapt, the more we shall have to give. By the harshness of English law Australia was first populated by white men, by the mother country's later liberalism the thriving child was led on to nationhood.

Space is another facet of distance. Australia is distant from her European world. Her first settlers found infinite and terrifying distances within the bounds of their new domicile. Only a thin rind of the coast was known; beyond that stretched what seemed a dark infinity. Captain Cook had only thought it worth while to take possession of half the continent, or as far as 135 degrees of east longitude. If you look at your map you will see that Great Britain thus claimed only the east of the continent as far as Eyre's Peninsula on the south and about a quarter of Arnhem Land on the north. This was repeated in Governor Phillip's instructions and the whole of Australia was not brought under the Crown until Sir George Murray was Secretary of State for the Colonies. The area was quite large enough to begin with.

The Navy was used to the seven seas, but the convicts were for the most part poor, ignorant men who at home had probably never moved more than ten miles from the place where they were born. Now an untamed, anything but cosy, continent stretched before them farther than their imaginations could reach. They could not conceive that there was so much land. Some even believed that China was only a few days' journey away, perhaps a hundred and fifty miles. On 1st November 1791 twenty men and one woman ran away from Parramatta with a swag of provisions and barter goods (stolen, of course) to walk there. They were caught and after a struggle brought back, but they would not believe in the fallacy of their dream and a few days later made another attempt which cost some of them their lives. Captain Tench tells the story in his *Complete Account of the Settlement at Port Jackson* (p. 106), and adds to the tragic and pathetic tale the amusing touch:

> I trust that no man would feel more reluctant than myself to cast an illiberal national reflection; particularly on a people whom I regard in an aggregate sense as brethren, and fellow citizens, and among whom I have the honour to number many of the most cordial and endearing intimacies, which a life passed in service could generate. But it is certain that all these people were *Irish*.

Governor Phillip's final remark in a dispatch dated 18th November 1791 was: "As these people work daily in the woods, the preventing such desertions is impossible, but this is an evil which will cure itself."[3] In so much space it was useless to run away, there was nowhere to go.

The quality of the space was different from anything that anyone had ever known before. The land was there and Englishmen had grown up to reverence land, but the land produced little that was of any use. Midshipman Southwell wrote:

> We meet with no thing that is deserving of the name of fruit, and its quad's are scarcely to be classed above vermin. There are no rivers of water, and we are indebted to the frequent rain that supply the little runs that furnish us with this article. . . . We find many salutary herbs that make wholesome drink, and of g't use to our sick. Balm is here in plenty, and sev'ral vegitables have been lately found that are of the same kind, tho' not so good, as at home. Here is spinach, parsley, a sort of b'd beans, sev'ral wholesome unknown vegitables. Many of the productions of the country are aromatic, and have medicinal virtues, and it yields a variety of things proper for foementa and other external application.[4]

I suspect that these items were wholesome only for convicts and that in any case young Southwell did not know anything about it. The trees, of which there were an unconscionable number, were "fit for no purpose of building or anything but fire" according to Surgeon Bowes.[5] The soil of the littoral plain was poor, crops did not flourish even when the trees could be cleared away sufficiently to plant the seed. Within earshot of his companions a man could be irrevocably lost. So little were their eyes attuned to the strange vegetation and repetitive scenery that no landmarks could be distinguished. Beyond the pin-point of light that was Sydney the country stretched as far as the Indian Ocean, for all they knew, in one vast monotone of grey-green foliage, tipped in spring with pentecostal red leaves, gum-trees and gnarled banksias, murmuring casuarinas, spiny undergrowth and outcrops of old grey rock. It was secret and it gave nothing. That was the first impression and stony welcome that the First Fleeters received.

Gradually, to later settlers, the continent was to unfold and to become a wonder book, but the fact remained that everything for use—except minerals and gold, pearls in the nor'-west, garnets in the inland so copious as to be valueless, hills of mica, silver-lead, tin, uranium—everything needed for a progressive society had to be brought in from outside. The aborigines had adapted themselves to the country as completely as the eucalypt, but they had attained only to a static society relentlessly patterned, a subsistence economy. They planted no crops, not because they were too stupid but because they had no means of bringing in seed. They lived off the country, but they could only do so by keeping their numbers small and by continually moving on so that the meagre resources of the land were not exhausted. In the last war commandos were taught to live off the country in case of necessity. It was just possible. To support a large mixed population would be quite impossible.

The continent was old and delicate, it had reached the end, or nearly the end, of an evolutionary cycle. Its vegetation, animals, and birds had become so perfectly adjusted that there was no need for change. It was immobile. It was sufficient unto itself. Fresh factors had to be brought in from outside to make it prosper and produce in the European sense.

The beauty, the variety, and the potential wealth of Australia were learnt slowly and in the hard way.

We can see the fugitive beauty of the gum-tree pencilled against the sky; our educated eyes can find a thousand nuances of colour in the bush; we can appreciate the native blooms and not even find them strange, flower cyphers, mechanic, functional, barbaric. Look if you have the opportunity at Margaret Preston's pictures of flowers and you will see what I mean. We have come to marvel at the fauna, species long extinct in other parts of the world, missing links like the platypus which is at once bird, mammal and fish. And with it all we can have the rose, the lily, the sparrow and the horse. We have grown to love the sunburnt brownness of our plains, the grape-blue mountains, the aromatic bush. . . . There is variety enough from the karri forests of south-west Western Australia to the rippled hills of glittering mica, the moving sand, red or gamboge, the gibber deserts of the Centre, to the cattle stations, the sugar-cane and the coral reefs of Queensland; from the classical landscape of the Riverina to the crocodile-

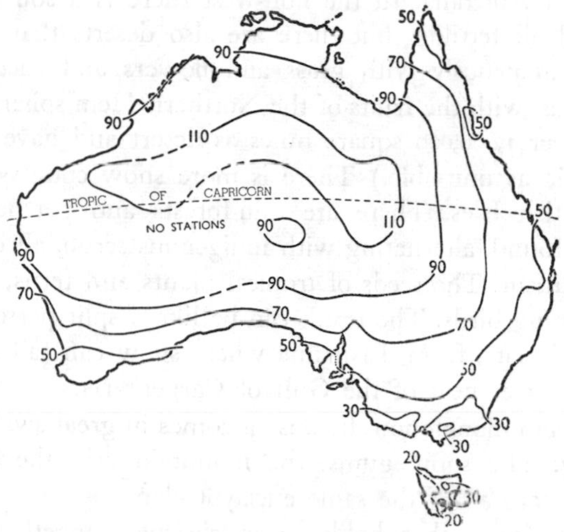

Map 1a (Annual evaporation)

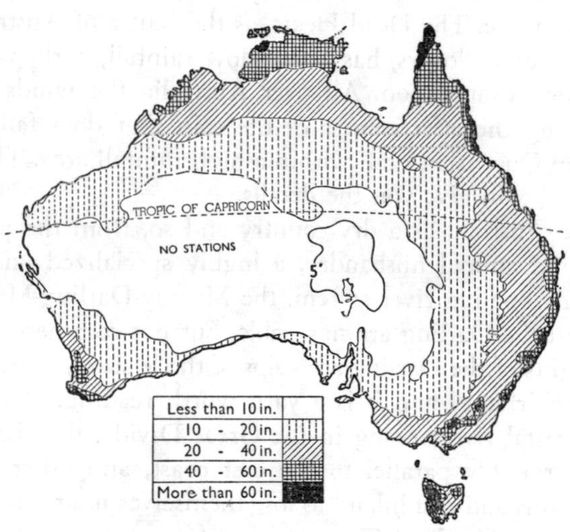

Map 1b (Annual Rainfall)

infested rivers of the Northern Territory. The oldest earth above sea level is to be found in Australia. In the nor'-west there is a soil called laterite which is beyond all fertility, but there are also deserts that, given water, will flourish spontaneously with grass and flowers and succulents or, in the irrigation areas, with the fruits of the Northern Hemisphere. (Geologists have classified over 1,000,000 square miles as desert and have labelled one-third of Australia as unusable.) There is more snow country in Australia than in the British Isles. There are rain-forests and patches of tropical vegetation to be found, alternating with indigenous scrub, all down the east coast of the continent. The seeds of tropical plants and ferns, it is said, are carried by migrating birds. The result can be like a split personality. There is every sort of climate, from Tasmania where snow can fall on Christmas Day to the heavy wet heat of the Gulf of Carpentaria.

Variety can seem monotonous because it comes in great swathes. There is unity in variety. The snow gums, the mountain ash, the coolabah, the gimlet, the karri, are all of the same eucalypt clan.

The common factor that holds so much space together in unity is rainfall. The average Australian rainfall is very difficult to arrive at with any accuracy. Thirty-seven per cent of the continent has a rainfall of less than ten inches and only fifteen per cent of thirty inches. It can sink as low as five and rise as high as seventy. Added to this, it is unreliable. The same district may vary widely from year to year. In the north there is a wet season and a dry season. The wet is very wet and the dry is very dry, which makes things awkward for the cattleman or anyone else who tries to establish a primary industry there. The Dead Heart, as the centre of Australia is called to the annoyance of its lovers, has a very low rainfall, perhaps five inches, coupled with high evaporation. All over Australia the winds dry out the moisture, lessening the effectiveness of the rain that does fall. Only parts of Tasmania and Queensland fall within a high rainfall area. The *Commonwealth Year Book* will give you the details.

By and large Australia is a dry country and so, from the point of view of agriculture and animal husbandry, a highly specialized and speculative one. She has only one big river system, the Murray-Darling-Murrumbidgee. The Murray and the Darling are navigable, but not commercially so today. The Dreadnoughts of the Darling are ships of the leisurely past. Dr C. E. W. Bean has told their story and it is a yarn worth reading.

There are coastal rivers rising in the Great Divide, the chain of mountains that runs roughly parallel to the east coast, and others that rise in the same mountains and run inland to lose themselves in arid country. There are big rivers in the Northern Territory, but for much of their length they are tidal and therefore salt. The nor'-west coast of Western Australia is dry to waterless, the Swan in the south is beautiful but not economically important. The Bight region of the southern coast is desert, and so we come round to the mouth of the Murray and Lake Alexandrina.

As the Australian soil lacks the leaf-mould from deciduous trees so, except in particular areas, the country lacks those reservoirs of permanent water that would make large scale irrigation possible, and provide transport as the river highways of Europe do.

Taking a quick glance at the continent as a whole, we see a moderately fertile east coast running the gamut from the humid tropical country of Cape York Peninsula through the sub-tropics of central and southern Queensland, growing bananas and pineapples and sugar-cane, to the milder New South Wales coast tapering into a cool climate in the far south, with dairying north and south of Sydney.

Beyond the Dividing Range, whose southern end provides the snow country, is the Bush. Here, reading from north to south, is the beef-cattle country, the sheep lands, the wheat belt, and again, in the western district of Victoria, Australia Felix, sheep again. The good lands fray out westward into semi-desert, halted for a moment by the irrigation area fed by the Murray, orchard and vineyard country. Then comes the desert. The shores of the Great Australian Bight are hopelessly dry, north is the Nullarbor Plain, a name often thought to be of aboriginal origin but really from the Latin *nulla arbor,* "no tree", which describes the region sufficiently. This is a hollow land of hidden limestone caves and long-dried lakes and their fossil remains.

North again is the Centre, brilliant, heart-break country, that with its winter climate, its curiosities, its survivals, attracts many tourists. It has no permanent rivers, for the Finke is only a sandy gulch. A train called "the Ghan" runs from Adelaide to Alice Springs (Alice was the wife of the South Australian Postmaster-General, Charles Todd, whose energy carried through the north-south telegraph line); a military road at perpetual attention, straight as a ramrod, carries on to Darwin. If you would like to make the acquaintance of the comic Northern Territory railway, which found it was better to be going somewhere than to arrive, read Xavier Herbert's *Capricornia.* Till the coming of the road the telegraph was the lifeline, the only one, across the continent from north to south.

The wealth is in minerals and a sparse, necessarily far-flung, cattle industry. The Birdsville Track is the old stock-route that served it. In this new atomic world space itself may be said to be a commodity. Australia's empty spaces are being turned to account for good or ill. Woomera Rocket Range has plenty of elbow room. The uranium of Rum Jungle, and who knows where else, enhances the wealth, the dangerous desirability of a continent that once seemed null and void.

Darwin is an outpost, an air terminal. Wyndham is the port from which the Government exports beef and has its roaring season when the experts arrive to slaughter and pack. Arnhem Land and the Territory hold out promise and then snatch it away. They have been the scene of many a chimera and may be the land of promise when the right key is found.

Between the dry lands of New South Wales and the Centre is Broken Hill, a mining centre of great importance. West again of the Alice are the gold-bearing lands of Western Australia, Kalgoorlie with its Golden Mile and famous water supply brought some 308 miles from Mundaring, 18 miles outside Perth, and Coolgardie, Siberia, and other desert lodes.

West of Perth is the Indian Ocean, to the south is Swan land with its tall timbers, to the north the lion-coloured waterless coast, Port Hedland and its hurricanes, Broome and its pearls. Here White Australia ceases.

There is wealth in this great land, but it has always been locked away. There were ideal pastures for sheep, but the sheep had to be imported and the land pioneered for them. There were wheat lands, but they were useless until railways were built to carry the grain to the ports. Dairy produce could be produced for export, but not until refrigerated ships were available. It needed irrigation before there could be a dried fruit industry, and so it goes on. . . . Land could be brought into use when artesian bores were sunk, pastures improved, soils analysed and if necessary their mineral content adjusted, beast and crop co-ordinated with earth and water, erosion combated, diseases, pests and noxious weeds conquered or ameliorated . . . all costing money either directly in plant and labour or indirectly in research.

To get results much beside hard work had to be put into the land. The population was, and is still, so small that only Governments can afford the outlay for railways, roads, irrigation, electricity works such as the vast Snowy Mountains Scheme, water conservation and supply like the Eildon Weir and its satellites in Victoria, and the long-term research that makes progress possible. The Commonwealth Scientific and Industrial Research Organization, the one large co-ordinated research project in Australia, is autonomous but government-financed. The States maintain agricultural schools and experiment stations, advisers and inspectors, and issue a spate of publications.

The citizens pay for all this, of course. The majority of them live in cities and pay, because they are more numerous, the greater part of the bill for opening up the country, yet in the bush one often finds resentment against the city as if it were a parasite. One could not do without the other. The bush, and in particular the wool industry, ultimately finances the cities, the cities act as clearing houses for the products of the bush.

Where rain is scant money must be poured in instead. Distance has a high price. This is not a continent where you only have to scratch the soil to get results or where markets are ready and near.

Transport and communication have been and always will be of the greatest importance for defence, for commerce, for the preservation of life. The largeness of the continent has made the Australian people amongst the most air-minded in the world. The aeroplane diminishes the miles to European standards. It facilitates intercourse and commerce. It spots for bushfires, floods, and sharks, it broadcasts seed and scatters fertilizer. The unique Royal Flying Doctor Service brings medical help to the Never Never Country. Even pigs can fly if necessary. There is an Air Beef scheme to bring meat to market from otherwise inaccessible country.

The aeroplane is only an instance. Railways and roads are important, too. More and more it becomes the custom to move stock, not by the old droving methods that are hard on man and beast, not by train which has its abuses, but by road transport, resting them each night and maintaining their condition. All except the worst droughts can be thwarted by the moving of stock. Quick transport stems waste and suffering. The history of the bush could be written in terms of transport, for transport, where there is plenty of space, is the answer to distance. Cattle King Kidman died a millionaire because his inland cattle stations were vast enough for his herds to move with the seasons and the rainfall.

Because Australia was cut off from the world and her scattered settlements and homesteads isolated again within herself, there has been enacted in the last 170 years, under practically test conditions, an evolution such as in the old world worked itself out either in prehistoric times or certainly before the age of scientific observation. The settlement began at scratch, and a close study of any activity—of agriculture, the pastoral industry, commerce, education, literature—reveals that it went through all the stages of evolution, though at an accelerated pace because Australia had the more advanced old world to draw upon for experience and supplies. This could be well illustrated in the development of the pastoral industry from the biblical simplicity of nomad shepherds to the scientific management and highly mechanized conditions of today.

The point I want to make is that an *evolution* did take place, that for all the awareness of the eighteenth century, civilization could not be imported, like the Olympic Torch, into a totally different context. It had to be relit, or, to use a better metaphor, to grow there as a plant grows from a seed, passing through all the natural stages from germination to blossom and fruit. Man set down anywhere on a virgin soil will develop his environment in much the same way. Australian history is an epitome of all social history. I hope in the chapters that follow that I shall make this clear.

This chapter, which could spread to volumes, has been necessarily short. I have made statements without a long, slow, scholarly building up of evidence. I believe them to be true and demonstrable. They are the stuff of which history is born, and for the understanding of history some assessment of natural factors is necessary. History itself grows out of the basic material of geography, climate, and human nature.

REFERENCE NOTES

[1] See *Commonwealth Year Book*, 1956, p. 924.

[2] The narrative may be read in full in the *Historical Records of New South Wales*, vol. ii, p. 755.

[3] *Historical Records of Australia*, ser. I, vol. i, p. 309.

[4] *Hist. Rec. N.S.W.*, vol. ii, p. 667.

[5] MS. in possession of the Trustees of the Mitchell Library.

CHAPTER II

DISCOVERY

Circumnavigations of the globe have been of late the universal topic of all companies.

—FORSTER'S *Voyage of Bougainville.*

NOW FOR A LITTLE WHILE we must cast our net over a great ocean and a long period of time. It is a matter of perspective. In writing or reading the history of Australia, or of any other country for that matter, it is easier and simpler to look on it as individual and separated from the rest of the world, as if it were a short story complete in itself and not only a chapter in a long and ever growing volume. Any such limited outlook would lead to distortion. It is not enough to say that Australia was discovered by Captain Cook in 1770. The finding of Australia was part of a pattern of world expansion, an integral part of the exploration of the Pacific, and it is a story that goes back a long way in time.

I. THE GREAT SOUTH LAND

The Greeks, who knew that the world was round, postulated a Great South Land. It was as much a myth as the Lost Atlantis, but like all myths it had its seed of truth. The idea lived on. It could not be verified or disproved, but it was never quite lost.

The Christian peoples of Europe in the Middle Ages no longer believed in a global world for religious reasons. The Tabernacle described in the Old Testament was flat and it, they believed, represented the world. The South Land was still vaguely sketched in on contemporary maps but it was believed to be uninhabited and uninhabitable. For was not the Equator a land of fire through which no man could pass and live? As, again according to the Bible, all men were descended from Adam, there could be no one on the far side of the fiery barrier. When any one thought of the South Land it was as we think of the moon.

The Arabs, who were not bound by such theories, and who, as great seafarers, had first-hand knowledge of India, Malaya, and the East Indies, believed in the existence of a South Land and may have had some hearsay knowledge of a land mass south of the Indies from the Malays, who were also adventurous sailors. They would hear no good of it. To the Malays the Great South Land, though not uninhabited, was the Land of the Dead.

In the Dark Ages, the centuries immediately following the fall of the Roman Empire, there was little intercourse between the East and the West and less sharing of knowledge. The Crusades, fought from the end of the eleventh century into the fourteenth, with as their main object the recovery of the Holy Sepulchre by Christendom, did much to bring together the two halves of the known world, to foster trade and to diffuse knowledge. Long before the fall of Constantinople in 1453 Greek scholars from that city, carrying the learning and knowledge of Greece and of the East, had reached Italy. In the thirteenth century at least one famous Venetian traveller, Marco Polo (*c.* 1254-1324) had visited China and Japan and in his voyage to Persia had sailed near "Sumatra", which he took to be the northern tip of an otherwise unknown continent.

The idea of a world-beyond-the-world floated dreamlike in the minds of geographers and philosophers. It remained for long a figment because the "known" world had no use for it. A few men might speculate and weave theories, a pastime men have always enjoyed, but that was all. Europe's aspirations for wealth and luxury were satisfied by the East. The spices of the Indies, the silks of China, and other luxuries came by long caravan routes to the Levant in the Mediterranean and were there sold to the merchants of Italian seaports like Venice, and thence were slowly diffused over Europe. The Norsemen had opened a long and dangerous trade route from Norway to the shores of the Black Sea. In either case trade had to be carried on through foreign lands and by grace of infidel traders and might at any time be interrupted by local wars or the caprice of princes.

With the Renaissance in the late fifteenth and early sixteenth centuries came a resurgence of the human spirit such as the world had not seen since the days of Pericles in Greece. The idea of progress was reborn and a new adventurousness sprang up in Western Europe. It was recognized that the world was a sphere and philosophers were sure that there must be a land mass in the Southern Hemisphere to balance that in the north.

We do not know with any exactitude what the population of Europe was at this time. Plagues and wars kept it small. There was no need for more space. Trade was acceptable, easy riches were welcomed, but colonization was not an issue.

The quickening of the Renaissance led on to the age of discovery and the revival of science. No matter how keen man's curiosity may have been, he had little chance of making long sea voyages before the invention, in the twelfth or thirteenth century, of the compass. The knowledge and use of the compass came to Western Europe from the Arabs as one of the results of the Crusades. Improvement in ship-building, the use of the astrolabe, the cross-staff and the log (actually a log attached to a rope, knotted at certain intervals and thrown overboard, by which distance run could be judged), and the division of maps by lines of latitude and longitude matched the new spirit of adventure and made exploration by sea possible. It was possible, but hazardous, for though latitude could be worked out fairly accurately longitude was very uncertain until after the invention in 1735 of the chronometer and its application to navigation over the following thirty or forty years. Logging or dead reckoning, as it was called, was also very sketchy. But ships could and did move out into the open seas with what would seem the most primitive equipment.

The Portuguese prince, Henry the Navigator, proved by the expeditions he launched that the Equator could be passed in safety. The Southern Hemisphere was opened to exploration by this knowledge. Mixed motives drove men on and on. Portugal wanted African slaves, Christians were in honour bound to convert the heathen; everybody wanted treasure; the few wanted knowledge. The East was El Dorado. The land route there was unsatisfactory and costly. Now men began to believe in a sea route. The explorers were coming south. In 1486 Bartholomew Diaz rounded the Cape of Good Hope and in 1498 another Portuguese, Vasco Da Gama, sailed up the east coast of Africa and reached the Indies. By 1512 Portugal had entrenched herself in the Moluccas. The Indian Ocean was hers and, she fondly hoped, hers alone. She brought back in her own ships the luxuries for which Europe was hungry, and the Italian cities, such as Genoa and Venice, which once had had a monopoly of the trade from the East began to feel the pinch.

No doubt the Portuguese heard from the peoples with whom they traded of another country to the south, but there is no evidence that they were interested. They already had what they wanted. They set up their trading posts, loaded their galleons, and profited exceedingly.

Spain was unwilling to be left behind in the race for riches. An Italian navigator, Christopher Columbus, in the service of the King and Queen of Spain, conceived the boldly imaginative plan of reaching the East by sailing west. This idea was founded on the work of Ptolemy, the Graeco-Egyptian astronomer, mathematician and geographer of the second century, and would have worked out as planned had not Ptolemy made a mistake of about one-seventh in the size of the globe. Sailing in 1492, Columbus discovered America instead of reaching Zipangu (Japan) and Cathay (China). He died without knowing his mistake. His discoveries were followed up, and the Americas were of great value, but to Spain the East still seemed better than a new world. Portuguese and Spaniards were bitter rivals, one had the Indies, the other the Americas. Both wanted all. The Pope, to avert war between two Christian States, arbitrarily divided the world between them. The Spaniards were nevertheless determined to have their share, or more, of the fabulous East. In 1519 Magellan sailed down the coast of South America, through the straits that bear his name, and into the Pacific, and so by a long, laborious route to the East. By 1565 the Spanish had colonized the Philippines, so named after the King of Spain, a jumping-off place in the Pacific. From there Andres de Urdaneta sailed back to Mexico on a northerly route, something which had been thought impossible.

It was the Spaniards who first set out intentionally to discover the Great South Land. In Peru there were Inca legends of islands to the westward rich in gold and silver, where a strange, exotic civilization existed. They sounded like the Islands of the Blest and had all the marks of the romantic legend, but the Spaniards thought that there might be something in the tale. There was a visionary streak in these men as well as a lust for wealth. They heeded the legend and embellished it. These fabled islands might be only the screen to the unknown continent, as Japan to China, the West Indies to America, and that continent could be of solid gold.

Alvaro de Mendana was sent out to find it in 1567, sailing from Callao in Peru. He found, not the golden South Land but the Solomons, an archipelago that stretches across six hundred miles of ocean, a name that in itself suggests a hope for treasure such as the biblical king lavished on his temple. The expedition lived to return, but only after great hardship. Mendana was eager to try again for he believed that beyond the Solomons lay the hoped-for continent. It was Santa Cruz.

It was 1595 before he was allowed to set out again, this time with Quiros as his pilot. The expedition found land, but it was not in the Solomons, nor yet was it the continent. Rebellion, native attack and sickness brought the Spaniards low. Mendana died, Quiros took command on the laborious and dangerous return to the Philippines.

The torch had passed to Quiros, a good pilot, a deeply religious man, but touched with the madness of a Don Quixote. In 1603 he won permission from the King of Spain to lead another expedition in search of the Great South Land. After a false start he sailed in 1605 with Torres as his pilot. He discovered those islands now called the New Hebrides. Optimistically he concluded that here was the tip of the continent he sought. He named the land Austrialia del Espiritu Santo (South Land of the Holy Spirit). The name Australia was on the map. Triumph was short. It is not known exactly what happened, but suddenly Quiros was heading for home with a mutinous crew. Torres was left behind. After fifteen days he made the heroic decision to sail on westward, though his company was unwilling and his stores almost exhausted. Sailing north-west he picked up the southern coast of New Guinea and passed through Torres Strait between Cape York Peninsula and that island and so to the Moluccas. Whether or not he saw Australia is unknown. He would probably have taken it for another island, and not a promising one either. His voyage was kept secret because, after all, he was poaching in the Portuguese sphere of influence. This was the last of the great Spanish voyages of discovery in the Pacific and the end of attempts to find the Great South Land by sailing west from South America and the Philippines.

If you look at a map of these voyages, say the excellent one in Beaglehole's *Exploration of the Pacific* (p. 128), there is something that will impress you. Setting out due west or even south-west, every expedition sailed north before it came within sight of the Australian coast. Torres at New Caledonia reached the most southerly point and the one nearest to the Great Barrier Reef. This northerly trend was neither accidental nor intentional. It was due to the logic of the prevailing winds with which the small sailing ships of the day could not argue. It was practically impossible to discover Australia by sailing west from Spanish bases, and so ends the early story of approach to the east coast of the continent.

Australia stands between two oceans, the Pacific and the Indian, so there were two reasons why she should be discovered eventually.

Another nation enters the story. The Dutch won their freedom from Spain in 1581 after a long struggle. The Dutch were a virile, progressive people, shrewd traders and brave seamen. They too were determined to have their share—that is, as much as they could take—of the wealth of the Indies. Since 1580 Spain and Portugal had become one kingdom and it suited the Dutch temper admirably to score off their old enemy by following the Portuguese route round Africa to the Moluccas and there to seize what they could. They were, too, a Protestant people and cared nothing for the Pope's division of the world between Spain and Portugal. In 1595 they sailed round the Cape of Good Hope and up the eastern coast of Africa. They travelled in large well-armed flotillas, and the Portuguese grown lax in fancied security, were no match for them. They mopped up the Portuguese forts and trading posts, aroused the already restless Mohammedans of Africa and the islands against the Spanish and Portuguese, and quickly established themselves in the East Indies. Sixty-five ships sailed out of Holland on this route between 1595 and 1601. In 1602 the United Dutch East India Company was formed. The Dutch were now in Australia's near north, but they, like the Portuguese before them, were contented with the prize that they had won and were not going to spend money and time looking for another, which might prove less profitable.

Nevertheless, they had heard local talk about the gold and silver of New Guinea, or the Papuas, as it was called. It was worth investigating. In 1605 *Duyfken*, a small ship sometimes referred to as a yacht or a pinnace, was commissioned to sail along the south coast of New Guinea. This she did for nearly nine hundred miles, then missed the strait which Torres was to discover the following year. She followed the western coast of Cape York Peninsula southward into the Gulf of Carpentaria to a point which was named Cape Keer-weer (literally "Turn again"). *Duyfken* found no gold or silver, only barren land and murderous black men. In this undramatic way was Australia discovered. It was still the unwanted continent.

That is not the end of the Dutch story. Something happened in 1611 which made the discovery of the west coast of Australia inevitable. In that year a Dutch navigator, Brouwer, pioneered a new route to the Indies. Instead of sailing up the east coast of Africa, he struck out due east from the Cape of Good Hope and then, after four thousand miles or so, due north. This proved a much faster route, cutting as much as ten months off the journey, so in future all the ships of the Dutch East India Company were ordered to follow it. A glance at the map will show you how close the regular traffic lanes now were to the coast of Western Australia.

It was in 1616 that the ship *Eendracht*, commanded by Dirk Hartog, made the inevitable miscalculation. She fell in with Dirk Hartog's Island, which was uninhabited. Here a post was driven into the ground and a pewter plate giving the name of the ship and her captain was nailed to it. *Eendracht* sailed on along the coast and her name began to appear on maps. Eendrachtsland is the stretch between North-west Cape and Gantheaume Bay on modern maps. Nobody was particularly interested, but in 1696 Willem de Vlamingh, another Dutch master, was instructed to have a look at the coast whilst on his regular sailing. The report on this investigation was not exciting: "Nothing of importance has been discovered on this exploratory voyage."

Meanwhile other Dutch ships had accidentally touched the coast at various spots and one Commander, Frederik de Houtman, in 1619 identified it as "the South-land of Beach". "Beach" frequently appears on old maps in connection with the Great South Land.

Houtman's Abrolhos (meaning "Open your eyes" in Portuguese) is his present-day memorial on the map.

It was clear to the Dutch that they had discovered a coastline of continental extent. But what of it? The place was barren. The lion-coloured sand was at first thought to be gold-bearing, but that was wishful thinking.

By 1622 the coast was known from Cape Leeuwin (the name of yet another Dutch ship) to Cape Gantheaume. The dangers of the coast, where the English ship *Trial* was wrecked in 1622, made it advisable to chart it. There was also an element of scientific curiosity. Governor-General Coen of the Indies planned a thorough exploration, which would circumnavigate the continent charting its coast. Two ships were even taken up, but they never set sail. In 1623 a more modest expedition under Jan Carstensz in *Arnhem* and *Pera* was sent to check on the findings of *Duyfken* nearly twenty years before. Cape York Peninsula Carstensz named Nova Guinea.

(You must get used to the way names floated round in the early days.) Carstensz wrote of the country:

> The land . . . is a barren and arid tract, without any fruit trees, and producing nothing fit for the use of man; it is low-lying and flat, without hills or mountains, in many places overgrown with brushwood and stunted wild trees; it has not much fresh water, and what little there is has to be collected in pits dug for the purpose; there is an utter absence of bays and inlets, with the exception of a few bights not sheltered from the sea wind; it has numerous *salt* rivers, extending into the interior, across which the natives drag their wives and children by means of dry sticks and boughs of trees. The natives are, in general, utter barbarians, coal-black; they are utterly unacquainted with gold, silver, tin, iron, lead and copper, nor do they know anything about nutmegs, cloves, and pepper. . . .[1]

Alas for El Dorado.

The name of the little ship *Arnhem* is still used for the land mass to the west of the Gulf which takes its name from the Governor of the Indies, Carpentier.

Carstensz's report should, one would have thought, have discouraged any further interest in the poor shrunken South Land. But no, in 1627 another Dutch ship, *Gulden Seepaart*, was cruising along the south coast of Australia discovering the equally unwelcoming shores of the Great Australian Bight, some thousand miles of barren country.

In 1629 *Batavia*, under François Pelsart, was wrecked on the treacherous Abrolhos, and then followed the epic story of Pelsart's voyage to Batavia to bring help after repeated landings on the coast had failed to find water. Whilst he was away the supercargo Jerome Cornelius murdered some forty of the stranded crew and set himself up as a pirate where there were none to rob. Pelsart, returning with help, was warned in time; he captured and executed the mutineers and rescued the few survivors.

Anthony Van Diemen, reported to be an adventurer who ended up as Governor-General of the Indies in 1636, provided, curiously enough, a link between his practical predecessor, Coen, and the idealist and dreamer, Quiros. He was fruitful in plans for the systematic sea exploration of the South Land which were touched with the fervour and even the style of the Spaniard.

In 1642 he found the sailor he was looking for in Abel Janssen Tasman. Tasman sailed from Mauritius due west till he found and skirted to the south the modern Tasmania, naming it, of course, Van Diemen's Land, then he struck boldly across the Tasman Sea, fell in with the South Island of New Zealand, went into, but not through, Cook Strait, and followed the North Island as far as Cape Maria Van Diemen, thence north and west in a wide sweep round the north of New Guinea and so home to Batavia. It was a remarkable voyage.

In 1644 he was off again, going from Batavia to pick up the Australian coast at a point a little south of North-west Cape and following the coast north and east to Arnhem Land, the Gulf of Carpentaria, and Cape York Peninsula, thence to the south coast of New Guinea and to Timor Laut, coming to port at the Dutch station of Banda.

The Dutch now knew the Australian coast from Fowler's Bay on the south to the tip of Cape York, with the south of Tasmania thrown in for good measure. The continent had taken shape, reality had replaced fantasy.

With Tasman's voyages the Age of Curiosity may be said to have begun.

II. The Age of Curiosity

The sixteenth century had belonged to Portuguese and Spanish explorers, the seventeenth to the Dutch. In the eighteenth the English and the French took up the story. Between the Age of Discovery and the Age of Curiosity there is a difference in climate.

The Age of Discovery was the active aftermath of the Renaissance, just as the Reformation and Counter-Reformation were its spiritual aftermath. It was a time of contradictions, of idealism, faith and fantasy, of avarice and bloodshed. Its feet were amongst the myths, its head among the stars, and its hands were picking up gold and silver.

The Age of Curiosity is modern, the curiosity is scientific. It was often heroic, for the means of exploration and voyaging called for heroism; it was also practical and prosaic, but rarely avaricious. The Dutch were really a buffer between the two well-defined ages. They wanted El Dorado, they were credulous about the Great South Land, Messer Marco Polo and all that, but they went about the business of exploration by sea in a dogged and common-sense fashion. Of Englishmen Drake, the circumnavigator, belonged to the Age of Discovery and Dampier (b. 1652) was a precursor of the Age of Curiosity, also called the Age of Reason.

Dampier was a buccaneer by trade—quite an honourable one, given the right time and place—a seaman, and by cast of mind an observer. In 1686 he was with Captain Swan in *Cygnet*, ranging the Pacific. In the course of the voyage Swan evolved a plan of entering the spice trade in opposition to the Dutch (the enemy) and founding a factory in the Philippines. Dampier liked the idea, thinking that pirates should make good merchants, and adding his own rider that on the way to the Philippines they should explore "Nova Hollandia", as the quondam Great South Land, or Terra Australis Incognita, was now commonly called. Instead they went to Timor and then south to see what Australia "would afford us". They were on the nor'-west coast at Cygnet Bay early in 1688. The group of islands off the coast were later named Buccaneer Archipelago in honour of the landfall.

Dampier grew tired of *Cygnet* and at the Nicobar Islands he deserted. After many adventures he returned to England in 1691. There in 1697 his journal was printed and attracted the attention of the President of the Royal Society (founded 1660). The Admiralty, with qualified generosity, gave him a very old ship of 290 tons burthen, the *Roebuck*, and sent him out to voyage, to discover, perhaps even to establish trade. He intended to investigate the eastern coast of Australia, but the weather was hostile, the season wrong. He sailed instead from the Cape of Good Hope to the Australian coast as the Dutch had done, and he sighted it very much where Dirk Hartog had. He coasted northwards and saw much what the Dutch had seen, but he did note that the bush flowers were beautiful, strange, and sweet-smelling.

He had Tasman's charts, but doubted if what he saw was a solid coastline. It might be no more than a labyrinth of islands with a way through. He could not find out because he ran out of water and provisions and had to hurry to Timor. Refreshed there, he was able to visit New Guinea, which he saw first on New Year's Day 1700. He discovered New Britain and sailed through Dampier Strait. He had some idea of circumnavigating the continent, but his ship was not fit for it, nor was his crew willing. The poor old tub finally fell to pieces and Dampier made his way home to face a court martial. He did not add very much to the world's knowledge of Australia, but his journals brought the country alive for the first time. Perhaps he was the first man to look at it for its own sake and not with an eye to possible advantage. His journals were read, but they did not, to the men of his time, seem to have any practical application.

The Dutch were not pleased by English interest. What if the land they had discovered had possibilities at present not apparent? The English were a colonizing nation and might step in and take what really belonged to Holland. There were those, Jean Pierre Purry, for example, who used to say that the Dutch East India Company should set up trading posts on the most likely part of the Australian coast, the southern shore discovered by the ship *Gulden Zeepaard* and called by her master Nuytsland. It was not only possession of the land that had to be considered. An enemy, French or English, could establish himself there and prey on Dutch shipping. Ships heavy-laden with spices from the Indies would be prizes worth taking. The canny Dutch East India Company thought about it, but decided not to take action. After all, New Holland might not be Terra Australis Incognita. Tasman had discovered New Zealand, Staten Landt as he named it, and *it* might be a northern promontory of the Great South Land.

One more great Dutch voyager, Roggeveen, set out with three ships and the backing of the Dutch West India Company to look for another, better Australia. He rounded Cape Horn far to the south and crossed the Pacific west and north. He found a vast sea studded with islands but no continent. He did not come anywhere near New Zealand or the east coast of Australia. He added very little to the voyage of Le Maire in 1616 and the knowledge he gathered was negative. The Pacific was vast, there was still hope that it hid a rich continent.

In particular England, coming late, was anxious for a new sphere of influence and trade. Of all the ocean-seas there was only the Pacific left. It had been crossed, but it was not known. In 1744 John Campbell was urging colonization in the Pacific. He was what we should probably call today a publicist. He published a collection of voyages and used them as propaganda in an effort to arouse merchants to take up the opportunities still open to them. He and the Dutchman Purry had similar ideas. Campbell went so far as to suggest that the Dutch decried their discoveries in order to discourage anyone else from visiting them.

The French were also becoming interested. They had their own legend of a rich, idyllic South Land accidentally discovered by de Gonneville in 1505 and then mislaid. They, too, had an East India Company and in 1738 it sent out two ships under Captain Bouvet to find the elusive land and harness it to trade. Bouvet thought that he discovered the misty outlines of a continent south of the Cape of Good Hope, but the season was so foggy that he could not be sure of anything.

Theorists like Maupertuis and Charles de Brosses pounced on the idea, the latter wrote his *History of Navigations* (1756) in which he listed forty-seven voyages in the South Seas and drew his own morals from them. France, from motives of philanthropy, national pride and business acumen should take advantage of the opportunities awaiting her in the South Seas. The more interested France became the more likely was her hereditary enemy, England, to turn her attention to the South Seas.

The battle for the Pacific was waged on paper. John Callander in his *Terra Australis Cognita* (1766), rehashed de Brosses's facts and arguments, directing them, of course, to the English reader. Alexander Dalrymple, the hydrographer and servant of the East India Company, took a hand and in 1767 published *Discoveries in the South Pacific to 1764*.

His researches had unearthed the secret voyage of Torres through the strait north of Australia. He believed fervently in a South Land and brought a great many arguments to bear on the problem.

The time for action was slowly ripening. In 1764-5 Commodore the Honourable John Byron, with two well-found ships, crossed the Pacific from Cape Horn to Batavia. It was the old story of a north-westerly passage, sea and islands.

In 1766 Captain Samuel Wallis, in Byron's flagship *Dolphin*, followed with variations much the same course. Philip Carteret was the second in command on this expedition and in his ship, *Swallow*, a slow and untrustworthy vessel, was soon separated from Wallis and made his own laborious way across the Pacific somewhat to the south of the routes taken by Byron and Wallis. It was a terrible voyage in a leaking ship, the crew racked by scurvy and weakened by hunger. Native spears accounted for some of them and it was only the doggedness of the commander that brought the ship at long last to Batavia, having discovered, amongst other islands, New Ireland and the strait between it and New Britain.

Also in 1766 the French had two ships in the Pacific under de Bougainville. He had endeavoured at his own expense to found a strategic colony in the Falkland Islands to guard the entry to the Pacific. England and Spain both claimed these islands. Bougainville was ordered by his Government to hand them over to Spain and himself to make a voyage of exploration across the Pacific. Owing to delays it was not until 26th January 1768 that the Pacific voyage actually began. Bougainville was able to hold a more westerly course than any of his predecessors and actually reached the outer fringe of the Great Barrier Reef off the coast of Queensland. Every sign told him that he was close to a great land mass, perhaps the desired continent. The chivalrous Frenchman, whose aim was scientific knowledge rather than commercial gain, might well have had the honour of discovering the east coast of Australia, but sickness was rife in his crew, provisions were running short, and, worst of all, the coastline was so dangerous, with its hidden coral reefs that could tear open the hull of a ship, that he too was forced to turn north, and, missing Torres Strait, zigzag through the Louisiade and Solomon groups, and make his way round the north of New Guinea, through the Moluccas to Batavia.

The wonder-book of the Pacific was open. Some of its pages were blood-stained, others scarred by incredible hardship. Stories were brought back to the old world as colourful and stimulating as any Marco Polo had had to tell. And these were true stories. The age of credulity had gone . . . well, it had receded as far as it ever does. King's ships were being employed and men skilled in observation and cultivated of mind. Dampier had been a brilliant amateur, now professionals were exploring and charting the last great ocean. Not only was the popular imagination stirred, but the scientists of the world were enlisted.

The Age of Curiosity reached its consummation in the first voyage of Captain James Cook, 1768-71. He was a Yorkshireman who had joined the Navy as an able seaman in 1755 and by sheer ability had worked his way up to the command of a King's ship. Not only was he a fine sailor, he was also a skilled cartographer and a competent astronomer. He was known to the Admiralty, and when for the honour of the nation, the Crown decided to finance an expedition to Tahiti to observe the transit of Venus there on 3rd June 1769, it was quite natural that he should be chosen to command H.M.S. *Endeavour*, which was to carry the scientific expedition and then to proceed on a voyage of discovery.

Cook followed the old route round Cape Horn, sailed to Tahiti, and thence, unlike any other sea-voyager of the Pacific, turned south, then west, till he fell in with the coast of New Zealand. He circumnavigated the islands, proving once and for all that they were not the peninsula oı continent but free in the ocean. From New Zealand he crossed the storn Tasman Sea and found, as he expected, the coast of New Holland, not as far south as he had intended, but at Cape Hicks, later called Cape Everard. He refitted in Botany Bay, and Sir Joseph Banks, the naturalist of the expedition, gathered strange plants. *Endeavour* sailed north, falling foul of the treacherous coral reef inside the Barrier Reef. Cook careened his ship near what is now the site of Cooktown, repaired her, sailed on through Torres Strait, and home round the Cape of Good Hope, having circumnavigated the world.

Except for part of the southern coast, the outline of Australia was now known. The Great South Land had shrunk to the size of the largest island in the world. Its wealth lay buried in the future. But curiosity was satisfied. Only one minor problem was left—was Van Diemen's Land part of New Holland or a separate island? Cook had meant to settle that question, too, but the winds and the currents had carried him northward of his objective.

It was at 6 a.m. on 20th April 1770 that the east coast of Australia was first seen.

In two later voyages Cook combed the seas south and east of New Holland and laid the ghost of Terra Australis Incognita.

REFERENCE NOTE

[1] Quoted, G. A. Wood, *Discovery of Australia*, p. 242.

CHAPTER III

BEGINNINGS

The beginnings of the settlement in Australia were both doctrinaire and sordid. The world had a spare continent. The Dutch had first claim to it, but saw no profit in it. The claim next in validity was England's, founded on the voyage of the *Roebuck*. She showed no signs of wanting the country either. Cook's discovery and accurate charting of the east coast brought the continent into focus. It ceased to be legendary, it was real, England had her navy's word for it. Cook, to be on the safe side, had formally taken possession of half the continent in the name of the Crown. Everything was shipshape and Bristol fashion, but still England found no use for her large and distant possession. It was a pity to waste it, but what could she do with it?

There were theorists who answered the question. As early as 1748, when only the west coast was known, John Campbell proposed a colony from which, drawing on his imagination and exaggerating the proximity of the Spice Islands, he expected great advantages. No one was impressed. In 1756 a Frenchman, Charles de Brosses, in one of those "instructive and entertaining" volumes of voyages so much the fashion in the eighteenth century, outlined with admirable logic a settlement on the Australian coast that would rid France of her felons, her foundlings, her beggars, vagabonds, and all other enemies of society. They would, he opined, support themselves in the new land and at home the worthy citizens would be unhampered by the expense and depredations of their useless or criminal brethren.

John Callander, from his name another Scot, translated de Brosses into English and added some touches of his own. He moved the locale of the Colony of Disgracefuls to New Britain as handier for the spice trade. Where these visionaries found evidence to support their theory that successful and profitable colonies could be founded by social misfits on a coast that all reports, except one, had described as barren, waterless, and dangerous, it is difficult to conceive.

A slightly more credible plan was put forward in 1783 by James Maria Matra, who had been a midshipman in *Endeavour* with Cook. He at least had seen the east coast of the continent and his scheme was supported by Sir Joseph Banks. Matra belonged to a loyalist American family and conceived the idea of finding a new home in Australia for British subjects driven out by the War of Independence. He gilded his theme:

> By the discoveries and enterprise of our officers many new countries have been found which know no sovereign, and that hold out the most enticing allurements to European adventurers. None are more inviting than New South Wales. . . . The climate and soil are so happily adapted to produce every various and valuable production of Europe, and of both the Indies, that with good management and a few settlers, in twenty or thirty years they might cause a revolution in the whole system of European commerce and secure to England a monopoly of some part of it, and a very large share in the whole.[1]

One senses here a certain jealousy of the Dutch. For good measure and to popularize his plan, Matra threw in flax of such exquisite delicacy that it could resemble cambric or silk, a trade in woollen goods with Japan, a depot for furs from China and Russia, and an outlet for convicts who, with Chinese and Otaheitans, would provide the labour necessary for the new plantation state. Expense he airily waved aside, tools could be drawn from Ordnance stores, the Navy had to keep ships in commission in any case, and they could pay for the voyages by picking up timber in New Zealand for spars. The plentiful soil would do the rest. Three thousand pounds would cover the whole expense. He also pointed out that it would be better for migrants to go to a British possession than to America. The only paragraph of all these that appealed to Lord Sydney at the Home Office to whom it was addressed was that regarding convicts. "Give them," wrote Matra, "a few acres of ground as soon as they arrive in New South Wales, in absolute property, with what assistance they may want to till them. Let it be here remarked that they cannot fly from the country, that they have no temptation to theft, and that they must work or starve." This sank into the official mind and can be traced in future policy.

Captain (later Admiral) Sir George Young also had a plan, like but less restricted than Matra's because he had never visited Australia. Judging from size and position, he took it for granted that New South Wales would produce "all kinds of spice . . . fine oriental cotton, indigo, coffee, tobacco, with every species of the sugar-cane, also tea, silk, and madder". Flax, of course, there would be to supply the current scarcity; convicts could be taken out as ballast in East Indiamen on their way to China and labour could also be brought in from China and the Friendly Islands. "The very heavy expence Government is annually put to for transporting and otherwise punishing the felons, together with the facility of their return, are evils long and much lamented." (You are telling me!—or words to that effect—remarked that dry and precise man, Lord Sydney.)

"Here is an asylum open that will considerably reduce the first and for ever prevent the latter."[2] Again Lord Sydney was only interested in the disposal of convicts, but he absorbed the idea of using East Indiamen (by the Company's Charter New South Wales was within its sphere of trade monopoly) and, in an edited form, the importation of Friendly Islanders.

These schemes, however influential their source, would have fallen on stony ground but for a most uncomfortable by-product of the American War of Independence. In the days of the Old Dominion England had got rid of her felons very easily and inexpensively by shipping them off to the plantations of Virginia. At first the Government paid contractors £5 a head to carry them across the Atlantic. Later it made a better bargain. The contractors made their profit at the American end. The services of a skilled man for the term of his punishment were sold for from £15 to £20. Women brought from £8 to £10 each. This showed a good profit, although the death-rate on the journey was heavy. There was no supervision either of the contractors (that is, the ship-owners) or of the masters. The convicts were slaves in all but name. Once they were handed over to the contractor the Government took no further interest in them, save devoutly to hope that they would never return. In the seventeenth century, as a matter of indulgence and to meet a scarcity of labour, prisoners might be pardoned on condition that they worked for five years in some of the King's plantations. At the end of that time they would be granted land, again on a condition, this time that they did not return to England without the King's licence. This more humane form of banishment was still on the Statute Book in 1718 when an Act of Parliament (4 Geo. I, c. 2) entitled "An Act for the further preventing robbery, burglary, and other felonies, and for the more effectual transportation of felons and unlawful exporters of wool etc." superseded it. The "effectualness" of this lay in the complete handing over of the convict to the ship-owner who undertook to take him out of the country. The land grant was quietly forgotten, the embargo on return was left to take care of itself as it was sufficiently difficult of achievement to prevent it from being an issue.

Everything was nicely settled when the American War of Independence ruined the contractors' business and left England with a fast accumulating number of felons on her hands. Prisoners had been sent to America at the rate of about a thousand a year. These, added to the short-term offenders, soon filled English jails to overflowing. In 1775 hulks (that is, ships no longer seaworthy) moored in the Thames were put into commission as prisons. They were even more unhealthy and depressing than the prisons on land. In that year, too, and in the next 746 convicts were transported to Gambia in West Africa as an experiment. It was an immediate and terrible failure; 334 died, 271 deserted and most probably perished, and of the remainder the Home Office had no record. These figures, being made public, aroused even the callous conscience of the day.

The nuisance continued to grow, public health was threatened by jail-fever and other maladies, the moral health of the community was also threatened by the depravity of prisoners released at the end of their sentence. Public opinion demanded that something be done. It was wrong that the just should suffer on account of the unjust. Hardened rogues must be sent out of the country, but not to equatorial Africa. That was murder, and a justice-loving people could not condone it. In March 1786 the Mayor and Corporation of London were petitioning the King for relief from this evil. They represented public opinion in general when they wrote:

> That your petitioners humbly conceive that this dreadful accumulation [about 4000 habitual criminals] is alone sufficient to account for all the evils that are so heavily felt and so justly complained of, both as to the overcrowded state of the gaols and the increase of crimes and of offenders.
>
> To what extent the mischiefs that are so severely felt already, and the fatal consequences so justly apprehended, may be carried by a longer continuance of so rapid and alarming an accumulation of convicts within the kingdom, no human wisdom can foresee.[3]

William Eden, Lord Auckland, in his scholarly *Discourse on Banishment* (1787) enunciated the legal principles behind transportation and revealed unconsciously the general social attitude towards the criminal. He was an outlaw and, having offended society, could expect no mercy. Punishment was a mixture of vengeance with a forlorn hope of deterring other potential criminals. Any idea of reform was only a pious gesture. Lord Auckland himself was not altogether in favour of transportation. He thought felons could be used more usefully at home, in the salt works and in mines, on dangerous enterprises when it would be wasteful to expend a valuable citizen, for experiments involving risk or to exchange them in Tunis and Algiers for the redemption of Christian slaves.

> . . . every effect of banishment, as practiced in England [he wrote] is often beneficial to the criminal, and always injurious to the community. The kingdom is deprived of a subject and renounces all the emoluments of his future existence. He is merely transferred to a new country; distant indeed, but as fertile, as happy, as civilized, and in general as healthy as that which he hath offended.

It is not clear what country Lord Auckland had in mind, possibly the Riviera. It could not have been New South Wales. There was actually nowhere left, unpossessed, distant, reasonably healthy, except in the Pacific.

Lord Auckland's *Discourse* is particularly interesting in that it illustrates the prevailing eighteenth-century attitude not only towards criminals but in general. There is a dry and polished hardness about it, a touch of cant as when he refers to "the devoted convict", an eye to the main chance in his so reasonable contention that a man who has put himself outside the pale by breaking the law should be turned somehow or other to profit. All the schemes for colonization of New South Wales already quoted have a neat, often unreasonably reasonable, profit motif, supported by deductions that smack of medieval dialectic.

Sir Joseph Banks, when asked if England would derive any advantage from a settlement in Australia, gave the acceptable answer: "If the people formed themselves a civil government, they would necessarily increase . . . and it was not to be doubted that a tract of land such as New Holland, which was larger than the whole of Europe, would furnish matter of advantageous return."[4] Again and again government dispatches to the colony strike the note of contrived profit, of doctrinaire arrangement that, reasonable within its premises, has very little to do with the facts of the situation. Your eighteenth-century official believed that event should conform to preconceived pattern and was offended when it did not. Apparently reason often functioned in a vacuum. Australia was to suffer again and again from the preconceptions of influential and intelligent men who knew nothing about the subject.

By harsh facts, by incipient fears, and by the pressure of public opinion, the Home Office was gradually brought to the sticking-point. It originally had three reasons for considering a new colony in the Pacific, heartily sick as the nation was of colonization after the American War of Independence. One had been the resettling of loyalist American families, but by masterly neglect they had resettled themselves in Canada and elsewhere.

The second was a vague but persistent suspicion of the French. They had made too many voyages of curiosity in the Pacific—Bougainville, Surville, Marion, and now La Pérouse. They might have intentions of colonization. If they had England preferred on principle to forestall them. The Dutch had beaten her to the East Indies and that rankled. A continent was going begging. England did not really want it, but less still did she wish to see it in French hands.

The third and most pressing reason for action was the superabundance of convicts. As long ago as 1779 a Parliamentary Committee had considered the need for and the location of a penal settlement. It had called on Sir Joseph Banks for an opinion and he had answered, "Botany Bay". Had he not spent eight days there nine years before? There was water and timber, the soil was "good enough", the climate was good. As a home for Englishmen he would not, on the evidence of his diary, have considered it, but for convicts, men and women who had forfeited all privileges, it was ideal. He did not suggest, as Matra had done and as Phillip would in vain, that an advance party should be sent ahead to plant crops and erect the necessary buildings. It was probably Banks's advice that clinched the matter. New Zealand does not seem to have been considered, probably because of the warlike character of the Maoris, possibly because if England made the supreme effort of planting a colony in the Pacific it was more prudent to take the largest island available.

The crucial date was 18th August 1786, for on that day not only had Lord Sydney made up his mind, but he had written to the Lords Commissioners of the Treasury:

> I am, therefore, commanded to signify to your Lordships his Majesty's pleasure that you do forthwith take such measures as may be necessary for providing a proper number of vessels for the conveyance of 750 convicts to Botany Bay, together with such provisions, necessaries, and implements for agriculture as may be necessary for their use after their arrival.

He enclosed the "Heads of a Plan"

> . . . for effectually disposing of convicts, and rendering their transportation reciprocally beneficial both to themselves and to the State, by the establishment of a colony in New South Wales, a country which, by the fertility and salubrity of the climate, connected with the remoteness of its situation (from whence it is hardly possible for persons to return without permission), seems peculiarly adapted to answer the views of Government. . . .

This insistence on the fineness of the climate which began with Banks and Matra ranks with the famous remark attributed to Marie Antoinette when she was told that the people lacked bread: "Let them eat cake." Climate does not sustain life, and Banks as a botanist should have known that the vegetation of Botany Bay would not. The Gambia tragedy was another reason why the Government was eager to reassure itself and the public as to the healthiness of the proposed site.

Lord Sydney's plan[5] is definite and practical, as were the instructions to the Captain-General which followed fast upon its heels. The voyage was to be a naval operation (and how, wondered Sir Charles Middleton, should the *Navy* know anything about convicts?) with two King's ships, three store-ships, and six transports. Following Sir George Young's suggestion, the transports taken up were East Indiamen which after depositing their loads at Botany Bay, could go on to China for tea, a considerable economy. A "discreet officer" was to be chosen as Captain-General and two companies of Marines were to be sent with the expedition for defence. No superintendents were to go with the convicts, but it was hoped that some of the Marines might be artisans or have some knowledge of farming. Expense had to be considered. More generous than Banks, Sydney planned to send two years' supply of food and clothing instead of one. In form the American usage of sending the prisoners under contract to the masters of the ships was followed, but now a certain sum—10s. a ton per month—was paid to the ship-owners. A contractor, William Richards, Jr., provided food for both Marines and convicts, but only whilst the ships were at sea. As soon as they reached a port the officers of the colony took over, buying fresh food and paying for it with notes on the Treasury. The officers of

Marines, one of whom at least sailed in each transport, were responsible for the health and discipline of the convicts. They shared out the water when it was rationed, and it devolved on them to inspect the food that was issued. When the ships arrived at Botany Bay the convicts and their papers were formally transferred to the Governor. This sounds cumbersome, but it was a matter of official habit and such is not easily broken. Phillip complained that he was neither consulted as to the arrangements made nor told of them. Some of the convicts' papers were left behind, which made it impossible to know when or if they should be released from servitude.

From Matra and Young Sydney accepted the idea of a supplementary population from the Pacific Islands, this time women to redress the balance of the sexes. They were never brought in, owing to the chronic state of famine which was to prevail in the settlement.

Sydney was too much of a realist or too chary of the American pattern to envisage another plantation State in the south. He fell back on the original idea of banishment in which the prisoner was bribed to stay where he was when his term expired by a grant of land. Matra in his revised scheme had included this idea. Land was abundant in New South Wales, it all belonged to the Government, it could be used at no expense to reward services and to provide for the time-expired convict. A State composed of small peasant holdings should give no trouble, and that was the sort of State the Governor was ordered to found and which he did found and maintain.

Neither did Sydney have illusions of riches or fantastic ideas about bases for the fur trade and all that. All he asked was hemp for the Navy and the gallows and perhaps some timber for masts and spars.

The aborigines were to be treated with kindness and led into the light of civilization. The Governor was to open barter with the natives of the mainland and of the adjacent islands as soon as possible.

The Governor had wide powers, civil and military, to constitute and appoint justices of the peace, coroners, constables, and other necessary officers and ministers, power to pass judgment on criminals, exact fines and forfeitures, to pardon, reprieve, and remit, to levy armed forces "for the resisting and withstanding of all enemies and rebels both at sea and on land", to execute martial law, to erect fortifications, to exercise sovereign naval powers, to control finances, to grant lands . . . and so it goes on, all decent and in order but mostly beside the point. In short, the Governor was to have absolute power only conditioned by circumstances, his own ability and conscience, the co-operation of his officers, and a number of other very real but unmentioned factors. The eighteenth-century façade was erected. Life would go on behind it.

The choice of Post Captain Arthur Phillip as Governor was most fortunate for the new settlement. He had gone into the Navy as a midshipman in 1755 and was now on half pay. His record of service was good but not distinguished. The choice of him to command a penal settlement was surprising. Admiral Lord Howe could not even spell his name; besides, he had a candidate of his own in Captain John Hunter. Phillip was not a protégé of Lord Sydney. The other government department involved was the Treasury, and there he had a friend and neighbour in Sir George Rose, an Under-secretary. It has been suggested that it was through Rose that the job came his way. It was a thankless, responsible, and inglorious task. His salary as Governor was £1000 a year, with allowances of £20 a year for stationery, and five shillings a day for a secretary; as a naval captain he received and retained £500 a year. Phillip was delicate and nervous, but his exterior covered a character of great determination, an incorruptible honesty, and an unexpected, imaginative vision. The very existence of the colony was to hinge on this man.

The choice of Major Ross as Commandant of the Marines was not so happy. He was an obstructionist of the first water and made Phillip's task even more difficult than it need have been. He stood upon the dignity of his service and refused to let his Marines, officers or men, do anything but their garrison duty. Modern research has, I believe, thrown a more comely light on him, but that there was ill feeling between the Governor and his commandant, the two men who should have stood together, there is ample proof in the records.

The other officers and men, naval and marine, were the mixture of good, bad, and indifferent that one would expect. The naval officers and sailors came out of it best, but then their lives were not as much changed. They had their ships and their routines. This was just another tour of service. There was not for them, as there was for the Marines, a deadly vacuum.

The eleven ships of the Fleet were a scratch lot. The flagship *Sirius* (600 tons burthen) built for the East India Company, had been burnt to the waterline whilst still in the shipyards and the remains had been sold to the Government cheaply, refitted still more cheaply, and sent on a couple of voyages to the West Indies as a victualler. Now, with a new name, twenty guns aboard, and, as her company was to discover at sea, a too perfunctory overhaul in the Naval Dockyards, she was dubbed a warship and handed over to Phillip, with John Hunter as second captain. She was only on loan, Phillip was to return her as soon as possible, but she did not live to see England again.

The other King's ship *Supply* (170 tons burthen) was described by Lieutenant Philip King in his journal as "much too small for so long a voyage, which, added to her not being able to carry any quantity of provisions, and to her sailing very ill renders her a very improper vessel for this service".

The transports *Alexander, Scarborough, Friendship, Prince of Wales, Charlotte*, and *Lady Penrhyn* were a poor lot, the two ladies being particularly heavy sailers. The total tonnage of the Fleet, including the store ships, was 3972 tons burthen. They were to travel some sixteen thousand miles by way of Rio de Janeiro on the coast of South America, the Cape of Good Hope in South Africa, the Antarctic Circle, then east to pick up the South Cape of Van Diemen's Land (Tasmania) and so up the Australian coast to a destination last visited eighteen years before by Captain Cook.

So much for the theory, the instructions, the officers and the ships of the quietly momentous expedition. What of the convicts themselves, the raw material of the colony to be? They were, like everybody else in this story, the product of their times. As a body of men they have been viewed from generation to generation through very different spectacles. Contemporarily it was taken for granted that they were the greatest collection of rogues in the world; later they were subjected to a succession of doctrinaire treatments, humanitarian and otherwise; after transportation had ceased they were shovelled out of sight and out of mind; later again they were exhumed and white-washed. They were the victims of an inhuman system—the man who had poached a rabbit because his children were starving, the little girl who in a spirit of fun had ridden a neighbour's horse and then was accused of horse-stealing, the nineteen-year-old boy who told the mutineers of the Nore that if they wanted to succeed they must stick together and only narrowly missed hanging for his words, the Tolpuddle Martyrs, or Dorchester Labourers, the Scottish Martyrs, many guiltless Irishmen who had only been agin the Government and couldn't quite talk themselves out of trouble. . . . These instances were all true, but not necessarily representative. Some convicts made a success of their lives in the new world, worked out their sentences or were pardoned, became useful and well-to-do citizens. They had, if they wanted to reform and had the necessary stamina, remarkable opportunities. As no free overseers, superintendents, or warders were sent out in the First Fleet, Phillip was forced to rely on the better-behaved convicts. If they had skills they were valuable men. The opportunity was real, but whether they could avail themselves of it or not could be a matter of chance as well as character.

On the whole the First-fleeters were a poor lot; many had already lain for years in the unspeakable prisons and had become depraved. Often the crime with which they were charged appeared trifling, but it could be, and often was, only one incident in a life of crime. There were certainly some first-class ruffians amongst them. Phillip, who was naturally lenient and hopeful of human nature, revised his opinions after close contact. They were probably much like petty and habitual criminals at any time in English history, ranging from the vicious and callous to the weak and unfortunate. They did come out of a particular world, however. The

Industrial Revolution was bringing men from country to town, robbing them of their former meagre security, breaking old ties, subjecting them to new temptations, fostering discontent with conditions and protests against them, offering a variable fortune, now wages that appeared good compared to the farm labourer's pittance, then unemployment and hard times, just such variations as provoke social protest or finally revolution. The common lands were being enclosed behind the migrating labour.

Criminal law and procedure were very different in the eighteenth century from today. There was no police force except London's Bow Street Runners, until Robert Peel founded one in the 1820s, much to the rage of a number of citizens who insulted and even attacked these guardians of their life and property. The Crown did not prosecute for theft and similar crimes. The onus was on the victim, who often could not afford or was afraid to prosecute. The law was harsh, the death penalty could be enacted for small offences like the theft of an object valued at more than a shilling or the inevitably quoted but mysterious crime of "impersonating Egyptians". Executions were gala occasions and the populace could expect one a week. Nevertheless the law's bark was worse than its bite. Many criminals escaped punishment, many others sentenced to death were transported instead to America, where labour was needed. Judges probably felt, like Lord Auckland, that it was a pity to waste men when they could be turned to profit. To the criminals of the British Isles it was a hit-or-miss matter whether they were punished or escaped. It was the weaker brethren who were most likely to come to court. The prisons, notoriously, made more criminals than they received. Reform was on its way. John Howard, a delicate but determined man, spent a large private fortune and travelled about 50,000 miles inspecting prisons in the British Isles and Europe. He published a massive treatise on them, *The State of the Prisons*. It was his efforts and those of Jeremy Bentham which led in 1779 to the passing of an Act of Parliament authorizing the construction of model prisons in which by a mixture of solitary confinement and hard labour the convict would be not only punished but reformed. The heavy expense entailed made the scheme a dead letter. The nuisance of the prisons continued and the plans for transportation came slowly to a head.

REFERENCE NOTES

1 *Hist. Rec. N.S.W.*, vol. i, part 2, pp. 1-5.
2 *Ibid.*, pp. 11-12.
3 *Ibid.*, vol. ii, p. 736.
4 Quoted, G. A. Wood, "The Plan of a Colony in New South Wales", *J. Roy. Aust. Hist. Soc.*, vol. vi, pp. 36-68.
5 It can be read in full in *Hist. Rec. N.S.W.*, vol. i, part 2, pp. 18-19.

CHAPTER IV

VOYAGE AND LANDFALL

ON 18TH AUGUST 1786 Lord Sydney wrote his "Heads of a Plan". In October Phillip received his first commission. The ships were to be taken up in November and Sydney expected the expedition to be on its way in December. It did not leave Portsmouth until 13th May 1787, and even then it was so hastily got together that, despite Phillip's care, some important items—for example, clothing for the women convicts—were left behind.

The voyage took eight months and one week, or six months' sailing time, for a week was spent in the Canaries and a month each in Rio and at the Cape. The voyage is very well documented, for most of the officers and some of the Marines kept diaries and a number of them have survived: Captain Hunter's, Lieutenant King's, Surgeon White's, Captain Tench's, Captain Collins's, Lieutenant Bradley's, Surgeon Arthur Bowes's, Second Lieutenant Ralph Clark's, Midshipman Southwell's, Sergeant Scott's, Marine John Easty's.[1] From them, taken together, there arises a lively and homely picture. The Fleet was a world in itself.

The treatment of the convicts varied during the voyage from ship to ship according to the character and humanity of the officer in charge. Phillip did his best for them before sailing and after, but each ship was a little world in itself and it was difficult for him to supervise what went on in them. Phillip was neither a weak man nor a sentimentalist. He had been bred to naval discipline and he showed himself able to keep his difficult colony in hand. We can still read, in the *Historical Records of New South Wales*, his reflections, made for his own guidance, on the policy he intended to follow. He remembered that convicts were human beings and that some at least were capable of redemption. He determined to give them justice and by a policy of segregation to keep the less guilty from being contaminated by the hardened rogues. This policy was thwarted by the Government. The ships' masters, and not Phillip received the convicts' papers, and the papers themselves did not supply the most important information, that is, the name of the crime for which the prisoner was transported. Name, place and date of trial, length of sentence, was all the information supplied. Only by questioning the convicts themselves could he find out more. How could he, except by some small adjustments after the voyage had begun, sort different types of convicts into the different ships? They were loaded like so much merchandise according to accommodation, convenience, or indifference.

Phillip fought their battles before sailing. This letter of 18th March 1787 to Under-secretary Nepean was only one of many.

> Tho' I have so often solicited that essence of malt or some anti-scorbutic may be allowed, I cannot help once more repeating the necessity of it; and, putting the convicts out of the question, which humanity forbids, the sending of the marines that are on board the transports such a voyage as they are going, in a worse state than ever troops were sent out of the Kingdom . . . cannot, I am certain, be the intention of his Majesty's Ministers, yet it is absolutely the case, and I have repeatedly stated this fact. . . .
>
> The giving cloaths to those convicts who have been embarked at Plymouth is so very necessary that I have ordered it to be done [from the stores of the *Sirius*], and presume the Navy Board will replace the cloathing, but as there are more convicts to be sent on board the different ships, unless orders are being given for their being washed and cloathed on their leaving the prison or the hulks, all that we may do will be to no purpose.
>
> These complaints, my dear sir, do not come unexpected, nor were they unavoidable. I foresaw them from the beginning, and repeatedly pointed them out, when they might have been so easily prevented, at a very small expense, and with little trouble to those who have had the conducting of this business. At present the evils complained of may be redressed, and the intentions of Government by this expedition answered. But if now neglected, it may be too late hereafter, and we may expect to see the seamen belonging to the transports run from the ships to avoid a fatal distemper, and may be refused entrance into a foreign port.
>
> The situation in which the magistrates sent the women on board the *Lady Penrhyn*, stamps them with infamy—tho' almost naked, and so very filthy, that nothing but clothing them could have prevented them from perishing, and which could not be done in time to prevent a fever, which is still on board that ship. . . .[2]

He fought tirelessly against overcrowding, unnecessary confinement, and all the abuses of carelessness. His victories were only partial.

When necessary Phillip punished effectively and with precision, but he took no pleasure in it. There was no cruelty in his nature. The same could not be said for all his officers. The naval officers obeyed him, the officers of Marines did not at any time feel the same tie of duty.

Phillip briefed his officers: strict cleanliness was to be maintained in the ships, the convicts were to be freed of their chains and allowed exercise and fresh air for their health's sake, major punishments were to be referred to him, women convicts were to be segregated from the male convicts and the crew, rations were to be handed out with scrupulous care, and in times of scarcity all convicts, crews, marines, and officers were to share alike. These were counsels of perfection and practice fell far short of them.

JAMES COOK

From the portrait by George Dance in the National Maritime Museum, Greenwich

ARTHUR PHILLIP

From the portrait by Francis Wheatley, R.A., in the National Portrait Gallery, London

Charlotte was a good ship, in which the discipline of the convicts was under the charge of Captain Tench. It was not until leaving Rio that the first punishment was given, twelve lashes to Thomas Brown for insolence.

Friendship was a bad ship. Captain Meredith was in charge with Faddy and Clark as his lieutenants. Punishments were frequent and heavy, the attitude of the officers was hostile, and no real effort was made to keep the crew out of the women convicts' quarters.

Lady Penrhyn was also one of the worst ships, if Surgeon Bowes's attitude is any indication. He thought that by Phillip's orders the convicts were treated far too well and they had no right, wicked as they were, to be so healthy.

> I wish I could with truth add that the behaviour of the convicts merited such extreme indulgence—but I believe I may venture to say there was never a more abandoned set of wretches collected in one place at any period than are now to be met with in this ship in particular. . . . The greater part of them are so totally abandoned and calloused to all sense of shame and even common decency that it frequently becomes indispensably necessary to inflict corporal punishment on them.[3]

Bowes acknowledged the use of the thumbscrew, iron fetters, and the shaving of the heads of women convicts, though he admitted that the practice of flogging them naked had been given up for reasons not of humanity but of decorum.

Scarborough was not a happy ship, and the master of *Alexander* disobeyed the regulations for cleanliness flagrantly. Even so, the health of the First Fleet was infinitely better than that of the Second Fleet and the prisoners more humanely treated.

It could hardly be said at this date that there was any convict *system*. Phillip would have systematized the whole business, but officialdom frustrated him at home and circumstance in the colony. But, by sheer force of character, he was able to do more towards shaping a state than any other Governor until Macquarie.

On 13th May the transports were mustered. *Sirius* hove to and the transports passed in procession within hailing distance of her, the masters shouting their reports. At night *Sirius* was put under an easy sail and a light attached to her mast so that stragglers could come up and the Fleet keep together. Phillip sent into each ship to find out how many farmers there were or men with knowledge of a trade and he gave his orders that all major punishments should be meted out by him personally. There was trouble in *Friendship* over the seamen's rations, they demanded two pounds of meat a day instead of one and a half, there was near mutiny in *Scarborough*.

After the formality of departure the pattern of everyday life asserted itself. The first accident happened on 15th May. Surgeon White recorded it:

An accident of a singular nature happened to-day. Corporal Baker of the Marines, on laying a musquet down, which he had just taken out of the arms chest, was wounded by it in the inner ankle of the right foot. The bones after being a good deal shattered, turned the ball, which taking another direction, had still force enough left to go through a harness cask full of beef, at some distance, and, after that, to kill two geese that were on the other side of it.[4]

And on the twenty-eighth he recorded the first death: "Departed this life Ishmael Coleman, a convict, who, worn out by lowness of spirits, and debility, brought on by long and close confinement, resigned his breath without a pang." Three days later Isabella Lawson, a mantua-maker, transported for "privately stealing", gave birth to a girl and Mr Watts's goat had two kids, one male and one female.

Teneriffe, where the Fleet stayed for a week, was a welcome break for the officers and meant green figs, onions, and pumpkin added to the convicts' diet. They, of course, did not go ashore, except for John Powers, who escaped for a few hours.

The Fleet sailed on towards Rio into the hot weather. The humidity bred fevers, an epidemic was nearly brought on in *Alexander* by the carelessness of the master in not keeping his ship clean. The women convicts who were battened down between decks at night fainted with the heat and even took fits. Water was rationed to three pints a day for all purposes, without respect of persons, and it was issued twice daily with due ceremony. The sea supplied plenty of fish, which was a change from salt ration. Even a devil-fish with horns over its eyes and three sucking fish attached to it was served in the cabin of *Sirius*, but "it was not found good". White, who was always interested in nature reported from *Charlotte*: ". . . at night the sea, all round the ship, exhibited a most delightful sight. This appearance was occasioned by the gambols of an incredible number of various kinds of fish who sported about us and whose sudden turnings caused an emanation which resembled flashes of lightning darting in quick succession."[5] There were the usual high jinks crossing the Line in serene weather. Then came storms. They swept the Fleet before them, *Sirius* carried away her fore top-gallant mast, a man was lost overboard and a woman convict was crushed to death by a ship's boat which broke loose. They spoke with an English ship *Remembrance* twelve weeks out from London and sighted other ships. Now eyes were raised from sea to sky, for land birds were seen. On 1st August 1787 Phillip hoisted his broad pennant for the first time to make his entry into the Portuguese port of Rio de Janeiro.

Here the officers, for again the convicts were kept mewed in their transports, saw a colony in the grand style of the Age of Discovery, with its closely guarded gold and diamond mines, fever and romance, flowers and nymphs; a rain of golden oranges, a *décor* of bright-plumaged birds, a display of piety that surprised the more reserved northerners, an old-world pomp and ceremony. Phillip was much embarrassed because every time he passed the Vice-King's palace the guard turned out and laid their colours at his feet in token of honour. It was an Hesperidean world, strange in every way to these prosaic sailors on their momentous but underrated enterprise, coming in from the sea.

Reading their journals you see gold-dust in the air.

> About two miles in the country we stepped into a grove of oranges when the gentleman asked us if we would walk in and offered us tiffin and go and eat oranges in the grove, he sent his servant with us to pull them off the trees for us, when we ate as many as we could and stuffed our pockets full and he would take nothing for them, his wife who is a true native is very dark like a Mulatto presented me with a nose gay for which I thanked her very much.[6]

One wonders what Ralph Clark used for speech, since he could not even cope with the syntax of his own language.

Surgeon Bowes, drawing a tooth for a beautiful Portuguese, was rewarded with a handful of rare beetles. Lieutenant Clark chased butterflies to send home to "Alicia, my virtuous wife". Surgeon White had a delicate idyll through a grille in a convent with one of the dark-eyed pupils.

Phillip, less susceptible, saw an excellent chance to stock up his fleet with fruit, vegetables and rum to face the voyage ahead. The chaplain, Richard Johnson, took the opportunity to visit the transports, preach in his usual gloomy vein, and baptize the children born on the voyage. Major Ross also toured the fleet uttering more military admonitions and threats.

On 4th September, to the tune of 21 guns, the Fleet left Rio. Now the real privations of the voyage began. Austerity was harder to bear because everyone, at least those who were in a position to be vocal, had been softened by the luxury of Rio. Nerves were soon on edge, punishments were numerous, the Fleet ran into equinoctial gales, dysentery broke out, a man was drowned overboard, meals were monotonous, the convicts had to be kept between decks because of the weather, and a general malaise spread through the ships. Mutiny welled up in *Alexander* and the ringleaders were transferred to *Sirius* to be quelled under Phillip's eye, and the convict who had incited the sailors, John Powers, he who had tried to escape at Teneriffe, was "very heavily Iron'd and now stapled down to the deck". The informer was removed to *Scarborough* for his own safety.

On 13th October the Fleet reached Cape Town. Lieutenant King went ashore to beg permission of the Dutch Governor to buy supplies and was politely rebuffed. This was a very different settlement from Rio. It belonged to the modern world, commercial and commonplace. Its function was to victual the Netherlands East Indiamen and its main attraction was a large garden of vegetables grown for them. It had the nickname of the Tavern of the Seas.

Phillip was eventually able to persuade the Governor to revictual him. Had he not, the Fleet's state would have been desperate indeed. The ships were a month in port, necessary repairs were made, livestock bought and potatoes, cabbages, barley, meat and whatever else was offering were taken on board. Phillip bought for the Government, the officers for themselves. Prices were high, "nor do I conceive," wrote Surgeon Bowes, "there is any part of the Dutch possessions better calculated to exemplify the character of Dutch avarice than Capetown. Every article while the fleet lay there was advanced to treble its usual price."[7]

When it left Cape Town the fleet was likened to Noah's Ark. Eight guns had been taken out of *Sirius* (they were unlikely to need them now) to make room for a bull, a bull calf and seven cows. A stallion, three mares and three colts were stowed in *Lady Penrhyn*; the women convicts were taken out of *Friendship* to make room for sheep, pigs, foals and poultry. Space was found for more in *Fishbourne* and the officers' private stock travelled in another store-ship, *Golden Grove*. The ships were now crowded to capacity as fodder and extra water had to be taken on for the livestock.

At the Cape the expedition had the first glimpse, had its members been aware of it, of the kind of country they were bound for, in its brownness, its barrenness, its strange mechanic flowers. The convicts were encouraged by seeing "many gallows and other implements of punishment erected along-shore in front of the town". There were also "many wheels for breaking felons upon, several of which were at this time occupied by the mangled bodies of the unhappy wretches who suffered upon them, their right hands were cut off and fixed by a large nail".[8] The Fleet departed in no very cheerful frame of mind, especially as two English ships which came in during their stay brought only two letters for them. They were forgotten indeed.

On 12th November, a calm day, the Fleet sailed into the unknown. The diarists wrote their melancholy reflections and hope sank to a low ebb. The livestock aboard, mostly poultry, had little reason to be cheerful either.

On 16th November Phillip divided the fleet into two sections. He moved into *Supply* and, with the three fastest transports and store-ships, into which he had moved all the more useful convicts, set off as an advance party. All the ships were so slow that he gained nothing by this manoeuvre and the story of the voyage remains one story, not two.

The ships ran into calms. "No wind, all the ships in company with their heads different ways," wrote Clark.[9] Then storms. "The brig labours much," wrote Lieutenant King of *Supply*, "and is very uncomfortable. It must be acknowledged that ease and convenience were not our errand on board this vessel." Many of the seas "wetted the head of ye forsail" and, of course, everything and everybody aboard. The ships were driven off course. The weather grew piercingly cold. The sea was full of whales, the sky of albatrosses and petrels. Sickness increased. On 28th December the dreaded scurvy made its appearance and such anti-scorbutics as the doctors had were of little use, for water was again scarce. The animals suffered and died of the buffeting and starvation. Snow, darkness, hail descended on the Fleet. The seas were so high that King reported that *Supply* was "almost constantly under water" and "the situation of everyone on board her truly uncomfortable".

The least articulate, the convicts, suffered most, and the sailors were not much better off; neither group could provide itself with any extras in the way of food, both had cramped quarters. The convicts were worst off, since they were unused to the sea, were under discipline, and had little hope of the future to sustain them.

In the midst of so much distress and danger perhaps the God who notes the fall of the sparrow remembered a little hawk.

> This afternoon [14th December] a little hawk came aboard and one of the men caught it, found it belonged to somebody on board the *Scarborough* who had let it fly away for its dirtyness, the man that caught it let it fly away again and the poor little thing, in endeavouring to reach the *Alexander*, it fell in the water. I suppose it was drowned.[10]

Christmas day was glum in *Sirius*. "We complied as far as was in our power, with the good old English custom, and partook of a better dinner this day than usual but the weather was too rough to admit of much social engagement."[11]

In *Lady Penrhyn* the Captain made a special issue of grog "to chear their hearts and to distinguish this day as being the most remarkable in the year, and which generally brings with it Mirth and Glee to the Hearts of all except the most Miserable".[12] In *Friendship* drunkenness was the only diversion. The year went out with a storm and the women in *Lady Penrhyn* were washed out of their bunks.

On 7th January the first division of the fleet sighted the coast of Van Diemen's Land. It was at least land, and only expert seamanship could have brought them to it through such storms and the great wastes of the sea. It was now reasonably certain that they would reach their destination, but they were not home and dry. There were still tribulations to be faced before they reached Botany Bay. "Hard-hearted" winds split *Friendship's* sails, carried away the mainsail of *Prince of Wales*; the cabin windows of *Golden Grove* were stove in by a heavy sea; fog enveloped them all so that they could only keep in touch by firing guns; Edward Thompson, a convict, died "worn out with melancholy and long confinement"; the boatswain on *Fishbourne* fell from the topsail yard and died of mortification. . . . But at last, at ten minutes to eight on 20th January 1788, *Sirius* entered Botany Bay, finding *Supply* and three other ships already anchored. The other ships straggled in. The voyage was ended and, by the standards of the day, very prosperously. The water butts were opened and everyone was free to wash his clothes.

Behind this official description there is another, told naïvely by Lieutenant Clark of the Marines, who sailed in *Friendship*, and glimpsed in the other unpublished diaries. Clark lived in a world of his own and his narrative is as innocent of varnish as of punctuation. Between his preoccupation with his "adored Alicia" and his "sweet boy Ralphie" and a sadistic attitude towards the convicts he sandwiches significant little glimpses of life unknown to and unsuspected by Phillip, aboard the smallest transport. His diary begins with a lament: "Can never forgive Captain Meredith for refusing me leave to sleep out of the ship last night. Oh, did he love as well as I do he would never have refused me", and to this he appends a prayer:

> Oh gracious God what a task I have gone through last night in taking leave of the dearest and best of wives and not seeing my boy God grant them health and welfare is the most sincere wish of an affectionate husband and fond father. Oh when ever I am restored to them again will never leave them bless them both.[13]

That and nothing else is what the sailing meant to him. By 28th May he had cheered up a little: "Flog this day John Bennet, a convict, with 87 lashes for breaking out of irons, a young man but an old rogue, read part of the story of the Humble Friend in the *Lady Magazine* for the year 1775 very much taken with it."[14] He was incensed that Phillip should order the convicts out of irons and again incensed when the seamen of *Friendship* asked for a larger ration of meat, "I never met with a parcel of more discontented fellows in my life. . . ."[15] All his sympathy was kept for Ralph Clark.

Being very hard up, he did not go ashore at Teneriffe, but as a man of appetite enjoyed the "very sweet" beef brought aboard. From boredom or some other reason he fell ill on 14th June and tells us all about it. "Exceedingly ill all this day, oh my God for your servant my dear Alicia's sake don't forsake me. Took an emetic by doctor's orders, very ill after it, the doctor very kind, gave me something else in the evening."[16] By the nineteenth the other facet of his character was uppermost.

> Capt. Meredith put the four convict women, Elizabeth Dudgeon, Margaret Hall, Elizabeth Pully, Charlotte Ware out of irons, whom I had put in irons on the 9th of this month for fighting . . . I am convinced they will not be long out of them, they are a disgrace to their whole sex, that they are. I wish all the women were out of the ship.[17]

The twenty-third of June being Clark's wedding anniversary, we hear a lot more about Alicia and his son, but he ends sensibly: "I could write about them for ever but must leave off and see about getting dinner."[18] That evening he, with Surgeon Arndell and Lieutenant Faddy, had a drinking party accompanied by songs. The next day he had a headache. In between these major occurrences he sandwiches the minor events, a convict had died and a marine's wife had given birth to a fine boy, for which she was rewarded by the gift of a shoulder of mutton.

Curiously, when he reports the routine allotted to him of serving out water both his manner, his prose and his punctuation improve out of sight, but he is soon back in the intimacies of his private life and preoccupations.

Captain Walton has given me a puppy, have called it Efford after the dear sweet place where first I came acquainted with my Alicia, my virtuous wife. Capt. Meredith ordered one of the corporals to flog with a rope Elizabeth Dudgeon for being impertinent to Captain Meredith, the corporal did not play with her, but laid it home, which I was very glad to see, then ordered her to be tied to the pump, she has been long fishing for it, which she has at last got, until her heart's content.[19]

Next Clark reports that Elizabeth Baker has been put in irons, flogged, and had her hands tied behind her back for two days and a night. As Phillip had ordered all major punishments to be left to him, these were evidently only little domestic corrections.

Nothing is so small as to escape the diary so long as it has to do with its hero. He got wet issuing the water and lost his pencil; he could not sleep; a dinner of salt pork, potatoes, and pumpkin pie displeased him. This was the harder to bear since in *Lady Penrhyn* they did much better with hot rolls for breakfast, home-brewed spruce beer, and salads grown on wet flannel; he had an ill-omened dream of Alicia; the little dog Efford was lost overboard and Clark, not surprisingly, attributed this to malice towards himself; he thanks God that he is not troubled by bugs as Lieutenant Faddy is; he gives a convict woman "some thread" from which she made (or knitted?) a pair of trousers; he works on a desk as a present for Alicia . . . we can follow his intellectual, as well as his emotional, life with breathtaking interest:

Read this day part of the *Tragedy of Douglas* oh what sincere love does Lady Randolph express herself for the death of Douglas and her lost child, and the timeless death of her brother, in the beginning of the first Act . . . I love the character of Anna but I am afraid that Glenalvon from his first speech, has some treachery in view, hope not but something foretells me he has. . . . Oh, it is a sweet play, what an innocent sweet spirit that is of young Norval when he informs Lord and Lady Randolph whom he is and where his father lives, on the Grampian Hills, my father feeds his flocks etc. and what are the emotions in the breast of Lady Randolph when she sees the features and shape of her lost and stained husband Douglas, in that of young Norval, little does she know, fond mother, that he is her long lost son, or she would not have let him go to the field with her Lord, what a villain Glenalvon is, if it had not been for him her son had lived and she, fond mother, had not taken the rash step which she did, but still I cannot think that she loved as my Betsy, my virtuous Alicia does, heaven knows how much she and I love, the tear of sorrow would not refrain from rolling down my cheek at the affecting scene in this play.[20]

At Rio Clark again determined not to go ashore and sat at his cabin window fishing. He feared a tropical fever that might widow Alicia, then again he would incur expense and perhaps—who knows?—fall into temptation. He must have been very bored, for he asked an officer off a Portuguese guard-boat to breakfast; "he came on board and drank only one dish of tea, he can neither speak French or English so we could not converse with one or the other but sat like posts".[21]

Clark eventually went ashore and had a small adventure in the best taste:

At a gentleman's house where I went in to rest myself and ask for a few oranges my tender beloved Alicia's picture swung out of my bosom when one of the ladies asked me what it was and begged me to let her see it, which I did on her father's promise that she should return it to me again, on my opening the case where all my treasure that I have here with me was, she said it was impossible that there could be so much beauty on earth, I told them that my Betsey was much more so than they had done in her picture, I was glad when it was safe in its little bag again for my heart fluttered all the while it was out of my hands like a little bird when the school boys are handling its young.[22]

(There is a miniature of Alicia Clark in the Mitchell Galleries which is probably the one her husband wore round his neck: it shows a very young, sweet, good-tempered but not memorable face.)

But all was not gold; going on shore one day, Clark's boat was caught in a squall, "very harrowing", and he caught a cold for which "the doctor ordered me some bark which I took a glass of before I went to bed"; he was also the victim of a practical joke. Major Ross told him that Phillip was opening and reading his letters from home, and in a rage Clark went aboard *Sirius* to demand his property, only to discover his mistake. He was infuriated again when Phillip took six of the best-behaved women convicts out of *Friendship* and exchanged them for six of *Charlotte's* black sheep, as a reward, presumably, for the latter ship's good record. Not a single punishment had been logged. Who would now do Lieutenant Clark's washing and mending?

Incidentally, it was Clark who initiated the rum trade which was to figure later so largely in Australian history. On 24th November he notes:

"Gave this afternoon a quart of rum to the boatswain and carpenter of the ship for the things they have done for me."[23] He was now busy making, or having made, a tea canister for Alicia.

From time to time Clark gives us a glimpse of the mess and the development there of barrack-room fever. His entry for 5th September reads

> Capt. M. [Meredith] and the doctor [Arndell] had some words about some wood the doctor told the Captain that he did not behave like a gentleman on which the Captain struck him, which the doctor did not return. I ordered them both to be quiet or I would confine them both so there the matter stands, have seen two friends fall out about a small piece of wood, so ends Wednesday night.[24]

When in port Lieutenant Faddy got very drunk and accused Clark of ungentlemanly conduct—the supreme insult in the officers' mess. Clark, incensed, demanded a court martial. Faddy, now sober and sick, pretended he remembered nothing; "but," says Clark, "I am not to be put off in that way". The quarrel was referred to Major Ross, who told them to settle it themselves. After an unofficial inquiry Faddy withdrew the words he did not remember. Clark was vindicated, but the atmosphere of the mess was not sweetened.

On a later date:

> The mess mates drew for something that could not be divided, there were three prizes and a blank and I was most lucky I drew the filtering stone, the doctor the mustard pot and Mr Faddy a rotten pumpkin, Capt. M. the blank. Capt. M. and Mr F. had some words again, Mr F. is the most selfish grumbling and bad hearted man I was ever shipmates with, I am glad he is going to leave our mess when we get to Botany. . . .[25]

In Cape Town Clark did not distinguish himself. He went ashore and bought two china basins for a shilling and, from a Dutch East Indiaman, a piece of nankeen "very fine for four shillings". He also bought two fowls as basis for a farming venture in New South Wales and was given some corn to plant there, a jar of sweetmeats, and a piece of ebony. An incident in port illustrated the stiffness of discipline in some directions whilst it was so lax in others. On 8th November "neither we marines have had, nor the convicts, anything to eat to-day, it blows too hard for a boat to live to send for any beef and soft bread and there is no order to give them any salt provisions".[26]

As the voyage progressed we hear less of Alicia and more about food. A religious streak also crops up, Clark objected to merrymaking on the Lord's day, and on 16th September he records: ". . . read the morning service and Psalms for the day, put clean sheets on my bed, hope that I will sleep well to-night".[27]

On 21st December Clark "wrote 8 prayers for the health and welfare of you my dear wife and sweet son, which I shall with the assistance of God repeat morning and evening before my rising from bed or going to it and hope in Almighty God that he will hear me".[28]

His mood sank lower and lower. "Dreamt of several things and cried very much in my sleep on account I thought two men had taken my beloved Alicia away." He was reduced to mending the holes in his tablecloth and had to have his old green coat "tailed again which is now the third time since I have been on board. It is now not much larger than a large waistcoat. . . ."[29] But it was food that really mattered:

Captain Walton killed his boar this afternoon and sent us a loin of it, I never lived so poor in my life as we do at this time, nothing every day except salt beef or salt pork, thank God that we have got some rice in the mess, otherwise I should starve for I don't like salt pork and beef every day, so ends Saturday evening.

On 25th November he repines: "For the first time in my life drinked my tea without sugar, which I intend to do all the voyage as my sugar begins to grow short, therefore will only drink tea and sugar now and then, after we get on shore on certain days." Again it is ". . . I am quite sick of salt beef and salt pork, but I must make the best of it."[30]

His reading depressed him, too. In December it was "the play of Jane Grey. Oh what a deep tragedy it is, poor Lady . . . I cannot rest, I wish that it was bedtime that I might have a hearty cry, that would ease the heavy load that at present is around my heart."[31]

The cold weather tried him sorely, it "being so cold that I have been obliged to put on a flannel waistcoat and in place of one pair of stockings, two pair, and obliged to keep my great coat on constantly all day".[32] His Christmas was doleful and on 25th December he exclaims: "Never was anybody so sick of the sea as I am." On New Year's Day: "It is now one o'clock and I am going to sit down to the poorest dinner ever I sat down to on New Year's Day, a piece of hard salt beef and a few musty pancakes."[33] Everything was getting very short, the ship had run out of oatmeal, there was no wood left and only a week's supply of coal. *Friendship* was still eight hundred miles from Botany Bay. At this darkest hour there was a flicker of light for Ralph Clark. "I killed one of the young pigs this afternoon, how I shall feast to-morrow, please God. I wish that you were here my beloved Betsey to have a piece of it for I know that you are as remarkably fond of pig as I am."[34] It was a flash in the pan. On 14th January Clark was hungrier than ever. "I wish that I had a piece of a goose, I would much rather sit down to it than the dinner which I am going to partake of to-day, pea soup and pork and rice pudding, I am quite tired of them all."[35]

His first sight of Australia did not cheer him. "It is very high land, I am glad that we have seen the land, I wish that I was going from it." He did not know then, either, that being ashore was going to make little difference to the commissariat.

Botany Bay proved disappointing. It was wide open to the sea and so gave little protection to shipping. The supply of fresh water which was ample for Cook's one ship, *Endeavour*, on investigation appeared far too scant for the needs of eleven ships and a permanent settlement. Sand dunes, swamps, scrub, low-lying land everywhere met the eye. No one to this day has found the "fine meadows" referred to by Cook.

The advance expedition with Phillip in *Supply* had arrived two days ahead of the rest of the Fleet, and in that time Phillip must have suffered all the bitterness of disillusionment. He knew that the place would not do. He had Cook's charts, but they did not offer much encouragement. There was an inlet a few miles to the north named Port Jackson by Cook, but it had not been entered and there was no particular reason to think that it would offer more amenities than Botany Bay. Farther north again was Broken Bay, another possibility. Phillip gave orders that neither stores nor convicts should be landed until he had made further investigations.

Lieutenant King, R.N., Phillip's friend, gives an account of the first landing.[36] That was on the afternoon of 18th January. The next day in the morning Phillip, King and three other officers set off with a party of sailors and Marines in three boats systematically to explore the north side of the bay. They had their midday meal ashore, the first Australian picnic, "ate our salt beef, and in a glass of porter drank ye healths of our friends in England".[37]

It was not a very cheerful picnic in the midsummer heat, with only the sparse shade of the strange trees and nothing to eat but the ration beef. The land seemed so incapable of producing any food that it was a wonder there was any life on it at all. The bush was another less fertile sea and they were becalmed upon it.

The aborigines provided the only relief from monotony and they, like the continent, were neither friendly nor hostile. They accepted the incongruous presents offered—beads and ribands and strips of baize—but were not impressed by them. A spear was thrown wide of the mark and an unloaded musket was let off. Phillip displayed his usual quiet courage.

> We relanded on Lance Point, and ye same body of natives appeared, brandishing their lances and defying us. However, we rowed close in shore, and ye Governor disembarked with some presents, which one of them came and received. Thus peace was re-established much to the satisfaction of all parties.[38]

Tench tells two charming little stories of his relations with the aborigines to which he even manages to impart a touch of elegance. They hold all the brightness that can be found in this unhappy journey's end.[39]

The next day Phillip and Hunter and a small party set out in ship's boats to explore the coast northward of Botany Bay, with Major Ross and his marines set to the thankless task of clearing Point Sutherland (so named for Forby Sutherland, one of Cook's seamen who was buried there), should the spot have to be used. Instead, Ross went exploring with Dr Arndell and Lieutenant Clark, "but did not see anything of the natives, after walking a great way, sat down to dinner with what we had brought with us when Arndell by accident ran the knife through his hand. I bound it up and stopped the blood."[40] Another not very successful picnic.

So far Botany Bay had only produced some fish and, living up to its first name, a stingray and everyone was disgruntled. Lieutenant Clark led all the rest. "I hope that the Commd. will find out a better place at Port Jackson for us to settle for if we are obliged to settle here at the place they intend there will not be a soul left in the course of a year."[41]

Phillip returned on the twenty-third with news that restored public confidence. As he was to write in his first dispatch to Lord Sydney: "We got into Port Jackson early in the afternoon and had the satisfaction of finding the finest harbour in the world, in which a thousand sail of the line may ride in the most perfect security."[42]

Security was hardly their first need—or was it? The next day a sailor looked up from his work to see two tall ships standing into the bay. Rumour went mad. England was at war and the enemy, having pursued them to the end of the earth, was about to attack. They were store-ships from home loaded down with all the necessities and luxuries they needed. Only Phillip guessed aright. It was the Comte de la Pérouse with his two ships *Boussole* and *Astrolabe*, sent out by Louis XVI in 1785 on a voyage of curiosity. The ships disappeared again, driven off by the wind, but just as the English party was departing for Port Jackson they made a successful entrance. They had only come for wood and water, La Pérouse explained. He had heard of the British expedition and expected to find a thriving settlement. Whether this was spoken with French politeness or equally French irony it is difficult to say. The two expeditions fraternized at a high level with great politeness. Phillip offered to send on La Pérouse's mail and the Comte punctiliously returned all the convicts who tried to desert to him. Small parties of officers tramped over the sand dunes to dine with the French and admire with some chagrin how well the Frenchmen were appointed, with three timekeepers to each ship, whilst the First Fleet only had one to serve eleven, and all the graceful living of a world now so far away. On 10th March La Pérouse sailed away to complete shipwreck in the New Hebrides, a fate that remained for many years a mystery.

Meanwhile at Port Jackson, on the shore of a cove named, as in duty bound, after Lord Sydney, about four miles up the harbour in a westerly direction, a permanent settlement was being sketched out. An unbiased spectator at the time would have believed La Pérouse was the one with the better chance of survival.

Sydney Cove was chosen because it afforded fresh water, the Tank Stream which for years was the settlement's main water supply, and because deep water right up to the shore enabled ships to unload without difficulty. Phillip had to make decisions quickly and to act on them at once. A working party under his personal supervision began to clear a camping place whilst *Sirius* shepherded the transports round from Botany Bay. In the first flush of the moment, not unmoved by the unexpected beauty of the harbour, David Collins, the Judge-Advocate-elect, described the creek

> . . . which stole silently along through a very thick wood, the stillness of which had then for the first time since the Creation, been interrupted by the rude sound of the labourer's axe and the downfall of its ancient inhabitants [trees not aboriginals]; a stillness and tranquillity which from that day were to give place to the voice of labour, the confusion of camps and towns, and "the busy hum of its new possessors".[43]

It is well to record the romantic mood, for it was very short-lived. It hardly appears again until the country was a paying proposition.

Collins goes on to describe the day we now celebrate as Australia Day.

> In the evening of this day (26th) the whole party that came round in the *Supply* were assembled at the point where they had first landed in the morning, and on which a flagstaff had been purposely erected, and an union jack displayed; when the marines fired several volleys, between which the Governor and the officers who accompanied him drank the healths of his Majesty and the Royal Family, and success to the new colony. The day, which had been uncommonly fine, concluded with the safe arrival of the *Sirius* and the convoy from Botany Bay thus terminating the voyage with the same good fortune that had from its commencement been so conspicuously their friend and companion.[44]

REFERENCE NOTES

[1] The Journals of King, Bradley, Bowes, and Clark are in the possession of the Mitchell Library; those of Southwell and Easty are in the Dixson Library.
[2] *Hist. Rec. N.S.W.*, vol. i, part 2, pp. 58-9. [3] Bowes's Journal.
[4] White, *Journal of a Voyage to New South Wales*, p. 11.
[5] *Ibid.*, p. 38. [6] Clark's Journal. [7] Bowes's Journal.
[8] *Ibid.* [9] Clark's Journal. [10] *Ibid.*, p. 71.
[11] D. Collins, *Account of the English Colony in New South Wales*, p. xxxvi.
[12] Bowes's Journal. [13] Clark's Journal, p. 1. [14] *Ibid.*, p. 16.
[15] *Ibid.*, p. 14. [16] *Ibid.*, pp. 19-23. [17] *Ibid.*
[18] *Ibid.*, p. 21. [19] *Ibid.*, pp. 23-7. [20] *Ibid.*
[21] *Ibid.*, p. 36. [22] *Ibid.*, p. 38. [23] *Ibid.*, pp. 65-6.
[24] *Ibid.*, p. 41. [25] *Ibid.*, p. 99. [26] *Ibid.*, p. 60.
[27] *Ibid.*, p. 44. [28] *Ibid.*, p. 73. [29] *Ibid.*, pp. 65-6.
[30] *Ibid.*, p. 47. [31] *Ibid.*, p. 69. [32] *Ibid.*, pp. 72-3.
[33] *Ibid.*, p. 76. [34] *Ibid.*, p. 77. [35] *Ibid.*, p. 80.
[36] *Hist. Rec. N.S.W.*, vol. ii, p. 539. [37] *Ibid.*, p. 540.
[38] *Ibid.*, p. 541. [39] W. Tench, *Narrative of the Expedition to Botany Bay*, pp. 55, 58.
[40] Clark's Journal, p. 83. [41] *Ibid.* [42] *Hist. Rec. Aust.*, ser. I, vol. i, p. 18.
[43] D. Collins, *Account of the English Colony in New South Wales*, p. 6. [44] *Ibid.*

CHAPTER V

TAKING SHAPE

THE NEW SETTLEMENT posed a number of problems. The first and most pressing was food. The country offered very little, the most useful being hauls of fish. These could not be relied on, sometimes they were plentiful, sometimes the nets came in empty. Despite everyone's hunger, Phillip insisted that the aborigines should have a share of the catch. If the fish belonged to anyone—except His Majesty, of course—it was theirs. The remainder went to feed the sick.

Kangaroos made good eating, but they were fast and shy. "When young the Kangaroo eats tender and very well flavoured, tasting like veal, but the old ones are more tough and stringy than bull beef," wrote Tench. The 8th February was a day to remember, Captain Shea shot the first of them. Another day to be remembered was when Phillip's "gamekeeper", or professional hunter, M'Entire, shot an emu seven feet two inches tall and the flesh was found to be "very well flavoured". Parrots and even crows were eaten, in stews or stuffed with the salt ration to give them flavour. But these pickings made very little difference. Everyone continued to eat salt beef and salt pork now nearly a year old. The weekly ration for everyone was 7 pounds of salt pork or 4 pounds of salt beef, 7 pounds of hard ship's biscuits, one pound of flour, 3 pints of peas, 6 ounces of butter. Women received two-thirds of this ration. The Marines in addition had an issue of spirits, this being laid down in army regulations. It was a crime to kill any of the stock without permission, as it was needed for breeding, but it was permissible to hunt in the bush for food so long as the convicts stayed near the camp. The only thing the bush yielded was a little vine which, when boiled, provided a herbal drink. The convicts were not allowed firearms and so could not bring down birds or animals.

Phillip knew only too well the delays of government and had little hope that any fresh stores would arrive soon. Farming was the answer, but it was so desperately slow. Much of the seed brought out had spoiled on the voyage and would not germinate. Some corn came up well, but withered away in the heat. The soil was an unknown quantity; the seasons were upside down; few in the colony knew anything about farming; tools were of the poorest quality, and broke easily or were deliberately lost by the convicts. There was not a plough in the settlement. The soil was poor and there was no way of manuring it. The trees were the greatest problem; they had to be felled and burnt on the spot, leaving the earth full of roots and stumps. Fruit-trees—oranges, lemons, limes, figs—flourished, but they were a long-time project.

The livestock strayed, were secretly killed and eaten, were struck by lightning or pulled down by dingoes. The hope of fresh meat from them receded.

In desperation, at the end of the first year, when nothing had come from England, Phillip sent *Sirius* to the Cape for provisions.

It was not until the middle of 1790 that any ship arrived from England. *Supply*, that tiny ship which was now the settlement's last hope, since *Sirius* had been wrecked on Norfolk Island, had sailed in April 1791 to Batavia for food. Lieutenant King went with her *en route* for London to plead the case of the colony and to carry Phillip's resignation.

The ration had gone down and down. It was now 2½ pounds of flour, 2 pounds of salt pork, one pint of peas and one pound of rice a week. Soon the peas gave out and there was no salt left except what was got from sea water. One of the surgeons has left a picture of these hungry days in his diary.

> It is now so long since we have heard from home that our clothes are worn threadbare. We begin to think the mother country has entirely forsaken us. As for shoes, my stock has been exhausted these six months and I have been obliged since that time to beg and borrow among the gentlemen, for no such article was to be bought. In this deplorable situation famine is staring us in the face. Two ounces of pork is the allowance of animal food for four and twenty hours, and happy is the man that can kill a rat or a crow to make him a dainty meal. We have raised some excellent vegetables but such food does not supply strength but keeps us lax and weakly. I dined most heartily the other day on a fine dog, and hope I shall again have an invitation to a similar repast. The animals that were meant to stock the country are almost all butchered. Hunger will be appeased while any eatable remains.[1]

A gleam of social life remained and Tench was the man to see it.

> If a lucky man, who had knocked down a dinner with his gun, or caught a fish by angling from the rocks, invited a neighbour to dine with him, the invitation always ran "bring your own bread". Even at the governor's table, this custom was constantly observed. Every man when he sat down pulled his bread out of his pocket, and laid it by his plate.[2]

Store-ships came with the Second Fleet, but since about a thousand convicts, many of them sick, came too the gain to the colony was small.

Shelter was another problem, but to begin with, since the weather was warm, not an acute one. The Governor had a prefabricated canvas house, costing £125. It was neither rain- nor wind-proof. The officers had marquees, the troops small tents, the convicts some condemned dockyard canvas and their own ingenuity. A hospital and storehouses were the first necessities, for now scurvy and dysentery had descended on the community with greater violence than at any time during the voyage. Phillip brought sailors ashore to help with the work. The sick must have fresh air and shelter; there were no blankets for them. A strong storehouse was very urgent because Phillip had to get the chartered ships away as quickly as possible. They were costing government money. To bring supplies ashore without adequate protection would be to beggar the colony in a night.

Phillip encouraged self-help. The convicts had to work part of the day for the Government, on piece work, the rest they would spend, it was hoped, in building themselves huts, planting vegetable gardens, and generally improving their situation. Garden Island, now the Naval Station, was given to the crew of *Sirius* to raise vegetables, and an enclosure was cleared and sown to supply the hospital. The Marines set to work to build themselves barracks. An observatory to house the valuable instruments with which the Astronomer Royal had entrusted Lieutenant Dawes was needed at once. Many public works had to be undertaken in a hurry, and the workers, through illness and unwillingness, were few.

Even the first Sydney was arranged to plan. The Marines were camped on the west side of the Tank Stream, the convicts on the east side. The hospital was on the waterfront of the west shore of the cove for the convenient landing of patients, Lieutenant Dawes was established on Observatory Hill. Government House was in the midst of the settlement, about where Macquarie Place now is, with huts, built by the sailors, near by for the more respectable women convicts. The east side of the cove (Fort Macquarie), was reserved for defence works and the storehouses, two establishments that were intimately connected. Reproductions of this plan can be seen in the Mitchell Library and it is obviously a workable one.

It was a flimsy little settlement to begin with. The convict huts, built from saplings driven into the ground with walls of wattle and clay and thatched roofs of cabbage-tree palm, were easily destroyed by fire, water, and time. Buildings of green wood cracked and crazed. By July bricks were being made, but as there were no beasts of burthen and no wheeled vehicles they had to be hauled to building sites by convict power. There was good building stone, but with brick and stone alike the same difficulty arose. There was no limestone for mortar. They had to be stuck together with clay and mud and the walls made very thick to support the weight of the roof. For over twenty years Government House was the only building of two storeys and boasted the only staircase.

Some confusion was inevitable at first. Tench has supplied the classical picture:

Business now sat on every brow and the scene, to an indifferent spectator, at leisure to contemplate it, would have been highly picturesque and amusing. In one place a party cutting down the woods; a second setting up a blacksmith's forge; a third dragging along a load of stores or provisions: here an officer pitching his marquee with a detachment of troops parading on one side of him and a cook's fire blazing upon the other. Through the unwearied diligence of those at the head of the different departments, regularity was, however, soon introduced and, as far as the unsettled state of matters would allow, confusion gave place to system.[3]

On 6th February, the day the women convicts were landed, notwithstanding all precautions and despite a violent thunderstorm, "scenes of Debauchery and Riot . . . ensued during the night". The ill-natured Surgeon Bowes remarks: "The anarchy and confusion which prevails throughout the camp and the Audacity of the Convicts both men and women is arrived to such a pitch as is not to be equalled I believe, by any set of Villains in any other spot upon the globe." Clark hoped piously that from such a den of iniquity he would be able to return unsmirched to his Alicia.

The land provided difficulties, its barrenness, its unnerving silence, the laborious task of clearing away the trees (only eight acres were cleared in the first year), its dryness, its ants and mosquitoes, but the most serious difficulties Phillip had to deal with, greater even than feeding his people, were the social problems inherent in such a community. Phillip believed that the settlement could be successful, even handicapped as it was, if everyone put out their maximum effort. It was reasonable to expect that they would, since survival depended on it. But no one, apparently, except Phillip himself and his naval officers, was reasonable. The Marines, led by Major Ross, were obstructionists. They had come out as soldiers and the one thing that was not needed was soldiering. During the voyage they had got on one another's nerves and on land it was even worse. They had no society but their own and they developed barrack-room fever. Quarrels were incessant. Through their commandant they refused to do any but ordinary garrison duty. If any of the rank and file helped with building or other works he had to be paid extra for it. They did not want to sink to the same level as the convicts, but there was no other society, no home life. Only the chaplain amongst the officers had been allowed to bring his wife, and only a small proportion of the Marines' wives were allowed to accompany their husbands. This disparity in the sexes was unhealthy. The Marines had not enough to do in a community that needed help from every member. Since Phillip could get no help from them he had to look to the convicts themselves for supervision of work and other positions of trust, a situation that had both good and bad results. The situation of the Marines, even if in the perspective of history it seems unworthy, was natural and pitiable enough. It affected their health and jaundiced their outlook. Captain Shea died of "a general decay", Lieutenant James Maxwell went out of his mind in the dark days of 1790, rowed himself about the harbour for two days, was rescued, but died on his way home to England. The quarrels between Major Ross and Captain Meredith reached such a pitch that the captain was sent home under arrest, only to be completely exonerated by a Court of Admiralty, the only one capable of dealing with such internecine strife.

In February 1790 Phillip in a dispatch to Lord Sydney summarized the tangled—not to say jangled—situation.

> Officers have been put under arrest by their commandant, and courts martial have been demanded, and which have likewise been requested by the officers in defence of their conduct, but no inquiry into the conduct of any individual above the rank of a non-commissioned officer can take place, and the consequences will be obvious to your Lordship, where so little harmony prevails between the Commandant and his officers. The strength of the detachment consists of only eighteen officers, one of whom is on duty at Norfolk Island, and a second has never done any duty since he was appointed by Major Ross; of the sixteen remaining for the duty of this settlement, five have been put under arrest by the commandant, and are only doing duty till a general court-martial can be assembled, in consequence of a sentence passed by them at a battalion court-martial, a sixth officer is suspended in consequence of a representation made by the corps of his unofficerlike behaviour, a seventh is suspended by his commandant for unofficerlike behaviour in taking a soldier who had been abused by a convict to make his complaint to the magistrates, without having first given information to his commandant; and both adjutant and quarter-master of the detachment have been equally under his displeasure, whilst the Judge-Advocate's conduct has been complained of by Major Ross, as commandant of the detachment, and as the Lieutenant-Governor, and the Judge-Advocate, in his turn, has represented his having been treated in such a manner by the Lieut. Governor and Captain Campbell, before convicts and others, that he wished to resign his office of Judge-Advocate; and Captain Hunter, who one day in the week, while the *Sirius* is in the harbour, assists the Judge-Advocate as a Justice of the Peace, thought himself treated on the same occasion so very improperly by the Lieutenant-Governor that he represented it to me, and desired to be excused from that weekly attendance as a magistrate; and had those two officers declined that duty I could not have replaced them, for though other officers have been appointed to act as civil magistrates I have found it necessary to avoid calling on them to act in that capacity.[4]

Any hornet's nest would have been an abode of love and peace by comparison with the Marines.

The convicts' situation was relatively less complicated. They had been brought to the country against their will, so it was hardly likely that they would display the zeal of the Pilgrim Fathers. They were an inert mass. Boredom and privation did not cure them of their moral failings, most lacked the intelligence and vitality to take advantage of the opportunities that the new life offered them. They stole as naturally as they breathed, but they had an excuse in hunger. Otherwise there was not as much crime as one would expect and most of the *al fresco* punishments were for "insolence" and similar offences that can only be a matter of opinion. Their resistance was generally passive. They ran away—"absconded" was the period term—though that got them quite literally nowhere. They lost their tools and sabotaged the work from which they would have benefited. The more ingenious ones created momentary excitement by bringing in tales of discoveries of rivers, precious stones, marble, or whatever they thought would be most popular. "At first," said Tench, "we harkened with avidity to such accounts but perpetual disappointments taught us to listen with caution and to believe from demonstration only." The most elaborate hoax was Daley's gold-mine. He even "salted" a mine with some scraps of gold and brass which he melted down.

Many thefts were committed but remained undetected by authority. The convicts stood by one another and even such great rewards as a bag of flour or a free pardon did not elicit information.

The aborigines were the last and least of Phillip's worries. It was not a matter of protecting the settlers from them but of protecting them from the settlers. He knew who were the aggressors and did his best to see justice done, to establish friendly relations, and to collect such information about them as might appeal to the intelligent curiosity of his masters at home.

His attitude towards them was benevolent but unscientific. What was anthropology to the Navy? He sought, by taking into his household such members of the tribe as he could catch, Arabanoo the noble savage, Colbee the wily savage, and Bennelong, to win their trust. He hoped to make of these boys ambassadors to their people, and by teaching them the outward habits of civilization to civilize them. He had little success, for the natives came less and less to the settlement. When finally he sailed for England he took Bennelong and Yem-mer-ra-wan-ine with him. Bennelong lived to return and to make his home (more or less) in the settlement as a privileged person. Bennelong Point, chosen for the National Opera House, is his memorial.

The manner in which Phillip coped with his difficulties is a lesson in government. The foundation of the matter was in his character and mind, but he also had a technique. Because of the clarity of his thinking and the steadfastness of his nature he could face his difficulties and accept the material he had to work with and not, as so many did, lament the unkindness of fate and put "should" in the place of "is". He kept his vision intact through four difficult years. He was no sentimentalist, but he believed in human endeavour as something that could conquer all difficulties. He believed this because he felt its truth in himself. In July 1788 he wrote his famous dispatch to Lord Sydney in which he spoke of "the little difficulties we have met with, which time, and additional force and proper people for cultivating the land will remove". He continued:

. . . your Lordship may be assured that anxious to render a very essential service to my country, by the establishment of a colony, which from its situation must hereafter be a valuable acquisition to Great Britain, no perseverance will be wanting on my part, and which consideration alone could make amends for the being surrounded by the most infamous of mankind, it is to your Lordship and to Nepean only that I make a declaration of this kind. . . . As to myself I am satisfied to remain as long as my services are wanted: I am serving my country and serving the cause of humanity.[5]

He gave complete loyalty to the terms of his commission and to his instructions, unless the circumstances on the spot made them obvious misfits. He was instructed to colonize Norfolk Island, so on 14th February he dispatched Lieutenant King there with a party of convicts and Marines and a commission as Lieutenant-Governor. He was to explore the coast and environs of the new settlement. This he did in a number of arduous expeditions, called by Ross "Parties of Pleasure", which he led himself, although ill. He was looking for more fertile land as well as gathering material for a report to the Home Office. He was to set the convicts to work at once for the public good, and this he was able to do because he sized up the situation at Sydney Cove quickly and intelligently and had a plan of work ready as soon as the convicts were disembarked. He was to grant land to emancipated convicts and "other free persons wanting to settle". He interpreted this as excluding those who held the King's commission. It was the will of the Home Government that he should found a peasant state of small holders. He did not depart from this. He realized that if he gave his officers land he would give them more power than was wholesome. The rank and file, on finishing their term of service, could have grants on slightly better terms than ex-convicts. He had been entrusted with wide powers, he had accepted the trust and for that reason he did not delegate them. The disaffected accused him of despotism. Because of his commission he never let public opinion—the often poisoned criticism of the men near him—affect his outlook or his actions.

Moving to his decisions quickly, Phillip knew how he should act in founding this difficult colony. He must establish morale as well as provide food and care. He must set up an ordered State and never let the settlement, whatever its hardships, degenerate into a confused scramble for survival. He had to find dignity where there was none.

His first formal act was to set up a flagstaff; his second, on 26th January 1788, to acknowledge his King with proper ceremony. On 7th February he inaugurated the State in the presence of the whole community. The convicts were brought to a cleared space early in the morning. The Marines marched in, their band playing, their colours paraded. Phillip arrived surrounded by his officers of state. The Judge-Advocate read aloud the Captain-General's commission, the Act of Parliament founding the Colony, and the Letters Patent setting up the Courts of Judicature. The Marines fired three salvos and Phillip made a speech. Tench, White, and Collins all gave a brief account of its substance, later biographers added some improbable prophetic flourishes; Midshipman Southwell claimed to report it verbatim and he could be nearest to the truth.

You have now been particularly inform'd of the nature of the laws by which you are to be gov'd, and also of the power with which I am invested to put them into full execution. There are amongst you, I am willing to believe, some who are not perfect'y abandon'd, and who, I hope and trust, will make the intend'd use of the g't indulgence and lenity their humane country has offer'd; but at the same time there are many, I am sorry to add, by far the great'r p't, who are inate villains and people of the m. abandon'd principles. To punish these shall be my constant care, and in this duty I ever will be indefatigable, however distress'g it may be to my feelings. Not to do so would be a piece of the m't cruel injustice to those who, as being the m't worthy, I have first nam'd; for shou'd I continue to pass by y'r enormity with an iljudged and ill-bestowed lenity, the consequence would be, to preserve the peace and safety of the settl't, some of the most deserving of you must suffer with the rest, who might otherways have shewn thems's orderly and useful members of our community. Therefore you have my sacred word of honor that whenever ye commit a fault you shall be punish'd, and m't severely. Lenity has been tried; to give it further trial would be vain. I am no stranger to the use you make of every indulgence. I speak of what comes under my particular observation; and again I add that a vigorous ex'n of the law (whatever it may cost my feeling) shall follow closely upon the heels of every offender.[6]

It must be remembered that the night before the convicts had thrown off all discipline in "scenes of Debauchery and Riot". It was necessary for Phillip to regain moral control, which he did on this impressive occasion. After his speech Phillip reviewed the troops and encouraged them. He and his officers then retired to a marquee to eat a "cold collation". Clark as usual supplied the earthy touch by remarking, "but the mutton which had been killed yesterday morning was full of maggots, nothing will keep in this country I find".[7]

On 11th February the first criminal court was held and three prisoners were convicted and given, for those days, mild doses of the lash. This was somewhat of an anticlimax after all the talk about abandoned criminals and perpetual crime that one reads in the diarists. The court had the appearance of a court martial because officers of the Navy or of the Marines were the only men available to sit with the Judge-Advocate. It was a civil court and applied the English codes. David Collins, the Judge-Advocate, was in a curious position. He was not versed in the law but his position and authority were made legal by the Letters Patent of 2nd April 1787. In criminal cases the Judge-Advocate sat with six officers, five having to be in agreement before an execution could be carried out. In the civil court only three sat on the bench. The Judge-Advocate ranked next in power to the Governor. His position would seem very peculiar today. He was president of both the criminal and civil courts. He prosecuted for the Crown, advised the prisoner on his defence, instructed the court in matters of law (he had copies of the English Statutes), and then voted with his colleagues on the verdict. He also had to do the secretarial work of the courts, take minutes and record verdicts. The Governor had the power to override both courts as, in theory, the King had in England, but here his power was more real.

Collins was a conscientious young man and justice was scrupulously done as far as he and Phillip could control it. There was a preconceived idea of discipline in both naval and military officers and they knew that they were dealing with already convicted criminals. Nevertheless punishments were not harsh by the standards of the day, and Marines and sailors were subjected to the same code as the convicts.

In April 1788 stealing was made, by order of the Governor, a hanging matter. It was, in the condition of the settlement, the most serious offence against society. Crimes that we would consider much worse were only punished by banishment to Norfolk Island. They were individual crimes and did not affect the general well-being. Early punishments, executions and floggings, were carried out with the greatest solemnity and publicity in the hope that they would prove a deterrent. Prisoners whom Phillip intended to reprieve were brought to the place of execution with halters round their necks to give them a salutary fright. If public need demanded severity it also demanded lenity. Men with special skills were too useful to be executed, no matter what their sins or how often committed. The superintendent of fishing was one of these. He was always in trouble, but he kept his job and his vertebrae intact. In meting out justice the settlement was more important than the individual and in that spirit it was done and everybody was satisfied, or as satisfied as anyone in that cantankerous community was likely to be, until the coming of the trained lawyers who had other ideas both about justice and the Governor's prerogatives.

The judicial arrangements, supported though they were by Act of Parliament, were to be after Phillip's time a constant source of trouble. David Collins accepted them, the legal men who came after him had other ideas.

On 12th February the Governor's commission and the other documents were read again with equal solemnity. Major Ross and Captain Collins were appointed justices of the peace and Lieutenant King was given his commission as Lieutenant-Governor of Norfolk Island. Nothing was hidden or kept secret, but it is doubtful if many understood what they heard, even the officers, for Clark commented: "I never heard of any one single person having so great a power vested in him as the Governor has by his Commissioners [*sic*]."[8]

Phillip knew the value of little ceremonies in keeping up the spirits and courage of the settlers. On 15th May it was laying the foundation stone of Government House with an inscribed copper plate let into it. On 4th June it was the King's birthday, on 12th August the Prince of Wales's. He also knew the value of "business as usual". Everything was done in an orderly way. When he made an appointment, and his first was on 26th January of a Provost-Marshal, it was drawn up in seemly and dignified terms and sealed with Phillip's private seal because the Great Seal of the Colony did not arrive until September 1791.

An even sharing of what there was to share, with protection for the weak and the sick, was another of Phillip's tenets. There was no privileged class. He himself drew only the same ration as everyone else, though he had a French chef to cook it. It must have broken the poor man's heart trying to lend elegance to salt pork that was two-thirds bone "and the remainder . . . was almost too far advanced in putrefaction for even hunger to get down" (according to Collins) and worm-eaten rice.

Unflaggingly Phillip fought the colony's battles with the Home Office. He kept its pressing needs before Lord Sydney. Firmly, persistently, respectfully, he asked for supplies of food, clothing, medicines, tools, stationery (for he reached a point at which there was not enough writing paper to carry on the business of the colony). He asked repeatedly for a few free settlers, say fifty families of farming people. Not only would they improve agriculture but they would leaven the substance of the population and improve morale. Above all, he entreated the Government to remove the fear, becoming widespread, that the colony was not only forgotten but intentionally abandoned. Against this fear even he could not maintain the morale of the settlement indefinitely.

He succeeded in his requests. *Guardian* had been sent loaded with most of the things he had asked for; it was ill fortune that she was wrecked. After the arrival of the transport *Lady Juliana* in July 1790 the colony was never again left in isolation. The Second Fleet brought its load of sick and dying convicts, its scanty stores, its problems, but it also brought news, letters, reassurance. The Home Government announced the policy of sending ships twice a year to Australia. With the arrival of *Gorgon*, man-of-war, on 8th September 1791, bringing provisions, livestock, garden seed, and the colony's seal (but no wax to impress it), the colony entered on a new era of relative prosperity. It believed in its own future; there were to be times of scarcity for years to come, but never again hopeless starvation. A small trickle of free settlers had been allowed to immigrate, there were now some overseers and supervisors, an established way of life was growing up.

Even in the dismal year 1790 Phillip had expressed his faith that "the settlement is now fixed" and he asked leave to be relieved of his commission. His health had broken down; he knew that it would be at least a year before he would receive permission to return to England, and he felt that by then his work would be done.

In March 1791 he was more confident. He wrote to Grenville, who had superseded Sydney at the Home Office: "The settlement is now so fully established that the great labour may be said to be passed; and it has, sir, been attained under every possible disadvantage, though it is not in that situation in which I should wish to leave it, for it is not independent for the necessaries of life. . . ."[9]

It was not until December 1792 that he sailed for home in *Atlantic*. He left a record of achievement behind him. The colony was founded and had survived starvation and every other distress of body and mind to which its isolation laid it open. It had come through a drought in 1791. So hot and parched was the country that at Rose Hill:

> An immense flight of bats [flying foxes?], driven before the wind, covered all the trees around the settlement, whence they every moment dropped dead, or in a dying state, unable longer to endure the burning state of the atmosphere. Nor did the *perroquettes*, though tropical birds, bear it better, the ground was strewed with them in the same condition as the bats.[10]

Crops failed; the Tank Stream gave anxiety, and the Surveyor-General deepened it; the struggling little farms were hard hit and the recorded temperature in Sydney rose to 105°F.

To survive was a positive achievement and to survival was added progress. A fairly flourishing satellite colony had been founded and maintained on Norfolk Island. A second centre had been established on the mainland, where the soil was better, Rose Hill, later called Parramatta after the river on which it stood. (This is reputed to be an aboriginal name meaning "The place where eels sit down".) Even in 1790, when Henry Edward Dodd, formerly Phillip's servant, was its uncrowned king, the place was flourishing and rivalled Sydney. Tench describes it in his *Complete Account of the Settlement at Port Jackson*.[11] There were 200 acres of cleared land, 55 under wheat, barley and oats, 30 under maize.

> Four inclosures of 20 acres each are planned for the reception of cattle. . . . In the centre of them is to be erected a house, for a person who will be fixed upon to take care of the cattle. All these inclosures are supplied with water; and only a part of the trees which grew in them being cut down, gives to them a very park-like and beautiful appearance. . . .

These enclosures became the Cumberland Park which Mrs Parker, who came out with her husband in *Gorgon*, was to admire, and which is today Parramatta Park.

Tench continues:

> The main street of the new town is already begun. It is to be a mile long, and of such breadth as will make Pall-Mall and Portland-Place "hide their diminished heads." It contains at present 32 houses completed, of 24 feet by 12 feet each, on a ground floor only, built of wattles plaistered with clay, and thatched. Each house is divided into two rooms, in one of which is a fire place and a brick chimney. These houses are designed for men only; and ten is the number of inhabitants allotted to each; but some of them now contain 12 or 14, for want of better accommodation. More are building; in a cross street stand nine houses for unmarried women; and exclusive of all these are several small huts where convict families of good character are allowed to reside. Of public buildings, besides the old wooden barrack and store, there is a house of lath and plaister, 44 feet long by 16 wide, for the governor . . . with excellent out-houses and appurtenances attached to it. A new brick store-house, covered with tiles, 100 feet long by 24 wide, is nearly completed, and a house for the store-keeper. The first stone of a barrack . . . to which are intended to be added wings for the officers, was laid to-day. The situation of the barrack is judicious, being close to the store-house, and within 150 yards of the wharf, where all boats from Sydney unload. To what I have already enumerated, must be added an excellent barn, a granary, an inclosed yard to rear stock in, a commodious blacksmith's shop, and a most wretched hospital, totally destitute of every conveniency.

This also gives some idea of how the community lived. The bachelor establishments were the rule, but a woman was generally allotted to each hut to keep it clean and to prepare the meals for the men. Other women were set to making clothes, but they were so indolent and careless that little good came of the enterprise.

Beyond Rose Hill there were other rudimentary settlements, at Toongabbie, Prospect Hill, and the Ponds. The last two were places of secondary punishment, that is of punishment for crimes committed after transportation. Forced labour there was dreaded more than the lash. George Thompson, a sailor in *Royal Admiral*, has left a very stark account of "Toongabby", which is preserved in the British Museum. The treatment there was brutal and brutalizing, the labour of clearing very hard, the working day long and the food sparse. "Many a one has died standing at the door of the storehouse waiting for his allowance of provisions, merely for want of sustenance and necessary food." They had neither beds nor bedding, nor any utensils save a small iron cooking pot each. It is possible that Thompson over-coloured the picture, but it is certain that the boredom of the place was devastating.[12]

During Phillip's governorship a road was made, sixteen miles long, between Sydney and Parramatta, usually referred to as the Path. It supplemented the water route up the Parramatta River, which was slow and laborious, for it took the Rose Hill Packet, alias "the Lump", two days and a night to reach the out-settlement from Sydney. It is true the night was spent by passengers ashore. The road brought the two settlements closer, but the more respectable citizens shook their heads. It offered too many opportunities for rogues to move from the hitherto safe distance of Parramatta to the town. This was the first road in Australia, and naturally a bad one.

Following his instructions, Phillip had granted land to such emancipated convicts and ex-soldiers as seemed likely to make a success of farming it. The first independent farmer was James Ruse, a convict who had worked out a seven-year sentence in August 1789. He married a well-behaved convict woman and they were given uncleared land at Rose Hill. This was an experiment. Ruse was given a convict to work for him for a time, he was supplied with tools, a hatchet, a tomahawk, two hoes, a spade, and a shovel, and he and his wife were fed and clothed by the Commissary until, in February 1791, Ruse declared himself self-supporting. From Tench, who visited his farm, we get a picture of the farming methods of this first settler, they were probably the common practice of the time.

On my wheat land I sowed three bushels of seed, the produce of this country, broad cast. I expect to reap about 12 or 13 bushels. I know nothing of the cultivation of maize, and cannot therefore guess so well at what I am likely to gather. I sowed part of my wheat in May, and part in June. That sown in May has thriven best. My maize I planted in the latter end of August, and the beginning of September. My land I prepared thus: having burnt the fallen timber off the ground, I dug in the ashes, and then hoed it up, never doing more than eight, or perhaps nine, rods in a day, by which means, it was not like the government-farm, just scratched over, but properly done; then I clod-moulded it, and dug in the grass and weeds:—this I think almost equal to ploughing. I then let it lie as long as I could, exposed to air and sun; and just before I sowed my seed, turned it all up afresh.—When I shall have reaped my crop, I purpose to hoe it again, and harrow it fine, and then sow it with turnip-seed, which will mellow and prepare it for next year.[13]

At the end of a year Ruse had eleven and a half acres in cultivation and had convicts working for him on the share-farming system; they cleared the land in their spare time and as payment had the first crop.

This first experiment was a success. There were three other free settlers, two sailors from *Sirius* with sixty acres each and a superintendent of convicts with 140 acres. The last, named Schaffer, was a good farmer who grew wheat, maize, vines, and tobacco.

From them Phillip was able to gather data for the settlement's first land policy. Its main features were: the land was granted in perpetuity provided the settler stayed on it and worked it for five years; he might not sell it in that time without permission; the public store would provide seed and a small selection of tools, such as had been allowed to Ruse, and would feed and clothe the settler and his family for eighteen months. The land was free for ten years, but after that the settler must pay a small quit rent to the Government.

At the end of 1791 there were 86 settlers, including those on Norfolk Island, 31 Marines, 11 sailors, 44 well-behaved ex-convicts, some better adapted to agriculture than others.

The Second Fleet brought out detailed instructions as to land grants. Ex-convicts were to have 30 acres if single, 50 if married, and 10 more for each child—the first baby bonus. Non-commissioned officers wishing to settle were to have 130 acres, privates 80 acres, both with the same additions for wives and children. Free settlers were to rank with non-commissioned officers. Phillip's ten years free of payment was reduced to five years, after which a shilling a year quit rent for every fifty acres would be demanded. Land grants could also be used as rewards for special services. Phillip was to see that the good lands and the river frontages were equably distributed and that Crown lands were reserved. The more convicts that were assigned to work for settlers the better, thought the Home Office.

A dispatch dated 16th October 1792 made a return of land under cultivation: 208½ acres of wheat, 24¼ acres of barley, 118½ acres of maize, half an acre of oats, 17¼ acres of vegetable garden, four acres under vines, an additional 100 acres cleared and ready for planting. This was the achievement of nearly five years. The Home Government could hardly have realized what it cost in effort. It was, at last and at least, something tangible.

As regards town lands, Phillip had other ideas. All town land, he thought, should remain the property of the Crown and only be leased under strictly binding regulations. In this way he hoped to control the development of towns and avoid the evils, such as slums, that attended them overseas. It was not to be as he hoped.

Settlers meant a market, for the Australian land was not versatile enough to lend itself to subsistence farming. So it fell to Phillip to initiate private trade. Settlers might bring their produce to the public store and receive a standard price for it. Settlers might also trade amongst themselves and markets were set up in Sydney and Parramatta. There was some difficulty in arriving at the standard price, since there was no outside competition. The Home Government had not expected the colony to need currency, so none was provided. Most trading was in the nature of barter. When money did appear in the colony it was generally the Spanish dollar, and Phillip had to intervene and stabilize its value at 5s.

Theoretically no convict might own property, either real or personal, but they had ways of earning and acquiring it. One example of this was the convict, who, found guilty of buying goods from a soldier, was offered the alternative of imprisonment or a fine of £5. He paid the fine, a considerable sum in those days.

External trade began. The masters of transports brought out goods for sale and set up shops whilst they were in port. Phillip did not approve, for were not the ships hired by the Government and should they not use all the space in them for government goods? The masters put up a good argument and the needs of the colony were so great that the Governor gave his permission for selling. There was evidently enough money in the colony to buy unless the prices were too avaricious.

For example, *Royal Admiral* sold £3600 worth of goods privately in the colony and left another £750 worth to be disposed of on commission. Whilst she was in port shops were opened at Sydney and Parramatta. From *Pitt* the Commissary bought £4000 worth of goods and Phillip wrote home protesting against the trade. Following a well-known economic law, ribands and fancy millinery were taking precedence over necessities.

An American brigantine, *Philadelphia*, the first foreigner to enter Port Jackson, arrived on 1st November 1792 with a cargo of beef, wine, gin, tobacco, pitch, and tar. Phillip spent £2829 on behalf of the Government, the officers purchased the rest of the cargo, and Phillip then hired the ship for £50 to make a voyage to Norfolk Island. This was in contradiction of his instructions and the Navigation Acts, but he could plead necessity.

Whaling had begun off the coast, prosecuted chiefly by Americans. The ships brought profit to the colony when it was able to water and victual them, but it offered an easy means of escape to the convicts and posed to the Governor what amounted to the first international problem. Ships in need must be assisted whatever the law, but was this trade becoming so regular that it was illegal?

Government was carried on mainly by orders issued as necessary by Phillip. As society grew more complex more and more regulations had to be made. Provision was made for orphan children or those whose parents were too disreputable to have charge of them. A constabulary, composed of convicts, of course, was formed to guard the settlement at night. In a dispatch Phillip related the story of this innovation and its consequences:

> The watch consisted of twelve convicts. They assembled immediately after the tap-too had beat, and patroll'd during the night. No complaint was ever made of them. They were particularly cautioned against having any dispute with a soldier or sailor. . . . Soldiers and sailors, when stopped by the watch, were left at the guard house till the next morning, when, if nothing criminal was laid to their charge, they were delivered to their proper officers. But a soldier being one night stopped by the watch in the convicts' camp and delivered, as usual, to the guard, Major Ross, the next morning, sent the adjutant to tell the Judge-Advocate (under whose direction I had placed the night-watch), "that

he considered a soldier being stopped, when not committing any unlawful act, as an insult offered to the corps, and that they would not suffer themselves to be treated in that manner, or be controuled by the convicts, while they had bayonets in their hands." (Here I must beg leave to observe to your Lordship that the last sentence, respecting the bayonets, was never mentioned to me till after this business was settled, for if it had I should not have been induced to have withdrawn the order, which directed the night-watch to stop a soldier, by so pointed a menace, for I should not have thought it could tend to the good of his Majesty's Service.)[14]

Captain Tench comments (lest you think that everything in the garden was lovely): "Nightly depredations became less frequent and alarming: the petty villains, at least, were restrained by it. And to keep even a garden unravaged was now become a subject of the deepest concern."[15]

All stock had to be penned at night for they, too, were hungry and robbed the gardens. A fine was imposed on owners for letting them run loose. And so on, in order to stop every leak . . . but still hunger found a way if villainy did not.

During the first five years population had increased greatly. The Second Fleet set out with forty-six military passengers accompanied by seven wives and eight children, about a thousand convicts with three wives, six children and one passenger, or about 1085 souls. So many died on the voyage or soon after that these figures are very shaky, nor do they take into account the women convicts who arrived in the *Lady Juliana*. The Third Fleet brought about 1900. Births, we are given to understand, outnumbered deaths in the colony but no accurate records were kept.

According to the *Official Year Book of New South Wales* (p. 223) the population in 1788 numbered 1024, in 1790 2800 and in 1795 4500. These figures are dependent on the periodical musters and no one would dare vouch for their accuracy.

Phillip encouraged marriage both by precept and by offering extra land to married settlers. The Government had given passages to the wives of some convicts. Others had married, sometimes bigamously, in the colony. Family life was taking slow root and existence was becoming more diverse, less boring and stark.

The first dramatic performance, on 4th June 1789 (the King's birthday), was Farquhar's comedy *The Recruiting Officer*. It had an all-convict cast and was put on as a benefit performance to help the wife and children of a soldier who had been drowned. The theatre was a barn decorated with coloured paper and lit by candles, with oil-lamps for footlights. About sixty people thronged to see it and the entrance money was in kind. David Collins in his *Account of the English Colony in New South Wales* (p. 70) notices the occasion and remarks of the actors: "They professed no higher aim than humbly to excite a smile, and their efforts to please were not unattended with applause." Officialdom did not encourage a repetition, it might be subversive of good order.

Dinners at Government House, hunting parties, a little music from Lieutenant Dawes's piano, gambling, drinking, and quarrelling were the entertainments of the upper class, and for the lower orders thieving would appear to have been the main diversion, together with the even more dangerous one of "absconding".

The colony by now had such a good name that, wonder of wonders, a quartermaster and six sailors deserted from *Royal Admiral* and were not discovered until after she had sailed. The sailors were given the hard job of rowing the longboat to and from Parramatta until they could be deported. No one was allowed to enter the colony without permission, foreshadowing later immigration laws. That they should want to stay is the interesting point.

The white men had moved into Australia and, like a burr in a sheep's fleece, they meant to stay.

These early years are of particular interest and significance. In them was laid the foundations of much that was to follow. The habit of looking to the Government for everything, whilst adopting an attitude of critical hostility, began then. The nature of the country with its great distances was to encourage the former habit and an infiltration of rebels was to keep alive the latter. Practicability at home and a doctrinaire attitude from overseas were characteristics of this first period, and how could it be otherwise when no one outside Australia knew anything about it and those on the spot had to tackle their problems empirically? The Welfare State was foreshadowed. Questions of land and justice had been raised. Pioneering, if reluctantly, had begun.

REFERENCE NOTES

1 *Hist. Rec. N.S.W.*, vol. ii, p. 770.
2 W. Tench, *Complete Account of the Settlement at Port Jackson*, p. 42.
3 W. Tench, *Narrative of the Expedition to Botany Bay*, p. 60.
4 *Hist. Rec. Aust.*, ser. I, vol. i, p. 137.
5 *Ibid.*, p. 67.
6 *Hist. Rec. N.S.W.*, vol. ii, p. 665.
7 Clark's Journal, p. 87.
8 *Ibid.*
9 *Hist. Rec. Aust.*, ser. I, vol. i, p. 262.
10 W. Tench, *Complete Account of the Settlement at Port Jackson*, p. 166.
11 *Ibid.*, pp. 75-9.
12 *Hist. Rec. N.S.W.*, vol. ii, pp. 794-6.
13 W. Tench, *Complete Account of the Settlement at Port Jackson*, pp. 80-1.
14 *Hist. Rec. Aust.*, ser. I, vol. i, pp. 134-5.
15 W. Tench, *Complete Account of the Settlement at Port Jackson*, p. 33.

CHAPTER VI

THE CORPS AND THE GOVERNORS

I. MILITARY RULE, 1792-5

THE DEPARTURE OF Governor Phillip meant, to use the words of Eris O'Brien, the "end of the national experiment in co-operative living". The last of the Marines sailed with him. Compared to the New South Wales Corps, which replaced them, they seem like old friends. The Marines were withdrawn because of their quarrelsomeness and their obstructive behaviour, but there had been able and well-disposed men amongst the officers, and Phillip had on several occasions praised the rank and file for their devotion to duty. The new Corps, raised when England was on the brink of war with France, was made up of the riff-raff of the Army, men who had been in trouble, even mutineers, who were misfits or so useless that their regiments wanted to be rid of them; the officers were either as unsuccessful as those they commanded or were anxious to leave England for some personal reason, such as debt. They lacked the tradition and *esprit de corps* of a regiment, being brought together at the last moment, and were the worst conceivable type of military guard for a penal settlement. Even before his departure Phillip had a sample of their mettle. He discovered that a ship, *Britannia*, ostensibly on her way to New Zealand, had been secretly chartered by the officers of the Corps for a private trading venture. This was in October 1792. Phillip was immediately suspicious and the Commandant, Major Grose, in a letter of explanation did little to quiet his fears, only made it more difficult for him to scotch what instinct told him would be a breach of discipline. Grose wrote:

> The situation of the soldiers under my command who at this time have scarcely shoes to their feet, and who have no other comforts than the reduced and unwholesome rations served from the stores, has induced me to assemble the Captains of my Corps for the purpose of consulting what could be done for their relief and accommodation. Amongst us we have raised a sufficient sum to take up the *Britannia* and as all money matters are already settled with the master, who is also an owner, I have now to request you will assist us to escape the miseries of that precarious existence we have hitherto been so constantly exposed to.[1]

To which Phillip answered acidly, "I cannot acquiesce with you in thinking that the ration served from the public stores is unwholesome; I see it daily at my own table", and he systematically disproved the other complaints. He reported the matter Home with the remark: "... I wished to prevent what may be supposed to affect the interest of the East India Company by opening a door to contraband trade . . .".

This was not an episode, it was the beginning of a monopolistic private enterprise that was to have a very bad effect on the colony and to set the tone for the next seventeen years until Governor Macquarie, backed by his own regiment, reshaped the settlement. Eleven officers between them put up £2000 for this first trading venture. The cargo brought back from the Cape of Good Hope by *Britannia* was not used to alleviate the sufferings of their men but to line their own pockets.

It was unfortunate that John Hunter was out of the colony on other service when Phillip surrendered his government. Had he been on the spot his dormant commission, overriding the powers of the commandant, would have made him acting Governor instead of Francis Grose, and three disastrous years of military rule would have been avoided.

Major Grose was very much under the influence of his officers, especially as they numbered amongst them one man of great drive and determination. Their influence was far stronger than that of the Imperial Government, 16,000 miles away, at war and passably indifferent. He confessed his own timidity in a dispatch to Dundas at the Home Office: ". . . I cannot but be alarmed at all I purchase and everything I do, being unaccustomed to business and fearful of acting from my own discretion."[2] Nevertheless he could show the Home Office the kind of results it liked and gloze over his own disobedience.

Within a month of Phillip's departure he had changed the whole tenor of the colony. Equality of ration was at once abolished in favour of the military. More serious still, he transferred the powers of the five civil magistrates in the colony into the hands of his officers. He issued an order "that all inquiries by the civil magistrate were in future to be dispensed with" until he remodelled the system and that he himself would undertake the punishment of all convicts. This amounted to substituting summary for legal punishment. His captains serving at Sydney and at Parramatta he elevated into petty tyrants.

It played into the hand of the Corps that shortly after Grose took power he received instructions from England to grant land, 100 acres, to officers and a relative parcel to non-commissioned officers. This was well intentioned, as it was hoped that with the assigned labour of two convicts each, supported by the Government for two years, the officers would help to open up the country, and it was indeed laid down that the land must be granted in such districts as would repay orderly settlement. There was, I think, another motive, one of those dexterous economies so often practised. When the officer

By courtesy of the Trustees

VISCOUNT SYDNEY

From the portrait by Gilbert Stuart in the Dixson Gallery, Sydney

WILLIAM BLIGH

From a portrait by J. A. Russell, R.A., in the possession of W. Bligh Nutting Esq.

left the colony he was free to sell his land, and that would serve instead of the money grants or pensions so often solicited for men retiring from, or invalided out of, the service.

The instruction was put into practice immediately and Grose reported to Dundas on 16th February 1793 that he had distributed grants to his officers:

Which, with great spirit, they, at their own expense, are clearing. Whether their efforts result from the novelty of the business, or the advantages they promise themselves, I cannot say, but their exertions are really astonishing, and I absolutely expect, if they continue as they begin, that in the space of six months the officers will have a track [*sic*] in cultivation more than equal to a third of all that has ever been cleared in the colony. As I am aware they are at this time the only description of settlers on whom reliance can be placed, I shall encourage their persuit as much as is in my power.[3]

Where the officers' "own expense" arose I, in turn, cannot say. The land was free for ten years and then only subject to a token quit rent, and even that the present holders would not be likely to have to meet. Not two convict labourers fed and clothed from the public store, but ten or more, were allowed to officers. So they had their labour for nothing. The only source of tools was the public store, and I have discovered no records of sales of them to the gentleman farmers, so no doubt they were supplied as to other types of settlers. Stock they had an opportunity of getting very cheaply. Grose to Dundas 9th January 1793:

I am much plagued with the people who became settlers, and who have evidently no other view than the purpose of raising a sufficient supply to pay their passages to England; and although Governor Phillip whilst here did everything in his power for their accommodation and assistance, they still persist in disposing of their stock; and a large flock of sheep which the Governor on his departure divided amongst them were, almost as soon as given, offered for sale; and I was absolutely obliged to encourage and promote the purchase of them by officers, dreading that, without this precaution the dissipation of a week would exterminate a stock that had been the work of years to collect.[4]

There is here and elsewhere an underlying note of scorn for Phillip. Eventually Grose received a mild reprimand for allowing the stock to be bought. He should, he was told, have prevented valuable breeding animals being turned into mutton by confiscating them for the Government. He had a legal right to do so if the settlers had not fulfilled their undertaking to farm for five years. It was by that time too late to do anything about it.

The officer-farmers had no difficulty or expense in marketing their produce. Phillip, to encourage settlers, had already arranged that their surplus grain would be bought by the Commissary. The officers had control of the public stores and so a priority of sale. The Commissary could and did safeguard their monopoly by opening and closing the store for their convenience, buying their grain and refusing that of the small settler so that he was forced to sell at a low price or to barter it away for rum. It was given in evidence at an inquiry instituted by Governor Hunter that "agents used to wait outside the stores and 'persuade' them to part with their grain in exchange for rum".

A ring of officers gave themselves a monopoly of the right to purchase all speculative cargoes brought into port. There was no longer any quibbling over the right of masters to bring out goods for their own profit or as to the welcome offered to foreign ships, generally Americans, who came in with trade goods. Although the Home Government still prohibited intercourse with foreigners, and although Australia was in the sphere of the East India Company, Grose could always plead necessity, as Phillip had done when buying from the American ship *Philadelphia*. Masters soon learnt that rum was the most welcome cargo, but unless they sold at a compromise price they could not sell at all but must take their goods elsewhere. The officers could sell the most desired commodities, rum, tobacco, sugar, at high prices making forty or fifty per cent or more profit. It would be a pity to spoil such splendid trade by excluding the most numerous customers, the convicts. It was against all discipline and instructions to sell anything to or to buy anything from convicts, or to let them have spirits on any condition. It was now sold to those convicts who could afford to pay for it or given to them in return for services.

For the moment at least everyone was pleased. The officers and their families were highly delighted. John Macarthur, writing to his brother, said:

> The changes that we have undergone since the departure of Governor Phillip are so great and extraordinary that to recite them all might create some suspicion of their truth. From a state of disponding poverty and threatened famine that this Settlement should be raised to its present aspect in so short a time is scarcely credible.

His wife, writing to Miss Kingdon in September 1795, remarked, amid family gossip:

> The officers in the Colony, with a few others possessed of money or credit in England, unite together and purchase the cargoes of such vessels as repair to this country from various quarters. Two or more are chosen from the number to bargain for the cargo offered for sale, which is then divided amongst them, in proportion to the amount of their subscriptions. This arrangement prevents monopoly, and the impositions that would be otherwise practiced by masters of ships. These details which may seem prolix are necessary to show you the mode in which we are in our infant condition compelled to proceed.

In another passage she remarks: "This country possesses numerous advantages to persons holding appointments under Government."[5]

These words may sound naive now in the light of history, but this intelligent woman was quite sincere in believing that the colony had benefited under the new régime and she certainly had no sense of guilt. Every man had a legitimate right to seek his own prosperity in the circumstances in which he found himself.

Her husband by his energy and address was doing well, the doubts that her family had entertained when she married him were amply disproved. He was the good provider, she his loyal wife and helpmate. It would not occur to her that the success of the officer class was founded on robbery and disobedience of the rankest kind. The officers drew their army pay, but they used their time to trade and to farm and their position of authority to monopolize trade, both buying and selling, robbing the Government, robbing the prisoners in their charge and the small holders whose welfare was part of their duty. Safe under cover of distance and England's preoccupation with the French war, they broke every rule of the colony and of their service.

Most of their critics were perforce silent, but the Governors did not hesitate to speak their minds about the officers' conduct and particularly of their leader in enterprise, John Macarthur. King was not slow to note that "Captain McArthur was £500 in debt when he left England but by 1801 he was said to have a fortune of £20,000".[6] All the early Governors quarrelled sooner or later with Macarthur, for he stood in the path of the reforms they hoped to make, but it should be recorded of him that, unlike some of his brother officers, he did not overstep the regulations governing convict labour and, self-seeking as he must have been, he was also a great benefactor to the colony when, with energy and foresight, he fostered the wool industry. Had his temper not been so fiery and his partisan spirit so marked, he might not have come in for as much criticism as he did. He was always confident of his own rectitude.

The Home Government was at first pleased by what appeared to be an improvement in the colony. Grose wrote smooth dispatches—for any irregularities he could plead necessity, the Home Office was used to such a cry—and he kept official statistics in a respectable state. From his returns and those of his successor, Colonel Paterson, land grants appeared very modest. Grose, on paper, granted 10,674 acres and Paterson 4965. These figures were not at all startling; with the expiration of convicts' sentences, which would year by year become more numerous, and with the new order allowing grants to officers and N.C.Os whilst still in the service, they were about what one would expect. What Grose did not disclose was that officers were receiving more than the hundred acres permitted, and were forcing settlers off the land by depriving them of markets and discouraging them in other ways. This did not apply to the misfits only, or Tench's "gentleman of *no trade* (his own words to me) [who] will, I apprehend, at the conclusion of the time when victualling from the store is to cease, have the honour of returning to drag a timber or brick cart, for his maintenance", or the attorney's clerk who found "cultivating his own land, not half so easy a task, as he formerly found that of stringing together volumes of tautology to encumber, or convey away that of his neighbour".[7] Some of them were sober, hard-working men, as Hunter's inquiries were to show later. The downpour of rum also helped to make dissolute, and so fair game, men who with encouragement and discipline might have become self-supporting settlers.

Nor did Grose report that land was being granted without system and that areas of Crown land were not being reserved near the towns as ordered. Officers selected without survey as a later generation of land-hungry men was to do. They took the best they could find either in the country or in the settlements. Grose's generosity is to blame for the narrow crooked streets of Sydney, they had to find their way as best they could round plots that had been taken up. No government rule ever allowed convicts to become settlers whilst they were still serving their sentences. Some of them were now put on the land with no better authority than a note of hand from one of the officers saying that they had permission. It is not difficult to believe that these irregular settlers were in reality adding to their patron's estates or in some other way working for him. The situation has some resemblance to conditions prevailing in Europe at the time of the break-up of the Roman Empire, when poor men surrendered their lands to richer and more powerful neighbours. A short-lived manorial system was growing up in Australia. There were manors even on the outskirts of Sydney. It was during this period that Commissary Palmer built up his property at Woolloomooloo. Inside a triple barricade of wall, ditch, and sweetbrier hedge, he set workshops, gardens, orchard, even a family vault. It was a little world of its own. Captain Harris of the Corps built Ultimo House in the part of the city that still carries its name, and there he had a deer park with two hundred spotted deer. Other men, amongst them John Piper, who came out as an ensign in 1792, carried on in the grand style until bankruptcy eclipsed them. A fragmentary and astonishingly luxurious plantation state existed. All the possible riches of this primitive world were concentrated in the hands of a few, and this was something that the Imperial Government had never envisaged when it set up a remote penal settlement with a possible peasant state as its aftermath to keep time-expired men from returning home.

Dundas, who was now in Lord Sydney's office, in a dispatch dated 31st June 1793, re-enunciated his instructions as to the granting of land and control of the traffic in spirits. Grose replied: "The orders relating to all future grants of land will be obeyed." He had by this time done most of his damage, for in May 1794 he asked for leave of absence on account of trouble he was having with old wounds. In December 1794 he left the country, and Captain Hunter was already named the second Governor. He arrived in September 1795 and in the interim Captain William Paterson allowed things to flow as they would.

Convicts on the whole preferred the military régime. Public farming, which they disliked intensely, came almost to a standstill. Instead, they were brought to Sydney and set to work on new barracks and they found their daily life more entertaining than at Toongabbie; or they were distributed as servants to private masters. This was a gamble. They might be treated well and "indulged" with tea, sugar, and tobacco, or, with a harsh master, they might be worse off than in the gangs. Discipline was in general relaxed, rum was plentiful and could be had at a price in service, usefulness, or money.

Spirits—and any spirit was called "rum"—were not only imported by the Corps, but stills, by courtesy called illicit, were busy turning wheat into rum at the rate of five quarts from each bushel. This sold, according to David Collins, or was bartered, at the rate of five or six shillings a quart when wheat bought in the market cost eight shillings a bushel. More magnificently, a gallon of home brew that cost 7s. 6d. to make could sometimes be sold for as much as £8.

The punishment motif had been replaced in high places by a consuming desire for profit. Justice was also relaxed and it was now thought quite in order for a master to punish his own assigned servants. From the convicts' angle much more was to be gained now by "sucking up" to the military. A man who played his cards well could be as good as free, or better.

It was hardly to be expected that the convicts should worry much over their increasing drunkenness and degeneracy, or over the scant attention Major Grose or his officers paid to religion.

Grose was on bad terms with the chaplain, the Reverend Richard Johnson, and in an unequal battle, heaped slights upon him. The chaplain was forced to hold services at six in the morning and in the short time allowed him was interrupted by the clatter of the convicts' guard. Gambling and drinking was allowed on Sundays under his very eyes. He had reproached Phillip for not putting a church on the list of buildings most urgently required, now he saw no likelihood of a church's ever being built. So he set to work to build one himself. He paid for material and work out of his own pocket, sometimes rewarding his helpers with rum. When the building was completed the bill was sent to Grose, it was for £67 12s. 11½d., to which in fairness to himself Johnson added another threepence. Grose was indignant and, on sending the bill to the Treasury, commented:

> His charge for this church is infinitely more than it ought to have cost, and his attempt to make a charge at all surprises me exceedingly: for on his applica-

tions to myself for a variety of little articles with which he has been furnished from the stores, he has invariably stated that as he was building this church at his own expense he hoped to be obliged, and on this account generally was accommodated with whatever he came to ask.[8]

So introduced, the bill was not paid by the Treasury. It was not until 1797 that Johnson was refunded the money. A year later the church was wilfully burnt down by convicts to escape Hunter's insistence on religious observance.

In April 1794 Grose was again complaining of Johnson in his dispatches. "I . . . have not always received the most grateful return, and was it not in pity to a large family I should represent the disorderly behaviour of the Rev. Mr Johnson, from whom I have received treatment very unbecoming his character as a clergyman to offer, and not very consistent with my situation to put up with."[9] Quarrels between officers were endemic but this was a particularly unfortunate one as it brought into disrepute one of the few elements in the colony that stood firmly for morality.

The people who suffered most from the military interregnum were the very class that the Government at home was most eager to foster, the settlers. They were being slowly squeezed dry of hope, just at the time when the rich river flats of the Hawkesbury were being opened to cultivation. Grose wrote in a dispatch (29th April 1794): "I have settled on the banks of the Hawkesbury 22 settlers who seem very much pleased with their farms. They describe the soil as particularly rich, and they inform me whatever they have planted has grown in the greatest luxuriance."[10]

The settlers had no redress. It was useless to complain to the Lieutenant-Governor and any appeal to the King would have had to go through him and would, of course, have been discredited, like Johnson's church.

Grose made a formidable enemy in Lieutenant King, who was still Lieutenant-Governor on Norfolk Island and making a success of it. By 1794 he was able to report the island self-supporting except for salt meat. This was just as well, for Grose left him a year without sending a ship to the island. This, however, was not the reason of the quarrel between them. It had other causes. King was dependent on the Corps for his guard. He found the soldiers sent unruly and troublesome. They assaulted free settlers. King's protests were so badly received on the mainland that he knew he would get no support from the Commandant. He took strong action, disarmed all the soldiers on the island, and sent them back to Sydney. He raised a guard of ex-marines and trustworthy settlers on the island. The delicate military pride of the Corps was irretrievably offended.

A second quarrel arose from King's interference with the officers' monopoly, an equally delicate subject. As harvests had been good on the island, King, following instructions, sent a cargo of grain to the mainland on the understanding that it would be bought by the Commissary. The colony was in need as usual, and Grose was sending to India for grain, but he refused to buy the cargo from Norfolk Island on the grounds that it would interfere with private enterprise. This, if nothing else, opened King's eyes to the real situation on the mainland.

King was a trusted officer and a personal friend of Phillip. He knew the colony and the manner in which Phillip had governed it in accordance with his instructions. He may have given Grose an uneasy feeling that distance was not quite such a good cover as he expected, and have prompted his retirement from the honourable reason of "old wounds".

Grose went, the Corps remained.

Apart from a revolution, not much happened in the three years between Phillip and Hunter. Four hundred and five convicts were sent out, most of them from Ireland, and they arrived in good health, for the Government had learnt the shocking lessons of the Second and Third Fleets. Transport of convicts was no longer left to be merely an occasion of profit for shipowners. A naval surgeon sailed in each ship to care for the health and the master received a bonus for every convict landed in health. It became good business to keep them alive and well. The changes were remarkable, though there could still be disastrous voyages, as, for instance, that of *Hillsborough*, which, setting out in 1799 with 300 convicts, lost 95 during the voyage and six after landing. The cause was typhus, which was already amongst the prisoners when they sailed.

Famine was still just round the corner. The corn crop "which once flattered us with the most luxuriant appearance, has, for want of timely rain, been parched and withered to almost nothing, and instead of the twenty bushels an acre which were expected, we must content ourselves with six".[11]

The cry is as of yore for tools and utensils. "If five hundred mills and a thousand pots were sent in the first ship, they will do away more distress than can be conceived."[12] This is a reminder that convicts, when issued with a ration, often had to grind their own flour. It could take half the night in the trumpery handmills issued. Not to have a handmill was to have no bread. In the same dispatch of 30th May 1793: "Tools are so much wanted that until the small supply we got in the *Daedalus* we had not an axe, and at this time we have not a cross-cutting saw in the stores."[13]

Two Spanish ships came into port on 13th March 1793 and stayed a month, receiving "every compliment and attention".

Some free settlers arrived and were granted land at Liberty Plains. Mr Boston arrived to cure fish and make salt, Samuel Marsden arrived as assistant Chaplain. The "Scottish Martyrs", political prisoners, began to arrive in 1794 and their luggage was searched for seditious literature.

The old guard were leaving: Surgeon Arndell retired on a pension of

£50 a year, Judge-Advocate Collins received permission to return to England, and Richard Atkins, a lesser man, took his place. Surgeon White was only waiting for relief to come before he, too, returned home.

The civil estimates for the year from October 1792 to October 1793 were £4657 18s. 0½d. and, of course, the difficulty of paying salaries of civil officers, whilst there was no coin in the colony, remained.

II. Governor John Hunter, 1795-1800

Hunter, who had always had the expectation of governing the colony, arrived in 1795. He was fifty-seven years old, "a pleasant, sensible old man", and had had no experience of administering a penal settlement such as his successor, Philip Gidley King had gained at Norfolk Island. He was too old and too mild for the difficult task set him. Phillip had a *tabula rasa,* Hunter faced an already complex settlement which was thoroughly out of hand. His commission and instructions, which can be read in the *Historical Records of Australia,*[14] were counsels of perfection on many levels. He was to enforce land-grant regulations strictly, he was to give particular attention to the curing of fish so that they could eke out the salt ration; he was to appoint justices of the peace, coroners, constables, and all other necessary officers; where possible he was to pay them with land or the services of convicts; he was to keep expenses down ("œconomy"); he was to build up the stock of breeding animals; he was to end the liquor traffic ("We do, therefore, strictly enjoin you, on pain of our utmost displeasure, to order and direct that no spirits shall be landed from any vessel coming to our said settlement without your consent");[15] timber was to be reserved to the Government; free settlers were to have every encouragement "without subjecting the public to expence"; for every thousand acres granted five hundred were to be kept as Crown land; he was to lay out towns, on "navigable rivers or on the coast for preference", to extend public agriculture, to explore the coasts, to cultivate flax, to send home detailed returns—and so it goes on. In short, he was to eradicate all the abuses that had grown up under the rule of the Corps, to observe strict economy, and to lead the settlement on the road to expansion. It is clear from the instructions that the Duke of Portland had a pretty good idea of what had been going on. The Secretary of State was "sorry to observe that the amount of public livestock and cultivated ground bears by no means that proportion to the private which might be expected from the nature of the case and the number of convicts employed, whose labours should be considered the property of the public by whom they are supported".

Hunter was foredoomed to failure. He was a naval Governor in a military colony. The only force he could call on to carry out his orders was the New South Wales Corps, whose privileges and profits he was to cut back.

There was little understanding of his difficulties in England and so no moral support. The settlement he had known had grown out of recognition; it had spread over roughly a radius of thirty miles. The population consisted of a mixture of convicts, expirees, emancipists, free settlers, and military landowners. Between 1793 and 1800, 1264 male convicts completed their sentences and became free. This number exceeded that of the convicts who had first been sent into the country. They could not be forcibly settled on the land. If they had no will or ability for it, it would be waste of government land and money to force them. Some of them supplied the need for labour in the towns, others continued their life of crime and ended up convicts again on Norfolk Island.

At the Select Committee on Transportation which heard evidence in England in 1812 expirees were investigated and some very different opinions of them were gathered in. Most witnesses considered them, with a few exceptions, beyond redemption. Hunter remembered some good qualities. Chaplain Johnson thought they might be reclaimed by clergymen with a *proper salary*. Lieutenant-Colonel George Johnston, who had come out with the First Fleet and had later transferred to the New South Wales Corps and become one of the better type of gentleman farmers, praised them: "Some of the people that were convicts and have been allowed to become settlers are the best people we have there, and far superior in point of industry to some that come from England as free settlers."

Even without the intervention of the New South Wales Corps the colony would not have developed on the lines laid down for it in England. The Government still wanted a docile community of peasant farmers, but the colony was well on the way to being a plantation state, that is, one with large estates worked by cheap labour. The nature of the land and soil made it likely that large properties would succeed where small plots would fail. Hunter was instructed to encourage enterprise and to make the country self-supporting as soon as possible and simultaneously bring it back to the condition it was in when Phillip departed. He was to sail his ship against wind and tide and that, fine sailor though he was, he could not do.

Hunter's governorship began badly. It was a time of scarcity. The colony was "destitute of every kind of tool used in agriculture as well as such as are necessary for carpenters and other artisans", he wrote in a dispatch, and he feared for the livestock in the current food shortage. The thriving settlement on the Hawkesbury, too, had been overwhelmed by floods. "The rise of the river was so rapid that one person, a settler, was unfortunately drowned, and I much fear that it would be the utmost imprudence to place any dependance on that settlement as a resource."[16] Soon Hunter quarrelled with Macarthur, the key man in the colony, and that boded very ill for the future.

In June 1797 in a dispatch Hunter expressed his opinion of Macarthur:

"There is not a person in this colony whose opinions I hold in greater contempt than I do this busybody's, because I have ever observed that under the most specious and plausible of them has always been cover'd a self-interested motive."[17]

A tour of private as well as government farms almost won the Governor over to the side of the military farmers. He saw, or someone pointed out to him, the difficulty of marketing surplus grain if government farms also came into production in a big way. "Your Grace"—this was the Duke of Portland, that dilatory man—he wrote,

> will notice that if Government were to continue to cultivate land sufficient for the maintenance of whatever number of convicts may be hereafter sent out, in such case there would be an effectual stop to the exertions of industrious farmers for want of a market for their crops, and that we shall soon have abundance, there is scarcely any reason to doubt, and this abundance of grain will of course promote the breed of cattle of different kinds.[18]

This began a series of compromises, none of them successful. Hunter attacked the liquor traffic by forbidding its importation except by the Government. He was disobeyed. He then tried to take it under government control by setting up licensed houses and forbidding distillation in the colony. He was disobeyed on the second count. He finally in despair allowed spirits to be imported and the officers of the Corps to "distribute" them. The colony was back in the old rut.

As for the other great evil, the monopoly of trade and labour, he made a good beginning by getting at the facts. He gave the settlers a chance to tell their story, but it was not until February 1798 that the full report was in his hands. It is a valuable historical document, for it shows just how the system worked. But that is all it remained.

Having no power, Hunter had no remedy. The licensed houses gave him a similar idea that the Government might compete with the officers by selling necessities to the settlers at a reasonable price. This plan was eventually put into action, but not by Hunter. In the meantime he bade the settlers be thrifty and buy neither spirits nor luxuries. He tried to fix wages and to limit the number of assigned servants any one class of settlers might have at government expense, thirteen for the gentleman farmer, two for the free settler, and one for the ex-convict.

He entreated the masters either to return to the Government all but the legal number of convicts assigned to them, or to support them. They were welcome to as many as they liked provided that they "took them off the store", that is, fed and clothed them at their own expense. Some officer farmers were quite correct in their attitude. Neither Macarthur nor George Johnston ever had more than two convict servants supplied by the Government.

Hunter's own attitude changed; at first he was wrath at the very idea of commissioned officers engaging in trade or spending His Majesty's time farming. Later he came to believe that the future of the settlement lay with the larger estates, and who was there to manage them except the officers? Free settlers were coming out in small numbers, but they were at this time men without capital and only such as could be spared at home. There was no class to replace the military and civil officers, and so if the land were to be developed they must do it. The Governor capitulated completely in June 1798 when he published a general order allowing the officers to act as "agents for the general benefit of the whole colony". The military caste was back in the saddle. The text of all general orders had to be sent to England. When Portland, who had never been understanding or helpful, read this one he recalled Hunter and named King as his successor.

Portland had another and perhaps deeper cause for discontent with Hunter. On 31st August 1797 he wrote:

> . . . I cannot observe without infinite surprize and regret the very heavy expences which have been incurred from the 1st of June, 1796 to the 31st August following, which I find amount to upwards of £40,000, exclusive of the very large supplies which have been sent from hence. From this it appears that the expence of maintaining the convicts in New South Wales, without including that of the civil and military establishments of the colony or the supplies sent from hence, is more than two-thirds of what they would have been kept for in this country.

Hunter had committed the blackest of sins, extravagance. It is not remarkable that Portland disapproved of spending £20 a year on each convict assigned. The officers' profitable enterprises were therefore costing the Government £260 a year each in free labour.[19]

Macarthur, too, was sedulously poisoning his mind against Hunter. This was a curious situation. Hunter was sent out to curb the privileges of the Corps, yet their most forceful officer had the Secretary of State's ear.[20]

Hunter was a well-intentioned man, loyal and honest, but he was not of the stuff of which Governors of penal settlements are made. He was easily convinced on the spot, he was disobeyed with impunity, and fraud took place even in his own office, where it was discovered that convict clerks, for a bribe of £10 or £20, were falsifying convict records so that men were getting their freedom and even sailing for England before their sentences had expired. It was said at the time, but how true it was I do not know, that his own servants were engaged in the liquor traffic.

Hunter tried to re-establish religion, but the convicts disliked church-going and made a mockery of it. When they burnt down Johnson's church Hunter set the worst of them to building another in their leisure time. Even this created a problem, for the system made it necessary for convicts to have time in which to earn some money. No lodging was provided for them, so they had to hire some sort of accommodation. Take away their earning time and they became a nuisance and a menace in the streets at night.

Hunter railed against the depravity of the convict and rather childishly asked that the more desperate characters be transported somewhere else. The women he found a sore trial and would, if he could, have refused to receive any more. Yet we hear the voice of the "pleasant old man" when he wrote, "If we estimate their merit by the charming children with which they have filled the Colony they well deserve our care."

He had ready sympathy even for the convicts and the picture of men working naked horrified him and remained long in his memory.

The colony expanded during his term of office. The cattle lost in 1788 were found again, increased to a fine herd, in 1795. Hunter in a dispatch to Portland gave an idyllic description.

> On the evening of my Arrival in those Parts, after a Short Search, was directed to the Place where the Herd was feeding, by their frequently calling to each other. Here to prevent being discovered, we ascended a Hill, from which we observed an Herd of Forty feeding in a beautiful Pasture in the Valley.

On trying to investigate their breed, Hunter was attacked by a very fierce bull, which had to be shot.

> I was now satisfied that they were the Cape of Good Hope Breed, and no Doubt the Offspring of those we had lost in 1788, at this Time we counted Sixty-one in number, young and old. They have chosen a beautiful Part of the Country to graze in, where I will do all in my Power to prevent their being disturbed, or in any way annoyed, by which means they may become hereafter a very great Advantage and Resource to this Colony.[21]

The "beautiful Part of the Country" is still called the Cowpastures and is in the Camden district. The herd was long cherished as a mobile larder, but in the end degenerated and was lost.

The law courts had been re-established and magistrates appointed. Various methods, such as passes and certificates, had been used to control the movements of convicts, but with only partial success. Hunter was an experimentalist who did not carry his experiments through; he was a kind man who inflicted terrible punishments in the vain hope that they would act as deterrents.

He spoke his own valediction: "I have no story to tell but a fair, honest and honourable tale."

III. Governor King, 1800-4

Philip Gidley King arrived in Sydney on 15th April 1800 and found Hunter not yet ready to relinquish his government. "I have been here three weeks," he was soon to complain, "and have not a place to put my head into, except depriving Coll. Paterson of a part of his quarters."[22] This invidious position with two Governors in the colony bred ill-will between them, expressed on King's side with little dignity. Amongst many complaints he called this the "most disagreeable and provoking part of my life". He little knew what the future held.

King had time to look about him. He found what he expected.

> Vice, dissipation, and a strange relaxation seems to pervade every class and order of people. One shipload of spirits is not more than half sold. Cellars, from the *better sort of people* in the colony to the blackest character among the convicts, are full of that fiery poison. The children are abandoned to misery, prostitution, and every vice of their parents, and, in short, nothing less than a total change in the system of administration must take place immediately I am left to myself. But it must be done by degrees. . . . I shall have to begin everything anew. . . .[23]

King was confident but he was also aware of the difficulties.

> I must count on having for decided enemies those from whom I ought to have support. Do not suppose that I am at all intimidated from my task and professions. . . . I shall have no private concerns whatever to warp my intentions or divert my views from the great object I hope to attain for the public benefit for the five years you were so good to say should be the term of my residence here. . . .[24]

King was at this time forty-two years old, he had been bred to the Navy and had had twelve years' experience, with a few breaks, in ruling the penal settlement on Norfolk Island. He had been successful there and had shown himself capable of firm and prompt action.

Frederick Watson, in his introduction to Volume iii of the *Historical Records of Australia*, Series I, sums up his character: ". . . a wayward temper, a suspicious and jealous disposition, and a self-satisfied manner which isolated him from his subordinates, and prevented him from taking or seeking advice when necessary". I have found nothing to support this disparagement except a trace of self-satisfaction. He was involved in a number of quarrels, but so was everyone else, including his two successors in office. Hunter had done nothing to improve the situation in the colony, so King, if he fulfilled his commission and obeyed his instructions, which closely resembled Hunter's and which to his chagrin he did not receive until October 1802, had a veritable Augean stable to cleanse with no more help from home or support on the spot than Hunter had had. He was energetic and threw himself whole-heartedly into the task of remaking the settlement. He had two weapons at his command—Government Orders, which he had difficulty in enforcing, and the raising of a numerically strong emancipist class (as distinct from expirees), who owed everything to him and on whose loyalty, as a counterbalance to the military caste, he could depend. Even his patron, Sir Joseph Banks, thought that he went too far in encouraging this class. New South Wales was, after all, a penal settlement.

His chief problem was to break the power of the officer-farmer-trader clique. Their fingers were in every activity of the State. King attacked from many angles. Government orders flowed from his pen in a desperate effort to stop up every avenue of privilege.

He forbade traffic in spirits, but that was not enough. He must control the entry of spirits into the country. "In future no person whatever is to have any communication with vessels arriving in this port until such permission is signified by an Union Jack being hoisted on board the vessel, excepting such persons as the Governor may authorize for that purpose."[25] All ships had to tie up at the government wharf where they would be most easily policed. The Government had first right of purchase over cargoes. Private individuals were restricted to twenty per cent of the residue. Smuggling was taken care of—or was it?—by granting the smuggled spirits to the informer. Anyone had the right to seize spirits if he knew them to be illegally imported.

King also used persuasion. He continued Hunter's licensed houses, rationed spirits to them, and visited any irregularities discovered with heavy fines and loss of licence. He encouraged the brewing of beer. He made it a crime to move liquor from one place to another without permission from a magistrate or other officer charged with this responsibility. The regulation read:

> There being much reason to suppose that spirits have been improperly landed and concealed at Farm Cove, and in other parts of the harbour, from whence they have been occasionally removed, no greater quantity of spirits or wine than half a gallon will be allowed to be removed from any one place or house to another without a permit.[26]

The strict carrying out of this rule involved the Governor in a quarrel with Macarthur. Macarthur made a present to his military company of provisions, including a gill of spirits for each man. A sergeant was caught conveying the refreshment to the mess and it was confiscated. The law went into action, and so did Macarthur. No one was allowed, except licensees, to have more rum in their houses than they needed for normal domestic use. Two officers, Wentworth and Balmain, immediately wrote to the Secretary of State to complain. They had "investments" and now they were not allowed to sell. No one seems to have seen anything amusing in their complaint to the man who inaugurated the action against them. King fixed the price of rum at 28s. a gallon. Illicit stills were strictly forbidden and heavy punishments named.

If paper were potent these regulations would have effectively scotched the rum trade, but King had the whole colony against him. The officers wanted their profit and the settlers and convicts wanted their rum. Distilling and smuggling were the answer. To stop smuggling King offered a curious bait. Anyone, as before mentioned, who seized smuggled rum might have it for his own. The man who seized the illicit spirit would then be breaking the law by having too much of the "fiery poison" in his possession. The Governor became somewhat entangled in his regulations. They had at last almost a frantic note. No debt for liquor over £1 could be recovered in the courts. (New South Wales now boasted a debtors' prison and it was well patronized.) Every farmer must make a return to government officers of wheat in his possession so that it could be compared with his sales and consumption. It was hoped that this would put a brake on the use of wheat for distilling.

The government continued to buy spirits because, by military regulations, every man in the Corps must have his ration. King did not object to normal domestic consumption if supplies were bought through the licensed houses. He did not, however, subscribe to the view that men could not work in so hot a climate without stimulants. Convicts must work without stimulation and would be the better, not the worse, for it. Since rum, like anything else, had to be bought when the chance came, King set up a bonded store, very strong and well guarded, in which he kept the spirits he had to buy in bulk for gradual doling out to the colony. King was not afraid to act. All the world had got the idea that New South Wales provided a good market for rum. Ship after ship came in with it and was sent away disgruntled. In March 1801 King was writing home in a dispatch:

> A dealer, or rather the agent of a dealer, is gone to England with an intention of prosecuting me for ordering about two hundred gallons of liquor to be staved, he having, in disobedience of orders, purchased some convicts salt provisions just as it was received from the stores, for spirits, the actual consequence of which was that the convict must either rob, or do worse, to maintain himself for the remainder of the week.[27]

King thought that Macarthur was the man with money behind this racket.

It is difficult to see what more anyone could have done without a loyal and trustworthy police force and without the backing of public opinion. King certainly made things more difficult for the Rum Corps, but he did not succeed in suppressing the traffic, and this was known in England as well as locally.

Rum was only one head of the hydra. There were also the trade monopoly and the grain monopoly to be dealt with. King broke up the officers' ring which had bought every speculative cargo coming into port. He enforced the Government's right to buy first. He also induced the Home

Government to send out general cargoes of goods for sale to settlers at cost price plus twenty per cent to cover the charges of handling and distribution. This was later increased to thirty per cent and finally, by the instruction of the Secretary of State, Lord Hobart, to fifty per cent. Even so, goods were selling at a far lower price than under the monopoly where four and five hundred per cent was considered a fair return. The idea had originally been Hunter's, but it was King who put it into operation. These trade goods were sold through the public stores. Lists of articles for sale with their prices were posted up outside the store. King knew the value of a fixed and published price in honest trading. Storekeepers were disciplined. "It is to be understood," King proclaimed, "that where the public interest suffers by the misconduct of those who have charge of the stores etc., the loss will be made good out of their respective salaries." The experiment was not an unqualified success, one reason being the uncertainty of supplies. More effective was permission to an independent merchant, Robert Campbell, to set up business, provided that his stocks of spirits were limited and that he sold his merchandise at a fair price. Campbell's venture was a success. He was experienced, a keen, honest business man. He and his family became prosperous and respected citizens for generations.

To break the farming monopoly King revived the government farms. Land cleared at Parramatta and Toongabbie, he found, had been distributed in grants. Clearing was a very big item and the men who had mopped up this ground had done well for themselves. It was not possible to repossess it, so King fixed on Castle Hill as the main government farm, and gangs were sent there to clear, burn and plant the land. For these operations King needed labour. Free or very cheap labour was the mainstay of the monopolists. By a general order the Governor demanded a return of all convict labour employed from every landholder. He took away from them all except the two servants supported by the Government that the regulations allowed them. They were, however, permitted to employ convicts if they fed and clothed them, or if they paid about fifteen guineas a year for every man, as that was reckoned his cost to the Government.

Labour at cost price was fair enough. It was an economy to the Government when masters supported convicts. In January 1801 the assignment system was temporarily suspended for overhaul. If at any time assigned servants were observed to be idle or if their masters hired them out and so made a profit on them, the Government reserved the right to take them back and put them in the labour gangs.

The price of grain was fixed, wheat 8s. to 10s. a bushel, maize 4s. to 6s. a bushel.

These means should have broken the power of the Corps, but somehow it continued to flourish. King tried to maintain good relations. He frequently, in the early days of his government, praised the officers and men of the Corps in a way that could only be interpreted as flattery. With Colonel Paterson, the commanding officer, he got on very well, though he knew Paterson was a weak man and that, under Macarthur's influence, he had written to England complaining of the Governor's conduct.

The officers had now, on paper at least, lost their privileges of rum-running, monopoly trading and free labour, and King was building up an emancipist class, a policy that his successor, Macquarie, was to carry further, to be the Governor's party in the State.

There was more to King's governorship than this battle with the Corps which was the main issue. King was a tidy man, like most naval officers. He tried to tidy up the convict system in particular and the settlement in general.

He found the system, if system it could be called, in a very confused and uneconomic state. Owing to gross carelessness many of the Irish convicts had been sent out without their papers, so that the authorities in New South Wales knew neither the length of their sentences nor when they expired. Also, through corruption in the Governor's office, many entries in the books had been falsified either for bribes or out of malice. The confusion was so great that Lord Hobart sent out a complete new list of convicts and their sentences. With the closing down of government agriculture and the very casual system of assignment the Government hardly knew where to lay its hand on its convicts. They moved from master to master and on their own occasions all over the fast extending colony. Hunter had made it a rule that convicts should only move from one place to another when they had a permit. King strengthened and extended this ruling in a general order which imposed a penalty of one hundred lashes and a year's imprisonment in the jail gang for convicts *or expirees not settled* who were found going from settlement to settlement without a pass signed by a magistrate. This was also applied to free men who were not settlers or in regular employment. This seems hard, but it must be remembered that expirees, or indeed anyone who was not *rangé*, was a charge on the store and in return the Government expected to keep control over them. Out of these magistrates' passes tickets of leave naturally developed. They allowed a convict of good behaviour to earn his own living before the expiration of his sentence. This was an economy for the Government and a contribution to the always starving labour market.

Justice was restored to the convicts. Their masters or overseers had been wont to punish them at will. King proclaimed:

> . . . as the Governor will not admit of any individual presuming to inflict that punishment, which must be openly awarded by a magistrate, he strictly forbids all officers, and every person, bond or free, from striking or ill-using any other person in this colony, on pain of being proceeded against according to law, or such other notice taken of the offence as the case may require.[28]

King also asked permission for civil officers to sit on the bench as well as military and naval ones.

The assignment system was overhauled and at the first muster in 1800 485 persons were struck off the rations at a saving of £10,488. When they qualified for it convicts were forced to take on the responsibility of providing for themselves.

The rest of the community was also tidied up. King found that free settlers were in arrears with their quit rents, token payments of sixpence or a shilling for fifty acres, that they were expected to pay yearly to the Government after a certain time. He made a drive to collect them, but was not outstandingly successful, since the settlers had been left in peace for so long that they considered this an imposition.

When the public store needed to buy grain King, on instructions from the Home Government, insisted that tenders be called and the lowest taken. He was himself dissatisfied with the running of the Commissariat, suspected Commissary Williamson of incompetence, and asked for an inquiry.

For government business he established regular hours and forbade anyone to approach him on Sundays or buttonhole him in the street on official matters.

He found Government House almost falling down about his ears and the Battery on the west side of Sydney Cove in a state of dilapidation. Government House he had to endure, and so had two of his successors, but he pulled the fortifications together, such as they were.

Dogs and goats had become a nuisance.

> . . . as the breeding stock of sheep is of the greatest consequence to the welfare of this colony, no person is to suffer any cur dogs to follow them, or any cart, wheelbarrow etc., the Governor having given permission to those who have flocks of sheep to order their herdsmen to kill any dogs that approach them, and the owners will forfeit treble the value of any stock killed by them. Persons who keep cur dogs that are in the habit of flying at horses are to destroy them, otherwise they will be indicted as a nuisance. It is recommended to those who have more dogs than one (except greyhounds or terriers) to kill them, as a tax will shortly be laid on all cur dogs.[29]

Goats unattended would be forfeit, cows and calves and other animals liable to prey on gardens must be tied up or yoked so that they could not get through fences. In King's time there were many gardens and orchards in what is now the city of Sydney and their products were a very necessary supplement to the ration.

King, like his predecessors, ran into difficulties because there was no legal specie in the colony. When the King's ship *Porpoise*, the second of that name, arrived she brought a cargo of copper coins on which King set the value of 2d., 1d., and ½d. They were legal tender up to £5. This did not really alter the situation. Small salaries presented a difficulty. King cited the case of Martin Timms, Superintendent of Convicts on Norfolk Island. He did the work of three men, but never saw his money. From July 1793 to January 1801 the Government's debt to him had mounted to £368 13s. 4d. His was not an isolated case. King, who had nothing except his salary, well understood these difficulties and he knew that he could not expect loyal service and rigid honesty from men who were not getting what was due to them. Any adjustments took a long time, for everything had to go through London and there was no such thing as petty cash, let alone a bank. In view of this it might appear unreasonable that King forbade the use of notes of hand in place of money.

King framed the first shipping regulations and established port dues. *Porpoise*, when she was in port, had the duty of stopping and searching every ship before she left the harbour. This was mainly to look for stowaways. No ship might leave the harbour and no person sail in her without giving a week's notice publicly. This was so that debts might be settled before departure.[30]

It was forbidden to cut down cedar-trees on the Hawkesbury. And so on and so on, until one would think that the Governor had provided for every possible emergency. It would be a great mistake, of course, to believe that because they were forbidden by government order the nuisances did not continue.

As instructed, King exercised every economy. He was particularly anxious to keep down the ration account. He emancipated, he gave tickets of leave, and he assigned servants, and each recipient of "indulgence" went off the store. Magistrates he paid with the services of four convicts. It had been usual to victual all the wives and daughters of soldiers, but King would ration only five in each company. In all things he protected government interests and, in the manner of his day, had many patent ideas for saving money. For example, he suggested that convicts and supplies should be sent out in whalers, which were coming in any case and so would be cheaper. He tried to get as much useful work out of the convicts as possible. He endeavoured to save the salt ration by using the wild cattle of the Cowpastures for beef. They were now to be numbered in thousands, but to get them to table was a difficult matter. The Governor sent out good marksmen, attended by a drummer, as it had been noticed that drumming attracted cattle. They came, but they made off again too fast for much execution to be done, so King finally decided to leave them alone to increase. There was not much fear that they would supply meat to fugitives in the bush. They knew only too well how to take care of themselves.

King gathered together a revenue from port dues and fines and confiscations. In this he had two prime objects, one was to build a new jail and the other to found two orphanages, one for boys and the other for girls.

As the father of a large family he was deeply troubled by the plight of children whose parents were either dead, gone out of the country, or too depraved to bring them up properly. The girls were in the greatest need of protection, so he bought Captain Kent's house at the corner of George and Bridge streets, with its orchard, for £1539. A public subscription was opened, money from port dues was allotted to it, and various fines were divided between the orphanage and the jail. There he established a group of girls nine to fourteen years old, but the situation was, alas, too near to the barracks, and when the orphanage for boys was completed at Parramatta the girls were sent there and the boys brought to Bridge Street. The orphanage theme weaves in and out of all King's dealings. It was the project nearest his heart. On Norfolk Island, whose system of government was now almost exactly similar to that on the mainland, courts, land grants and all, he instructed the commandant to finance an orphanage out of the quit rents. In other ways we find King very thoughtful for children. For instance, when there was some molasses in store he ordered that it should be issued every week to the children of the non-commissioned officers and privates.

It was rather a blow to the colony's financial structure to find that Governor Phillip's pension of £613 13s. 10¼d. a year was to come out of its revenues.[31]

King had the misfortune to run into troubled times. The many Irish sent out for political crimes proved a source of danger. There was a bond between them and they had the will to resist. The trouble began in September 1800 when a plot was uncovered complete with secret signs and passwords. Pikes had been forged as weapons, it was believed, but they were not found. The plan was to take Parramatta by surprise, gather recruits there and from the Hawkesbury, capture the barracks at Sydney, and send a ship to France, with whom England was at war. Joseph Holt, a gentleman convict, was named as their general, and though he was innocent he was punished with the rest. The rebellion was stillborn but the threat remained. A voluntary association was raised, trained, and armed to meet the danger. In 1804 the Irish rose again, this time at Castle Hill. Parramatta had a night of fear when the free population realized that it was sitting on a keg of gunpowder, but it was a pitiful affair and easily quelled, more by address than by force of arms, by Major Johnston, the hero of the hour. King asked for reinforcements and "well behaved English convicts who have been light horsemen and sent here for crimes which are but too common among the lower orders".

There were minor troubles, robberies so numerous that a curfew had to be imposed and a band of watchmen reorganized. There were disorders at Green Hills on the Hawkesbury. Convicts escaped to the bush to be the first bushrangers or wanderers in the bush. Their only means of subsistence being raids on lonely settlers or on the sparse traffic of the roads, the term soon acquired its modern meaning. Even nature was against the settlement, for the Hawkesbury flooded repeatedly, destroying crops and beasts in the colony's most thriving agricultural area.

And there were incessant quarrels. King began his term of office under strained relations with Hunter and bitterness towards Major Johnston over the pasturing of government herds. His most spectacular quarrel was with Macarthur. Macarthur roused his brother officers to boycott the Governor. Colonel Paterson dined with King and in consequence was insulted by Macarthur to the point at which Paterson challenged him to a duel. There were some irregularities about this affair of honour and Paterson was dangerously wounded. Since it was useless to try Macarthur in the colony, he was sent to England under arrest. King prepared the way for him in a dispatch:

> His employment during the eleven years he has been here has been that of making a large fortune, helping his brother officers to make small ones (mostly at the publick expence), and sewing discord and strife. . . . Experience has convinced every man in this colony that there are no resources which art, cunning, impudence, and a pair of baselisk eyes can afford that he does not put in practice to obtain any point he undertakes.[32]

This quarrel went deeper than personalities. It was the New South Wales Corps against the Governor.

More damaging to King was his later and less dignified quarrel with Captain Colnett of H.M.S. *Glatton*, and an unfortunate episode involving the officers of a French ship. Barrack-room fever still raged.

Under King, if not necessarily because of him, the colony made great strides. Whaling brought profit to its shores, for the ships came into Sydney to refit. King referred to whaling as the only "staple" and saw visions of secondary profits. A tiny export trade began in coal from Coal Harbour (Newcastle), which was worked by the Government with convict labour. It was sent to India and the Cape. The camp there was later closed for lack of miners and a suitable superintendent. A little timber was exported, but being different did not get a good reception. A source of cheap salt pork was found at Tahiti. The difficulty was salt, as Mr Boston's efforts to make it fell below expectation. However, a cargo of salt arrived unexpectedly and was bought up, and *Porpoise* made two successful trips for meat.

"The manufacture of linen and woolen goods is begun with some success," King announced in August 1800. In 1801 472 yards of linen were woven from flax in five months. Twopence a pound was paid for wool and it was woven into blankets, of which the colony was perennially short. In one year 306 yards were produced, part of this going to the owners of the wool in payment for it. Unfortunately a master weaver who was sent out was drowned on the passage.

The most important thing that happened, though it was hardly recognized then, was the beginning of the wool industry. In a dispatch of 21st August 1801 King wrote: "I have had the honor of informing your Grace that every endeavour is making by individuals who own so great a proportion of the sheep in the colony to improve the hair into wool by means of three Spanish rams brought here in 1797, and that no pains would be spared to obtain the same object with Government's flock."[33]

The colony was growing more sophisticated. It had a Naval Officer (or Harbour Master), and a licensed auctioneer who paid an annual fee of £2 to the Orphan School and 5s. to the clerk who drew up the licence. One and a half per cent of the sales, which had to be reported, also went to the Orphan School. Two vignerons had been sent out, though so far grapes had been grown only for eating. Bakeries were inspected and there was a standard loaf. Two natural-history painters and botanists were adding a touch of culture and science to the primitive community.

The Governor had a bodyguard, a luxury that the Home Government did its best to take from him. For the first time a man of legal training, Richard Dore, held the position of Judge-Advocate, but he died untimely and insolvent and again Atkins, an amateur, was called on to fill the office. He was described by King as exceedingly clever, but "unfortunately addicted to liquor".[34]

Ships came more frequently, so commodities were more plentiful and there was more money, or its equivalent, to spend on them.

Exploration flourished, too. Bass had already explored the coast to the south in a tiny cockleshell of a boat, *Tom Thumb*, finding a coal seam at Bulli. In June 1797 he had sailed through the strait that bears his name, proving that Van Diemen's Land was a separate island. In 1798, with Flinders he made assurance doubly sure by circumnavigating Van Diemen's Land. In 1801 Flinders returned to the attack in the sloop *Investigator*, which Sir Joseph Banks had persuaded the Admiralty to put at his disposal. He explored and charted the southern coast of Australia from King George's Sound to Sydney, where he arrived in February 1802. In May he set off northward, threading the difficult waters of the Great Barrier Reef, then called the Labyrinth, and finally circumnavigated the continent. At last the complete outline of Australia was known and mapped. Later it fell to Governor King's son, Phillip Parker King, also a naval officer, to re-chart the north of Australia and make more detailed discoveries there. But this was not until 1817. It was an assignment that took more than four years to complete.

On land Caley and Barrallier, an officer of the New South Wales Corps, made separate attacks on the mountain chain that hemmed the colony in, but they were unable to cross it. They made the mistake of following the valleys instead of the crests and every time they were brought to a standstill by sheer cliffs, impervious to climbing irons and mountaineering skill.

It was King who in 1803 first colonized Van Diemen's Land, planting a small settlement on the Derwent at Risdon under Lieutenant Bowen.

All in all, King's governorship was a time of expansion.

The reasons behind King's recall—for recall it was, though he had served the five years promised to him at the time of his appointment—lay in his quarrelsomeness (especially that disastrous quarrel with Captain Colnett, which had its roots in a number of small incidents and an underlying jealousy because Colnett was King's superior in the Navy), in his annoying habit of writing long dispatches full of complaints and of referring to England a number of matters which he should have settled on the spot where the evidence was accessible. King, falling over backwards to do his duty and to justify himself, became a nuisance, and how the Colonial Office hated such long-winded and troublesome fellows! Much of his zeal in prosecuting his government had leaked away in the five years of effort and disappointments. He was letting all but personal quarrels slide. It is doubtful, however, if this was a conscious accusation on the part of the Colonial Office. The Lords of Whitehall wanted a strong, silent ruler for their penal settlement. They were disappointed in King.

IV. Governor Bligh, 1806-8

The Secretary of State for the Colonies was now determined to settle the troublesome colony by giving it a strong man as Governor. Commodore William Bligh had proved himself a man of exceptional courage and a good seaman. He had been exonerated of all blame attached to the mutiny which had occurred in his ship, *Bounty*. He had, however, proved quarrelsome and had figured in at least one court martial, from which he emerged with a caution. He was, one suspects, at once a worthy and a troublesome officer. What could be more suitable than to send him as Governor to an unworthy and troublesome colony where his strength of character and courage would be useful in suppressing abuses and his quarrelsomeness be insulated by sixteen thousand miles of sea?

He arrived in the King's ship *Porpoise* on 6th August 1806. On the voyage he had quarrelled with the ship's commander, Joseph Short. It played into his hands when Lieutenant Tetley brought accusations against Short of using ship's stores for his own benefit, of "cruel oppression" and of "unofficerlike" language". Tetley ended his complaint pathetically: "I beg leave to say that in consequence of ill usage I have received from Captain Short, my peace of mind is broken and my health much injured." Another man with the unfortunate name of Lye accused Short of drunkenness. Both Tetley and Lye were put under arrest, one for inciting a mutiny, the other for disobedience. Bligh when appealed to sent three officers to inquire into the charges. They reported adversely to Short and Bligh sent him to England under arrest. He was court-martialled and acquitted. In the meantime Bligh had received instructions to grant Short six hundred acres wherever he chose to take it. This was petrol on the fire. Such was the prelude to his governorship.

It is all the more remarkable, after such a beginning, that Bligh restrained himself for six months whilst he looked into the affairs of the colony. Like his predecessors, he found it in a poor way; the granaries were empty following a disastrous flooding of the Hawkesbury River, the public buildings were falling down, morale was low.

> In the customs and manners of the people here a great deal is to be corrected. The Settlers in general, and particularly those from Prisoners, are not honest, have no prudence and little industry, besides being burthened with debts; great chicanery is used in all their dealings, and much litigation. All this will require a vast deal of attention on my part to remove, to which end the rising generation shall be watched over and educated, while the pernicious customs of the place shall be checked by every means in my power.[35]

The strivings and reforms of Hunter and King had evidently left everything just where it was. Bligh was as confident of success as they had been and as Macquarie was to be in his turn.

He was formally welcomed by John Macarthur on behalf of the free citizens, and then by the free settlers, who to a man repudiated Macarthur as their representative. This little unpleasantness passed off.

Bligh bestirred himself to feed his hungry people and his prompt relief measures won him the respect and affection of the settlers on the Hawkesbury. They remained his only friends. Soon he clashed with D'Arcy Wentworth, who was powerful, and then with Macarthur, the richest and most influential man in the colony. This was inevitable. Bligh's instructions bade him suppress the use of spirits in barter. He issued a proclamation forbidding it and threatening heavy penalties: for convicts 100 lashes and a year's imprisonment; for free settlers three months in prison, the withdrawal of government assistance, and a fine of £20; for "all others", by whom he meant officers and gentry, a fine of £50 and loss of "indulgences". He tried to suppress the rum trade without offering anything, such as specie, to take its place. He was no respecter of persons, though he followed the usual course of adjusting penalties to social standing. He forbade importation and distillation of spirits. He made many enemies and few friends by this direct attack on a profitable racket. He offended the merchants by restricting trade, he stirred up trouble by investigating town leases and evicting six families for irregularities. His manners were rough and his speech violent. He soon had plenty of trouble on his hands. Joseph Short was taking away his character in England. Collins in Van Diemen's Land was complaining bitterly to the Secretary of State, Windham, that he received no supplies, and Windham was surprised and perturbed because Bligh had arrived with ample provisions but had not distributed them. Bligh had probably expended them on the distress in New South Wales, without taking into consideration the more distant distress in Van Diemen's Land.

D'Arcy Wentworth and John Macarthur were soon bitter enemies of the Governor, and each had his faction. George Johnston, the commandant, was alienated and with him, as he was very popular, the regiment. Settlers like the Blaxlands had early come in for caustic comment from the fiery Governor and they did not forget. There was hardly a man of any prominence in the colony with whom he did not quarrel. Interested in farming and knowledgeable on the subject, Bligh had no time for sheep. If graziers had their way, he thought, it would be the end of agriculture, and by agriculture alone, so he believed, could the colony thrive.

Stories began to circulate to the discredit of the Governor. On his arrival Governor King had given him three substantial land grants, one south of the town which he called Camperdown, having fought in that naval engagement, one of 105 acres at Parramatta, which led, years later, to a claim by his six daughters to a great part of that thriving settlement, and one on the Hawkesbury for a farm. In return Bligh made a grant of 750 acres to Mrs King, which she tactlessly named "Thanks". Worse still, Andrew Thompson, Bligh's overseer at the Hawkesbury farm, declared on oath—and he was a man of good repute with nothing more serious on his conscience than a little illicit distilling—that buildings worth £1000 had been erected there at government expense, that the implements used were from the government store and the livestock from government flocks and herds. It was not very convincing when Bligh explained that his sole intention was to set up a model experimental farm to improve agricultural standards.

Bligh's reign was short and full of trouble. His commission gave him the same powers as earlier Governors. He was in the same position as Hunter and King had been, a naval Governor dependent on a military force. Macarthur had come home from exile to lead the opposition. Bligh underrated Macarthur just as he underrated the importance of wool.

Incidents began to build up, all centring on Macarthur, which led to the events of 26th January 1808. There is more than a suggestion of provocation. There was the matter of the receipt for wheat issued when wheat was 9s. 3d. a bushel. After the floods the price of wheat rose to 13s. 9d. and finally to 28s. a bushel. Macarthur thought, or appeared to think, that the value of his receipt rose, too. He tried to recover in a civil court and lost the case. The receipt, the court held "was an expression of value and not of quantity of produce".

This was only an opening gambit. More serious was the trouble over the two stills for making spirits from grain, which arrived in the ship *Dart*. One belonged to Captain Abbott, one to Macarthur. Bligh ordered them both to be returned to England. Macarthur asked leave to sell the stills to the master of the ship or preferably to keep the copper for household use. Bligh did not reply to Macarthur, but ordered the stills to be seized. The Naval Officer put himself in the wrong by sending his nephew, an unauthorized person, to take them. Macarthur saw his opportunity and sued for wrongful seizure. He won his case on a point.

An article, no doubt inspired, appeared in the Press announcing that Bligh was to be recalled and that Grose, now a general, was to succeed him.

As the soil was prepared other incidents followed, the colony in any case being rife with irregularities. In June 1807 a small colonial ship *Parramatta,* of which Macarthur was part owner, carried away a stowaway, a lifer, who at Tahiti transhipped into *General Wellesley* for India. It was, of course, an offence to take a convict under sentence out of the country, and all masters had to enter into a bond of £800 with two other sureties of £50 each. Macarthur was one of the sureties for *Parramatta.* He was sued for the bond, lost his case, and appealed. The ship had returned to Port Jackson and was arrested. Macarthur abandoned it, making no provision for the crew, who after a week were driven ashore by hunger. By regulation crews were not allowed to leave their ships. The Judge-Advocate, Richard Atkins, a poor creature, a drunkard and, more dangerous, a debtor to Macarthur, issued a writ, with the Governor's approval, for Macarthur's arrest. Macarthur knew more law than he did. As he had not been summonsed first he could not be arrested. The warrant was issued the next day, Macarthur was haled before Atkins and committed for trial on 25th January 1808. Macarthur riposted by demanding the money Atkins owed him but could not pay. He appealed to Bligh, who treated him curtly and told him to seek restitution in the Civil Court, a difficult matter with Atkins on the Bench. Macarthur now did everything he could think of to provoke Bligh. He began to fence a lease in the town which he had asked for but had not yet been granted. His fence cut the townsfolk off from a public well. Bligh stopped the soldiers who were working on it. The field-pieces at Government House were tampered with and a soldier admitted unscrewing them, but pleaded orders from Lieutenant Minchin, one of the Macarthur entourage. The Governor was badgered and furious. Macarthur behaved like a conspirator. Bligh could not fail to know that a cabal was working against him.

Macarthur went to his trial on the twenty-fifth and, with a great display of insolence, abused the Judge-Advocate and declared him an improper person to try the case. Bligh sent for Johnston in his capacity as commandant; Johnston excused himself on the ground of having met with an accident. The next morning, the twenty-sixth, Macarthur was served with a warrant for his arrest. He escaped custody. Bligh lost his head and charged Macarthur and six officers with treason. Johnston, too ill to visit the Governor, hurried to the barracks, declared himself Lieutenant-Governor, signed a warrant to release Macarthur, and with his regiment marched on Government House. Bligh could not defend himself; there was in any case no intention of shedding blood. The whole affair was artificial, the righteous indignation which the Corps managed to pump up was only a veneer covering their calculated intention to defend their financial interests. As a rebellion it was a poor affair. Macarthur was the guiding spirit, but because of his unpopularity he could never have given the undertaking the colour of a popular rising against a tyrant. George Johnston, well bred, amiable, the idol of his soldiers, was just the man for the job. How he was prevailed upon to do it is not known. Like Colonel Paterson, he was easily swayed.

Foveaux provided the blurb:

> . . . I have already perfectly satisfied myself that Captain Bligh has been acting on a settled plan to destroy and ruin the better Class of Inhabitants, and that Major Johnston is in possession of incontrovertable proofs of his being guided in the most important concerns of the Colony by the advice of Crossley, your knowledge of whom will enable you to judge in what a dreadful State the whole Settlement must have been involved previous to the change which Major Johnston was called upon to effect.[36]

Crossley was an ex-convict lawyer suspected of roguery, but never caught in it after the expiration of his sentence. It is possible that Bligh consulted him on a point of law as the only man in the colony likely to have the requisite knowledge.

And Bligh, of course, spoke his piece: "The insolence, wickedness and duplicity of the principal rebels exceed all description. The People see, with great concern, how much the colony is injured, Government plundered, and beggary making hasty strides to their utter ruin."[37] And much more to the same effect.

The rebellion resolved a deadlock. It could not be disregarded even in an age which applauded Nelson for putting the telescope to his blind eye, but nevertheless it was not taken as seriously by the Home Government as one would expect.

An undignified and prolonged wrangling between the deposed Governor and his captors ensued. Bligh retired to Van Diemen's Land, the victors quarrelled amongst themselves, and Macarthur ruled. Delay and indifference marked the conduct of the Colonial Office.

The short governorship of Bligh was productive of little except sound and fury. When Macquarie arrived he found the colony in a degenerate state. He, too, set to work to regularize it. Change and regeneration were not to come from the exertions of any man, but from a more fundamental impulse.

REFERENCE NOTES

[1] *Hist. Rec. Aust.*, ser. I, vol. i, p. 381.
[2] *Ibid.*, p. 44. [3] *Ibid.*, p. 416. [4] *Ibid.*, p. 414.
[5] R. S. Macarthur Onslow, *Some Early Records of the Macarthurs of Camden*, pp. 45, 46, 51.
[6] *Hist. Rec. Aust.*, ser. I, vol. ii, p. 321.
[7] W. Tench, *Complete Account of the Settlement at Port Jackson*, p. 152.
[8] *Hist. Rec. Aust.*, ser. I, vol. i, p. 451.
[9] *Ibid.*, p. 469. [10] *Ibid.*, p. 470. [11] *Ibid.*, p. 433.
[12] *Ibid.*, p. 434. [13] *Ibid.* [14] *Ibid.*, pp. 513-27.
[15] *Ibid.*, p. 523. [16] *Ibid.*, p. 529. [17] *Ibid.*, vol. ii, p. 11.
[18] *Ibid.*, vol. i, p. 533. [19] *Ibid.*, vol. ii, p. 107. [20] *Ibid.*, pp. 89 *et seq.*
[21] *Ibid.*, vol. i, pp. 550-1. [22] *Ibid.*, vol. ii, p. 505. [23] *Ibid.*
[24] *Ibid.*, p. 506. [25] *Ibid.*, p. 622. [26] *Ibid.*, vol. iii, p. 36.
[27] *Ibid.*, p. 74. [28] *Ibid.*, p. 43. [29] *Ibid.*, p. 50.
[30] *Ibid.*, pp. 34, 384, 622, 712. [31] *Ibid.*, p. 108. [32] *Ibid.*, p. 322.
[33] *Ibid.*, p. 125. [34] *Ibid.*, p. 246. [35] *Ibid.*, vol. vi, p. 27.
[36] *Ibid.*, pp. 633-4. [37] *Ibid.*, pp. 671-2.

CHAPTER VII

MACQUARIE: "JAIL INTO COLONY"

The Government in England took surprisingly little notice of the rebellion in New South Wales. The Corps ruled undisturbed, except by its internecine feuds, for another two years, during which the colony degenerated. England turned on the rebels a frosty indifference that in the long run was more effective and less expensive than sending a King's ship to subdue them. No store-ships came, nothing. Macarthur, the only man capable of ruling, was too strict to please his brother officers. As usual quarrels broke out and the population, feeling itself again forgotten, grew heartily tired of the military régime. The Rum Rebellion was an end, not a beginning.

When the new Governor, Lachlan Macquarie, arrived on 31st December 1809 there was no spirit of resistance left. The whole population turned out to greet him and tar barrels burned by way of rude illumination in the streets on New Year's night. Bligh was in Van Diemen's Land, the Commandant, Paterson, was at Parramatta, and the genial Colonel Foveaux was at Macquarie's elbow. Two King's ships, *Dromedary* and *Hindostan*, escorted Macquarie. It may have looked like a show of force, but none was needed.

The officers must have asked: "What next?" and wondered if this was another Bligh. They were soon to know. The Corps was recalled. It became the 102nd Regiment and, its tour of service in New South Wales over, it was given other duties. Macquarie brought with him his own Regiment, the 73rd Highlanders, and for the first time a Governor had reliable support. Only two men went home for court martial: Johnston, who was cashiered but allowed to return to his large and undiminished estates, and Macarthur, who was simply refused permission to return for eight years, a time which he used to advantage. Unfortunately, any officers or men of the Corps who wished to stay in Australia were given permission to do so and in this way kept alive its unfortunate spirit. For form's sake Macquarie had instructions to reinstate Bligh for one day, to convey the King's displeasure to all and sundry, and to revoke all appointments, leases, land grants, pardons, and sentences of the rebel government. In practice this proved impossible. So ended, like a very damp squib, the Rum Rebellion.

The reign of Macquarie is often looked upon as a new beginning in Australian history, a turning-point. In reality it marked the end of a policy.

Macquarie was sent on a fool's errand. The colony was changing, but his commission and instructions followed the old pattern. He was to break the trade monopoly, suppress the rum traffic, encourage and foster a community of peasant farmers, to economize, to exercise a list of formidable powers. The one new factor was the presence of his own regiment. The honour was originally intended for Colonel Nightingall, but, his health being unequal to it, it was passed to his second in command. Macquarie had seen considerable service as a soldier in America, India, and Egypt; he had had experience in administration as military secretary to the Governor of Bengal. His record was good, he had integrity, high-mindedness, a distinguished bearing, a massive style in prose and speech, considerable vanity, no tact, no sense of humour, and he was delighted with his appointment. He believed every word of his commission and, whilst taking his obedience to his superiors as much for granted as he did that of his inferiors to himself, he interpreted his instructions in the light of his powers. He liked the idea of power, but he intended to exercise it in the most gracious and benevolent manner. He underrated the colony he came to govern, for he thought of it as still a blank sheet on which he could set his impress. He was wrong; a great deal of history had been packed into twenty-two years, a compendium of experience, so that in retrospect it is the Governor, with his good intentions and patent remedies, who appears naive.

Like Phillip, Macquarie came prepared for his charge, but not solely by his own reflections. He arrived well armoured in preconceived ideas, which even in the face of reality he did not lay aside. One of the strongest influences was a letter, given to Macquarie for perusal on the voyage out, from T. W. Plummer, a theorist who, although he had never visited New South Wales, had evolved a simple scheme to make the colony prosper. What Australia needed, thought Mr Plummer, was markets. Geographically there was no handy market, but one could easily and inexpensively be created if the Government gave the monopoly of distilling spirits to a private company. Excess wheat could be turned into spirits, but in times of scarcity the Government should have the power to stop the distillation and divert the grain to the Commissariat. In this way good and bad seasons would be equalized. A high tax could be levied on spirits and they would still be cheaper than the imported article. Money would be kept in the colony, revenue would accrue, and the traffic though a monopoly could be easily regulated. This was a curious idea to take root in the mind of a man, one of whose duties it was to suppress the rum trade, for naturally the monopoly could not prosper and the revenue would not roll in unless consumption were high. Nevertheless we find this motif continually cropping up in Macquarie's administration. Another idea of

Plummer's which appealed to the Governor-elect was that land in towns should in future be granted on a freehold instead of a leasehold tenure and that a building clause be inserted in each grant binding the recipient to erect buildings of a certain standard. This, Macquarie felt, would be a cheap way of beautifying his capital.

There were two other known influences affecting Macquarie before he took up his duties. One was the spectacle of a colonial bank operating successfully at the Cape, the second was the impact of Foveaux, the first officer to greet him on arrival. It was Foveaux who supplied him with first-hand information about the colony and its inhabitants, who with just the correct shade of deference, praised some and warned him against others. Macquarie was impressionable and impressed. Foveaux always remained for him an authority and a pattern of what an officer should be. Colonel Paterson, the once intrepid traveller, was now old, sick, and on the point of retirement. For that reason probably the Home Government did not think it worth while to take any action against him for condoning the rebellion.

When on 17th January 1810 Bligh returned from Van Diemen's Land in *Porpoise* Macquarie received him with every courtesy. He could afford to, and the salutes, parades, compliments must have infuriated the old sea-dog more than insults. He was the failure, Macquarie was urbanely sure of easy success. They hated one another at sight, and the three months before Bligh got himself off with his entourage, his evidence, his cloud of witnesses, Macquarie found trying in the extreme. He even wrote to Lord Castlereagh at the Colonial Office: ". . . I must acknowledge that he is a most unsatisfactory Man to transact business with, from his want of candor and decision, in so much that it is impossible to place the smallest reliance on the fulfillment of any engagement he enters into."[1]

There were incidents. Macquarie had sealed the room at Government House where Bligh had perforce left his papers. When it was unsealed the papers had gone and Johnston was suspected of having taken them for his defence. Bligh took with him to England sixteen people, including Judge-Advocate Atkins and Commissary Palmer, to the great inconvenience of colonial business. And, what is more, he quite filled up *Hindostan* and *Dromedary*, which Macquarie had hoped to use for sending home the 102nd Regiment, a formidable task as in its long sojourn it had acquired 105 wives and 98 children. The expense of it all was great, and Lord Castlereagh did not like expense.

Correct to the last, Macquarie gave a farewell (or thanksgiving) ball. The *Sydney Gazette*, which King had founded in 1803 and of which Macquarie was to make considerable use, described it.

Government House was neatly decorated and brilliantly lighted; the ball room hung round with festoons of flowers encircling the initials of Mrs Putland and Commodore Bligh in a very neat device. In the evening a ball was given, which was supported with uncommon vivacity until "the twinkling stars gave notice of approaching day"; a handsome firework was also displayed on the occasion between the hours of 10 and 11; and no single circumstance was omitted that could convey an idea of the respect entertained by His Excellency, for the distinguished persons in Compliment of whom the entertainment had been given.

Four days later Bligh really departed with excessive pomp and ceremony, but unfortunately his widowed daughter, Mary Putland, stayed behind to marry Colonel O'Connell and keep alive her father's wrongs.

Macquarie declared a general amnesty and got to work. He surveyed his domain and found the stores empty. Besides sending urgent and copious requests home he caused 200 acres to be sown with potatoes and ordered 200 tons of wheat from Bengal through local merchants. He was able to get a cut price by giving them leave to import 20,000 gallons of rum. He was putting Plummer's ideas into effect in a small way.

He turned his attention to "Morality, Virtue and Temperance". Not only did he exhort, but he reduced the licensed public houses in Sydney from 75 to 20. Like King, he endeavoured to substitute beer for spirits. He insisted that all convicts go to church. He encouraged marriage by pardoning convict women who could find respectable husbands. He paid especial attention to the assigning of women so that their morals would be safeguarded. He set up a co-educational charity school. . . .

Then he set to work to clean up his capital, which he found in a deplorable condition. He widened the streets and had them cleared of stumps, set up a scavenging service, forbade the erection of the old-style temporary and unsightly buildings, and gave the streets dignified names: George after the King, Pitt after the Prime Minister, York, Essex, Sussex, Cumberland after the Royal Dukes, Castlereagh after the Secretary of State for the Colonies, Phillip, Hunter, King, and Bligh, after former Governors, Macquarie after himself, Campbell and Elizabeth in compliment to his wife, and Bent after his Judge-Advocate, who had come out in *Hindostan* with him and with whom he was still friendly. Park, Spring, Barrack, and Market streets were purely functional names. Macquarie gave Sydney the form it has today, though the appearance was very different. He began to build a new granary, barracks to hold 1000 soldiers, a market on the present site of the Queen Victoria Buildings, handy to Cockle Bay (later Darling Harbour), whither boats brought produce from settlements on the Parramatta. But the hospital was his masterpiece. Three merchants, Simeon Lord, Garnham Blaxcell and D'Arcy Wentworth, undertook to build a large hospital in Macquarie Street free in return for a monopoly in the rum trade. They were a little hampered because there was no archi-

JOHN MACARTHUR

From a portrait in the possession of Lady Stanham at Camden Park

By courtesy of the Trustees

LACHLAN MACQUARIE

From the portrait by John Opie, R.A., in the possession of the Mitchell Library, Sydney

tect in the colony, but the series of buildings they erected are still standing and still in use, though not as a hospital. It was too big for the colony's requirements, but Macquarie liked everything big and, besides, some spare space was likely to come in useful. News of this clever business deal did not reach England for some time; pleased as he was himself, Macquarie seemed to have a suspicion that Lord Castlereagh would not approve. Instead he asked for a Government Architect, and the Colonial Office did not see the need for one.

In 1814 when Francis Greenway arrived, a convict but recommended by Phillip, Macquarie found he had the services of a first-class architect and he was really possessed by building fever. Greenway built a lighthouse and on the occasion of its opening in 1817 received his pardon. He built St James's Church, churches at Liverpool and Windsor whose simplicity is dateless, the "Female Factory" at Parramatta, the hospital at Liverpool. . . . Together the Governor and architect planned a city, as Phillip had before, but this was more grandiose. It was to have a cathedral set in a circus of radiating streets, a palace of justice, a new Government House "like Thornbury Castle, only better", an ornate fort, a workhouse, a convict barracks. Of these only the stables of Government House, today's Conservatorium of Music, Fort Macquarie, and the convict barracks were built. Imperial displeasure overtook Macquarie before the rest could be executed.

Hyde Park Macquarie allotted to the citizens as a common, and the Domain, which Bligh, in the teeth of commercial interests, had saved for the people, he surrounded with one of those high walls which he thought so efficacious for morals, and opened to all for their pleasure, but by day only. It was then the beginning of the bush and the end of the town and belated kangaroos, wallabies and emus were still to be found in it.

Macquarie was also a road-builder. First he repaired the Parramatta Road, which already existed, but only just. Macquarie had it levelled and the stumps taken out. It was an earth road, dressed where necessary with crushed stone. All his roads were to be of the same pattern. Despite free labour the project was expensive, so Macquarie set up a toll to pay for it in the region of the modern Railway Square. Pedestrians passed through free, a horseman paid threepence, and vehicles various sums, more for a carriage than a cart.

Later he carried Parramatta Road through another twenty miles to Windsor, then came the Liverpool road, and finally a cross-road from Liverpool to Parramatta with its eight bridges, once called the Dog-trap Road, now Woodville Road. To the south he ran a road to Appin and the Cowpastures. An obelisk in Macquarie Place, then the centre of the town, commemorates the starting point of these roads. There was another road replacing a track to Watson's Bay, the Old South Head Road, built by public subscription and the 73rd Regiment, which, having few duties, was glad of a little pin money. There was also a couple of miles of road built in the direction of Botany Bay and various stretches of private road. They were good roads—except in wet weather. The upkeep of the roads was in the hands of commissioners. Two of them, Simeon Lord and Andrew Thompson, were ex-convicts, and for this reason Samuel Marsden, the Chaplain, refused to accept an appointment and was replaced by D'Arcy Wentworth, who, though not a convict, was not on the highest rung of society. The Colonial Office was not enthusiastic about roads. If the public was not ready to pay for them, Lord Liverpool opined, they were not necessary.

As a soldier, Macquarie was particularly interested in the fortifications. He found them deplorable. Fort Phillip was dilapidated and its enclosure used for a vegetable garden; had its guns been fired the town would have been destroyed. Of Dawes Battery and its fourteen guns Wentworth remarked, ". . . the carriages of the guns are in a bad state of repair, and the embrasures are so low that a single broadside of grape would sweep off all who had the courage or temerity to defend it." The guns on Garden Island were sunk in sand. Sydney was undefended. There was a French scare in 1813 and Macquarie was told to prepare for attack. He had no means of doing so. Fortunately nothing happened. Eventually he built Fort Macquarie, in which his taste triumphed over Greenway's, but even then the town could not have stood up against the enemy who never came.

Everywhere the Governor was pleased to find confusion on which he could exercise his talent for organization. He regularized the revenue, still using King's Jail Fund and Orphan School Fund, which now became the Police Fund and the Orphan Fund. The Police Fund, which supported jails and police and financed public works, was the beginning of consolidated revenue. Into it went three-quarters of the customs duties, of which the backbone was the duty on spirits, and licensing fees. It is a happy thought that the more the citizens drank, the more money there was to control them. The Orphan Fund was for education and poor relief. Other moneys, such as fees for drawing up documents, generally paid the clerks who did the work.

The police force was overhauled, the civil service tidied up with regular hours, and a new Chief Superintendent of Convicts was appointed, the energetic Isaac Nichols, an ex-convict, who was also the Postmaster of the colony. It was Macquarie who set up the first post office. It was what would now be called an agency. Nichols had been assistant to the Naval Officer and as such had brought letters ashore. They were distributed in an irregular and neighbourly way. The *Rose Hill Packet* carried them at twopence each to Parramatta, constables going into the bush would obligingly take letters with them. Now Nichols opened a post-office shop in George Street.

He advertised letters received in the *Gazette* and later listed them at his office. They could be reclaimed at eightpence each. To the more important inhabitants he delivered letters. Convicts, because they moved from place to place and because they very often lacked the eightpence, frequently did not receive their letters. These arrangements applied to mail from England. Internal communications were generally by hand. Dispatches and government orders were carried by constables or members of the Governor's bodyguard. The people at large were informed by a town crier, notices prominently displayed, and a sturdy local grape-vine.

The *Sydney Gazette* had had a struggling existence since 1803. It was not strictly an official organ but it was subject to government censorship. Macquarie set it on its feet by giving the editor, George Howe, a salary. The *Gazette* was very useful to him, for he published in its columns not only his proclamations and government orders but his personal views. It was a handy source of publicity, under his immediate control, in the numerous quarrels that were to come.

Most persistently Macquarie asked permission to set up a colonial bank as the only means of regulating the financial chaos. The Colonial Office thought it unnecessary, but despite this the Bank of New South Wales opened its doors in 1817 with a subscribed capital of £3625. It was to cost the Government nothing, the initial capital was to be put up by private subscribers, but it would handle government business. It had a stabilizing effect and its own paper money, backed by sufficient reserves, replaced the confusion of promissory notes, store receipts, and more doubtful papers that did duty for currency. As England would not send out a colonial coinage Macquarie made his own. He bought up Spanish dollars, had the centres (called "dumps") cut out of them, and so had money of two denominations, on which he fixed arbitrary values. A savings bank was already in operation to safeguard any money convicts might have. It was little used, since they preferred to hand over their valuables to untrustworthy individuals rather than to trust authority.

Macquarie was always writing to the Colonial Office asking for something—the usual supplies, two small colonial vessels (very much cheaper than a King's ship, as he pointed out), advancement and higher salaries for the deserving, promotion for himself—but most important was a dispatch written in April 1810 to Lord Castlereagh, for in it he enunciated a policy that was to colour the eleven years of his governorship.

I was very much surprised and concerned, on my arrival here, at the extraordinary and illiberal Policy I found had been adopted by the Persons who had preceded me in office respecting those Men who had been originally sent out to this country as Convicts but who, by long Habits of Industry and total Reformation of Manners, had not only become respectable, but by many degrees the most useful members of the community. These persons have never been countenanced or received into Society. I have, nevertheless, taken upon myself to adopt a new Line of Conduct, conceiving that Emancipation, when united with Rectitude and long-tried good Conduct, should lead a man back to that Rank of Society which he had forfeited, and do away, in so far as the Case will admit, All Retrospect of former bad conduct. This appears to me to be the greatest Inducement that can be held out towards the Reformation of the Manners of the Inhabitants and I think it is consistent with the gracious and humane intentions of His Majesty and his Ministers in favour of this Class of People. I am aware it is a measure which must be resorted to with great Caution and Delicacy, but I am hopeful that in time it may be extended beyond the Line within which I must restrict myself for the present.[2]

Macquarie had the courage of his convictions, but he lacked the "Caution and Delicacy". He appointed emancipists to positions of trust, even to the magistracy; he steadfastly upheld their right, since they had paid for their sins, to be treated on their merits like any other free citizens; he invited them to dine at Government House; he took Redfern to be his honoured friend and on his behalf suffered the last of many humiliations. He was sincere in his belief that, after serving his sentence and reforming, a convict should be received back into society. Combined with this humane principle there was a policy.

It had been proved that danger to the State and to its peace and well-being came from the officer class rather than from the convicts. Macquarie, like King, saw that the best way to offset their power was by raising up a numerous and well-to-do middle class who, owing everything to the Government, would be loyal and who would supply a useful and moderate public opinion. To the peasant farmer Macquarie added the idea of the independent trader and honest artisan. He had little time for the grazier who claimed so much land and who was carrying settlement beyond the limits of his authority. The grazier, who was inevitably an officer or man of means, was the intruder in this colony whose rightful citizens were peasant farmers and the convicts for which it was founded.

Out of the Governor's attitude there sprang a sharp and acrimonious division of society. Before it had been the bond and the free. Now it was the emancipists and the exclusionists, or the "pure Merinos", as they came to be called. The exclusionists were the well-to-do minority who had come free to the colony, the officers of the regiment, ex-officers, the higher civil officials, the merchants, the privileged. The emancipists were the more respectable and successful of the ex-convicts; below them in the hierarchy came the expirees, convicts who had worked out their sentences; and below these the convicts. Amongst the convicts there were many degrees, the clerk, the overseer, the assigned servant, the desperate and hopeless felon in the chain gang. . . . Foveaux seems to have been of Macquarie's opinion and to have recommended to him some men who had been convicted and to have warned him against some, like the chaplain Marsden, in the exclusionist camp. The exclusionists felt about the emancipists much as in America the white Southerner feels about the negroes. They were determined not to touch pitch. They were a small minority and had much to lose; they secretly feared the convicts, especially when, after the battle of Waterloo, times were bad in England, crime increased, and convicts were sent out in greater numbers than ever before. In eleven years some 22,000 convicts arrived in Australia. Actually, the emancipists were the exclusionists' natural allies for they, too, had a good deal to lose. Of competition there was little, for the two classes diverged along natural lines. Grazing and officialdom was for the exclusionist, farming and small trading was for the emancipist. It was very difficult for anyone, even with the Governor's patronage, to cross the dividing line. Three men did—Lieutenant Bellasis who killed a man in a duel fought for a woman's honour, Sir Henry Brown Hayes who committed the equally gentlemanly sin of abducting an heiress, and the Reverend Mr Fulton, sent out for his politics, whose cloth and simple goodness made him acceptable. Captain John Piper married a convict's daughter and survived socially.

King had made tentative efforts to raise up an emancipist class, but he did not make a social issue of it. He merely found it expedient, Macquarie raised it to the height of a moral issue. Before him the cleavage had been accepted but dormant, now it became a matter of first importance. The Governor was left on the wrong side of the door.

For two and a half years everything went smoothly. If Macquarie had enemies they kept quiet. On 27th October 1810, when St Phillip's was consecrated, he wrote to the Colonial Secretary: "I am rejoiced to have it in my power to inform your Lordship that there is already within the Short Period of my Government a very apparent Change for the better in the Religious Tendency and Morals of All the different Classes of this Community."[3]

Macquarie worked very hard, he had no taste for delegating authority, he liked to attend to things himself. He kept regular office hours when he was not touring the country with a nabob's camp equipage, costing £551 10s. 7d. for which unauthorized expenditure he was duly reproved by his masters in Whitehall. He exhorted, he advised, he patronized. He was in his element. He paid special attention to the Hawkesbury, the most fertile part of the country but subject to floods. He planned five towns on high ground whither the farmers could retire, as into medieval fortresses, in times of danger. In each he set aside land for a church and a school, the proceeds from which should maintain parson and schoolmaster without expense to the Government. He was sorry to see the slackness of the farmers. He read them a lecture. They must build "commodious residences for themselves, and suitable housing for the reception of their grain and cattle"; they must be temperate and thrifty and improve the manner of their dress. He promised them livestock from the government herds to be paid for on a hire-purchase system in grain, "but none need apply for such indulgence except those who can bring unquestionable vouchers for their honesty and industry and are ready to give good security for their retaining such cow and her offspring in their possession for the course of three years from the time of receiving her"—or so he is reported in the *Sydney Gazette*. In November 1811 he visited Van Diemen's Land, which was nominally under his control, but through distance was practically independent. David Collins had died suddenly and been buried with unnecessary expense, and now, without Macquarie's sanction and to his annoyance, Colonel Davey had been appointed Lieutenant-Governor.

The year 1812 was a halcyon one and Macquarie wrote to the Colonial Secretary:

> I may safely assert that no Governor since Governor Phillip first established the Colony, ever arrived here under such inauspicious and untoward circumstances and difficulties as I have done and had to labor through and overcome; and I believe I may also without vanity and with great truth assert that I have already done more for the general amelioration of this colony, the improvement of the manners, morals, industry, and religion of its Inhabitants, than my three last predecessors, during the Several years they governed it.[4]

(This dispatch was addressed to Lord Liverpool, for Macquarie had not yet received the news that there was a new Colonial Secretary, Lord Bathurst.)

Next year the mountain barrier that for 25 years had restricted the settlement to the coastal plain was crossed. It was not an official expedition. On 11th May Gregory Blaxland, a wealthy free settler, Lieutenant Lawson, and William Charles Wentworth, the son of D'Arcy, set out with four convict servants, four packhorses and five dogs. They had worked out a new approach to the problem. They would follow the crests. It was an epic journey. The bush was so thick that they had to hack their way through and then return for their gear, making it a double journey. Above all the silence demoralized them so that they dared not stop. Grass for the horses was sparse and when found had to be cut and carried to the next camp. A pile of rocks which they called Caley's Repulse marked the farthest point that any other explorer had reached. After that they were in an untouched world. It took seventeen days to reach Mount York and the little party was at the end of its resources, ill, starving, and the horses perishing with thirst. There was no way back. They had to lead the horses down the pass in the dusk in the hope that they would find water. There *was* water and grass "enough to support the stock of the Colony for the next thirty years".

This feat of exploration had been in the interests of sheep; Macquarie had treated it coolly when it was preparing, but the triumphant result pleased him. He sent his assistant surveyor, George William Evans, to ratify the discoveries. His report had a Biblical ring: "I came on a fine Plain of rich land, the handsomest Country I ever saw; it surpasseth Port Dalrymple; this place is worth speaking of as good and beautiful. . . ."[5] It was a land of plenty at last, sunlit, empty, infinite. Only rarely did he meet aborigines, once a party of two women and four children to whom he gave fish and fish-hooks. The children cried, but Evans played with them till they laughed. On the first Christmas Day in the New Country he opened his "tin case of Roasted Beef" and ate it in the flowering wilderness.

He turned back and recrossed the mountains. It had rained on his outward journey, now they were ablaze with bushfires. He was back in Sydney on 8th January 1815.

By April 1815—the year of Waterloo—William Cox, sometime paymaster of the New South Wales Corps, had built a road over the mountains without the loss of a single life. This was truly a feat, and the convicts who had worked on it were rewarded with their liberty.

Macquarie, with his lady and entourage, made a grand progress over it, scattering names as he went. Evans had already named Mitchell Plains, O'Connell Plains—"on which we saw a number of wild Geese"—and Macquarie Plains, which were vaster.

On the banks of the Macquarie River on 7th May he unfurled a Union Jack and solemnly proclaimed the town of Bathurst. He camped there for seven days and found everything good. He gazed on the New Country and planned its future. There was to be a town of his usual pattern, with provision for church and school; in fact, two centres, one for free settlers, the other for convicts. The rich river flats were to be apportioned in grants of fifty or one hundred acres. At first fifty settlers were to be sent and supported by the Government for eighteen months, then after two years a hundred more would be sent and provisioned for six months, after which it was hoped the first group would be able to supply the needs of the second. Graziers could have land farther out, but no support from the Government. It was all very neat and, of course, it did not work out to plan.

Had Macquarie known it, the breaching of the mountains meant the end of his dream, which he also believed to be the Colonial Office's plan, of a compact community of small holders. There would be no holding the sheep now, and for the next fifty-five years the Golden Fleece was to rule the country.

Macquarie had a proprietary interest in the New Country. He sent Evans out again to follow the Macquarie River to the Western Ocean, a grandiose assignment. He succeeded only in finding the Lachlan River, named after Macquarie's young son. It was curious that the rivers should flow away from the sea. The Surveyor-General, Oxley, followed, pushing west beyond the fertile country into a wilderness of swamps and reeds. He turned back within two days' march of the Murrumbidgee. In 1818 he looked for the outfall of the Macquarie with the same result. Was he on the verge of an inland sea? Evans, sent on a detour from the main party, discovered the Castlereagh, crossed the mountains, and came down to the sea at Port Macquarie, at the mouth of the Hastings. No one was any the wiser about the vast interior of the continent. William Charles Wentworth had a vision, rose-coloured by wishful thinking. The Macquarie, he thought, was the head-waters of a great river rivalling the Amazon. "It will surpass all the rivers in the world in variety of climate," he wrote, "since reckoning merely from the spot where Mr Oxley discovered it to its conjectural embouchure, there will be a difference of latitude of 20°." Every product of nature could be grown on some part of its banks and its waters would provide a highway of commerce. Here there would grow up a new civilization, free from all the taints of the old world, and a golden age would begin. He was right in believing that a river system was the answer, as future explorations were to show, but the millennium was as far away as ever.

Meanwhile private enterprise was opening up the bush in the south and south-west. Hamilton Hume beat his way through to the Wingecarribee, Charles Throsby out beyond Sutton Forest. Together they made a wide inland sweep from Liverpool to Jervis Bay, and in 1819 Throsby made his way from the Cowpastures to Bathurst. In 1820 Lake George and the site of Canberra were known and in the next year white men were on the Murrumbidgee. It pleased Macquarie to see his realm enlarged; he issued instructions and made plans for the new territory as if he were dealing in English counties; he appointed the aboriginal Bookoogong, who had guided Throsby, chief of his tribe and gave him a brass collar inscribed with his name.

The twenty-eighth of July 1814 marks the turning-point in Macquarie's story. Before this time he had made enemies in the colony, but thought nothing of it. He had also, mingled with praise, received an intimation from the Colonial Secretary warning him not to carry his emancipist policy too far and not by "unnecessary enterprise" to involve the Home Government in expense. In 1812 he should have been warned, for he received a very broad hint:

I am Commanded by His Royal Highness the Prince Regent to acquaint you that the Burden of the Colony of New South Wales upon the Mother Country has been so much increased Since the period of your assumption of the

Government of it, that it becomes necessary that you should transmit a more Satisfactory explanation than any that has yet been received of the Grounds upon which the unusual Expenditure has been Sanctioned by you.[6]

Macquarie did not take the hint. The immediate present was more insistent than any words written sixteen thousand miles and eight months distant. In the colony his power was absolute. His Commission said so.

On that day in July 1814 Jeffery Hart Bent, brother of the Judge-Advocate Ellis Bent, stepped ashore. He had been appointed Judge of the Supreme Court newly set up at Macquarie's most urgent request.

I understand Mr Jeffery Bent is a Man of Considerable Eminence as a Lawyer, good Sense and Conciliatory Manners; and as such would be a great Acquisition to the Colony. It is also very desireable that Unanimity should prevail in the Courts of Civil and Criminal Judicature in Such a Colony as this is, and the Appointment of Mr Jeffery Bent to be the Assistant Judge Could not fail of producing so desirable an Object, when United with the Mild and Conciliatory Manners of his Brother, Mr Ellis Bent.[7]

No sooner had he landed than Macquarie had a taste of his "Conciliatory Manners". He demanded an official residence. Macquarie told him that there were no instructions to that effect and offered him an allowance until the matter was settled in England. Jeffery Bent refused and joined his brother's household, to poison his already irritated mind against the Governor. This irritation had had small beginnings. Ellis Bent had complained that his court-house was too small; Macquarie did nothing about it. He in turn had complained that the Judge-Advocate did not rise when he, the King's representative, came into church. In November 1813 an order went forth that no civil or military officer might leave Sydney without the Governor's permission. In those day of slow, bad transport and great distances, Macquarie naturally wanted to know where to put his hand on his key officers. Bent took no notice. Macquarie hurt his dignity by telling him that it was his duty to come to Government House daily for orders. A conflict of powers immediately arose. Macquarie thought his power absolute. Bent held the high ideal that the judiciary should be independent of political power. He was willing to co-operate, but not to take "orders". His brother took an equally high attitude on his appointment but was unwilling to co-operate. Both were inevitably sucked into the exclusionist attitude of their friends and associates. They looked on New South Wales as no more and no less than a penal settlement.

Macquarie had quarrelled also with the Chaplain, Samuel Marsden, another dominant man. Foveaux had warned him against Marsden. At first relations had been amicable enough, but temporal and spiritual power eventually clashed. There was a scarcity, owing to droughts, in the colony, and because Macquarie had fixed the price of wheat below its scarcity market value, farmers were not bringing their grain to the store. Macquarie countered this, as his way was, with a government order, commanding farmers to sell their wheat to the Government on pain of having their debts to the Government called in. The chaplains were sent this order to read from their pulpits. Marsden, a farmer himself, refused. He would not have politics brought into his church, it was for the worship of God and not for the Governor's convenience. It was again a clash of professional ideals, but underneath it, too, was the emancipist question which divided them. Marsden had shown, when he refused to sit on the Roads Commission with two ex-convicts, where his sympathies lay.

More seriously still, Macquarie was losing the support of his own regiment. The officers' professional pride forbade them to mix with men who had been convicted felons. The presence of his regiment had given Macquarie an advantage no other Governor had enjoyed. He was losing it.

Three regiments served in New South Wales during Macquarie's governorship. The first was his own, the 73rd Highlanders, under Colonel O'Connell whose tour of duty lasted from 1810 to 1814. By this time Macquarie and O'Connell were bad friends and the rank and file were out of hand. Macquarie writes of their "gross irregularity of behaviour and alarming degree of licentiousness . . . exhibiting scenes of disgraceful riot and confusion to the dread and terror of peaceful inhabitants".[8] On the emancipist question the officers accepted socially the ex-convicts they met at the Governor's table, but their general attitude was made clear when they court-martialled a young officer for "conduct unbecoming to a gentleman" because he unknowingly sat down to a game of cards with an emancipist.

It was at Macquarie's own request that the 73rd was withdrawn. He asked that no regiment be sent to serve for more than three years in the colony because both officers and men, having not enough to do and too many temptations, became demoralized. He was against giving land grants to officers, though out of a kind heart he sometimes broke his own rule. He asked for a specific instruction on the subject. He also very sensibly asked that when a regiment was moved none of its officers or men should be granted leave to stay behind. He had seen the trouble that came from the remnant of the New South Wales Corps which remained.[9]

The second regiment was the 46th Regiment of Foot (South Devon) under Colonel Molle. They gave considerable trouble, because before they even arrived the officers took a vow that they would have no dealings with convicts. The 73rd had lost caste, they would not. The regiment took sides against the Governor and amongst other occurrences was the caricature of Macquarie drawn by an ensign on the guardroom wall. Other officers amused themselves by adding unseemly embellishments and "scurrelous labels". Macquarie heard of it and was furious. Molle reproved the ensign, but did not punish the others. Macquarie allowed the now terrified and abject ensign to return to England under circumstances that would not ruin his career, but he got no satisfaction from the commandant. Molle himself suffered the vexations of unpopularity, was lampooned, suspected his officers, and most unconstitutionally had their desks broken open and searched. As a military man, Macquarie was horrified. D'Arcy Wentworth discovered that at least one of the lampoons had been written by his son William Charles, now on the way to England. He told Molle, there was a *rapprochement* in the mess, and an Address of Affectionate Esteem was offered by the officers to the colonel. It was a barely veiled attack on Macquarie. Molle then tried to court-martial D'Arcy Wentworth for a crime he had neither committed nor hidden.

All this, in great detail, was reported to the Colonial Office. In the colony the regiment was popular, it provided so much amusement.

The third regiment was the 48th (Northamptonshire), under Colonel Erskine, which arrived in 1817. The colonel and his two senior officers were loyal to the Governor, accepted the emancipists they met at Government House, and even tried to introduce Dr Redfern to the mess. The trouble now was internecine, subalterns *versus* senior officers. This was an improvement on the 46th, but neither comfortable nor tranquil.

The absence of Macarthur, that scourge of Governors, for the first eight years of his rule was an advantage to Macquarie, but in place of Macarthur he had Bent and Marsden.

Such was the state of things when the stormy petrel Jeffery Bent arrived. Subsequent events were grotesque, comic, futile, and, for Macquarie, tragic. Quarrels snowballed until they became an avalanche.

A new and larger court-house was necessary. Macquarie, having room to spare in his new hospital, conceived the idea of using part of it as a court. When the Bents found that they were to work under the same roof, though in offices otherwise entirely separated from convict patients, the dignity of the law was affronted. They wrote to the Colonial Office about it. So did Macquarie. Macquarie won that round.

In December 1814 Ellis Bent decided that it would be improper for him as a judge to preside any longer over the Bench of Magistrates in the police court. He had done so because there was no one else suitable to fill the position. On 14th December Macquarie, in the *Sydney Gazette*, reprimanded magistrates for their carelessness in giving certificates for pardons. Ellis Bent took this as an insult to himself. Without telling the Governor he withdrew from the Bench. Macquarie sent for him and reprimanded him in a stormy scene. The Governor announced in the *Gazette* that the Judge-Advocate refused to sit on the Bench. This was a pyrrhic victory. Bent, to whom Macquarie had sent his codification of the Port

Regulations, not for a legal opinion but simply to have them vetted as to proper legal terminology, returned them with the report:

> I cannot in the due discharge of My Duty to my Sovereign, or to my own conscience, consent to attempt to give legal form to that which is illegal, or to frame or draw up regulations, many of which, in the due exercise of my functions as a Judge, and with proper regard to My Oath to administer Justice according to Law, I cannot enforce in my Judicial capacity. . . . Your Excellency will excuse me for saying that Your Order would be no justification to me in my own eyes or in the Opinion of His Majesty's Ministers, more particularly if I am right in my Opinion that it is no part of my Official duty to draw up Your Excellency's regulations.[10]

This was pure obstructiveness, because when sent to the Crown Law Office in London the regulations were not considered incompatible with English law, but for the moment Macquarie could do nothing except write to Lord Bathurst.

The gilt was off Macquarie's gingerbread world. A three-year drought blasted the land, the harvests were poor, the cattle dying. As Macquarie had suspected, Davey was too lax and things were going badly in Van Diemen's Land. In dispatches Macquarie accused him of dissipation, profligacy, malversation, disobedience, and even smuggling. The Governor and Colonel O'Connell had fallen out, and the reason is clear from Macquarie's accusations. The colonel was now described as a man of "irritable temper and overbearing disposition" and of "illiberal prejudices". The lesser civil officers were ill-disposed because Macquarie, in an economy campaign, had cut down their privileges. Convicts were arriving faster than the colony could absorb them. Even the aborigines were murdering shepherds on the outskirts of the settlement. Nearer home, Mrs Macquarie's coachman ran over and killed a child. When the coroner brought in a verdict of accidental death Macquarie's enemies spread the report that he had been coerced.

In 1815 everything went wrong. Macquarie had got the two colonial vessels he asked for, *Kangaroo* and *Emu,* but they were unsuitable and the naval officers commanding them were a cut above carrying coals and other such chores. One proved obliging, but Jeffreys of the *Kangaroo* was, according to Macquarie, incompetent, insolent, and ruled by his wife. Eventually both ships were returned to England, *Kangaroo* taking aboard, against orders, a merchant in debt to the Government.

The other disturbances are too numerous and petty to retail. The main trouble arose when the two judges refused to convene their courts. When the judiciary was reformed and the Supreme Court set up, it was the Government's intention to furnish the colony with two solicitors. One, Moore, arrived safely, but the other, Garling, was captured by the Americans during the 1812 war. No legal business, the Bents argued, could be conducted with justice until there were two solicitors, one to represent each side in a case. Macquarie pointed out that there were already three other solicitors in the colony. They had all come as convicts, but the most formidable of them, George Crossley, had been free and in practice for twelve years. He had never been in trouble since his arrival, he was competent and understood court procedure. The other two were more doubtful. All three petitioned Macquarie; he sent their petition to the judges with the request that they might be allowed to act in the public interest in the cases already in hand. He laid himself open to a bitter retort that he "in an unprecedented and unprofessional manner" was trying to "exercise an undue influence with the Supreme Court in their favour, thereby insinuating most unworthily and manifestly that the court would grant to the recommendation of your Excellency what they would not grant to the merits of their respective cases".[11]

The Supreme Court was scheduled to open on 18th May 1815, the Governor's Court on the eighth. Macquarie named two magistrates to sit with the judge in the Supreme Court and two respectable citizens to sit with Ellis Bent. Not unnaturally he chose men who, acceptable themselves, were supporters of his emancipist policy. The court was twice adjourned whilst the judge and the magistrates fought out the issue in private. The magistrates were for admitting one ex-convict solicitor, Crossley, on the grounds that men who had worked out their sentences should be received back into society, that emancipists had held many responsible positions under the Government, and that great inconvenience and damage was being suffered by the public from having no courts. Jeffery Bent quoted legal decisions in England and the damage to the court's dignity if emancipists were allowed to plead. Tempers ran high. The court was opened, but Bent refused to hear the petitions. There was a violent quarrel in the open court between the judge and the magistrates. Crossley said he would appeal to the Governor, which was oil on the fire. The court was adjourned, but recriminations went on. A month was lost in bickering. Macquarie reminded the judge that there had been no civil court for ten months; no debts had been recovered and those in prison for debt had had no relief. Bent replied with venom. Macquarie sent the correspondence to England and each of the Bents wrote his account to the Colonial Secretary. Lord Bathurst wearily recalled the brothers, but explained in his dispatch to Macquarie that it was on account of their behaviour and not of their principles, which he found quite correct. This took a long time and whilst an answer was awaited no courts were held, to the confusion and damage of this particularly litigious society.

For two years Jeffery Bent remained and was fertile in ways of annoying the Governor. He was angry that he had not, like his brother, been given the right to use the turnpikes without paying toll. At first he was not asked to pay the threepence for himself and horse, but when the men on the gates knew that Governor and judge had quarrelled they demanded it. Bent declared the tolls illegal and the money misappropriated, since it was not used for upkeep of roads. He refused to pay and crashed through the gates, using "language natural to an angry Englishman on such an occasion". The toll-gatherers reported to D'Arcy Wentworth, the police magistrate, who in turn, on meeting Bent in the street, expostulated with him. There was a scene which no doubt delighted all spectators. Bent declared that as judge of the Supreme Court he was not amenable to criminal jurisdiction. He did not appear. He was fined £2. He did not pay it nor did he use the turnpike again.

Ellis Bent was now fatally ill. He asked leave to make a sea voyage for his health. Jeffery Bent offered to act in his place. Macquarie refused this offer and called on the Solicitor, Frederick Garling, who had now arrived, to be his legal adviser and preside in the Governor's Court. During the wrangling Ellis Bent died, aged thirty-one, and was canonized by the Governor's opponents. Macquarie, though praising him formally in his dispatches, reproved Marsden for blasphemy, so highly did he laud "the saint of the Exclusionists".

Garling, as Acting Judge-Advocate, admitted two emancipist solicitors, for now again the colony had only one free solicitor. Bent immediately spread the story that Garling was bought. There is no evidence of this, but Garling's harsh judgments were later used against Macquarie.

Another fish soon fell into Bent's net in the shape of a discontented and unhappy young chaplain, Benjamin Vale. He had expected much of the colony, but what he received was ten shillings a day and the military equivalent of a curacy. He had a wife and family to support and the cost of living was high; he longed to return to England, but Macquarie could not release him from his military commission. Suddenly the colony was electrified to hear that Mr Vale, invoking the Navigation Acts, had seized as a prize an American ship, *Traveller*, which had come in with a much needed cargo of tea. Forty-two American ships, beginning with *Philadelphia* in Phillip's time, had come to the colony, eight of them during Macquarie's government. No one had questioned the legality of trading with them, though the East India Company had a nominal trade monopoly and the Governor's instructions always automatically forbade intercourse with foreign ships. The government solicitor, Moore, acted as Vale's agent and they were seen going from Jeffery Bent's house to the ship. Macquarie, as soon as he heard of it, released the ship and scolded the chaplain. Vale took his admonition in bad part and was put under arrest. He was tried and found guilty of "conduct subversive to good order and discipline", a small matter compared with the charges Macquarie had made against him. As punishment he was to be "publicly and severely reprimanded". On account of his cloth, Macquarie waived the publicity and delivered the reprimand with no greater audience than his personal and military staff, and the Major of Brigade. Lord Bathurst was, of course, told the whole story. It crossed with a dispatch from him warning Macquarie that under the Navigation Acts it was illegal for him to admit any foreign ships. It had been condoned in the past because of necessity, it would not be again. Macquarie was under no compulsion to publish his dispatches. To find himself at fault may have been painful, but it did not deter him. To punish Moore for his part in the affair Macquarie stopped his salary and ration. Moore wrote to the Colonial Office complaining and setting out a formidable list of illegal acts which he attributed to the Governor. Vale, still smarting, drew up a petition to the House of Commons indicting Macquarie. Bent no doubt supplied the ammunition.

One prime scandal was the summary flogging of three men who were caught trespassing in the Domain at night. Macquarie had claimed that they were of bad character and as a magistrate he had the right to punish them. They were now represented as the innocent victims of a tyrant. It was implied that this arbitrary behaviour was a habit with Macquarie and that every citizen feared for his liberty. Two of the men went to Bent and made a statement, and the flogger went to Marsden and made a statement. This was exhumed, and Macquarie was also charged with selling pardons and rigging the inquest when his wife's coachman ran over a child.

Macquarie heard of the petition through an informer and only after Vale had taken it out of the country in *Emu*. He lost his head and cancelled land grants to those reputed to have signed it, for which reason some of them recanted. A saturnalia of abuse followed and all the parties wrote to the Colonial Office. Macquarie it was claimed had now tried to deprive citizens of their legal right of petition.

The whole imbroglio became more and more petty. Bent refused to give up the official set of Statutes, the only one in the colony. With a trumped-up charge he landed Macquarie's staunch adherent, Commissary Broughton, in prison and it took the Bench of Magistrates a week to exonerate him. When Judge-Advocate Wylde arrived armed with a dispatch recalling Bent he ignored it, and even in December 1816 attempted to open the Supreme Court. He ignored communications from the Governor, so Macquarie published in the *Sydney Gazette* an excerpt from Bathurst's dispatch dismissing the judge.

Bent now had nothing but a nuisance value. His sister-in-law refused to move out of the official residence and when, after a most acrimonious correspondence, she finally left, an equally long and equally acrimonious correspondence began over payment for the improvements she claimed to have added to the house. In the end Macquarie paid her £249 1s. She then asked for her husband's body to be removed from the churchyard to the church. Macquarie refused. Jeffery Bent retorted:

> If your Excellency notwithstanding shall persist in the refusal . . . I will cause the request and denial to be inscribed on the present tomb, that when those who knew my brother shall chance to read the inscription the sigh they breathe over departed worth, may bear a silent malediction upon what I shall be authorised to call, and ever shall consider, your despicable Conduct.[12]

Macquarie won the last trick. When the Bents were about to embark two detainers were lodged against them, one by a carpenter asking payment for work done years before, the other by a magistrate for money he had lent to Ellis Bent. Departures were always advertised in the *Gazette* so that creditors could collect money due to them before it was too late. Jeffery Bent declared the claims to be false. Their ship was about to sail, the courts were not sitting. (That was a particularly good touch.) They would have to forfeit their passage money or pay the debts. In this situation they asked Macquarie for help. They were told through his secretary that they must abide by the law. At last, however, he let them go.

The Colonial Office now had a taste of Jeffery Bent's mettle. He pestered the Government incessantly for compensation, for expenses, for a statement that his recall was political. . . . He even offered his services as Governor of New South Wales.

Quarrels with Marsden, all petty, filled in the blank left by Jeffery Bent. The Bents were gone, but the damage was done. Macquarie had lost the high confidence that he brought to his governorship. He kept up the pace. His building programme went on and, indeed, he could not stop, for more and more convicts arrived, product of the depression in England, and they must be put to work. The year 1818 was a bad one; there was scarcity in the colony; the settlers could not support assigned servants and were sending them back to the store. They must not remain idle. Public works were the only answer, but public works cost money, manipulate them as Macquarie might.

He flogged himself with an appearance of his old energy. He founded his Native Institution at Parramatta in the hope of "civilizing" aboriginal children. It prospered and then faded. He poured out dispatches, letters, journals, but energy was not enough. Every mistake he had ever made was catching up on him. He had too many enemies. Lord Bathurst was displeased with him. His greatest crime was extravagance. Macquarie promised retrenchment, but could not carry it out. A disgruntled friend of Marsden's, Nicholas Bayly, wrote to Bathurst blaming Macquarie for misdemeanours that happened in transports, for treating convicts laxly, for Garling's harsh sentences, for desecration of the sabbath and other disorders. Bathurst was impressed and sent the letter to Macquarie without the signature. Macquarie had to defend himself. Lord Bathurst was annoyed by the long tale of quarrels which had come to him. Macquarie had acted against the Navigation Acts in allowing *Traveller* to land tea; his court martial of Vale was illegal, for chaplains could only be court-martialled for offences pertaining to their sacred calling.

> The whole of your proceedings against him were consequently illegal and it is therefore utterly out of my power to give them any sanction of approbation. . . . I have only to lament that you should, in a moment of irritation, have been betrayed into an act which, at the same time that it exposes you personally to considerable risk, cannot fail to diminish your Influence among the more respectable part of the Community, who justly look upon the Law as the only true foundation of authority.[13]

It might have been Macquarie himself speaking to a defaulting inferior, only Macquarie would have been more sonorous.

Then came the matter of the petition. He had acted unconstitutionally. He was instructed to restore Moore's salary at once.

Cut to the heart, Macquarie sent in his resignation.

> I lose all I have been so long labouring for, with so much Anxiety, fatigue of Body, and distress of Mind, for I have certainly *not added to either my Rank or Fortune* by my eight years of hard Service in New South Wales; Consequently all that is now left to console me is an approving Conscience.[14]

After a long pause Bathurst asked Macquarie to reconsider his resignation. His character and intentions had never been in doubt; he had been blamed only for the rashness of some of his actions. Macquarie stayed on, but he had lost the illusion of absolute power.

In 1818 Macquarie disposed of his adversary Marsden. Judge-Advocate Wylde reported to him that Parramatta jail was so overcrowded as to become a danger and suggested that some of the minor offenders be released. Macquarie acted on the suggestion without consulting Marsden, the chief magistrate of the district. Marsden in a fury wrote his resignation. Macquarie took no notice, but in the *Sydney Gazette* there appeared a paragraph saying that His Excellency had been pleased to dispense with the services of the Reverend Samuel Marsden as Justice of the Peace and Magistrate at Parramatta.

But it profited him nothing, nor could any other local victory. Lord Bathurst was seriously displeased. Macquarie had been attacked in the Commons; colonial expenses were hard to explain, especially at a time when the Home Government was beginning to look to its ugly duckling for some return. In 1812 a Select Committee of the House of Commons had investigated the system of transportation. The mother country was attentive as never before to the deeds and needs of New South Wales. Bathurst decided to investigate on the spot Macquarie's government of which he had had so many complaints. He had come to suspect that the colony was not fulfilling its true function as a penal settlement. The Governor's emancipist policy was against his grain, too. These were only surface reasons. Macquarie's mistakes gave him a colourable excuse for investigation. In John Thomas Bigge, a barrister and sometime Chief Justice of Trinidad, he had a man of incisive character who could be trusted to bring home the right answers. He was appointed Commissioner in January 1819 and arrived in Sydney on 26th September. His commission was read on 7th October. He was already hand in glove with the leaders of the exclusionist party.

Very soon Macquarie was instructed in his powerlessness. The test case was that of Dr Redfern, who had come to the colony in 1801 with a life sentence for no greater crime than advising the mutineers of the *Nore* to stick together. A surgeon's mate, he had been given the duties of a doctor at Norfolk Island from necessity. He proved himself skilful, and had offered himself for examination before a group of naval surgeons—the first examination held in Australia, and a successful one. He had undertaken vaccination against smallpox; he had reported sensibly and usefully on health and hygiene in transports. Governor King granted him an absolute pardon. He had become the best surgeon in the country, numbering the Governor amongst his patients. He was a respected citizen, a director of the Bank of New South Wales. Macquarie said of him, "Mr Redfern, as a Professional Man, is a very great Acquisition to this Colony, his Talents as a Surgeon being far superior to those of any other Person of that Description in this Country, and perhaps equal to those of the Most Skilful Medical Men in any other Country." Despite his talents, he was passed over when the position of Surgeon-General fell vacant. Now, having been a successful landowner also, he wished to retire to his property at Airds and asked his friend Macquarie to make him magistrate for the district. Macquarie was only too glad to make him this return for his services and drew up his commission on 30th October. There was nothing new in elevating an emancipist to the Bench. Andrew Thompson and Simeon Lord, for instance, had both served. But Bigge was scandalized. He first remonstrated and then he commanded. In vain did Macquarie turn on his loftiest sentiments and most sonorous periods. Both parties wrote to Lord Bathurst. In the interval Macquarie had his way, but when Lord Bathurst's answer arrived the Governor was instructed to omit Redfern's name from the new Commission of the Peace which by law must be proclaimed on the accession of George IV. This time Macquarie was forced to obey.[15]

A pamphlet published in England, *Letter to Lord Sidmouth on the*

Transportation Laws, the State of the Hulks and of the Colony of New South Wales attacked his administration bitterly. For his defence Macquarie circulated a questionnaire to all magistrates and chaplains, asking their opinion on certain measures and including a crucial question: Did they think that the colony had improved under his governorship? Bigge took exception to this and vented his rage on Macquarie. From that day ordinary social relations were broken off. Bigge was openly contemptuous of the Governor. Macquarie wrote to the magistrates and chaplains saying that he would not after all require their answers. This was not enough. In February 1820 he sent in his resignation once more. "I am now heartily tired of my situation here," he wrote, "and anxiously wish to retire from Public Life as soon as possible." In July a dispatch was written accepting it. The interval before his possible departure dragged out. Bigge's departure in February made little difference. Macquarie kept up appearances. He visited Van Diemen's Land again, where bushrangers were giving trouble. He reluctantly signed twenty-six death-warrants for their extirpation. Had not his own death-warrant been signed? There were quarrels, but the bite had gone out of them. Old friends were dying, he had been forced to humiliate Redfern, his whole policy was shattered. The emancipists petitioned the King asking for their legal status to be regularized. Macquarie supported them to the last. On 7th November Sir Thomas Brisbane, the Governor elect, arrived and his Commission was read on 1st December. Macquarie left Government House and spent most of the two months until a passage home could be arranged for him in touring the country, making his farewells. The gentlemen of Sydney presented him with a piece of plate valued at five hundred guineas. Did he remember that he had been in the country a fortnight before they presented him with an address of welcome?

In February he sailed in the transport *Surry*. He had come in a King's ship and Bigge had returned in one. He was discredited and had not much longer to live. He had already spoken his own epitaph: "I found New South Wales a jail and left it a Colony; I found a population of idle prisoners, paupers and paid officials, and left a large free community thriving in the produce of flocks and the labour of convicts."

There is a curious likeness—or perhaps not so curious since they faced similar conditions—between King and Macquarie, though in character the two men were poles apart. Both had great energy, both made a good beginning that tailed off into a quagmire of quarrels. Both had a passion for tidiness and both leant heavily on government orders; both were artists in employing patent devices for saving government expense. Macquarie took over a number of ideas from King and developed them. For example, King had endeavoured to raise up an emancipist class to balance the monopolists. Macquarie made this the cornerstone of his policy. King divided revenue into the Jail Fund and the Orphan School Fund, under Macquarie they became the Police Fund (consolidated revenue) and the Orphan Fund devoted to education and charity. King set out Port Regulations, Macquarie codified them. . . . More superficially, each had trouble with his predecessor. This may be no more than "times makyth the man", but it is an interesting point and a link in continuity.

The Macquarie period is more fully and variously documented than any earlier time. There is ample evidence to show how life was lived then in city and in the bush, for it was then that the cleavage began.

Macquarie's world was predominantly urban and he wished to keep it so, for he liked everything under his own eye and, in a penal settlement, dispersion was dangerous. The life of the white man in Australia, in spite of the bush and the great open spaces, has always been predominantly urban. It began with the little settlements huddled together at the water's edge. The bush was as trackless as the sea. To survive the inhabitants must cling together. Twenty-two years later, when Macquarie arrived, Sydney was still the centre. It was the seat of government, but it was more than that, it was the focal point, the Mecca. Most of the prisoners were from London or the provincial cities of England. The bush had no attractions for them. As soon as they received their ticket of leave or their freedom most of them managed to stay in the town. By 1820 there were 12,079 men, women and children in Sydney, or more than half the total population. Parramatta was another urban centre. It was government policy to keep the convicts together; the assignment system dispersed them, but their masters were responsible for their discipline and in a less degree for their well-being.

The Sydney of Phillip's day, with its huts of wattle and bark, had disappeared entirely except for a few names scattered round the harbour. Under the Corps a haphazard settlement grew up without beauty or dignity. Macquarie left a pleasant little town whose general shape is still discernible today. We have its specification. In 1820 there were 1840 buildings in the town, 259 were of brick, 68 of stone, the rest of wood with a few pisé huts. The walls were whitewashed, the roofs of wooden shingle or slates, or of colonial tiles. Until 1815 there had been no architect, so the houses were simple in structure, square, with lean-to kitchens and small windows with tiny panes of glass. The doors were solid, with heavy bolts, as if fear walked the streets. Every place of business was also a home and most of them had gardens full of English flowers and hedges of geraniums.

The whole of the town was held in the arms of a bay. On its western tip was the slaughter-house, convenient to the water for disposal of refuse and happy rendezvous for the seagulls. Beside it was Dawes Battery, and on the high ground above was old Fort Phillip, built ruggedly of stone and now in disrepair. Below the Fort was a ragged area called the Rocks, "more like the abode of a horde of savages than the residence of a civilised community", said William Charles Wentworth. Tatterdemalion huts and cottages were built at all angles where the ground allowed. They were reached by flights of crazy steps. The area was undrained, unlit, unpatrolled. Its reputation was so unsavoury that the watchmen and constables left it alone, the licensing laws did not run, and escaped convicts, criminals of all descriptions, and the lower type of sailor made it their stamping ground. Not far away was the first church, St Phillip's, with its pepper-castor tower and its bells, familiarly called "the pots". Where Wynyard Station is today was the long line of the barracks and their high-walled parade ground. The Tank Stream, the water supply, ran through the centre of the town and its banks were reserved to save it from pollution, so that there was a green strip. The wooden bridge crossing it is commemorated by Bridge Street. Merchants had their premises on the inner side of the west cape. Here were Robert Campbell's wharf, warehouse, home, and orchard. Near the top of the bay were the Commissariat Stores, where the Maritime Services building stands today. The government wharf was close by and from it a wide road led up to Government House. This stood on a hill studded with springs and was a tranquil, if already crumbling, two-storeyed house, white, with columns supporting a veranda. It had a reception room 50 by 18½ feet and a noble dining-room, but Macquarie was most displeased with it. It had been built by Phillip and, to quote Macquarie, was

> . . . in point of Size Altogether Inadequate to the Residence and Accommodation of even a private Gentleman's Family and Much less that of the Governor in Chief. All the Offices, exclusive of being in a decayed and rotten State, are ill Constructed in regard to Plan and on Much too Small a Scale; they now Exhibit a Most ruinous Mean Shabby Appearance. No private Gentleman in the Colony is so Very ill Accommodated with Offices as I am at this Moment, Not having Sufficient Room in them to lodge a Very Small Establishment of Servants; the Stables, if possible, are still worse . . . it having been of late frequently Necessary to prop them up with Timber Posts to prevent their falling, or being blown down by the Winds.[16]

Macquarie got new stables but nothing else. In front of Government House was a great Norfolk Island pine from which on gala occasions resinous branches were torn and used as flambeaux. And grand parties there were. Macquarie showed Sydney how to celebrate the King's birthday. Between eighty and ninety people sat down to dinner at three o'clock in the afternoon, following a review of the troops and a levee. Nineteen toasts were drunk and "the general style of elegance of the entertainment afforded the utmost gratification to all the partakers of its distinguished festivity". The merry-making went on into the evening when the populace gathered on the lawn

> . . . to behold the decorations of the verandah, which was hung with festoons of

the richest foliage interspersed with a number of lamps and producing a most pleasing and enchanting effect when beheld at a distance, especially as the branches of oranges in full growth that appeared suspended throughout the whole, gave it altogether the air of an illuminated orange grove; and the fascination was rendered complete at the time by the numerous airs and pieces of music performed by the band of the 73rd Regiment which was stationed in the hall of Government House.[17]

The gardens of Government House were under the care of Charles Fraser, a botanist who acclimatized plants from all over the world and distributed useful plants and grasses to anyone who could make good use of them.

Most of the higher officials and successful merchants lived in houses round Macquarie Place and here on a summer evening the band would play.

The Government workshops or lumber-yard, a great square enclosed by a high wall, stood beside the Tank Stream. Here the carpenters, harness-makers, coopers, sawyers, and other tradesmen worked, and here, too, were stored the timber and other raw materials needed.

The markets were like the lumber-yard, another hollow square surrounded by a high wall, against which booths and pens offered vegetables and animals for sale. Here were set up the standard scales, weights, and measures.

Beyond the markets, where the Town Hall now stands, was the burial ground—already, the living thought, too close to their homes.

Bridge Street was practically on the waterfront. The town stretched as far as modern Park Street and beyond were the brickfields. When a southerly wind blew it carried clouds of dust into the town, from which it was called "the brickfielder".

The skyline was low, broken on the high ground, not by spires, but by windmills for grinding corn. On three sides the bush hemmed in the town. It came up to Macquarie Street. To the west the great house of Annandale, Major Johnston's "seat", was an outpost of civilization. On the north Cockle Bay poked a blue finger between the town and the wilderness.

The hinterland could not yet feed this little town, most of whose inhabitants drew rations from the Government Store. The salt meat and even grain, in bad seasons, came from Ireland or the Cape. The citizens enjoyed vegetables and fruit in plenty, unless there was a drought, or a flood on the Hawkesbury, that Arcadia where peaches were fed to hogs to the breath-taking surprise of a newly arrived immigrant, Alexander Harris.

Every manufactured object—if you except a few hundred yards of blanket, some exceedingly rough boots, and the short pipes or dudeens that sold at a penny each—had to be brought in by ship. Tobacco came from Rio or the Cape, sugar, soap, and rum from Bengal, tea and candies from China. Wine, clothing and all other luxuries came from England.

Prices were high in proportion to wages. Fresh meat was 1s. 6d. a pound, poultry 5s. or 6s. a bird, butter 5s. or even 7s. a pound, bread 1s. for a two-pound loaf, wine £3 to £4 for a dozen bottles or £41 for a pipe. The coarsest woollen cloth was 15s. a yard. The rent of a very ordinary house ran into £100 a year. Naturally over eleven years there were fluctuations, but these figures will give a general idea.

Salaries and wages were small. The Governor received £2000 a year, the Judge-Advocate £1200, both with a residence thrown in. The Supreme Court Judge had £800 and no house, the two government solicitors £300 each, a schoolmaster might get £10 or £15 a year with rations, a chaplain 10s. a day. Petty officials were often paid in kind and clerks by fees.

With larger salaries paid to agents in London and little specie in the colony there were often money difficulties.

These figures, however, do not give a true picture, for there were many perquisites, and anyone free and able was sure to engage in trade of some sort, whether or no he was employed by the government. The Reverend Samuel Marsden, for instance, besides being Chief Chaplain and a magistrate, was also a farmer, a merchant, and a grazier, and did very well. Officers were forbidden to trade, but it seems that to a man they did so, personally or through agents. Soldiers earned extra money helping to bring in harvests or by road-building. There were, too, shady sources of income, such as illicit distilling. In the troubled waters there were many opportunities.

The settlement was still artificial and dependent, but it was full of life and growing fast.

It generated its own activity. It was full of anomalies. There were rich men like Alexander Riley who spent £5000 on a house and Captain John Piper who spent £10,000 and furnished it with great luxury; there were many who lived on the lowest subsistence level. Many homes lacked the common necessities, but their fittings were of cedar. There was rigid discipline and much confusion; many regulations and as many ways of evading them; there was an official policy of scrupulous justice and humanity to the aborigines side by side with a callous brutality which commanded convicts to carry sacks of quicklime through the surf on their bare shoulders at Newcastle; gentility and sensitive pride in the privileged found no difficulty in condoning punishments of a thousand lashes.

There were many rungs to the social ladder. The regimental mess rather than Government House was the social arbiter. The officers were more royalist than viceroyalty. The Governor was secure, but they had to look to their pride and keep it bright in the doubtful surroundings of a penal colony. The officers were by no means all blue-bloods, but they had colonial rank as aristocrats and society consisted of those accepted by the military caste. On the other side of the pale were the wealthy emancipists like Simeon Lord. He arrived in the colony in August 1791 with nothing but a seven-year sentence. He was assigned to Captain Rowley and endeared himself to that gentleman by making money for him, and also, in a quiet way, for himself. When he was freed he owned two houses. It was a beginning. His manners were rough, his domestic morals far from strict, but he had drive and imagination. His interests grew and spread. He was a landowner, but that was never his main interest. The processes of nature were too slow, probably. He became auctioneer, storekeeper, ship-owner, general agent, merchant-venturer with interests in pearl-fishing, mining in Van Diemen's Land, sandalwood cutting in the South Seas, flax-growing in New Zealand. He manufactured rope, extracted soda from seaweed and tannin from bark, and at his Waterloo Mills at Botany made cloth and hats. He had been recommended to Macquarie by Foveaux, and since success appealed to the Governor he was favoured and even raised, rather incongruously, to the magistracy.

Andrew Thompson was perhaps the pattern of the good emancipist. He arrived, aged sixteen, during Phillip's governorship and at once was given a clerical job. The Hawkesbury became his sphere of influence where he became constable, boat-builder, landowner. His enterprises included salt works, the building of a toll bridge over the Hawkesbury, and sealing. He had two hundred acres under cultivation and employed from 80 to 120 men. He was described as "a father and a patron" to his neighbours. He gave his life for them, dying from an illness, probably tuberculosis, contracted through prolonged exposure and over-fatigue during Hawkesbury floods. His estate was valued at £20,000, a quarter of which he left to Macquarie.

There is an entry in Macquarie's diary:

> After Service drove for about a mile to the new burying ground, to view the tomb where the remains of our late worthy and highly esteemed good friend Mr Andrew Thompson are deposited, and whose loss we both sincerely lament and deplore; and from whose superior and judicious advice I once fondly flattered myself I should derive good benefit and advantage during my present tour of inspection through the Colony.[18]

Gossip, perhaps malicious, said that Thompson ran an illicit still on Scotland Island.

Francis Greenway, the architect, sent out, it is commonly believed, for concealing assets in bankruptcy, left his mark on the town. Some of his buildings still stand in timeless grace. He was the first architect and he set badly needed standards in workmanship and materials. He was happy, one supposes, in planning a town where architecturally speaking there was at yet nothing. Macquarie was happy, too. He even managed to get Greenway a tiny salary as Government Architect. But the cold wind blew; Macquarie was ordered to dismiss him; Bigge found his buildings far too ornate for a penal settlement, stripped them down, altered the uses of buildings begun, vetoed those not yet started. Greenway was no business man and quite incapable of making a fortune on the side. He sank into poverty and died in 1837.

There were other emancipists who brought gifts, but, lacking acumen, were unable to succeed; amongst them was John Hutchinson, a clever chemist. His crime was forgery, his sentence was for life, but it would seem that he was unworldly rather than felonious. The Society of Arts in England petitioned that he might be allowed to continue his experiments into dyes from wood. Even in the hulks he had tried to carry on his work. The Colonial Office passed the petition on to Macquarie with a recommendation that he act on it. Macquarie was not interested, but he assigned Hutchinson to Simeon Lord and when that did not work gave him a conditional pardon and told him to go out into the woods and discover valuable dyes. Not satisfied with this indulgence, "he asked for a laboratory, chymerical apparatus", a couple of assistants, a kiln, a boat. This, Macquarie thought, was nothing but megalomania.

Hutchinson pleaded—how could he work when Simeon Lord held his instruments and papers against a debt? Macquarie would not help him until he gave proof of his ability. He could do nothing without help. His voice grew weak and soon was no more heard.

Among the emancipists it was the few who succeeded spectacularly, many made comfortable and more or less honest livings, many others sank back into the misery from which they came and were indistinguishable from expirees, just as the free settler without capital on his small land grant became indistinguishable from his ex-convict neighbour, and their assigned servants became part of the family, and propinquity being what it is, as likely as not married their masters' daughters. It was obvious by the time Macquarie left that the land and its future belonged to the grazier and that the settler, while he filled a need in the community, could not expect any of the big prizes.

There was gaiety and colour in Macquarie's Sydney. Apart from the gangs of manacled convicts occasionally seen, it was not obviously a penal settlement. Many uniforms enlivened the streets, not only the scarlet of the regiment on garrison duty—and as a safeguard Macquarie insisted that the soldiers always wore their uniforms—but the red and white of the Veteran Company, a scattering of uniforms from Indian regiments, officers on furlough recruiting their health in the mild climate. The ladies as far as possible followed the English fashions, but also wore silks from China and muslins from India. Those below that status wore print frocks of black and white or red, for so far those were the only dyes that stood up to washing. Gentlemen not in uniform wore the clothes in fashion in England at the time. Petty officials were issued by the Government with duck trousers, blue jackets, check shirts; farmers when they came to town with their produce were to be seen in smocks or fustian jackets, blue trousers, straw hats or caps of kangaroo hide. The regulation dress for convicts was trousers and jackets of coarse yellow material, but this was not always available, so they wore grey or natural woollen slops from home-grown wool, or, if they were undergoing special punishment, a conspicuous black-and-white garment or canvas jacket embellished with a large R. For economy old uniforms, red and blue, were sent out for them from the military stores in England. For decency's sake they were dyed maroon and added to the general patchwork of colour. Outside the town they went almost naked or were clothed like scarecrows. Another touch of colour, the aborigines still hawked fish in the streets.

Ticket-of-leave men, assigned servants, and convict clerks wore their own clothing and looked just like men of their station in England. There was no regulation dress for women convicts and they were much addicted to finery. It was possible to place anyone you met by what he or she wore.

The shops, as David Mann, a schoolmaster, reported at the time of Macquarie's arrival, "are particularly respectable and decorated with much taste. Articles of female apparel and ornament are greedily purchased for the European women in the settlement spare no expence in ornamenting their persons and in dress each seems to vie with the other in extravagance."

There was no public entertainment, but the colony amused itself with dinner, supper and card parties, picnics, excursions on the harbour, excursions by boat to the still thickly timbered North Shore for the macabre entertainment of a corroboree. The fashionable afternoon outing for ladies in their carriages and men on horseback was to Watson's Bay and the Macquarie Light. Dinner was eaten at four or five o'clock and afterwards it was customary to walk in Hyde Park whilst the regimental band played light airs until the summer dusk drove people home and the darkness of an unlighted town, with its dangers of theft and assault, descended. This promenade was so much a matter of routine that in January 1817 the *Sydney Gazette* announced that, on account of the heat, it would begin at half past six instead of half past five.

Apart from Macquarie's grand official celebrations, there were occasional subscription dances.

The really important annual event was the races. In October 1810 a course was laid down in Hyde Park; two purses of fifty guineas were subscribed. The bachelors gave a pre-race ball and festivities went on for a week. Gentleman riders only competed. A special gala dinner was served each evening at five at the Sydney Tavern. There were two balls during the week under viceregal patronage. "The full band of the 73rd played 'God Save the King' in exquisite style and between the country dances filled the room with other melodious and appropriate airs." Thus the *Sydney Gazette*. Macquarie exceeded himself in issuing orders to ensure decorum.

All dogs were to be tied up during the races, no booths to be erected, no intoxicating liquor sold, no gaming, swearing, quarrelling, fighting or boxing, no noise or disturbance. . . .

Merrier were the proceedings at Parramatta in April 1810, where there were trotting races, cockfighting, and "feats of humour". The *Sydney Gazette* in its unmistakable style described it:

> Then succeeded the motley mirth of foot-racing, wheelbarrow races, or rather shamblings, for the heroes who had charge of these wooden concerns were blindfolded to give them the fairer chance of effecting by accident which they had no *visible* means of doing. Jumping in sacks came next in order; and a venerable host gave the calculated complement of calico for a chemise to be run for by these vestals of the *current* order; this was a very warm contest, and was obstinately kept up as long as the fair competitors could themselves keep up.

Litigation, gambling, and hard drinking were common to men of all classes. Horse-play and indulgence in the rough pleasures of the Rocks was not unusual among the younger officers, and amongst the convict population thieving was endemic.

There was no public transport, ladies drove in carriages, gentlemen rode horseback, farmers had their carts, the others walked.

Macquarie favoured education, but was not able to do much about it. There were two government-assisted schools in Sydney, accounting on an average for 103 boys and 83 girls. The regiment had its own school. When Macquarie departed there were eleven private schools in the colony. Most amazing of them was Laurence Halloran's Establishment for Classical, Mathematical and Commercial Education. Halloran had come out as a convict from the Cape in 1819 for the ugly crime of writing threatening letters. Despite this, rigidly exclusionist families sent their sons to him. The very best families sent their sons and even their daughters to England to be educated.

Commissioner Bigge in 1820 estimated that of the 7568 children in the colony only 895 were receiving any education at all.

For those stricken with illness the outlook was also poor. The only medical men, with one exception, were those paid by the Government to attend the convicts. The only hospitals were for convicts, the free poor were also admitted by special permission. Patients brought their own rations with them until Dr Bowman about 1820 arranged to substitute milk, vegetables and fresh meat for flour and salt meat. Sago was the principal "medical comfort". The orderlies were all convicts, chosen usually because they were useful for nothing else. Other people were treated in their homes or not treated at all. All drugs and medicines in the colony were the property of the Government. Nevertheless Sydney was a healthy place.

The poor and unfortunate were cared for by the Government, but the

Colonial Office looked coldly on Macquarie's assistance to victims of the Hawkesbury floods. It was taken for granted that ex-convicts unable through age and infirmity to maintain themselves should be rationed from the store. Macquarie had a kind heart and charity ranked high in his calendar of virtues. He founded the Benevolent Society in 1813 and by 1818 it had helped 1075 people. He also built a house, but not a workhouse, on the edge of the town as a refuge for old people.

Taking things all round, life was very pleasant for a privileged few, though they did their best to poison it with their quarrels and feuds. For a large section of the community it was tolerable. There were opportunities for those who could take them. For convicts still in the gangs, for those who were old, sick and poor, there was nothing but a thin trickle of charity. Even for them, the outcasts and misfits, life would have been harder still in England.

A new generation was growing up, the cornstalks, the currency lads and lasses, who were Australian born, healthy, vigorous, and, Bigge admitted, with no marked tendency to crime.

With Macquarie an old order ended. The Colonial Office had changed its mind and its policy. It no longer wanted a community of peasant farmers. Macarthur with his samples of Australian-grown wool, with his militant confidence, had convinced the powers that graziers and not small landholders were the men to foster. It was unfortunate that they were identical with the men who had caused so much trouble with their monopolies and their rebellions. Macquarie had been sent to curb them. His instructions were silently scrapped.

A new era was initiated by Commissioner Bigge's report. It was more important by far than the Rum Rebellion, which was, after all, only a colonial episode.

REFERENCE NOTES

1 *Hist. Rec. Aust.*, ser. I, vol. vii, p. 331.
2 *Ibid.*, pp. 275-6. 3 *Ibid.*, p. 346. 4 *Ibid.*, p. 532.
5 His journals may be read in *Hist. Rec. Aust.*, ser. I, vol. viii, pp. 165-77, 611-19.
6 *Hist. Rec. Aust.*, ser. I, vol. vii, p. 476. 7 *Ibid.*, p. 777.
8 *Ibid.*, vol. viii, pp. 1-2. 9 *Ibid.*, p. 4. 10 *Ibid.*, p. 424.
11 *Ibid.*, p. 496. 12 *Ibid.*, vol. ix, p. 279. 13 *Ibid.*, p. 207.
14 *Ibid.*, p. 500. 15 *Ibid.*, vol. x, p. 226. 16 *Ibid.*, vol. ix, p. 70.
17 Quoted from the *Sydney Gazette.*
18 From the MS. in the Mitchell Library.

CHAPTER VIII

THE PASTORAL AGE

WHEN MACQUARIE left Australia the age of absolute power vested in the Governor was over. The jail had became a colony, more than that, it was becoming an entity in its own right. It was no longer, as it had been in its first years, an artificial settlement, fed from without, producing no wealth except for a few and then only by manipulation and monopoly, governed by a legal despotism, its future a matter of faith rather than of deeds. Now behind the façade of Macquarie's world a new age was evolving, based on the final reality of the earth. The sheep had moved in.

Sheep had been brought into the settlement by the First Fleet. They were hairy goat-like animals. All that was expected of them was that their progeny would eventually produce mutton to help out the ration. They did not thrive particularly well. After a miserable passage, when fodder ran out and they had to be fed on a paste of flour and water, the rank grass of Sydney Cove killed most of them.

There is some controversy about who first actually brought the fine-woolled Merino sheep into New South Wales, but there is no doubt as to who was the father of the sheep industry. John Macarthur, born in Devon in 1767, entered the army, volunteered for service in the newly formed New South Wales Corps, and sailed for Australia at the age of twenty-four with the rank of ensign.

He was in debt and undecided what he wanted to do with his life. Farmer, lawyer, soldier? His wife, Elizabeth, who was to prove his trusty partner, was still an unformed girl. The voyage was unpropitious, their quarters cramped and uncomfortable; quarrels with the master of the ship made things worse, and after leaving the Cape Macarthur was stricken with rheumatic fever. Elizabeth had her hands full with a sick husband and a young child. She learned to be indomitable.

On arrival Macarthur was stationed first at Parramatta and then at Sydney. It was not until early in 1794 that he was singled out as a man of ability. Grose made him Supervisor of Public Works. On 12th February 1793 he had received his first land grant of a hundred acres in the Parramatta district. In April he acquired another hundred acres as a prize for good farming. From the first he was a remarkably successful farmer. Within two years his whole property was cleared and he had a hundred acres under crop, his granaries were full, and he had made £400 from selling his farm's produce.

Like other settlers he had been given a cow by the Government, a great blessing where there was a young family. He also had 130 goats, 100 hogs, and two mares. By 1801 he had bought up neighbouring properties at Parramatta and 1770 acres at Toongabbie, on which he ran 1350 sheep. He was also a member of the officers' trading ring and a participant in the rum racket. He was known as a rich man; Governor King assessed his fortune at £20,000, but this is not necessarily accurate.

Macarthur quarrelled with Hunter and King and later more decisively still with Bligh. But for him there would have been no Rum Rebellion. His was the driving force that brought the easy-going Johnston to the sticking point. More remarkable, he was not then even an officer of the Corps. He had been sent to England in 1801 for fighting a duel with his commanding officer, the basic reason being that Colonel Paterson refused to boycott Governor King. He had been rebuked by the Duke of York, the Commander-in-Chief, and bidden return to the colony and obey the Governor's orders. He had then resigned his commission. The time in England had not been wasted, he had talked wool.

In 1810 he was in England again under arrest for his part in the Rebellion, and it was eight years before he was allowed to return. His wife managed the property and Macarthur talked wool again in high places. He now really had something to talk about.

It was in 1794 that he began to breed sheep for wool with sixty Indian rams and ewes and two ewes and a ram from Ireland. By careful cross-breeding, even with this unlikely stock, he improved the fleeces. His interest was aroused. When Colonel Gordon's Merino flock was sold at the Cape, Macarthur bought four ewes and two rams.

The Merino was a native of Spain, renowned for its fine wool. It was a crime punishable with death to export these sheep, but the King of Spain gave a few to the Elector of Saxony, and Saxony in time became an exporter of fine wool. The King of England acquired a small flock, but manufacturers of woollen goods looked to Spain and Saxony for their raw materials. With expanding markets the supply was insufficient and liable to be cut off by war. Spain and Australia are not unlike. They are both wide brown lands with arid pastures. Australia suited the Merino. In 1801 Macarthur took home samples of wool. Their quality eclipsed the fact that he was under arrest. He brought back eight Merino sheep, culled from George III's flock, for which he had paid £135 7s., and an order for a grant of five thousand acres—an unprecedentedly large grant at this time, and it would have been ten thousand had he not quarrelled with Sir Joseph Banks—wherever he chose to take them up.

To the Governor's rage he chose the Cowpastures, a tract which King hoped to keep for the Government's herd of wild cattle. He called his estate Camden after the Secretary of State by whose order he received the grant. He also had a reserve in his favour of five thousand acres adjoining. During his next exile he was able to convince the people who mattered, except Sir Joseph Banks, that Australia was a valuable new source of raw material for the woollen industry. On this slender string of coincidences the future of the colony depended.

The tenor of life in England had been changed by the Industrial Revolution. As she became the leading manufacturer in the world her cities grew. Work in factories lured men from the land, the Enclosure Acts forced them from it. Population began to exceed the capacity of the country to support it. Industry and the carrying trade brought wealth. Most raw materials had to be imported. Markets both to buy and to sell became of crucial importance. No longer was England a tight little island living of and to herself. To her secure and stationary aristocracy, with wealth from land and little necessity to exert itself, was added an energetic and successful middle class whose undertakings must grow or perish. Competition reinforced the natural law of survival of the fittest. Wealth became a badge of success and so wealth became a psychological necessity. Capital was increasing and looking for a market.

The current economic philosophy of laissez-faire, or "go as you please", left those with initiative and money, opportunity to pursue their business untrammelled by anything except the criminal law.

There was also now surplus population. In times of change there are always those who cannot adjust themselves. England no longer feared the loss of population. She was willing to export her poor, and the merchant-venturer spirit was alive again and ready to carry men to the ends of the earth for profit.

Land had always been a magic word in England and now it was realized that there was plenty of land in Australia. Its different quality and type were not so clearly recognized. All the land belonged to the Crown by simple act of possession. It should and could be made to pay. No one who had not visited the fifth continent quite understood that grazing in England was one thing, a tame pursuit, and in Australia quite different.

Australia rose above the threshold of consciousness into this alerted world. The woollen industry was one of the most important. The raw-material market was out of its control. Now came Macarthur with his sample fleeces grown in a British possession and equal in quality to anything procurable from the continent. Australia was sixteen thousand miles away, but the English were a seafaring people. Convicts and supplies had to be sent out, a return cargo of wool dovetailed in nicely with the scheme of things.

The Colonial Office—it was now the Colonial Office and not the Home

Office which had charge of the settlement—reorientated its views. This happened quietly and slowly. There was no proclamation, no declaration of policy. The original idea, conceived in a time of disillusionment, of a penal settlement in which time-expired felons were bribed to stay on by small land grants, was now replaced by a tentative vision of a plantation-style colony where men of capital grew wool for English mills and convicts provided them with cheap labour. Without any help from the Government something of the kind had already happened. The Colonial Office did not have to create it, it only had to foster it. This it set about doing in a roundabout way.

When the New South Wales Corps was recalled it was not pulled out in disgrace. Members were allowed to resign and stay on as settlers under generous terms. Those who had made fortunes and acquired large estates naturally elected to stay. They were, of course, just the men who had, allegedly, caused the trouble. Macquarie was instructed to quell trade monopoly, suppress the rum traffic, and implement the peasant state; but had this been the Government's real policy these key men, so well entrenched, would not have been allowed to remain in the colony. Open rebellion had called for a gesture. It was a very mild one. Already in 1807 Macarthur had sent one bale of wool to England and it brought 10s. 4d. a pound, a price that was not to be bettered for over a century. When Macquarie arrived it is estimated that there were 25,000 sheep in the colony—not, of course, all Merinos. His "extravagance" and the hornet's nest of quarrels which buzzed loudly enough to be heard in England gave the Colonial Office a reason for investigating his government and recalling him.

Commissioner Bigge made a thorough survey of the colony, but it is clear that he arrived with preconceived ideas. He had picked up the trend in the Colonial Office. It was no secret from the first that he sided with the exclusionist faction to which the graziers belonged. His reports were, at one remove, the first overt indication of the Government's change of heart. They became the foundation of future policy. New South Wales was no longer a penal settlement but a plantation-state to which convicts were sent to provide labour.

In the swirl of the turning tide there was some confusion. Wool is inedible, and it was most desirable that the settlement should become self-supporting in foodstuffs, therefore the small farmer must still be encouraged. New South Wales was still a receptacle for convicts, and so those in authority naturally wished to keep settlement compact and the prisoners under control.

It was useless for the small farmer to occupy land except near Sydney, Parramatta, or some other settlement, otherwise he would have no market for his produce. A disgruntled would-be settler who wanted permission to

By courtesy of the Trustees

SIR RICHARD BOURKE

From a contemporary print in the Mitchell Library, Sydney

HAMILTON HUME

Statue on the Lands Department Building, Sydney

set up a "warehouse" or granary at Liverpool pointed out to Governor Brisbane:

> At present the Settlers of that neighbourhood are compelled to carry the principal part of their produce to Sydney, where too many fall a prey to the temptations of contagious example of their own inflamed appetites, absenting themselves from their families for many days together, and consuming in drunkenness and every species of debauchery that pittance which must be replaced by many days starvation or the mortgaging their land.[1]

As for the debauchery, one can only assume that it was very cheap.

Farming was very primitive. The first great difficulty was clearing the land. The trees had to be cut down and burnt, hard, slow labour. Governor Brisbane helped the settlers by organizing clearing gangs of convicts. Each gang consisted of an overseer and twenty-two men. The overseer was paid 3s. 6d. an acre and the men received issues of tea, sugar, and tobacco. For this service the settler was charged six bushels of wheat, valued at 8s. 6d. a bushel for every acre cleared. It was well worth it to him, and by this means 11,503 acres were cleared in two years. Hard work in the open air was also deemed beneficial to the convicts' morals.

John Macarthur was the first man to import and use a plough. Cultivation was generally by hoeing between the stumps, which it was impracticable to grub out except on very lightly timbered stretches. Convict labourers on government farms were required to do a certain amount of hoeing each day and generally only scratched the surface of the ground. There were no manures or fertilizers. Rotation of crops was practised to some extent, but the soil after the fillip given by the ash from the timber burnt on it, was quickly exhausted. It was usual for the farmer to move on to another plot. It was only on the large and well-farmed estates, such as Macarthur's, that the cultivation was continuous.

It was under Brisbane, who was a man of science and born on a landed estate in Scotland, that an Agricultural Training College was formed in the particular hope that the colonial born would learn to farm better than their fathers. He also made an effort to classify land as good, moderate, and bad, so that some settlers should not have too great an advantage over others.

The Agricultural Society of New South Wales was founded at a public meeting held on 5th July 1822. The Governor was patron and Sir John Jamison president. The subscription was five guineas a year and members were further expected to take up shares of £25 each to finance a scheme of importing livestock, so on closer investigation, despite its title, the Society would seem more in the interests of the graziers than the farmers.

Despite official countenance, privileges accorded to the small holder gradually dwindled and those accorded to the grazier increased. On Bigge's advice cattle were no longer issued or lent to settlers from the government herds "except under the circumstances of Loans of Cattle to the Sons of persons who have been Convicts, and are alive and settled in the Colony". The ex-convict himself, apparently, was to have no such assistance. In November 1824 Lord Bathurst instructed Brisbane to cut down the time that new settlers were victualled from the store to four months. Land could not possibly be brought into production in so short a time. At first settlers had been victualled for eighteen months or two years. The reduction of assistance meant that to start farming now a man must have capital.

In 1824 the sale of Crown lands began, but as Brisbane wrote in a dispatch of July 1824, ". . . whilst the system of free Grants exists, there is little chance of extensive improvement taking place generally in the Colony, as the improver of land can never enter the Market in competition with the individual who gets his Land for nothing".[2]

The system of both granting and selling was for a time maintained, but in January 1825 Lord Bathurst was writing to Brisbane stressing the desirability of a property qualification. In this dispatch the Secretary of State outlined a scheme covering the whole land problem. Grants were suspended, except in special circumstances. An upset price of five shillings an acre was placed on all government land irrespective of its quality. It was to be auctioned and to go to the highest bidder. It was, wrote Bathurst, ". . . to be constantly borne in mind that the possession, or at least the command of Capital, are essential qualifications of every Agricultural Settler in New South Wales", and that it was "desirable that men of real capital be encouraged".[3] When grants were given their recipients must be able to spend a sum equal to a quarter of the land's value on improving it.

No longer were settlers allowed convict servants "on the store", they were required to undertake the maintenance of at least one convict. Convict mechanics were no longer to be assigned to settlers, they were to be hired out at a profit by the Government.[4] To employ one would cost the settler 3s. 6d. a week and the man's keep. In one year this brought in to revenue £3712 16s., apart from the saving in the maintenance of 408 convicts at £16 a year.

Government farms which had been allowed to lapse were again brought into production following Bigge's advice. The main one was at Emu Plains, where production was stepped up by fixing the overseer's pay at ten per cent of the profits. The big men had moved to other fields and the Government was competing with the farmer.

Government buying was by tender, which introduced competitive selling, and this bore hardly on the farmer when he needed money, his continual state.

Thus the poor man was, in theory at least, shut out from the land, but one must always remember that the colony did not conform slavishly to the patterns laid down in dispatches. Its size, its distance, the constant need for improvisation, the cross-currents of interest, the nature of the population —these and other reasons, all prevented it from becoming stereotyped. It was still a troubled water in which many fished, some of them most successfully.

Grazing began on the outskirts of Parramatta where Macarthur, Cox, Marsden, Foveaux and others ran their flocks. It was soon evident that there was not enough room east of the mountains for grazing. It took, Brisbane computed, 2000 acres to support 200 head of cattle or two flocks of sheep each 300 in number. Every three years, given reasonable seasons, stock doubled its numbers; "it is quite impossible to suppose that the liberality of the Crown can keep pace in extending grants with the increase of stock",[5] the Governor pointed out.

The Australian sheep needed a great deal of country; waterholes were scarce and far between, the natural pastures were delicate and easily eaten out. So the sheep became an explorer. He was the motive force behind the crossing of the Blue Mountains. It was in his interests that explorers—official, unofficial, and just casual—moved south and west. By 1823 flocks had crossed the Murrumbidgee and Captain Currie had found the Monaro. In 1824 Hume and Hovell reached Port Phillip by the overland route. The great drought of 1826-8 gave impetus to exploration. Allan Cunningham, who had pioneered the route from Liverpool to Bathurst, in 1827 discovered the infinity of rolling country which he called the Darling Downs, and the year after, through Cunningham's Gap, made his way to the sea at Moreton Bay. Captain Charles Sturt, Surveyors-General Oxley and Mitchell, and settler Hume, between them worked out the riddle of the rivers which, running westward from the mountains, had suggested an inland sea. This was resolved into the Murrumbidgee-Darling-Murray river system.

Major Mitchell found the good lands of Victoria's Western District, which he called "Australia Felix". Angus McMillan pushed down the Snowy and Tambo rivers to Port Albert. Strzelecki, overlanding to Western Port, named Gippsland. Hawdon, Eyre, Sturt, and Bonney linked up Port Phillip and South Australia. . . .

These were the official, or publicized, explorers; there were many more, anonymous men moving from waterhole to waterhole and from grass to grass farther out. As pastures were discovered so they were occupied. The sheep crossed Bass Strait from Van Diemen's Land and founded the settlement at Port Phillip. Without the sheep it would not have been necessary or desirable to pioneer the country beyond the littoral. There was land enough on the coast and the Hawkesbury to supply the needs of a small settlement. The mild sheep was the explosive element.

An effort was made at first by the Government to keep the pastoral industry within "the bounds of location", or the "nineteen counties", an area from the Manning River in the north to the Goulburn Plains in the south, from the sea west to Wellington Valley, a radius of about one hundred and fifty miles from Sydney.

The area was too restricted. There was no means of holding the sheep or the men who owned them. They passed over the invisible line and became trespassers on Crown lands. They were outlaws and they were called "squatters". Governors were ordered to restrain them, but they could not and, being on the spot, they saw where the wealth of the country lay.

The Colonial Office fumed. "It were as unauthorised an act of presumption for an Australian squatter to drive his flocks into the recesses of the untrodden wilderness, without Her Majesty's express sanction first obtained, as for a Berkshire farmer to feed his oxen, without rent or licence, in the Queen's demesne of Hampton Court."[6] All of which shows how little a Secretary of State could understand local conditions.

Governor Bourke was better informed. He wrote to the Secretary of State, Spring Rice: ". . . the sheep must wander or they will not thrive and . . . the colonists must have sheep or they will not continue to be wealthy. Sheep are erratic animals and the doctrine of concentration is ill applied to them. Our wool is our wealth, and I am disposed to give ample runs."[7]

Governor Gipps wrote in December 1840:

> As well might it be attempted to confine the Arabs of the Desert within a circle, traced upon their sands, as to confine the Graziers or Woolgrowers of New South Wales within any bounds that can possibly be assigned to them; and as certainly as the Arabs would be starved, so also would the flocks and herds of New South Wales, if they were so confined, and the prosperity of the Country be at an end.[8]

By 1830 it was probable that half the colony's flocks were depastured beyond the boundaries. The legend runs that one squatter alone roved over five million acres.

A formula had to be found for what had already happened. In 1836 the position of the squatter was legalized. He paid £10 a year and for this he could run as many sheep as he wished, or had, in any part of the interior he chose. It was impossible to police these licences, or tickets of occupation as they were called, for there was no authority outside the nineteen counties. It was, however, in their interests for the squatters to pay the £10, for it protected them from their rivals.

Articulate public opinion in Australia was with the squatters. The Legislative Council, now in existence, was a squatters' council leavened by officials who generally saw eye to eye with them, as they had at an earlier date, and for the same reasons, with the exclusionists.

Judge Stephen without hesitation ranged the law in support of the squatter, once he had been recognized by the Crown.

A man passed into the interior and took possession of a tract of country, established his huts, sheep and shepherds in various directions; the tract of country so occupied by himself and his establishments was said to be in his possession and he could bring an action against any person who would intrude upon him. He was not bound to show his title. He simply said . . . "I had possession before you came in."

The system began very simply, no red tape, no rules, just the working out of a natural law. The shepherds of the Bible were not less trammelled. But it could not stay as it was in 1839.

Governor Darling replaced tickets of occupation by grazing licences, first at the rate of £1 a year for every hundred acres, which was later reduced to 2s. 6d. a year. Now, in theory at least, the squatters were confined to particular areas.

There was considerable obscure lawlessness and the squatters were dissatisfied. Now that their stations had been crystallized, they felt insecure. They could not buy their land, nor did the Crown wish to alienate it. It was the people's future heritage, and by the people the Colonial Office meant not only the citizens of Australia but those of Great Britain as well. So much land was required for grazing that no squatter could afford to pay the fixed price of twelve shillings an acre. It would not be worth as many pence to him.

It was expressly stated that in April 1839

. . . the temporary occupancy of the land under the Licence is expressly declared to give no permanent right over it whatever. The country being entirely unsurveyed, and indeed very imperfectly explored, except on the Banks of a few of the principal Rivers, it would have been impossible to define the limits which are to be occupied by the Flocks or Herds of any individual. The Licence gives only a general right to depasture Cattle or Sheep on the Crown Lands, in the same way as a right of Common is enjoyed in England or as Licences to cut Timber are granted in Canada.[9]

A right of occupancy was good against everybody but the Crown. A commissioner was appointed to decide disputes between rival squatters and to define what was and what was not occupancy.

In 1840 Sir George Gipps expressed himself strongly against the sale of any land outside the "area of location" or the nominal boundaries of inhabited territory.

. . . if any price whatever were fixed at which the first claimants might take such portion of land as he chose, a complete scramble would ensue; that every acre of good land would be immediately bought up by great Capitalists, at whose mercy all newly arrived Emigrants would be placed; that the System of Sale at an uniform price with unrestricted liberty of appropriation would lead to complete confusion if adopted anywhere within the 22 Counties of N.S.Wales, and that the system would lead to a still greater confusion if extended beyond these limits.[10]

A residence clause went with the licence, and that in the nature of things led to injustice. A squatter, called William Lee, in the Western District of what is now Victoria had his licence taken away on the grounds that he had abandoned his station. He explained in vain that in his temporary absence his overseer had been forced to move the stock because drought had withered the pasture in that area and to stay was to lose his flock by starvation or aboriginal attack. Eight magistrates and the great majority of the squatters upheld Lee. It was a test case. For the first time the squatters came together as a body, held a conference at Bathurst in August 1842, and petitioned the Legislative Council. Whilst they were at it they aired all their grievances. They pointed out the anomalies of the licensing system, how it bore more heavily on the small man than on the big man. For instance, three squatters held between them 305,920 acres under three licences, that is, for £30 a year or a rental of a shilling a year for every 510 acres. On the bottom rung three men with small properties paid between them £30 a year for 13,440 acres or one shilling annual rental for 22 acres. Insecurity of tenure was their worst grievance. Gipps stated it for them in a dispatch of December 1840.

If unsurveyed lands are to be open to selection . . . all . . . the houses or huts, folds and stockyards which they have built, the provision fields which they have cultivated, the streams or pools at which they water their cattle, may henceforward be wrested from them by anyone who can run faster than they to the Land Office and there deposit a few pounds.[11]

There was in the colony a constant demand that new lands be opened for sale because the best had already been bought and occupied in the settled areas. The nineteen counties had increased to twenty-two.

A licence lasted for one year only, and at the end of any year the Crown could turn a squatter off as if he were a naughty boy, or could open his run to sale. The squatter might not be able to buy it, for, however numerous his flocks, drought and depressions sometimes left him embarrassed for ready money. Whilst he had no security he was unwilling to put in any expensive improvements, to build a homestead, dig dams, conserve fodder. . . .

The problem of the waste lands, as the uncharted interior was called, had a three-way stretch. The squatters themselves knew what they wanted. It was security in the use of the land at a cheap rate. They alone brought wealth into the colony. They were using land unsuitable and too distant for agriculture, they were undertaking the grinding toil and risk of pioneering. Surely the country owed them something. They were willing to pay the £10 licence, for it was understood that the proceeds would be used to bring out suitable immigrants, that is, suitable as servants in the pastoral industry. They were also presumably willing to pay a tax on their flocks and herds, for that money was ear-marked to support border police for their protection. They were well represented on the Legislative Council sitting in Sydney. They exercised their right of petition and they formed in April 1844 the Pastoral Association of New South Wales with money to back it. Meetings were held all over the country, nineteen petitions with some 6500 signatures were sent to the Queen. The Queen's reply on 15th May 1846 was brief and highly unsatisfactory to her petitioners: "Her Majesty did not think it necessary or advisable to state the course which she might be advised to pursue."[12]

Neither the Council nor the Governor had the last word when it was a matter of Crown lands. The Governor was in the difficult position of serving two masters. He reported to and advised the Colonial Office. He could do no more. Bourke, Darling, Gipps were all in favour of liberal terms for the squatter and reported the total impossibility of controlling him from Sydney.

In October 1835 Governor Bourke wrote in a dispatch to the Colonial Office:

> The Wool of New South Wales forms at present, and is likely long to continue, its chief wealth. It is only by a free range over the wide expanse of native Herbage, which the Colony affords, that the production of this staple article can be upheld at its present rate of increase in quantity, or standard of value in quality. The proprietors of thousands of acres already find it necessary, equally with the poorer settlers, to send large flocks beyond the present boundary of location to preserve them in health throughout the year. The Colonists must otherwise restrain the increase, or endeavor to raise artificial food for their Stock. Whilst Nature presents all around an unlimited supply of the most wholesome nutriment, either course would seem a perverse rejection of the Bounty of Providence, and the latter would certainly require more labor than can at present be obtained in the Colony, or Immigration profitably supply. Independently of these powerful reasons for allowing dispersion, it is not to be disguised that the Government is unable to prevent it. No adequate measures could be resorted to for the general and permanent removal of intruders from waste Lands, without incurring probably a greater expence than would be sufficient to extend a large share of the control and protection of Government over the country they desire to occupy.[13]

The Bishop of Australia produced a plan, Governor Gipps produced another, for the pacification of the squatters, but the third party, the Crown, remained obdurate. The management of Crown land remained a matter for the Imperial Government to decide. When in 1842 New South Wales was given a measure of self-government the disposal of Crown lands was not handed over to the Legislature. This aroused so much anger in the colony that there was even talk of rebellion. In an effort to further regularize squatting Gipps quarrelled irreparably with his Council in July 1846. And there the matter rested until an Order in Council came from England, drawn up in March 1847, which at last gave the squatter a measure of security, a fourteen-year lease of the land he occupied with the option of purchasing 324-acre blocks for their homesteads. After fourteen years it would be very difficult to dislodge any man, especially if he had purchased the most valuable parts of his run.

It may seem curious that the Imperial Government, having recognized that Australia was producing a valuable staple in wool, should appear hostile to the graziers, the men who produced the wealth. There were various reasons. One was, of course, a misunderstanding of the nature of the country and a doctrinaire insistence that the industry should develop according to rules laid down for it in England. There was also a conflict between English capital and colonial effort. From 1820 capital had begun to flow into Australia from the mother country. In 1824 two big companies, the Australian Agricultural Company and the Van Diemen's Land Company, were chartered in England. The Australian Agricultural Company, despite its name, was concerned more with the Merino than with tillage. For a million pounds raised in capital the British Government promised a million acres of land, provided the Company stocked it and brought out immigrant labour to work it. Behind this huge grant (or what appeared in those days to be huge), was the idea of monopoly. The officers of the New South Wales Corps had created a monopoly in little and it had worked. It had extracted wealth where the possibilities had appeared almost nil. Perhaps that lesson, though derogated at the time, had not been forgotten. Perhaps in the Australian Agricultural Company we see the ghost of the East India Company, that recipe for ruling without responsibility or expense and of increasing national wealth by allowing capital an open go under the protection of tacit power. Unlike the East India Company, the Australian Agricultural Company had not only to organize and distribute wealth already in existence, but to create it. It lacked, too, the advantages of coolie labour. Convicts were not quite the same thing; there were not enough of them, their services were not permanent, nor were they to the same degree expendable.

The Australian Agricultural Company, for all its flying start, its legality and security of tenure, was not the success it was expected to be. Its original land grant in the Port Stephens district did not come up to expectation. The Imperial Government transferred its holdings to the Liverpool Plains, overriding the acquired rights of earlier settlers. Still it struggled. A coal monopoly for thirty-one years was thrown into the balance. At the end of the 1840s the Company reorganized, reduced its capital, and turned from wool to mining. In 1914 it sold out the last of its interests.

Other companies financed in England entered the pastoral industry on a smaller scale with no pretensions to monopoly. They flourished and continue to flourish side by side with private enterprise, but it was the squatters who developed the industry and won the hard victory.

Who actually were the squatters? Most of the well-to-do men and the higher officials in Sydney were squatters. Their overseers or their sons ran their flocks in the bush. When wealth could only be in kind they had accumulated flocks and herds, and nothing could have been more natural, as these grew too large for their land grants, than to drive them into the New Country. Squatting was practically thrust upon them. Other squatters were men of capital who came out from England, or perhaps more often Scotland, to enter the pastoral industry. There were men of little capital also who got together a small flock and went out to try their luck. There were men of no capital at all who depastured flocks, not as employees but on the "thirds system". They supplied the labour whilst the Crown supplied the land gratis and a capitalist the stock and equipment, for which he took one-third of the profit. Others again came by their flocks and herds in nefarious ways in parts where the Queen's justice did not run. The colonial Government drew a distinction between the respectable and substantial pastoralist who had moved over the boundaries and the less reputable men who were taking advantage of a boom and the waste lands. They were a mixed lot. Of them Governor Gipps said in 1846, "Among the Squatters of New South Wales are the wealthiest of the Land, occupying with the permission of Government thousands and tens of thousands of acres; Young men of good Family and connections in England, Officers of the Army and Navy. Graduates of Oxford and Cambridge are also in no small number amongst them."[14]

At the end of 1839 Gipps reported that there were depastured under tickets of occupation 1,334,593 sheep, 371,699 cattle, 7085 horses. Under the various tenures between 1820 and 1850, the Pastoral Age in Australia, 73,000,000 acres came under licence or lease in New South Wales (which still included the Port Phillip district), and 4,500,000 in Van Diemen's Land. The average run in New South Wales was 30,000 acres, the squatters being only some 2000 strong.[15]

By 1830 Australian wool was established on the English market, over 2,000,000 pounds of it being exported. In 1834 the amount had doubled. In 1841 8,000,000 pounds went to England, in 1850 39,000,000 pounds or half the total English import of wool.[16]

In money this meant during the 1830s from 2s. to 3s. 6d. a pound in London and in the depression of the 1840s about 1s. 3d. a pound. This was gross, out of it had to come duties, which fortunately had been lowered, and freight, which in the 1830s, owing to competition for cargoes, was as low as 1d. or 1½d. a pound. This sounds as if the squatters were on Tom Tiddler's ground picking up gold and silver.

Professor Edward Shann, in his lively *Economic History of Australia*, estimates the cost of producing wool. The land the squatters at first had for nothing, then for £10 a year, and later again at varied, but of course greater, capital cost. Convict shepherds were to be had for their keep, but free men employed as shepherds earned at the most £25 a year, a hut-keeper received £15 to £25 a year, both with rations. Shearing and sheep-washing was done by itinerant seasonal workers. The shearers received 3s. for every twenty sheep, which the graziers thought exorbitant, and 700 sheep were washed a day for £1 a week and rations. A sheep, it was estimated, could be run for a shilling a year, washed for ¾d. and shorn for 4d.

Alfred Joyce, a settler who came to Melbourne in 1843, gives the figures for the depression years. A shepherd, he said, earned 15s., hut-keepers 12s. a week, shearing was 10s. for 100 sheep, reaping 10s. an acre, threshing 6d. a bushel, and strong three-railed fences were put up at 2s. 6d. a rod. Hurdles were 5s. a hundred. He also gives prices of commodities. Flour £6 to £7 a ton, brown sugar £14 a ton, tea £3 a chest, potatoes 30s. a ton, tobacco, in long twisted sticks (like old-fashioned barley-sugar, one imagines), was 6s. to 8s. a pound.[17]

Sturt, the explorer, opined in 1835 that £2814 invested in sheep would in five years show a capital increase to £9845 whilst paying 7½ per cent annually. Why he chose such a curious sum I do not know, unless he was thinking of a particular investment. These figures can, of course, only be approximations.

At first all wool was sold in England, but in 1843 small parcels found local buyers. I cannot do better than quote Professor Shann as to the method:

> Wool might reach the coastal parts at any time throughout the year. A bullock team seldom averaged more than twelve miles a day, and rains might make the black soil plains impassable for weeks at a time. . . . As soon as word came of bullock-waggons toiling in with wool, the cash buyers rode out to "Jack Ireland's Corner", at the junction of the Parramatta and Liverpool roads, or to "Bark Huts" on the way to Liverpool. Having satisfied the owner-driver that his accoster was not a bushranger—though the distinction seems to have been a conventional one—the buyer would clamber on the waggon and slash the bales to inspect them, the owner pretending utter indifference and refusing the first offer, as of course. An atmosphere more favourable to business might be reached in the bar-parlour of the "Farmer's Home"; "The Woolpack": the "Emu Inn" or the "Square and Compass", while the working bullocks were being watered at the Haymarket waterhole.[18]

This manner of business appears to have been short-lived, for in the same year wool auctions began and the first wool store was set up by Thomas Sutcliffe Mort beside the Tank Stream. (An additional reason to wonder concerning the purity of the water supply.) It was primitive enough, an iron roof, four wooden posts, a dump and scales that would take one bale at a time.

In Melbourne a Yorkshireman, bred to the wool trade, Richard Goldsbrough, set up the first wool store in 1848, on the corner of Flinders and William streets. This was a weatherboard shed, perhaps not quite as primitive as his future partner's in Sydney.

The wool industry was taking shape, its essential features were already there. Taken by and large, grazing was very profitable, but there were many obstacles to overcome, both natural and artificial.

There were recurrent droughts which reduced the flocks and herds, and wiped out the life-work of many a grazier. There were economic depressions that stole the value from wool.

In 1827 there was a financial crisis owing to over-confidence. Capital brought into the country by the Australian Agricultural Company led to over-speculation in stock and upon this there descended a drought. Recovery was fairly quick. The 1830s were very prosperous. Capital was abundant, prices rose, banks sprang up like mushrooms, and over-speculation began again.

In 1837 a drought began which lasted until 1839. At the same time there was a financial crisis in London and down came the price of wool. Suddenly sheep were as cheap as a shilling a dozen, fat cattle brought 7s. 6d. each, horses 10s. Bankruptcies became so common that imprisonment for debt was suspended and in 1843 an Insolvency Act allowed a bankrupt to continue to manage his property if there was any possibility of his reclaiming himself. Banks discovered that the securities on which they had cheerfully lent money were now worthless. They had given too much credit. In 1843 the Bank of Australia closed its doors, and its assets, including its handsome new premises, were disposed of by means of a lottery. The Colonial Office unwillingly allowed a lien on wool, since that was the only commodity that seemed likely to regain its value.

The Colonial Government in the general *débâcle* was not able very greatly to alleviate the situation. It did support the Savings Bank and increase the note issue, but the banks were left with £2,500,000 worth of discounted bills on their hands. In the midst of this trouble transportation of convicts ended. This had been desired and fought for particularly by the city populations. Now it came as an added blow. It meant that the squatter lost his supply of cheap labour, and it meant also that the Imperial Government would spend far less money in Australia, thus reducing her national income. In 1839 the Commissariat spent £170,000 for support of the convicts. By 1842 this had fallen to £90,000 and in 1843 to £70,000.

Providentially a new use was found for sheep and cattle. They could be boiled down for tallow. This was the tragic postscript to the years of high prosperity. There were fifty-six boiling-down or tallow houses in New South Wales alone.

Alfred Joyce describes the process in detail.

The operation, like shearing, being paid for by the hundred, was very rapidly performed, the dressed appearance being of no importance whatever. The following day when the meat was set they were quartered and thrown into large wooden vats which, when full, had their manholes securely fastened down against the escape of steam which was then let in from a boiler at a somewhat high pressure. After a certain time the meat was completely disintegrated and all the fat was drawn out through several taps at different heights, lower taps were opened in succession while the clear white fat flowed through them until the gravy appeared, when the flow was stopped; the residue was then emptied out through openings in the bottom and put, minus the bones, into gunny bags and subjected to screw pressure to get the last of the fat squeezed out, the gravy and fat being put into receptacles with tops to settle and have the remaining fat drawn off.

The meat residue, void of all its fats, was then conveyed to adjoining yards, where, with the entrails, it formed a fine wallowing mess for a herd of pigs. . . .[19]

The boiling-down works were kept busy from 1842 to 1850, when with the gold-rushes the price of meat soared so high that they were put out of business.

In 1840 20 tons of tallow were exported, in 1844 3000 tons worth £84,000. Two and a half million sheep and 260,000 cattle were being sacrificed each year. In 1844 the price of wool began to rise again. The crisis was over, the flocks had been culled very thoroughly, and so had the squatters. The strongest of them were stronger than ever, and within three years they were to attain that security of tenure, through the Order in Council of 1847, for which they had been battling.

The life of the pioneering squatter was hard, laborious, and hazardous. In the early days, when flocks were driven at will through the vast interior, drought was not the serious scourge it became later. Just as at a future time the great cattle stations of the inland throve because in their extent there was always water and grass, so when the sheep was a nomad he could generally, except in universal drought, move to new pastures and new waterholes without exhausting the country, in much the same way as the aboriginal tribes followed their food supplies and survived.

Their worst enemy was the native dog, the dingo. Once one of these got into a flock it might kill thirty or forty sheep before the shepherd could come to their rescue. The aborigines sometimes speared sheep, for they were game in a hungry land, but this trouble never reached serious proportions.

Man's worst enemies were loneliness and isolation. There were no roads, only the tracks worn or cleared by the squatters themselves, no bridges, no surveys, however rough. The squatter went into the wilderness driving his sheep at their own pace, hoping to find grass and water not already annexed. He had generally made an advance trip and with secrecy marked out a run, but there was no certainty about it. Everything in those days went slowly. When he had selected his run, perhaps misled by a good season into thinking he would have permanent water, he must make himself a shelter, a bark or slab hut with holes for windows, protected by flaps of bark; in exceptional circumstances there was a fire-place and chimney built of stones and clay. The furnishings were hessian bunks with sheepskin blankets, a slab table, a log to sit on, a pannikin for tea, an iron pot for cooking, and when the thousand-mile darkness closed down there was a wick floating in mutton fat to lighten it.

His workmates were his horses and dogs. Without them he would have been lost indeed. A new breed of working dog appeared in the interior, called a kelpie after a bitch who was the reputed ancestress of the whole tribe. The kelpie is a genuine folk dog, whichever way you look at him. Some believe that this breed had its origin in a collie-dingo cross, but Robert Kaleski, in his *Australian Barkers and Biters*, tells a different story: that kelpies are of Scottish origin, having been secretly bred by a gipsy from a collie-fox cross. The result was a poacher's dream. Imported into Australia, acclimatized and improved, they became sheep-dogs.

Less near to the settler were his convict shepherds, and his sheep were so many that, having no individuality, they were to all but the exceptional man nothing but entries of profit and loss.

Contact with civilization was a yearly journey to Sydney, at first by pack-horse and later by bullock-wagon, taking in the clip and bringing back the necessary supplies. The journey could take months. In illustration there is the story of Alan Macpherson, a Scot who needed all his stamina. In 1848 he set out from the Gwydir in the north of New South Wales with his dray and ten working bullocks, two "bullockies" or drivers, and a black boy, to carry provisions to his station on Mount Abundance three hundred miles away. The first hundred miles was easy going and accomplished in three weeks. Then he struck trouble. There had been rain, the country was boggy, and progress became very slow. When he arrived at the Boomai River it was in flood. He unloaded the dray and ferried some of the stores over in a tub. The flour, wrapped in tarpaulins, was left on the dray and the bullocks were driven into the water. They crossed the river, but became bogged in the far bank; to extricate them the dray was lightened by having the flour taken off, a difficult business requiring all hands. Whilst it was being safely stowed the bullocks disentangled themselves from the mud and swam back across the river, submerging the dray. They had to be persuaded to return. Alan

Macpherson swam the river twenty-one times before he got all his stores across, and then a thunderstorm caught him with the sugar uncovered. In ten days the dray travelled twelve miles; after that the pace improved and he reached Mount Abundance three months out from Gwydir. It was a short journey as they went, and, of course, the stores had had to be brought to the Gwydir first by sea and then across country by bullock-wagon. When on the road it was usual to sleep under the bullock-wagon or in a tent made by throwing a tarpaulin across the pole. Halts were made where there was water and grass for the animals, and not where convenient for man. Grass-stealing from other men's properties passed on the trek later became quite an industry.

The wool was less troublesome to carry than the supplies. The bales stood up to bad roads, exposure, and wetting more successfully than any other product could have done. Delay did not spoil it. These are reasons why wool could be successfully grown in the Never Never Land and carried twelve thousand miles to its market.

The interior in the early days was almost exclusively a man's world, which made it the lonelier and robbed robust men of home, wife, and children. It was no place for women and children, for there was no medical service of any kind, and a laudanum mixture called "pain-killer" was the cure-all for everything short of broken bones. Alfred Joyce tells how he suffered from "a most excruciating, deep-seated whitlow" and lost a joint of his finger through it. Later matters improved. Doctors who came out with immigrant ships and were not wanted on the return voyage often stayed on and, making their headquarters on one of the stations, where they were welcomed and lived board free, attended patients within a radius of about twenty-five miles. In these days of luxury an urgent case was likely to receive medical attention within a fortnight.

Food was extremely monotonous: damper, tea, and mutton (or beef as the case might be). Sugar and tobacco were luxuries that were almost necessities. Occasionally pumpkins were grown—good old ironbarks—and put up on the roofs of the huts to be mellowed by frost. The winters were cold, the summers hot (as they still are), and there was continuous trial by insects. Mosquitoes bred in the dams and the only protection from them was the acrid, eyewatering smoke of dung. When the mosquitoes gave up the flies took over. "You seldom lift a piece of food to your mouth," wrote the author of the Hobler Papers,[20] "without one hand driving away flies to make room for it. Anything like gravy in your plate is a sort of fly-trap, and most successful in its operations." These discomforts went on and on, the major calamities of drought, bushfire, flood, and aboriginal attack were occasional. All these things undoubtedly happened and yet, looking at the bush today, one can imagine that even in the most primitive times the life of the squatter had its compensations, a free open-air life in the morning of the world, following the seasons and reaping their harvest.

After the Order in Council of 1847, which did not take full effect until the fifties, conditions improved. The squatter had security and it was worth his while to build himself a home; more wives ventured into the bush, and with them necessities that had formerly been unobtainable luxuries began to arrive on the bullock-wagons. A semblance of normal, even of social, life began. Neighbours were neighbours, even if they were twenty miles away; anyone going up the country was a welcome visitor, sure of food and lodging. Each station was a rallying point in the wilderness; the money earned in the bush was trickling back into the bush.

That is the story of the squatter, behind him are other stories, for, from the first, life in the bush was stratified. The first shepherds and hut-keepers were almost always convicts; they received food and clothing but no money, their life was perhaps the loneliest in the world of the nineteenth century. They inherited all the privations and discomforts their masters had had to begin with. Many of them were petty criminals from cities or from provincial towns and the loneliness and silence of the bush bore heavily upon them. In theory, life up the country was supposed to improve their morals by keeping them away from evil associates and out of temptation. In reality they were, by and large, a class without hope, and many became crazed with loneliness, the "hatters" of the bush. From the first there was often bad blood between them and their masters, particularly when their sentence had expired, or they had acquired tickets of leave, and had to be paid a small wage. The squatter was used to free land and free labour. Any payment on either he felt to be an unjust imposition.

In the days of unrestricted grazing a normal flock consisted of four hundred sheep; when labour was short, as it nearly always was, the shepherd was required to look after seven or eight hundred. His duties were to lead the sheep to grass in the morning, to watch over them, to gather them together in the evening, and erect a fold for them out of hurdles. Then he must sleep beside them to protect them from the dingoes. "To protect the sheep in the fold," wrote Alfred Joyce, "a dog was tied up at each corner and a shepherd or hut keeper slept in a wretched box in between the folds, which was shifted with them every day."[21]

> He must look after the ewes at lambing time, as was customary with the small flocks in England, putting each mother with her new born lamb in a separate pen and making sure that she mothered it. . . . If scab got into the flock the shepherd must treat it . . . the animal was immersed in a large tub of corrosive sublimate and then laid on a sheet of bark and scraped down with an iron hoop.[22]

At first, until the flocks grew too large, he also washed the sheep before shearing. This took place in a waterhole by means of a race. They were afterwards put to dry in pens where the ground was thickly covered with boughs.

Alexander Harris, who was looking for work in the bush in the 1820s and 1830s describes the unhappy lot of the shepherd.

The master grumbles if the flock is not allowed to spread; he says the shepherd must be keeping them together by severe dogging, and that running so close they cannot fill their bellies; for this, if the shepherd is a free man, he will often refuse to pay him his wages; if he is a prisoner, he takes him before some other sheep-holding settler in the commission of the peace and flogs him. On the other hand, if the shepherd suffers the flock to spread, in these mountainous runs especially, they get into creeks and hollows; and he loses sight of them and leaves them behind; or a native dog sneaks in among them, and, as it is the habit of these animals to bite as many as they can before beginning to prey, 20, 30, 50 get bitten, most of them mortally, before the shepherd sees or hears the stir and comes to their rescue. By this time the whole flock perhaps is scattered in all directions by the panic to which sheep are so liable. For these mishaps again, if the shepherd is free, the master refuses to pay his wages, and tells him to go to law and get them if he can; which he knows, in nine cases out of ten, the man will not do from want of confidence in the administration of justice; if he is a prisoner he flogs him. And this flogging answers two purposes, he supposes . . . he imagines that it spurs the man to a sort of nervous and extranatural watchfulness from terror of the lash; and then again he knows . . . that this intimation of ill demeanour will impede the man with the authorities in getting his ticket of leave to work for himself; and so he shall retain for some time longer than he otherwise could a servant whose cost is not half what he must give a free man.[23]

Another trap for the shepherd or drover is described by Joyce:

It occasionally happened, when the shepherd of one station approached too closely the shepherd of an adjoining station, with their respective flocks on the boundary, that the one flock would run with the other and become what was colonially called "boxed". The two flocks thus mixed would be taken to the nearer of the two stations and the other station intimated of the disaster. All available hands from both stations would then be mustered at the yards and the smaller of the two flocks, probably about a thousand sheep, drawn out by the leg and passed through another yard or on to the open ground and kept near at hand till all were out.

It is not surprising to learn that this was a very dirty job on account of "fine manureal dust, which adhering to our perspiring faces, would give us more the appearance of black fellows than white men and choke us so with the dust that our expectoration would be somewhat of the colour of coffee".[24]

Unwatched, the shepherds often found means to revenge themselves that could not be sheeted home. Shepherding and hut-keeping were not professions that usually led the convict to better things. The Government hoped to protect convicts from the viciousness of their masters by making it illegal for a man to punish his own servants. He must take them before a Justice of the Peace to be legally sentenced. The Reverend Dr John Dunmore Lang points out in his *Historical and Statistical Account of New South Wales,* what a mockery this was in practice, since the magistrate was of the same class as the master and saw eye to eye with him.

On arriving at the magistrate's, the settler, who is a remarkably good Protestant, kisses the book and swears that the man spoke to him insolently; the overseer, who is a stanch Roman Catholic, confirms his master's deposition by kissing the same book on the other side; on which the worthy magistrate—who knows that the Bible was sent him for kissing and not for reading—has religiously pasted a bit of whity-brown paper, cut with a pair of scissors, in the form of a cross. When this *religious* ceremony has been gone through, the magistrate, assuming a very grave aspect, sentences the convict to receive twenty-five lashes for insolence to his master, and he is accordingly delivered over to the scourger of the district.[25]

For free men there was the Master and Servant Act by which a man could be arrested for leaving his employment. In the structure of that society the poor free man was in a not much better position than the convict or ticket-of-leave man.

More fortunate and independent than the shepherd was the itinerant bush worker, a class that increased as the growing flocks made outside seasonal workers necessary. These were the shearers, drovers, bullockies, the horse-breakers, the travelling blacksmiths and shoemakers, and later the fencers and dam-diggers, who went from station to station, working under contract.

The shearers, as described by Joyce, are in quite startling contrast to the professionals of today:

There were two classes of shearers, the Derwenters from Van Diemen's Land and the Sydneyites. The former were the better shearers but the latter were the faster. The Derwenters were distinguished by their tall hats and kangaroo knapsacks, or Derwent drums as they were called, and the Sydneyites by their quart pots and blanket swags.[26]

The wild colonial boys, the native-born, were rarely to be found as shepherds; they preferred the life of the itinerant bush worker. Often they had a little place of their own, but, to eke out its scanty returns, spent part of the year on contract work. The very nature of the pastoral industry, which supplied, and supplies, regular work all the year round for only a few men, with rushes at shearing time (which in the 1830s and 1840s was in March), and odd jobs from time to time, fostered this band of nomads, free, self-respecting, and the accomplished drivers of hard bargains. There was a class war in the bush from earliest times, though in a crisis of fire or flood it was the unwritten rule that every man turned out.

The first shops of the bush were the Afghan or Syrian hawkers. Patrick White in *The Aunt's Story* gives a picture of one such:

Down the road from the direction of the hills the Syrian came from time to time. He came into sight at the bend of the road, where his wheels thrashed splashing the brown water of the ford. From a good distance you could see the dirty canvas swaying and toppling above the cart, and there was time to shout a warning, to call: "The Syrian! Here comes the Syr-i-urn!"

This made everyone run out of the house, everyone from the back of the house, that is. . . . Everyone ran out. It made quite a scattering of fowls.

Gertie said the Syrian sold trash, but everybody liked to buy, and Gertie even, to touch, to choose. It was exciting as the cart grated through the yard. Turkeys gobbled, dogs barked. The day was changed, which once had been flat as a pastry board. Now it was full of talk, and laughing, and the whining of the Syrian's mangy dog, and the jingled harness of his old blue horse. Now there was no question of work, now that the Syrian had come.

The Syrian himself was dry and brown, with blue tattoo marks on his hands. The eyes were deep and dark in the bones of his face. But they did not tell much, nor did his voice, in the language that he talked. When the Syrian became intelligible, he spoke in shillings, or with his brown hands. He uncovered his brown teeth in a clockwork smile. Out of the cart, from under the old tarpaulin, he brought the openwork stockings, the ribbons, the shawls, the mouth organs, the safety pins, and the pen knives that he sold.[27]

This actually is of a later time but the picture it evokes is immemorial.

It is not so many years since an itinerant vendor of tombstones was travelling round the countryside with his slabs ready for engraving as required.

The nature of the land tried to press white men into the same mould as the aborigines. A scarcity economy made them nomads also.

Out of all classes arose the bushman, more at home in the saddle than on his feet, able to find his way in trackless country, to hold out against silence and loneliness. He had his particular vocabulary, his bushcrafts, like the plaiting of stockwhips, his endurance, his sardonic humour.

For squatters and bush workers alike there grew up an indigenous life. The ruts of the bullock drays became tracks and then rough bush roads and beside them sprang up settlers' huts. Harris describes such a one in the Illawarra:

It was one of those huts which must be ranked among the remarkable objects of Australian life. Situated on some main track and alone in the midst of the wilderness, one of these little "cribs" necessarily becomes the nightly rendezvous of numbers of travellers. If the traveller have no food with him, a share of what there is is always freely offered him. . . . The same hospitality is maintained in accommodations for rest. Those who have a blanket with them contribute it to the general stock; those who have none have equal share with those who have. These customs lead very naturally to a great degree of frankness and cordiality among the persons, most of whom are thus meeting for the first time, and the evenings consequently are for the most part spent in cheerful conversation and merriment. This species of arrangement extends throughout the colony; with this difference, that off the main lines of road, and still more so the farther you advance into the bush, the usual run of travellers are not only not expected to make any recompense, but in many places it would be treated as an insult to offer it. As full two-thirds of the labouring population of the country are in perpetual migration, the custom is a very proper one. It probably originated in the first place from the smallness of the community, almost every one knowing almost every other; and there is no doubt that the great scarcity of cash in the up country parts has principally maintained it.[28]

You can imagine the settlers, in such lonely times, planting their little bark or slab huts beside some track for the very purpose of human intercourse, so rare and valuable a thing was it.

The hand-outs at the stations, that even owners with the inevitable nickname of "hungry-guts" were compelled by public opinion to give, the hospitality of the wayside hut where mutton and damper were bartered for company and news, were the transmutation into more generous terms of the early social state in which everyone was fed by the Government and where, though money might be totally lacking, food was generally plentiful.

Later, less pleasing and devouringly commercial, appeared the bush "shanty", the precursor of the public house. Under a barrage of rough bonhomie and a pretence of providing accommodation for wayfarers, the main business of the shanty-keeper was to sell liquor and he was the inheritor of many a shearer's or drover's cheque. It was understandable that men leading hard and often lonely lives, without any sort of entertainment or relaxation, such as was the lot of shepherd or boundary rider, on receiving their money would celebrate their momentary freedom. The celebration too often ran away with them and left them confused as to what had happened to their money and penniless once more. This state was seasonal, like their work. The shanty-keeper was to the bush worker what the rum merchant was to the penal settlement in the days of the New South Wales Corps.

Behind the men were the animals, the dogs who worked the sheep and the cattle, the grass-fed horses whose descendants carried the light-horsemen in the desert warfare of 1914-18, never to return. The cattle and the sheep, as much as the men, bore the brunt of drought, fire, flood, and depression. In the dry spells the sheep ate the scant foliage of the trees, dug the bare earth with their hooves for roots, and then they died. The cattle stood like painted beasts on the parched earth until they fell dead. In bushfires sheep have died slowly in their smouldering wool. They have gone meekly to the slaughter-yards, travelling in waterless trains, trampling one another to death. They went in their tens of thousands to the tallow factories. In floods the flocks and herds have been too numerous to save. They have been martyred to the greed that overstocked the pastures for immediate gain.

Australia has been a hard stepmother to the animals who have made her wealth. A hungry sheep still gave fine wool. It has been cheaper to let animals die than to save them. Dealing in thousands, it has been difficult for the average squatter to think of his stock as living creatures, subject to pain, thirst, fear. . . . Profit too often has calloused him. Their sufferings are unregarded except by the very few.

In good seasons the life of the flocks and herds can be idyllic, in wide well-watered pastures, saved by man from the dangers that beset them, such as the dingo and blow-fly strike. Pedigree stock has always been in a class by itself, better tended than the men who bred them as like as not. With the advance of science so will the health and welfare of animals improve.

We have seen the sheep as explorer, as money-spinner, and as an arbiter of a way of life. He was also a political force. It was in his interests that a policy of migration was adopted by the Government. Particularly after the supply of convicts was cut off by the cessation of transportation in 1840, the squatters were in acute need of labour. Unfenced, unmechanized, and with much more individual, if less skilful, attention paid to the sheep than in later days, the squatters could not carry on without shepherds, hut-keepers, drovers, and the rest of their retinue. Money paid for depasturing licences was ear-marked to provide immigrant labour. When this was insufficient there was talk of bringing in Asiatics, or of petitioning England to restore transportation.

In a wider and different sense the sheep was also responsible for the coming of self-government in 1850. The pastoral industry attracted men of capital to the country, it brought in wealth, it gave importance and dignity to the former Colony of Disgracefuls. This new type of settler, who was not an official, felt that he had as much right in Australia as at home to his traditional liberties and institutions. He brought his politics and his standing with him. Though not numerous, this class was articulate. The British Government was now more anxious to get rid of its poor and its unemployed than its criminals. It was obvious that Australia, if by reason of its growing wealth alone, must receive political autonomy in increasing measure. It would have been absurd to give self-government to a penal settlement, so transportation had to stop.

Again we strike the anomaly that the very people, the rich and thriving squattocracy, for whom liberal institutions had to be provided, were also the people who would have liked an unchecked stream of convicts to provide them with cheap labour. They favoured a plantation state in which there was a privileged minority with a pool of semi-slave labour to draw upon. It was the clamorous townsmen, also living at one remove on the wool industry, who insisted on democratic government. They far outnumbered the squatters and they made themselves heard. It was logical. If England insisted that colonial law should be in accord with English law, she must give to her Antipodean subjects the same rights and privileges as the true-born Briton enjoyed at home. A gulf had opened between the city and the bush. With which party did Australia's future lie? With profit or with liberalism? The Home Government was probably unaware of all the cross-currents.

At the end of the 1840s the sheep was triumphant, and the very measure of its triumph seemed to have embayed the colony in a pastoral tranquillity—or would have, but for the gadfly of the city. Agriculture grew less except in South Australia. Population was drifting away. The sheep needed only grass and water, and less attention than any other major industry. Although the pastoral industry was never to lose its importance, the dramatic discovery of gold in 1851 was to bring new life and diversity into the colony and to set in motion another prolonged struggle for the land.

REFERENCE NOTES

1 *Hist. Rec. Aust.*, ser. I, vol. xi, p. 54.
2 *Ibid.*, p. 331.
3 *Ibid.*, p. 440.
4 *Ibid.*, p. 681.
5 *Ibid.*, p. 331.
6 Quoted by W. K. Hancock, *Australia*, p. 15.
7 Quoted by R. M. Hartwell in *Australia: a Social and Political History* (ed. Greenwood). p. 81.
8 *Hist. Rec. Aust.*, ser. I, vol. xxi, p. 127.
9 *Ibid.*, vol. xx, pp. 90-1.
10 *Ibid.*, p. 695.
11 *Ibid.*, vol. xxi, p. 130.
12 *Ibid.*, vol. xx, p. xxii (Introduction).
13 *Ibid.*, vol. xviii, p. 156.
14 *Ibid.*, vol. xxi, p. 130.
15 Figures from S. H. Roberts, *The Squatting Age in Australia*, Appendix V, p. 418.
16 Figures from A. G. L. Shaw, *Economic Development of Australia*, p. 49.
17 A. Joyce, *A Homestead History*, p. 41.
18 E. O. G. Shann, *An Economic History of Australia*, pp. 130-1.
19 A. Joyce, *A Homestead History*, p. 98.
20 MS. in possession of the Mitchell Library.
21 A. Joyce, *A Homestead History*, p. 45.
22 *Ibid.*, p. 41.
23 A. Harris, *Settlers and Convicts*, pp. 329-30.
24 A. Joyce, *A Homestead History*, p. 63.
25 J. D. Lang, *An Historical and Statistical Account of New South Wales* (2nd ed.), vol. ii, pp. 12-13.
26 A. Joyce, *A Homestead History*, p. 58.
27 P. White, *The Aunt's Story*, pp. 25-6.
28 A. Harris, *Settlers and Convicts*, pp. 43-5.

CHAPTER IX

VOYAGE IN THE BUSH

I could not use the quadrant, but I set out trusting to my compass, my knowledge of bush travelling, a stout heart, and a hardy constitution.—HAMILTON HUME, *A Brief Statement of Facts in connection with an Overland Expedition from Lake George to Port Phillip in 1824.*

THE BUSH was like the sea, a rooted, tideless sea. It presented to the first settlers the same anonymity, wild and strange. Its dangers, more passive, were just as real. It closed like water over those who penetrated it. It went on and on across a continent as unlimited as an ocean. A specialized knowledge was needed to navigate it, but it could not be learnt at a marine college. A generation had to grow up to it. Many explorations, it is true, were led by men not born in Australia, army officers like Sturt and Mitchell, officers of the Surveying Department like Oxley and Evans, or amateurs like Leichhardt, but when they made their journeys a knowledge of the country, of the bush and bushcraft, existed. It took exactly a generation before a way over the mountains was found and the interior unsealed. This may not sound reasonable, but it has its own logic.

Scientific curiosity played its part in the opening up of the country. Governors might ponder the riddle of the westward-flowing rivers, but the real impetus behind it was the need of sheep for grass and water. With flocks and herds doubling their numbers every three years, if seasons were propitious, the necessity for new pastures was imperative and insatiable. Official parties with definite objectives were sent forth from time to time by the Government, but at the same time unofficial and often unrecorded explorations were being carried out by squatters and their sons or shepherds. There was a natural and inevitable expansion into the bush. Exploration is part of the story of the pastoral age and cannot be separated from it.

The tale of exploration by land has been told and retold. There has even been a noticeable effort to play it up in the hope of adding a spice of adventure to the reputedly dull history of Australia. It would not be possible to relate here in detail the many expeditions with their successes, heroism, and failures. It seems to me better to take one exploration and use it as an illustration. The journey of Hume and Hovell in 1824-5 from Lake George to Port Phillip, or more particularly to Corio Bay and the site of present day Geelong, is very closely woven into the general pattern of Australian life and history.

This expedition did not just happen along the lines of the old joke: "It's a nice day, let's have a war." It had an interesting prelude and a tragicomic codicil.

In the short Australian story the Hume family has assumed a touch of folklore. It is claimed that they were descended from the Earls of Dunbar, with a dash of royal blood on the side, and in or about the thirteenth century assumed the family name of Home, which in due course was corrupted to Hume. More certainly they were of an old Border family. In 1746 the Reverend James Hume went to Ireland as the Presbyterian Minister of Moira. Here he married a sister of Major Hamilton of County Down. His eldest son, Andrew, born on 24th June 1762, his descendants claim, first made the Army his career like his grandfather. In 1782 he held a commission in the Moira Regiment of Volunteers, which is slightly different from, but not exclusive of, this theory. In 1786 he fought a duel at Greenwich and this may or may not have been the reason for a sudden *volte face* in his career.

In December 1789 he sailed for Australia, as a superintendent of convicts and agricultural instructor, in the ill-fated ship *Guardian*. When she was wrecked south of the Cape of Good Hope he had the good fortune to be in the only ship's boat which survived the disaster. He resumed his voyage in *Lady Juliana*, transport, and finally reached Sydney in June 1790.

Andrew Hume was recommended to Governor Phillip for his knowledge of flax, its cultivation and dressing, and for that reason was sent to Norfolk Island where flax grew wild and persistent attempts were made to turn it to the advantage of the Navy. There is little reason to believe that Hume had more success with the obstinate plant than others. In 1792 he was back on the mainland and was given charge of government livestock at Toongabbie. Men had to be versatile in those days. Free men were at a premium and to be a superintendent in government service was not as lowly as it sounds.

Presumably before he left England Andrew Hume had married Elizabeth More Kennedy, daughter of the Rector of Nettlestead in Kent. It is unlikely that she was with him in *Guardian*, but she joined him later and they made their home at Parramatta where Andrew did a little farming on his own account, along with his official duties. Here on 18th June 1797 their eldest son Hamilton was born. There were two other sons—John Kennedy Hume, who was killed by bushrangers near Gunning when he was thirty-nine years old and the father of nine children, and Francis Rawdon Hume, who acquired the property of Castlesteads—and a daughter, who married George Barber of Glenrock.

In 1800 Governor King dismissed Andrew Hume. Captain J. H. Watson alleges that this was in order to replace him by one of his own protégés. The truth of the matter is not easy to come by. Watson disliked King and was apt to attribute the worst motives to him. Andrew Hume may well have been a difficult man; his descendants admit the hot Hume temper. Major George Johnston reinstated him after the Rum Rebellion, which looks as if he supported the rebels. Foveaux dismissed him again in the same year.

In about 1814 the Humes moved into the bush, to a grant in the Appin district given by Macquarie. This was the very outpost of civilization. The children were educated by their mother and the boys at least ran wild in the bush, learning its ways from practical experience and from the aborigines, who were still numerous. Young Hamilton was bred to exploration.

This prelude is typical of the early days, a life of change, improvisation, uncertainty and self-help, of freedom and limitations, of government service and private enterprise, of new class values and new skills. Into Hamilton Hume, the cornstalk, was woven the Scottish ancestry so frequently found amongst the early graziers, the echo of Ireland as vibrant in the colony as the sound of the sea in a shell, and the absence of any nostalgia for a world he had never known.

At seventeen, with his younger brother John and an aboriginal boy, Hamilton was making excursions south into the unknown country which was to become known as Berrima, Picton, Mittagong, Bowral, and Bong Bong. His skill as a bushman was so well known that in 1816 Dr Charles Throsby enlisted his services as a guide when he decided to settle in the new country. The Throsbys were a Parramatta family and had probably known young Hume as a child. This was a valuable connection, which brought him to the notice of Governor Macquarie. He asked him to go on an official exploring expedition with Surveyor Meehan and Dr Throsby, to what was now "his own country". The partnership broke up near Bungonia, before they had gone far. Meehan and Throsby quarrelled. Throsby struck off to Jervis Bay and Meehan and Hume went on to discover Lake Bathurst and the Goulburn Plains. For this Hume was rewarded by a grant of 300 acres. The next year, 1818, he went with the Surveyor-General, John Oxley, and Meehan to Jervis Bay by a land route. Oxley returned by sea, but the other two came back by land, passing through Berrima, then called Toomboong.

In 1821, at Throsby's request, Hamilton Hume, his brother John, his brother-in-law, George Barber, and W. H. Broughton went south to look the country over. Hamilton Hume was now the leader. It was a successful journey, for he discovered the fertile plains lying between the present site of Yass and the Murrumbidgee. Some authorities believe that Yass is a corruption of the aboriginal name for the place, Yahrs. There is another story (of the oldest inhabitant vintage). Hume is said to have told one of his convict servants to climb a tree. The man went up and there was a long silence. Impatiently Hume asked: "Well, can you see anything?" To which the man replied in a drawl, "Ya-a-ss, plains."[1]

Hume was now much in demand. Alexander Berry, the well-known pioneer of the South Coast, asked the young man to help him mark out and set up his new grant of 10,000 acres on the Shoalhaven River. This done, they set out to explore the district and discovered the Clyde River, which they followed to the present site of Braidwood, whence they returned cross-country to Sydney.

Hamilton Hume had now served his apprenticeship.

It was of him that Governor Brisbane thought when he conceived the novel idea of landing a party of convicts at Cape Howe or Wilson's Promontory to find their way back to Sydney, where, if they reached it, they would receive emancipation as a reward. This appealed to the Governor, as it would have to Lord Auckland, as a cheap way of opening up the country. Brisbane, however, was a humane man and did not want to condemn his unfortunate guinea-pigs to death. He considered asking a competent bushman, Hume, to lead them. He, or his friends, convinced the Governor that the plan was impracticable and another one was substituted for it.

Surveyor Oxley had declared that the country round Western Port was "utterly useless for every purpose of civilized man". Brisbane wanted to test this opinion. Prompted by Alexander Berry, he suggested that Hume should lead a party overland from Lake George to Western Port and report on the country. He did not want to give more than his blessing. When Hume asked for six men, six bullocks, six packhorses and the necessary provisions, he found that all the Governor was prepared to contribute was

> . . . six pack saddles and gear, one tent of Parramatta cloth, two tarpaulins, a suit of slops each for the men, a few bush utensils, a small quantity of arms and ammunition, and *two* skeleton charts for the tracing of our journey. With the exception of the articles just mentioned, we were thrown entirely on our own resources. For my own part I had to dispose of a very fine imported iron plough (no small consideration in the days of which I speak) to help to raise money sufficient to purchase my supplies for the journey.[2]

Hume wanted to make the journey, but he could not afford to, and the Governor, on whom the strictest economy was enjoined by Whitehall, would not relent. Alexander Berry produced a solution in the person of William Hilton Hovell of Minto, a master mariner turned landowner, who wanted to go on the expedition and was willing to share the expense.

Hovell (pronounced not in the manner of a broken-down hut but with the accent on the last syllable) was born in the English seaport of Yarmouth in 1786. He went to sea as a boy and in the early 1800s was captain of a ship trading with South America. He married the daughter of Thomas Arndell, a surgeon in the First Fleet. Dr Arndell retired in 1796 to live on his property at Parramatta and later moved to the Hawkesbury. It was probably this connection which induced Hovell to come to New South Wales in 1813. He arrived with an investment of £500 in merchandise and a letter of recommendation from the Secretary of State for the Colonies. He was given, in 1816, a grant of 700 acres near Narellan, where he settled in 1819. In the meantime he commanded Simeon Lord's ship *Trial* and *The Brothers*, which was wrecked in Bass Strait in 1816. After this experience Hovell retired from the sea. He, too, by 1824, although not a cornstalk, was well woven into the colonial pattern.

Hovell was so eager to join the expedition to Western Port that he sold all his land, except the original grant, to finance his share. Each of the partners took three convict servants and supplies for four months. Hovell in his journal[3] enumerated them: 640 pounds of flour, 200 pounds of pork, 100 pounds of sugar, 14 pounds of tea, 8 pounds of tobacco, 12 pounds of soap, salt, coffee, etc. In addition each had packhorses, bullocks, hunting dogs, a cart, a tarpaulin and between them, a "perambulator"—that is, a species of pedometer for the dead reckoning of distances—and a small supply of medicines, including snake-bite cures.

The party gathered on the Hume property at Appin on 3rd October 1824. As Hovell had only two convict servants, Hume found him a third one, Boyd, whose loyalty, it subsequently appeared, was all for Hume.

On 17th October the real start was made from Hume's station beside Lake George. The next day they crossed the Dividing Range between Gunning and Yass and came to the plains Hume had discovered. Hovell

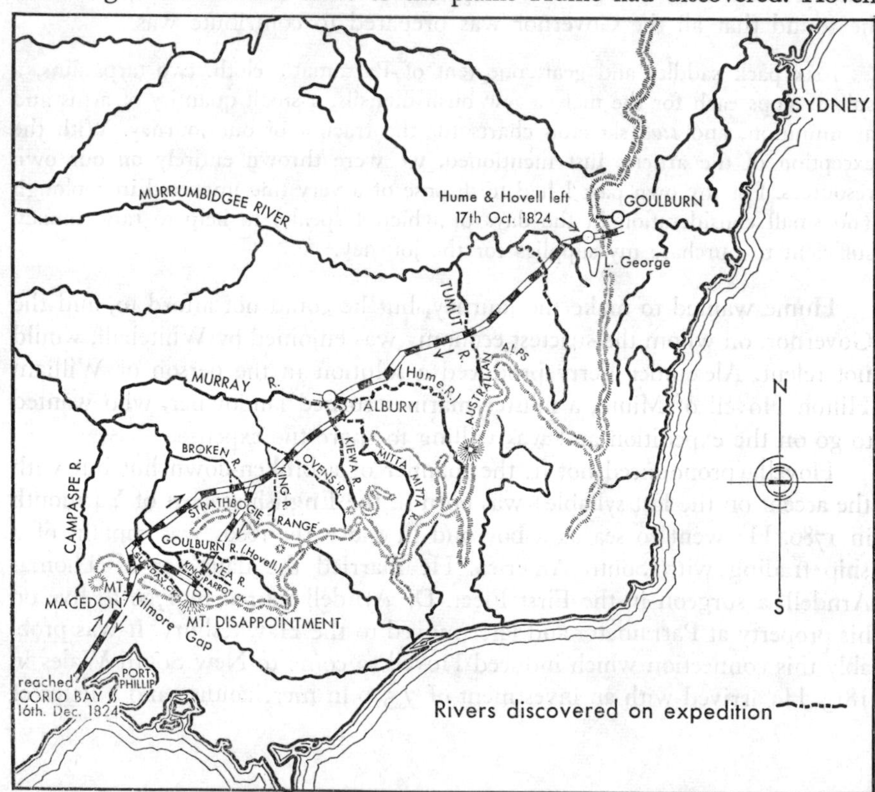

began blazing the trees, a practice Hume held in poor esteem, though he had used it in his youth.

The first big obstacle was the Murrumbidgee, which was in flood and running fast. They waited four days, but the river showed no sign of falling. Hume tried to make canoes of bark as he had seen the aborigines do, but the season was now too late. The sap was down, making the bark brittle and it cracked when he bent it. He then, according to his own account, took the wheels off one of the carts, passed a tarpaulin round it and converted it into a punt, as he had seen Meehan do on an earlier expedition. He and Boyd swam across the river with "a line in our teeth, and thus established communication between either bank; when, with much trouble and not a little danger, the whole party, with the cattle and stores, were safely landed on the other side".[4]

Beyond the river, Hovell reported, "The whole locality has a fine appearance, and looks like meadow land in England, or as if it had been cultivated for grapes; and the high mountains on all sides give it a grand appearance. Killed one kangaroo today."[5]

The party camped for two nights on the Narrengullen Meadows, reconnoitring a way through the tangle of high mountains which hemmed them in. On 24th October they agreed to split the party to double their chances of finding a pass. Hovell's account reads:

> In the direction that I went the whole country was impossible, for upon following each small watercourse, it would receive perhaps twenty others, until at last it would end in a deep ravine, and fall into the river. . . . On going the dogs killed an emu; we hung it on a tree, with the intention to take it on our return, but it being dusk before we got to it, and losing time in looking for it, we had the satisfaction of sleeping in the bush for our pains, besides going to bed supperless.[6]

Hume found a way round. His comment on Hovell is: "He lost himself and his road. I did not."[7]

On 26th October they crossed the Coodradigby River, now usually spelled "Goodradigbee", and the going became so hard that they decided to leave their carts, harness, and part of the provisions. They hid them, as they hoped successfully, from the aborigines, and pressed on. Pack-saddles were put on the bullocks who, being unused to them, gave trouble. Hovell's journal and Hume's *Brief Statement* here disagree on one small but important point. Hovell says that Hume's tarpaulin was left behind in the cache, whilst Hume declares that Hovell would not take his own tarpaulin, and adds: "One cause of our success, simple as it may appear, was my sticking to my tarpaulin, and lugging it along through all our weary journey."[8]

They crossed the Tumut River and found their way blocked by the Snowy Mountains. It is here that the famous quarrel was said, thirty years after the event, to have occurred. Hume wanted to go west to round the mountains, Hovell proposed to go south. They parted, but not before, according to one account, they had torn the tent of Parramatta cloth in half and broken the handle of the frying-pan in a battle for possession. Hovell says nothing of this unedifying incident in his journal; Hume's statement is supported by the doubtful evidence of his convict servants. It appears more likely that they agreed to part as they had done earlier, to improve their chances of finding a road through and that Hume, the better bushman, was again successful and Hovell had to return upon his tracks.

In those high altitudes they suffered a new misery.

> . . . to describe the way in which we were tormented by the small fly and the mosquitoes is almost impossible. Suffice it to say, to write, to read, to sleep or to rest in any place we got to, was impossible; our whole time was employed in grumbling, scratching or beating them away with our handkerchiefs.[9]

The horses suffered as much as the men, and stood almost in the campfires to get the benefit of the smoke. The dogs took refuge in a waterhole and the bullocks lay in the long grass. By day the going was dangerous because of the wombat holes and the fallen timber on the mountainsides.

It was a time of testing, and, according to Bland, the bullocks proved more serviceable than the horses.

> Never was the great superiority of bullocks to horses (in some respects) for journeys of this description more observable than in the progress of this difficult and dangerous descent. The horses, it had become indispensable to unload, and to conduct each separately with great care; but if one of the bullocks be led, the rest follow; the horse is timid and hurried in its action, in places where there is danger; the bullock is steady and cautious. If the latter slip in its ascent, or if the acclivity be too steep for its usual mode of progression, the animal kneels down, and scrambles up in this posture. If it be descending, and it becomes placed in a similar predicament, it sits down, and turns its head round towards the ascent, as if to balance the body. For the crossing of unsound or boggy ground, the structure of its hoof is particularly adapted, while the foot of the horse, on the contrary, is ill suited for this purpose, and for which the fears, and consequent agitation of the animal, render it unfit.[10]

Game was scarce and "we are under the necessity of feeding our poor dogs on boiled flour".[11] As they grew weaker the dogs were less able to hunt. Kangaroos are fast and powerful and the dogs were often wounded and one by one they fell out and were lost. Hovell mourned for his dog Rolla.

After coming through the Alps, Hovell, the more sensitive observer, noted:

> There is also an evident change in the countenances of our men since we have come into the fine country. When among the mountains, we had so frequently to turn back to take another road, or an unfavourable looking mountain to ascend or descend, that I have seen them with faces similar to those I have

seen of sailors when on a seashore in a gale of wind, feeling great doubts whether it is possible the ship can get off or not, but as soon as it is known that the ship is out of danger a change is perceived immediately in the countenance of every person aboard.

The party began "amusing themselves by singing all together, not one song, but each man a different song and tune, and evidently not paying the least attention or even a thought on his neighbour's song".[12]

Across the good lands they came to the River Murray. "This I named Hume's River, he being the first that saw it," wrote Hovell in his journal,[13] but Hume has a different story: "I named it the 'Hume' in compliment to my father."[14]

It was Sturt who renamed it the Murray after the current Secretary of State for the Colonies. In lieu, Hume received, posthumously, the Hume Reservoir and the Hume Highway.

The Murray was crossed by swimming the animals over and piloting the dwindling provisions on a raft of saplings covered with the tarpaulin.

The land was pleasant, the river ran "serpentine" with lagoons or billabongs on its banks. The little hills flowered. Bellbirds chimed. The aborigines were numerous but rarely seen. There were fine fish in the river. But there were snakes in this paradise as they were later to discover.

. . . in the evening . . . Mr Hume's mare was bitten on the nose by a snake, and became immediately a shocking spectacle, the head swelling so much that the eyes were quite closed. An attempt to bleed having failed, half a pint of spirits of turpentine with some water was given, and about twenty minutes after, at which time the swelling had began to subside, some *eau de luce* properly diluted was also administered . . . in order to prevent the animal from sleeping, she was kept walking gently during the whole night.[15]

Brisbane had wanted rivers. Hume and Hovell found plenty for him. After the Murray it was the Little River, which although it was in flood, they crossed by means of a fallen tree. Then it was the Ovens (after Major Ovens) and they unknowingly trod the future goldfield, then the Goulburn, named after the Colonial Secretary, not to be confused with the Secretary of State for the Colonies.

The country became difficult again, with dense undergrowth through which they had to hack their way. Hume was injured by a fall, staking his leg, and the party had to turn back from Mount Disappointment and return to their camp on King Parrot Creek.

Everyone, including the animals, was in bad shape. The backs of the beasts were sore from their loads and had to be washed with warm water and soap every time the packs were taken off. The horses were crippled for want of shoes.

Stores, too, were running low and anything was welcome in the pot. "The flesh of the Native Companions," wrote Hovell, "when boiled, resembles beef, both in appearance and flavour, but there is no fat. . . ."[16]

They nearly lost their precious supply of flour. "When we were crossing one of the creeks the bank gave way, and Mr Hume's mare fell upon her back into it, and her load, which was flour, was not halfway in the bags before we could get her on her legs again."[17]

It is not surprising that nerves were frayed and discontent began to work like yeast amongst the men. At Sunday Creek, which was marshy and difficult to cross, on 13th December, the discontent became articulate. Hume promised that if they did not reach the coast in three days he would turn back. They crossed the Main Divide again and at an aboriginal camp saw oyster shells, sure sign that they were near the sea. One 16th December they camped on the beach of what they took to be Western Port. It was a cheerless camp without water. The next day they found Kennedy's Creek, but had trouble with the aborigines which was settled peaceably.

Of them Hovell wrote:

> Those are the people we generally call "miserable wretches", but in my opinion the word is misapplied, for I cannot for a moment consider them so. They have neither house rent nor taxes to provide, for nearly every tree will furnish them with a house, and perhaps the same tree will supply them with food (the opossum). Their only employment is providing their food. They are happy within themselves; they have their amusements and but little cares; and above all they have their free liberty.[18]

Whilst on the beach the party heard what appeared to be a cannon shot; Hume also understood from the aborigines that there were white men on the coast, if he interpreted their sign language aright. He wanted to go on, but no one else was willing. Supplies were so low that they feared to stay any longer. There were only 150 pounds of flour and 6 pounds of tea left, no sugar or salt, and game was uncertain, particularly without the dogs. They saw a high hill and called it Mount Wentworth—the Mount Macedon of today.

The outward journey had been 670 miles, almost all of it through unknown country. Those who have seen the mighty Snowy Mountains Scheme under construction will have some imaginative understanding of the immensities through which these eight men moved. On the return journey the way they came was a long and weary one, even if they managed to shorten their route by 150 miles. On the 8th January the last of the rations was served out, six pounds of flour to each man, and there were at least 150 miles to travel before they could reach their supplies beside the Coodradigby. They were able to supplement the ration with fish from time to time, and on 13th January 1825 they shot a kangaroo. They ate the meat and out of the skin made "mocassins" for the bullocks who had been lamed on the stony ground. The men also were without shoes by this time.

On 16th January 1825 they reached the spot on Coodradigby River where they had hidden their carts and supplies. Everything was intact except for a spear tear in the tarpaulin. The bullocks were foundering and had to be turned loose. All but one of them died at the place where they were left. The men were worn out, too.

They had gone out in flood, they returned in drought.

The reward for so much effort was small. The Government did not even pay for the bullocks lost. Hume was given a land grant of 1200 acres, but he had to sell it "for my means at the time were very slender".[19] From the census of 1828 we learn something of Hamilton Hume's financial status. The entry reads: "Hamilton Hume, 31 years, farmer, Appin. Total acres 2200, 12 cleared and cultivated. 5 horses, 372 horned cattle, 1500 sheep. Wife, Elizabeth, 26. Total acres 1580, cleared 115, cultivated 75. 6 horses, 90 horned cattle, 700 sheep."[20] Between them they were not, apparently, doing badly. They had no children.

Hovell also received a grant, but it, too, was absorbed in expenses. In 1826 he went with Captain Wright's party to Western Port and immediately discovered the mistake that they made in confusing Port Phillip with it. He explored the district between Cape Paterson and Koo-wee-rup Swamp, found the first coal in Victoria, and presented a report to the Governor which led to the winding up of the Western Port settlement in 1828. In 1829 Hovell was financially just where he was before he went overlanding with Hume, farming his 700 acres at Narellan. He petitioned Governor Darling for more land, but was refused. The Colonial Office intervened on his behalf and in 1837 Governor Bourke forgave him a debt, probably for quit rents, which he owed to the Crown. After that he moved to the Goulburn district. In 1853 he revisited Port Phillip, where he was lionized, an incident which precipitated a bitter quarrel with Hume. He died in Sydney on 9th November 1875.

As for the six convicts who accompanied the expedition, it was only after delay and difficulty that they were given their tickets of leave as reward. The *Australian* commented on the "miserable cold-water-like encouragement given to Messrs Hume and Hovell".

Hume undertook two more pieces of exploration. Governor Darling offered a reward to anyone who could find an alternative route over the mountains to Bathurst, avoiding, if possible, Mounts York and Blaxland, which were very dangerous. Hume set out in September 1828 and on 1st November his plan for "Darling's Causeway" was in the hands of the Surveyor-General, Sir Thomas Mitchell. Mitchell reported that "as a line of road to Bathurst, which should avoid Mounts York and Blaxland, and also Cox's River, the line of Mr Hume seems to me the most eligible that can be found". Unfortunately, as it would not serve the settlers already established on O'Connell Plains and the Fish River, it was impracticable, but Hume received the reward of 1286 acres of land to be selected by himself.

In the same year, 1828, Hume accompanied Captain Charles Sturt on the expedition which led to the discovery of the Darling River.

After this Hume retired from exploration; his health was impaired and he could not afford to leave his property, called Cooma, and situated two miles from Yass, for long periods.

Here the story would have ended on a note of *succès d'estime* but for the quarrel which broke out in 1853 and which is still faintly a-simmer among historians. Animadversions of more than a century ago make poor reading, but this particular quarrel, being deeply embedded in source material, is worth a glance.

The heads of the quarrel were ostensibly, first, who led the expedition, and, second, did Hume mistake Port Phillip for Western Port or was it Hovell's error alone? These questions carried long trailers of bitterness.

As for leadership, Hume was first approached and was obviously the finer and more experienced bushman, but he took Hovell as a partner, mainly for financial reasons, not as a subordinate. Hume speaks of him as providing the necessary material "jointly". It was an equal outlay. Hovell was eleven years older than Hume and in the early days of their association Hume insisted that for this reason Hovell should be the first to sign any letter written jointly. The expedition which is now commonly called that of Hume and Hovell was in earlier days sometimes referred to as the journey of Hovell and Hume. Pinpricks, but they were to fester.

Captain J. H. Watson, strongly partisan, claimed that the whole journey was "unpleasant" on account of quarrels, that Hovell was "unfit to be a leader". "In fact," wrote the captain, "he was an encumbrance and incubus on the Expedition. There is no doubt but that Hamilton Hume led the expedition through the unknown wilds which separated Yass Plains from Port Phillip Bay, and brought it safely back, which Hovell could never have done."[21] Watson had evidently been reading Hume's venomous *Brief Statement* to the exclusion of other source material. He may not have had access to Hovell's journal, which was not printed, by the Royal Australian Historical Society, until 1921.

As for mistaking Port Phillip Bay for Western Port, there is evidence that Hume was as much misled as Hovell. In writing to the Governor (24th January 1825) and to the Secretary of State for the Colonies (April 1826) Hume referred to their journey's end as Western Port, nor did he correct articles in the *Australian* and the *Sydney Gazette* when they named Western Port. It was not until the end of 1826 that Hume learned of their mistake, and then it was through Hovell, who had been sent to Western Port on Government business.

The general allegations of cowardice, laziness, and incompetence which Hume hurled at Hovell in his *Brief Statement*, first published in 1853 and reprinted, with a fresh infusion of acid, in 1873, just after Hume's death, are another matter and more difficult to disprove. Hovell's journal, written in the field, shows no signs of rancour and, more important, makes no effort at self-justification. In his rebuttal of the 1873 edition of the *Brief Statement*, Hovell stated: "No word of complaint was uttered by him nor did he ever tax me with laying claim to any credit that was not my due." They met from time to time in a friendly way.

> Then came my visit to Melbourne and Geelong in 1853, during which the people of Victoria may, in their exuberant kindness and hospitality, have paid me more attention than my services deserved, but if they did so, Mr Hume would have shared that attention with me, had he had the good fortune to accompany me, and that he did not, was entirely due to himself.

The last sentence is a little misleading. Hovell explains that he had considered inviting Hume to accompany him and had asked the advice of one of Hume's relatives on the advisability of doing so. They had decided between them that Hume's personal "habits" put it out of the question. If this leaked back to Hume his anger is understandable.

A garbled Press version of Hovell's speech at a banquet given in his honour made it appear that he claimed all the credit for the discoveries. When the full text of the speech was examined this was seen to be untrue, but the damage had been done.

The length of time Hume allowed to elapse, nearly thirty years, before he made his accusations, and the time at which he made them, do something to discredit them. It is unlikely that on such an arduous journey there was never a difference of opinion or a quarrel between the leaders, and no doubt there were incidents which, seen in their true perspective at the time, began to rankle when Hume had time to brood upon them. For instance, when Dr William Bland brought out a book, delayed until 1831 because the publishers had run out of paper, rehashing in the manner of the time the story of the expedition from the journals of the leaders, he used Hovell's journal more freely than Hume's because the latter was so "scanty". The Bland narrative does not, otherwise, take sides between the two men.

So much effort and striving, so much bitterness, so many words and what did it all amount to? The route of the journey lay like a thread, often a tangled thread, across the map which till than had been blank. A whole system of rivers flowing into the Murray was discovered and some excellent pastures, such as the Iramoo Downs, were revealed. The Snowy Mountains as barrier and watershed were put on the map. Hume claimed, and he may well have been right, that his account of the land about Geelong, published in the *Sydney Morning Herald* in 1833, attracted great attention in Van Diemen's Land and led on to the settlement of Port Phillip by Batman and others.

REFERENCE NOTES

1 Quoted by J. H. Watson in the *Scottish Australasian*, vol. x (1919), p. 7193.
2 Hume's *Brief Statement* (2nd ed.), pp. 30-1.
3 Hovell's Journal, *J. Roy. Aust. Hist. Soc.*, vol. vii, pp. 307 *et seq.*
4 Hume's *Brief Statement* (2nd ed.), p. 34.
5 Hovell's Journal, *J. Roy. Aust. Hist. Soc.*, vol. vii, p. 313.
6 *Ibid.*
7 Hume's *Brief Statement* (2nd ed.), p. 36.
8 *Ibid.*, p. 37.
9 Hovell's Journal, *J. Roy. Aust. Hist. Soc.*, vol. vii, p. 327.
10 W. Bland, *Journey of Discovery to Port Phillip, New South Wales, by Messrs W. H. Hovell and Hamilton Hume*, pp. 25-6.
11 Hovell's Journal, *J. Roy. Aust. Hist. Soc.*, vol. vii, p. 328.
12 *Ibid.*, p. 331.
13 *Ibid.*
14 Hume's *Brief Statement* (2nd ed.), p. 39.
15 W. Bland, *Journey of Discovery to Port Phillip, etc.*, pp. 74-5.
16 Hovell's Journal, *J. Roy. Aust. Hist. Soc.*, vol. vii, p. 339.
17 *Ibid.*, p. 345.
18 *Ibid.*, p. 347.
19 Hume's *Brief Statement* (2nd ed.), p. 31.
20 Quoted by E. S. Yeo, *Hamilton Hume and the Hume Family of New South Wales.*
21 J. H. Watson in the *Scottish Australasian*, vol. x, p. 7195.

CHAPTER X

COLONIZATION, SCIENTIFIC AND OTHERWISE

I. Natural Growth

The British were not content with one *pied-à-terre* on the continent of Australia. Having annexed it peacefully and without rivals, various motives drove them on to assimilate the whole—defence, the hope of bigger profits farther out, the need of expansion, the psychological effect on English theorists of great quantities of undefended land.

1. *Norfolk Island*

In the month of February 1788 the colony's first colony was founded. Phillip, acting on his instructions, sent his right-hand man, Lieutenant Philip Gidley King, to Norfolk Island, about a thousand miles east of Sydney. King took with him a surgeon and his mate, four other free men, two Marines, and fifteen well-behaved convicts, six of them women. Also of the party were six ewes, two boars, three sows, a goat, four hens, one cock, three ducks and a drake.

The island was as unprepared to receive them as New South Wales had been. This was another act of faith on a smaller scale. Cook had discovered and praised Norfolk Island in October 1774. It was five miles long, three miles wide on an average, with an area of about thirteen square miles of mountainous, thickly timbered, surf-girt land.

King described it as "one intire [*sic*] wood, without a single acre of clear land. . . . The pine-trees rise fifty and sixty feet before they shoot out any branches. . . . The trees are so bound together by a kind of supple-jack that the penetrating into the interior parts of the island was very difficult."[1]

Such was the young lieutenant's kingdom. His salary was £250 a year and nothing to spend it on.

The Home Office had had two motives for its colonization, defence of the infant settlement on the mainland and the cultivation of hemp, which was said by Cook to grow prolifically on the island. The defence motive was the first manifestation of the "screen of islands" policy of today, the germ of the later theory that Australia, with her long coastline, her many unmanned beach-heads, could never be defended on her own soil and that her only chance of survival in times of peril was to prevent the enemy from reaching it. Australia was saved in 1943 in the Coral Sea, the Solomons, and the jungles of New Guinea, but in 1788 any such contingency was distant and unthinkable. Yet the idea in embryonic form was there. With no desire for colonies and still smarting under the loss of America, England was yet aware of French interest in the Pacific and, once she had planted a settlement, was jealous enough to guard it. La Pérouse, for instance, was known to be somewhere in the Pacific on a voyage of curiosity, but was curiosity all his intension? To secure New South Wales, a settlement as token of ownership should be set up on the nearest habitable island. It is true that one warship could have extinguished the tiny flicker of life on the desert island, for it had no means of ready communication with any British force. However, in peace-time, when even hereditary enemies could be expected to play the game, occupation by a lieutenant of the King's Navy should be enough and always was. Danger came not only from the inquisitive French but from pirates. Norfolk Island would make a nice private hide-out for them from which they could attack store-ships and where they could hide plunder.

In 1785 a scheme had been put up to establish a factory there (factory in those days meant various things, in this instance an armed trading post), to be a half-way house to China for the East India Company, a depot for the Alaska fur trade, a manufactory for hemp, and a jumping-off place for attack on the Spanish colonies in the Pacific in event of war. The whole idea smacked of piracy, and Alexander Dalrymple, the East India Company's hydrographer, reported against it. It showed however that the idea was loose in the world.

Hemp seems to have been a fixed idea with the Home Office—hemp for the Navy and the hangman. It was scarce, and requests for hemp sprinkle thickly the early years. It was as if Secretary of State after Secretary of State pointed out all that had been done for this outpost, all the money that had been spent on colonizing it, and asked plaintively for just some hemp in return. The wild flax did grow on Norfolk Island, but no one knew how to dress it. Several Maoris were kidnapped, without violence, and brought to Norfolk Island. All that was asked of them was that they should teach the convicts how to make hemp from the flax. Unfortunately it turned out that in New Zealand the industry was entirely in the hands of women, the warriors knew nothing about it. They were taken home again.

Phillip had his own reasons for colonizing the island and sent to it more and more convicts as conditions worsened on the mainland. It partook of the south-sea fertility and Port Jackson did not. Men could live there much more easily. Crops throve, the sea was full of fish, the trees of birds. It was a relief to Phillip to send some of the hungry mouths there, knowing that they would be filled.

After the arid terrain of Port Jackson the island was as balm. King wrote:

The climate is pure, salubrious and delightful, preserved from oppressive heats by constant breezes from the sea, and of so mild a temperature throughout the winter, that vegetation continues there without interruption, one crop succeeding another. Refreshing showers from time to time maintain perpetual verdure: not indeed of grass, for none has yet been seen upon the island, but of the trees, shrubs, and other vegetables which in all parts grow abundantly. On the leaves of these, and of some kinds in particular, the sheep, hogs and goats not only live, but thrive and fatten very much. To the salubrity of the air every individual in this little colony can bear ample testimony, from the uninterrupted state of good health which has been in general enjoyed.[2]

Encouraged, Phillip sent *Golden Grove* in October 1788 with 21 male and 11 female convicts, two seamen, and a small posse of Marines. (He also sent some dogs and cats to cope with the rats on the island.) The population was steadily increased. In March 1789 there were 51 male and 23 women convicts, 16 free settlers and four children on the island. More and more were sent.

King made a very fair success of his governorship, building up a small community along the lines laid down for New South Wales. The days were not without incident, as the stories of the rising of the convicts and a mutiny of the soldiers illustrate.

On another occasion, 7th November 1804, when Captain Piper was relieving commandant, there was a scare. Nine large sailing ships in formation appeared off the coast. With great presence of mind Piper clapped all the disaffected Irish convicts into jail and furbished up his defences. The heavy surf that was nearly always running prevented the fleet approaching, but next morning it was off Cascade Bay. "At Seven O'Clock the Fleet were standing into the Bay; they fired a Gun to leeward, and hoisted English Colours." Piper thought it might be a trap and remained on guard, but the colours were genuine. It was the East India Company's China Fleet seeking refreshment. The crews were hungry and sick. Piper was able to send them twelve sheep, twelve goats, and some lemons, and so they sailed away.[3]

The psychological climate was much happier than at Sydney Cove, but not for long. Barrack-room fever broke out. The community was too restricted, life too monotonous. The officers quarrelled bitterly, and so, I suppose, did other ranks. Harsh punishments were meted out to the convicts. No supply ships came until after the arrival of the Second Fleet. There was no meat to issue and all must live on birds and fish. Four thousand birds and one hundred and eighty large snapper were caught on one Sunday alone. Ralph Clark, when doing his tour of duty there, wrote in his diary: "I have not . . . drank a dish of tea or drank a glass of wine these six months. Our breakfast is dry bread and coffee made from burnt wheat, and we are glad even to be able to get that God help us."[4]

Major Ross, the Lieutenant-Governor, sent to relieve King, was not successful in his governorship. His arrival in a bad temper, because he was not accorded the honours he expected, was further marred by the wreck of *Sirius,* a great loss, since now little *Supply* was the only ship left to serve the two settlements.

Ross let the allocation of land fall into confusion. "From the total ignorance of the surveyor, and from his inattention to the King's instructions in that behalf, the allotments for the different settlers are made out in the most irregular manner, and so situated as to interfere with and to intersect each other in many instances."[5] The only remedy was to indemnify settlers out of adjacent Crown reserves and take up other land for the Crown.

Nevertheless, Ross was very pleased with himself. He instituted a system of economy. He gave each convict a tract of land, a pig between three, and two days' "holiday" a week for cultivation. At the end of three months his ration of flour was to be reduced by a quarter, after six months by half, and on 1st March 1792 the flour ration was to be discontinued altogether. The meat ration also was to be stopped a year after the sow farrowed for the first time. So, if a man did not want to starve, he must work. If he worked very hard and brought grain to the store he was rewarded, not with money, but with extra "holidays" to produce more grain. The women were to keep house for the men, who were expected to provide for them, and help on the farms; their services would be requisitioned by the Government only in emergencies, as when rain threatened the public harvest.

This arrangement was both unpopular and impracticable. It did not take bad seasons or Acts of God, like plagues of caterpillars, into consideration. When King returned in November 1791 he pacified the island, but irreparable damage had been done to morale.

Norfolk Island suffered from its remoteness and the difficulties of communication. It had no safe harbour. It was dependent on England for many of its needs, all clothing, tools, salt meat . . . and although it was suggested that ships go there direct this was rarely done. The Governor in Sydney had to charter vessels to carry supplies there, when, and if, he had the chance.

Grose, writing to Dundas, did not mince matters:

> The danger in this passage [to Norfolk Island] of losing both the ship and her cargo is a business always to be dreaded. I never discovered the advantages proposed from the possession of the island; there is not herbage sufficient to feed cattle of any description, consequently the probability of the inhabitants being ever able to maintain themselves is out of the question. The progress of this settlement [New South Wales] has been greatly interrupted by sending working people there whose labour could have been better employed here, and sooner or later some unpleasant consequence will certainly attend the conveyance of supplies to it.[6]

The gilt was already off the earthly paradise in 1794. And Grose contributed his own special brand of difficulties. Whilst in office he neglected to draw bills on the Treasury for the expenses of the island, leaving it without funds and Governor Hunter with heavy debts to settle.

Sometimes the island was a year without any communication with the world. Then, too, there were, to begin with, no law-courts on the island and offenders had to be sent, with witnesses to Sydney for trial, a cumbersome business.

Conditions improved somewhat with the development of the whaling industry in the South Seas. But there was a catch in it. Whalers not only put into Norfolk Island for refreshment, thus providing a market for surplus products, but they illicitly landed spirits, especially the Americans, and obligingly stowed away convicts desirous of leaving the island. King optimistically thought that the whalers could be turned to good use, especially those fishing off New Zealand. They could take pigs, of which Norfolk Island had a surplus, to New Zealand and bring back the flax plant. With the importation of rope-making machinery he foresaw "an amusement to the People and a double Object gained, as the leakage of the Oil [in the Whalers] would not damage that Rope but on the contrary strengthen it".[7]

In 1794 a Judge-Advocate was appointed by Act of Parliament and one of the worst inconveniences was cured, but it remained an expensive and, as conditions improved on the mainland, a not very useful little settlement. In 1805 the Home Government decided to abandon it and transfer its population to Van Diemen's Land. This was a slow business and it was not until 1813, after Macquarie had arrived, that the evacuation was completed.

The settlers were unwilling to go, many of them were expirees and had their own small farms. Only ten out of forty settlers expressed willingness to leave. Shipping had to be found to take them, their wives and children, and their livestock to Port Dalrymple or to the Derwent, where they had to begin all over again in a less benign climate and in a colony more backward than Norfolk Island. Van Diemen's Land was not yet able to feed itself. True, they were given four acres for every one they had cultivated on Norfolk Island and two for every uncultivated one they had owned, together with rations for twelve months and the labour of two convicts.[8] King was against abandoning Norfolk Island. As his first and successful command it had become dear to him.

The island lay fallow except for a few families, the most loath to go, who maintained the settlement as a post of refreshment for whalers and an emergency larder for New South Wales.

In 1825 Governor Brisbane was instructed to use it as a place of secondary punishment. Now, not well-behaved convicts, but only the incorrigibles, the most hardened and desperate characters, were sent there.

The mainland wanted to be rid of them and from surf-girt Norfolk Island they would have little chance of escape.

On the island fertility had run wild, the old government buildings were overgrown, the farms had fallen into ruins, and pigs, left behind for want of space in the ships, had multiplied exceedingly. All that had been done in the way of clearing, with much labour, now must be done again.

Gone were the idyllic days of an earthly paradise. The new régime was severe to the point of brutality. No women were to be allowed on the island for fear of their softening influence and the men were under such harsh discipline that they begged to be hanged rather than sent there. They worked in irons (but only, it is pointed out, to prevent escape) from sunrise to sunset. Good behaviour might win them tobacco, but this was later disallowed.

In 1839 another new era began, Norfolk Island was now to become a model prison. Convicts were to go there direct from England and to serve a probationary period of not more than fifteen years, generally much less, and their treatment was to be carefully adjusted to their conduct. After conditioning they would be considered fit to be assigned as servants on the mainland. The Superintendent was to be an officer of the highest character. "He should," wrote Lord Normanby, "feel a deep interest in the moral improvement of the Convicts, and be disposed to devote his whole energies to this important object. The opposite faults of over-severity and over-indulgence should be carefully avoided, as alike destructive of any good effect on the prisoners."[9] For his "whole energies" he was to receive £800 a year and a residence. The idea was not new. Plummer, read by Macquarie on his voyage out, proposed segregation of convicts and the slow return to society by fixed stages. Bigge in his report suggested five stages of punishment and regeneration. The Colonial Office modified the plan, and as usual it proved impossible to carry even this out in its entirety. The Old Hands, the men who had been on the island for rigorous punishment, remained. There was nowhere else to send them. Captain Maconochie, a zealot with a system of reform through encouragement and hope, was appointed commandant with instructions to keep the two types of convicts, the newcomers and the Old Hands, separated. But, wrote Governor Gipps, he "extended to all a system of extreme indulgence, and held out hopes, almost indiscriminately, to them of being speedily restored to freedom".[10] "The whole Convict population of the Island was on the occasion of Her Majesty's Birthday regaled with Punch and entertained with the performance of a Play."[11]

Maconochie had a remarkable system characteristic of the humanitarian spirit of the 1830s and 1840s and of the doctrinaire approach so usual to Australian affairs. He issued tickets of leave to nearly every convict on the island regardless of his status. He had a system of marks. To every man he gave eleven marks a day in place of rations and to men working for the Government thirty-six marks a day. The marks were currency at the store. Six marks would buy a pound of pork or beef, three a pound of maize, five a pound of sugar, twenty-four a pound of tobacco. Marks would also buy freedom. If a man saved half his marks for a year he could buy, not a ticket of leave, but a conditional pardon. Whilst the men bought at the store with marks they were paid for any produce they brought in in money, threepence a pound for pork, and so on. When a man left the island any marks he had saved over and above those necessary for his freedom were changed into money so that he had something in his pocket to begin his new life. Music and reading were encouraged as refining influences.

Gipps was not impressed. He saw that the convicts were cheating their benefactor, or rather the Government. The maintenance of a convict now cost £37 3s. 11d. instead of £17 a year. Convicts sold back to the store for money the pork they had bought for marks. Agriculture had fallen off. Maconochie said it was the fault of the seasons; the Commissary, who disapproved of the whole system, declared that it was the result of too great lenity. Gipps found Maconochie popular, the convicts quiet and respectful in manner, but listless at their work. Petty crimes abounded and the Old Hands were restless. By bad management timber and firewood were running out and the island fast losing its prosperity. To top it all, the convicts during the Governor's visit tried to seize the brig *Governor Phillip* whilst it was unloading. They were in possession of the brig for half an hour and it was only recaptured at the loss of five convicts' lives, a soldier drowned and two severely wounded.

Gipps reported to the Colonial Office that it was time that the experiment ended, it had had two and a half years' trial. The inhabitants of Sydney were in a panic at the thought of a flood of hardened criminals soon to be loosed upon them. Van Diemen's Land was not anxious to take the Old Hands, but Gipps determined that they should go there and the prison be kept on only for transportees direct from England. Maconochie fought hard for his system, but in the end he was disillusioned. Out of respect for his obvious sincerity the Colonial Office hesitated to recall him.

Transportation had ceased in 1840, but prisoners were working out their sentences on Norfolk Island until 1856. After that the island lived and still lives a quiet life thrown clear of the world. Maconochie's experiment was the one curiosity in its history and stands apart by reason of its bizarre nature from the convict system in general.

2. *Van Diemen's Land*

In the earliest days a death sentence was sometimes transmuted to transportation to South Cape, that is to the most southerly cape of Van Diemen's

Land, or Tasmania, as it was rechristened in 1856. The sentences were never carried out because of the impracticability of landing the offenders on that distant and inhospitable spot. Ships rounded South Cape on their way up the coast of New South Wales from England, but from Port Jackson they usually went north to China or India for trade. The hangman would have been kinder than such a fate in any case.

It was again fear of the French that forced the settlement of Van Diemen's Land. During the lull in the Napoleonic wars, after the Peace of Amiens in 1802, French ships again took up their pursuit of curiosity in the Pacific. Admiral Nicolas Baudin was known to be off the coast of Tasmania and southern Australia with his ships *Géographe* and *Naturaliste*. Flinders, circumnavigating the continent in *Investigator,* met him at Encounter Bay on 8th April 1802. There was friendly intercourse between the two explorers and, indeed, Baudin was quite sincere in his claim that his interest was entirely scientific. Suspicion, however, was aroused when it was found that a map published in Paris named the land between Wilson's Promontory and Spencer's Gulf "Terre Napoléon". Moreover, Baudin was supposed to have told Colonel Paterson that the French intended to plant a settlement in Van Diemen's Land. This was later denied, but the damage was done.

Thanks to the coastal discoveries of George Bass early in 1798, it was now known that a strait existed between the mainland and Van Diemen's Land. Both in England and Sydney it was felt that it would be most unwise to allow the French to establish themselves in Bass Strait or anywhere on Van Diemen's Land. It would be more awkward to have them planted on the sea route between New South Wales and England than, more hypothetically, on Norfolk Island. France was the protagonist in the long-drawn-out Napoleonic wars and it would be very serious if she were in the position to cut the lifeline between England and her most distant, and still struggling, colony. King's ships could hardly be spared, and in any case possession was nine points of the law. As regards discovery, honours were about equal between the French and English.

Governor King, the man on the spot, sent a young naval lieutenant, Robbins, in the thirty-ton ship *Cumberland* to the danger area. Robbins had two commissions, a public one to explore the coast and bring back samples of rock and soil and generally to behave, after the manner of the French, in an innocently curious manner. His secret commission bade him keep his eyes open for the French ships and forestall Baudin by taking formal possession of Bass Strait.

Robbins fell in with the French at King Island, a dot on the map at the easterly end of the Strait. He landed with three Marines, formally proclaimed the island British territory, ran up the Union Jack (upside down in his haste) over the very heads of the astonished French, fired a volley, gave three cheers, and retired. Robbins was then to visit Port Phillip on the mainland and the Derwent in Van Diemen's Land, leaving two soldiers in each place as token colonists. *Porpoise* was to follow him and consolidate what he had begun.

In England the matter was given more mature consideration. Port Phillip, named and praised by Lieutenant Murray in *Lady Nelson* in 1802, was chosen as the site of a settlement. David Collins, once Judge-Advocate at Sydney, was put in charge of an expedition so well found and carefully thought out that Phillip must have been green with envy. There were three hundred male convicts in the party, all carefully chosen for their skills as farmers and mechanics and for their good behaviour. Thirty wives were allowed to accompany their husbands.

Cloth, leather, and knitting wool were provided on the voyage for occupational therapy. Collins was given a civil staff so that it would not be necessary to put convicts in positions of trust. He had instructions to conciliate the natives, practise economy, send home regular returns of births, marriages, and deaths, of the increase of his stock and of the products of convict labour. . . . He was to set up a police force and guard against the introduction of intoxicating liquors. Should this be impracticable he might issue two or three licences and exercise rigorous control over the licensees. Religion was to be observed and so were the privileges of the East India Company. King Island was to be a satellite colony, just as Norfolk Island was to Port Jackson, and for the same reasons. Free settlers were also sent out and were to be encouraged by six months' longer support from the public store than their counterparts could expect in New South Wales. Lord Hobart regretted that he could not persuade men of substance to settle. It is clear some lessons had been learnt from the first Australian settlement and that the Colonial Office was consciously aiming at a model community planted on untainted ground.

If Port Phillip proved unsuitable Collins might choose another site in consultation with the Governor of New South Wales, "but", his instructions continued, "you must understand that you are not to delay the disembarkation of the persons under your command upon your arrival on the coast, with a view to searching for a more eligible place. . . ."[12] Every least detail was thought out. Governor King was instructed to equip Collins with stock for breeding and to give him every possible support. One guesses that there was not much cordiality between the two men and, in any case, the Secretary of State, as usual, underestimated Australian distances. There was little that King could do for Collins. Besides the distance between Port Jackson and the proposed settlement, there was a chronic lack of ships. Collins was unwilling to look to King as his superior for advice and help.

Collins had not the staunch heart of Phillip. He quickly formed a poor opinion of the land at Port Phillip and was nervous about the water supply.

The settlers went in terror of the aborigines. After only three months' trial he decided that the place was impossible. Without referring to King—and, indeed, King could hardly have advised him, as he had no local knowledge—Collins departed to try his luck in Van Dieman's Land, where he arrived on 9th October 1804. He chose the estuary of the Derwent and landed on the site of modern Hobart.

Near by at Risdon Cove he found a small, struggling settlement already entrenched under a nineteen-year-old naval lieutenant, John Bowen.

King, in March 1803, had issued a proclamation: "It being expedient to establish His Majesty's Right to Van Dieman's [*sic*] Land, His Excellency has been pleased to direct Lieut. John Bowen, of His Majesty's ship *Glatton*, to form an Establishment on that island and has appointed him Commandant and Superintendent of the Settlement so formed."[13]

Bowen had volunteered. His settlement was not well formed. It consisted of 49 souls, of whom 10 were women and 3 children. They had eight months' provisions, 32 sheep, 10 cattle, one horse, some goats, pigs, and fowls. It was a wretched, discontented, disorderly little community. Seven of the twenty-four convicts escaped. The soldiers were little better than the convicts. Bowen got himself into bad odour by being shipwrecked and costing the Government £500 for his rescue.

The two settlements existed side by side for a short time in sulky rivalry. Risdon was doomed; after seven months Bowen left for Sydney and most of his settlers followed suit.

Collins, with a new access of energy, set to work clearing the land, erecting Government House, setting aside land for a government farm, and establishing his free settlers at Newtown. Amongst them was a boy of eleven, John Pascoe Fawkner, who was destined to return to Port Phillip and leave his mark on Australian history.

The usual struggles ensued, but Hobart Town was fortunate in that it very quickly found a staple. The estuary of the Derwent swarmed with whales and a whaling industry began. A Dane, who had learnt the trade in New Zealand, claimed to have inaugurated whaling in Van Diemen's Land when he harpooned the first whale in the Derwent in 1804. Whaling made Hobart Town a thriving port with a ship-building industry. Whales also brought the Americans. Even whilst it was starving or living on kangaroo and emu meat the little port had an international flavour. It was not until 1810 that the threat of extinction by famine was finally overcome.

It was a blow to the young settlement when the Home Government decided to send convicts and settlers there from Norfolk Island. The population was doubled before the island was ready for it.

After a bad beginning Collins made a good administrator and saw the settlement through its early troubles. He held office until his sudden death, whilst drinking a cup of tea, in 1810. Even his funeral was attended with trouble. Lieutenant Edward Lord, on whom the government fell, misguidedly spent £500 on the last rites. Macquarie refused to pay it, and the bill was relayed to London where it had a cold reception, but was eventually settled.

The Commandant at Hobart Town had much to contend against. Although Van Diemen's Land was on the route from England to Port Jackson store-ships sailed round the island without calling in. Their cargoes were carried to Sydney. The share for Hobart Town was then shipped back when opportunity offered. Collins wrote to England complaining of the infrequency with which he received supplies and of their quality. Technically he was still a Lieutenant-Governor, responsible to the Governor at Sydney, but whilst resentful of the treatment he received, he always considered himself independent and wrote direct to the Colonial Office. King, answering the charge of neglect, replied that he had sent *Lady Barlow* with a year's supplies. It was not his fault that much of the cargo was condemned. The food was from the same consignment as that being eaten in Sydney, meat that had come from the Cape in March 1803 and flour from England in 1802. It was unreasonable to expect it to be in good condition in 1805. It was true, too, that some of the meat had not been pickled, and so was bad, and that the flour had weevils, but there were no complaints in Sydney, so why should Collins be so pernickety?[14]

Transport by sailing ship was always difficult. On one occasion *Sophia* left Sydney with a full cargo for Van Diemen's Land, but she was caught in a storm and had to throw overboard twenty-eight tierces of salt pork. There was also mismanagement and a mistake in the Commissary's returns credited Van Diemen's Land with more stores than she had. All might have starved to death had not a whaler come unexpectedly into port with food for sale.

Kangaroo meat was taken into the store in Hobart Town as a regular thing and sold in the market at from 8d. to 1s. 6d. a pound.

Years later, in 1826, we still hear of complaints, this time of shoes. They were old army boots of superseded pattern. "As at the end of a War a very great store of shoes was on hand, they were to a large extent sent to New South Wales and doubtless in part must have reached Van Diemen's Land." (Army disposals is no new thing.) They were old when they arrived, they were held up in Sydney for want of shipping for perhaps six months. They had heated in the holds of ships and the stitching had perished. Or else they had been made by prisoners in jails in a very slovenly manner and at a contract price of 4s. 7d. a pair. What could one expect?[15] After this, but not because of it, Van Diemen's Land received her supplies direct. This is to illustrate the early difficulties of a remote colony in the age of sail.

There was much on the credit side, too. The soil about Hobart Town was much better than that about Sydney. By 1813 there were 300 farmers and 2000 acres under cultivation; by 1819 there was a population of 4000, with 8000 acres cultivated and 200,000 sheep grazed. Van Diemen's Land was already being called "The Granary of Australia". The main trouble was still communication with Sydney. The settlement there had for the service only small colonial ships that were often turned back by bad weather.

As mentioned before, whaling and sealing were the main industry. It centred on Hobart Town and the islands in Bass Strait, where, far from authority, the whalers set up barbaric and primitive states, whaling in the season and cultivating the land in the off season.

The whaling and sealing industry was quite unregulated, with the result that whales and seals were well-nigh exterminated. In 1806 one ship alone brought 66,000 sealskins into Hobart Town. Nothing was wasted. The flesh of the seals after they had been skinned was traded to the aborigines for kangaroo skins.

High duties on whale-oil, whalebone, and sealskins entering the United Kingdom, the Navigation Acts which forbade trading with foreign nations (many of the sealers were American, coming into Hobart to refit and so bringing prosperity), and the monopoly of the East India Company in all trade in the Southern Hemisphere, between them brought the industry to a standstill—or would have, had the laws been obeyed.

The high duties drove local whalers to seek their markets in the East. Only English ships with capital behind them could make it pay in the face of the duties. These were relaxed in 1828. By that time the far cheaper method of bay whaling had been developed. This meant that small ships harpooned the whales off the coast and towed them to stations on land. One station could serve many ships. Costly equipment need no longer be installed in each ship for treating the carcasses at sea. The years 1836 to 1838 marked the peak of the industry, and in 1836 there were nine stations in and about Hobart. By 1840 prosperity from the sea was exhausted. Greed had destroyed it. As early as 1826 a Court of Inquiry into the industry had suggested a closed season be observed. Whalers and sealers ignored the recommendation. The massacre went on. By 1832 the seals had disappeared and by 1840 so had the black whales. Franklin, the Arctic explorer, who was Governor of Van Diemen's Land from 1837 to 1843, tried in vain to revive the industry.

Meanwhile Hobart Town had created a ship-building and repairing industry and her staunch little ships were trading far and wide in the Pacific, to Chile, Batavia, China, New Zealand and the islands. Eventually, like New South Wales, Van Diemen's Land turned away from the sea and looked inwards for her wealth.

Hobart Town was not the only settlement in Van Diemen's Land. When Collins left Bass Strait unguarded by his withdrawal from Port Phillip Governor King sent Colonel Paterson to the north coast of the island. He sailed on 15th October 1804 with a party of 67 soldiers, 74 convicts, and 40 free settlers to Port Dalrymple, named after the famous hydrographer, and situated on the River Tamar. The site had been discovered and named by Bass and Flinders when they circumnavigated the island in 1798. Paterson's expedition was not as simple as it sounds. At first Governor King had been in a quandary over his instructions. The Secretary of State had told him to colonize Port Dalrymple on the *south* coast of Van Diemen's Land. It is, of course, on the north coast. The south was already being taken care of by Bowen and Collins, so King finally decided that there had been a slip of the pen. The north coast was, moreover, the logical place for a new settlement. Paterson set out forthwith in *Integrity*, a ship too small for such a voyage, and bad weather forced him to return to Port Jackson. When he sailed again it was in the King's ship *Buffalo* with the colonial vessels *Lady Nelson, Francis,* and *Integrity* in attendance. They had a stormy but successful passage.

Paterson's interest had long been in exploration, he was a seasoned traveller in wild places, so just the man to pioneer new, or almost new country, for Bass, Flinders and David Collins had been there before him. Port Dalrymple did not please Paterson, the aborigines were hostile, the land less fertile than he had hoped. He moved his settlement to Yorktown, which was even less suitable, and in 1806 to the present site of Launceston, which, for a short time, was called Patersonia.

To avoid trouble between Collins and Paterson, King divided the island into two counties; Paterson reigned in the northern one, County Cornwall, and Collins in Buckinghamshire. Governor King was a Cornishman, hence the names scattered round the north of Van Diemen's Land. The Governor seems to have favoured the northern settlement, spending £15,350 to stock it with cattle alone.

Despite careful fostering, the settlement progressed very slowly. By 1810 there were only sixteen settlers. Those transferred from Norfolk Island and given the choice of Port Dalrymple or the Derwent almost universally chose the latter. Macquarie on his visit of inspection to the island in 1811 was not impressed by Launceston and ordered the seat of Government to be moved to George Town (named after the King), because it was more accessible to the sea. Nature defeated the Governor's plans.

In 1807 Lieutenant Laycock pioneered a land route to the Derwent, but it was not until 1812 that the whole island was brought under one Governor.

In the Rum Rebellion Paterson sided with his Corps, and Collins with Bligh, who took refuge with him. He came as a private citizen, however, not wishing to upset Collins's government. They soon fell out, and Collins threw in his lot with the *de facto* government in Sydney.[16]

It was not until 1813 that a new Lieutenant-Governor was appointed with his seat at Hobart Town. He was Colonel Thomas Davey, generally called

"Mad Tom". Roy Bridges tells an anecdote of him which bears out the nickname. On the day of official landing Mrs Davey and her daughter donned their best clothes to make a good impression.

Her husband, drunk as usual, ruined the poor lady's best bonnet and her hope to impress the colonists with her elegance. The day of the official landing at Hobart Town was 4th February, 1813. By the time for them to be rowed ashore Davey was drunk, sitting in his cabin with a bottle and a glass before him. He blinked at Mrs Davey when, in her best dress and the charming bonnet, she dared to remind him that the boat was waiting. Pointing to the bonnet, he issued his first order in the Colony: "You are not going ashore in that bonnet!"

She protested that it was the latest word from Paris; she thought only to do him credit on his landing in the colony. Port wine on a hot day had inflamed his temper. He insisted. She resisted. He persisted. Her tears and entreaties weighed with dear Thomas not at all. He snatched the bonnet from her head and poured the port wine over it. He refused flatly to go ashore with her.

In despair, and with the second-best bonnet, Mrs Davey was rowed ashore with her daughter to receive the welcome of officialdom and the colonists. The drunken dictator settled down to another bottle. Later in the day he, too, was rowed ashore. He was found wandering about the little settlement, in his shirt-sleeves.[17]

Davey sober was a different man from Davey drunk. Unfortunately he was very often intoxicated. One suspects that because of his little failing and his powerful patron, Lord Harrowby, he had been stowed away at the end of the earth.

Certainly Colonel Davey was not a man to appeal to the correct and upright Governor Macquarie, his titular chief. Nevertheless he fitted into the picture well enough. He went his own way with a studied independence of Sydney. He fostered the whaling industry, legal or not, exported the first corn to the mainland, and in 1815 declared martial law in the settlement and took strong measures against bushrangers. These were escaped convicts who, running away into the bush, could not live, unless they joined forces with the aborigines. This meant raids on the farms and on travellers. They existed and became a terror, because they had secret allies amongst convicts and ex-convicts or were able to frighten them into giving them food. It was a frontier society and these marauders became such a menace that every farmhouse was barricaded against them, every farmer was armed and had loopholes in his walls for defence. The very arms he was issued with were a lure for the bushranger.

In 1817 Macquarie contrived Mad Tom's recall. After a pause of two years a man of very different calibre, Lieutenant-Colonel William Sorell, arrived and governed until 1824. He continued the war against the bushrangers, whose ranks were continually increased by the harshness of this most remote prison whither all the worst offenders gravitated. Harsher and harsher measures only aggravated the trouble by brutalizing men and making them even more desperate.

In these early years Van Diemen's Land enjoyed greater prosperity than New South Wales. The mainland's need was her opportunity. By 1820, sixteen years after her foundation, Van Diemen's Land was exporting wheat and salt meat to New South Wales. She had a population of about 5500, 2588 convicts and 2880 free men, of whom all but 712 were ex-convicts. It is estimated that there were 30,000 cattle and 180,000 sheep in the island.[18]

In 1820 the wool industry was founded when Governor Sorell imported Merinos bought from Macarthur. Governor King had already sent eight Merinos to the island, but the great mass of the sheep—Teeswaters and Bengals and what-have-yous—were bred for mutton and the number of crosses was not important. Widowson described them in his *Present State of Van Diemen's Land*:

> Their form, as near as possible, is this: a very large head, Roman nose, slouch ears, extremely narrow in the chest, plain narrow shoulders, very high curved backs, and a coarse hairy fleece; these bad qualities, with four tremendous long legs, give a faithful representation of the native sheep. . . .[19]

Their wool, if used at all, was for stuffing mattresses. It was this type of fleece that was sold to New South Wales for 4d. a pound in 1820, 10,000 pounds of it, for manufacture of rough woollen clothing for convicts, the home-grown article being by then too good for the purpose. Sorell tidied up the wool industry, improved methods, and, besides the Macarthur rams, brought in English and Saxon Merinos. Of the 300 rams from New South Wales 119 died on the sea journey. The remainder lived to sire profitable flocks. He distributed them to "deserving" flockmasters. By 1830 about a million pounds of wool was exported to London. Wool was now the staple, and this was fortunate because the whaling and sealing industries were dying and the market for grain and meat on the mainland had shrunk as New South Wales became self-supporting. Other markets there were none.

Van Diemen's Land was even better suited to the wool industry than New South Wales, pastures were better, disease less frequent, and methods better. Pastures were improved and runs fenced in Van Diemen's Land long before they were on the mainland.

The Van Diemen's Land Company was formed in 1825 along the lines of the Australian Agricultural Company. But already before this English capital had arrived and Sorell encouraged free immigrants. Other industries were also springing up. Potatoes were exported to New South Wales in 1817, hops for beer in about 1820, and the apple industry began in 1827. The island was a fertile garden, only markets were lacking. When New South Wales could look after herself and the Commissariat Stores were full there was no other outlet for surplus. Agriculture declined and wool with its oversea market throve. Van Diemen's Land was only small, 26,215 square miles and some of that area useless for grazing, so the pastoral industry could not expand indefinitely. In 1832 it had reached saturation point.

Sorell also endeavoured to regularize the convict system and to segregate the worst criminals at Macquarie Harbour. This settlement on the west coast was in actuality almost as distant from Hobart as Norfolk Island from Sydney, and there, out of sight and out of mind, terrible brutalities were perpetrated, and men who escaped and had the stamina to cross the island provided a far more savage type of bushranger than was ever known on the mainland.

Sorell's successor, Governor Arthur (1824-36), saw the formal separation of Van Diemen's Land from New South Wales in December 1825. For years the lieutenant-governors had been independent owing to the difficulties of communication. Now Van Diemen's Land had the convenience of her own courts, on the early New South Wales pattern, and her governors were left in absolute and unrestrained power. Melville in his *History of the Island of Van Diemen's Land, 1824-1835* wrote of Arthur: "The despotism of the chief authority is superior to the power of any prince in Christendom. Scarcely is there a single settler in the Island, who is not dependent upon His Excellency's will and pleasure, either for his grant, or for his decision in some dispute about boundary lines."[20]

The governors were more absolute in their power than any governors of New South Wales had the opportunity to be. The population was more heavily loaded with convicts and so there was less public opinion and more claim to exercise untrammelled authority. Between 1817 and 1850 60,000 convicts arrived and only 20,000 free emigrants. The place was more remote, smaller, less noticed by the Colonial Office. The Legislative Council set up in 1825 was nominee. There was a Supreme Court from 1824, but there does not seem to have been the bitter struggle for power between the Governor and the judiciary that there was in New South Wales.

Van Diemen's Land followed the same pattern as New South Wales, but the accent fell differently. The land-grant system was the same, so were the land-sale regulations. English law ran. Progress towards self-government was parallel and the same economic depressions afflicted both colonies.

Government was similar but slower to develop, because transportation continued longer to Van Diemen's Land. By 1850, however, she was on the same rung of the ladder as the other colonies. The convict system had been in theory identically ordered by the Colonial Office, but local conditions were different. This was more nearly a plantation society. The big landowners held their place, there was less opportunity for the ex-convict. The moral level of the prisoners was lower and the measures taken against them more severe.

It was never said of Van Diemen's Land, as far as I know, that the advantages of being transported there outweighed the punishment. Shocking as Macquarie Harbour was, its successor, Port Arthur, could not have been much better. Segregation was complete. It was guarded by dogs and sharks, both perpetually hungry, and soldiers perpetually alert. For their own redemption the convicts were set to building a church. Before it could be consecrated a murder was committed within its walls, and so it still stands today, half finished. The tourist is shown the leg-irons, the fetters, the black cells for solitary confinement. . . . It is still, deserted, a place of ill omen. It would be wrong, however, to remember Arthur's convict policy only by Port Arthur. He sincerely believed in transportation as a cure for crime and set himself to bring order out of the still confused system in Van Diemen's Land. He believed it was in the interests of the Government, the settlers, and the convicts themselves to disperse them as assigned servants. The Government was saved the expense of their keep, the landowners got cheap labour, and by hard work, preferably on the land, the convict could redeem himself. Arthur saw to it that both masters and assigned servants obeyed the law. The convicts were to be kept under strict discipline, but they were also to be fed and clothed according to government standards. In 1829 he replaced honorary magistrates with paid officials, who were likely to be more nearly impartial. Idleness, drunkenness, and insolence were punished by the convict's being sent to the chain gang. It was these gangs that carried out public works such as road-making. More serious crimes were punished by incarceration at Port Arthur. Boy delinquents were segregated at Point Puer after 1835, taught a trade, and later apprenticed to it. This was praised as a humane arrangement, "an oasis in the desert of penal government".

Governor Arthur put down the bushrangers. In 1821 Macquarie had signed twenty-six death sentences, but still there were more to be caught and hanged, Alexander Pierce the cannibal, Brady and his gang who burnt, robbed, and murdered, and others less spectacular. Only Brady showed any of the spirit that made Ned Kelly a folk hero. When he heard that there was a price on his head he offered twenty gallons of rum for Governor Arthur's body and expressed "concern that a person known as George Arthur is at large". Brady kept his precarious liberty for two years.

Arthur was unpopular, not on account of the Black War or the severities of Port Arthur, but for his high-handedness towards his free subjects. He sacked incompetent officials (as if incompetence mattered in a penal settlement!), ordered the lives of the free as well as the bond, took away the power of the magistracy from the settlers, and controlled the Press in a way that would have delighted Governor Darling. By 1850 the island carried a population of 70,000, of which roughly two-thirds were free or freed by servitude. Of its land, 4,250,000 acres had been granted or sold, about 170,000 of them being used for farming of one kind or another; 1,750,000 sheep and 80,000 cattle were being grazed. Transportation ended and so did cheap labour and government expenditure. No gold was found. The land seemed to be already fully exploited and the colony lost its place as second in importance among the Australian colonies to the settlement of Port Phillip which, like Adam's rib, had been taken out of its side.

Except in its beginnings the story of Van Diemen's Land is much the same story as that of the other Australian colonies. They all began differently, they were all pressed into the same mould.

3. *Port Phillip*

As flocks increased and pastures were taken up in Van Diemen's Land graziers looked across Bass Strait to the unoccupied southern shores of the mainland. Everyone had not agreed with Collins that the land round Port Phillip was impossible. Now that necessity drove, it looked like the promised land. In 1835 three parties had crossed over. The Henty family, father and seven sons, were discovered at Portland Bay by Major Mitchell in his overland journey of 1836. They were already a thriving little community. Prosperous farmers in England, they had migrated to Western Australia, found conditions there very different from what they had expected, and moved on to Van Diemen's Land. They petitioned the Government asking to exchange their 80,000 useless acres in Western Australia for a grant at Portland Bay. The answer was so long in coming that they did not wait, but squatted in 1834, combining grazing with whaling. In 1835 a party led by John Pascoe Fawkner and another under John Batman selected land at Port Phillip. Batman, with fourteen other free settlers, crossed the Strait in May 1835 in a little ship, *Rebecca*, of 23 tons. He bought 600,000 acres—100,000 of them near the present Geelong, the remainder on the site of Melbourne—from the aborigines for a yearly tribute of 100 blankets, 50 knives, 50 tomahawks, two tons of flour, and some less useful trade goods, in all to the value of about £200. All was done decently and in order, a document was drawn up by Gellibrand, the lawyer of the group. The settlers signed it and the aborigines set their marks on it. This has been described as sharp practice, but in reality it was much more honest than just seizing the land, which was the usual practice. Governor Arthur, who had been informed of the settlers' plans and methods, thought them good and saw an enlargement of his own power. Lord Glenelg at the Home Office and Governor Bourke in Sydney viewed the matter differently. Bourke disallowed the treaty. "I have considered it incumbent on me immediately to protest against any consequences derogatory to the Rights of the British Crown that might be imagined to flow from the alleged Treaty."[21] The land, of course, legally belonged, not to the aborigines, but to the

Crown, and it was nothing to do with Governor Arthur. Bourke issued a proclamation declaring the settlers trespassers and intruders. Meanwhile they organized themselves. They meant to stay, and Bourke knew that he could not turn them away. He felt it his duty to regularize the settlement, bringing it under the same laws as New South Wales. In June 1835 Batman and his associates formed the Port Phillip Association. The subscription was 500 good breeding rams to be delivered within six months and 500 more within twelve months. The members allotted the land between themselves after it had been surveyed by J. H. Wedge, one of their number. They made their own laws. No member was to sell his land for at least five years, each was to pay his own overseers, no convicts and no liquor were to be admitted.

All disputes, except as regards land, were to be submitted to James Simpson, who could name two impartial settlers to help him. This "court" had the power to impose fines. The aborigines were to be protected and 5s. a head to be paid for the destruction of dingoes.

Batman handed over the land to Swanston, Gellibrand, and Simpson as trustees for the Association. There seems no reason to believe, as Bourke did, that: "The undertaking must sooner or later prove a total failure unless supported by the interference and protection of Government."[22] The colonists were well organized, but they had their troubles, for when Batman was absent in Van Diemen's Land preparing to bring over more stock they in turn suffered trespass from Fawkner and his party.

Fawkner stated his case long after the event in the *Port Phillip Patriot*, 30th August 1845:

We, in conjunction with Messrs. Samuel and William Jackson (all now of Port Phillip) and Captain Lancey (deceased), planned to form a settlement upon these shores in April, 1835. There was some difficulty in finding a vessel to bring us over to examine the country. . . . In the month of May, 1835, we purchased the "Enterprise" schooner, for this purpose, but she did not arrive from Sydney until July following. Thus between our plan and its execution, Messrs. Batman and others formed a similar plan, and Mr. Batman did actually come over in June, and looked at the land—saw some natives at 20 or 30 miles distance—and at that great distance obtained their signatures to a Deed conveying half Port Phillip to Governor Arthur, in the name of his nephew and to Messrs. Solomons, Gellibrand, Swanston, and others—in all 15; two shares were reserved for the British Ministers, by way of bribe. Mr. Batman returned to Launceston on the 6th or 8th of June. Ourselves and Messrs. Lancey, Evans, Marr and S. Jackson in July started in the "Enterprise". A gale of wind drove the vessel back to the Tamar, and we gave written directions for the voyage and survey of these shores, and returned to Launceston. The journal of the voyage kept both by Captain Lancey and Captain Hunter, states that after carefully examining all Western Port and the Eastern coast of this Bay, they selected the present site of Melbourne as a resting place. On the 30th August, 1835, our horses and cattle, and men were landed, and a hut built; our fruit trees and garden plants planted—ground ploughed, seeds sown—and upon our own arrival in October, we found fine acres of promising wheat, grown most surprisingly for the time, and enjoyed cress, lettuce, and radishes, the first grown at Melbourne.[23]

The note of malice is unmistakable and no doubt it was reciprocated.

In June 1836 there were at Port Phillip 142 men, 35 women, 26,500 sheep, 100 cattle, and 57 horses. Its wealth was assessed at £80,000. Bourke sent a magistrate, G. Stewart, to survey the settlement and was impressed by his reports. He thought it would be "more desirable to impose reasonable conditions on Mr Batman and his associates than to insist on their abandoning their undertaking".[24]

He decided, with the permission of the Colonial Office, to set up two new centres under his administration, one at Port Phillip (a *fait accompli* in any case) and one at Twofold Bay, the latter to be a port for the "Minaro Plains", to "provide, though but imperfectly, centres of Civilization and Government, and thus gradually to extend the power of order and social union to the most distant parts of the wilderness".[25]

The Port Phillip Association was now ready to accept a Resident appointed in Sydney. Bourke's conciliatory attitude had borne fruit.

On 9th September 1836 Bourke issued a proclamation acknowledging the settlement and sending to it, not a Resident, but a police magistrate, Captain William Lonsdale, three surveyors, a customs officer and a guard consisting of a lieutenant and thirteen soldiers.[26] Taxation now entered this near-Eden, for Bourke found it "but reasonable that the Settlement should contribute to the Revenue of the Government, which upholds it, and that its Lands should be acquired under the general Regulations of this Colony".[27]

In March 1837 Bourke visited Port Phillip, renamed its "capital" (curiously called Bearbrass) after the Prime Minister, Lord Melbourne, and a settlement on the bay William's Town, in honour of King William IV.

In the following June a hundred allotments were put up for sale in Melbourne and a few in William's Town. The treaty with the aborigines was declared void, but those who had occupied and improved the land were given preferential terms for purchase. The Port Phillip Association continued to exist, and in January 1836 its representative in London was agitating for separation from New South Wales on the grounds that, since it was not a convict settlement, land could not be obtained as advantageously. The law at that time allowed easier terms in purchasing land to those who employed and maintained convicts. The representative, G. Mercer, also pointed out that there were no convicts to build roads, bridges, and other public works. The settlers had to provide them. It was, he said, in England's interest to have a "free and useful colony founded on principles of conciliation and civilization, of philanthropy, morality and temperance". New South Wales, the penal colony, and Port Phillip, the free settlement, had little in common. Let them be separated. Port Phillip was so prosperous it would not be a burden, all it asked was land grants with quit rents spent on immigration to provide free labour in place of convicts. This plea foundered on the Home Government's land policy. Glenelg stood firm. Port Phillip was part of New South Wales and the same land laws obtained. The Crown still had the power to oust the settlers as trespassers. The settlers were willing to purchase outright. It was at last decided that land in the Port Phillip district should be sold at auction on "moderate and easy terms" with preference to first settlers.[28]

The progress of Port Phillip was phenomenal. It was founded on sheep and private enterprise. It was fed by immigration of graziers from Van Diemen's Land and squatters overlanding their flocks to the good pastures discovered by Major Mitchell and others. Distance made it difficult to rule from Sydney. In 1839 the police magistrate was superseded by a Superintendent who was virtually a Lieutenant-Governor. The first Superintendent was C. J. La Trobe. He was an able man and under him the district prospered. Batman died in 1839, but Fawkner lived to see separation. By 1845 all grazing land to the Murray River was occupied, and in 1850, the year of the long desired separation from New South Wales, there were some 77,000 settlers in the area and over 5,000,000 sheep.

The Port Phillip district in the fifteen years of its dependent life shared the legislative and judicial progress of New South Wales. In 1842, when an elected Legislature was granted to New South Wales, the Port Phillip district was allotted six members. Distance made this nugatory. Members were not paid, and even if they had been it would have been difficult to persuade the right sort of men—that is, men acceptable to the "Shepherd Kings"—to leave their estates, affairs, and families to represent their district in Sydney. Nor would their sacrifice have been effective, for they would always have been in a hopeless minority. The alternative was to elect men resident in Sydney and it was not a palatable one. The electors drew attention to their situation and feeling by electing Earl Grey, the Secretary of State for the Colonies, and the Duke of Wellington.

When in 1850 New South Wales achieved self-government the Port Phillip district was separated and also became autonomous under the name of Victoria. Fifteen years does not seem very long to have to wait for such an achievement, but it generated much discontent and ill-feeling.

4. *Queensland*

The Queensland coast was first charted by Captain Cook, who sighted Stradbroke Island on 17th May 1770, and it was at a point a little south of the modern Rockhampton that he first landed. On the extreme tip of Cape York Peninsula Cook landed and took formal possession of the whole east coast in the name of the Crown. Actually this ceremony took place on an island in Endeavour Strait, Possession Island. In 1799 Flinders followed the great master up the east coast and entered Moreton Bay. In 1802 he was there again and stayed a fortnight. He failed to find the river flowing into the bay, but deduced it from the colour of the water. He named it Pumistone River. Phillip Parker King, son of Governor King, also visited Moreton Bay when circumnavigating Australia in 1817.

There were long pauses between visits. Until the 1820s there was little incentive to expand northward. Allan Cunningham's land explorations between 1823 and 1827 led to the discovery of the Darling Downs and a way through Cunningham's Gap to the sea at Moreton Bay. New and excellent grazing country was opened for sheep. In 1823 it was not only sheep that needed more room; the Governor, Sir Thomas Brisbane, was looking for a remote place to send twice convicted and incorrigible convicts. The Hunter Valley had been used for this purpose, but the soil was too good for convicts and it was too easy for them to escape to "civilization". The establishment was closed and the Hunter thrown open for free settlement. Port Stephens and Port Macquarie had also proved insufficiently remote. Surveyor Oxley was sent north in *Mermaid* to look for a more suitable place. First he went to Port Curtis, was unimpressed, and returned to Moreton Bay. Here he found two white men, Finnigan and Pamphlet, who had been timber-getters in the Illawarra. They had put to sea in a tiny boat without a compass, meaning to return to Sydney; a storm blew them out to sea, and when at last they struggled back to the coast they had completely lost their bearings. They still thought that they were south of Sydney and so, enduring great hardships, they went north, ending up at Moreton Bay. But for the help of the aborigines they would have died. They were taken into the tribe and in their wanderings discovered a river. They told this tale to Oxley, who after verification named the Brisbane River in honour of the Governor. He brought back good reports and it was determined to found a penal settlement there. Bigge had suggested some such settlements on the Queensland coast in the interests of segregation and to purify the air of Sydney.

Brisbane himself visited Moreton Bay and approved. He held the theory that dangerous pioneering should be done by convicts, whose lives were less valuable than those of free men. He had probably been reading Lord Auckland.

A small party was sent in the brig *Amity* to prepare the site in September 1824. It consisted of thirty prisoners to do the hard work, a guard, Oxley as guide, and Lieutenant Miller as commandant. After a false start the site of modern Brisbane was chosen for the settlement.

Miller's instructions were definite. "The principal object in view in forming the establishment is to provide a place of security for the runaways from Port Macquarie." He was to choose an "airy situation close to fresh water",[29] erected a palisade, huts, a guard-house and jail. It was hoped, as usual, that the settlement would soon be self-supporting. Pigs for breeding and maize for planting were provided. There was to be no communication with the outside world, except when a government ship came every second month, no liquor, plenty of hard work, and a meagre ration of four pounds of salt meat and 10½ pounds of flour a week. There was also to be no corporal punishment, only docked rations and solitary confinement for offenders.

Remoteness worked both ways; it segregated the worst characters amongst the convicts, but it also made abuse of their power easy for commandant and guards. It is generally believed that Moreton Bay became a hell on earth following the pattern of Macquarie Harbour and Norfolk Island in its worst days. The second commandant, Captain Logan, was murdered whilst on a botanizing excursion. Aborigines were blamed, but many thought that it was done by convicts in revenge for his harsh treatment.

Deadly monotony, small pay, and the lack of normal social life were enough to deprave the keepers as well as the prisoners. In 1830 there were approximately 1000 convicts and 100 soldiers at Moreton Bay. A school with 33 pupils, a surgeon, and a chaplain were the only concessions to humanity.

Already in 1832 there was talk of abandoning the penal settlement, and in 1837 Governor Bourke reduced its numbers to 300. It was now a depot for women who had been re-convicted in New South Wales. Governor Gipps wrote to Lord Glenelg on 1st July 1839: ". . . I am happy to be able to report to your Lordship the further measures which I have adopted for reducing the Establishment at that place [Moreton Bay], and for throwing the District open to Settlers."[30] In this dispatch and another written on the same day he recounts his meticulous arrangements for winding up the prison and safeguarding government property. The herd of 900 cattle and the flock of 4500 sheep and "all moveables or implements of husbandry" were to be sold, and the buildings, such as they were, kept for military use. The women convicts, who had been employed in agriculture, were to go to the Female Factory at Parramatta. Three surveyors were to be sent to Moreton Bay, the land surveyed and sold in the usual way, and Brisbane, at first called Edenglassie, was planned and allotments sold in Sydney.

The penal settlement had existed for fifteen years and, as regards food production, it had thriven very well.

As the convicts moved out the squatters moved in, and history repeated itself. Governor Gipps wrote in April 1844:

Beyond the Boundaries, the Country never having been surveyed, there is no division, either real or pretended, into allotments or sections of square miles; the quantity of Land, therefore, occupied by any Squatter under the denomination of a "Station", or a "Run", is altogether indefinite; and the price of a Licence is equally £10 for every body, whatever may be the extent of his Run, or the number of his Sheep or Cattle depastured on it.[31]

Life was wide and free, but already, as in the Port Phillip district, resentment was building up against Sydney. The north was being neglected and the squatters were not getting their fair share of the labour available. A movement towards separation was already beginning.

William Coote has left a picture of Brisbane as it was at the end of the convict era:

At the time when the convict rule was supposed to be nigh its end, Brisbane existed almost only in name. There were no streets, and nothing that could by any stretch of the imagination, be tortured into a town. Fronting the river, adjoining what is now called William Street, stood the modest wooden residence of the Commandant. In its rear was a long row of old rubble buildings for the minor officials and servants immediately attached to him. . . . At some distance further up the river were the commissariat quarters, now the office of the Colonial Secretary, and next to them the military barracks, at present occupied by the Colonial Treasurer and a host of the Civil Service. The hospital, transformed into a police barracks, has recently been removed for our new Law Courts. The old prisoners' barracks, which successively accommodated our legislature, our law courts, and I know not what besides, were as, until recently, we saw them —odd-looking and ugly. The wind-mill usefully occupied the building now called the Observatory, and on another and slighter eminence, stood the female factory, until of late the Police Court and Lock-up, now removed to make way for the Telegraph Office. Farther on the road to Breakfast Creek—for Fortitude Valley then had no name—was the house of the clerk of the works. Beyond these and a few temporary huts, there was nothing to indicate a town. . . .[32]

The wealth was in the bush. Stations were already thriving on the Darling Downs and a muted Black War had broken out with the aborigines. There was a pitched battle at Helidon and many murders were committed by both sides.

Victoria became the golden colony, New South Wales remained the wool colony; but its northern area proved more suitable for cattle. New South Wales, whilst it included the present Queensland, was far too cumbersome. Transport and communication were bad, interests diverged, and ill-feeling ran high. New South Wales was loath to lose rich lands, the northern citizens were determined to live their lives as they wished and not according to the views of politicians in Sydney. The Home Government was bombarded by both parties. By Letters Patent dated 6th June 1859 the northern part of New South Wales became a separate colony and chose the name Queensland. It is very large, some 670,500 square miles, and includes so many diverse climates and interests that there is always a sporadic attempt by the northern portions to break away.

II. The Doctrinaire Settlements

Norfolk Island and Van Diemen's Land had been settled as outposts of defence and tokens of occupation. Victoria and Queensland were the results of natural expansion, pasture for the sheep and segregation for the convicts. Now we come to a group of settlements artificial, if not strictly doctrinaire in origin.

1. *The North*

The old dream of the Indies and their wealth died hard, fear of the French was more concrete. Both wove together to produce a series of settlements in the north of Australia. It was really one idea: there was an Eldarado, or, if not a treasure-land itself, a good jumping-off place for the exploration of the Spice Islands, in northern Australia. The French must not be allowed to snap it up.

In 1810 France had overrun Holland and Dutch interests in the East had thus become virtually French interests. The East India Company for this reason, and in that same year of 1810, planned the conquest of Java. Lord Minto's expedition was successful and Stamford Raffles was Governor of the island for five years, until it was returned to Holland after the fall of Napoleon. This was a bitter blow to Raffles. He knew the commercial value of Java, and once it was lost to the Crown he looked about him for a substitute. He believed that northern Australia would be suitable. He urged the British Government to annex it. Eventually he found a better spot in Singapore, where he established a British settlement in despite of both the East India Company and the British Government, but with the support of English mercantile interests.

A seed had been sown, however, and in 1817 Lieutenant Phillip Parker King, R.N. was instructed to survey the northern coast of Australia very carefully. It is significant that he named a bay which he discovered in April 1818 Raffles Bay. W. S. Campbell in his "Earliest Settlements in the Northern Territory of Australia"[33] narrates how Raffles had privately briefed King and had given him a letter in Malay as one of his credentials in that region. King was well impressed by the northern coastline. His was the point of view of a naval officer, not a settler. He thought that Raffles Bay, Port Essington (named after Admiral Sir William Essington), and Melville and Bathurst islands would all be suitable trading posts.

Acting on King's report, the Home Government ordered Captain

Gordon Bremer to found a settlement at Port Essington in 1824. His base was Sydney, half a continent away. He was given forty-eight, or some authorities say forty-four, convicts to do the hard work and sailed north in *Tamar*. He arrived at his destination in August 1824, but as he could find no fresh water he transferred the settlement to Melville Island. It was Bremer who took formal possession of the north between 130° and 135°.

In 1823 the Colonial Office had received another memorial proposing a settlement in the north. It was from William Barnes (or Barns). He suggested a settlement in the Gulf of Carpentaria with himself as commandant, and painted a glowing account of the riches to be won by fishing for trepang and whales and the trade that could be opened with the Malays. Shrewdly, he played on jealousy of the Dutch, who were gathering all the profits of the Indies back into their own hands. The Colonial Office listened sceptically and slowly made up its mind to act, but not through William Barnes. He was a trader. This was a job for the Navy.

Much the same pattern emerges in the north as in the south-east. The Colonial Office chewed over various schemes and then made its own arrangements.

To return to Bremer, there was fresh water on Melville Island, but the little expedition suffered many hardships. The land was difficult, no trade developed, no supplies arrived, the aborigines were hostile, scurvy and other diseases broke out. *Lady Nelson,* Bremer's store ship, sent to Timor for supplies, was never heard of again. Another ship, *Stedcombe*, captained by William Barnes, was chartered, but she, too, disappeared into the blue, captured by pirates. Barnes, however, was not in her. He had remained on Melville Island and became a troubling influence. He gaily instituted the rum trade.

The garrison was relieved in 1826, further convicts, stores, and livestock being brought from Sydney. The new commandant, Major Campbell, was not disturbed by the gloomy reports he received.

> I was, however, not of a temperament to be cast down by these accounts, but on the contrary, rejoiced that I had been placed in so novel and interesting a situation and looked forward with a pleasing anticipation that patience, exertion and industry would soon bring the settlement to answer the intentions of government in having formed it.[34]

In a year's time Campbell was disillusioned.

In 1827 a new settlement was planned for Croker's Island in Raffles Bay, to be commanded by Captain Stirling, R.N. The objects were the same as before. He found the island impossible and moved to the shores of Raffles Bay. The Colonial Office decided to abandon Melville Island and this was finally accomplished in March 1829. The Raffles Bay Settlement, under Captain Collet Barker, flourished for a time and intercourse was opened up with the Malays. It came as a shock to the little colony when word arrived that it, too, was to be abandoned. This was done in August 1829.

Eight years later another expedition to settle Port Essington sailed from England and left Sydney in September 1838. It was thought that the French had designs on it. Again Bremer was in command. A few months after their arrival at Port Essington aborigines brought in a tale of ships in Raffles Bay. It was the French under Dumont d'Urville and a French flag was flying over the remains of the deserted settlement there. Bremer treated d'Urville with every courtesy. It was, the Frenchman claimed, just another voyage of curiosity, and after three days they sailed away and whether they were disappointed or not we do not know. Bremer had called his new settlement Victoria after the Queen.

This was a better found settlement than the earlier ones. There were two Queen's ships, *Alligator* and *Britomart*, and a transport *Orontes*. Adequate water was now found at Port Essington, indeed the little community was nearly overwhelmed by the wet season. Bremer was as enthusiastic about the port as Phillip had been over Sydney Harbour. An "admirable little town" grew up and there seems to have been no lack of food, vegetable or animal. The colony was equipped with greyhounds to hunt kangaroos, and with buffaloes as beasts of burthen. These last, and some ponies, were brought from Timor. With a few which had been taken to Melville Island they became the ancestors of the present herds in the north.

In 1839 Port Essington received a visit from H.M.S. *Beagle* on a surveying voyage. The name of this ship is connected with Charles Darwin, who travelled in her as official scientist from 1831 to 1839. The next visitor of distinction was Dr Ludwig Leichhardt, who performed a remarkable journey, crossing the continent from Queensland to Port Essington through untouched and difficult country in 1845. He travelled more than three thousand miles in fifteen months and discovered some of the northern rivers, such as the Roper.

Bremer had sailed away to India long ago. Hopes of trade and wealth had slowly died, and in 1849 it was decided to close this settlement too.

Fifteen miles to the westward *Beagle* had discovered and named Port Darwin (after the captain's former shipmate) and the Victoria River.

It was not until 1863 that any further attempt was made to settle the north. In that year the territory had been put under the control of South Australia. A Resident was sent to Port Darwin and a small settlement made there, named Palmerston after the Prime Minister. Dreams of trade with the East Indies or Malaya had faded. In any case the Navy was not trade-minded. Nevertheless, there were still men who felt that the hidden treasure of the future was to be found in the north. The heroic project of the Overland Telegraph, some 1800 miles of it, went through in 1872 following the south-north route of the explorer McDouall Stuart, first to cross the continent. The small colony of South Australia, with a population of some 130,000, bore the expense. Gold and other metals were found, but it was baffling country. It promised, but it did not reward. South Australia had the enterprise but not the wealth to develop it. In 1911 the Territory was handed over to the Commonwealth and Palmerston became the modern Darwin.

It is curious that this old, old land is, in its way, with its uranium deposits at Rum Jungle, its air link with the world, and who as yet knows what other possibilities, the most modern part of Australia. The past failed in it; the future, with its different needs and technique, may succeed.

2. *Western Australia*

Western Australia, the first of the really "doctrinaire" settlements in Australia, sprang from the outpost at Raffles Bay. On Captain Stirling, R.N., of *Success* was laid the duty of establishing a colony there, and he became the apostle of the Swan River. When Raffles Bay was abandoned it was to the Swan that many of the settlers went.

In 1827 Captain Stirling had put into the Swan River, which had been discovered by the Dutch in 1697. Coming in from the sea and going on to the more barren north, he was delighted by its beauty and fertility; so was his companion, Fraser, the botanist. It reminded Stirling, one wonders why, of the Lombard Plain. Perhaps it was his private symbol for all good things, just as Columbus likened any fair country he saw to "spring in Andalusia". The old tale of trade with the East was thrown in for good weight. Stirling's excessive praise fell on fertile ground in England, where capital was looking for opportunities. A speculator, Thomas Peel, a relation of Sir Robert Peel's, with a number of associates was eager to form a syndicate to plant a colony there. They approached the British Government with a plan. It was another of these paper schemes, for it does not seem to have occurred to them to send experts to evaluate the land and its possibilities. They asked for four million acres at 1s. 6d. an acre; the syndicate would supply the capital for development and the settlers, ten thousand of them. They expected a monopoly. They were the commercial heirs of the East India Company and the Australian Agricultural Company and the rest. The thing that no one took into consideration was the nature of the land itself.

The British Government was cautious. It accepted the scheme, cut it down, but did not recognize its impracticability. Another thing it did not take into consideration was that Western Australia had never been declared a British possession. Both Cook and Phillip had only claimed half the continent for the Crown. It was Governor Darling who called the attention of the Colonial Office to this discrepancy. In strict legality the land on the Swan River was not in the Government's gift. This oversight was corrected. In 1828 Captain Fremantle in the King's ship *Challenger*, was

. . . directed to proceed immediately . . . to the Swan River on the Western Coast of New South Wales, where you will on your arrival take formal possession of that part of the coast in the name of His Majesty, which possession is meant to be extended to the whole of the Western Coast.

You will remain with the *Challenger* in Cockburn Sound or some other safe Anchorage in that neighbourhood until you are in Receipt of further Orders, and in the mean time employ working Parties on shore in constructing Huts or other commodious Dwellings for reception of Troops, which may be weekly expected after your arrival there; You will endeavour to find Springs of Water as near to the River as may be, and instruct those under your Orders on shore to be constantly on the alert to prevent surprize from the natives, and especially to be very guarded with respect to the Women.[35]

Peel and his partners, notably Solomon Levey, were offered a million acres, to be issued in two parcels. Their monopoly was disallowed (but this was a principle rather than a fact) and, apart from sending a few soldiers, the British Government disclaimed all responsibility and liability for the colony. "Regulations for the guidance of those who may propose to embark, as Settlers, for the new Settlement on the Western Coast of New Holland" (England had not even made up her mind as to the name of the place!), published in January 1829, began uncompromisingly:

His Majesty's Government do not intend to incur any expense, in conveying Settlers to the new Colony on the Swan River, and will not feel bound to defray the *expense* (cost) of supplying them with Provisions, or other Necessaries, after their arrival there, nor to assist their removal to England, or *elsewhere*, should they be desirous of quitting the Colony.[36]

The lion, however, showed some sketchy desire to keep his paw on the land. The same instructions lay down penalties for not improving it and offer grants as reward for importing labour or bringing in children.

Captain Stirling was appointed Governor in May 1829. His position was obviously difficult, for he was responsible to the Home Government in a settlement in which it professed no interest. A dispatch dated 20th January 1830 at "Perth, Western Australia", shows him battling on optimistically.

As soon as the difficulty attendant on landing and housing the establishment was surmounted, I caused an exploration of the country immediately in the neighbourhood of the port to be made, and two towns to be laid out; one, named Freemantle, at the entrance of Swan River; the other, Perth, about nine miles higher up, on its right or Northern bank. Allotments in these towns were speedily occupied by the first settlers, who arrived in August, and the more diligent among them commenced the erection of temporary buildings. On the

1st of October, I found it necessary to open a district of country for location. In the first instance, I selected for that purpose the banks of the Swan River; and, being urged by further applications for land, on the 2d of November I threw open the country extending between the sea and the mountains fifty miles southward from Perth, including the district originally reserved for Mr Thomas Peel. In these districts, the first comers found suitable locations, and, acting under the impulse of novelty, there were many who at once established themselves on their lands, regardless of danger from the natives and of the difficulty they encountered in removing their goods from the coast. This adventurous and laudable spirit, which it was politic to encourage, I am happy in saying met with no check; and single individuals have traversed the country freely, at great distances from the towns, hitherto without interruption or injury.[37]

This all sounds very smooth, but there were other factors not mentioned.

Peel's partners had withdrawn, but Peel accepted the Government's terms and sank a fortune of £50,000 in the venture. He hoped to bring out four hundred settlers by November 1829, but settlers were difficult to get, particularly those suited to the hard labour of pioneering virgin country. The British Government had an assisted immigration scheme to New South Wales, but its benefits were not extended to Western Australia. Those who came—and twenty-five ships had reached Fremantle by January 1830—had to finance their own passages and find ships to carry them, for naturally there was no regular, or irregular, service. The colonists were drawn from a class of people with some capital but often no experience of farming, let alone pioneering. They were attracted by the idea of receiving forty acres of land for every £3 in capital that they brought into the country. This capital need not even be in cash, it could be in kind—anything from implements of agriculture to children, servants, and objets d'art.

To most, Australia meant the pastoral eastern colonies with their growing prosperity. They had no conception of the distance separating west from east or of the kind of country that lay between. Peel brought his workers with him, many of the others did not. They arrived in an alien land where no preparations had been made to receive them. The land was there, but nothing else. Those with most capital received their grants first. Half a million acres were allotted to seventy settlers within eighteen months. The others must take land farther and farther from the coast, with no roads to take them to it, no survey to identify it. Salaries were paid in land. Month by month estates grew larger but remained inaccessible. Even Stirling's salary was paid in land, 100,000 acres of it, and he was hoist with his own petard.

In 1831 twenty instead of forty acres were granted for every £3 in capital, but the whole scheme remained unmanageable. The value of capital, whether in money or goods, depreciated because it could not be used. Grand pianos and other such objects that were valuable in England rotted on the beaches.

By 1832 a million acres had been granted, but the owners were disillusioned. The land was not fertile by English standards. To clear it of its hardwood timber was a Herculean task. There was no convict labour. The aborigines, far from providing a labour pool, were indifferent or hostile. Even experienced farmers, like the Henty family, could not make a living and migrated to Van Diemen's Land before they were ruined. The most anyone could hope for was a hut of his own building and, if fortunate, a subsistence farm.

Population in 1830 was 4000, in 1832 it had fallen to 1500.

Peel himself encountered many difficulties, some of them due to his incompetence. To begin with, he was so slow in getting his expedition under way that he risked losing his promised land grant from the Government. His ship *Gilmore* arrived at Cockburn Sound on 15th December 1829. Inertia again overtook him.

After disembarking from the *Gilmore*, the settlers and workmen settled down to a miserable life on the beach at Clarence, waiting for direction from Peel. The settlers looked to him for their farms, whilst the labourers and artizans expected employment. They looked in vain, for Peel did practically nothing either to alleviate their miserable conditions or to carry out his promises to them. He seemed utterly incapable of the ability to organize the settlement of his settlers or to provide productive employment for his workmen.

The result was that they remained at Clarence living in the crude shelters on the beach, and depending on the supplies which had been brought out with them. At the end of each month when their wages fell due, Peel made them take either his own paper money or else stores consisting chiefly of salted meat.[38]

Sickness broke out, occasioned by poor diet; Peel ran out of credit as well as of ready cash. The management of the settlement devolved more and more on Stirling. It was 1832 before Peel even applied to Stirling for his land; 250,000 acres were granted to him. He was embroiled with the aborigines, his wife and daughters returned to England, one tribulation followed another. By 1841 he felt constrained to retire from the magistracy and to resign his seat on the Council. Archdeacon Wollaston gives a picture of Peel's property at Mandurah, where he stayed in 1842:

He lives in a miserable hut built of stone, and covered with rushes. Everything about him shows the broken-down gentleman—clay floors and handsome plate, curtains for doors; windows without glass; and costly china; hardly any utensil put to its proper use; odd cups and saucers; coffee in a mug; a handsome china bowl for washing; the only looking glass the size of a hand; a whole pig hanging under the verandah. He has beautiful summer and winter gardens and an extensive grapery, but in utter neglect. I got a good bed on a sofa in the dining hut, and in the respect was quite as well off as my host for he sleeps on one himself, having no bedroom exclusively as such.[39]

This picture illuminates the general state of the unpractical experiment. It is said that it had cost £50,000 to land three hundred settlers, and when they were landed it needed more and more capital to bring the land slowly into bearing. Levey supplied much of this and lost it.

A handful of settlers lived on and took root. In 1848 the population index was rising towards 5000, but there was no impetus in the colony to make it a success. Whaling and jarrah and karri timbers were its main support. In 1849 the dream was over. Western Australia became a Crown Colony of standard pattern and petitioned the boon of convicts. This suited the Imperial Government very well. Transportation to New South Wales had ceased in 1840 and a new market for convicts was becoming increasingly desirable. At least Western Australia now had labour and a transfusion of government money spent on the convict establishment. Lessons had been learnt in New South Wales and the convict system as applied to Western Australia was better regulated, less brutal and more beneficial. Free settlers in equal numbers to the convicts were brought in by assisted immigration. From then onward progress if slow was steady. Western Australia did not share in the increasing self-government of the eastern colonies because she was a penal settlement. In 1868 transportation was abolished. Ahead lay gold and prosperity.

3. *South Australia*

The most spectacular of the doctrinaire colonies was South Australia, founded in 1834 by Act of Parliament. It was backed by specious theory, but not as specious as that behind Western Australia. The story of Western Australia was of a get-rich-quick experiment that failed. It was based on faith, but faith of the wrong kind. It was a typical example of shrewdness without intelligence. The Age of Reason did not include a scientific approach, and in any case in the 1820s the Age of Reason was almost over and was being succeeded by a blend of the commercial and the romantic born of the prosperity that now had conquered the depression following the Napoleonic wars.

South Australia was founded on a theory which had no connection with the character of the earth. Flinders in *Investigator* had sailed into Spencer's Gulf in 1802 looking for a passage through the continent to the Arafura Sea. Captain Collet Barker of Raffles Bay fame had explored St Vincent's Gulf from the sea and had climbed Mount Lofty, to lose his life when exploring Lake Alexandrina. South Australia was on the map and that was all.

In 1829 Edward Gibbon Wakefield, of Quaker origin, was lying in Newgate prison for the crime of abducting a schoolgirl who was also an heiress. It was the second time that this had happened. The first time no action had been taken. The marriage was happy but short. A second offence was viewed differently. He was tried and sent to prison. His incarceration, one imagines, was a nuisance, but not insupportable, for he had money and influential friends. It gave him time to think. The results of his cogitations were eleven "Letters from Sydney" published in the *Morning Chronicle* in 1829. He had never visited Sydney or any other part of Australia, but he had ideas on colonization and a persuasive pen. Possibly, to begin with, he did not take himself too seriously, his address was not edifying and he added a touch of drama and verisimilitude to his opinions by putting them allegedly into the mouth of a settler in New South Wales.

Land and labour were burning questions at that time and Wakefield thought he had found a solution for both. Land was the key to the situation, but not if it were granted *ad lib.*, as in Western Australia. That robbed it of its value. It should be sold for a "sufficient price", say from 12s. to £1 an acre. This would mean that only men of capital could buy it, men who would have a stake in the country. The money from land sales should then be used to bring out agricultural labourers. The price of land would make it impossible for them to become landowners themselves, except after years of diligent saving, during which time the large landowners would have their services. As more land was sold more useful migrants would be brought out. The market for products would be increased whilst the supply of labour was kept up. The high price of land would prevent its too rapid disposal, so that the Western Australian *débâcle* could not be repeated. No land was to be granted. It should all be sold or auctioned. This was logical and should have worked like clockwork. Wakefield's articles attracted attention, he soon had influential backers for his foolproof scheme. It appealed to capitalists looking for an investment and it appealed to the Government. To sell land and use the proceeds for immigration was better business than to give it away, with a highly problematical quit rent attached, and then to assist immigrants with the equally problematical expectation that they would ever repay their passage money. Wakefield's theories were to colour land policy in New South Wales for years to come. In the meantime there was a move to try the plan, not in New South Wales, where there would be many complications, such as vested interests, convict population, a body of government orders and the habits and customs of the inhabitants, but on untouched country where it could be put into effect in all its logical purity.

The first scheme was to undertake colonization by an autonomous chartered company. The Colonial Office knew only too well the dangers of this and vetoed it. The South Australian Association, founded in 1833, was therefore wound up in 1834 for lack of government support. The South Australian Act of 1834 set up a Crown colony on the usual pattern, except that land sales, at a "sufficient price", were to be vested in a Board of Commissioners. These were originally to be ten in number of whom only one was required to live in South Australia. As none of them wished to do so an eleventh Commissioner, Fraser, was appointed to fulfil the requirement.

The Government expected to profit by this arrangement. The sale of land, besides all the other advantages claimed, would relieve the British taxpayer of the expense of founding and maintaining a colony.

Among the Commissioners was G. F. Angas, who saw possibilities of profit within the new framework. He was instrumental in founding the South Australian Company with a capital of £320,000. He became its chairman on resigning from the Board of Commissioners. The Company's object was to buy land at 12s. an acre for reselling and for development. The scheme attracted a very different type of settler from Peel's in Western Australia. It did not offer exorbitant gains for nothing. It was taken for granted that the land would be bought and developed in the normal way with hard work and the expenditure of capital. It drew to it men who wanted a respectable investment and also a number of idealists who hoped for a fresh start in a land uncontaminated by the evils of the old world. There were many nonconformists amongst them, solid citizens with some of the spirit of the Pilgrim Fathers. This settlement was, of course, to be unpolluted by convicts. By comparison with these sensible plans the unlucky experiment in Western Australia appeared frivolous.

The soil was far kinder, too. South Australia began as a farming community and has kept many rural interests. The land around Adelaide is fertile and suited to small holdings. The settlers could hardly, in the whole of Australia, have chosen a better site. Colonel Light, a colourful figure, was sent with an advance party in May 1836 to explore and survey the land, divide it into farms and lay out a town. The Adelaide of today still carries the print of the colonel's set square.

So far, so good. The plan appeared to be workable, but the compromise between Government, Commissioners, and Company very nearly ruined it. Control was not only divided but, with most of the Commissioners and shareholders in England, remote. The Colonial Office appointed a Governor, Sir John Hindmarsh, who shared his powers with the Commissioners. Law and order were the province of the Governor. The Commissioners controlled the sale of land and the use of moneys from it for immigration. Loans were to be raised in expectation of revenue. These loans remained unsecured.

In December 1836 Hindmarsh arrived with the first settlers, numbering 546. Of course, in so short a time Light and his too small team had not been able to survey sufficient land to accommodate them. The territory was larger than anyone had envisaged. He had only made a beginning. He was blamed for not having made more preparation. He had chosen a site for the capital, named Adelaide in honour of William IV's Queen, and the Governor did not approve of the situation. Soon Hindmarsh and Fisher were quarrelling over their respective powers. The settlers were disappointed, for life in the colony was much harder than they expected. It was also so very different from anything that they were used to. They huddled together in Adelaide, consuming their capital because their land was not yet surveyed and because that was the line of least resistance. The price of land was reduced to 12s. an acre, but that made little difference. Cultivation was disappointingly slow and supplies had to be brought in from Sydney and Van Diemen's Land. In 1837 there were only four acres under crop, though 3700 acres had been sold. In 1839 443 acres out of 170,500 sold were cultivated and there were 100,000 sheep. Imports rose in 1839 to £346,600, whilst exports totalled only £22,500. The settlers had expected self-government from the beginning, but they were told by the Colonial Office that it would only be granted when they numbered fifty thousand. They could not see the logic of this. They were all free-born British citizens and they did not see why they should not enjoy in Australia the rights they had exercised in England. Moreover, self-government was part of the Wakefield plan. Was not Lord Durham his friend and supporter?

Many nonconformists hoped for greater religious liberty, but the established Church of England came with them. Hindmarsh was a military disciplinarian and had no sympathy with his subjects' aspirations. His quarrels with Commissioner Fisher racked the colony with discord.

The Colonial Office always found these colonial disagreements tedious and hard to understand. Its scepticism had been justified. The colony was in confusion and soon it would become an expense. To close the breach Hindmarsh's successor, Gawler, was both Governor and Commissioner. He had two masters and although he did much for the colony he pleased neither of them. He found, as early governors anywhere in Australia always did, muddle and retrogression, and he saw that he must reorganize the whole colony. He found it apathetic; he left it hopeful. His remedy was to start capital circulating and to get the population out of Adelaide, where speculation in land was the only industry, and onto the land itself. He sent surveyors out into the country districts, and by the time he was recalled in disgrace in 1841, five thousand farmers were settled and 200,000 sheep were being grazed. The unemployed had been set to work building roads and on other public works. It all cost money. Between 1839 and 1841 he spent £357,615. Colonial revenue was only £75,773. For the balance he called on the Commissioners.

He wrote to G. F. Angas in rebuttal of charges of extravagance.

The firm and solid establishment of the Colony has been the great object of my hopes, my anxieties, and my system. Extravagance did not characterise either my public or private career. Solid, liberal expenditure may have distinguished it. It was what I intended. No other system would have met the circumstances of the Colony and have brought it to what it is.[40]

Gawler had established the colony on a good basis, but he was unfortunate. The depression of the 1840s struck it early and hard. Land sales fell off, the Commissioners had no money, the bills he had drawn were dishonoured, and South Australia found itself bankrupt.

The British Government took over the colony, paid its debts amounting to £155,000, and tried, as it did when Bligh was sent to New South Wales, the remedy of a strong man, but with less drastic results. Sir George Grey (1841-5), a vigorous soldier of twenty-nine, followed a system diametrically opposite to Gawler's. He cut government expense to the bone, decreasing it from Gawler's £170,000 in 1840 to £30,000 in 1843. He raised taxes, lowered wages, and increased working hours. There were no more relief works for unemployed. Adelaide being now nearly as bare as Mother Hubbard's cupboard, the population that had banked up there sought work on the farms, the real growing point of the colony.

Grey was so unpopular that his effigy was burnt in the streets of Adelaide. He was by nature an autocrat and at that juncture of history he needed to be to get results. He was given a nominee council, such as New South Wales had had in 1824, but if it in any way represented public opinion he was able to override it.

Both Gawler and Grey served South Australia well; one raised confidence and the other acted as an astringent. Neither was responsible for the depression which affected the whole of Australia in the early 1840s. By 1846 prosperity had returned to the continent and South Australia was flourishing. The sheep population was over a million and wool was being exported to England. In 1850 41,000 acres were producing wheat. Bull and Ridley's automatic harvester, or "stripper", had revolutionized the wheat industry. Copper mines were one of the crucial factors in recovery. South Australia, which had never reached the low ebb of Western Australia, was now one of the most prosperous colonies. By 1850 the population exceeded 63,000 and she was ripe for, and received, self-government.

There was nothing left of Wakefield's state.

4. *Australind*

The influence of Wakefield and his theories should not be minimized. His doctrines, well suited to the times, seem to have become diffused through the air of the continent. They crop up here, there, and everywhere. Although South Australia was the most ambitious project to grow out of them, another attempt to put them into practice, in a small way, was made in the early 1840s at Australind. This is a tract of land in Western Australia at the mouth of the Collie River which flows into Leschenault Inlet. It was originally a ten-thousand-acre grant to Colonel Lautour, and before the scheme began was a whaling depot and a centre for breeding horses for India.

A company was formed, the Western Australian Company, to buy this land and inaugurate a model settlement. It did not lack subscribers. A fine town complete with all amenities was planned in London. This was to serve a rural subdivision into hundred-acre blocks. Although the town was laid out, everyone seemed to forget that its prosperity would depend on the surrounding land. Allotments were sold at a "sufficient price" and labourers were brought out only to find that the land they were expected to till was virgin bush. The labourers left for the other colonies as fast as they could. The owners farmed in a desultory way. Within three years, that is by 1843, the settlement had dwindled almost to nothing, though the Company was not wound up until 1875. Australind was small and fugitive, one of the curiosities of history, but for a brief moment men believed in it.

III. Envoi

As the bush by its vastness and emptiness brought out the creative spirit in the men who lived in it, so the *tabula rasa* of a continent with apparently inexhaustible land for the taking stimulated the imaginations of many people who never visited it. It was empty, primitive, it must be malleable. That mistake was made over and over again. The individuality and resistance that was in that emptiness was inconceivable to Englishmen. From Matra and Young to Peel and Wakefield, dreamer, doctrinaire, philosopher, capitalist, all tried to impose their schemes on it.

Australia suffered from the fantasies of the Age of Reason. Reasons, without investigation, could always be found why it should fulfil any wish. The continent was mistaken for Aladdin's Lamp. Australian history grew under the shadow of the legends of Eldorado, of the Spice Islands, of the South Sea paradise. But the country was outside the orbit of them all.

The Colonial Office acted as a brake on the wilder and more expensive schemes, yet it, too, half believed. Governors received solemn injunctions to grow hemp, rice, indigo, and were told that the country must be ideally suited for such products. They were bidden to confine the population within strict limits, to segregate convicts, to civilize the aborigines, and generally to achieve off-hand any result that the Home Government thought desirable, without reference to the nature of the country or even to human nature.

There was no tangible opposition to the white man in Australia, therefore he could do with it as he wished. (That this sort of creative thinking is not extinct is witnessed by the Ground-nut Scheme of recent fame.) Slowly we came to understand that the continent could only be possessed on its own terms.

REFERENCE NOTES

[1] *Hist. Rec. Aust.*, ser. I, vol. i, p. 21.
[2] Quoted, *Voyage of Governor Phillip to Botany Bay,* p. 76.
[3] *Hist. Rec. Aust.*, ser. I, vol. v, p. 326.
[4] Clark's Journal, p. 158.
[5] *Hist. Rec. Aust.*, ser. I, vol. i, p. 457.
[6] *Ibid.*, p. 479.
[7] *Ibid.*, vol. v, p. 322.
[8] *Ibid.*, vol. iv, p. 304.
[9] *Ibid.*, vol. xx, p. 153.
[10] *Ibid.*, p. 689.
[11] *Ibid.*, p. 690.
[12] *Ibid.*, vol. iv, p. 15.
[13] *Ibid.*, p. 338.
[14] *Ibid.*, vol. v, p. 155.
[15] *Ibid.*, vol. xii, pp. 709 *et seq.*
[16] The Reverend W. R. Barrett has written a most delightful *History of Tasmania to the Death of Lieutenant-Governor Collins in 1810,* which is not only good reading but is very thoroughly documented.
[17] R. Bridges, *That Yesterday Was Home,* pp. 25-6.
[18] R. M. Hartwell, *Economic Development of Van Diemen's Land 1820-1850,* p. 11.
[19] H. Widowson, *Present State of Van Diemen's Land,* p. 142.
[20] H. Melville, *History of the Island of Van Diemen's Land 1824-1835,* p. 212.
[21] *Hist. Rec. Aust.*, ser. I, vol. xviii, p. 153.
[22] *Ibid.*, p. 155.
[23] Quoted, *Australia: a Social and Political History* (ed. Greenwood), p. 77.
[24] *Hist. Rec. Aust.*, ser. I, vol. xviii, p. 157.
[25] *Ibid.*, p. 156.
[26] *Ibid.*, note 149.
[27] *Ibid.*, p. 155.
[28] *Ibid.*, p. 391.
[29] Quoted from an unpublished source by J. Jervis, *J. Roy. Aust. Hist. Soc.*, vol. xxi, p. 12.
[30] *Hist. Rec. Aust.*, ser. I, vol. xx, p. 209.
[31] *Ibid.*, vol. xxiii, p. 509.
[32] W. Coote, *History of the Colony of Queensland,* pp. 29-30.
[33] *J. Roy. Aust. Hist. Soc.*, vol. iii, p. 85.
[34] *Ibid.*, p. 90.
[35] *Hist. Rec. Aust.*, ser. III, vol. vi, p. 614.
[36] *Ibid.*, p. 606.
[37] *Ibid.*, p. 615.
[38] W. C. Smart, *Mandurah and Pinjarrah: History of Thomas Peel and the Peel Estates 1829-1865,* pp. 12-13.
[39] *Ibid.*, quoted, pp. 42-3.
[40] Gawler to Angas, September 1841. Quoted by R. M. Hartwell in *Australia: a Social and Political History* (ed. Greenwood), p. 75.

CHAPTER XI

THE SYSTEM: A RETROSPECT

". . . the devoted convict. . . ."

—Lord Auckland, *Treatise on Banishment.*

The transportation of criminals or political offenders was no new thing. Banishment of the politically dangerous was an old and useful expedient practised at all times when simple assassination appeared for one reason or another to be unwise or impracticable. It came down in the world when in 1597, in the reign of Elizabeth I, an Act of Parliament setting up laws for the relief of the poor—or perhaps more rightly for the relief of society from the poor—enumerated punishments for "Rogues, Vagabonds and Sturdy Beggars". The Privy Council was given the right of banishing the Rogues "beyond the seas". When in 1606 Virginia was colonized there was a ready market for labour and it was only practical to ship off felons to the plantations. It was not so much a punishment as a conditional reprieve. The East India Company accepted such material also. Under the Stuarts shipments of convicted persons and prisoners of war to Virginia and elsewhere were frequent and normal. It continued until the loss of the American colonies, and by that time had been systematized into a profitable trade. Contractors carried away the troublesome and the unwanted without cost to the Government and sold their services to the planters. With the cessation of this traffic English prisons, not built to accommodate large numbers, overflowed and hulks moored in the Thames and the Severn were used as prisons. They, too, overflowed.

Crime was prevalent amongst "the lower orders". The curious phrase "poor but honest" may have had its rise at this time. There was great disparity of wealth. The poor had little reason to be honest. They had lost their security on the land and they had little or none in the new industrial world. The principle of laissez-faire was so well entrenched that no government would intervene to raise wages or set a living standard. It was regrettable, of course, that machine knitters should only get six shillings a week, but impossible to prevent the employer from making the best bargain as to wages that he could. The poor-laws could only patch the situation, and by doing so make it possible for starvation wages to continue. Vagabonds could be whipped, and anyone reduced to complete poverty was a vagabond.

Combinations of workmen to better their condition were regarded as seditious and treated as such. The Church was at a low ebb and took no responsibility for social injustices and distress. The laws, particularly those protecting property, were harsh. On paper they were much harsher than in application. Humanity and charity were not dead. There were men like John Howard, the Fieldings, Jeremy Bentham, and Patrick Colquhoun, who diagnosed the disease and fought for reform. Conditions in England were bad, but they never equalled those that led up to the Revolution in France. Justice was not summary and many magistrates and juries were humane in their findings, but in the turn of the tide in the nation's history, and in agriculture and industry and commerce, there were many victims who turned criminal. The children of the dispossessed were growing up, knowing nothing but the law of the jungle.

And so the prisons were filling and the danger of contamination, moral and physical, aroused public opinion. Something had to be done. An effort to continue transportation to America was rebuffed. Somewhere else must be found.

Transportation of felons was put on a new, secure legal basis when an Act of Parliament (24 Geo. III, c.56) "for the effectual transportation of felons and other offenders" was passed in 1784. The place to which they were to be transported was left to the King in Council to determine. The first choice was Africa, Gambia in particular and Lemane Island, where it was proposed to turn them loose with supplies and tools to set up their own state, with only a guard ship down river to prevent escape. Some were sent to Africa with disastrous results. A member of the House of Commons, the orator Edmund Burke, made it impossible for a Government ever to try Gambia again. He could

> . . . not reconcile it with justice that persons respited from death should, after a mock display of mercy, be compelled to undergo it, by being sent to a country where they could not live, and where the manner of their death might be singularly horrid, so that the apparent mercy might with justice be called cruelty, as the merciful gallows of England would rid them of their lives in a far less dreadful manner than the climate or the savages of Africa.

This and a great deal more in the same vein saw to it that penal settlements in Africa were sealed off by public opinion. In August 1786 Lord Sydney was driven, apparently unwillingly, to advise the King to select New South Wales for his penal settlement, and an Order in Council in agreement with the terms of the Act was made. The machinery was set in motion. The colony was founded in England.

Seven hundred and eighty is the generally accepted number of convicts who sailed in the First Fleet. In 1787-8, according to John Howard, there was an aggregate of 7482 prisoners in England and Wales, but 2197 were debtors and 1412 had committed crimes too petty to merit transportation. That leaves 3873 transportable offenders.[1] The numbers were not so great as the public outcry had indicated, and 780 was a beginning.

The great majority of them were under sentence for seven years, which indicates that, under the prevailing laws, their crimes were not very serious. However, they included a number of men with death or life sentences whose terms had been reduced as they were going overseas. The method of selection to begin with was haphazard. Men were not then specifically sentenced to transportation to New South Wales. Some offences could carry transportation, this generally meant convicts under sentence for seven to fourteen years, or for life. Prisoners on shorter terms did not come into the scheme. All convicts sent out had one or other of these terms, though some by the time they were embarked had already served part of their sentences in prisons or hulks. From those eligible the governors of jails liked to get rid of prisoners with long terms and those who gave the most trouble. There was a general rule that men should be under fifty and women under forty-five years old. This was not strictly followed. There were old people, like Ishmael Coleman, who died worn out with age and suffering, and a woman of eighty-two, sent out in the First Fleet. The real rule was convenience.

Indent papers accompanied the convicts, or in theory they did. They gave the name, age, place of trial and length of sentence, but never the crime committed. This made it impossible to segregate them, but there were some, like Macquarie, who thought it a circumstance in the convict's favour. He left his crime behind him whilst he worked out his sentence. As a convict he would be policed, but not in a special way. For instance, the forger would not be continually suspected of repeating his crime or the perjurer's word for ever be discredited. This may be good psychology, but it also made many difficulties. It was, for example, unfortunate when the expert forger was employed on clerical work because he was intelligent and literate. When convicts had been going to work on plantations in Virginia the niceties of their crimes mattered little, their strength and endurance were what mattered. In New South Wales, where at first most offices had to be filled from the convict ranks, trust had to be placed in them and it was important to know as much as possible of their antecedents. The forms to which government officials were used continued to be followed. Convicts coming from Ireland direct, as a large proportion of them did after 1791, were often sent without any papers at all, so that no one knew, except from the convict himself, a discredited source, when his sentence expired. This was all the harder as an Irish convict was only deemed to have begun his sentence on the day he embarked on the transport, even though he had already lain one or two years or longer in jail. They were helpless, they could prove nothing, governors were chary of liberating them, particularly as more lifers, generally men reprieved from death, were sent from Ireland than from England.

The cost of sending a prisoner to New South Wales with supplies for one year was in the early years of transportation from £14 to £17 each, according to O'Brien and Bigge, and as more and more convicts poured in from Ireland there was some talk of Ireland sharing the overhead expense, in particular raising and supporting one company of the New South Wales Corps. With the Act of Union these difficulties disappeared.

Transportation to New South Wales lasted from 1786 to 1840 and was continued to other parts of Australia until 1869. In all some 160,000 convicts were sent out. This is the figure determined by Eris O'Brien in his *Foundation of Australia*, a work of great and careful scholarship. Other authorities, for example A. G. L. Shaw, put the number at 130,000. Governor Gipps gives the figure at about 102,000 at the time transportation ended in New South Wales.[2]

The convict beginning was looked upon as a disgrace—not, of course, to England, but to Australia. "It is a shameful and unblessed thing to take the scum of people, and wicked condemned men to be the people with whom you plant," wrote Francis Bacon in another context, and it looked as if those words had become engraved on the portals of Australian history. The arithmetic of immigration and a more rational approach to crime have erased the sense of inferiority. Depravity may run in families, as witness the notorious Jukes, but there is little reason to believe that law-breaking is hereditary. Commissioner Bigge remarked of the first generation Australian born that they showed no taint of their parents' crimes, and since those days there has been a greater dilution of original stock than in any other country, because settlers, like everything else, have had to be imported into Australia.

The convict system as first conceived was very simple. It was securely founded on Act of Parliament and implemented by an Order in Council. The Home Office, and later the Colonial Office, issued the directives, the Navy supplied the first four governors and King's ships did convoy duty. The transports were generally East Indiamen, because this meshed in with John Company's eastern trade. Some tatters of the Lemane Island scheme clung to the project. The convicts were set down on virgin soil and with a Governor, a guard of Marines, and their initial supplies, were more or less expected to make their own way. There were no superintendents, overseers, instructors, jailers or civil officials. There were no fantasies about a model settlement or scientific reformation. If they reformed in communion with nature and from lack of temptation so much the better; if they did not then they could only prey on one another and the civilized world was well rid of them. Escape was almost, but not quite, impossible. All communication was in theory controlled by the British Government and the East

India Company, in whose trade monopoly Australia was included. It seemed like perfect insulation, but it was not. Necessity and profit attended to that. There was no currency, and as late as 1817 the Home Government opposed the establishment of a bank on the grounds that a penal settlement did not need either. To feed, clothe, and shelter themselves should fill their whole need. An artificially primitive world was to be inserted into the complex structure of modern times.

The system grew in two, often incompatible, directions. Theory changed in England, regeneration became a more important object in the humanitarian 1830s. The Colonial Office gave more and more thought to punishment and reform. Various schemes, beginning with Bigge's plans for segregation and filtering of convicts, were handed out to the governors for implementation. The developing colony changed the system. It had to be adapted when the two incompatibles, the world of free, prospering men and the penal settlement, became incongruous and a half-way measure of dividing the convict establishment and the civil government into two entities was adopted. The Governor was the pivot between the Colonial Office and the System. He had to devise and improvise. He had to obey his masters at Whitehall and he had to make the colony in his charge work. The Legislative Council was never in the same position. It was not responsible to the Home Government. It always represented, even when nominated, the interests of the free settlers. The Governor was again a buffer between his council and the unrepresented majority. The settlement was planned and re-planned, but circumstance and necessity were the strongest factors in its growth. New South Wales very early ceased to be for the "benefit" of the convicts. The day Governor Phillip quitted his government, 10th December 1792, marks the end locally of the convict's prime importance. From that time onwards the colony existed primarily for those who could make a profit out of it, by trading monopoly and presently by wool-growing. Under Grose it began an independent life of its own which the convicts were made to serve. Macquarie came nearest to re-establishing Phillip's penal settlement and was recalled for his trouble.

The convicts were the only labour force. Not only was the settlement unattractive to free labourers to begin with, but the Government controlled all entries and exits. It was only in King's ships or in transports that anyone could travel to Australia, and to board either they must have permission. Later—when for instance, the Blaxland brothers chartered their own ship to come out—it was by grace and favour. Labour was a commodity of which, like land, the settlement had an ample supply. It was essential that convicts should not be idle. The work that was done on the public account or for the officers and other free men was done by convict labour. It was of poor quality. The majority of the prisoners had come from cities or provincial towns, they were neither husbandmen nor artificers. The few who had skills were so valuable to the infant settlement that if they were villains it was overlooked or only punished, say with a flogging, in such a way as not to impair their usefulness for long. The majority were unwilling workers, listless, without pride or interest in anything they did. Their overseers were drawn from their own ranks and had little influence over them. When an overseer of a different type was available the quality of their work improved. Such a man was Henry Edward Dodd, who came free to the country as Phillip's servant. More useful work was soon found for him. He knew a little about agriculture and he had the gift of controlling and disciplining men whilst he kept their respect. He was made superintendent at Rose Hill and he was soon in charge of the government store there, acted as a quasi-magistrate and even deputized for the captain in charge of Marines. Under him the government farm yielded 200 bushels of wheat and 35 of barley in 1789, as against 25 bushels of barley grown on the farm at Sydney. He also achieved by his personal exertion a cabbage weighing 26 pounds. Unfortunately he died in the course of duty on 28th January 1791. In the night he heard thieves in the garden and, although he was ill at the time, he got up and gave chase for several hours, clad only in his nightshirt. He had a relapse of his illness and died. Judge-Advocate Collins described him as attentive, quiet, competent. He had complete ascendancy over the convicts without being hated by them.[3] All that brought him a reward of three shillings a day over and above his rations. This is only by the way.

The convicts worked badly because they did not want to work, because they were often undernourished, and because they did not have the right men to encourage their efforts. It is not surprising that they, situated as they were, were apathetic. Still, looking at their work as a whole, they did not do badly by the settlement. They built roads—bad ones, of course—including the first road over the Blue Mountains; they erected Macquarie's buildings and many others less notable; they supplied most of the essential labour for the wool industry up to about 1850. They did all the fatigues of the colony. They were the "cannon fodder" of the new world.

The fact remains that on their labour and on the money that the British Government spent upon them, the colony was founded. Governor Gipps did some arithmetic.[4] If the average sentence expiated in Australia was four years (most of the convicts had seven-year sentences, but part was expired by the time they arrived), and the Home Government spent £10 a year in the Colony on each of 51,000 convicts, that would amount to £2,040,000. Add to this the public works executed by convict labour—roads, bridges, buildings—which became the property of the community and you have another £1,000,000 value in kind. Half the convicts had been assigned and agriculture and grazing had been encouraged by cheap labour. It was, he pointed out, a flying start, for a land in which all the means of wealth had to be created.

The system took shape gradually.

The actual transportation by ship from England or Ireland to Australia was one of the worst ordeals the convicts had to face. The story of the First Fleet, already told, cannot be taken as a fair sample of the voyage in transports. Everyone agreed that, with all its inconveniences, it was a prosperous voyage and that the convicts were well treated—too well, some of the candid diarists of the day thought. Only forty persons of all ranks and grades died on the voyage, and some of these deaths were accidental or inevitable. The Second Fleet was a sad and sorry affair. It was made up of three ships, *Surprize, Neptune,* and *Scarborough,* bringing 1017 convicts. Of them 267, or 26 per cent, died on the journey and more than 400 sick were landed, some of them dying as they were taken out of the ship; about 81 others died in the emergency hospital accommodation that had to be rigged up to receive them. Most of the survivors never fully recovered their health after their ordeal. Both the Reverend Richard Johnson and Surgeon White have left harrowing accounts of the sufferings of these unfortunate men and women who were emaciated, starving, racked with fever, defaced by scurvy, and with not even a blanket to cover them. So great was the callousness of the masters that the bodies of those who died on the passage up the harbour were thrown "into the harbour and their dead bodies cast upon the shore, and were seen lying naked on the rocks".

A convict woman who witnessed the disembarkation wrote home and her letter, published in the *Morning Chronicle*, 4th August 1791, can be seen in the collection of Australian papers in the British Museum.

> Oh! if you had but seen the shocking sight of the poor creatures that came out in the three ships it would make your heart bleed; they were almost dead, very few could stand, and they were obliged to fling them as you would goods, and hoist them out of the ships, they were so feeble; and they died ten or twelve of a day when they first landed; but some of them are getting better. There died on their way on board the *Neptune*, 183 men and 12 women, and in the *Scarborough*, 67 men, and in the *Surprize*, 85. They were not so long as we were in coming here, but they were confined and had bad victuals and stinking water. The Governor was very angry, and scolded the captains a great deal, and, I heard, intended to write to London about it, for I heard him say it was murdering them.[5]

The reason for the difference between the two fleets was that with the Second Fleet the Government had reverted to the old bad system of handing the convicts over to contractors, who in turn passed them to the masters of the transports. Payment, in this instance £17 7s. 6d. a head, was to be made on the convicts embarked in England, not on those landed in Sydney. It was more profitable to the masters for convicts to die than to live, for the surplus rations could then be sold at a high profit in Sydney. The Home Government had made a generous contract setting out the rations to be issued. These, on paper, were better than those allowed the prisoners on the First Fleet. A Government representative sailed with the Second Fleet, but as he died during the passage there was no check on the avarice of the masters. The worst of these was Donald Trail of *Neptune*. Soldiers coming out in *Neptune* lodged an information against him and he was tried in England as soon as he could be caught.

Governor Phillip made sure that the Home Government should know the enormity of the crime against humanity. As the chief excuse of the masters was that the convicts had been sick when taken aboard, he was also angry because no notice had been taken of his reasonable request that only strong, healthy, useful prisoners should be sent whilst the colony was in a precarious condition. He did not mince matters. "The sending out the disordered and helpless clears the jails, and may ease the parishes from which they are sent; but sir, it is obvious that this settlement, instead of being a colony which is to support itself, will, if the practice is continued, remain for years a burthen to the mother country."[6]

As the Third Fleet, which arrived in August and October 1791, had sailed before the scandal broke, the same conditions prevailed but the results were not as disastrous. It was composed of eleven transports with 1864 prisoners aboard; 196 of them died on the voyage and the rest arrived in poor shape. They had been overcrowded because the masters were bringing out speculative cargoes and to do so stole space. Phillip reported this and was ordered to seize any "illegal cargoes". It is interesting to note that the ship on which the Government's agent sailed was the most healthy.

These bad conditions did not always prevail, even when the contracting system was at its laxest. *Lady Juliana* arrived in June 1790 after a voyage lasting ten months with 221 female convicts, only five having died on the way, and those landed were very healthy.

The reforms that followed Phillip's protests were not as effective as might have been expected. In future contractors were to be paid not on the basis of the number of convicts carried but on the tonnage of their ships. Separate contracts were made for rations. Each transport was supposed to carry a doctor, but this was sometimes evaded. The convicts were inspected medically before they sailed in the hope of preventing contagious diseases from being carried out in the ships. This was not always successful. *Hillsborough* in 1799 sailed with jail fever, a malignant form of typhus, on board, brought from Langston Harbour prison. Of 300 convicts aboard only 205 survived the voyage and they in a miserable condition with no garments fit to bring on shore. This was all the more flagrant as the Inspector-General of Health had protested against the sailing.

Bonuses were to be given both to master and surgeon for landing the convicts in health, but these were not large enough and too uncertain to distract their attention from the greater profit to be earned by selling unexpended rations or from speculative cargoes illicitly shipped but condoned because the colony had so many unsupplied needs. The bonus might be a lump sum of £50 or a guinea each for every convict landed. The superintendent and surgeon in *Surprize*, 1794, did get this substantial reward on the Governor's certificate.

In 1801 the Transport Commissioners, set up to regulate the carrying of convicts and safeguard their health, issued instructions to masters of transports setting out the treatment of convicts at sea, their right to time on deck daily, measures for cleanliness, records of sickness, issue of medicines and many other details. Payment would only be made on the Governor's certificate of good conduct, neglect would be prosecuted. It was only when naval surgeons, used to combating illness at sea and taking the proper precautions, were in 1815 put in charge of convicts that really good results were achieved. They were generally men of good standing and professional pride who were unlikely to conspire with masters to rob and neglect their charges. They were directly responsible to the Transport Board and the blame for neglect could be fastened on them. The human element remained and from time to time there were scandals. That these became known was the convict's greatest safeguard.

The prisoners in transit fell victims to other things beside greed and neglect. There is the story of *Lady Shore*. She sailed from England in 1797 with 66 female convicts and, as their guards, recruits for the New South Wales Corps made up of military prisoners from the Savoy, disaffected Irish and French deserters. Ten Frenchmen, seven of the Irish, and some of the crew mutinied, killed the captain and mate, seized the ship, and sailed for South America. Twenty-nine persons, including children, were cast adrift in the longboat and eventually reached the Rio Grande. The mutineers sailed into Montevideo without knowing that England was at war with Spain. They were interned as prisoners of war, the ship was sold as a prize, and the female convicts were assigned as servants to the Spanish ladies of the city.

Then too, convicts easily became victims of fear. There were frequent rumours that they were on the point of revolt. Ships' masters feared them and treated them accordingly.

The story of the ship *Chapman*, which arrived from Ireland on the 26th of July 1817, with 200 convicts underlines the possibilities that still existed. The

Chapman was an uneasy ship from the first. Before she sailed there was trouble with the crew. The convicts had a bad report from the hulks, Captain Drake and Surgeon Dewar decided to keep them in double irons. The *Chapman* sailed on the 15th of March. On the 25th the first alarm was given. The sentry at the fore hatch reported that the convicts were picking the locks. The guards found all quiet. On the 13th of April a second alarm was given. The convicts had escaped on to the deck and were rushing the ship. The crew was put under arms. It proved another mare's nest, but a number of convicts and two seamen, suspected of helping them, were punished. Four days later Michael Collins, an informer, told the master there was a plot to seize the ship and sail away to America. The next day was very hot, everyone's nerves were on edge. Arms were piled on the deck ready for use. The prisoners were confined between decks. The day passed in sullen quiet. Five prisoners were flogged on suspicion. At 8 o'clock, when it was dark, the ship's cook standing on a grating of the starboard forescuttle felt it lift under him. He gave the alarm that the prisoners were forcing the scuttles. He heard, or thought he heard, them rushing the hospital bulkhead. The third mate, Baxter, and a party of soldiers opened fire on the prisoners through the loopholes in a bulkhead. The convicts were just going to bed, some of them on the floor because of the heat. The firing lasted perhaps half an hour. Three were killed and 22 injured. The surgeon was afraid to go into the prison and they remained uncared for until the morning.

As punishment all the convicts were put on half rations till the end of the voyage, and from 70 to 100 of them were chained every night to an iron cable in the prison; four lengths of chain were passed over each hatch. Baxter threatened to suffocate them all where they lay with brimstone and charcoal. And the punishments continued, floggings for rattling chains, for speaking Irish, for coughing, for laughing; stabbings, beatings with cutlasses, chainings and starvings. On the 30th of April there was another outburst of hysteria and firing down the hatches, two killed, four wounded. Soldiers and seamen began to suspect one another, and two seamen were killed in a third outbreak of shooting, this time on deck. On the 24th of May another man was killed and three wounded. In all, twelve men died and thirty were wounded, the rest brought starving to port.[7]

Convicts did seize the colonial ship *Norfolk*, but that was a different matter. In 1801 there was an alleged plot to seize the transport *Anne* from Ireland. The captain shot one ringleader, hanged another, was tried for it before a Court of Vice-Admiralty and honourably acquitted. A master who honestly believed his ship to be threatened was always deemed right if he took strong measures for her safety. Open mutiny was very rare. There was little cohesion amongst the convicts—in such a gathering there was always one informer.

Through fear, no employment was ever found for male convicts during the voyages, because tools of any kind could be turned into weapons. Women were allowed to sew or knit, but Bigge did not approve of even this. "All employments that have a tendency to encourage a passion for dress should be studiously avoided," said he. Gambling, thieving, and quarrelling were the main alleviations to boredom.

Even with scrupulous attention to cleanliness, conditions were uncomfortable and unhygienic. In the prison which was between decks, the walls were lined with bunks and five boys or four men slept in each. Every convict was allowed eighteen inches of space for sleeping. The ration consisted of salt meat and flour, with a little lime-juice or wine as an anti-scorbutic, and sometimes butter and pease. It had to be cooked in the prison. The convicts were divided into groups or messes for this purpose. Water was often short in the tropics. The hospital, to which only the worst cases were removed, was located in the fore part of the ship and could only be reached through the prison. The patients suffered from smells, leakages, and the rolling of the ship, but they were, thus isolated, unlikely to pass their diseases on to the crew.

In the 1830s there was a marked improvement in the conditions of transportation and a sharp fall in mortality.

Year	*Convicts sent*	*Deaths*	*Proportion of deaths*
1830	4981	45	1/111
1831	5303	41	1/129
1832	5117	54	1/96
1833	5560	63	1/85
1834	6190	61	1/101
1835	5315	37	1/145

To the issue of chocolate regularly during the voyage was attributed, rightly or wrongly, the low death-rate in 1835.

Arrival in the colony was generally marked by some ceremony. Phillip assembled the convicts as well as the Marines to hear his commission read and then to witness the formal founding of the colony. Governor King sent the Naval Officer and a surgeon aboard each transport as it arrived, primarily to check the health of the convicts. The Governor then went aboard himself, made inquiries as to the prisoners' behaviour on the voyage and asked them if they had any complaints to make. Macquarie, as one would expect, developed the theme. The Governor's secretary and the Chief Superintendent of Convicts first went aboard. The convicts were mustered on deck in the presence of the ship's master and surgeon. They were checked against the records and each man was questioned individually as to his treatment, whether he had received his rations, had he any complaints, had he any illness or infirmity, had he a trade or what could he do. This detailed check might take two days. The convicts were then clad in new clothes, landed, and marched to the jail yard where Macquarie inspected them and addressed them, exhorting them to good behaviour and promising rewards for industry and sobriety. The Judge-Advocate then gave them more good advice, suggesting that they deposit any money or valuables they might have in a savings bank which he had organized for them. He could not compel them to do this and on the whole they were too suspicious to take advantage of it. After this the Superintendent, working on the data he had collected, made his choice of those required for public works and government farming. The remainder were then allotted as assigned servants. Margarot, giving evidence before the Select Committee on Transportation in 1812, said that wealthy settlers got the pick of the convicts by bribery. But this was something Macquarie would not tolerate. In theory at least they were allotted impartially and, in times when labour was very scarce, by the drawing of lots. Later governors treated the matter in a more coolly official manner. Under Darling the convicts were kept in the transports until assigned lists were made out. They were then sent straight to their masters. The object of this was to keep them out of Sydney and prevent them from communicating with the convict population already established.

The convicts were now inhabitants of a penal settlement. During Phillip's governorship the prisoners worked for the public good, on the government farms, erecting the necessary buildings and, to a certain extent, fending for themselves in the hope of eking out the dwindling supplies. They were not assigned as servants at first.

During the interregnum, with Grose in power, assignment of convicts to individuals for farming, trading, domestic and other purposes became so much the usual thing that there were none left except a few incorrigibles, to carry on public works and to farm the government establishments.

In a dispatch from Dundas to Grose, dated 31st (*sic*) June 1793, he was empowered to allow every civil and military officer two assigned servants, maintained by the public store for two years. After that the officers were expected to maintain them. If, however, an officer, still receiving his military pay, was granted land and convicts were assigned to him to till it, he must provide their food and clothing.[8] Grose interpreted this permission in a very liberal way indeed.

Assignment was no new idea. Convicts sent to America had been assigned as servants to their masters. Now in New South Wales they were assigned to the officers who, beside their military duties, were soon farming and breeding stock on their new grants, and carrying on trade. They were building up self-supporting estates, like miniature manors, and for all this they needed labour. The convicts provided the labour, the Government continued to feed and clothe them, often buying the fruits of their labour in order to do so.

Since his generosity could not be concealed, Grose excused himself in a dispatch of 29th April 1794:

> When the gentlemen were first indulged with grants I gave them ten servants each, less than that number not being equal to the cultivation of the ground allotted them. The public labour is very little interrupted by their accommodation, as nine hundred and sixty (960) acres of ground have been cleared in one year by the officers only, and as the produce of that ground has been of much publick utility, I have some hope that on this representation they may [be] suffered to keep their convicts.[9]

Governor Hunter's instructions repeated explicitly that he might allow "any number of convicts as assigned servants," so long as their employer fed and clothed them satisfactorily. Hunter, too, dodged the issue when he pointed out that were servants withdrawn from the officer-farmers there would be no harvest.

In a government order dated 15th October 1795 Hunter made a direct statement of his policy. Officers were to be allowed three domestic servants and ten for agriculture. Superintendents, constables, and storekeepers were to have four servants, free settlers two, expirees one, sergeants of the New South Wales Corps one. Artificers must be turned over to the Government. Servants must not be allowed to come into the Town. There is not a word about who feeds and clothes them.[10]

In vain did Hunter try to extract £20 a year for every assigned servant, additional to the legal two. The colony was dependent for its life on grain raised by officers, so they were in a position to make their own terms.

Governor King made an effort to regulate assignment. He drew up a proper contract which ensured to the Government some control, for their protection and other reasons, over convicts after assignment. He called together all employers of assigned servants and issued them with a printed statement of the terms of assignment so that none could plead ignorance. If they did not keep to the rules he threatened to take away their servants. The Government was willing to feed and clothe assigned servants if their masters paid £13 13s. a year, that is, the assessed price of their rations and clothing plus 25 per cent.

Portland at the Colonial Office thought that officers who farmed should not be allowed any servants unless they kept them, that five maintained by the Government was too many to allot to magistrates as a return for their services, that government farming should be revived. On 1st March 1802 King announced to Portland that officers were no longer allowed any assigned servants at government expense and that magistrates had been reduced to four, "which is the least recompense they can have for their useful services",[11] and that he was reviving public agriculture at Castle Hill.

In October 1800 he struck 450 persons off the ration, saving the Government, according to his estimate, £10,488. In 1804 it was all to do again, and he reported that he had reduced officers' servants from 124 to 58, and assigned servants, kept by the Government, from 3216 to 233. In April 1803 Lord Hobart had directed King to take away the two convict servants, maintained by the Government, from eleven officers who had received increases in pay. Frederick Watson gives us a curious sidelight on this:

> The twenty-two convict servants of the eleven officials, who received increases in salaries were worth £858 *per annum* at Hobart's estimate. The recipients of increases in salaries thus collectively suffered an actual loss of £65.5.0d *per annum* and the officials, who received no increases, experienced a loss by these changes of £78 *per annum* each.
>
> It will be clear therefore that Lord Hobart effected a large saving to the crown by granting these increases in salaries, and by the withdrawal of the allowance of two convict servants.[12]

In February 1803 civil officers were allowed six assigned servants, and convicts were being hired out by the Government to help bring in the harvest. If they did not return in three weeks they were flogged and jailed. By the following December one assigned servant, kept by the Government, was allowed each officer to draw his water and haul his firewood.

Under cover of the conflicting, copious, and ever-changing regulations issued by the Secretary of State for the Colonies in England and by the Governor on the spot, the exasperated officers felt themselves grievously ill-used and continued much as before.

King became intensely unpopular on account of his policy of curtailing privileges, and there is no doubt that his government orders were evaded. He had nothing but paper for ammunition. In any case the student of Australian history is ill advised to believe that dispatches and government orders represent immutable fact. They are essays in, and expressions of, hope and good intention. The orders and proclamations may have had some effect, but the colony was moved by far stronger impulses than obedience. It was extremely difficult to police and, Governor or no Governor, it went its own irregular way. It is useless to say, "Look at what Governor King did to regularize assignment, and suppress the liquor traffic. . . ." He tried to do these things, he did not succeed. He was a nuisance to the privileged and the powerful and that is about all.

By the time Macquarie was Governor policy seemed to have defeated privilege. Assigned servants were not only kept by their masters but they received an annual wage of £10. As this was usually paid in kind at inflated colonial prices they benefited very little. The principle of payment was established, however. It was, of course, a contradiction of the firmly established principle that no convict might receive or own any money, other than what he brought with him. This, in theory, was held in safe keeping for him until his sentence expired or he was granted a ticket of leave and was entitled to use it. A convict in servitude was not allowed to buy or to sell. On the supposition that he owned nothing he could not be imprisoned for debts.[13]

In February 1822 Lord Bathurst, in a dispatch outlining the findings of Commissioner Bigge, warned Governor Brisbane not to allow convict clerks and overseers to have assigned servants and ordered him not to monopolize mechanics for government service but to assign them with other convicts to "the more opulent settlers who have the means of employing and supporting them".[14]

In 1827 the Colonial Office was very suspicious about the expenses of the convict establishment. Lord Bathurst wrote of "the difficulty I feel in reconciling the scarcity of assignable Convicts . . . with the enormous and increasing expense with which this Country is still charged, on account of the Prisoners who are transported to that part of the World".[15] The nigger was still in the woodpile.

The Home Government's attitude to assignment was confused. One thing all governments and parties had in common was the desire to save expense. Assignment of convicts to officers and settlers was a saving so long as their masters fed and clothed them. The assignment system then was to be encouraged. At the same time Lord Portland and other Secretaries of State for the Colonies ordered that agriculture for the public good be increased, since they also considered that a saving of money. What was not realized in England was that in so small a colony these policies were incompatible. The public store was the only large market for grain. If its granaries were filled from government farms, officer-farmers would be put out of business and would not require large numbers of assigned servants. It was government farming that was discontinued.

The encouragement of assignment was not altogether influenced by financial considerations. Lord Bathurst believed that it was beneficial to the convicts' morals. He wrote:

> . . . the utmost care must be exerted that the situation of the Convict, when taken off the Store by the Colonists, must be one of laborious employment, tempered at the same time with every consideration of proper humanity, and with every corrective principle of reformation; and I need scarcely observe that this reformation is likely to be accomplished, in proportion to the distance which the Convict is removed from the Towns, where no precautionary

measures can prevent the contagion arising from evil association and connections.[16]

Again, in September 1826, he told Darling to distribute the convicts through the country, out of reach "of pleasures, which are open to those who reside in the Town of Sydney, and which prevent Transportation from being either an object of terror or the means of reformation".[17] He felt that hard agricultural labour was curative, and this chimed in very nicely with the needs of the colony.

Assignment was not only encouraged, the taking of prisoners off the Government's hands was made one of the conditions of a land grant. When the Australian Agricultural Company was formed in 1825 it was granted huge tracts of land and 1400 assigned servants at a saving of £30,800 a year to the Government in maintenance.[18]

Under Brisbane, when land was granted the recipient was required to maintain one convict per hundred acres. In issuing this instruction Lord Bathurst wrote tentatively:

> . . . I am not sanguine enough to anticipate that many Grants will be accepted upon the terms proposed, for, considering it in the light of a tax, its operation must be most unequal, as the quality of the land will necessarily vary both as to fertility and convenience of situation, and consequently the invariableness of the condition imposed must in many instances prevent its fulfilment.

Brisbane could use his own judgment and not press the matter.[19]

It did produce an outcry, but, remarked Brisbane, "clamour . . . is no where a long liver, and its day is past here already".[20]

Later settlers were offered a bonus or a remission of part of the price of land if they took convicts on assignment. Governor Darling pointed out that this inducement was quite unnecessary, since the labour of convicts was indispensable.

In 1826 Darling set up an Assignment Board to allot convict labour. He was unpopular already and he did not want to call down on his head accusations of favouritism or malice. Also the colony was now so large that the Governor had not time to attend to all its details personally in the way that had delighted Macquarie. Darling had a gift for organization and the old haphazard method of assignment appeared wasteful to him. All was now to be done in a much more regular way. With the setting up of the Board the Governor lost all rights of personal patronage. New arrivals were to be classified according to trade and capacity and assigned where they would be most useful. No master might ask for any particular convict nor were wives to be assigned to husbands or husbands to wives any longer. New settlers were to have preference and absentee landowners were not to be allowed any convicts unless they employed a free bailiff of good character. The morals of employers were also looked into, and if they were inhumane or fed their convicts badly, or kept sending them back to store, they were either allowed no assigned servants or made to wait until all other claims had been satisfied.[21] The Principal Chaplain, Samuel Marsden, was amongst the masters who were disciplined.

Towards the end of 1826 the conditions of assignment were again made more rigorous. The master was bound to pay 18s. a year to the Government for each servant, of which 6s. was for divine worship if a church, chapel, or chaplain was within five miles, 6s. for medical care and 6s. towards the maintenance of good order and justice.[22] Servants were now always taken to their masters and, if necessary, brought back again by constables, no matter what the distance.[23]

In 1827 the law as personified by Chief Justice Forbes took a hand. He declared that once a convict was assigned, the Government had no further control over him and that his master must keep him until his sentence expired. Darling could not have agreed less. The Government, he felt, must continue to protect the convict and society. He wrote to Lord Bathurst: "There are many Masters here, who would connive at the absence of a troublesome character in order to get rid of the expence of his maintenance, though they could have no doubt he was plundering and preying on the Public." He asked for the law to be modified.[24]

Darling's own idea of convict discipline had been to put all newly arrived male convicts into the chain-gangs to work on the roads under the supervision of soldiers for a certain time and then assign them. "Their employment on the Roads in Irons, in the first instance, would have rendered their assignment to the Settlers a desirable release from a painful and degraded situation; and, in proportion to their dread of being so employed, they would have behaved to their Masters so as to avoid at least being returned to Government."[25] Forbes pointed out that the convicts had only been sentenced to transportation and that it was illegal to put them in irons. It was also illegal for the Government to hire out mechanics or indeed any other convicts. The situation was becoming very complicated. Darling was angered by what he felt to be plain obstruction. "When I took charge of the Government," he wrote in a dispatch, "there was no Order or Rule for the disposal of the convicts. They were given at the caprice of the Civil engineer, to whomsoever and in such numbers as he pleased." He had established the Assignment Board, regulated conditions, called in clearing gangs, and in one year 3350 convicts had been assigned. Now his good work was being destroyed by the legal quibbles of his Chief Justice and the attitude of a section of the Press which, right or wrong, espoused the cause of the convicts.

By a government order of 16th March 1827 all assignment of convicts as servants in Sydney was stopped.[26] A rural life was better for their morals as it offered fewer temptations; it was also better for the community, because it was on farms that the vital work was done. There were now enough expirees to supply servants to the town.

In 1839, however, there were still convict servants in Sydney. Governor Gipps reported:

> Although Assignments for the purposes of Luxury are discontinued, the Convicts formerly assigned for such purposes have not been withdrawn. The Domestic Servants, Grooms, Coachmen and Footmen of the gentlemen of greatest wealth and of most importance in the Colony are still Convicts, and it will certainly require all the power of Government to enforce the wearing of a Convict Badge over their Liveries.[27]

The Home Government upheld the Governor in his claim to retain control over all convicts whether assigned or not, and a Statute was passed in the House of Commons to put it beyond question.[28] But at long last, in 1835, the order came from England to take the irons off convicts.

Meanwhile the assignment system followed its tortuous course. In 1831 the Secretary of State, Goderich, was suggesting a tax on assigned servants of 10s. a year to reduce their competition with the paupers he was sending out as free labourers. A questionnaire was sent to settlers to find out their labour requirements and also to test out whether they would still take assigned servants if the tax were imposed. In 1831 there were 13,400 assigned servants. If the numbers fell to 12,000 the tax would still bring in £6000 a year.[29] The money would be used to bring out immigrants. Governor Bourke thought the idea impracticable. As it was, with their maintenance, the charges for medical treatment, time lost one way and another, and the general poor quality of convict labour, they were not getting cheap servants and a further tax would make it impossible for settlers in a small way to employ any convicts at all. The plan was dropped.

By 1831 a stable code for assignment had been established and it was continued until the end of transportation and all sentences had been worked out. Bourke favoured the abolition of the assignment system, but the economy of the country could not stand this.

Assignment was necessary for the development of the country. As regards the convict it worked variously, sometimes to his advantage, sometimes not. Acting Commissary-General Maddox, reporting in November 1827, was in favour of assignment because it dispersed the convicts; their food was likely to be much better than those in government employ received, for it was natural to suppose that on farms they were given milk, vegetables, and fresh meat. He also supposed that they were kindly and indulgently treated. (This was a change of wind from earlier days when the fear was always that humanity would take the sting out of transportation.) Moreover, Maddox thought that the convict population of New South Wales, unless assigned, would cost the Government more than £80,000 a year for food and clothing alone.[30]

If the assignment system supplied regular labour, tickets of leave, granting the convict near-freedom in return for maintaining himself at no expense to the Government, created a pool of casual labour. It was also an inducement to the convict to be of good behaviour.

Tickets were at first granted by the Governor at his pleasure. Some types of convict were given tickets as soon as they landed, others received them as rewards for good conduct. In the early days a ticket of exemption was issued occasionally for periods of a year. It meant nothing, except that the convict did not have to work for the Government and might live in the house of someone who would be responsible for his conduct. These were soon superseded by tickets of leave. By 1813 their issue was regularized. They became a reward for three years' work either as an assigned servant or for the Government, without incurring a "black mark".

The man with a ticket was still a convict. He was mustered every Sunday and sent to church with other convicts, and if he committed any offence he was punished as a convict and went back to the foot of the ladder. His ticket could be taken from him at any time. He earned his own living, wore his own clothes, had access to any money he might have in the savings bank, and, within certain restrictions, could move about the colony. The granting of tickets was regularized by Brisbane and became an established right. A convict with a seven-year sentence must work for four years for the Government or a master, one with a fourteen-year sentence must work for six years, and a lifer for eight years. Their conduct during the probationary time must have been good and they must have worked under not more than three masters. A convict who was continually being returned to the Government got a bad name. At the end of these probationary periods he had to produce a certificate of good conduct signed by a magistrate, a clergyman, and each of his masters. A master could withhold his certificate in order to retain the use of a good worker.

Governor Darling found the system falling into abuse, as all systems did in a colony where irregularity was the rule. He wrote to Bathurst in May 1826:

> The pretensions of the "Ticket of Leave men" having been encouraged by the indulgences they had been accustomed to receive, and their cause having been advocated by the Newspapers, it appeared to me adviseable to declare the principle, on which it was my intention to act with respect to them, that no individual of that Class would in future be licensed as a Publican or have a Convict assigned to him as a servant.[31]

In January 1827 he published new regulations. Convicts with seven-year sentences were eligible for their tickets after four years with one master or five with two; those with fourteen-year sentences, after six years with one master, eight years with two, or ten years with three; lifers must serve eight years with one master, ten years with two, or twelve with three, unless they could prove that the changes of employment were no fault of their own. Remissions of from six months to two years in these periods were given for catching runaway convicts, bushrangers, and receivers of stolen goods. If all these good deeds were performed the ticket would be granted at once—but it is doubtful if the recipient would greatly enjoy his freedom. The master's certificate of good conduct was no longer indispensable if three magistrates of the district where he worked recommended the prisoner. The recommendation would then go to the Chief Superintendent of Convicts, who would check his records and police records. If after this thorough investigation nothing was found against the man, he received his ticket, but it was valid only in the district where he lived unless he obtained a special pass from a magistrate. He could lose it again if he blotted his copy-book, if he failed to report to the magistrate every quarter, if he did not go to church regularly. Darling felt that now he had drawn the net so tightly that the privilege could not be abused.[32]

In 1831 the number of convicts holding tickets of leave was assessed at 2750, of whom 750 were in Sydney. By the time of Governor Gipps the Governor had no control over the granting of tickets of leave; the whole process was regulated by Statute. After holding a ticket blamelessly for six years a man was eligible for a conditional pardon, and he became free within New South Wales, but might not leave the country. Free, or unconditional pardons, which allowed convicts to return to England whenever they could get a passage, were only given in special circumstances, as when a miscarriage of justice had been discovered, or when a man's conduct had been so exemplary that he won the Governor's favour. Free pardons had to be ratified in England under the Great Seal and were always a matter of grace.

Conditional pardons were used as rewards, particularly in the early days. The first conditional pardon or emancipation was issued to Bloodworth, who founded the brick-making industry in Phillip's time. Arscott, who put out a fire in *Sirius* at the risk of his life, was also emancipated, so were the fourteen convict survivors of the wreck of *Guardian,* and the men who built the first road over the Mountains. The number of pardons varied with the character of each Governor. Macquarie, as one would expect, was a liberal distributor of pardons. In the eleven years of his governorship he granted 352 absolute and 1164 conditional pardons. With the establishment of regular steps to ticket of leave and emancipation, absolute pardons became less frequent.

The great majority of convicts only attained their freedom by working out their sentences, and this was often delayed because indent papers showing the length of sentence had not been sent to Australia. As late as 1828 it was still happening.[33]

So much for the road upwards to reinstatement in society; there was also the road down. Transportation itself was intended as a punishment, and the breaking of all ties, the almost hopeless and very monotonous life led by even the more fortunate and better behaved made it a severe one. To it were added the punishments of hard labour, often in chains, for misdemeanours, and for more serious crimes floggings, re-transportation to a place of secondary punishment, or execution.

From the first foundation of the colony civil courts were set up and convicts committing offences were tried in a correct and legal manner. It is true that the courts had the appearance of courts martial because the only men qualified to sit on the bench were naval and military officers, but justice was not summary or according to military law. (It is also true that magistrates could order "small" punishments for minor offences, as was the rule in England.)

The first Judge-Advocate was not trained to the law, but he followed as far as possible the procedure of English courts. The punishments meted out during Phillip's governorship were mostly very moderate. Stealing was made punishable by death, and that applied also to Marines or any other free persons who robbed the store. In the prevailing famine theft of food was a more serious social offence than it would have been in happier circumstances. The sentence was more often commuted than carried out.

At first justice was even-handed, but by the time of Governor King there was one law for the bond and another for the free. Nevertheless, convicts were always subject to *legal* punishment and, in theory, to no other.

In a government order of 19th February 1802 it is set out that any prisoner who strikes a free man, if convicted before two magistrates, is liable to 200 lashes, whereas any free man who strikes a convict is liable to a fine of £2 and must make a bond of £50, with two sureties of £25 each, to keep the peace.[34] Convicts, having no money, had to pay with their backs.

Convicts who left government work without permission were to have 500 lashes. Sheep-stealing was a hanging matter, but one such thief, caught on 25th December 1802, was reprieved and sent to Norfolk Island for life, because it was Christmas.

Lord Bathurst, writing to Governor Brisbane, instructed him to order corporal punishment *"in special Cases only"* under the Governor's warrant or after conviction before magistrates, "but in no case where milder means can be resorted to with due Effect".[35] A new humanitarian outlook was penetrating officialdom; but even so this was a counsel of perfection and there is no doubt that many sentences were severe to the point of brutality. Chaplain Marsden and Hannibal Macarthur were both known as "flogging" magistrates and justice was all too probably taken into their own hands by some masters. Nicholas Bayly and a man called Matthews, to name only two, were so flagrant in this respect that they were not allowed any more assigned servants. What we know of happenings in transports at sea is a pretty good indication of what went on in the bush. The convict's chief safeguard was that he was more valuable alive than dead and that it was uneconomic to punish him so severely that he could not work, or to feed him so badly that he lost his strength.

Darling found the proceedings of magistrates "irregular", sometimes too harsh, sometimes too lenient. In 1833 there were 1149 floggings with a gross total of 53,038 lashes.[36]

In 1840 Gipps was accused by his enemies of too great lenity,

> . . . the laxity of convict discipline, has increased to such a degree that life and property are exposed to the greatest peril even in the most populous districts. In the more distant parts, bands of Bush rangers plunder and lay waste the Country with impunity. During the late Maitland races, there were upwards of thirty highway Robberies committed within three miles of the Town, most of them between it and the Green hills, and many of them accompanied with bloodshed. On three successive nights, no less than seven burglaries were committed within a mile of the same spot; and it is by no means uncommon for eight or ten fellows well armed and mounted to ride up to a farm in open day, "Call up" the occupants and their servants, and carry off all the valuable property they can find. This has actually happened to three different settlers within 12 Miles of me in the last month.[37]

One must allow for malice in this account, of course. Laxity was the least likely failing to attribute to this able, just, and energetic Governor. There is no doubt, however, that there was endemic lawlessness.

The "milder" punishments advocated by Lord Bathurst would include the treadmill, a useful punishment since the convict laboured for the public good whilst expiating his sins,[38] the wearing of special clothing, like canvas smocks marked with an R for "rogue", the shaving of women's heads, and the stocks.

Flogging was the punishment in ordinary, and was supposed to be carried out with a doctor in attendance. Convicts with heavy sentences, say 1000 lashes, would be flogged, sent to hospital to recover, flogged again, sent to hospital, and so on until the sentence was completed.

More dreaded than the lash, more even than a death sentence, was transportation to a place of secondary punishment, to Norfolk Island, to Port Stephens, to Port Macquarie, to Moreton Bay in New South Wales, or to Macquarie Harbour or Port Arthur in Van Diemen's Land. In these secluded places anything might happen and life quickly became insupportable, breeding crime even worse than that which they were established to punish.

We have the figures for death sentences in 1825 and 1826 and they are not, considering the nature of the colony, particularly high.

	1825	*1826*
Murder	11	8
Burglary	15	8
Rape	2	0
Other felonies	62	30
	90	46

Contemporary sources habitually described the colony as a "sink of iniquity" or peopled by the "worst rascals in the world". Such crimes as petty theft and "absconding" were certainly rife, but the commentators are often a little reminiscent of the fine gentleman delicately holding his none too clean lace handkerchief to his nose as he steps over a gutter.

For incorrigibles or desperate characters unsuited for assignment there were the jail and road gangs. By night they slept in hulks—of these there were at least two, *Supply*, when she became unseaworthy, and *Phoenix*—and by day they worked, heavily chained, hoeing the ground, repairing and building roads, scavenging. . . .

If their work was in the bush they were confined at night in stockades, or "prisoners' boxes", huts on wheels in which from 18 to 24 men were packed and which could be moved from site to site as the road work progressed. The very refuse of the system were employed in the "ironed gangs" on the roads. Darling pointed out that this was a very economical arrangement, since 1260 of the worst prisoners, for whom a new penal settlement would have had to be set up at great cost or who "would have been eating the Bread of Idleness", were thus employed.[39] Their lives were anonymous and miserable in the extreme. To find overseers for these gangs was always a problem. Convict overseers had no authority and were slack, military overseers soon lost their "character as soldiers" from consorting with convicts and had to be withdrawn. The gangs did the hard work the hard way. The problem of these men really began when their sentences ended and they had to be released, without skills and mentally and morally debauched.

The punishment of assigned servants differed a little from that of those in government employ. Their masters were forbidden to punish them, but must take them before a magistrate who would hear the accusation and make such inquiries as he thought necessary. There was often collusion between the magistrate, or Justice of the Peace, and his fellow landowner, the employer of assigned labour. The definition of misdemeanours cited, such as "insolence" which might be by word, act or even intention, was open to abuse. Governor Bourke clipped the power of these magistrates by ruling that one magistrate sitting alone could not sentence a convict to more than fifty lashes. Too much severity, he thought, only made crime worse.[40]

As a supplement to punishment there was a large body of regulations, added to by each Governor, to keep the convicts in order. They were not to move from place to place without the written permission of a magistrate, they must not be abroad at night except on their master's business, they must not sell their clothing or any part of their ration, they must not either buy, sell, or otherwise obtain intoxicating liquor, they must not absent themselves from work, they were not permitted the use of boats under any circumstances . . . and so on and so on. The net was drawn tighter and tighter, but they still found ways to drink, to gamble, to wander, to idle, and to do all the other things they were supposed not to do. In particular they "absconded", or ran away, but rarely successfully. The nature of the country did not lend itself to escape, the aborigines did not want to be burdened with men who lacked the skill to find their own food. He who ran away had three alternatives: to return if he could find his way, to die in the bush, or to turn bushranger, eking out a short and precarious living by theft.

The management of convicts was complicated by the different types of prisoner. The ones who gave the most trouble were the women. There was a great scarcity of women in the colony and the Home Government was very worried about it. The disparity between the sexes could only lead to more trouble. Phillip was empowered to bring in women from the Friendly Islands, but did not do so because he already had too many mouths to feed. In 1820 it was claimed that there were still fifteen men to every woman in the colony.[41] The women in the First Fleet seem to have been an abandoned lot, to any who had shreds of decency left Phillip offered his personal protection. Those who came later were not much better, with exceptions, of course, such as Elizabeth Parry, who is described as of "exemplary behaviour" and was given her freedom when she married James Ruse, the first settler. Governors were always anxious to get rid of the women convicts either by assigning them as servants or by marriage. Marriage was encouraged and married convicts were given children in their own huts. Many of the marriages solemnized were illegal certain indulgences, including the right to live with their wives and because one or other party was already married in England. Steps had to be taken to prevent emancipated or time-expired convicts from returning to England, leaving their colonial families to be a burthen on the Government.

There was always a residue of women convicts who were unsuitable either for marriage or assignment. Governor Hunter complained that the "vast number of women for whom we have little work are a heavy weight upon the store of Government".[42] They were set to sewing, which they did badly; they were employed as hut-keepers to prepare the meals and do the cleaning for groups of working convicts. This, naturally, was open to abuse.

A Female Factory was built at Parramatta for reception of the women who could not be placed and as a temporary residence for those who had just landed, a refuge of sorts between one assignment and another. This factory, or prison, was very primitive.

> The old Female Factory was a plague spot. It consisted of a long room over the gaol, a few sheds and the upper floor of a small wooden house. The long room was used for spinning; it had a fireplace where the women cooked their food and here some of them, who could find no other roof, slept on heaps of greasy wool beside their work. There were two windows at each end of the room with wooden bars, looking into the prison yards. The boards of the floor were warped and open in large cracks through which the women could talk to the prisoners below, and down which the water fell if an attempt to wash the floors were made. Walls and floor were perpetually filthy. Nor were conditions any better in the wooden house. Here new arrivals might lay down their bedding while they looked for lodging. Men convicts occupied the ground floor and nothing but their absent chivalry kept them from mounting the stairs. By night the supervision of the factory was left to a constable, himself a convict, whose pay consisted of a ration and a half, insufficient reward to guarantee much vigilance. . . . The squalor and promiscuity of these arrangements can be imagined. . . .[43]

Macquarie, with the co-operation of Greenway, the architect, built a new factory over the river.

> It was a large three-storied building designed to house 300 women. There were dormitories with twenty double beds in each of them, two large bare "living" rooms in the basement, a library without books, two small rooms and a dispensary called the hospital, weaving, spinning and carding rooms, cells for solitary confinement and a cupola in the roof for ventilation and ornament. It was "dry, healthy, cheerful," but the laundries and wash houses had been forgotten, the privies drained into the river and so much loam had been mixed in the cement that the building was crumbling before it was finished. It cost some £6000 and was built by contract. Greenway had designed it and had intended adding to its architectural interest with a handsome circular staircase—that little bit of sweetness that he tried to slip into even his most prosaic buildings—but Commissioner

Bigge vetoed it as too ornamental and costly. In any case he felt that the building was far too fine and did not smack sufficiently of punishment. It stood on the edge of its large barren grounds as if straining across the river to the settlement. In summer the river was often nearly dry, and at most times was fordable, so the factory's isolation was not as complete as desired. The women washed in the stream the cloth they wove and spread it to bleach on the sunburnt grass.[44]

The convict women themselves preferred the noisome old factory; it offered more opportunities for entertainment.

Governor Brisbane gives a depressing picture of the women. "On the day of debarkation, they have always been dressed in their Navy board clothing; the petticoats of which are so short, however, as to oblige them for decency to wear their own clothes underneath." Those who committed crimes after landing were sent to the Factory and the Governor proposed "to lodge these in a secluded apartment, and employ them on a tread-wheel".[45]

There were frequently riots at the Factory and it had a very ill name. If the women got drunk "all the Soldiers here would not keep them in Order", Brisbane reported. There were at that time six hundred of them at the Factory, many with young children, living in squalor and without a proper water supply.

Elizabeth Fry, the Quakeress famous for her good work amongst prisoners, wrote to Under-Secretary Horton about the female convicts in Van Diemen's Land. They should be housed in a new building, she said, presided over by a matron and equipped with a school. She was particularly interested in their clothing. It should be "strong and decent", not particoloured. "We consider that it would be a great advantage . . . that the women should wear a simple uniform dress; and we think it *indispensable* for establishing of order and for enforcing the needful regulations on board the ship that a Matron be stationed constantly therein. . . ."[46] Mrs Fry had not visited Australia.

Governor Darling placed the Factory under a board; staff salaries were to be paid in money and not augmented with percentages of work done by the inmates, and the women's rations were to be improved and divided into three classes according to the virtue, or lack of it, of the recipients. A hospital was to be attached to the Factory. Children over four years were to be taken from the Factory and put in the Orphan School. He was also determined to marry off as many of the women as possible, preferably to mechanics in government employ.

The Factory by 1822 was established as the first "weaving establishment" in the colony and the Government Auditor was worrying about costs.

Inspired by Elizabeth Fry, a committee of ladies was formed to help women convicts along the road to reformation. It did not last long. The convicts were too tough. The board of management was replaced by a committee of gentlemen, including the surgeon and chaplain resident in Parramatta. Discipline remained bad and strong measures were taken, the worst women being set to break stones for the roads.[47]

In 1828 Lord Glenelg expressed himself as "deeply impressed with the importance of rendering the existing system of transportation as effectual as possible for the reformation of the Offenders", and being

> . . . sensible how great must be the effect on the general interests of the Colony of women were all together in a spacious yard, surrounded with sheds or out-acquire a permanent settlement among the free Inhabitants, I feel it an imperative duty to leave no means untried, by which the moral discipline to which they are subjected while convicts, may be rendered as effectual as possible.[48]

These were creditable sentiments, but they boiled down to appointing in England a matron for the Factory.

Conditions continued as before. Gipps found fifty women herded into each room of the factory and hoped that a new matron would improve the situation. In 1838, on a visit of inspection, he was impressed by the cleanliness and manners of the women, *but*:

> With the exception of a few employed in cooking, washing, or other such necessary employment, they were all in absolute idleness. The 3rd or penal class of the character and habits of the Females, who after a limited term of servitude buildings, into and out of which they passed freely and at their pleasure. In another yard, there was a considerable heap of stones, which had been brought there for the purpose of being broken up for the repair of roads; but I was informed they could not be employed on this work for want of hammers, or rather for the want of handles to their hammers, as they destroyed them faster than they could be supplied. The women of the 2nd class, or those who have children under their charge, were in a separate yard, smaller than that of the 3rd class, but differing from it very little in other respects. And the women of the 1st Class, or those who are eligible for assignment, were in a third yard.[49]

They lived in miserable discomfort.

> On three sides of each room [dormitory] . . . there are numerous windows; but, as scarcely a pane of glass remains in any one of them, the floors are wetted to a considerable distance whenever rain falls, and, if there happen to be a drifting wind accompanying the rain, it is necessary to huddle the mattresses together as closely as possible on the opposite side from that by which it enters, in order to keep them dry.[50]

Gipps with his usual energy set to work to remedy the situation. He built a new block containing 72 single cells, costing £2580 or £36 for each cell. He surrounded the building with a new high wall. His aim was to establish the "American Separate System", at that time the last word in penitentiary reform. He announced that "order, cleanliness, perfect obedience and *silence* may be said to prevail in the Establishment to a degree scarcely surpassed in any Prison in England".[51] He put the women to work. They made nets out of twine for fishing and for throwing over fruit-trees to save the fruit from the birds. But no one bought them, so that idea was abandoned. Lady Gipps and her housekeeper instructed them in needlework, but at this they earned only £30 in three months. They made clothes to order, straw hats and bonnets, and about a third of them were so employed. Gipps suggested that no more slops be sent from England, only the cloth, and the women convicts could make it up. The best behaved women were organized into groups of nine, elected their forewomen, and gave an account of their work every Saturday. They earned about £700 a year and one-sixth of this was returned to them, in the form of tea, sugar, and other luxuries, to encourage them. The rougher women were still unemployed. From the beginning of 1839 they were put to doing the washing from the barracks and hospital. If there was time to spare they could take in private washing. In the last resort they were to pick oakum. In October 1840 there were 970 women in the factory. The female establishment at Moreton Bay had been broken up and its inmates brought to Parramatta. Competition from free labour and the prevailing drought and its consequent depression made it difficult to assign them. Their children were numerous and an infant school was set up at the factory to teach them, or at least keep them out of mischief and leave their mothers free to work. They went to this school when they were a year old and stayed until they were three or four or whenever the overcrowded Orphan School could take them.

It was always difficult to get suitable staff, whether sent from England or appointed locally. They got in league with the contractors and robbed the Government or they became involved in scandals. In 1847 Mr and Mrs Smythe, the storekeeper and matron at Parramatta, were dismissed because they had "committed a gross breach of the Regulations of the Factory by giving a Ball within its precincts, which led to scenes of intoxication, riot and insubordination among the women under confinement".[52]

Gipps disapproved of the assignment of women convicts, and Lord Stanley at the Colonial Office was concerned about their welfare. It was very difficult to get them respectable employment. When it was known that they were convicts they were all too likely to be subjected to insults and violence. The safest thing seemed to be to keep them in an institution where the Government could "throw the shield of its protection around them".[53] Yet in the factories regeneration was almost impossible. Many of the women were hardened and violent criminals and they led the others astray. On one occasion a section of the women rioted at Parramatta.

The police could not control them and the military had to be called in. But for heavy rain, the buildings would probably have been burnt down. The institution and its inhabitants were a source of fear and loathing to the free, respectable citizens.

The female factories in Hobart and Launceston were even worse, overcrowded and ill-managed.

The secret was that there was never enough money or sufficient personnel of the right type to turn the female factories into model institutions. The inmates beat the system. The redeemable amongst the women convicts married or became steady servants, and, as their sentences expired, were lost to view in the colony's increasingly free population. The incorrigibles, too, had in time to be released upon the community and find their own level therein.

Another class of convict that was looked at askance by authority was the few educated men. They were not fit for work in the gangs or on government farms; employed as clerks they often turned out badly. Special treatment caused discontent. As a sample, Michael Robinson, a Cambridge undergraduate, was sent out for writing threatening letters. Hunter gave him a ticket of leave, Macquarie favoured him even to the extent of inviting him to Government House, where on the King's birthday he recited odes of his own composition. Judge-Advocate Richard Dore took him as his clerk and solicited a conditional pardon for him. Yet, with all to gain, he continued his career as a criminal. He was convicted of perjury intended to pervert the course of justice and sentenced to transportation to Norfolk Island for seven years. Some, of course, like Greenway, proved an asset to the colony. Governor Brisbane took no risks, he segregated the educated convicts at Bathurst.

Governor Gipps employed them as keepers of the Meteorological Journal in stations at South Head, Port Macquarie, and Melbourne. For this work they were each paid 1s. 6d. a day, in lieu of rations. An argument eventually arose as to who should pay the 1s. 6d. The Colonial Government thought it should fall on the Home Government, as the journals were sent to England for use there. The Home Government thought that the Colonial Government should pay, as the stations were local establishments and the information collated was published in the Government Gazette. It was just another of those interminable disagreements.

Political prisoners belonged to the same class, but were not criminal. The danger with them was not that of lapsing into felony but, more seriously, of combining together and inciting others to sedition.

The Scottish Martyrs were the first of this class to be sent out.[54] They arrived in 1794 and Grose received instructions to search their baggage for seditious literature and "keep a watchful eye over their conduct".[55] They were not to be assigned, neither were they to be a burden on the store. Hunter found them living lives "quiet, retired and as much at their ease as men in their circumstances can be supposed to be; yet they do not appear satisfied with their situation here considered as compulsory. They can have no other cause for dislike."[56]

Their fires were not even banked down. They considered the "vindication of our personal and absolute freedom to be our bounden duty", and, "Even freedom as an indulgence we would spurn."[57]

Muir escaped in the American ship *Otter*. Joseph Gerrald died of a broken heart. He was given permission to buy a small house and garden. "Here he saw his friends, and was visited by the surgeon, but he was soon pronounced in a rapid consumption, of which he died on the 16th day of March, 1796."[58] "Mr William Skirving, a very decent, quiet, and industrious man, who had purchased a farm already cleared, and was indefatigable in his attentions to its improvement, just as the labour of the harvest was near over, was seized with a violent dysentery of which he died on 19th of March, 1796."[59] The remaining martyrs, Fyshe Palmer and Margarot, "who live quiet and retired",[60] had the added humiliation of being charitably taken onto the store, for no help came from friends at home. Margarot, the fiery one, lived to give evidence in England before the Select Committee on Transportation in 1812.

The Irish, who came out in droves after 1791, were for the most part ignorant, credulous, and truculent. Hunter complained of them in February 1798. They were

> . . . so turbulent, so dissatisfied with their situation here, so extremely insolent, refractory, and troublesome, that, without the most rigid and severe treatment, it is impossible for us to receive any labour whatever from them. Your Grace will see the inconvenience which so large a proportion of that ignorant, obstinate and depraved set of transports occasion in this country. . . .[61]

They brought excitement and fantasy into the drab scene. Some of them believed that there was, somewhere in the interior, an earthly paradise where white men lived but did not work. Was this a last faint echo from Marco Polo? They stole two mares and tried to escape, but were brought back. Sixty more conceived the idea of reaching China overland and put it into action. Twenty of them were caught and brought back. "Some of these fellows had been provided with a figure of a compass drawn upon paper, which, with written instructions, was to have assisted them as their guide."[62] Caught, they tried again. Hunter, to disillusion them, sent the hardiest of them on a journey of exploration into the country "with three experienced guides". But the dream still held, they plotted to murder the guides and go off with the supplies.[63] Hunter sent them again, this time with soldiers. They saw the country and how little it had to offer, but faith lived on. Another party of Irish made a break, this time for Botany Bay, and would have perished there but for the hundred-to-one chance of a boat's being in the bay.[64] All through Hunter's governorship and until 1804 they simmered with rebellion. There were rumours of ploughshares turned into pikes, of plots with secret signs and passwords and all the panoply of intrigue, nights of terror in Parramatta, the arming of a Volunteer Association, plotters caught and punished, others taking their place, romantic, reckless and inept. At last it came in 1804, a rising at Castle Hill, suppressed by Brevet-Major Johnston more by guile than feat of arms.[65] Then came the punishments. Joseph Holt, an Irish aristocrat, was named their general and, protesting his innocence—What would he have to do with such canaille? He was not even of their faith—was punished with the rest. It was all nebulous, but the punishments were real. After that the Irish lost heart. Though still numerous, their warhead was lost in the increasing population.

Boys—and some as young as eleven were sent out under sentence—were given preferential treatment. In New South Wales they were kept in Sydney at the carters' barracks near the Brickfields. Here there were a carpenter, a shoemaker, a stone-cutter, a blacksmith, and other tradesmen, and to them the boys were apprenticed. The product of their labour went into the public store and a small pool of much needed mechanics was created.[66] In Van Diemen's Land Governor Arthur set up a similar establishment, Point Puer, near Port Arthur, which was described as a model prison.

Men who were old and infirm were set to work with the women or, like them, made hut-keepers. In theory no man over fifty or suffering from any incurable disease was to be transported, but like all rules this one was frequently broken.

There was great diversity amongst the convicts; some came from India, some from the Cape; there were Frenchmen left over from the wars, even Negroes, including the redoubtable Caesar. And some of them had very curious stories, like that of the two John Gradys, one a lifer, the other on a seven-year sentence. Naturally the sentences were switched over in the records. There was the stranger case of Alexander Lockage, alias William Edwards. He came out in 1819 in the ship *Atlas* and for crimes committed on shipboard was sent to Newcastle, then a place of secondary punishment. He met with an accident, being crushed by a log of cedar, which incapacitated him for hard labour. He was brought to hospital in Sydney and when he had recovered worked as a clerk in the lumber-yard and at the prisoners' barracks. He was trusted and finally entered the service of Judge Wylde. On the night of Wylde's death he escaped with a lot of money and was not found. Years later a convict, William Edwards, was sent from the Cape. He was identified by his scars as Lockage,[67] and was sent to Port Macquarie, and then to Wellington

Valley as punishment for absconding. Sherwell, "An English gentleman", then confessed that he had recently met the real Lockage. Edwards ran away from Wellington Valley in an effort to reach Sydney and prove that he was not Lockage. His wife pleaded his cause in vain, even writing to the Secretary of State. No one believed Edwards, who was sent to Norfolk Island where, in despair, he committed suicide. Darling granted the penniless widow £80 so that she could return to the Cape.[68] The case was a very curious one and engaged the attention of Sir George Murray, the Secretary of State for the Colonies, himself. Darling was ordered to make a very close examination, but to this day it is not certain that Lockage and Edwards were identical.

The sorrows of Henry Russell were brought to light by Marsden, who recommended him for pardon.

> This Petitioner was recommended to me by the Proctor of the University of Oxford. His crime was for passing a one pound forged Note. Mr Pearson informed me that it was the opinion of the University that Russell did not know the note was forged, and he was detained in Oxford Castle for six years, in the hope of procuring his pardon; but the Bank of England interfered, and prevented this being done. Russell has been an industrious man in the Colony.[69]

These are only glimpses; the stories could be multiplied a hundredfold.

The daily life of convicts differed so much according to circumstances and from decade to decade that it is difficult to give a picture of it.

The majority worked for the Government in the early days of the system, but there were fewer and fewer so employed as assignment became almost universal and public works were carried out by contract. The status of the assigned servant, as of the Roman slaves, varied infinitely, and his treatment ran the whole gamut from brutality to a benevolence that made his lot as comfortable as that of a free man.

We have a fairly comprehensive picture of the work of those in government employment contained in a report drawn up by Major Ovens in 1824. There was, at that time, a great concentration of convicts in Sydney, employed in two big workshops, the lumber-yard and the timber-yard adjoining it. In the lumber-yard the metal-working trades were carried on and government materials were stored. The convicts worked on a task, or piece, system. In the timber-yard beams and floor-boards were sawn and prepared, also by piece-work, and all wood had to be accounted for to a storekeeper. Any excess products were sold at auction. It was more difficult, Major Ovens pointed out, to fix the tasks for outdoor gangs, since the weather and the accessibility of timber had to be taken into account. Besides, since a convict only received half a free man's ration, very much exertion could not be expected of him.

At the dockyard about seventy men were employed, mainly in ship repairs. In addition there were a number of gangs classified by trades, for example, the carpenters' gang of about fifty men, including cabinet-makers, turners, shinglers; the bricklayers' gang, which was small, varying between five and ten men (each bricklayer was expected to lay 4500 bricks a week); the sawyers' gang of up to twenty-five men who worked in two pits in the timber-yard stacking the timber in the middle of the yard to season; the brick-makers' gang of about fifteen men, with boy assistants, which operated a kiln 22 feet long by 18 feet high producing 24,000 bricks at one raking; the pasterers' gang, which also undertook whitewashing and stucco work; the quarry gang, which worked at the government quarries in the "Domain and at Cockle Creek", producing flagstones, hearth-stones, and mantelpieces, as well as building blocks; the wheelwrights' gang with coopers attached; the shoemakers' gang of about eight men, each of whom was supposed to produce a pair of shoes a day from leather tanned at the government establishment at Cawdor; a brass-founders' gang, and a tailors' gang. Gangs were also sent out to garden, cut grass, dig foundations, carry grain. . . .

This was the moment of highest organization. From 1825 onwards the policy was to get convicts out of the town and to disperse them amongst private masters. All gangs were gradually abandoned, except the "ironed gang", which was retained for punishment.

In 1824 a convict's weekly ration was 7 pounds of beef or 4 pounds of pork, 7 pounds of flour or wheaten meal, 3 pounds of maize meal, and half a pound of sugar. A woman received half this ration and a child a quarter of it. Every six months clothing was issued: a pair of trousers, a jacket or frock, a pair of shoes. Each convict had a hammock and a blanket.[70] Working hours were from 5 a.m. in summer or daylight in winter until 3 p.m. At places of secondary punishment it was from dawn to dark. The £10 a year paid to assigned servants in Macquarie's time was overtime, the value of their work from 3 p.m. to dark.

All these factors were variable. In times of scarcity the ration was reduced and less work was expected of the convicts. As time went on the ration was improved and included salt and soap. Often, most particularly during Hunter's governorship, the store ran out of clothing and the convicts, and the soldiery as well, were reduced to rags. Rations were always issued raw and the convict must find some means of cooking them, sometimes of grinding wheat into flour as well.

Until 1819 there was no provision for housing convicts except those that were being punished in jail. After 3 p.m. they were free to work for themselves and earn the 5s. or 10s. a week to rent sleeping space in another convict's hut, or they might be allowed to sleep in a free settler's outhouse in return for cutting wood, gardening, or some such service. The most feckless sheltered under rocks or in any other cranny they could find. Macquarie built four convict barracks, the largest, the Hyde Park barracks, in Macquarie Street. There were smaller barracks at the brick-fields (the carters' barracks), and adjoining the timber-yard, and one at Parramatta. In December 1819 there were about a thousand convicts living in barracks in Sydney and another 594, mostly married men with families, finding their own lodgings, generally huts or shanties that they had built themselves. Sydney was safer at night with most of its criminal population locked up, but their labour was a sad loss to the citizens, for, logically, when they did not have to pay rent the Government claimed their services until sunset.

All convicts, regardless of creed, had to attend church every week unless they were more than five miles from a place of worship. This was impossible, of course, even had they not used their wiles to dodge this duty. There were not enough churches or big enough ones to hold them all. If seen wandering during church time they could be arrested.

Life in the places of secondary punishment was very much harder and more monotonous than in Sydney. It was less easy to evade the rules, there were no diversions, and spirits were unprocurable. Nor did the convict have any support from public opinion. The rigorous life told on the nerves of the guards as surely as it did on the convicts', but they could find relief in drinking and in punishing those in their power. Assignment had one great thing in its favour. Under it, convicts were part of a normal life. Even if they were themselves restricted, more in theory than in fact, they were not cut off from the living world.

When a convict had been pardoned or had served his sentence he still remained a problem. Technically ex-convicts fell into the two classes of emancipists and expirees, but they coalesced in the face of free men into one party. In theory, having expiated their crimes, they were again free men, but society in a penal settlement was very tetchy about such matters. Those who had come to Australia free looked on the fact as a valuable asset. They, if they had any capital or the wit to make it, were the aristocracy. Macquarie, in an effort to break the monopoly of the officer class, built up the emancipists. The community was soon sharply divided into exclusionists and emancipists. The exclusionists not only would not have any social dealings with ex-convicts, but wished to keep all privileges and opportunities for their own class. To Macquarie it was the exclusionists who were the intruders in the penal settlement. Again and again he insisted on the rights of the emancipist:

It has been my Invariable Opinion and upon that Opinion I have acted ever since I came to this Colony, that, Once a convict has become a Free Man, either by Servitude, Free Pardon or Emancipation, he should in All Respects be Considered on a footing with every other Man in the Colony, according to his Rank in Life and Character. In Short, that no Retrospect should in any case be had to his having been a Convict. . . .[71]

The Secretary of State agreed, but coolly. Legally what Macquarie said was true, but was his policy expedient? Feeling ran very high indeed. The exclusionist party comprised officers, officials, wealthy free men and merchants; the emancipists were the farmers, the traders, the adventurers. It would seem that never the twain would meet. There were curious exceptions, of course. The fashionable school to which most of the exclusionists sent their sons was run by a mealy-mouthed ex-convict, Dr Halloran, who had been, and continued, a rogue.

Lord Bathurst, in a dispatch of 29th July 1823, took up the vexed question with Governor Brisbane.

. . . I must advert to the very delicate point of the manner and degree in which those persons who have been in the situation of Convicts should be received into Society, and called upon to exercise the various functions which attach to the possession of property; I allude to the Magistracy, and such other duties as they may be entitled to discharge by law, but which they can only be called upon to perform by the appointment of the Executive Government.

His lordship felt that it would be unpolitic to discourage the now powerful emancipist class. In principle, their members were entitled to sit on the bench, but Brisbane would be well advised not to appoint them. "The only positive direction, that I feel disposed to give, would be that, in order to uphold the magistracy of the settlement, you will not appoint any person, who has been a Convict to that important situation, until he shall have acquired weight and consideration by the meritorious dicharge of other civil employments." The Governor must be discreet and not make it an issue. Time would heal the factions, as indeed it did.[72]

In 1845 there was still in practice, though perhaps not in theory, one law for the free and another for ex-convicts, whether emancipists or ex-pirees. If one of the latter committed an offence he could be, and was, more heavily punished than a man who had never been a convict. He was imprisoned when a free settler was only fined. He could even be sent to the "ironed gang", as if he were still a convict.[73]

Emancipists had to win their right to lesser offices and to sit on juries. However, in a dispatch dated 13th May 1846, Gladstone, then at the Colonial Office, gave a definite ruling. The ex-convict was to be treated in the courts no differently from any other free man. This was six years after transportation had ceased.

A new class, the native-born, was coming into existence and it gradually brought together the two sections. The great wave of migrants brought by gold washed the slate clean at last.

Public opinion as a brake on the treatment of convicts was never quite lacking. As the emancipists and expirees increased in numbers they formed, if not exactly a convict party, at least a body of men, some of them wealthy, able and vocal, who could understand and sympathize with the lot of the prisoners. When in the 1820s a free and very outspoken Press grew up in Sydney at least one of the newspapers, the *Monitor,* espoused the cause of the convicts and advertised their wrongs.

More important was the attitude of the liberal-minded Chief Justice, Francis Forbes. He attacked the legality of sending convicts to places of secondary punishment and of working them in irons. Their sentences had been given in England; it was not for the Governor, or anyone else, to change them. Had it been the intention of the English or Irish Courts to sentence them to hard labour in irons it would have been recorded. Judge Stephen took up the cudgels too. The *Monitor,* delighted, quoted him as saying "that the rights of Prisoners were as sacred in the Eye of the Law as those of Free Men, and, while he had the honor of sitting where he did, he would never allow them to be impugned or treated carelessly".[74] Forbes's attitude was legalistic. Whilst he supported the convicts' rights in certain directions he also deemed it illegal for the Governor to exercise any control over them once they had been assigned as servants, thus taking from them their only protection against unjust and brutal masters. He went on to declare tickets of leave and conditional pardons illegal for the same reasons. In a strictly legal sense no doubt he was right, but had he had his way the convict would have been deprived of any hope of bettering his condition before the expiration of his sentence and the labour market in the colony would have been seriously affected.

The Governors were, with some reservations regarding Bligh and King, a fine set of men, none of whom threw in their lot with the exclusionist or anti-convict party. Their personal influence was on the side of lenity and humanity, they restrained the powerful and protected the weak. The penal colony was exceptionally fortunate in having the services of such men. Instances of brutality can easily be collected, but it was never condoned in high places. An assigned servant had redress against the master who ill-treated him if he commanded the courage and intelligence to seek it. The governors had poor material to work with and were often forced to nominate men as magistrates and justices of the peace who would never have been appointed in England, for the simple reason that their choice was very limited. Free settlers were often adventurers, or get-rich-quick experts, who in no way resembled the landed gentry of England from whom the magistracy was chosen. Naval and military officers, particularly the former, were more impartial than the landowners, but they had their duties to attend to. There was no leisured and secure class from which the governors could expect co-operation and honorary service. Yet they were expected to carry on as if Australia were as well equipped as

England. Quarrels between magistrates and other public figures were wholesome in that they dragged a lot of dirty linen out into the light of day. Abuses were exposed, often for no higher motive than the satisfaction of a private grudge, but exposed they were.

Assistance came to the convict from the Imperial Government. To Lord Bathurst, eighteen years Secretary of State for the Colonies, redemption and reform were matters of moment in which he differed considerably from Lord Sydney, whose one intention seemed to be to rid England of her surplus convicts. Lord Stanley showed himself anxious for reform regardless of expense, and so did many other Secretaries of State. Awareness of the problems of the penal settlement was constantly growing and found expression in the Select Committee on Transportation of 1812, whose proceedings give an instructive picture of the settlement from a number of angles. In 1838 another Select Committee examined the question and resulted in the abandonment of transportation to New South Wales in 1840. A Select Committee on Finance in 1798 looked into the affairs of the colony *inter alia*. Bigge's reports following his inspection of 1819, biased though they were, provided a general stock-taking.

The general attitude of the Home Government to its ugly duckling was liberal, if doctrinaire. Official ideas of reformation were curiously artificial, they swing between Bigge's recommendation of five stages of purification, beginning with the harshest conditions and gradually working towards a normal life, and schemes for segregation and the benefits to be received from country life.

In 1827 the convict establishment was separated from the civil establishment in New South Wales; in short, it ceased to be a penal settlement and became a colony in which His Majesty's Government maintained an open-air jail.[75] There was a complicated parting of brass rags. The colony was to become financially self-supporting and the Home Government was to continue to pay for the convicts.

In 1827 the colony had a revenue of approximately £77,072 0s. 9d.; the estimated cost of the convict establishment was £51,106 3s. 4d. a year, and of the military £52,226 18s. 11d. a year. There were £20,000 worth of commissariat stores in hand.[76] The Military Chest became the treasury for the convict establishment and any money earned by convicts was paid into it. Parliamentary estimates were abolished. The colonial legislature was to manage its own revenue.

It took years to disentangle the two establishments, the main contention being the upkeep of jails and police. The Home Government unloaded these on the Colonial Government, and the citizens were wrath. It was the convicts and expirees who made it necessary to employ so many police. It remained a sore subject until the end of transportation. The Governor was the head of both establishments.

This separation was the prelude to the abolition of transportation. The colony had become a source of wealth, the sheep industry had attracted well-to-do and educated settlers who were unwilling to resign the social and political rights which they had enjoyed in England. The whole free population, whether imported or native born, was the more anxious for self-government, because of the convicts in their midst. Agitation for an elected assembly began as early as 1825, a free Press kept the issue alive in the public mind. The Imperial Government had learnt a lesson in America, it did not want to lose Australia now that it was a valuable source of raw material. The will to conciliate and advance was not entirely, perhaps not even mostly, pecuniary. England had swung towards liberalism. She believed, with the rest of Europe, in the efficacy of constitutional self-government. It was impossible to give it to a penal settlement. The alternative was to abolish transportation. Governor Bourke advised it. He realized that the Legislative Council represented only one party in the colony and was outmoded.[77] The population of the towns, already far outnumbering the rural population, was eager to be rid of transportation, which they felt as an insult. There were many free workers, and they, too, wished to be rid of convict competition in the labour market. The squatters naturally wanted a continuing supply of cheap labour and its quality mattered little. It is curious that the men who by grazing the Merino made Australia a fit subject for self-government were the ones who desired the continuance of a system which made self-government impossible. They were overridden. In 1840 by an Order in Council, as it had begun, so was transportation to New South Wales abolished.

When Governor Gipps announced in November 1839 to the Legislative Council that transportation was about to cease and published the information in the *Sydney Gazette*:

> The Settlers in general were so well prepared for the event that but little excitement was produced by the announcement of it; the Public Press affected for the most part to rejoice at it; and the discontent of those, who have always been the advocates of Transportation, was manifested principally in reproaches against the Government for having made the support of the Police and Gaol a charge upon the Land Fund, instead of appropriating it, as they assert the Government was pledged to do, to the importation of Free Laborers, who will now more than ever be required in the Colony.[78]

The momentous news was, when it came, a damp squib.

Transportation did not stop as suddenly as it began. The Home Government still wanted to get rid of convicts, sections of the community in Australia still wanted their labour. The various schemes to continue it in another form generally had a gloze upon them. In 1842 Sir James Graham and Lord Stanley, the Secretary of State for the Colonies, planned to send out boy convicts (juvenile delinquents were still unknown), after disciplining at Parkhurst Jail, because, Stanley remarked rather naively, they "should not be turned loose upon the world in England". They would be pardoned before embarkation, but they were to be kept at Point Puer where, it was hoped, the disciplinary routines of Parkhurst would be copied. A year later the scheme was re-presented in a slightly different form. The Legislative Council thought these settlers would be "by no means beneficial to the Colony" and the idea had to be dropped.[79]

In 1844 the Home Government was suggesting "exiles" to relieve the labour shortage. They were really convicts, hastily pardoned and transported. They were to go straight to a labour pool, or separate community, and be held there until work was found for them. "Such a Community, though seldom consisting long of the same numerical strength, might yet be always numerous enough to demand superintendence, Medical care, and Religious Instruction. . . . The fundamental principle of every such Settlement should be that it is the temporary receptacle, not the permanent abode, of its Inmates."[80] Thereafter it was hoped that they would be fused with the population. This plan did not appeal to Governor Gipps. He was anxious that nothing should be done which would affront his subjects' moral sense.[81] As labour was scarcer in Port Phillip district, it was decided to send some "exiles" there.[82] The need was so great that some 1600 men in all were snapped up by employers and disappeared into the population.

In 1846 Gladstone approached the subject again with a profusion of tact;

> Her Majesty's Government sympathise with the impatience of the Colonists of New South Wales under the system which prevailed there some years ago; and can well understand that the recurrence of that system, the resumption of transportation to that Colony on a scale even faintly resembling the former one must be regarded with a just jealousy and alarm. But the question is essentially and entirely different. Whether it might not be a measure favorable to the material fortunes of New South Wales, and unattended with injury to its higher interests to introduce either directly from England at the commencement of their sentences, or from Van D. Land at some period during their course, a number of Prisoners, small in comparison with the number which was carried to the Colony under the former system of transportation, and smaller still of course relatively to the augmented population among whom they would now be dispersed.

The colonists would receive material, the convicts moral, advantage. If the Legislative Council wished they could be kept in gangs under close supervision, releasing free labour from road work and other heavy toil.[83]

The Legislative Council declined the sugared pill. The Home Government returned to the attack, suggesting just a few ticket-of-leave men to relieve the labour shortage.[84] Only hand-picked men were offered, of course. The question of the "exiles" was being thrashed out right up until 1850.

The arrival of the ship *Hashemy* with convicts caused, in 1848, a near-riot in Sydney. The citizens of the towns, who far outnumbered those who lived in the bush, had a deep-rooted repugnance for any type of semi-slave labour. There was now a large body of free workers who resented any suggestion that convict labour should be brought out to compete with them. The Legislative Council, having embarked on a policy of free immigration, believed, and with reason, that it would be difficult to induce immigrants to come out if they thought transportation was to be re-introduced.

The discovery of gold laid the ghost of the system in the eastern colonies for ever. The Imperial Government now resigned all intention of sending "exiles", or any other type of convict, to New South Wales. Why give felons a free ticket to Eldorado?

The squatters, who would have liked a mild form of transportation to continue, enough to supply their fairly low labour requirements, had to look elsewhere. In 1841 the assignment system was abolished, which meant that they could not keep even their convict shepherds as cheap labour. Foreseeing this, in 1840 they were petitioning for permission to import hill coolies from India. The Land and Emigration Board opposed the idea. It would be nearly as expensive to bring coolie labour from India or China as free workmen from England, and the coolies would have to be taken home again when their indentures ran out. They would come without their womenfolk and the disproportion of the sexes would be still further increased. Most important, they would lower the standard of living and impair "the tone of activity and enterprise which has hitherto so eminently characterised this colony".[85]

Once more Australia escaped the embarrassment of a brindled population.

Meanwhile the convict establishments were being wound up. Goat Island, in Sydney Harbour, where numbers of convicts had been employed building a powder magazine, ceased to be a convict depot about 1840. It was too small to accommodate many and once the magazine was built there was no work for them.

All those of good behaviour were given their tickets of leave and for some of them the Government brought their wives and children from England, in the hope that this would induce them to reform and to live normal lives.

Convicts to whom this indulgence could not be given were confined at Cockatoo Island at the mouth of the Parramatta River. Here they worked in irons excavating "siloes . . . in the solid rock, shaped like a large bottle, and capable of holding from 3,000 to 5,000 bushels [of wheat] each",[86] cutting building stone to be used in Sydney, and constructing a dockyard. Being surrounded by deep water, only one of these men, loaded with irons as they were, ever escaped from this prison. In 1847 there were still about 213 prisoners on the island.[87]

In 1847 Norfolk Island ceased to be a penitentiary and Van Diemen's Land had reached saturation point. Governor Sir Charles FitzRoy was told that he must punish all convicts who needed it locally and not get rid of his incorrigibles by sending them to the unfortunate island.

In 1846 the treadmill had been closed down in Sydney and the Government was saved £500 a year for its upkeep. It was removed to the new Darlinghurst Jail. The establishment at the carters' barracks had already been broken up and convict buildings everywhere were being annexed for military and government purposes. In 1848 the Female Factory at Parramatta was converted into a hospital for paupers and lunatics. Only Cockatoo Island remained a convict station and it was at vanishing point. The Secretary of State for the Colonies decided that the remnant could be treated as ordinary criminals and be absorbed into the colony's prisons.

The system had ended in a whimper.

REFERENCE NOTES

1 Quoted, Eris O'Brien, *The Foundation of Australia*, p. 97.
2 *Hist. Rec. Aust.*, ser. I, vol. xxiv, p. 250.
3 D. Collins, *Account of the English Colony in New South Wales, 1798-1802*, p. 148.
4 *Hist. Rec. Aust.*, ser. I, vol. xxiv, pp. 250-1.
5 *Hist. Rec. N.S.W.*, vol. ii, p. 768.
6 *Hist. Rec. Aust.*, ser. I, vol. i, p. 197.
7 M. Barnard, *Macquarie's World*, pp. 103-4.
8 *Hist. Rec. Aust.*, ser. I, vol. i, p. 442.
9 *Ibid.*, p. 470.
10 *Ibid.*, pp. 679-80.
11 *Ibid.*, vol. iii, p. 399.
12 *Ibid.*, vol. iv, note 22.
13 *Ibid.*, vol. iii, p. 260.
14 *Ibid.*, vol. x, p. 787.
15 *Ibid.*, vol. xiii, p. 221.
16 *Ibid.*, vol. xi, p. 85.
17 *Ibid.*, vol. xii, p. 585.
18 *Ibid.*, vol. xi, p. 591.
19 *Ibid.*, p. 84.
20 *Ibid.*, p. 183.
21 *Ibid.*, vol. xii, pp. 252-3.
22 *Ibid.*, vol. xii, p. 794.
23 *Ibid.*, vol. xiii, p. 137.
24 *Ibid.*, p. 138.
25 *Ibid.*, pp. 139-40.
26 *Ibid.*, p. 166.
27 *Ibid.*, vol. xx, p. 76.
28 *Ibid.*, vol. xiv, p. 270.
29 *Ibid.*, vol. xvi, p. 349.
30 *Ibid.*, vol. xiv, pp. 173-5.
31 *Ibid.*, vol. xii, p. 248.
32 *Ibid.*, vol. xiii, pp. 3-4.
33 *Ibid.*, vol. xiv, p. 116.
34 *Ibid.*, vol. iii, p. 473.
35 *Ibid.*, vol. x, p. 785.
36 For a table setting out crimes and their punishment in lashes see *Hist. Rec. Aust.*, ser. I, vol. xix, p. 654.
37 *Hist. Rec. Aust.*, ser. I, vol. xx, p. 586.
38 *Ibid.*, vol. xii, p. 142.
39 *Ibid.*, vol. xiv, p. 70.
40 For Governor Bourke's outline of the system, see his dispatch of 15th January 1834 (*Hist. Rec. Aust.*, ser. I, vol. xvii, pp. 313-30).
41 *Hist. Rec. Aust.*, ser. I, vol. xi, p. 598.
42 *Ibid.*, vol. ii, p. 24.
43 M. Barnard, *Macquarie's World*, p. 70.
44 *Ibid.*, p. 69.
45 *Hist. Rec. Aust.*, ser. I, vol. xi, p. 76.
46 *Ibid.*, pp. 114-15.
47 *Ibid.*, vol. xviii, p. 533.
48 *Ibid.*, p. 612.
49 *Ibid.*, vol. xix, p. 319.
50 *Ibid.*, p. 320.
51 *Ibid.*, vol. xxi, p. 2.
52 *Ibid.*, vol. xxv, p. 479.
53 *Ibid.*, vol. xxii, p. 525.
54 *Ibid.*, vol. i, note 245.
55 *Ibid.*, p. 463.
56 *Ibid.*, p. 542.
57 *Ibid.*, pp. 543, 545.
58 *Ibid.*, p. 568.
59 *Ibid.*
60 *Ibid.*, p. 569.

[61] *Ibid.*, vol. ii, p. 129. [62] *Ibid.*, p. 130. [63] *Ibid.*, p. 134.
[64] *Ibid.*, p. 131. [65] *Ibid.*, vol. iv, pp. 564 *et seq.*
[66] *Ibid.*, vol. x, p. 21. [67] *Ibid.*, vol. xii, pp. 242-3.
[68] *Ibid.*, vol. xiv, pp. 165, 170, 445, 730 *et seq.*, 857. [69] *Ibid.*, vol. xii, p. 292.
[70] *Ibid.*, vol. xi, pp. 650 *et seq.* [71] *Ibid.*, vol. vii, p. 775.
[72] *Ibid.*, vol. xi, pp. 91-2. [73] *Ibid.*, vol. xxiv, p. 602. [74] *Ibid.*, vol. xiii, p. 189.
[75] *Ibid.*, pp. 143 *et seq.*, 470 *et seq.* [76] *Ibid.*, p. 470.
[77] *Ibid.*, vol. xvii, p. 304. [78] *Ibid.*, vol. xx, p. 400.
[79] *Ibid.*, vol. xxii, pp. 75-7, 500-2.
[80] *Ibid.*, vol. xxiv, pp. 59-61. [81] *Ibid.*, p. 127.
[82] *Ibid.*, pp. 256, 275, 382. [83] *Ibid.*, vol. xxv, p. 35.
[84] *Ibid.*, vol. xxvi, pp. 587-96. [85] *Ibid.*, vol. xxi, p. 7. [86] *Ibid.*, p. 91.
[87] For an account of Cockatoo Island see J. F. Campbell, "Cockatoo (Biloela) Island" *J. Roy. Aust. Hist. Soc.*, vol. xviii, pp. 338-43.

CHAPTER XII

GOLD

"Put it away or we shall have our throats cut."

—Governor Gipps.

From the very beginning gold and rumours of gold haunted the Australian story. The first "find" was a tragic-comic fiasco. In August 1788 a convict named Daley reported that he had found gold and to prove it produced a clod of earth in which glittered some particles of yellow metal. A goldsmith pronounced it gold and amid general excitement Captain Campbell and a party of Marines took Daley down the harbour to the site. He led them into the bush and whilst they were eagerly looking for gold he slipped back to the boats, seized one, and rowed himself back to the settlement. He announced that Captain Campbell was amazed by the richness of the strike and had sent him back for a strong guard. Everyone believed him, he was the hero of the hour and no doubt was as liberally refreshed as the circumstances of the colony permitted. Just as the guard was setting out Captain Campbell returned, tired and angry, having found nothing. Daley fled before his wrath, but after a night in the bush returned hungry to the camp. He still swore that there was a mine. Officers and convicts alike wanted to believe him. Now he had the less credulous Phillip to deal with. He was sent back to the supposed mine under arrest. Lieutenant Johnston was prepared to shoot him if he tried to slip away again. The party searched and searched, there was no gold. Daley at length broke down and confessed that he had manufactured his specimens by melting down some fragments of old gold and mixing them with earth in the hope that he would be rewarded by a pardon and a free passage home. Instead he received three hundred lashes and had to wear a canvas coat emblazoned with the letter R for rogue. He came to no good. The following December he was executed for thieving.

Later there were authentic discoveries, but they were not welcome in a penal settlement. In 1823 a surveyor, James McBrien, noted in his field book that there was gold in the sand near the Fish River, in the Bathurst district. In 1830 a convict found it in the same locality and was promptly flogged on the suspicion that he had stolen it. In 1839 Strzelecki found gold near Hartley, between the Blue Mountains and Bathurst, and was anxious to press for its exploitation in the teeth of Governor Gipps's disapproval. He even wrote to the papers about it. In 1841 a clergyman with a geological turn of mind, W. B. Clarke, found gold on the banks of Cox's River and later beside the Wollondilly. Specimens were sent to England, and Sir Roderick Murchison in 1844, testing rock samples and talking to Strzelecki, gave it as his considered opinion that Australia was auriferous and that it would be a good scheme to send out unemployed tin-miners from Cornwall to work the putative mines. Nothing came of this, nor of the lump of gold exhibited by a man called Smith in 1849. He would not reveal where he found it unless the Government gave him a reward. The Government would not pay unless it had the information first and there the matter rested. The time was not ripe, but Murchison had not forgotten. He urged the Colonial Office to undertake a scientific mineral survey of New South Wales. Earl Grey refused on the grounds that it might be prejudicial to the wool industry if gold were found. In 1851, however, a government geologist was appointed.

By 1851, far from resenting the suggestion, the Colonial Government was eager to find a new source of wealth and develop mines, if any. It was then ten years since transportation had ended. New South Wales, Victoria, Tasmania, and South Australia had achieved self-government. They had just emerged from a period of economic depression and their governments were deploring the drift of population to the gold fields of California and other lands of promise.

The hour brought the man in the person of Edward Hammond Hargraves. He stepped onto the stage with appropriate theatrical gestures. He was an Englishman born in 1816, he came to Australia as a sailor in 1832, fished for bêche-de-mer and tortoise-shell in Torres Strait, then turned to the land and became a squatter in a small way on the Manning River and later in the Illawarra. At one time he kept an inn out of Gosford. When the Californian diggings were opened he felt the lure of gold and sailed away to look for it in 1849. He was moderately successful, but always he was haunted by the similarity between the auriferous hills of California and those he had known so well in Australia. Simpson Davidson, who had found gold at Wellington, New South Wales, was his mate and that may have influenced him, too. According to his own account, he talked so much of the gold in Australia that he drew on himself a gibe, "There is no gold in the country you are going to, and if there were that darned Queen wouldn't let you dig for it." Whereupon he took off his hat and declared with dignity, "There is as much gold in the country I'm going to as there is in California, and Her Most Gracious Majesty the Queen, God bless her, will appoint me one of her Gold Commissioners."

He returned to Australia in the ship *Emma* in January 1851. He made no secret of his purpose and everyone thought he was mad. On 5th February he set out alone on horseback to prove that he was right. He lost himself in the bush, but on the eleventh he arrived at Guyong Inn and enlisted the licensee's eighteen-year-old-son, John Lister, as his guide. They reached the Lewis Ponds Creek and Hargraves dramatically announced that they were now on a goldfield. But the creek was dry and it was with difficulty that he found a waterhole in which to wash some dirt. It showed colour. He announced grandiloquently to his young companion: "This is a memorable day in the history of New South Wales, I shall be a baron, you will be knighted, and my old horse will be stuffed, put in a glass case, and sent to the British Museum."

Hargraves prospected further at Wellington and on the Macquarie River, then he returned to Guyong and had a cradle made to his specification. With this improved equipment he worked on the Summer Hill Creek. This was the real thing. He recovered four ounces of gold and on 20th March 1851 he waited on the Colonial Secretary, E. Deas Thomson. He was well received. Thomson saw that gold was a trump card, it would end for ever attempts to re-introduce transportation under one name or another; it would re-establish prosperity and stop the drift to California. The Government Geologist, Stutchbury, was sent to confirm the finds. Hargraves, as he had boasted, was made a Commissioner for Lands, eventually he received a reward of £10,000 and a life pension and was presented to Queen Victoria in 1854. He was never a baron, and who knows where the bones of his old horse lie? Hargraves himself died at Forest Lodge, a suburb of Sydney, in October 1891. He had been treated as the man with the Midas touch and had been set to seeking for gold in Tasmania and Western Australia, fruitlessly in both places.

No sooner was the news published than the gold-rushes began. In a fortnight six hundred men were on the Summer Hill Creek. It was Bathurst that felt the first shock of excitement, as the *Bathurst Free Press* phrased it: "A Complete mental madness appears to have seized almost every member of the community, and as a natural consequence, there has been a universal rush to the digging [*sic*]."

Excitement rose when a boy found an eleven-ounce nugget and reached fever heat when Dr Kerr's aboriginal shepherd picked up a solid mass of gold weighing 106 pounds, the largest nugget in the world, Kerr's Hundredweight. The shepherd was rewarded by the gift of a flock of sheep and land to run them on.

The discovery of gold in New South Wales was sporadic. Turon, Araluen, Adelong Creek, Hanging Rock, Kiandra, Grenfell, Lambing Flat, Lucknow, Hill End . . . right up to the last major strike at Wyalong in 1893.

Meanwhile the Governor, Sir Charles FitzRoy, was called on to deal with a completely new set of circumstances. On 22nd May 1851 he issued a proclamation that all gold found on Crown land was the property of the Queen. It was an empty gesture. More practically, the next day he followed it with another proclamation naming a gold commissioner for the new Ophir field, as Hargraves had named it, and establishing a monthly licence costing 30s. In the general excitement and the quick profits that most prospectors made this was not resented or considered exorbitant. Later, as the number of diggers increased it was reduced to 30s. a quarter. In an effort to keep order, the sale of liquor on the fields was at first prohibited, but this rule could not be maintained. Illicit home brews were too disastrous in their effects.

In November 1851 the first gold escorts were established to bring the precious metal in safety to Sydney.

The social changes were great, and suddenly, almost over night, it seemed as if the whole population was in a state of flux. The road over the mountains was crowded with a motley throng, old and young, on horseback, on foot, pushing wheelbarrows or simply walking with their gear—shovel, pick, dish, tucker—slung about their persons. Traders quickly recognized that there was gold in other places besides the creeks. The price of all commodities soared. Cradles for washing gold cost 25s. or £2 each. Supplies of every kind rose in price, for high wages had to be offered to keep workmen at their jobs. Even so, many preferred the gamble of the diggings. The cost of transport over the mountains was high, too, and in the recklessness of the moment those with money were willing to pay almost anything to equip themselves to go prospecting. Sydney was practically emptied of able-bodied men, and some not so able, who hopefully took to the track. The lure of wealth possessed everyone like a fever even down to the man who advertised: "To Persons that want to go to the Gold mines, a large sized English feather bed weighing 100 pounds for the sum of £6."[1]

Even the aborigines cashed in by selling sheets of bark to construct rough huts on the diggings, the current price being 10s. for 40 sheets. Landowners charged rent, for example, 15s. a month for each claim pegged out on private property at Araluen. Poor but canny men sometimes sold their services to dig at 15s. a day, a very high wage for those times. Itinerant vendors of every sort of commodity down to "lollipops and nuts" quickly made their appearance, and storekeepers started business in bark huts on the more setttled diggings, taking gold in payment for their wares.

The prevailing architecture of the diggings was executed in canvas, for who knew whether tomorrow he would be folding his tent and moving on somewhere else, to a better, richer field?

A few women accompanied their husbands or fathers, but on the whole the diggings were a man's world. Law and order was good. Everyone was too busy to get into mischief and too tired at the end of the day to roister. Public opinion was very strong on the subject of theft. Health was good, too, and just as well, with pills selling at a shilling each.

The discovery of gold in New South Wales was only the prelude. As in most things, the colonies followed in one another's footsteps. South Australia, after enjoying the mild honour of being the first colony to mine gold, in a small field ten miles from Adelaide discovered in 1846, petered out as gold-bearing country but made money instead out of feeding the Victorian diggers. Victoria followed New South Wales with bigger, better, brighter, longer-lived deposits. In 1851 she produced £851,596 worth of gold, in 1853 it was valued at £10,976,392, in 1855 at £11,277,152, in 1856 at £12,214,976, in both 1857 and 1858 at more than £11,000,000. Thereafter the output slowly decreased until in 1909 it was £2,778,956. The highest yield in New South Wales was £2,660,946 in 1852. In 1862 it was £2,467,780, with a drop to £869,540 in 1909.

Queensland's gold history began in the 1860s at Canal Creek, Gladstone, Crocodile Creek, Ridgelands, Rosewood, Gympie, and the Gilbert River fields. The 1870s saw the opening of the Charters Towers, Palmer and Hodgkinson River fields. But it was not until 1882 that the northern colony found her bonanza at Mount Morgan, that most geologically curious of all Australian gold-mines.

Later again, in the 1890s, Western Australia took up the golden story. There were the usual rumours of gold found and lost again by shepherds as early as 1848, and there was mining in a desultory way in heart-break country during the 1880s. It was not until 1892 that Bayley and Ford discovered Coolgardie, far out in the dry country east of Perth. There in one afternoon, using only a tomahawk, they collected 500 ounces. The next year it was alluvial gold at the Ninety Mile, and in June Flanagan and Hannan discovered Kalgoorlie, at first called Hannan's, with its Golden Mile.

Nothing could be more prosaic than Paddy Hannan's story as he dictated it to Sir John Kirwan:

Early in June, 1893, I was in Coolgardie. News arrived of a rich discovery at a place called Mt. Youle somewhere to the east or north-east and parties had left in search of the new find. My mate, Thomas Flanagan and myself left on June 7, a few days after the report of the discovery was received. We would have gone earlier, but we had no horses. . . . My mate and I had made up our minds not to travel with the teams, but to form a separate party of our own as we wanted to be free to travel how and when we liked. By this arrangement we could prospect any promising country we passed through.

On June 10, three days after leaving Coolgardie we reached what is now known as Kalgoorlie. The other prospecting parties had gone on in the direction of the reported find. My mate and I found some colours of gold near Mt. Charlotte, so we determined to stop and prospect the country round about. On the

14th we shifted our camp and got good gold more or less from the north end of Mt. Charlotte to down south of Maritana Hill. . . . As we were getting excellent gold we decided to apply for a reward claim, and on June 17 I left for the return journey to Coolgardie. Rain began to fall as I was on my way and continued for some time. The fall was exceptionally heavy, and extremely welcome as it solved the water difficulty which just then was beginning to get grave. I reached Coolgardie on Saturday night. The news of our find soon got abroad. There was much excitement and men set out for the scene. In fact most of the men who had got beyond Southern Cross found their way quickly to our find. Hundreds of claims were being worked outside our pegs. Before Christmas two hotels were open.

I left on January 20, 1894, for a holiday as I had then been on the Goldfields for some years, and had not seen the sea since my arrival in Western Australia. I was not in the best of health, and I felt it was necessary that I should take a brief spell away from the fields where life was trying. We lived mostly on tinned food. The water sometimes was not too good and we scarcely ever got fresh meat, except during winter when we occasionally secured it.[2]

A couple of miles to the south of Hannan's Find a syndicate, the Ivanhoe Goldmining Company, pegged out a series of claims which they called Great Boulder. These became the famous Golden Mile and in half a century £100,000,000 worth of gold was taken from them.

The strikes came thick and fast—Bardoc, Siberia, Kanowna, Wealth of Nations (where J. D. Dunn obtained £20,000 worth of gold in a few days), Niagara, Hands-Across-the-Sea, Kunanalling, Blackboy Hill, Donnybrook, Nore, and names that read like those of syndicates on lottery tickets. This was highly rewarding treasure, but in such difficult, waterless country that the gold-seekers paid dearly for what they won and many a prospector died of thirst and heat. Rich as the mines proved, they were far behind the Victorian fields, the peak year being 1903, which produced £8,770,719 worth of gold.[3]

The Northern Territory had its day in the 1900s with a rush at Tanami, 200 miles from Hall's Creek, 450 from Wyndham. Or is its day still to come? It is a land of hope and hope deferred, a mirage of riches. When the current Commonwealth survey of the Territory is completed perhaps we shall know what is there and what not to expect, and if some future miracle of engineering brings water to the dry country it may be forced to yield up its wealth. It is likely to be mineral wealth, perhaps gold, perhaps other things.

As Victoria was pre-eminently the "golden" colony it seems more profitable to follow its story, in some detail, than any other.

As soon as the gold-rushes began in New South Wales, Victoria saw herself losing population and wealth. The Government, at that time in the hands of La Trobe and a Legislative Council, part elected, part nominee, offered a reward of 200 guineas to anyone who discovered payable gold within two hundred miles of Melbourne. A Gold Discovery Committee was set up to look into claims. The response was instant. William Campbell found it at Clunes, L. J. Michel at Anderson's Creek, T. Hiscock at Ballarat, H. Frencham at Bendigo, all between July and December 1851. Mount Alexander in the Castlemaine district, the Ovens River and Korong, fifty miles east of Bendigo, became gold-mining districts in the next year and McIvor's Creek, thirty miles from Bendigo, was discovered in 1853. The finds were rich. The precious stuff was in the form of easily collected alluvial gold and embedded in quartz reefs which required machinery to crush and extract it. It was finer and purer than in New South Wales.

The Victorian Government soon had more on its hands than it had bargained for. The population of Victoria was, at the beginning of 1851 only about 77,000, it was pastoral in character, and the Government was quite unable to stand the shock of the gold discoveries. It had few police and no machinery to cope with changed conditions. Melbourne was practically depopulated or left to the old, the sick, the women and children. Public services came to a standstill. According to a report submitted to La Trobe in December 1851:

> The postmaster apprehends an entire disruption of the business of his Department, unless remedial measures can be taken. The Surveyor-General is of a similar opinion. The Deputy-Registrar thinks that all his subordinates will leave their occupation. The Superintendent of Police states that, though in accordance with authority he offered high rates of pay to his force, fifty out of fifty-five constables have determined to go to the gold-fields, but his clerk and chief constables will remain. . . . The Crown Solicitor apprehends complete embarrassment. The Denominational School Board fears loss of teachers. . . .

The rushes were far larger than in New South Wales. It was nothing for 20,000 men to congregate on one goldfield. The news had spread overseas. Ships coming into port were promptly deserted by their crews and masters were forced to the expedient of manning them from the jails—when, indeed, they could induce the jailbirds to accept their offers.

Caroline Chisholm, the immigrant's friend, came forward with advice to those about to sail for Australia and gold. They should equip themselves, she said, with "knife and fork, ladle and spoons, metal plate, hook pot, drinking mug, meat dish, water can, washing basin, half a gallon of sand, flour-bag, half a bath brick, two sheets of sandpaper, two coarse canvas aprons, hammer, tacks, leathern straps with buckle, to secure the beds neatly on deck when required to be aired, three pounds of marine soap. . . ." She further advised them: "Passengers, by placing their shoes in a cabbage-net and tying the net to the rigging, dry them without the risk of their going overboard, which frequently happens when suspended by the shoestrings." They would need white clothes for the tropics and "all that was necessary in cold weather was to protect the joints, not to load the body with great amount of extra clothing. An old blanket cut up and sewed inside the waistcoat or trousers would be found very useful."[4] How much notice was taken of the good lady's advice it is impossible to say.

The squatters immediately raised the cry that they were ruined. There were no shepherds, no shearers. Crops, too, could not be harvested for lack of labour. Farmers were paying 13s. an acre with rations for harvesting barley or offering the produce of every second acre to anyone who would reap their wheat. R. S. Anderson recounts how: "The Lieutenant-Governor, during his visit to Ballarat had proposed to the miners that they should withdraw for two months, their claims being meanwhile guarded, in order that the crops of the colony should not be destroyed. This, it is said, was warmly responded to by a very large majority, so that our harvest may now be considered safe."[5]

The squatters soon found that they could do without much of their labour, and the farmers, if they were at all well placed, that they could find an excellent market on the diggings for their produce. Alfred Joyce, whose property was on the Ovens, sold vegetables and milk to the diggers and, having built a bridge that they must cross, reaped in a steady toll.

There are plenty of contemporary pictures of the goldfields. William Hall, in his *Practical Experience at the Diggings of the Gold Fields of Victoria* (1852), describes both the diggers and the diggings: "Old Golden Point was like a honeycomb, and the men were clustered together on this spot like bees."[6] He continues:

> The scene around us was singularly picturesque and striking—thousands of tents of every possible shape and size, whose snowy whiteness contrasted strongly with the dark thickly wooded hills in the background. In front of the tents the cooks for the day were seen busily occupied at the fires preparing supper for their parties who returned tired and hungry. The appearance of the men as they came home, their shirts and trousers stained with clay, one carrying the tools, another the gold, and the others armed to the teeth, escorting the latter [*sic*]. Their sun-burnt countenances, large whiskers and moustaches, and cone-shaped hats, gave them the appearance of Italian Brigands, and the broken, hilly, and mountainous country around seemed to confirm that impression. As night approached rockets and blue-lights ascended in every direction, and for upwards of an hour the discharge of fire-arms was incessant, then all became silent, silent as the city of the dead;—not a footstep or voice was heard in that vast assemblage, in whose breasts one all-absorbing passion prevailed—the acquisition of gold—nothing but the shrill amorous cry of the male cricket, or the low, melancholy but pleasing cry of the Mope-hawk, broke the unearthly silence.[7]

A dandy of the diggings caught the author's eye.

He was dressed in a red Guernsey frock, a broad glazed belt, while a large brass S hook encircled his waist, and a pair of silver-mounted pistols were stuck in it; his hat was made of cabbage tree, with a very low crown, and a broad black ribbon attached to it, the ends of which hung over his shoulders, and was worn jauntily; his handsome black whiskers and moustache were carefully brushed, and curled after the most approved fashion. After taking a minute survey of his person, with which he seemed much pleased, he stepped forward and asked a digger, who happened to pass at that moment, to carry a bag of sugar from the cart to his tent, a distance of thirty yards, and he would give him a shilling. The man looked at him with the most withering scorn, and placing his foot on a piece of stone, said—"I say, my fine fellow, if you will tie my boot-lace, I will give you a crown." This quite paralysed the dandy digger, who sneaked off amid the boisterous laughter of the by-standers.[8]

Whenever a digger "struck it rich" he drew his pistol and fired into the air, an innocent testimony to his trust in his fellows.

There was more to it all than an engaging picturesqueness. The young schoolmaster, James Bonwick, a prolific writer on many subjects, described from his own experience the hard work involved. First the claim must be selected, an agonizing job for any but an expert. Then it must be worked.

The tunnelling work now follows. The head stuff is removed for you to get under, to work at the latent treasure of specs, nuggets and washing stuff. The constraint of body in work, the damp, the closeness of the atmosphere, the gloom, the fear of impending rocks, with occasional raps of knuckles and skull against the sides and roof, altogether make this wombatting not the most amusing operation in life. . . .[9]

Often there was moral anguish thrown in as a promising vein disappeared into a neighbour's claim—"honesty says 'stop', and self interest cries 'go on' ". Then came the washing. There was generally a water shortage and the earth had to be either carted from "three to nine miles from the hole, paying, perhaps, one shilling a bucket for cartage. . . . Unless, therefore, you immediately require cash, you prefer carting the stuff home to your tent beside the dried up creek, waiting for the time of rains. When that joyous harvest of diggers does come, all is bustle and merriment." The washing was highly skilled and very laborious, first with the cradle and then with a tin dish.

The day's work over, you put your gold into the digger's treasure chamber, a matchbox; and you retire to your home to get dry clothes and your supper. But the gold has to be dried. A spade is put on the fire, the contents of the box poured on it, and the moisture soon disappears. The dust is then carefully blown away, the magnet is passed over to take up the iron particles, the little gathering is weighed and the result is known.[10]

A horse was necessary to a digger's outfit and its keep cost £3 to

£5 a week. "Some men close their work early, and take the beasts perhaps four or five miles to some scanty pasture, and stopping there in their 'possum rug for the night, bring them in the next morning."[11]

Living was hard. A bark hut or a tent with "free ventilation . . . on Hygean principles" provided shelter. "Our furniture is of a simple character. A box, a block of wood, or a bit of paling across a pail, serves as a table; though a few among us scorn such indulgence . . . the chops can be picked out of the frying pan, placed on a lump of bread, and cut with a clasp knife that has done good service in fossicking during the day."[12] Bonwick throws in a recipe for damper:

> Taking a washing tin dish, and clearing off the dirt a little, six or eight pannicans of flour are thrown in; a half table spoonful of carbonate of soda, the like quantity of tartaric acid, and a spoonful of salt are mixed together in a pannican, and then well mingled with dry flour. Water is then poured in, the whole thoroughly knuckled, rolled into a good shaped loaf, and tumbled at once into the warmed camp oven. Fire is applied beneath and above the oven in a way to insure uniform heat, and a couple of hours or less will turn out a loaf fit to set before the queen.[13]

Meat, he tells us, was seldom more than fourpence a pound. "Cheese, butter, pickles, ham, bacon, sardines, and eau de Cologne, are enjoyed only by successful miners."[14]

"A good fire, a short pipe and a long story are the usual evening accompaniments." For the rest it was dust, mud and flies. The diggings were "salubrious", but illness was common enough. Doctors charged 10s. a visit at their own tents and anything from £1 to £5 if they were called out. There were no comforts, no special food for the sick and, if it came to that, only a nameless grave.

As in New South Wales, there was little crime on the diggings and practically every observer remarked how creditably Sunday was observed. Is it fair to suggest that perhaps utter weariness had something to do with the "quietude and propriety" that prevailed? It is not surprising to learn, in the same breath, that "swearing is an almost all prevailing vice". "Even gentlemen of refinement and education," Bonwick sadly points out, "have been so oppressed by the circumstances around them, as to become reckless of their personal appearance, and even their language and demeanour."[15] But, he concludes, "There are not wanting pleasing moral features of the Diggings."[16] Above all a spirit of mateship flourished and equality reigned.

Life was colourful, but it was also very hard. The fortunate digger whose wife had accompanied him had a modicum of comfort, but life for a woman—even though all authorities agree that those who dared the hardships were treated with universal respect—was more difficult than most would face. There was throughout the summers generally an acute water shortage so that cleanliness was impossible. There was endless monotony and a husband too tired to give her any company or even attention. In sickness she was far from help and if there were children they could not be schooled. The insects, too, were no respecters of persons. Bonwick gives flies pride of place:

. . . *the* nuisance is the flies, the little fly and the stinging monster March fly. O! the tortures these wretches give! In the hole, out of the hole, at meals or walking, it is all the same with these winged plagues. When washing at a waterhole, the March flies will settle upon the arms and face, and worry to that degree, that I have known men pitch down their dishes, and stamp and growl with agony. The fleas, too, are not of the Tom Thumb order of creation, and they begin their blood-thirsty work when the flies are tired of their recreation.[17]

All these things were borne in the hope of profit. Sometimes it was very great and the rich claims were called "jewellers' shops". Gold brought up to £3 an ounce or a little more. Buyers set up their tents on the fields and, like storekeepers, took out licences in order to have the protection of the police. Many diggers preferred to hoard their gains and take them themselves to Melbourne, which was quickly transformed by the wealth flowing in. The quiet and dignified town became garish and the publicans there and on the roads—if roads the rough and rutted bush tracks could be called—flourished exceedingly. The innkeeper at Kyneton made £6000 in three months when gold was first found at Mount Alexander.[18]

Under the influence of gold the jealousy between Melbourne and Sydney flared up.

It should be borne in mind that two-thirds of the gold shipped at Sydney, for London, is purchased at Melbourne, by the agents of houses in Sydney, and forwarded to that place by the Steamer *Shamrock* . . . no doubt a very great part of it has been purchased by the Capitalists of Sydney to deceive the people of England, and induce them to emigrate to that place, in preference to Melbourne.[19]

There were, of course, unfortunate diggers who spent all their substance and found no gold. A party of these offered to drown Hargraves in the Nepean as the man who had falsely raised their hopes. These disappointed men were to increase in numbers until they became a problem. At first all was hope and their voices were hardly heard.

The discovery of gold meant more than high adventure. It was also a problem in organization. Lieutenant-Governor La Trobe was handicapped by lack of money and of police. Victoria, as a point of honour, had wanted gold when it was found in her elder-sister colony, New South Wales, but no one foresaw that the finds would be so rich or the diggers attracted so numerous. The independent government was very new. La Trobe, once the rush had begun, had only five policemen and forty-four soldiers to maintain order. FitzRoy lent him thirty more soldiers from New South Wales and in 1853 fifty London bobbies were sent to the goldfields. In the meantime La Trobe managed as best he could. He enlisted a volunteer police force. Men of the better type were not offering, he had to recruit ex-convicts from Tasmania and anyone on the spot who was willing. In this way he collected a force of one hundred and thirty. All the time new fields were opening up and the rich ones growing and spreading. Like FitzRoy he collected, or tried to collect, a licence fee of 30s. a month. He himself felt this to be unjust and would have preferred a tax on gold won or exported. This he could not carry out because it would have to be passed by his Legislative Council, which, as in New South Wales, was controlled by the squatters. Crown lands being still in the hands of the Governor, as the Queen's representative, he could collect a licence fee and use it for the policing and other needs of the diggings. The squatter Council was bitterly opposed to the diggers, who, they thought, would ruin the wool industry. If the Council collected the money as customs it was safe to suspect that it would not be used for the benefit of the goldfields and there would be no money for police, roads, or any of the other objects now urgently necessary. The 30s. licence was unpopular and when La Trobe, in dire straits for money, proposed to double it there were violent protests. At Forest Hill a crowd of more then fourteen thousand threatened rebellion and the other fields were not far behind. The diggers thought it was a plot to tax them off the fields because the squatters wanted labour. This and the rough methods employed by the special constables in collecting the licence fee angered the miners. The diggers resolved to stick together and to refuse to pay their licences. An amendment to the Vagrant Act was proclaimed. By it every miner, servant, storekeeper, or other able-bodied man on the fields was to be sworn in as a special constable, "to assist the Government in carrying out their measures, however much they might militate against the best interests of the colonists, or the liberty of the subject, under the penalty of fine and imprisonment, as rogues and vagabonds".[20] The miners organized, La Trobe capitulated, but the damage was done. The licence fee had become a political issue, the deepest feelings of true-born Britons were aroused. Hall becomes eloquent:

> Who ever heard of such an absurd and unjust tax as the one in question? The man that obtains no gold is taxed to the same amount as he that obtains a hundredweight! Is this politic, statesmanlike, or just? Is it in accordance with our recognised principle of taxation? There can be but one opinion as to the mode of levying it; and the sooner it is discontinued the better.[21]

The "honour system" failed, and in the face of public opinion the Amendment had to be withdrawn and the licence fee reduced again to

30s. It still rankled, and the man who avoided paying it had the support and even admiration of his fellows.

The whole economy was upset. Property in Melbourne was thrown suddenly on the market to be bought up at a hundredth part of its value by speculators. Wages rose a hundred per cent or more in a week or so. Grazing properties were put up for sale for what they would fetch and then eagerly bought up when it was realized that there was a fortune to be made in meat and grain. Prices rose because there was money to spend. Inflation set in. Bread rose 100 per cent, potatoes 300 per cent, flour rose to £30 a ton and then to £70, water became valuable, boots were at a premium and so were beasts of burthen.

It was all very unsettling, particularly to the people who did not participate in the new prosperity. They joined the malcontents. The liquor laws and the seizure of private stocks were another exasperation.

There was no lack of amusing incidents, however. Sir William Denison, the Governor of Tasmania, wrote in his journal: "The Bishop who keeps a little yacht has no longer a man left to take care of it; so he absolutely now paddles himself off to the yacht every night, and sleeps on board and paddles back in the morning", to prevent convicts stealing it to get to the goldfields.[22]

Despite prosperity and despite the remarkably good order that prevailed on the diggings there was much latent unrest, the tinder was dry, a spark could cause a conflagration. In 1853 a Select Committee considered the problems of the goldfields, but little came of its recommendations since the Legislative Council remained obstinate. La Trobe appealed to the miners, pointing out that the cost to the colony of the diggings was £136,000 more than the revenue brought in by the licences. Not only must they be policed, but each field had its commissioner, assistant commissioner, magistrates, surgeons, postmaster, chaplains, coroners, and clerks—a bureaucracy that had to be paid. The miners were not impressed, they felt that they could do very nicely without these functionaries.

It did not improve matters when the Chinese began to arrive in 1853. Many of them were coolies sent by their masters at a low wage to mine in Australia. All the gold they won went out of the country. Their industry, their frugal habit of life, their unwillingness to take any part in the community, all offended the diggers. They accused them of immorality, of wasting water, of making no contribution to the common weal.

Alluvial gold was beginning to peter out. That meant that mining would soon require capital and expensive machinery. The little man began to feel insecure.

Sir Charles Hotham replaced La Trobe. He toured the diggings, was well received, made various promises to the diggers that they should have the vote and be given "a chance to settle down". But he was firm. They must pay for these privileges. The collection of licence fees was tightened up. Disappointment fostered discontent. The time was ripe for an explosion.

It came on 6th October 1854. A miner was killed at the Eureka Hotel, Ballarat. It was a disreputable house and the licensee, Bentley, fell under suspicion. He was an ex-convict and so were his wife and alleged accomplices. When they were acquitted mob fury broke out and the hotel was burnt down. The ringleaders in this demonstration were arrested. The Governor took a hand, Bentley was re-tried and convicted but the miners were not pacified. All their grievances coalesced. They formed the Ballarat Reform League, which issued an ultimatum. They demanded the abolition of licences, the vote, manhood suffrage, payment of members of parliament, no property qualifications for either members or electors. It was, in fact, very like the Chartist platform.

Hotham was conciliatory, but not conciliatory enough. He promised the miners the vote if they held licences. The plan under consideration was for a goldfields electorate for which all miners would elect one representative. This was not enough. Nor was the Governor's offer to nominate a miner to the Council there and then. The deputation that had waited on him returned disgruntled to Ballarat.

It was probably mistaken of Hotham to mass troops there. The appearance of violence was the last straw. The diggers stoned the troops and the next day, 29th November, they held a meeting at which inflammatory speeches were made and licences burnt on a gigantic bonfire. This was riot and treated as such. The miners elected Peter Lalor as their leader and prepared to resist. They commandeered arms from the storekeepers, giving receipts for what they took. They built a stockade and ran up a pale-blue flag adorned with the Southern Cross. The volunteers were bound by an oath: "We swear by the Southern Cross to stand truly by each other and fight to defend our rights and liberties." There was a strong tincture of idealism in it all, but this was open rebellion and the soldiers knew their duty. Captain Thomas, anxious to save bloodshed, attacked the Eureka stockade with his 276 troops early on the morning of 2nd December. It was a Sunday and many of the "rebels" had gone home for the week-end. The engagement was short and decisive. It lasted about fifteen minutes. Thirty-four were killed, thirty of them diggers, and one hundred and twenty, or according to some accounts, one hundred and twenty-eight, were taken prisoner; others were "on the run". For two days Ballarat was under martial law and then everything returned to normal.

A great deal, perhaps too much, has been made of Eureka. Today we feel that justice lay with the miners because they were fighting for liberties that we take for granted. The short engagement did good because it drew attention to injustices on the fields, public sympathy was enlisted, and authority recognized that something must be done. The pathetic little rebellion was a very minor occurrence. It was heroic and doomed to failure.

No jury would condemn the leaders of the rebellion.

The Governor appointed a commission to look into the miners' grievances and it made its report in March 1855. It recommended that the hated licences be abolished and a miner's right costing £1 a year be substituted, and that the revenue necessary for the upkeep of the fields should be raised by a duty of 2s. 6d. an ounce on the export of gold. This was equitable and became law in June 1855. Every digger with a miner's right could vote, but it is on record that comparatively few of them exercised the privilege.

In 1857 New South Wales also replaced the licence with a miner's right and a tax on gold leaving the country. The fields in both colonies were pacified, except for the presence of the Chinese. In Victoria in 1855 an Act was passed imposing a poll tax of £10 on every Chinese entering the country. This may be said to be the beginning of the White Australia Policy. The £10 did little to stop the flood of unwanted immigrants. In 1853 they were a trickle. In 1854 there were roughly 2000 in Victoria alone, in March 1857 there were 25,370, in December 1857 35,000 and in 1859 42,000. A Restriction Act in Victoria tried to stem the flow in 1855. The Chinese were accused, often unjustly, of crimes against society. Their real crimes were a ceaseless industry and the export to China of all the gold they won. They did not profit Australia, for they spent very little and lived with the utmost frugality.

From 1855 onwards the Chinese were hedged about with restrictions, but it was not until after the Commonwealth was established that their entry was prohibited.

Gold in Australia, particularly in Victoria, brought great changes. Most spectacular was the growth of population. In 1851 the population of Australia was 437,665 of which some 77,000 lived in Victoria. In 1860 there were 1,145,585 people in the continent and the increase was largely due to gold.[23] The country turned the million mark in 1858, seventy years after Phillip landed; its second million in 1877, its third million in 1889, its fourth in 1905. Most of the increase was in Victoria and New South Wales. Much has been said about the influx of foreigners. C. B. Newling in a careful analysis of population figures in his article "The Gold Diggers"[24] has discounted some of the popular fallacies. Most of the gold-diggers were British subjects. In 1852, for instance, only thirteen men came from the United States and twenty-nine from other foreign countries. In 1861 in Victoria, where the intake was greatest, there were only 46,338 foreigners in a population of 540,322—that is, 8.57 per cent—and 24,732 of them were Chinese, 10,211 Germans, 2554 Americans and 1250 French. In New South Wales the figures were lower. In the same year Newling estimates, on the evidence of the census, that nine-tenths of the population had been born in the United Kingdom or Australia.

Representative government had been granted in 1850 before the discovery of gold, but the great increase of population and its nature, free, male, and spirited, had a strong influence for democracy. Australia ceased to be penal and pastoral. In the sweep of history gold was transient, but it left its mark.

Riches, too, left their mark. Between 1851 and 1861 gold worth £124,000,000 at least was taken from the Australian earth. That could hardly fail to impress the world. Wool had offered fortunes to the few, gold to the many. It was a great gamble, but all the world, it would seem, loves a gamble. After 1851 Australia had a new and exciting label.

Gold expedited but did not radically change the course of Australia's development. Wool re-instated itself as the staple, but the old pastoral days could not come back. Men had had a taste of high wages, they had learnt to co-operate, from the isolation of bush life they had moved into the crowds of the diggings. The land could no longer be a monopoly. The digger vote was to swamp the squatter vote. Nothing could be quite the same again.

REFERENCE NOTES

1 Quoted by James Jervis in *Gold in Australia* (ed. C. Barrett), p. 10.
2 *Early Days* (*J. West Aust. Hist. Soc.*), December 1942, p. 7.
3 All figures are from the *Commonwealth Year Book*, no. 4 (1911).
4 Quoted by R. S. Anderson, *Australian Gold Fields* (ed. G. Mackaness), p. 17.
5 *Ibid.*, p. 12.
6 W. Hall, *Practical Experience at the Diggings of the Gold Fields of Victoria*, p. 16.
7 *Ibid.*, p. 22.
8 *Ibid.*, pp. 20-1.
9 J. Bonwick, *Notes of a Gold Digger*, p. 12.
10 *Ibid.*, p. 14.
11 *Ibid.*, p. 16.
12 *Ibid.*, p. 19.
13 *Ibid.*, p. 20.
14 *Ibid.*, p. 21.
15 *Ibid.*, p. 28.
16 *Ibid.*, p. 30.
17 *Ibid.*, pp. 22-3.
18 W. Hall, *Practical Experience at the Diggings of the Gold Fields of Victoria*, p. 16.
19 *Ibid.*, pp. iv-v.
20 *Ibid.*, p. 38.
21 *Ibid.*, p. 39.
22 Sir William Denison, *Varieties of Vice-Regal Life*, vol. i, p. 184.
23 *Commonwealth Year Book*, no. 4 (1911), pp. 126-7.
24 *J. Roy. Aust. Hist. Soc.*, vol. xi, pp. 262 *et seq.*

CHAPTER XIII

LAND

The desire to be possessed of a portion of this solid Globe is showing in all men; and the additional importance, which is given to a man in New South Wales as elsewhere by being ranked as a landed Proprietor, is found quite sufficient to ensure the sale of land faster than in all probability it could be sold, if the price to be paid for it were not produced on the land itself.

—GOVERNOR GIPPS to Lord John Russell, 19th December 1840.

THE HISTORY of the white man's Australia is short, but it makes up for that in complexity. For this there are three reasons.

Progress was necessarily rapid. The colony, despite its meagre beginnings, belonged to the Western world and to the, in some respects, highly civilized eighteenth century. It had Great Britain to draw on. When it became a contributor it also became a junior partner in the Empire. An asset was discovered in Australia with the development of the wool industry and that asset had to be preserved. It brought its rewards. Progress was imported with capital and settlers. Economic self-interest coalesced with nineteenth-century liberalism to bring on the once backward child at a fast pace. In comparison with European history, development from autocracy to responsible government, from dependence to independence, was rapid in the extreme. Progress was hard, brittle, and involved, not a slowly unwinding evolution. It was forced by circumstance and sometimes against the grain of the land. All institutions had to be consciously founded, there was no local tradition, that amalgam of earth and habit. Progress and development were by necessity experimental and empirical.

Again, as a Crown Colony New South Wales was always changing her master. With every new government a new Secretary of State for the Colonies took over. None of them had ever visited Australia, each had his ideas, tinctured generally by what had been done in Canada or South Africa or India or some other place, and each had the power to force their acceptance up to the point where practicability broke down. The Governor was responsible to the Colonial Office and must attempt to implement his master's orders, generally in the face of bitter opposition on the home front. The changing personnel in the Colonial Office, the changing ideals, panaceas and catch-cries of Europe account for the many twists and turns of policy. Behind personality and fashion there were always various delimiting considerations, the greatest of which was expense. The expenses of the colony had to be kept down, its resources, particularly its land, had to be put to the best economic use. Suggestions for economies, sometimes bizarre, issued from the highest level, and this attitude undoubtedly had a distorting effect on progress, driving development into winding channels, whilst it produced much of the humour of Australian history.

Lastly, the apparent nullity of the country was a challenge. In Australia there was no old established civilization as in India, no earlier colonizing power which had to be ousted as in Canada, no warlike indigenous inhabitants to compare with the Red Indians of America, no savage animals, no climatic excesses, no entrenched diseases as in Africa, no overt riches as in all the Eldorados. It had nothing to give but space and distance, clean air, sunshine, and unlimited land. And the last of these alone was profitable. This temperate, highly evolved country without a label was the natural victim of every theorist, every doctrinaire reformer. The Great South Land was a sententious myth. Once discovered, Australia, diminished but still large, became the host to many plans, schemes and fables left over from its predecessor. The Colonial Office certainly acted as a brake on these, but it was nevertheless influenced by them, especially by Bigge as regards general management and by Wakefield as regards its land policy.

The empty space, the virgin land, the *tabula rasa* that was Australia drew men to scribble their dreams and their hypotheses upon it as surely as the blank surface of a desk or the smooth bole of a tree entices the schoolboy to cut his name or the lover to carve a heart. Unfortunately—or is it fortunately?—Australian timber is mostly hardwood, and few of the attempts to carve it were successful. Cure-all plans came from without and from within. The colonizing schemes of Matra, Young, de Brosses, Callander have already been outlined, and so have the curiously inflated hopes of Thomas Peel and the pedantry of Wakefield and the illusions of the East India Company. Hemp haunted the brains of Secretaries of State in the early days as persistently as a mythical Cathay, a day's march over the hills, obsessed the Irish transportees. Maconochie's method of reforming convicts has already been glanced at. It was one of many, differing only in that he had the opportunity to put it into effect. Edward Macarthur saw salvation in steam navigation. Four vessels of 500 tons each, paid for by England, would "give vastly augmented energy to the central Government at Sydney; the Laws would be better and more equally administered by the facilities afforded by establishing circuits for the judges". Religion would spread its light; the aborigines could be protected; land, because more accessible, would sell faster and at a better price, and in consequence more immigrants could be brought into the country. A larger, wealthier population would mean more trade with, and profit for, England. . . .[1] This panacea was not immediately put to the test of hard facts.

Adventurers felt the lure of the unknown country where all things were possible.

There was the tragi-comedy of Jonathan Burke McHugo, who arrived in Port Dalrymple in 1811 in the 100-ton brig *Active* with a cargo for sale. In confidence he persuaded the commandant, Colonel Gordon, that he was a member of the royal family travelling incognito. Colonel Gordon, so Macquarie reported, imagined him possessed "of Authority at pleasure to supersede All Governors Commanders, etca, etca, wherever he pleased to visit. In this Belief, Lieut. Col. Gordon had Actually Surrendered his Command to Mr McHugo, who was likely to have made a Very Alarming Use of the Power so Yielded to him, had not the Other Officers found it Necessary, to their personal Safety and to the Duty they owed their Sovereign, to remonstrate with Col. Gordon, whereby they at length Effected the Measure of sending Mr McHugo hither under a Military Guard." Thwarted, the poor man became violent and was very obviously, when Dr. Redfern examined him, "in a state of Outrageous Insanity." His brig and cargo were auctioned in Sydney and the proceeds sent back with him to India. Here he lay for two and a half years in an asylum before, probably on the strength of his winning manners, he made his way to London. There he importuned Lord Sidmouth early and late, asking for his brig and signing himself "Prince of Scotland (by birth) and (by Constitutional Laws) of Great Britain and Ireland." He pointed out that the throne was rightly his, but he would be content with a "moderate Subsistence." His appeal was touched with pathos—"if the members of Government possessed the real feelings of Gentlemen, they would not subject a Man, whom they know to be their King de jure, altho' He is an Irishman, to this humiliating Necessity." McHugo, who believed himself descended from Mary, Queen of Scots, and Bothwell, was the son of a Dublin tobacconist. His brig and cargo he had on credit.[2]

There was the international adventurer Jorgen Jorgensen, whaler, sailor, King of Iceland, convict, historian of Van Diemen's Land, sometime protégé of Sir Joseph Banks, who died in an Australian ditch.

There was the hard-headed, shadowy Captain Barnes who dreamed of an empire in Australia's north and peddled rum.

There was the fantasy of Captain John Piper who made in Australia his private Eldorado and whose possessions, sold in bankruptcy, read like a legend. The Catalogue of his effects, price 1s. 6d. read in part:

ALL the GENUINE ELEGANT FURNITURE and other valuable Effects, consisting of sofas, lounges, chairs and tables of rosewood, inlaid with buhl, elegant sets of dining tables, claw, loo, Pembrook and dressing ditto, brilliant pier, chimney and dressing glasses, of great dimensions, in rich gilt frames . . . elegant cut glass chandeliers . . . lofty four post, canopy, and other bedsteads, with rich hangings. . . . Splendid dinner services, breakfast and tea ditto, rich cut glassware, silver plate, comprising large cups and covers, hash dishes, gravy, table, and tea-spoons, four prong table and desert forks. . . . A cellar of valuable and choice wines consisting of Champagne, Claret, Madeira, Constantia, Saturn &c. &c. A most substantial London built carriage, with double sets of harness for four horses, in the most perfect state, a capital London built curricle, with excellent harness, about thirty horses, well known for their breed and quality, six boats with sails, awning, cushions and oars, brass and iron guns &c. &c. . . .[3]

And all this was in 1827. Captain Piper was an amiable, honest gentleman who, in a harsh world, became involved in dreams of luxury and splendour.

There was the prince of adventurers, Ben Boyd (1803-51), who arrived in 1842 with his own fleet of four ships flying his own "two bees" flag. He was banker, whaler, pastoralist (with eight hundred square miles of grazing land on the Murray). He built Boyd Town on Twofold Bay and for a time all went merrily, then came the cold wind. His bank failed and the shareholders found themselves in debt to the tune of £80,000. Public opinion was shocked to learn that his Kanaka labour was ill used. His empire melted away and he, still with mounting dreams, departed to California. Thence he sailed to the Solomons in his yacht *Wanderer* where he came to a mysterious and tragic end. The bones of his yacht are scattered on the sea-bed at Port Macquarie. His legend persisted.

There were other fishers in troubled waters and hunters in empty lands. They were all products and exploiters of the inevitable confusion of growth and distance. Land was the basis of the speculative "manias" of the late 1830s and early 1890s.

As land was the one definite asset Australia had, apart from providing a *distant* receptacle for convicts, it was the subject of more theories, changes, and experiments than any other strand of her history.

The history of land tenure in Australia began very simply with one assumption: all land was the property of the Crown. The aborigines alone might have been supposed to have some claim upon it and they, probably, at that time no more thought of a right to the earth they trod than to the air they breathed. Their rights were not considered and it barely entered their heads to defend them. In a penal settlement where a convict under servitude had in theory no right to possess anything, and where the official and military castes were not expected to have any interest in a permanent footing in the country, it appeared as if the asset would remain unexpended, but Governor Phillip was given the power to grant land in small parcels to ex-convicts. His instructions read:

> To every male shall be granted 30 acres of land, and in case he shall be married, 20 acres more; and for every child who may be with them at the settlement at the time of making the said grant, a further quantity of 10 acres, free of all fees, taxes, quit rents, or other acknowledgements whatsoever, for the space of ten years . . . Such persons . . . to be supplied with such a quantity of provisions as may be sufficient for the subsistence of himself, and also of his family, for twelve months, together with an assortment of tools and utensils, and such a proportion of seed-grain, cattle, sheep, hogs, etc., as may be proper.[4]

The Imperial Government's motives are plain. A convict, having completed his sentence, had a legal right to return to England. Some at least could do so, and did, by filling vacancies in the crews of transports, store ships, or such trading vessels and whalers as visited the coast. England preferred them not to return, and by giving to those who could profit by it—and this was necessarily left to the discretion of the Governor—a grant of land it was hoped that they could be induced to remain willingly in the settlement for the rest of their lives. It was also hoped that ex-convicts on the land would not only be able to support themselves and their families, but by supplementing public agriculture help fill the Government's granaries, building up provision for further instalments of convicts.

In the next paragraph of his instructions Phillip was vaguely told to give "every reasonable encouragement" to soldiers and other free persons wanting to settle.

Actually when Phillip discovered the hard row the settlement would have to hoe anyone who could and would cultivate land was welcome to do so, provided there was any seed to give him. The first settler he planted out under the terms of his instructions was James Ruse. In December 1789 he was given a grant at Rose Hill and a free pardon. At the end of 1790 he had an acre and a half under wheat, half an acre under maize, and a small kitchen garden. Three months later, when he had got in his harvest, he declared that he was able to support himself and his wife and was taken off the books of the store. The experiment had been a success and a formal grant of thirty acres was made to Ruse. Three other grants were made at the same time to free men, two seamen out of *Sirius*, Robert Webb and William Reed, 60 acres each, and 140 acres to Philip Schaffer, a German superintendent of convicts. By the end of 1791 44 ex-convicts, 31 marines, and 11 seamen were settled on grants on the mainland and on Norfolk Island. They were bound to work their land for five years and no rent was to be levied on it by the government for ten years, after which each grant was to pay an annual quit rent of a shilling. This is the debut of the quit rent, or token payment in lieu of rent, which in the future was to cause so much trouble. The theory behind it is difficult to deduce. It was hardly revenue and, since there was no coinage or intention of establishing one, it would have after ten years to be paid in kind. As a further small irritation the quit rent was apt to vary with time, place and person, but was never less than sixpence or more than a shilling for every fifty acres. It was really in the nature of a tribute, a perpetual small reminder that although the grants were given in perpetuity to a man and his heirs, provided he fulfilled the conditions, the Crown was still his suzerain. There is something feudal about the arrangement.

There was also a moral hurdle. No man, unless he gave evidence of having reformed, was allowed to become a settler. The Government was sternly paternal. Land was offered as a bribe. It was never quite given. It is interesting to note, too, that from the beginning there were nearly as many free men settled on the land as ex-convicts.

The small settlements of free, or freed, farmers were Phillip's particular pride and interest. He saw in them the growing point of the colony which he still believed, after all the vicissitudes of the early years, would some day be a proud possession of the Crown. When he left his government at the end of 1792 there were about sixty-seven settlers planted out.[5] He gave his own private possessions in livestock to be distributed amongst them as breeding animals.

It was Phillip, ironically, who first advised the Home Office[6] to allow land grants to military and civil officers, but it would be unfair to blame him for what came of it. The Marines and then the New South Wales Corps were sent out, not for any specified tour of duty, but indefinitely. The Marines were recalled because of their incessant quarrelling. Phillip may well have thought that an interest in the land would relieve some of the strain whilst it increased the colony's resources of grain. He did not envisage any but an agricultural future for New South Wales and had he remained Governor the privilege would not have been abused.

Phillip had no instructions as to granting or leasing land in Sydney itself, but with an eye to future development, he thought all land in it should be reserved to the Crown. He drew a line from Cockle Bay (today's Darling Harbour) to Garden Cove (Woolloomooloo Bay) and one of his last Government Orders read: "It is the orders of Government that no ground within the boundary line is ever granted or let on lease, and all houses built within the boundary line are to remain the property of the Crown."[7]

The self-interested abuse of land grants made by the New South Wales Corps and the system of privilege built on it has already been dealt with in Chapter VI. Macquarie was sent to suppress these abuses, which to some extent he was able to do, but an indelible character had been stamped upon the colony. The habits formed went too deeply and suited too many of the inhabitants—above all they suited the sheep, who were now the leading citizens—for him to be able to eradicate them. From a Welfare State Australia had been changed to a capitalist State and that could not be undone. The basis of wealth was land plus sheep.

By 1794 the Government had expanded the idea of grants. Land was to be used as payment. "Planters" were to be settled in "townships" for mutual aid and for security. The word "township" had then a different meaning from that attached to it today. It signified an agricultural community served by a small town or centre. In each such town land was to be reserved for public buildings, a site for a church with 400 acres of glebe attached to it for the support of the incumbent, a plot for a school with two hundred acres to maintain the schoolmaster. . . .

Any timber that would be useful to the Navy was to be reserved to the Crown on every grant. The grantee was to pay fees at the time the grant was given and these fees were to recompense the officials—the Governor's secretary, the surveyor, the registrar—who prepared the documents and delineated the land.[8] This was not only an economy, but it raised the land grant out of reach of the newly emancipated convict. At the same time the leasing of Crown land for periods of up to fourteen years was permitted. This was a sop to the crescent pastoral industry. These new regulations were straws which showed the way the wind was blowing.

The Home Government always claimed the right to make the rules for the granting, and later for the selling, of land, but as rules were also drawn up in the colony as expediency dictated and as many of the inhabitants were artists in both legal and illegal methods of self-help the ownership of land was in perpetual confusion.

When Hunter mustered the settlers in 1797 he found that one hundred and fifty of them had taken up land without grant or authority. There may well have been more, the canny ones who dodged the muster. Some of the illicit landowners were found to be lifers or still serving their sentences. Those who were making a success of farming and who had not called attention to themselves by bad conduct were allowed to continue in the possession of the land, the others were taken back into government gangs. One thing was obvious, land tenure already needed to be straightened out.[9]

On 9th April 1802 Governor King issued a proclamation:

> Whereas great confusion will occur hereafter in ascertaining the boundaries of the Allotments of Lands granted to individuals, owing to the smallness of the scale on which they have hitherto been delineated, and the different hands through which the writings have passed (many of which are totally effaced), and many allotments being partially or totally connected together by the verbal agreements of the possessors, which must in a short time cause that confusion and litigation which it is so necessary to provide against, as well for the present and future interests of the colony as for securing to each person the property he has acquired or become possessed of. . . .[10]

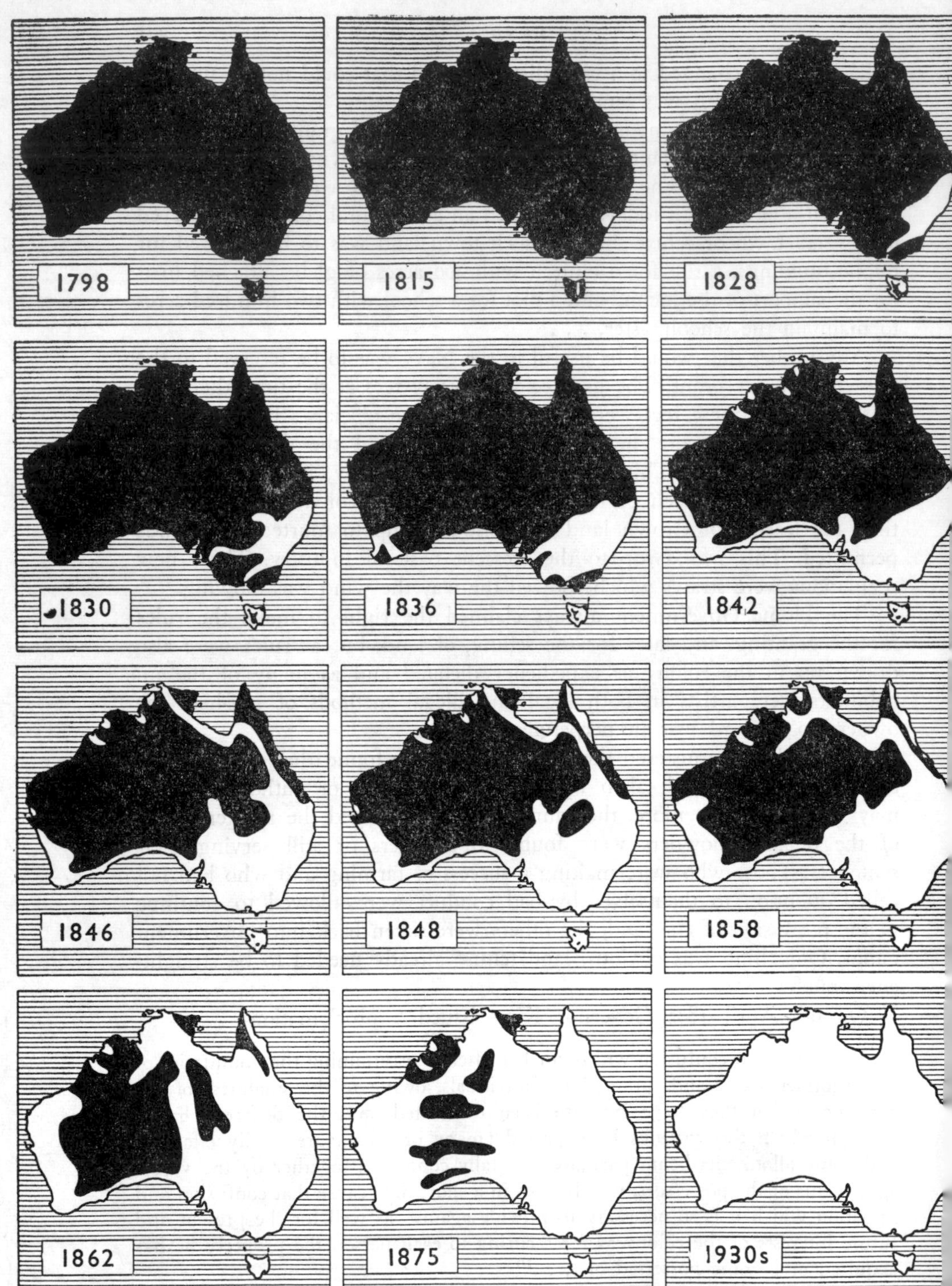

Map 3 (Opening Up the Continent)

In other words, the lands granted had not been properly surveyed, in many instances not surveyed at all; titles were either falsified intentionally or allowed to become effaced by the neglect or illiteracy of the holders; the conditions of the grants, such as five-year occupancy, had not been observed. King discovered that settlers were selling their grants even before they received them.[11]

The government surveyors were now ordered to make maps, scale one inch to the mile, of each district, showing all grants. Copies of these maps were to be lodged in the Surveyor's Office and in the Office of the Governor's Secretary, so that disputes could be easily settled by reference to them.

The following July two parishes were set up.

His Excellency is pleased to direct that in all Spiritual, Judicial, and Parochial Proceedings, Transactions, Deeds, Instruments, and Registers, that the Districts of Sydney, Petersham, Bulanaming [an area on Cook's River near Botany Bay, including the modern Mascot], Concord, and Liberty Plains [Strathfield-Homebush area], be comprised with a Parish to be henceforth named "Saint Phillip", in honor of the first Governor of this Territory; and that the Districts of Parramatta, Banks' Town, Prospect Hill, Toongabbie, Seven Hills, Castle Hill, Eastern Farms [Ryde], Field of Mars, Northern Boundaries [area north of Parramatta], Ponds, and Kissing Point, be comprised with a Parish to be henceforward named "St John's" in honor of the late Governor, Captain John Hunter; and that the Churches now building at Sydney and Parramatta be respectively named Saint Phillip and Saint John.[12]

Taking things at their paper value, it would appear that all was now shipshape, but no, confusion continued, the Survey Department was quite unable to keep pace with the granting of land and frauds were practised almost as a matter of course.

Brisbane in 1822 found even worse confusion than King had found in 1797. He wrote to the Colonial Office on 3rd September:

Soon after I had reached the Colony, I perceived that the lands in the towns were holden almost wholly by permissive occupants. Scarcely a crown grant or a crown lease in being; every tenanted allotment almost having been purchased from some obscure individual, who had exercised the right to sell, under an old verbal permission to occupy, given him by a magistrate or the surveyor. I did not then know, nor have I since been able to discover, any means of reducing this confusion into order, except by directing the Surveying department to draw a plan of each town with the divisions of prescriptive property actually subsisting; then, to frame a lease establishing a quit rent of such an amount that no more applications for allotments would be made than there were allotments to be let; and afterwards, to notify to these permissive occupants that they must take leases of the new form, or relinquish their claims. It was not until this had all been completed, which required a long time, that I could properly ascertain what allotments were disposable. This nevertheless has been accomplished for Parramatta and Newcastle; and I will venture to assert that applications for leases in these towns are answered now with every readiness. But neither Liverpool nor Sydney have been reduced into order as yet, which cannot be deemed surprising, if we couple the extreme irregularity of the boundaries of all their allotments with the various other duties of the Surveying department.[13]

Outside the towns things were no better. Brisbane goes on:

On obtaining the promise of a grant, the settler formerly went and located himself. Many, who had thus established themselves in the year 1811, have not to this hour had their boundaries so marked as to be able to fence; while some, bringing to the colony the commodity too often imported of a litigious disposition, have under this system purposely seated themselves on the same acre of ground; next quarrelled about boundaries, and then one of them has proposed to Government to forego his claim on receiving the compensation perhaps of two thousand acres in addition.[14]

He was sure that deceptions were being practised on the Government to obtain huge land grants.[15]

The Surveying Department was the bottle-neck. The staff was always too small to cope with the work and it was difficult to find, or induce to come to Australia, men with the required skill. Sometimes men impressed for the service turned out badly, as Assistant Surveyor Dangar did. In 1827 he quietly appropriated 1300 acres for himself and his brother. Governor Darling ruled that if his conduct was to be noticed "at all", he should be dismissed, but surveyors being so short this was thought too drastic.[16] An irregularity like this was only an excrescence. The real troubles were the size of the country, the confusion in grants already existing, the rapidity with which settlement was spreading, and the small number of surveyors. It did not help matters when in January 1825 Lord Bathurst sent Governor Brisbane a directive to divide the colony into counties, hundreds, and parishes, and to survey the whole forthwith. The machinery for this Herculean task was to be a commission of three members headed by the Surveyor-General. Each county was to be about forty miles square, each hundred a hundred square miles, each parish twenty-five square miles. Reports, charts, and maps were to be sent regularly to the Governor and the commissioner was at the same time to value all land, to mark out roads, government reserves, church and school lands, and allot extensions for townships.[17]

This was impossible of achievement and is an index of the complete incomprehension of land problems that existed in England. Lord Bathurst later explained that he had not meant a trigonometrical survey, but some sort of rough but orderly division of the land.

In 1828 the Surveyor-General, Major Mitchell, estimated that an "effective" survey of the 33,180 square miles that then comprised the colony, would with his present staff of ten surveyors and four draftsmen, take twenty-four years to complete if they had no other work to do and if the land were cleared. The "woods" made survey impracticable.[18]

The lag in survey caused much discontent amongst settlers, they were kept waiting, eating up their resources, whilst their land was measured.

An agricultural future was at first the only one envisaged for Australia. If the convicts would stay there after their sentences had expired and if by their efforts and by the produce of government farms the settlement could be made self-supporting in foodstuffs at least, it was all that the Home Government asked. The birth of the pastoral industry modified its ideas, but Secretaries of State saw nothing incompatible in simultaneously encouraging grazing and farming, private enterprise and government production.

Naturally with the free granting of land and assignment of convict servants public agriculture declined. When both fell into the hands of the monopolists the government farms withered away, as the Duke of Portland at the Colonial Office was "sorry to observe".[19] Governor Hunter pointed out to him that the increase of agriculture meant not only an increase of grain and livestock but the necessity for a market. The colony could afford a surplus as little as it could afford a shortage.

Not only were the officers busy tilling their land, but Grose had opened up in 1794 a new farming district. "I have settled on the banks of the Hawkesbury twenty-two settlers, who seem very much pleased with their farms. They describe the soil as particularly rich, and they inform me whatever they have planted has grown in the greatest luxuriance."[20]

Within a year there were four hundred settlers and the farms extended "near thirty miles along the banks on both sides of the river".[21] Pride in this achievement was short-lived. Aborigines harried the settlers and troops had to be sent to protect them, but far more serious was the repeated flooding of the river.

> The rise of the river was so rapid that one person, a settler, was unfortunately drowned, and I much fear that it would be the utmost imprudence to place any dependance on that settlement as a resource. The soil certainly is uncommonly fertile, and no doubt considerably aided by those occasional overflowings of the river, but the settlers are at present alarmed, and many have offered their grants again to the Crown. It would be a work of more labour and expense than we can at present command to throw up banks capable of resisting the force of the torrent, but without some such expedient the settlers never will be perfectly secure.[22]

They were insecure in another sense not here stressed. Grose did not put himself to the trouble of drawing up proper grants but simply issued a chit: "A.B. has my permission to settle."[23]

Paterson's prognostications were not fulfilled. The settlers returned to their land. Again and again and again they were flooded out and the Government had to come to their assistance.

The Hawkesbury was not one of the preserves of the officer-farmers. It was too far out of town for them to combine its cultivation with their military duties. It remained a settlement of small holders and they suffered the fate of other small holders at the hands of the Corps. King, just before assuming his governorship, found them very depressed, with fifty writs for debt issued against settlers in that one district. He appealed to Hunter, who was still Governor, but Hunter was deeply disillusioned.

> It may perhaps be said they have had too much consideration and attention paid to their interest, and sometimes at the public expence; and their subsequent conduct has but too often manifested how little such humanity was merited. If you can suggest any means of less'ning the exhorbitant demands of creditors which the law will admit I shall be much pleased, and will give it all the authority I hold.[24]

The wolf, rum, was in the fold, too.

> Charles Scoldwell, a convict, is now keeping a most disorderly hutt on the Green Hills, at Hawkesbury, and retailing spirits at a most exhorbitant rate without licence or authority. The settlers, from these irresistable lures, are prevented from cropping their grounds, and what remains in their stacks falls into the hands of three or four bloodsuckers. . . .[25]

So wrote King in the days of his reforming zeal. But the Hawkesbury settlement struggled on in the pattern of that peasant farming community which Phillip had hoped to establish and that Macquarie tried to re-establish. These farmers were the only part of the population with whom Bligh, by the help he gave them in flood time, won popularity. Macquarie was shocked by the wretchedness of their homes and, to encourage them to live above flood level and to have safe places to which to drive their stock in times of peril, founded five towns on the surrounding hills.

It might be said that such a trying ground did something to alienate the Home Government from its system of small land grants to ex-convicts. In 1801, when in eight months there had been four floodings of the Hawkesbury, "many farms [were] totally deserted for want of ability in the possessor to cultivate them".[26] Yet an acre of land there could produce 25 to 35 bushels of wheat while elsewhere only 12 to 14 were reaped.

In Governor King's instructions, which arrived some time after he had assumed the governorship, emphasis was laid on grants to free settlers to whom he could assign convict servants at his discretion on the understanding that they would maintain them. Lord Portland also made the proviso that for every 1000 acres granted 500 should be kept as a reserve for the Crown.

So far, that is up till 1805, the grants were given solely for agricultural purposes and were therefore relatively small. In that year John Macarthur returned from England with an order from Lord Camden for a grant of 5000 acres (he had asked for 10,000) for the purpose of breeding sheep. The wool-growing industry was under way and needed larger and larger tracts of land. Until the crossing of the Blue Mountains in 1813, when the vast interior of the continent became available, the graziers were within the grant system and their needs expanded it. John Macarthur's grant was one of the first and certainly the largest specifically ordered in England. It meant that the granting of land was changing from expediency to policy.

King, meanwhile, was continuing to settle land, as systematically as circumstances would permit, between Prospect and the Nepean, and was offering prizes for good farming, renting out oxen at 10 bushels of wheat a year to approved settlers with ploughs or carts, or selling them at 70 bushels and cows for the equivalent of £28, under the proviso that they should not be alienated till the third generation.[27] He also gave livestock as prizes for good husbandry, thus ensuring that they came into the hands of the more capable farmers.[28]

Meanwhile the colony was growing and spreading and the land was supporting the people. At the beginning of King's governorship the whole population of 4936 (2959 of them victualled by the Government) was contained within the County of Cumberland. There were two towns, Sydney and Parramatta, with farming areas at Petersham, Concord, Homebush, Hunter's Hill, the vicinity of Parramatta, Prospect, Toongabbie and along the Hawkesbury River from Richmond to Windsor. Four hundred and one landowners had absorbed 43,786 acres under grant. By 1806, when he left Australia, the settlement had expanded north, west and south; the population had increased to 7052 (30 per cent of whom were rationed); 84,465 acres had been alienated and there were 646 landowners.[29]

In the same period sheep had increased significantly from 6124 to 21,457, cattle from 1044 to 5286.

It did not take much to rock the ship, however. The bankruptcy of William Cox, Paymaster of the New South Wales Corps, led to a wide distribution of his stock and King, to accommodate them, made fresh grants in every district.

This I have done, with an intention of encouraging the rearing of stock at the bankruptcy of the Paymaster of the New South Wales Corps, who had monopolised a great quantity of stock, which had been bartered and exchanged by Government, has distributed the stock so that every industrious settler possesses some of one kind or another. To feed this increasing stock requires pasturage. To give all two or three hundred acres each would soon alienate all the disposable land adjacent to the settlers, and to give particular people three or four hundred acres each in places of their own selection would soon reduce the small farmer to sell his farm and stock, because he cannot feed them, to the person who can command money or its worth.[30]

In the history of land grants the devious proceedings of Governors King and Bligh were an innovation. Before he left office King made three grants of 240, 150, and 1000 acres respectively to Bligh, and as soon as he assumed office Bligh made a grant of 790 acres to Anna Josepha King, the Governor's strong-minded wife, which she called "Thanks". Bligh's land grant was to make trouble in the future when his six heiresses claimed a large part of Parramatta on the strength of it. The exchange of grants was not resorted to by any other governors and found little favour at Home.

Macquarie, as might be expected, was generous with land. When he departed there were claims for 340,000 acres promised, but the formal grants for which had not been executed. Sir Thomas Brisbane, his successor, as usual found land tenure in confusion. He wrote to the Secretary of State: "Surprised, no doubt, would Your Lordship have been to have witnessed the avidity with which the Major General was pressed for promises of land to the very last moment of his Government." Brisbane found that "an unsupported assertion, under the signature of the Convict clerk in the Surveying Department, that such a promise had been made, has been known to pass current with as much confidence in the public market as a Spanish Dollar".[31]

So the new Governor set to work to tidy the situation. In future chits signed by irresponsible persons would not be accepted as valid titles. He claimed for the Crown the right to annul any grant over a certain size if there were any irregularity in its title.[32] Land grants to emancipists were not to exceed ten acres unless they could prove that they had sufficient capital to develop more. The period of victualling from the store was dropped, in theory at least, from six to four months for all types of settlers. The property qualification was now well entrenched.

Brisbane inserted a new clause in each deed of grant by which the owner must maintain one convict for every hundred acres received. Lord Bathurst was dubious about this.[33] He would have preferred a quit rent of 1½ per cent on current estimated value of the land. This, however, was rather too complex an arrangement for the young and fluctuating colony. It would have been very difficult to discover the value in money of any plot of land.

In two years 107 grantees accepted land with the obligation of maintaining convicts.[34] Brisbane had it all neatly worked out:

> The Six months provisions for seven persons that are allowed to a proprietor, promised, for instance, two thousand acres of land, if expended with good husbandry, would soon enable him to raise a sufficiency of grain for the twenty he will be obliged to support ultimately; and a very small sum of ready money, laid out in swine, would ensure him a Stock of meat more than adequate to the wants of his men in a climate favourable to the multiplication of this most prolific animal. The mimosa would manufacture the leather required for the shoes of his servants with a facility unknown in the northern hemisphere; the straw of his wheat would be plaited into hats for light coverings to their heads; while the european flax, growing with luxuriance in a latitude requiring clothes of linen only, would readily supply every other want. . . . they would soon cost him nothing besides the trouble of Superintendence; and his outlay at the Beginning would be ultimately restored.

The superintendence would fix the owner's residence on his estate "instead of living in a dissipated Capital and thereby giving the reins to that course of stock plunder which from this very cause has run to such lengths in Van Diemen's Land".[35] Brisbane was playing the old, smooth game of make-believe. Lord Bathurst was now granting land in large parcels fairly freely, for example, 10,000 acres to T. P. Macqueen on the plea that times were bad and that he could plant out his indigent tenants on an Australian estate.[36] The absentee owner began to be one of Brisbane's worries. So, too, were the land-owning public servants. "So long as public Servants are permitted to become landed proprietors, the opposition I have hitherto encountered from the legitimate supporters of my government, must ever continue to be experienced in the execution of every measure of economy."[37] Perhaps he did not fully appreciate that men could hardly be persuaded to come out from England to serve in a remote penal colony for no more than their salaries. It was the expectation of becoming landowners that drew them.

Bigge had recommended in his report that Crown land should be sold in the colony. To Brisbane was given the task of implementing the new policy. Grants and sales were to continue side by side. The grant was a valuable piece of patronage, and as it became evident that the future of the colony lay with grazing, and as flocks doubled their numbers every three years, it was evident that no proprietor could afford to buy enough land for his flocks and herds. He must be encouraged by the Government with grants for which Lord Bathurst was determined that an annual quit rent of 1½ per cent a year was to be paid.

Macarthur was asking for all the ungranted land in the Camden district bounded on the north by the Nepean, west by Mount Hunter

Creek, south by Brisbane [*sic*] and on the east by West Camden.[38] He was willing to buy or to pay quit rent as Lord Bathurst pleased. In 1823 Bathurst ordered him further grants. He and his family already had 15,498 acres in the Cowpastures.[39] When Brisbane offered him another 5000 acres south of a grant he had named Brisbane he was dissatisfied. "Nothing," wrote Brisbane, "would satisfy Mr Macarthur, however, except the Cancellation of this deed . . . and the surrender into his hands of the Government establishment at Cawdor, and the grounds which had been always reserved for a Church, a School, and a Town. As I considered it impossible to Yield to this demand, Mr Macarthur is in consequence daily displaying irritation. . . ."[40] Brisbane was reproved by Lord Bathurst and Macarthur was given the 10,700 acres he desired at an annual quit rent of £142 10s. He had learnt that it was profitable to bypass local authority and make his requests direct to the Secretary of State. Lord Bathurst developed quite a taste for patronage and was unmoved by colonial regulations and reservations.

Macarthur was not the only one who had an insatiable appetite for land. "Not a Cow calves in the colony but her owner applies for an additional grant in consequence of the encrease of his stock. Every person to whom a grant is made receives it as the payment of a debt; every one to whom one is refused turns my implacable enemy," wrote Brisbane to Bathurst in November 1823.[41]

Squatting in the interior, which has already been discussed, eventually solved this problem. Two land policies had to be worked out, one for the squatter and the other for lands within the "bounds of location", that is within areas voluntarily released by the Government for settlement.

In 1824 the sale of land began. The graziers could look after themselves. Grants were retained for the maintenance of churches and clergy, for supplying dowries to the penniless daughters of clergymen, for rewards (though this use of land quickly fell out of favour with the Colonial Office), for settlers newly come from England. . . . In January 1827 Governor Darling was writing to Lord Bathurst that there were numerous applicants for land, "but the Executive Council advised that none but persons arriving from England with authority from your Lordship should receive Grants, until your Lordship's pleasure should be known".[42]

Lord Bathurst had already made history by ordering a grant for a single woman, Miss Eliza Walsh. "I am not aware of any reason why females, who are unmarried, should be secluded from holding Lands in the Colony, provided they possess sufficient funds for the purpose, intend *bonâ fide* to reside on their Lands and to fulfill any other stipulations. . . ."[43] Miss Walsh had been angling for a grant since 1801.

Grants also were still being made to settlers already established, but only if they maintained an additional convict, beyond the one kept for each 100 acres they already possessed. The average expense of a convict was £25 a year, the average price of land 5s. an acre. Oxley, the surveyor, pointed out that this arrangement would need policing. A certificate from the Colonial Secretary as to the average number of convicts employed by each landowner applying for the "indulgence" was absolutely necessary. "It would also be an important point towards attaining a Correct Knowledge of the Convicts in the employment of Settlers, if, on the discharge (for whatever reason) of the Convict, a Certificate thereof was transmitted by the master to the Office of the Colonial Secretary."[44] The only trouble was that with the increase of book work the chances of mistakes and corruption also increased. Brisbane found himself involved in another difficulty. The extra grants allowed to established landholders were also asked for by their sons on the same terms. Brisbane played safe and asked for a ruling from the Colonial Office. Brisbane was nothing if not impartial; he had not, as Macquarie had had, any political reason for building up one party in the State against another. His whole endeavour was to carry out his instructions, but not slavishly.

He doubted from the first the wisdom of mixing grants and sales and wrote to Lord Bathurst: ". . . whilst the system of free Grants exists, there is but little chance of extensive improvement taking place generally in the Colony, as the improver of Land can never enter the Market in competition with the Individual who gets His Land for nothing."[45] As a source of revenue the sale of Crown lands was in the long run illusory unless the money was, in one way or another, dug back into it. The asset simply decreased. In 1825 the value of ungranted land in the County of Cumberland was assessed at £33,588 and in the County of Camden at £10,550.[46]

The price of land to be sold was one of the first considerations. Bathurst's plan was that all land be classified into three classes: (i) the best land, which should fetch 10s. an acre, (ii) moderately good land for 7s. 6d. an acre, and (iii) inferior land at 5s. an acre. This was referred to Brisbane as the man on the spot. Bathurst's intention was to strike a just and liberal price. It was a difficult question. The classification of land would take time and, in any case, it could only be considered good, medium, or indifferent in relation to the use to which it was to be put. Much land had changed hands privately, but the prices received were not a safe criterion of value. Many of the sales were forced and in others considerations other than money—for example, exchange of lands and transfers of stock—came into the transaction. The Government's price boiled down to what it could get for any particular area.

In a dispatch of 1st January 1825 Lord Bathurst clarified his theories. As new counties were opened up church lands were to be allotted first. The remainder of the land would then be made available for private enterprise. The worst thing that could happen, Bathurst thought, was that large tracts of land should fall into the hands of men with insufficient capital to develop them or who acquired grants only for the purpose of speculation. Men might be led in good faith to ask for grants and accept the condition of maintaining a convict for every hundred acres, only to find that their servants were useless as agricultural labourers and did not make their keep, and so they would be ruined. Penniless (and therefore undesirable) persons were apt to camp on unimproved tracts and become a menace.

Crown reserves turned out to be a nuisance, for the estates of the richer or more enterprising colonists became separated from each other by intervening tracts of the "Original Wilderness". It was time, evidently, that the Original Wilderness was tamed. Capital would be the cure for all these troubles. "It is therefore to be constantly borne in mind that the possession, or at least the command of Capital, are essential qualifications of every Agricultural Settler in New South Wales."[47] The evidence of that capital was the ability to purchase land and pay for it. "The Local Government will be authorized and required to accept the upset price, if offered, unless within one Calendar month afterwards, a higher and better offer shall be made."[48] If there were no offer at the Government's price—that is, 10s., 7s. 6d., or 5s. an acre according to value of the land—in three years, then it could be sold for what it would fetch. The cash purchaser was to receive ten per cent discount and the whole of the purchase money was to be refunded if the landholder could show that in ten years he had supported convicts whose maintenance, at £1 12s. a year each, added up to ten times the amount of purchase money. Each parish was to be charted and divided into lots each of 640 acres. Each lot was to be numbered and to be sold by its number on the chart. No man was to have more than 9600 acres in one tract except by special order from the Colonial Office. Grants were to be suspended until the scheme for selling land was organized and put into practice except—there were always exceptions—in special circumstances.

This important dispatch of January 1825 goes on to bring grantees into line with purchasers. They, too, must have capital and be able to spend on the land granted them a quarter of its value. After seven years they must be able to prove that they have done this or the grant would be cancelled. After seven years a quit rent of five per cent of the average value of the land would have to be paid yearly. The land would be redeemable at any time up to twenty-five years by paying twenty times the annual quit rent. On additional grants quit rents had to be paid immediately. Grantees would be credited, as were purchasers, with the maintenance of convicts at £1 12s. a year each. The largest grant must not exceed 2560 acres nor the smallest be less than 320 acres.

This was all very complex and the Governor and his surveying department were not able to put it into force. It had to shake down into something simpler. Surveyor Oxley, writing to Major Ovens in May 1825,[49] showed what that something simpler was. Five shillings an acre was too much, 3s. was a more likely figure. It was impossible to put unsurveyed and "undescribed" (that is, land that had not been classified into Bathurst's three classes) land up for public sale. Instead, private contracts were made; £270 might be paid for 10,000 acres at 3s. an acre, less ten per cent for prompt payment, the purchase money to be returned in two years time if a certain number of convicts were maintained. Applications to purchase had already been accepted for 230,000 acres, and within a week of the warrants' being issued ten per cent of the payment for 40,000 acres had been paid.

Brisbane was of the opinion that grants and sales should be run in double harness. He suspected that deceptions were being practised on the Government to obtain large grants.

> I should, therefore, take the liberty of suggesting, in order to frustrate this, that the Individual should be required to purchase a quantity of Land, equal to what He solicits the grant of, at one Dollar per Acre payable in three Years; that no grant should be made to Him until the last instalment should be paid, which would operate as a pledge of his real object in cultivating and improving the Land, and certainly will never bear hard on the Individual.

Not only would land sales yield a good revenue but they would "put down the traffic in land, as few Persons would choose to purchase it with a questionable title who could obtain it with a good one. I am of opinion that 100,000 Acres of Land might annually be sold at one Dollar per Acre, which would materially aid in the reduction of the expenditure."[50]

In Governor Darling's instructions (1825) Lord Bathurst, still at the Colonial Office, suggested the establishment of a Land Board "for your assistance, to whom you may refer Applications for Grants of Land, and from whom you may receive Reports on the various Claims of the different Applicants".[51] It should consist of three members, preferably officials, and their pay for this service should not exceed £100 a year. The idea had probably grown out of his earlier one of a group of three officials headed by the Surveyor-General to classify all land. He left it to Darling to determine whether this Board were necessary. Darling duly set up the Board.

The Governor had now lost what had been a valuable asset in the past, the power and the patronage of granting land. Control had always rested ultimately in England with the Secretary of State for the Colonies, but it was Lord Bathurst who made this power a reality. He dictated the rules down to the last detail such as the onus on the grantee or purchaser to yield up land for roads passing through his property. If he failed to cultivate it he must pay for the roads that would give access to land further out.[52] The Land Board took over the Governor's role locally. He simply set the rubber stamp of authority on its decisions.

It was the Land Board that disagreed with the Colonial Secretary. The Board favoured a system of grants rather than purchase because it felt that in granting land and collecting quit rents the Government retained more control than in outright sale. Lord Bathurst was not particularly interested in control. The convict nature of the colony was even more present in the mind of the Board. Bathurst wanted the land opened up by men of substance. The proof of their substance was their ability to buy, and their having sunk money in the land was the best assurance that they would make good use of it. To cultivate they would need labour, and in supplying labour convicts would be kept and employed without cost to the Government. It would arrange itself. He had the wider, Englishman's view, that the sum of individual prosperity equalled national prosperity.

The quit rents on grants were a constant nuisance. They were resented by the grantees. They were perpetually in arrears and it was very difficult for the Government to extort the money. A Collector of Land Revenue was to be appointed, preferably from the Surveyor-General's Department, but since surveyors were at a premium it would have to be someone poor at his job but honest and trustworthy.[53] Petitions for relief from quit rents were numerous even from men in the strong financial position of Hannibal Macarthur. There was always a drought or a flood or a blight. The nominee Legislative Council, made up almost entirely of landowners, sympathized.

Lord Bathurst preferred the less complicated business of sale. It was impossible to demand the whole purchase price immediately, so he allowed purchasers seven years to pay for their land, with rebates for cultivation and permission to buy larger areas if they could prove they could use them. Leases of Crown land equal to their grants or purchases were also allowed to graziers who remained within the limits of location. Gradually grants and sales came to mean one and the same thing. Both strongly resembled a hire-purchase system.

In 1827 another effort was made to regulate the land question.[54] Purchasers and grantees were both allowed to select land before it was surveyed. The land was then advertised for sale, within a month of the application, and went to the highest bidder. If there were no bids or they were below the Government's reserve, or upset price as it was called, the land was sold or granted to the original applicant at the minimum price.

The Executive Council discussed the price of land at its meeting on 14th June 1828 and different members set the average at from 1s. 6d. to

5s. an acre. The minimum price recommended after deliberation was 4s. 2d. an acre, later reduced to 3s. 4d.[55]

An effort was made to clear up the quit rent question at the same time. Grants were held under a great diversity of regulations. Within one parish landowners might pay 2s., 15s. or 20s. as quit rent for every hundred acres. Now, Oxley, the Surveyor-General, remarked optimistically, "each Settler knew the Quit Rent he would be charged with, and, selecting his own land, he was satisfied".[56] Governor Darling, a methodical man, would have liked the grant system retained with quit rents payable for twenty years on each grant. It would have made taxation unnecessary and no doubt he felt himself unpopular enough without bringing in any new levies.

He could not have his way. As the Home Government had determined to sell land, he proposed in April 1827 that it should be put up to auction, subject to a reserved price.[57] This was approved in a dispatch dated 9th November of the same year.[58]

It was under Governor Sir Richard Bourke that sweeping changes were made. In an economy campaign the Land Board was abolished in 1831.[59]

Government land reserves were opened for sale and, calamity of calamities, the already inadequate Survey Department was reduced. The Governor was strictly forbidden to follow the time-honoured practice of giving land in lieu of pensions or as a reward for services. Lord Goderich, now at the Colonial Office, wrote: "You will, therefore, understand that you are not at liberty to sanction the remission of any purchase money on the ground of public services without special authority from home."[60]

In January 1831 Goderich abolished land grants altogether and substituted the Goderich Regulations. By 1837 the practice of selling Crown lands by auction with a minimum price of 5s. an acre was firmly established and Lord Glenelg was worried lest there should not be sufficient competition in the Port Phillip district. He wrote to Bourke:

> I must also impress on you the importance of adhering rigidly to the principle of the existing Regulations as to the disposal of Land, and of fixing such a minimum price for its Sale as, in the possible absence of the same degree of competition which exists elsewhere, will afford a security against improvident appropriation of Crown Land at an inadequate price.[61]

In 1840 Lord John Russell, at the Colonial Office, remodelled land policy. He divided New South Wales into three districts, the northern, middle, and southern. Land auctions were restricted to the older settled areas where much of the land was already alienated. Here only the best land, because it had been reserved to the Government, and the worst was still available, and a fixed price was not practical. Auctions continued with an upset price of 12s. an acre. In the outer areas, he argued, sale by auction could only mean delay and uncertainty and a fixed price for all land, irrespective of quality, was the best arrangement. The purchaser knew where he stood and how much land he could afford, and naturally would choose the best lands, those which would bring the greatest profit to himself and to society generally, rather than be lured by a lower price into taking inferior land with a probable disastrous result.

In the still new Port Phillip district the rules were a little different. The Government was to make reservations for utilities and defence. In Melbourne and William's Town land was to be sold by auction. Two other towns could be set up if necessary, otherwise villages and centres would be left to private enterprise. Outside the towns the minimum price of all lands was to be £1 an acre so that policy would be brought into line with the adjacent Wakefieldian colony of South Australia.

In 1841 the Imperial Parliament passed an Act for "Regulation of Sale of Waste Lands in the Australian Colonies". Its aim was "stability and consistency" and its main provision was that the control of land was transferred from the Queen to the House of Commons. This meant, or was intended to mean, that the granting or selling of land was no longer a matter of grace and favour, that conditions were stable on the Statute Book. The Act suggests that the Imperial Government was taking its Australian colonies more seriously than ever before. There were other clauses in the Act: for example, the minimum price was set at £1 an acre. The Governor was given power to raise it but not to lower it. The revenue was to be used for immigration, for the protection of aborigines, on main roads and bridges. Sales and conveyances were through the Governor under Parliament.[62]

The Act was framed following the findings of a Select Committee of the House of Commons. After the Act a local Select Committee was set up to protest. It protested against the high minimum price and advised a remission of £80 to cabin passengers, £40 to intermediate passengers, and £25 to those who arrived steerage as *bona fide* settlers. Governor Gipps did not support these findings.[63] He was heartily glad to be rid of the responsibility for land policy.

The land question continued to seethe with Select Committees, petitions and reconstructions. In 1848 Earl Grey at the Colonial Office brought forward one plan for all colonial lands, thus integrating Australia with the rest of the Empire. He wrote: "An increasing progress of Sales, however, can only be effected by contriving some system, which should oppose almost no obstacle at all to any one who may form any wish to possess Crown Lands."[64] This statement brings the official land policy almost full circle. The earliest policy had been to get men onto the land and the land into production as fast as possible.

Two new yeasts were at work. One was the Wakefield theory of a "sufficient price" for land, which was being tried out during the 1830s in South Australia (*vide* Chapter X). Although never formally accepted as government policy, Wakefield's tenets had worked their way under the skin of the Colonial Office. The end of the transportation system was already in sight and with it, everyone recognized, would come more acute labour difficulties. The sale of land and the intake of labour to work it must be made to balance. The price of land must be kept high. The minimum price rose from 5s. in 1831 to 12s. in 1839 and to £1 an acre in 1843, and the practice of distinguishing between good, bad, and indifferent land had been dropped, revived, and dropped again. It had settled down on a flat minimum rate. This was more than most of the land was worth, certainly more than it was worth for grazing, but it was adjusted to put a brake on speculation, to conserve Crown land, and to bring in a substantial revenue.

In September 1837 Governor Bourke was writing:

> Every day is increasing in this Colony the influence of competition. *Bona fide* Settlers seeking to purchase land are continually uttering the bitterest complaints against mere speculative buyers, who bid against them at the public auctions and who sometimes endeavour to exact money as the price of their withdrawal. Such persons are popularly stigmatized as Land Sharks and Land Jobbers; and, whatever opinion may be formed of their proceedings, their existence is a pregnant proof of the vigorous spirit of competition prevalent at the Government Sales.[65]

The brake was as necessary as the anti-inflation measures of a later day. It was ineffective. After the boom came the crash. (It would seem that high prices stimulate rather than retard booms.) The country was headed for its deepest and darkest depression to date, for which the Governor blamed the "mania" of land speculation.

Wakefield had not seen salvation only in a "sufficient" price for land which was geared to ensure that it came into the hands of purchasers who, because of their capital, could use it to the best effect; he also laid down the opinion that revenue from land sales should be used for the good of the land, primarily in bringing out suitable immigrants, such as agricultural labourers and artisans. The high price of land would prevent these men from themselves becoming landowners for at least several years and in that way would keep the plug in the labour market. It is difficult, as with all fashions, to know whether Wakefield liberated a new idea or merely crystallized something that was in the air. His influence was far-reaching and it is interesting to see his theories appearing as official dogma.

The other ferment originated within the colony. The Constitution of

1842 gave the colony many of the reforms for which it had asked, including representative government, but the Home Government retained control of Crown lands and so of the principal source of revenue. Since the new legislators, like their predecessors, were drawn almost exclusively from the landowning class, it was felt to be unwise to give them control of land, the most controversial subject of the day. It would mean giving the squatting interest a free hand. Although the Colonial Office appreciated the value of wool, it retained a lingering suspicion that these men were outlaws and that, with power to distribute land, they would not only rule but devour the State. The ghost of the small holder continued dimly to haunt Whitehall just as "closer settlement" has been a recurrent demand and policy in Australia ever since. By reserving to itself all rights in Crown lands the Home Government retained economic control of the colony. Its despotism was benevolent. It thought not only of the Queen's rights but of the future of Australian citizens. The land was their heritage, in fact it was the heritage of the whole British Empire, and it could not be allowed to fall into a few hands or to be subject to the political vagaries of the moment. It must be conserved, for it was the only asset; it must be distributed "scientifically" and not according to the self-interest of one group within the State. In the 1840s Australia was pastoral and the graziers were the most politically powerful group in the state. They were numerous because practically every man, be he official or merchant or a member of one of the professions or a tradesman, added, if he could possibly afford it, grazing interests to his other sources of income. It was the get-rich-quick way until drought and depression clamped down on it.

The colonials, even if they ran no sheep, did not see eye to eye with the Home Government. They were bitter and rebellious because control of the Crown, or "waste", lands was denied to them.

It was the sore point to which everything came back. Harassed Governors attributed all their troubles to this withholding of the final sovereign right, even whilst they agreed with Imperial policy.

Governor Bourke expressed grave doubts as to the advisability of handing over control of Crown lands to the Legislative Council. He wrote in a dispatch dated 25th December 1833:

> It appears then to be deserving of the fullest consideration whether a power, so large in itself and in its exercise by the unofficial Members attended with so little responsibility, can with Safety or advantage be lodged in their Hands. The experience I have had during the last Session, and the disposition manifested by the Council in certain cases have tended strongly to increase a Mistrust, which I had previously formed of the expediency of confiding so much irresponsible power to so small a number of Persons, who by combination may at least defeat the objects of Government, if they cannot secure their own.[66]

In 1850 Governor FitzRoy was also, though more tentatively, against the local control of land.[67]

Short of control, the colonists demanded that revenue from land be spent on immigration. The almost equally curly question of immigration will be discussed in Chapter XXI. It locks in with land and they are separated only for convenience and clarity.

The foregoing is by no means a detailed account of the land question prior to the discovery of gold. Its complexity is due to a number of factors. Policy was framed in England where local conditions were neither known nor understood; had it been framed locally it would have been by one interested section of the community and the result would hardly have been better. The lag in surveying was a constant hindrance to the smooth working of any scheme. Confusion was caused and fostered by the simultaneous working of a number of different plans; when purchase replaced grants it was not, could not be, retrospective; sale was by tender or by auction, and the upset price and conditions of sale were in perpetual flux. There were at least two classes of land-user, the farmer and the grazier, whose needs could not be encompassed by the same rules, and there were other classes of landowners, such as retired military men, who had special concessions. Behind official land policy and in competition with it was the open market, in no way regulated. Anything could and did happen and the oftentimes careless or dishonest keeping of records by convict clerks or semi-literate persons added its quota to the pervading irregularity.

As an illustration of the confusion that could arise, take the Maziere-O'Brien land tangle. In 1824 Michael O'Brien, a convict still under sentence, though the Governor did not know this, obtained the promise of a grant of 500 acres near Parramatta from Sir Thomas Brisbane. It was not until 1831 that the deed was issued after being advertised "in the Official Newspaper of the time, according to the usual practice", so that anyone thinking he had a better claim might, during the following month, make his protest. The time for protest ran out on 14th September 1831 and the deed in favour of O'Brien was executed on 19th October following.

Meanwhile the land, which had lain idle so long, was advertised for sale by auction by the Sheriff on 13th October 1831. It was bought by David Maziere. His papers came through on 29th October and he took possession on the thirty-first. He remained in unquestioned possession until 1843 and put in many improvements. In fact, he sank his capital in the land, for he is subsequently described as a "very poor man". In 1843 O'Brien appeared on the scene again and "by action of Ejectment ousted Mr Maziere from the land which has since passed into other hands for valuable consideration".

Maziere applied to the Supreme Court, but the ejectment was upheld on a quibble. The sale of "right, title, and interest" was made on 13th October, but came into O'Brien's possession through his set of papers on the nineteenth. This was held to make the sale invalid. The reason O'Brien did not claim his land earlier lay in the fact that he was working out his sentence on Norfolk Island. The Legislative Council upheld the ruling of the Supreme Court. Maziere applied to the Executive Council for compensation as the costly mistake was the fault of the Government. Legal opinion was taken from the Attorney-General and Solicitor-General. Their final decision, although they admitted the hardship, was that "Mr Maziere has no title, legal or equitable, to the property in question", and so was not eligible for compensation.[68]

In 1851 gold in richly payable quantities was discovered in Australia. This event was more dramatic, though less stable, than the discovery that Merino sheep throve here. Gold is a nexus, a turning-point in Australian history, as I have already pointed out, not so much for the wealth it brought as for the social changes it precipitated. For the first time Australia had a glamorous label. It was Eldorado after all. There was for a few years a staple that challenged wool. The depression in the 1840s had forced the wool industry to reorganize. Gold not only robbed the grazier of his necessary labour but forced another reorganization, which had far-reaching results, on him.

The end of transportation had cleared the way for responsible government. In October 1852, Sir John Pakington, Earl Grey's successor at the Colonial Office, relinquished control of the "waste lands" to the colonial legislatures. It was ironic that this should happen at the very moment when the squattocracy was losing its political dominance, in the face of a greatly increased population and a changed social balance.

Grey, whilst withholding control of Crown lands from the Australian colonies, was proclaiming an Empire policy of autonomy and had handed over their lands, in the Queen's name, to Canada and to other North American possessions, and to New Zealand. The Council in Sydney did not fail to observe this disparity and to note that it was not founded on population figures, for in the early 1850s, New Zealand, a younger, less advanced colony, had only about thirty thousand white inhabitants. Grey's reply was that if the Australian colonies had united, or had set up, as he had advocated, district councils (a strong form of local government) he would have advised Parliament to release the land. The Australian colonies wanted neither union nor local government. They wanted to control Crown lands. From Sydney came a petition so strong and determined as to be almost threatening. Pakington bowed to the storm before it burst. He had neither the grasp nor the interest of Grey. New South Wales, the newly formed Victoria, and South Australia received control of their lands and so, presently, did Van Diemen's Land, or, I should now say, Tasmania.

It is at this point that the two stories already narrated, that of the graziers beyond the bounds of location and that of land policy within the stricter control of Government, become one story. The Australian colonies, so eager to control the land, so sure, apparently, that they could do so, now found themselves in a thorny thicket of problems.

When the easily won alluvial gold petered out and it could only be mined by expensive quartz-crushing plants and dredges many diggers discovered that they could not make a living. They could not afford to return whence they came, or they had acquired such a taste for a free, open-air life in which, even if it was hard, they were their own masters, that they wanted to remain in Australia. The community was hard put to it to absorb them.

Squatters who had bitterly lamented the scarcity of labour and had felt they faced ruin when their shepherds and hut-keepers left for the diggings and they saw no hope of future convict labour, adjusted themselves to the new circumstances.

Alfred Joyce, for instance, took a sour view of gold: "I wish now I were safe out of it and in England, as I am afraid the colony is ruined in the social point of view by these gold mines."[69]

His station was on the Loddon in gold-bearing country. Joyce took miners' horses on agistment and sold wheat to the diggers at £25 a ton and hay at from £15 to £18 a ton, as well as mutton, dairy produce, fresh vegetables, and candles made from his sheep's tallow. He was in an advantageous position because, being near the diggings, there were always men down on their luck who were glad enough to work for him. He built a bridge over the river and, securing it with chain and padlock, charged toll which in one month put him on the credit side. He grudgingly admitted that he did well, but he still did not like the changed circumstances.

> Although our property has nearly doubled in value since the discovery of the gold, I would myself rather have back the olden times when labour was plentiful and everything went on regularly and steady. We were then at least tranquil and easy in our minds, whereas we are now nearly worried to death with cares for the present and anxiety for the future, but I suppose must keep on hoping, even if it ends in despair.

Other squatters were not so fortunate, they could not get labour to shear their sheep and often had to drove them to the diggings, wool and all, to be turned into mutton. Scab, too, was brought over from Van Diemen's Land in sheep exported to the Mount Alexander fields for mutton, and it was ten years before any remedy could be found for it.

Graziers discovered that in the Australian climate their sheep and cattle did not need the individual care given to them in England. Had it not been for the dingo they would have needed no protection except in times of flood or bushfire. They lambed without assistance; shearing, dipping, and occasional droving were all that was essential. It was now, perhaps, that the grazier lost all contact with his animals as living creatures. They were so numerous, if some were lost what did it matter? Individually they had no entity, they were corporately a source of wealth, a very different situation from the flocks of five or ten sheep in Norway today, where each beast is known and valued.

The Order in Council of 1847 had given the pastoral industry a measure of security. Lacking labour, it was in the pastoralist's interest to fence his run. Once it was fenced he no longer needed shepherds, a boundary rider sufficed.

In any case the ex-diggers were not looking for jobs as shepherds. Many gravitated to the towns, set up businesses, or moved restlessly from job to job. Many more demanded land. There was plenty of it, but "unlocking the lands" was no simple matter. Few of the applicants had substantial capital, they had oversea ideas of a nice little farm and they looked to the Government to make land available for purchase in reasonably small parcels. Crown land seemed to be the answer. Near the towns the farm lands were taken up and would have to be bought in the open market. In the bush there was ample land, sketchily but tenaciously held by the sheep and cattle men. Especially in New South Wales and Victoria, closer settlement could only be at the expense of the grazier.

The approach was political, not scientific. The land had been roughly graded from time to time as good, medium, and bad, but it had not been scientifically classified as suitable to its various uses. Land was land and it was taken for granted that the squatters were using and keeping in its unimproved state vast areas that the Statute Book could transform into a myriad happy little farms. There had always been a party division in the State, between bond and free, emancipist and exclusionist, town and bush. The squatters had been treated as outlaws and yet they had been the *élite*. They had had power without security. They had resented the influx of diggers and the resentment was being returned, for they monopolized the land and the diggers were clamouring for it. There was a treasury of bad feeling to begin with and now in the 1860s there began a veritable land war. It was in reality economic, though it paraded as militant democracy versus hard-shell conservatism. A political remedy was sought and applied.

In 1861 the Minister for Lands of New South Wales, John Robertson, who had himself been a squatter, brought forward two Bills in Parliament which became the Crown Lands Alienation Act and the Crown Lands Occupation Act. Between them they opened all Crown lands, whether they were under lease or not, to purchase in blocks of from 40 to 320 acres. The time-honoured practice of allowing men to choose their own land was retained and, since the Survey Department was, as ever, inadequate to the great amount of work expected of it, they were allowed to select and take possession of their blocks before survey.

With the turmoil of the gold-rushes, the lack of labour, the need to reconstruct, the squatters had barely had the advantage of the Order in Council of 1847 giving them longer leases and pre-emptive rights. Now their leases were reduced to one year in the intermediate areas and five years in the unsettled areas, when they came up for renewal, nor was a lease any protection against purchase. Squatters were given the right to buy without competition, at £1 an acre, one twenty-fifth of their runs; they might buy more land at auction and they had the same rights as any other citizen—man, woman, or child—of selecting before survey.

The selectors must pay a quarter of their purchase money, that is, 5s. an acre, at once and the other 15s. within three years. There were various conditions, such as residence for three years and the improvement of the property, by sinking dams, etc., at the rate of £1 an acre. The selector would then be in possession of a freehold property with grass rights to three times its area—provided no one bought the land.

The crux of the whole situation was water. Whoever secured the waterholes, creeks, or river frontages (if any) possessed the land. Without water neither farmer nor grazier could exist. There was no effort to divide up the water supplies equably. It was catch-as-catch-can.

The Acts which were greeted with such enthusiasm by the would-be farmers and by the city-dwellers generally, as fine democratic measures, landed both the squatter and the selector in difficulties. The squatter was in the better position. Having already lent him money, the banks were willing to advance more money to safeguard their investment. Loans, whilst they crippled him, perhaps only temporarily, enabled him to secure the best parts of his run as freehold. He could and did take up blocks in the names of his wife, his children (probably numerous), his station hands, and anyone else he could use as a "dummy". He could buy out selectors who had been too smart for him and had taken up desirable situations with that very object.

The selector also had to find money and for him it was more difficult. Generally banks did not care for the risk. They had backed the other horse. He was driven to seek loans from the local storekeeper—it being an old Australian custom for the storekeeper to "carry" the farmer in times of need—or from money-lenders of the more extortionate kind. Often, if he were honest and intended to farm his land, he chose badly, knew little of farming conditions in Australia, and had marketing and transport troubles. If he were dishonest and shrewd he could make money out of his selection by blackmailing a squatter into buying him out, by over-cropping the land and when it was ruined abandoning it without having completed the purchase, or, if he were in the timber business, he could pay his 5s. an acre, take off all the timber, and depart. In any case the Government found it very difficult to get any payment out of most selectors after the first, just as it had been unable to collect quit rents.

The Acts were amended, but only as to detail. They failed in their purpose to establish a large class of sturdy yeomen farmers. Part of the failure was due to human frailty and part to the nature of the country. Much of the land forcibly settled was unsuited to small farming. Without experience and the aid of science and machinery the selectors had no hope of survival. Those who made a success of it were generally men with some money behind them who settled on good land, better fitted for agriculture than grazing. The statistical result was very disappointing. I. D. McNaughtan gives the figures: "Between 1861 and 1883 a total of 29 million acres of Crown land had been sold whilst the area under crop had increased by less than half a million acres."[70]

More damaging still was the effect on national morale. Great bitterness was engendered on both sides, dishonesty was rife and condoned, a state of class war became endemic and its emotions were carried into the unions by selectors forced off the land by squatters and spread its venom through the shearing sheds. The legislation was probably well meant, but no section of the community involved came out of the land war with clean hands.

In 1883 a Royal Commission investigated the land question. It found that most of the pastoral land selected for farming had slipped back to grazing, that for a variety of reasons many farmers had failed, that the smaller graziers had gone to the wall, and that many properties had passed out of private hands into the possession of banks or pastoral and finance companies. Officials were exercising the patronage that had once been in the steadier hand of the Governor and only an illusion remained in the minds of men in the street, the voters, that for a very small outlay they could become landed proprietors.

In Victoria the story was much the same. The Nicholson Act of 1860 provided for selection after survey, with pre-emptive rights over three times the area purchased and penalties for leaving the land unimproved. It was followed by Duffy's Act in 1862 and Grant's Act in 1865. These Acts were more strictly policed than in New South Wales. The Minister for Lands could eject unsatisfactory selectors and a Land Board supervised the system. In 1869 selection before survey had to be allowed. By 1884 practically all the Crown lands, except the Mallee, had been alienated. Still there was no yeomanry.

In Queensland, which had become a separate colony in 1859, Acts of

SIR JAMES STIRLING

From a portrait in the possession of Mrs David Clarke Guthrie

By courtesy of the Trustees

SIR FRANCIS FORBES

From a portrait by Rodius in the Dixson Gallery, Sydney

Parliament dealing with land were passed between 1860 and 1884, each patching the one before, always ineffectively.

Tasmania began unlocking her lands in 1858. The picture was much the same, though some of the land was really suitable for closer settlement and orchards and hop-gardens throve. Western Australia, lagging behind the other colonies again, passed her land legislation in 1872. Her large semi-arid areas made small farms an obviously unprofitable venture, except in the south-west corner. There was more trouble and disappointment. The pattern repeated itself in every colony except South Australia, which was already a yeoman community. Much of its land was suited to farming and the spirit of its people, a fair section of whom had arrived in search of religious liberty rather than of fortunes, was more attuned to a way of life offering security but not the gamble of a great fortune. Here, certainly with the assistance of legislation, good lands gravitated naturally to agriculture and the grazier occupied the poorer country farther out.

It would appear reasonable to suppose that with the alienation of most of the useful Crown land in Australia the land would cease to be a matter of political controversy and would simply come under the common laws governing property and ownership, that it would be bought and sold between citizens or organizations and limited areas occasionally resumed with compensation by the Government for special purposes, such as water conservation. It was not so. The idea or ideal of closer settlement remained firmly wedged in the public consciousness and recurrently expressed itself in legislation. "Forty acres and a cow" continued to be a popular slogan. A predominantly urban community has always had a romantic hankering to be "on the land". There is so much land that it dominates the population as the mountains dominate Switzerland and the fjords Norway.

For reconstruction after war or economic depression the popular answer has always been to plant men on the land. After the depression of the early 1890s the Closer Settlement Acts began again, in 1895 in New South Wales and 1898 in Victoria, but now the Government had to buy back land and resell it on easy terms to would-be farmers. The Rural and State Savings Banks, together with local government bodies, were the instruments used. It was a bureaucratic operation with, one guesses, more attention paid to political opinion than to economic and agricultural experts.

Some of the settlements were co-operative. An estate was bought by the Government and a group of families settled on it. In Queensland there were autonomous little settlements with the power to divide up the land by common consent according to need. The accepted idea was that they would assist one another. In New South Wales the Government was willing to lend each settler £25, in Queensland £20, to help pay for the seed, implements, and other necessities of the farm. This mirrored, in a small way, the ideals of benevolent socialism and co-operation current in the nineties. It was a phase of Australian "mateship", so often celebrated in the literature of the day. Unfortunately the experiments were not very successful. They did relieve unemployment for the time, but behind them was just one more theory born in offices, of good intentions, that did not take the land into consideration. Some authorities claim that it was the beginning of the system of bounties to farmers. This is not true. From Phillip's time onwards farmers have received government assistance, not in cash certainly, but in its equivalent of rations, breeding stock, labour. . . . Closer settlement Acts were sporadic in the eastern States from 1895 to 1906. Under all the Acts the land was sold cheaply on easy terms (or leased) with conditions of residence and improvement. Paternalism lived on.

So did suspicion of large runs. The electorate was largely urban, "unlocking the lands" was a catchword not easily forgotten, idealistic democracy, which did not exclude paternalism fast changing into bureaucracy, championed the "little man". Moreover, the large sheep and cattle runs had, in the nature of things, the appearance of being unimproved waste land and the squatter a dog in the manger. An attempt to break up large holdings was made from another angle. They were to be taxed on their unimproved value. South Australia led the way in 1884 with a tax of ½d. in the £1. This measure did not have the same popular appeal in New South Wales and Victoria as planting out settlers had had. There is no romance in taxes and the average citizen reacts automatically against them. But in 1895 Sir George Reid's Government successfully got an act through both Houses imposing a 1d. in the £1 tax on improved land values. The Labour Party supported the measure more, I think, from their general underdoggery than because they wanted the revenue. As far as the squatters were concerned the tax had more a nuisance value than anything else. It cannot but recall the quit rents of an earlier time.

More *bona fide* farmers settled, or tried to settle, on the land at this time. There was not the chicanery associated with the land war of the 1860s, but a great many of them failed at public expense. Their blocks of land, except in the most favoured areas, were too small for Australian conditions, they began loaded with debts which they were never able to pay and which governments often had in the end to cancel. Too often the new farmers lacked practical experience and had not the substance to weather even one bad season.

The so-called "proletarian" literature of the 1890s bristles with experiences of the selector from the hilarious and ever fresh slapstick of Steele Rudd's *On Our Selection* to more sombre efforts in which the daughter would have been sacrificed to the ubiquitous mortgage, in the good old Victorian way, but for the intervention of some young Lochinvar in moleskins, against a background of drought, bushfire, and flood.

However, the movement was not without effect. "Between 1891 and 1914 the area under crop rose from less than 850,000 acres to 3,400,000 acres in New South Wales; from two million to nearly four million acres in Victoria, and from almost nothing to over one million acres in Western Australia", according to A. G. L. Shaw.[71]

It was fortunate that with the greater dispersal of land a new and much simpler method of registering and conveyancing its title had come into common use. This was the Torrens system, described as "a statutory system of registration of title, designed to facilitate and simplify the transfer of land". It was embodied in a Bill introduced by Sir Robert Torrens during his premiership of South Australia, which lasted only a month. It became law in that colony in 1857. Under this system the slow and costly procedure of verifying a title by tracing it back to the original grant or purchase, much of the evidence for which was, to say the least of it, shaky, was replaced by the issue of a single ratified document on which all transfers, mortgages, etc. could be registered and which was taken as legally definitive. The law was proclaimed in South Australia in 1858, adopted in Queensland in 1861, and in New South Wales, Victoria, and Tasmania, the next year. Western Australia fell into line in 1874. The slow process of transferring the confused old titles into Torrens began. The decks were cleared for all new purchases and in an advertisement the words "Torrens title" meant as much as "vacant possession" came to mean in the era of housing shortages.

In 1901 there began a new wave of intensive "closer settlement" and series of Acts were passed in all States.

This action had been building up since the 1880s when the failure of the Robertson Land Acts was obvious and a more scientific approach to the land was making itself felt in irrigation, classification of land, and similar activities. Also by this time there was a greater, but not sufficiently great, practical knowledge of the Australian earth. The Acts empowered Governments to purchase grazing properties where the land was suitable for more intensive use, subdivide them, and sell the land, generally on terms of conditional purchase. Areas of Crown land were reserved for agistment of stock, irrigation works and other purposes beneficial to the country at large.

The *Commonwealth Year Book* for 1956 (p. 97) states succinctly:

> From the inception of closer settlement in 1905 to 30th June, 1954 2,385 estates totalling 6,511,156 acres had been purchased by the Crown at a cost of £28,123,107 for purposes of closer settlement of civilians and returned service personnel.
>
> Closer settlement is now being effected entirely under perpetual leasehold tenure. . . .

These figures refer to New South Wales and are a "spot check" only. Further reliable information may be easily culled from the *Year Book*.

The pattern was already laid down and the need to settle on the land ex-servicemen from two wars was fitted into it with adaptations to meet the circumstances.

The War of 1914-18 was followed by the problem of repatriating returned soldiers in a "world fit for heroes". Many of them had gone straight from school into the forces; they had no profession, trade, or job to return to, or were now disinclined for their former, probably dull, occupations. The return of the "diggers" was like a new mass migration. Government and public sentiment were pledged to take care of the men who had sacrificed so much for their country. Rather than seek employment, many of the returned soldiers were willing to work ten times harder than any employer would require them to do, in order to remain their own masters. The answer tc their needs seemed to be to put them on the land, and we had Soldier Settlements, financed by the Government on easy terms.

Unfortunately nearly all the old mistakes were repeated, and the farmers-to-be were given no agricultural training before they set about working their too small and often difficult blocks. The end result was another costly failure. It must be remembered that although land was administered by the Lands Office, under the control of a Minister, in each State, rehabilitation was and is a Commonwealth responsibility.

No one could sum up the land settlement policy before World War II better than Professor Keith Hancock in his now classic *Australia*. Looking naturally to his native state, Victoria, he estimated that £34,000,000, or a quarter of her National Debt, had been spent in putting men on the land and that the total loss would be not less than £8,000,000.

At the same time there has arisen a curious personal relationship between the settler and the State. The Government "habitually has more money in the farm than has the settler," with the result that the latter frequently becomes its "veritable child"—very frequently a discontented child; for the Government has told him what his land will grow, has fixed the size of his farm and the payments which he must make for it—and surely all this amounts to a kind of pledge that he will be able to meet his debts and make a living? Therefore the settler who is failing or who fears failure is tempted to raise the cry that he has been deceived. Very frequently he has been deceived. But the chances are that, the more he is himself to blame (and many of the schemes have appeared to be so generous that they have attracted men with no real enthusiasm or aptitude for farming), the more loudly will he blame the Government. The Government is only too conscious that it has made mistakes, and has not the courage to be brutal. Nor can it afford to be magnificently generous. And so these land settlement ventures begin to slip down a sticky slope of benevolence and bad temper, of wrangling and wangling, into a bog of bankruptcy. Still, there is a visible result. If land settlement schemes have involved the State of Victoria in extraordinary losses, they have, at any rate, put on the land nearly 15,000 settlers—with their dependents about 50,000 souls.[72]

Came the years of unrest in Europe culminating in the Second World War. The unrest brought the refugees, the end of the war the problem of rehabilitating with justice and generosity the returning service men and women. On their heels came the migrants from a shattered and disillusioned world. Society was better able to place them as the needs of war and the years of isolation it brought had encouraged local industry. There were many openings and opportunities, but there was still land-hunger, and room had to be found for those who wished to settle. The Commonwealth Government was determined not to repeat the mistakes of a generation before. One great advance was the training, under the Commonwealth Reconstruction Training Scheme, of ex-service men and women for the work they wanted to take up. This was a very much more adequate service than the vocational guidance provided after 1918.

Again there was the land, and it must be unlocked for ex-servicemen. Under the War Service Land Settlement Agreements Act of 1945 the Commonwealth arranged with the various States that land should be made available for the scheme. Each State formally ratified the Act and the expense and responsibility of implementing it was divided. Both land and settlers were chosen with far greater care than formerly, the size of the blocks was adjusted to the productivity of the soil, and the land was developed by the Government before it was occupied, so that it would bring reasonable returns within a reasonable time. The settler was allowed an "assistance period" of a year during which no repayment was required and a living allowance was made if necessary. Every applicant had to attend a course on the principles of farm management. All this, with the exception of the course of instruction, is very similar to the conditions on which the land grants were given, if for "ability" you substitute "worthiness".

Loans up to £1000 were made to settlers by the Government, repayable over thirty years with interest ranging from 2 to 3½ per cent. The land had also to be paid for eventually, but on very easy terms. The novelty lies in the careful selection of the land and the adjustment to it of the settler.

By June 1952 over seven million acres had been acquired and distributed by the States with the approval of the Commonwealth at a cost of more than £2,500,000.

The States also have closer settlement policies for the benefit of civilians. Land may be allotted by ballot between approved candidates and a loan policy is implemented by the Rural Bank.

While purely political action may be said to have failed sadly in opening up the land to the farmer because it was not realistic, the scientific or, if you like, politico-scientific approach was another matter. A process of adaptation, invention, and scientific research has done more to keep men on the land and to make land profitable than all the Acts in the Statute Book.

At first the farmer's attitude to his land was empirical. He either knew nothing about agriculture or he tried to force on the Australian earth the traditional procedures of English farming, hampered by the lack of implements, of manure, and of leaf-mould from deciduous trees. Farming was often enough, in the beginning, nomadic. As soon as the fertility of one plot of ground was exhausted the farmer moved on to another where the soil was temporarily enriched by the ashes of the trees and scrub that had grown on it. The difficulty with this was not lack of land but the thick pelt of timber and undergrowth which the land carried, making clearing a slow and discouraging affair. Governor Brisbane in 1823 organized clearing gangs, composed of convicts under an overseer. In each gang there were about twenty-three men and they were expected to clear the land at the rate of fifteen acres a month. This meant felling the trees and generally burning them together with the scrub. It did not include grubbing out the stumps. The land was then hoed, it being impracticable to use ploughs, except in the limited areas that carried no trees, because of the stumps. The earth was scratched and the crop sown. It took its chance with the suitability of the soil, the rainfall and other factors.

It was not until the 1840s that invention took a hand and the growing point was in South Australia, the farming state. Here the stump-jump plough was invented and greatly improved cultivation. In 1843 Ridley invented his stripper which in one action harvested and threshed wheat, reducing the cost of getting in the crop from 3s. to 3½d. a bushel. This was the ancestor of the more complex and thorough harvesters of today. The conservative farmer was slow to adopt it, but scarcity of labour forced his hand. Clearing was made easier, cheaper and more effective by the "Mullenizer", forebear of the modern bulldozer, which rolled down the scrub. It could then be burnt. This machine could not tackle large trees, which had to be felled; their stumps were at first burnt out but later extracted mechanically.

It was not until the 1890s that the cultivation of wheat made great strides. By that time science had been brought to bear on its problems. Professor Custance of Roseworthy Agricultural College in South Australia, by experiment, discovered that most Australian wheat lands suffered from a deficiency of phosphates and preached the use of superphosphates, already well known in England. Exhausted land, which was going back to grazing, was rehabilitated by their use. Sowing became mechanical and fertilizer was planted with each seed.

In 1886 William James Farrer, a Cambridge graduate, had begun experimenting with wheat to produce strains suitable to the Australian climate and resistant to rust and other diseases which were then rife. The result of his, at first neglected, experiments was to increase greatly the areas in which wheat could be grown.

Nothing could be done about rainfall, and Surveyor Goyder drew a line at the fourteen-inch annual average fall beyond which it would be unsafe to farm. When, attracted by exceptionally good seasons, farmers moved across Goyder's Line they were often sorry.

The disadvantages of low rainfall were minimized by dry farming, a system of fallowing and working the soil so that it retained its moisture and built up its nitrates. Irrigation in the 1880s brought the Murray Valley and other limited areas, once semi-desert, under cultivation. Much Australian soil only needs water to make it fertile, but with only one considerable river system, the Murray-Darling-Murrumbidgee, possibilities there are restricted.

As early as 1879 the presence of artesian water was discovered, and it is now known that there are at least six basins underlying about 950,000 square miles of the continent's surface. The water is mineralized but suitable for stock. It provides permanent water in the dry country. The problems associated with the tapping of bore water were investigated in a series of conferences of engineers between 1912 and 1924. Paddocks are channelled from bores so that sheep do not have to be brought to water but drink where they feed, a saving in labour and hardship. Some authorities predict that the supply of artesian water is not inexhaustible and advise that it should be used with care.

In 1890 New South Wales created a Department of Agriculture to administer and to advise in all matters connected with the land. In 1944 a Ministry for Conservation was set up and its work covered soil and water conservation, forestry and irrigation. The other States were providing similar facilities for farmers and graziers.

In 1920 the Commonwealth Government entered the research field in earnest when it founded the Institute of Science and Industry, the progenitor of the Commonwealth Scientific and Industrial Research Organization, incorporated by Act of Parliament in 1949. It is now a very large organization indeed, with stations and laboratories scattered all over the Commonwealth, covering almost every phase of primary and secondary industry. The nation owes much to this organization, particularly on its primary side, for its ceaseless work towards adjusting production to Australian conditions, with its soil surveys, its pasture improvement, costly but effective in reducing the size of properties by stepping up their fertility, its plant acclimatization, its investigation of plant and animal diseases, its war against pests (for example, the extermination of prickly pear by the introduction of the insect cactoblastis and the curbing of the rabbit menace by the myxomatosis injection), and many other projects, including the still problematically useful science of rain-making.

The States have further assisted their farmers and graziers by the setting up of agricultural colleges, the publication and free dissemination of brochures bringing the latest results of research to the farmhouse and homestead, the employment of inspectors and advisers and the use of mobile demonstration units, to name only a few activities.

The intelligent man on the land—grazier, wheat-farmer, orchardist, dairy-farmer—is assisted to get the most out of his property whilst maintaining its fertility.

This is only part of the story. It is not enough to produce, the product must be transported to marketing centres and then sold to advantage. From the building of railways and roads, to the establishing of marketing boards and price equalization schemes and the giving of bounties to enable Australian products to compete in the world markets without lowering the Australian standard of living, the Government has helped the primary producer. Only wool has not received or needed any such assistance.

The full story of this belongs more to science and economics, but in any history of Australia a space must be kept for it, for it is vital to the history of the whole.

REFERENCE NOTES

1 *Hist. Rec. Aust.*, ser. I, vol. xx, pp. 219-23.

2 M. Barnard, *Macquarie's World*, pp. 167-8. See also *Hist. Rec. Aust.*, ser. I, vol. ix, p. 545.

3 See *Hist. Rec. Aust.*, ser. I, vol. xiii, note 62.

4 *Hist. Rec. Aust.*, ser. I, vol. i, pp. 14-15.

5 *Ibid.*, pp. 401-2.

6 *Ibid.*, p. 35.

7 Commonwealth Parliamentary Library Committee, *Beginnings of Government in Australia*, p. 16.

8 *Hist. Rec. Aust.*, ser. I, vol. i, p. 527.

9 *Ibid.*, vol. ii, p. 18.
10 *Ibid.*, vol. iii, p. 620.
11 *Ibid.*, vol. iv, p. 485.

12 *Ibid.*, vol. iii, pp. 630-1. See also J. F. Campbell, "The Dawn of Rural Settlement in Australia", *J. Roy. Aust. Hist. Soc.*, vol. xi, pp. 83 *et seq.*, for a detailed analysis of early settlement.

13 *Hist. Rec. Aust.*, ser. I, vol. xi, p. 121.
14 *Ibid.*, p. 122.

15 *Ibid.*, p. 303.
16 *Ibid.*, vol. xiii, p. 149.
17 *Ibid.*, vol. xi, pp. 434-5.

18 *Ibid.*, vol. xiv, pp. 178-9, Major Mitchell's memorandum dated 29th April 1828.

19 *Ibid.*, vol. i, p. 495.
20 *Ibid.*, p. 470.
21 *Ibid.*, p. 499.

22 *Ibid.*, p. 529.
23 See *J. Roy. Aust. Hist. Soc.*, vol. xi, p. 105.

24 *Hist. Rec. Aust.*, ser. I, vol. ii, p. 653.
25 *Ibid.*, p. 654.

26 *Ibid.*, vol. iii, p. 426.
27 *Ibid.*, vol. iv, p. 500.
28 *Ibid.*, pp. 501-2.

29 See Frederick Watson, Introduction, *Hist. Rec. Aust.*, ser. I, vol. v, pp. vii *et seq.*

30 *Hist. Rec. Aust.*, ser. I, vol. v, p. 6.

31 *Ibid.*, vol. x, p. 630.

32 *Ibid*, p. 631.
33 *Ibid.*, vol. xi, p. 84.
34 *Ibid.*, p. 179.

35 *Ibid.*, pp. 180-1.
36 *Ibid.*, p. 141.
37 *Ibid.*, vol. x, p. 730.

38 *Ibid.*, vol. xi, p. 94.
39 *Ibid.*, p. 182.
40 *Ibid.*

41 *Ibid.*
42 *Ibid.*, vol. xiii, p. 5.
43 *Ibid.*, vol. xii, p. 348.

[44] *Ibid.*, p. 398.
[45] *Ibid.*, vol. xi, p. 331.
[46] *Ibid.*, vol. xii, pp. 394-5.
[47] *Ibid.*, vol. xi, p. 440.
[48] *Ibid.*, p. 441.
[49] *Ibid.*, p. 692.
[50] *Ibid.*, p. 303.
[51] *Ibid.*, vol. xii, p. 20.
[52] *Ibid.*, vol. xiii, p. 223.
[53] *Ibid.*, p. 229.
[54] *Ibid.*, vol. xiv, p. 307.
[55] *Ibid.*, p. 311.
[56] *Ibid.*, p. 306.
[57] *Ibid.*, vol. xiii, p. 256.
[58] *Ibid.*, p. 614.
[59] *Ibid.*, vol. xvi, p. 391.
[60] *Ibid.*, p. 639.
[61] *Ibid.*, vol. xviii, p. 765.
[62] *Ibid.*, vol. xxii, pp. 279 *et seq.*
[63] *Ibid.*, vol. xxiii, p. 336.
[64] *Ibid.*, vol. xxvi, p. 541.
[65] *Ibid.*, vol. xix, p. 77.
[66] *Ibid.*, vol. xvii, p. 304.
[67] *Ibid.*, vol. xxvi, p. xvi (Introduction), also an unpublished dispatch dated 12th April 1850.
[68] *Ibid.*, vol. xxv, pp. 662-7.
[69] A. Joyce, *A Homestead History*, p. 122.
[70] *Australia: a Social and Political History* (ed. Greenwood), p. 118.
[71] A. G. L. Shaw, *The Story of Australia*, p. 207.
[72] W. K. Hancock, *Australia*, pp. 117 *et seq.* (Pocket Edition).

CHAPTER XIV

THE ROAD TO RESPONSIBILITY

I need scarcely add, that it will be a source of the highest gratification to me if, under the authority of Parliament, the Colonial Government of Australia can be settled on a basis, on which the Colonists may, under the blessing of Divine Providence, themselves erect Institutions worthy of the Empire to which they belong, and of the people from whom they are descended.

—Earl Grey to Sir Charles FitzRoy, 31st July 1847.

Australia developed quickly from a penal settlement autocratically governed to a sovereign state with responsible self-government, though to her citizens progress often seemed to be slow. The evolution was accomplished in a lifetime, in seventy years.

The colony was never wholly penal, like France's Devil's Island, for instance, nor was it intended to be. Perhaps the desire that it should show a profit, however small, accounted in part for this. It was not expected to remain a supine mass of criminals guarded by soldiers, it was in due course to be balanced by freed men, their children, and such other settlers, soldiers, seamen and the like who cared to take the reward for their services in land, of which the Crown had a superfluity. Life became progressively more normal and the State developed accordingly in a manner suitable to its inhabitants.

Very soon after the foundation of the colony it found a useful staple in wool. This added considerably to its respectability. It was fortunate, too, in its Governors, a succession of men of probity and intelligence. Most important of all, the Imperial Government, the final authority, had learnt a sharp lesson from the loss of the American colonies. Obstinacy did not pay. Empire was a business to be conducted reasonably, not a dream of grandeur.

In the days of Lord Sydney and his immediate successors the doctrine of laissez-faire was in full flower. The Governors were briefed and rules were laid down for the prison, otherwise the colony could grow naturally as it would. Lord Sydney was not particularly interested. Little matters like trading with foreign ships and so breaking the East India Company's monopoly were overlooked on the grounds of necessity. Illicit trading by the masters of transports was condoned, so were many other things. The old lion was not watching her latest cub of doubtful breeding.

When in time Secretaries of State took more interest in Australia, the swing to liberalism had been accomplished in England. Reformers like Lord John Russell and Mr Gladstone came to the Colonial Office. In the 1830s and 1840s the whole of Europe was clamouring for constitutions and saw in them the panaceas for all ills. England had her traditions and laws and felt no need for a written constitution, but her forward-looking statesmen could not but be influenced by current political philosophy. The new land had no slowly evolved tradition; that of England, although the presiding genius, did not cover the new situation. It would have been obviously absurd to raise up replicas of the House of Commons and the House of Lords in a society just emerging from tutelage. A constitution and a judiciary along English lines, together with the institutions to which free-born Britons were accustomed, were conceded with, in the perspective of history, extraordinary alacrity, even though the more articulate citizens in their importunity railed against the slowness and conservatism of the British Government.

Actually, New South Wales suffered very little from being a penal settlement and was fortunate in that her first unpromising colonizing material was early swamped by infusions of new blood, that wool, land grants, and then gold attracted free colonists. There was no foreign element to arouse Imperial suspicion, no subject race to put what might have been considered a necessary brake on progress.

The purpose of this chapter is to outline the formal development of the Australian colonies, which all followed substantially the same pattern, constitutionally, in administration, in the development of the judiciary, in finance, and finally in local government, the freedom of the Press, and other such liberties, from the beginning until the realization of responsible self-government.

I. The Government and Constitution to 1856

The early Governors were, on paper at least, complete autocrats. Distance, convenience, the nature of the settlement, all made this the natural, the inevitable, arrangement. The Home Office was willing enough, having equipped an expedition and chosen a Governor, to leave him the entire responsibility.

Even at the reading of Phillip's commission there were some murmurings amongst the officers at the wide and autocratic powers conferred on him. Phillip was not a man to become debauched by power and he was the only Governor to "enjoy it in anything but name".

After Phillip quitted his governorship in 1792 power passed to an oligarchy, the New South Wales Corps. This was *de facto,* not *de jure,* as the power was vested in the acting Governors only, who let it slip through their fingers to their officers. An aristocracy of greed, none the less powerful because it had no legal standing, entrenched itself so firmly between the departure of Phillip in December 1792 and the arrival of Hunter in 1795 that, although it changed its form from time to time, it was not eradicated until the discovery of gold in 1851, if then.

Hunter, with a commission comparable to Phillip's, found himself to be an autocrat divested of power. His successor, King, was in the same position, with waning support from the Home Government. Neither he nor Hunter had the means of implementing his power. Bligh, asserting his authority in the quarter-deck manner, was deposed. In the idiom of slang, the Home Government could hardly have cared less. After another interregnum Macquarie made a bid, not wholly unsuccessful, to reinstate the Governor's absolute power. He had his own regiment to back him up.

All the early Governors from Hunter to Bourke ran into trouble locally, but, as Professor Crawford points out: "The early opposition to the Governors contained no constructive quality, no germ of constitutional government, but remained particular and personal, relying on the influence of powerful friends at home with the British Government to defeat those actions of the Colonial Governors which were disliked."[1]

They were also frequently in trouble with their masters in Whitehall, the Home Office, the Colonial Office, the Admiralty and the Commander-in-Chief, all of whom had fingers in the Australian pie. The two main causes of this kind of trouble were doctrinaire views which had little or no connection with the actual circumstances of the colony, and the perennial trouble over money. No Governor of an expanding community in which few settlers could even make a start without government assistance, and in which practically all those incapacitated through age or illness became necessarily a charge on the State, could achieve the economy demanded by Whitehall.

Until 1823 the entire responsibility for the settlement rested on the Governor. Upon him was bestowed, formally, a power which, in the face of active opposition, a take-it-for-granted lawlessness in all ranks of society, even his officials, and the scattering of small settlements over ever increasing distances, he was unable to exercise effectively.

The manner of government was by proclamation. The Governor announced his will in a series of orders which covered every aspect of the colony's life. He fixed the price of wheat, he ordered observance of the Sabbath, he established a curfew, announced royal marriages, births, and deaths with suitable rejoicing or lamentation, long after their occurrence, tried to control the quality of bread and the validity of weights and measures, forbade loitering on public wharves, made rules for aliens, announced musters and the inspection of clothes and so on and so on. . . .[2]

These orders and proclamations were prominently displayed in writing so that those who could read, might, and they were often given out from the pulpit in church, for the chaplains were government officials. After 1804 they were published in the *Sydney Gazette,* a convenient vehicle but not an official organ.

Regarding New South Wales as an extension of England, this manner of government was not strictly legal, and when at one stage it was discovered that over several years the Governors' proclamations had not been ratified in England the whole fabric collapsed into illegality.

A retiring Governor, Macquarie for instance, as soon as he left the protection of his office (for no one could bring a suit against the Governor in the exercise of his power), could be sued by disgruntled parties who felt he had wronged them. Acts of Indemnity were passed from time to time by the Imperial Government to protect governors from the consequences of acts which, although expedient, might not be legal.

The situation was never simple. The Governor was always a harassed man. Writing to Under-secretary King in November 1798, Hunter pointed out: "The multiplied duties of the Governor are far, very far, beyond any idea you can possibly form of his situation, and, unless some means are fallen upon to lessen them, losses in various ways are unavoidable."[3]

In December 1823, long after Hunter's departure in disgrace, a way was found of assisting, and that doubtfully, the Governor in his many duties. A nominee Council was set up by warrant under the New South Wales Judicature Act (4 Geo. IV, c. 96). This is commonly referred to as the New South Wales Act and in it principles worked out for Canada were applied to Australia. It was passed for a limited period only, so that when it came up for renewal there was an opportunity to revise its provisions to meet expanding conditions in the colony.

The Council consisted of from five to seven members, including the Governor, who convened it, presided over it, and introduced all legislation. The warrant named as members the Lieutenant-Governor, the Chief Justice, the Colonial Secretary, the principal surgeon and the Surveyor General, who was often absent from Sydney, and was replaced by the head of the Anglican Church in Australia at that time, Archdeacon Thomas Hobbes Scott.

The Council had little power, but it was a beginning. It was only necessary for one member to support the Governor for an act to be carried. Every member, except the Chief Justice and the Archdeacon, was his subordinate, Colonial laws replaced the Governor's proclamations on all subjects of any importance. All Acts had to be submitted to the House of Commons and ratified by Royal approval. The most important clause in the constitution of the Council was that every enactment had to be certified by the Chief Justice as "not repugnant" to English law, and the most curious that all members of the Council were bound to strict secrecy as to its proceedings. The latter condition robbed the new body of any value as an outlet for, or educator of, public opinion.

The Council advised the Governor but could not overrule him. In times of emergency he could take back all power into his own hands. In any case the Governor remained the chief executive officer.

According to Frederick Watson, this Council under Governor Brisbane was workable. "The deliberations of the council under his fostering care were ideal in character; they were calm and thorough, and during his government the council was the one institution free from faction and party disputes."[4]

The first meeting of the Council was held on the 25th August 1824, when there was already a new warrant on its way from England changing the Council's composition. In future it was to be made up of three government officials, the Archdeacon representing the Church, two landowners (John Macarthur and Charles Throsby), and one merchant (Robert Campbell). Its functions were now rigidly laid down and its purely local character stressed. It was prohibited from enacting any laws that touched the prerogatives of the Crown or the rights of British citizens or which were prejudicial to trade. Nor must it pass any laws "of an unusual and extraordinary nature", a curious provision that at a pinch could be construed to cover almost any enactment. Any private laws or those affecting property must be read in church on three consecutive Sundays, just like the banns for marriage, before they were brought before the Council. This at least had the virtue of breaking down some of the secrecy that had hedged proceedings. The Council might vote taxes, but only taxes for particular purposes. Once money was voted, the Governor had control of spending it.

The colonists were not pleased. As a young student in England, William Charles Wentworth had dreamed of Australia as a new home for freedom and glory.

May this, thy last-born infant, then arise,
To glad thy heart and greet thy parent eyes;
And Australasia float, with flag unfurl'd,
A New Britannia in another world.

His was a lone voice. Now there were others, not as idealistic, who felt that mere residence in Australia was not sufficient reason for losing their rights as British citizens.

In January 1827, when Governor Darling arrived, he was presented with an address of welcome which was really a statement of grievances.

. . . Your Excellency may rest fully assured that a Legislature, founded on the same basis as the Legislatures of the American and West Indian Colonies, can alone make us a happy and contented People; and we further beg solemnly to assure Your Excellency that any compromising measures on this head, which by possibility may hereafter be adopted by His Majesty's Ministers, will only serve to increase and perpetuate beyond remedy those internal dissensions, which unfortunately have disturbed our Community ever since the arrival and departure of the late Commissioner of Enquiry [Bigge]. . . .

Then comes a famous passage that, had it stood alone, might have passed for nobility of sentiment: ". . . there exists . . . in the Territory a race of Men, already arrived at an adult state, who, scattered in the distant and silent woods of their country, unknown, unfelt and unheard of as a political body, are yet destined to be the Fathers of the succeeding generation and the inheritors of our Lands." It turned out, of course, that what the petitioners wanted was control of land in the squatting interests. "The patronage of Office they have always disregarded; but Grants of Land, which they consider their own as it were by natural inheritance, and which they have seen of late years . . . lavishly bestowed upon Strangers without capability of improving it . . . has had a baneful influence on their minds . . ."

The vested interests of Trade were not forgotten either.

Numbers are now indispensable in the Legislature of New South Wales to collect those various data and that variety of information with respect to our Agriculture, Commerce, Manufactures and Revenue, which are essential to a sound and healthy Legislature in every country, but particularly in this Colony, where the Legislature ought to be purged of all party spirit, private interests and family-jobbing.[5]

Can this last have been a thrust at the Macarthurs?

This was followed up by a petition to the King for a representative assembly and trial by jury. The cry of "No taxation without representation" was raised.

Both the Governor and the Chief Justice, Francis Forbes, a man of liberal opinion, felt that the colonists had a case. The Governor recommended an enlarged but still nominee Council of six officials, three landowners, and three merchants. The casting vote would still be in his own hands. He disliked the undemocratic secrecy that surrounded the Council. It was his practice to convene the Council, bring before it the legislation he thought necessary, and then to withdraw so that the members could have greater freedom of discussion. Their recommendations came back to him, but the oath of secrecy prevented even him from knowing what arguments had been raised. It was a ridiculous situation.

Forbes went further than the Governor. Not only did he want to see the Council enlarged, but he suggested that the Governor should be bound by the decisions of the majority.

To have a council at all had a salutary effect. Interest was aroused and both parties, the exclusionists and the emancipists, wanted more control of the government, the former, free, landed and prosperous, because they believed it to be their right and because their main interest was avowedly in land and its distribution; the latter because, as ex-convicts, their right to own and to will away property had been questioned. Their prosperity and standing depended on the recognition of their full return to citizenship. It behoved them to look to the matter themselves.

There were a few influential men in the colony who took a long and impartial view. They felt that the constitution of the Council had grave weaknesses and, in particular, that the Chief Justice should not be a member of it, because in his right of veto over all legislation he already exercised great power. This veto consisted in his duty to give every piece of legislation a certificate vouching that it was in accord with English law. If he withheld this certificate the Bill was null. Council meetings took up too much of his already overloaded time and his attendance made for conflict with the Governor. The colony had already suffered enough from these collisions of power. If the Chief Justice were to be the embodied law he should be withdrawn from politics.

In January 1829 the Council was remodelled. It was to consist of ten to fifteen members of whom five were to be landowners and two merchants. The Governor must take the advice of his Council just as the king must abide by the decisions of Parliament.[6] There was to be no more secrecy, and a précis of the general object of proposed legislation was published at least a week before a Bill came before the Council. This, in effect, meant that the temperature of public opinion was taken before discussion even began in the Council. Any member had the right to introduce Bills, but the "prerogatives of the Crown" were still safeguarded, meaning in particular Crown land and its distribution. Whilst Bills were in draft the judges, not the Chief Justice alone, considered them and gave their opinion as to their legality.

The year 1829 marks the beginning of something that resembles self-government. The autocracy of the Governor was curbed. More important, the power of the exclusionists, the heirs of the New South Wales Corps oligarchy, was also restricted by public opinion and in theory, if not in practice, by the loading of officials, deemed, sometimes mistakenly, to be above self-interest, in the Council.

Here constitutional progress rested until 1842. The New South Wales Act was due for revision in 1836, but it was renewed with only slight amendment. During the 1830s the agitation for representative government grew and grew. Not only was it fed from the old world, where Chartism was an issue, but now that Sydney had a Press, and an extremely articulate one, there were rallying points for all shades of opinion. The extreme unpopularity of Governor Ralph Darling (1825-31), an able and honest man but a martinet whose opinions often ran counter to popular taste, became entangled with the fight for liberty. It is one of those exasperating stories in which personalities, Press campaigns, transitory and often pumped-up grievances are mistaken for, or passed off as, liberalism. It is so much easier to be angry and to hunt down scapegoats than to set one's mind to clear and constructive thinking.

The ignoble quarrel of the People versus the Governor may have had some good results in awakening political consciousness and have made many aware, through shock treatment, of the democratic platform, who would otherwise have taken no interest in it. If so, it resembles the old story of the roué who reformed his manners and morals in order to marry an heiress and then, having achieved his object, found that his assumed virtues had become a habit which he could not break.

"The People," wrote Darling, "are taught by the Papers to talk about the rights of Englishmen and the free Institutions of the Mother Country, Many of them forgetting their actual Condition. Besides, it is evident that, altho' this is an English Colony, there is no similarity whatever in its Composition to that of England."[7]

This was a period, like the latter half of Macquarie's governorship, of quarrels and recriminations. Any stick was good enough to beat a dog. The whole issue was as petty, but the public, through the newspapers and the courts, had more opportunities of participating and taking sides.

Darling's relationship with the liberal-minded Chief Justice, Francis Forbes, was unfortunately bad. He repeatedly accused the judge of obstructing him and of serious breaches of official behaviour, such as amassing unacknowledged estates. In addition, Darling made many enemies when he carried out overdue reforms in the public service, and he fell foul of the Press. In this last he was unwise and harried enough to accept the challenge, to involve himself in libel suits and to attempt to use his power as Governor to suppress or ruin the hostile newspapers. Finally he was unfortunate enough to give his enemies a chance to attack him on the grounds of cruelty. The story has been often told, but it will sharpen the point here.

Two privates, Sudds and Thompson, seeing a better future for themselves as settlers than as soldiers, were anxious to leave the Army. They could find no better way than to commit a crime. Taking good care that they were observed, they stole from a shop in Market Street in broad daylight. They made no secret of their object. They were court-martialled. This sort of thing had happened before. Two men had even shot off their arms in the hope of escaping their military duty. It had done them no good, for they had been kept in the regiment but sent to Norfolk Island to act as scavengers. The morale of the regiment was low. The soldiers were sinking to the same level as the convicts. Normally the Governor would not have taken a hand in such a petty military matter, but on this occasion he felt he should make an example.

The crime was really one of desertion. The two men, wearing chains and spiked collars of iron, were publicly and ceremonially drummed out of the regiment. Their sentence of transportation to Norfolk Island was changed by the Governor to work on the roads. At this stage Dr Wardell's paper, the *Australian*, foreseeing no political capital to be made out of the incident, remarked that no more suitable punishment "could have been adopted than their being ordered to be worked in an iron gang",[8] and that it was "requisite both that extraordinary ceremonies should be observed in discarding them from the regiment, and that somewhat of unusual severity in their sentence should be ordered". The matter would have ended there if Sudds had not fallen seriously ill. His chains were struck off and he was sent to hospital, where he died on 27th November 1826. The Chief Surgeon, Bowman, did not even report to the Governor that the man was ill. Reports spread that he had died of shame or from tortures inflicted by the Governor's orders. Actually his death was caused by a kidney complaint from which he had suffered before his trial, but the Chief Surgeon does not seem to have made this public. In any case the rumours were much more savoury. Sudds became a martyr. The Press, including the *Australian*, launched a violent attack against the Governor. W. C. Wentworth, no longer a patriotic young student but the co-editor of the *Australian*, a barrister with a reputation, leader of the so-called Whig Party, unacceptable to the "Pure Merino", Exclusionist or Tory Party, but with very much the same platform, was the spearhead of the attack. He pressed for an impeachment of Governor Darling. He did not allow the issue to die until in 1835 a Select Committee of the House of Commons investigated the Governor's conduct as regards the sentence on Sudds. He was completely exonerated from blame. The only point on which his conduct was not entirely correct was in changing the soldiers' sentence from transportation to a penal settlement to work on the roads, and this erred on the side of leniency. The Chief Surgeon came in for a measure of blame because he had not reported Sudds's illness, whilst awaiting trial, to the Governor.

Although Darling left his governorship with clean hands on this and all the other matters in which he had quarrelled with the Press and, it would seem from the accounts in the newspapers, had outraged the feelings of all citizens, and although he had done some excellent work in reorganizing government departments, some of the mud thrown stuck to him. His military career continued to develop, but the Home Government, warned that he was a trouble-maker, never offered him another governorship.

This may at first appear like a simple tale of malice in which a few disaffected men used an unfortunate incident to whip up feeling against an already unpopular Governor. It was more than that. It was a piece of clever political strategy. The dates are interesting. The New South Wales Act came up for revision periodically and had to be re-enacted in the House of Commons. These redraftings were the times when citizens who wanted an elected assembly and other liberal reforms might hope to achieve them constitutionally. The New South Wales Act came up for revision in 1827, Sudds died late in 1826. With the time-lag of the journey to England this was the right moment for a demonstration. In January 1827 a petition went from New South Wales to the King and to both Houses of Parliament. Its main request was for an elected assembly. The showmanship of the gentlemen of the Press, who were also the prime movers at that time in the fight for "liberties", persuaded them that some dramatic event, like an act of gross oppression, would highlight the petition, gain signatures, and emphasize the evils of autocratic government. It was known that Darling, though he favoured some reforms, did not think that the time was ripe for an elected assembly and that he would advise the Home Government to that effect. There were plenty of precedents to show that Governors, and others, could be broken by a record of quarrels and disturbances. The Home Government was intensely bored by petty squabbles in the colonies and the long dispatches, reports, and petitions that arose out of them. It was hoped to make Darling the scapegoat for all the autocrats, even perhaps to buy reforms for the sake of peace.

Wentworth and his confrères failed in their objective. The new New South Wales Act of 1827 went through with some reforms, but not such as would satisfy the agitators, for they were in method only, not in principle. The Sudds scandal was such an excellent weapon that Wentworth could not bear to abandon it. He kept it tightly clutched in his hand until 1835, a remarkable effort. The New South Wales Act was due for revision in 1836. Again definite action was postponed in England, for it was already decided to abolish transportation to New South Wales. It would be time enough then to consider representative government. The time came in 1842.

This, I think, is the historical inwardness of the story of Sudds and its long trailers. In the late 1820s the agitation for popular government was not general. The squatters knew exactly what they wanted and were going to be content if they got it. It was land and a supply of cheap labour. The mass of the population, convicts, ex-convicts, and poor men almost indistinguishable from the latter in the manner of their lives, was not articulate. There were opportunities for them. What they wanted was security. A representative assembly was not likely to affect them greatly, not yet. Individuals were interested, particularly those who had been sent out for political "crimes", but not enough to make a movement.

". . . the people in general," Darling wrote home with reference to the Legislative Assembly, "are perfectly indifferent on the subject."[9]

At this stage personalities are inevitable. Without William Charles Wentworth it is doubtful if there would have been much organized agitation. He had the brains and the continuing drive for it. The circumstances of his birth and his social position could have had something to do with his early liberalism, which was to change into conservatism in the latter part of his life. He belonged to a small group of men who had money or influence or a flair for politics, but who did not fit into either of the main parties, the exclusionists and emancipists. William Charles was born on Norfolk Island in 1793. There were then no free women on the island. His father, D'Arcy Wentworth, though never a convict, had come to the country under a cloud. He did well for himself, made money, played a number of roles, but the Wentworths were not entirely acceptable to the exclusionists. The son was educated in England and absorbed the English liberal ideals of the day. There is little doubt but that he had a strong romantic attachment to his country. He returned to it with ambitions for leadership to find no niche for himself except the as yet unfilled one of head of a liberal, or Whig, party. How conscious he was of the workings of circumstance it is impossible to guess. You might say that he became the first professional politician in Australia. He wished to lead, he did lead. He fought for an Australian constitution and he came to be called the Father of the Australian Constitution. He was not a creative political thinker, his desire was to transplant the English political model to Australia. Having achieved a constitution, he found that it refused to remain static and the innate Tory under the Whig superstructure came to the surface.

His co-editor on the *Australian*, Dr Wardell (1793-1834), had met Wentworth when they were both young barristers in England. Wardell was then editor of the *Statesman*. They agreed to join forces and capital, come to Australia, and found a paper in competition with the *Sydney Gazette*. Wardell became a leading counsel at the Sydney bar, ran the *Australian*, from which Wentworth eventually withdrew, and farmed at Petersham. Under Wentworth's influence he was a violent opponent of Darling, but later under pressure from the Colonial Office, the breach was healed, the paper moderated its policy, and Wardell even acted in court for the Governor who had sued him for libel. He was murdered by bushrangers.

Edward Smith Hall, editor of the *Monitor*, established in April 1827 and equally opposed to the administration, seems to have been a man with a grudge. He had been refused a grant of five thousand acres, he had been denied permission to practise as an attorney. He was given the inferior post of coroner.

On the lighter side he is remembered for his spectacular quarrel with Archdeacon Scott over the occupation of a pew at St James's. Hall was prosecuted for trespass. He proceeded to libel the Archdeacon in his paper and was convicted in the Supreme Court of "indecent", "scandalous" libel "emanating from personal motives". It was on the strength of this conviction that he was refused the land. He had at first supported Darling's administration in the *Monitor*, but later became his bitter enemy. He paid dearly for his opposition. He was sued for libel, committed to jail, his convict servants were taken from him, and his paper was brought to a standstill, since he had no printery of his own and the Governor could restrain the employees of the Government Printer from printing it.

Hall was a man of genuine liberal principles, a disciple of Wilberforce and of charitable character (he was secretary of the Benevolent Society), but he lacked both the adroitness and the financial stamina of Darling's other newspaper opponents.

Sheriff Mackaness was also one of their number; "his friends, Mr Wentworth and Doctor Wardell, will always give him the full benefit of their influence and assistance," Darling wrote bitterly.[10]

There were others of course, but it was a small coterie. Of their number only one, Bland, had ever been a convict.

These men and others, most of them displaced in some way or bearing a grudge, tried to float hard-headed ideas on what Darling called their "golden dreams".

The character of the Governor himself was another pivot of history. He was able, just according to his code, well intentioned, but narrow in outlook and severe and unbending in his handling of men. "Golden dreams" and democratic aspirations unbacked by facts were anathema to him. Conflict with the group of which Wentworth was leader was inevitable. A Legislative Assembly was all very well, he said, if the country could sustain it, but in his opinion a hundred men could not be found to sit in one.

> Men, who have to provide for their Families, would not neglect their Farms and reside in Sydney at a great expence to attend as Members of the House of Assembly. The honor and novelty of the thing might induce them to do so once; but they would not repeat it. The Members of Parliament are Men of Fortune, who are put to no inconvenience by residing in London for a period. Here the case is exactly the reverse. Where the Servants are *All Convicts*, the immediate, the constant Superintendence of the Master is indispensible to the preservation of his Property. I am satisfied there are not three Settlers in the Colony, who would or could give up their time to the necessary attendance on a Legislative Assembly.[11]

This steely common sense was particularly wounding to the small bud of national pride and awareness.

Darling went his way and was succeeded by Sir Richard Bourke, a popular and liberal-minded Governor, who was, ironically, thwarted by the attitude of his Council and of government officials. "You are, in short," wrote Chief Justice Forbes, "a Whig Governor in the midst of High Tory Counsellors."[12] Professor R. M. Hartwell sums up: "The New South Wales council, for example, was from 1828 to 1842 an exclusive body, anti-emancipist, anti-Bourke and anti-Gipps and consistently self-interested in outlook. . . . In all colonies the Councils were the forcing grounds of constitutional change."[13]

Forbes, C.J., was himself an important piece in the pattern. Born in Bermuda in 1784, he had studied law in England and had been called to the Bar there. Whilst still a young man, in 1813 he was sent back to Bermuda by the Colonial Office as Attorney-General. Three years later he became Chief Justice of Newfoundland. By 1822 the severities of the climate had driven him back to England. Although he had had no Australian experience Lord Bathurst called him into consultation on the New South Wales Judicature Bill, then in preparation. His advice was taken on many points, but not on all. In 1823 he came to Australia as Chief Justice under the Act he had helped to frame. As has been seen, the very nature of the New South Wales Act placed Governor and Chief Justice in the position of antagonists. The Governor alone could initiate legislation and with him rested the power to force through any Bill he thought necessary. The Chief Justice had the ultimate power to veto or to refer back to England, any legislation that he believed to be repugnant to English law. The law is a labyrinth, the most conscientious and impartial men may differ as to its interpretation. Relations between Forbes and Governor Brisbane, founded on mutual respect, were unfailingly good. With Darling it was very different. There was a long and bitter controversy between the two most powerful men in the colony. Darling, considering himself authorized by the Colonial Office, brought forward measures in the Legislative Council to curb his critics in the Press, Forbes vetoed the Bill as not in accordance with English law. This happened at a tempestuous moment in English political history and three rapid changes at the Colonial Office meant that neither side received support. The quarrel undermined the Chief Justice's always uncertain health. When Sir Richard Bourke became Governor peace was restored and Forbes and Bourke worked together, in the teeth of opposition from the conservative Legislative Council, to bring about the liberal reforms, such as a fully developed system of trial by jury, which they both advocated. In 1837 Forbes was forced to retire by illness and died in Sydney at the end of 1841.

Gipps had succeeded Bourke as Governor when in 1842 the Imperial Government decided that, transportation having been abolished for two years and the Councils, particularly in New South Wales, having become anachronisms, it was time to give the colonies a measure of representative government.

The new Act provided for a Council of thirty-six members, twenty-four of whom were to be elected on a high property qualification, namely £1000 or more in freehold, or proportionate rentals, for a member and £200 in freehold for an elector. Emancipists and ex-convicts might vote if they satisfied the property qualification. A grazing licence was soon taken as an adequate property qualification to vote. Of the twelve nominee members only six might be government officials. The Governor's power in the Council was much reduced. He had, it is true, to give his assent to all Bills before they became law and could withhold it, an action which could only lead to a deadlock. He remained in control of administration.

The Act was unpopular with every section of the community. It was a really aggravating piece of legislation. "'Mother may I go in to swim?' 'Yes, my darling daughter. Hang your clothes on the mulberry bush, but don't go near the water.'"

First of all, the Crown retained control of the colony's most valuable asset, the land. The bush was displeased and disappointed. The main interest of landowners in constitutional change was to gain control of the land. Though they predominated in the new Council and were still easily the most powerful party in the colony, this profited them little.

The towns were disappointed, too, for they felt that their representation was inadequate. Country districts monopolized three-quarters of the elected members. For example, Sydney with 2823 electors returned only two members, and Cumberland with 1344 electors returned two also. Melbourne with 591 electors, Durham with 345, Camden with 586, and Northumberland with 369, returned one each. In this way 5858 electors were represented by eight members and 2619 electors in eleven districts by sixteen members.[14]

The residents of the Port Phillip district were more than disappointed. They were allotted six members, but they soon found how right Darling had been when he said there would be difficulty in finding men to serve in a distant capital in what was, of course, in those days a strictly honorary capacity.

Those who had asked to be freed from the autocratic power of the Governor found that, although his wings appeared to be clipped, he had really escaped practically unscathed. The Act made a schedule of about £81,000 the first claim on revenues. This was for the expenses of administration and the support of the Church. The real power to control the Governor by refusing to vote him supplies was denied to the representatives' Council. The Council could make laws, but the Governor administered them. Colonial pride, as well as party interests, was hurt.

Finally the Act created a system of local government through district councils with power to raise money for local objects. Nobody wanted these district councils. They were regarded with suspicion as another device to raise money from citizens. They were stonewalled.

The Act of 1842 was a sop and Lord Stanley, Secretary of State for the Colonies, instructed Governor Gipps to "pack" the new Council with officials or "safe men, as far as possible".[15] "It will be, of course, desirable that some of the Officers of Government should owe their Seats to popular Election." To do Stanley justice, he considered the Act as only a temporary measure to be followed by a more liberal division of power.

Gipps, like Bourke, had been in favour of a system of representative government and had submitted a plan to the Imperial Government in January 1839.[16] In some ways this plan was less, in others more, liberal than the Act. It suggested a smaller Council, part nominee, part elected, with one member only for Port Phillip district, a lower property qualification, multiple voting for men with land in different districts, full civic rights for emancipists and expirees, triennial elections, exclusion of the Governor, Chief Justice, and Archdeacon from the presidency, and effective control over nominee members, who could be removed by the Governor at will, provision for representation of minorities, and polling on the same day throughout the colony. The Governor, like the citizens, did not get what he asked for, and if he had the latter still would not have been satisfied. He had the unpalatable task of implementing this unpalatable Act. He came in for a large share of the opprobrium.

The Act was proclaimed in the colony on 5th January 1843. The retiring Council had carved out the electorates and the first elections were held in July 1843.

> The Elections in general went off very well, and the Act of the last session, 6th Vict., No. 16, passed for the purpose of regulating them, was found to work in a satisfactory manner; some rioting however took place, both in Sydney and Melbourne, as also in the Country Towns of Windsor and Paterson. One life was lost in Sydney, and one in Paterson, the chief polling place of the County of Durham.[17]

So wrote Governor Gipps to Lord Stanley.

There were some curious sidelights. For example, James Macarthur, the son of John, stood for election but was defeated on a religious issue. He had supported a Catholic for one of the Camden seats. When offered a nominee seat he refused it. The fiery Presbyterian minister, John Dunmore Lang was elected for the Port Phillip district. A problem arose: could a clergyman sit as an elected member? But then Lang had just been expelled from the Church by its synod. So was he a clergyman? Splitting legal hairs was a popular pastime. No party system had developed as yet. The high property qualification did something towards ensuring that all members had similar interests. The pull was not between differing ideologies but between supporters and critics of the administration. By and large the nominees and those officials who obtained election were government men and out of a sense of duty, or out of caution, stood with the Governor.

There was no means, however, of forcing them to vote in any particular way. The non-official elected members were the potential opposition.

The first result of the Act of 1842 was an agitation for responsible government. A Select Committee of the new council was formed to investigate grievances. They were many. Added to those already listed were others which appeared on closer investigation. These fell mainly under two headings, the gulf between the legislature and the administration, and the expenditure of colonial revenue. The Legislative Council wanted to control the executive by assuming the right to hire and fire the heads of government departments. It also wanted to set up a tribunal for impeachment; that is, a disciplinary body.

The trouble over revenue bit deeply. Up till 1835 the cost of jails, police, and the convict establishment was paid by the Home Government. It amounted to about £25,000 a year. This had now been unshipped onto the colonial revenue. True, transportation had ceased, but there was still a large convict population working out its sentences, and a larger one of ex-convicts. It was these two classes, it was claimed, that made police and jails necessary, and it was grossly unfair that the civil government should be saddled with the expense of them. The Select Committee also found that £793,034 10s. 8d. had been spent by the Colonial Treasury directly on convicts.

The only thing that the Select Committee could do about grievances was to petition the Crown. This was felt to be ineffective, for petitions must go first through the Governor and then through the Secretary of State for the Colonies. The Governor advised the Secretary, the Secretary advised the Queen. The colonists were dissatisfied.

The struggle for freedom was always confused. The demands of the powerful squatting interests for security on the lands they grazed were allied with the agitation for responsible self-government. For them it was a means, not an end. William Charles Wentworth was the link between those who supported the movement for responsible government as a necessary basis of their political creed and those who desired it in order to further their own ends. Both issues, although essentially different and separate, were dear to him. He could persuade the squatters that their security lay in responsible government, which they might expect to control, as they had controlled representative government. He could also persuade many of the people that their cause and that of the squatters was one freedom.

The squatters had money and influence. They could afford to employ agents to lobby in London, first Charles Buller and later Francis Scott. Through them the powerful wool trade in England could be brought to exercise pressure on Parliament. Archibald Boyd, squatter, was sent to England on a special political mission. The Order in Council of 1847, giving the squatters something of what they wanted, was won.

There was a change in the kaleidoscope. Robert Lowe, later Viscount Sherbrooke, drove a wedge into the popular front. He made it clear that the interests of townsmen and workers were not the same as those of the squattocracy. The first definite split was over transportation. It had ceased, but convicts and exiles were still seeping in because one section of the community wanted cheap labour. The working man could readily understand the danger to him, both in status and employment, of this. Transportation under any name ceased by popular demand. The many overruled the few.

A conception of modern democracy, of which Lowe and Henry Parkes were the prophets, replaced Wentworth's "Whig principles", which cloaked aristocratic control. The first plank of any such platform must be responsible self-government.

The Act of 1842 was never a success because those governed did not consent to it, because the local government clauses never came into effect, and because the Legislative Council did all in its power to nullify its own constitution. For instance, in 1847 it made a bold bid to gather revenue into its own hands by passing an Act to that effect. This drew down a sharp reprimand from Earl Grey, who described it as

> . . . an attempted usurpation of a function belonging exclusively to Parliament, an attempt on the part of the local Legislature to define and determine the limits of the Constitutional Authority with which Parliament has entrusted them, a precedent for diverting from the Legal Tribunals to the Legislative Council the right of interpreting the Act of Parliament. A more serious objection in principle can hardly be supposed; and yet you [Governor Sir Charles FitzRoy] report yourself to have informed the Legislative Council that you had not been induced to withhold your assent from any objection to the principle of the measure . . . it is indispensable that the Constitutional limits of that franchise should be respected and observed.[18]

The genuine and widespread desire of the Australian colonies for responsible government, their material progress and increasing population, together with a more integrated and enlightened policy at the Colonial Office, came to fruition in 1851. Experience in Canada reacted on policy towards Australia, and Australians were ready to point to and claim the liberties given to that and other colonial dominions. The Act of 1842 had, nevertheless, been a necessary apprenticeship to fuller self-government. If it had done nothing else it had generated political consciousness.

In 1850 Earl Grey was at the Colonial Office, Sir Charles FitzRoy was Governor of New South Wales, which still included the unwilling Port Phillip district. Grey avowed that it had always been his object to find out what Australians wanted and what would be most suited to colonial conditions and then to embody his findings in legislation.

He spoke of "My anxiety not to act without being fully in possession of the views of the Inhabitants of New South Wales on the question of their future Government".[19]

FitzRoy was asked for his views. He recommended responsible self-government with a bicameral system, the Lower House elected, the Upper (nominee) House to act as a brake, election through the revived district councils (this idea was not original to the Governor but had been mooted before), and an overall local power, "a superior functionary", to prevent or deal with friction between the Australian colonies, since there were already some family quarrels in progress.

Earl Grey also took the opinions of leading citizens. They were uncompromising. They did not want a "superior functionary"; they did not want district councils; they were apathetic about the bicameral system. But they did want responsible self-government with control of revenue and of the Crown lands.

As usual, the Colonial Office received suggestions, thought things over, and made its own arrangements. These deliberations issued in an Act for "the Better Government of Her Majesty's Australian Colonies", passed by the Imperial Parliament in 1850. This is sometimes referred to as the Act of 1851 because it was not proclaimed in Australia until the year after it was passed in England.

It was an enabling Act. It made few changes, but it opened the way for the future. It formally separated the Port Phillip district, henceforward to be called Victoria, from New South Wales. Actually, this only made definite and legal a state of affairs that had existed since 1840. Victoria had been for most practical purposes separate, with her own courts and financial arrangements, but that was not enough. The Act gave Van Diemen's Land (now Tasmania), Victoria, and South Australia the type of representative government current in New South Wales since 1842 and promised it to Western Australia when she should be able to pay her way. The representative councils set up in these colonies shared with New South Wales one important additional power. They could frame their own constitutions. In New South Wales, where the control of Crown lands was still withheld, the old Legislative Council virtually turned into a committee for framing a new constitution. This was responsible government at one remove.

The Legislative Council took up its option and passed an Act "to Confer a Constitution on New South Wales and to Grant a Civil List to Her Majesty". This Act was drawn up under the prevailing influence of William Charles Wentworth. He was chairman of the Select Committee which drafted the Bill, in fact, he had a draft ready for just such an opportunity. A room in his home, Wentworth House, Vaucluse, where it was discussed and beaten into shape, is open to the public as a historic exhibit.

FitzRoy did not feel that he could give his assent to so important an Act, nor had he the constitutional right to do so. He reserved it, that is, he sent it Home for ratification. The Act lay before the Commons and then before the Lords for thirty days. It was finally passed by both Houses and received Royal assent.

The four constitutions, framed independently under the Act of 1851, were very similar. In each a bicameral legislature was set up. Both Houses were to be elected in Victoria, Tasmania, and South Australia. In New South Wales, and later in Queensland, when it became a separate colony, the Upper House was nominee. This was due to Wentworth's influence. He abhorred "democracy" as much as some people today abhor communism. He believed that those who contributed most to the country's prosperity should have the greatest influence in governing it. The unwritten English Constitution was to him the model for all constitutions. In England, the realities of government were still in the hands of the ruling class, that is, the landed gentry and the wealthy in other sections of the community. He wanted to see this reproduced in Australia, even to an improvised House of Lords. The democratic and egalitarian spirit, now so well entrenched, defeated him. Even his nominee Upper House turned out to be a less formidable opponent of democratic legislation than the elected Upper Houses in other colonies.

The property qualification for voters was everywhere so greatly reduced that it was a poor man indeed who had no vote. To the propertied classes were added wage-earners who received £100 a year and upwards, and those who paid £10 a year for lodgings or £40 a year for board and lodging. The property qualification was down for members also, but as members of Parliament received no salaries it was only men of substance and independence who could afford the luxury.

In New South Wales any amendment of the Constitution required a two-thirds majority in favour. This was another of Wentworth's devices to assure stability. It was ineffective, for the clause could be repealed by a simple majority vote in the Legislature. This was promptly done.

The vexed question of district councils had been dropped. It was felt that the citizens had the right to set up municipal councils when they felt the need to do so.

In the meantime, in 1852, Sir John Pakington, as already noticed, had conceded to the Australian colonies the long desired right to control Crown lands.

Politically the Home Government had surrendered all control over the Australian colonies. Economic and sentimental bonds, both strong, remained. There was still much to do before full democracy was attained, but after 1856 Australia's political development was in her own hands.

II. Administration

Long after he had a Council, first to advise him and then to legislate, the Governor remained the executive head of the State. He implemented instructions from the Colonial Office, issued his own orders and proclamations covering every aspect of life, and later administered the colonial Acts. Administration is an unspectacular field and its power and importance are likely to be underrated. Executive powers must back up legislation or statutes fall dead at the portals of Parliament. The executive is the "carry-through". It is the practical side of government where the weaknesses of laws or edicts are discovered. The executive may be bound to carry out the law, but inevitably a certain sifting takes place, winnowing the practical from the impracticable. For example, it is a punishable offence to attach a postage stamp on a letter so that the Queen's head is upside down. Yet I have never heard of anyone being accused or condemned for this. Traitors would not be caught so, only the careless, the untidy, the hasty and the short-sighted. To come nearer to our subject matter, the Governor was strictly enjoined by the Home Government to forbid and prevent graziers from trespassing on Crown land beyond the boundaries of location. It proved impossible to execute this order and the Governor of the day knew it. Those who carry out a law can, of course, change its intention or climate. For example, when laws were enacted to provide old-age pensions the intention was to give financial help to men and women who, through age, were no longer able to work, a far more humane arrangement than putting them into institutions. However, in applying the means test and in the general attitude to the pensioner, officials and others too often made of a citizen's right a humiliating charity. Examples could be multiplied. The law-makers get the limelight, but the State's other arm is just as important.

The law envisages the end, the executive is the means, and the means, in a highly developed bureaucracy, can become an end in itself. It should therefore be interesting, having outlined constitutional development in Australia, to consider the growth of the public service and the power that has come to lodge in it.

To begin with, there was no public service. Phillip had absolute power within the limits of circumstance. He was the law-maker and the executive head. Neither secretary nor clerk was appointed to assist him. He wrote his own dispatches and copied them out at least twice, a copy for his own file and a copy to send home by a second conveyance lest the original be lost. Dispatches usually had to make a formidable journey by way of China or India and were transhipped several times with all the attendant dangers of shipwreck, piracy, or mutiny, all much more frequent at the time than today. If an officer were being invalided home or was returning on furlough they were usually entrusted to him; failing any other fit and proper person, they were delivered into the care of the master of the ship. A trusted officer, such as Lieutenant King, was occasionally sent home to carry dispatches and to supply the Colonial Office with first-hand information. In 1822 Robert Lethbridge saved the dispatches entrusted to him by Governor Macquarie when the ship he was travelling in caught fire. All his own property was lost. Lord Bathurst ordered him a land grant of 1000 acres as reward and reimbursement.[20]

If the Governor had the assistance of a secretary it was because one of the officers acting as his aide-de-camp took on the duties without pay. Any clerical work that was done was done by literate convicts, too often working out a sentence for forgery.

Under Phillip the mass of routine business was not great. The settlement was small and tight, communications were by word of mouth. The Governor's orders were posted in convenient places and read out by the chaplain. A large proportion of the convicts were illiterate in any case.

In 1803 the *Sydney Gazette* began publication and provided a useful means of disseminating the Governor's orders and proclamations.

By the time that Macquarie came to the governorship public business had increased enormously. The necessary personnel was still being drawn, economically, from the regiment and the convicts. The Commanding Officer was *ex officio* the Lieutenant-Governor, the chaplains and the surgeons were either on the strength of the regiment or pressed into service from the upper ranks of the convicts, like the Reverend Mr Fulton and Surgeon Redfern. The judiciary was only just emerging as a separate entity. Any gentleman who came to the colony free and had any pretensions to means and standing almost inevitably became a magistrate, for which service he would receive no payment, but certain indulgences, such as the labour of convicts.

The Governor's office, where he attended at certain hours every weekday to receive and consider the requests of his subjects, to take the reports of his officers and generally to transact the colony's business, was the administrative centre.

It is important to understand that there was a *civil* government from the very beginning.

Together with the two companies of Marines sent as guards, the Home Office provided the new settlement with a skeleton civil service, or rather with several officers who combined civil duties with their military ones. The office of Judge-Advocate was a civil one, but was held by a Captain of Marines, David Collins. The Surgeon, John White, twenty-one years old at the time of his appointment, was a naval surgeon appointed to his new position by Letters Patent. The Chaplain, Richard Johnson, was a recruit from the secular clergy who came under the final authority of the Commander-in-Chief.

The colony was provided with a surveyor in the person of Augustus Theodore Henry Alt, Baron of Hesse Cassel, an army officer of considerable experience. Unlike most of the officials, who were very young, Alt was fifty-eight when he arrived in the colony. His salary was fixed at £182 10s. a year, to be supplemented by fees for land grants delineated, that is, 2s. 6d. for every 110 acres, 5s. for grants from 110 to 501 acres, and 7s. 6d. for larger grants. It is estimated that from this source he would have received 12s. 6d. in 1791. Although his salary was on the estimates, it was paid irregularly. At one time he received nothing for four years. When land grants were available to officers he received one in the present day suburb of Ashfield, where a street still bears his name. In 1797 he asked leave to retire because of failing health, but it was not until 1803 that he was allowed to go on half pay. He died in 1815 "universally regretted by all his friends, who lost in the Baron a most compleat gentleman, and a man who never told an untruth to the injury of any man", to quote his tombstone, which can still be seen in the old cemetery at Parramatta.

In 1791 a second surveyor, Charles Grimes, was sent out for service on Norfolk Island. His pay was 5s. a day. He had to be recalled to the mainland when Alt became too blind to fulfil his duties. These, beside the delineation of grants, included general surveys, boat surveys, and the measuring of roads which, when once marked out, the settlers were expected to make. The settlers were not on the whole co-operative, and road-making became a government function. There is an amusing government order dated 30th June 1806 which reads:

> In consequence of the bad state of the road leading from Sydney to Parramatta, and the danger of horses being lamed in the deep ruts near Sydney, it is hereby directed that all public and private carts and wagons passing that way (not otherwise loaded) do take a load of brickbats from the brickfields and drop them in the places appointed by the overseers of the roads, provided it does not lie out of the way of the place to which the cart or wagon is going.

A staff of two surveyors was, of course, totally inadequate. They were also expected to act in other capacities. Alt, for instance, was also a Justice of the Peace. Anyone with the slightest knowledge or capacity was roped in for the work, from Lieutenant Dawes, who as a military officer had some knowledge of surveying, to superintendents of convicts, to a gardener.

Charles Grimes was the second Surveyor-General, with the increased salary of £277 10s. a year, but he did not enjoy it long. He was a hard-working man, who among his achievements numbered the first survey of Port Phillip, but he made the fatal mistake of throwing in his lot with Macarthur in the Rum Rebellion. Johnston made him Judge-Advocate in place of Richard Atkins, Collins's ignoble successor, and his first duty was to try and, of course, acquit John Macarthur. He was also created a magistrate and notary public with the power to solemnize marriages. He had no knowledge of the law and was soon discarded by his patrons as incompetent. Johnston, rather unkindly one feels, sent him to England with dispatches. Here he was kept dangling for three years without salary and was finally forced to resign owing to his part in the rebellion.

The colony was without a trained surveyor just at the time when the land-grant system was really getting into its stride. James Meehan, who had acted as assistant to Grimes, was pushed into the position of Acting Surveyor-General. He had been implicated in the Irish rebellion of 1798 and had been sent out as a convict for a minor political crime. He was what was called a "bog surveyor", having no qualifications but some practical knowledge.

Macquarie described him as "a most useful, deserving, meritorious man" and not only appointed him Surveyor-General but made him a magistrate and nominated him Collector of Quit Rents at an additional 7s. a day. The Home Government thought otherwise. Macquarie's appointment was brushed aside and the position of Surveyor was given to John Oxley, a naval officer. Macquarie, not to be beaten, appointed Meehan Inspector of Roads and Bridges and paid his salary out of local revenue.

Oxley had not sufficient experience to delineate land grants, so back came Meehan as assistant. He worked at Bathurst and on the Hunter River and was the first surveyor in Van Diemen's Land. He also made a plan of Sydney. Macquarie openly preferred him to Oxley.

George William Evans, who was to explore the New Country beyond the mountains, was Meehan's assistant and another "practical" man. He was retained in the department.

Bigge in his Report found much confusion and incompetence in the Survey department, but no dishonesty, something which appeared to him remarkable as the opportunities were great.

It was not until Sir Thomas Mitchell arrived as Surveyor-General in 1827 that the department was put on a proper professional footing. Mitchell was a major in the Army, a difficult man to get on with and more interested in exploration than in the duller routine of his position.[21]

The most important department was naturally the Commissariat. The First Commissary, as its head was called, was Andrew Miller, who sailed in *Sirius* with Phillip. He also acted as the Governor's secretary. By June 1788 he was forced to leave the colony by illness and died on the voyage home. His place as Commissary was taken by Zachariah Clark and as

By courtesy of the Trustees

WILLIAM CHARLES WENTWORTH

From a portrait in the Mitchell Library

By courtesy of the Trustees

SIR HENRY PARKES

From a photograph in the Mitchell Library

secretary by David Collins. Zachariah Clark received 3s. a day. He had originally been the agent of the contractors who brought out the convicts. William Broughton, who came with the First Fleet, was storekeeper at Parramatta from February 1789.

Perhaps the best known of the early Commissaries was John Palmer, purser of *Sirius,* who was appointed in 1791 after the loss of the ship in the previous year. He held office until 1819. In the Rum Rebellion he supported Bligh and suffered for it during the interregnum. He was later reinstated, but found no favour with Macquarie and was gradually ousted. He was landowner, trader, and magistrate, and later in life enjoyed the dangerous friendship of the Macarthur group. He outlived all other officers of the First Fleet, dying in 1833.

The Commissariat had charge under the Governor of all stores and provisions. It acquired locally produced supplies, but the importation of food, clothing, and other necessities from overseas was the responsibility of the Home Office, and, in emergency, of the Governor.

The Commissariat was the store and as such became the financial centre of the colony, where all transactions were by barter or note of hand. The only note in which there could be universal faith was that issued by the Commissariat as a receipt for goods received into the store. The department, you might say, was the proto-treasury. When a Colonial Treasury was set up the Commissariat remained for the provisioning of the convicts and only withered away with the end of transportation.

The Commissariat was always in a state of being reformed; Macquarie reformed it twice, Brisbane reformed it, and so did Darling. It was always closely connected with the regiment and the Commissary came in time to be responsible to the Commissary-General of the Army in England.

It was the intention of the Home Office to provide Phillip with a Provost-Marshal, and George Alexander was appointed to the office. He did not sail in the First Fleet and Phillip appointed James Brewer, a middle-aged midshipman in *Sirius*, to perform the duties. Brewer's commission was signed on 26th January 1788. His duties, which he seems to have carried out satisfactorily, despite his eccentricities, were analogous to those of a sheriff.

Such were Phillip's formally appointed assistants in his civil government.

Nightwatchmen and other such rudimentary police were drawn from amongst the better-behaved convicts. It was only by good fortune that someone other than a convict could be found to superintend government agriculture or workshops. Macquarie, in his effort to create a middle class that would balance and finally disintegrate the monopoly of the Corps and its adherents, was only too willing to appoint ex-convicts, or those who had been pardoned or emancipated, to positions of trust. He even made himself ridiculous by naming a thorough rogue, Michael

Robinson, who had once been at Oxford, his poet laureate. His effort to appoint a Government Architect in the person of Francis Greenway, at a salary of 3s. a day with a proposed rise, was finally quashed by the Home Government as an unnecessary luxury. An engineer was always chosen from the officers of the regiment, Lieutenant Dawes being the first. Macquarie was a dragon for work, he liked to do everything himself, to tour the colony, to oversee every government activity, to inspect and exhort every shipload of convicts, to meet and talk with and advise all his subjects. Like the Roi Soleil he could say, "*L'état c'est moi.*" He had a secretary, but the correspondence issuing in floods from Government House always bore the stamp of the Governor's unmistakable style. So voluminous was this correspondence, often with officers with whom he was no longer on speaking terms, that there were repeated crises when the supply of stationery ran out and letters had to be written on wrapping paper or anything available.

This improvised and often unpaid public service was supported, as everyone had to be in the earliest days, by the Commissariat. Its members received rations for themselves and their families, government-owned houses to live in gratis, firewood, and other perquisites. On 2nd September 1815 the Governor published an order regulating the issue of fuel. On the summer schedule the Lieutenant-Governor might have four fires, and 14 bushels of coals weekly; field officers, the Governor's secretary, the Commissary and the commissioned officers' guard, captains, paymasters and surgeons, one fire and 3½ bushels; "others", probably N.C.Os, 3½ bushels of coals weekly but, curious distinction, no fires. Privates were allowed a quarter bushel of coals weekly.

In the winter schedule the Judge-Advocate, the Judge of the Supreme Court, and the Chief Engineer received 14 bushels of coals weekly, the Chief Surgeon 10½, and so on down the scale. The coals were issued every second Saturday from the dockyard. Henceforward no one was to receive a ration of wood.[22] The summer issue, or what remained after cooking, one can only suppose, supplied barter goods in winter.

It was not until the advent of Governor Sir Thomas Brisbane, Macquarie's successor, that an Executive Council was formed and a public service began to take shape.

The Executive Council was set up at the same time as the nominee Legislative Council. The difference between the two bodies is so clearly delineated by Professor R. M. Hartwell that I could not do better than to quote him:

> The governor was assisted in administration by an executive, and in legislation by a legislative council. The sources of authority in each case were different, the executive council derived its powers direct from the Crown and its members

were officers of the crown; the legislative council was established by statute, and its power was statutory . . . thereafter all governors in Australia had the advice and assistance of executive councils, consisting of the chief executive officers of the Colony. The executive council was concerned with the general administration of the Colony, so that its range of activities was very wide. No where, however, was its influence decisive. Its functions were mainly administrative and advisory, although, in theory, it was also a policy making body. It supervised the administration of the Colony and reported to the governor on all matters that interested him. . . . The extent to which the executive council was important in policy-making depended almost entirely on the governor. For this reason the executive council was not like a cabinet; it determined policy only to the extent that the governor allowed it to do so; its allegiance was to the governor and the Crown, it was not responsible to the legislative council or to the colonists.[23]

Naturally the principal officers of, or departmental heads in, the colony sat in the executive council. The shortage of suitable personnel was so great that the same men had to be called on to fill the nominee seats in the Legislative Council. This meant that government nominees had a double share of power.

New South Wales was now a Crown Colony. In 1821 Frederick Goulburn was sent from England with a commission as Colonial Secretary, not to be confused with the Governor's private secretary. In the civil hierarchy he was next in rank to the Governor, with a salary of £282 10s.[24] His standing immediately caused trouble, for Mr Justice Wylde, a self-opinionated young man, refused to hand over to Goulburn the records of the criminal courts and it took a Royal direction to force him to do so.[25] Brisbane was at first willing to let much of the executive power pass into Goulburn's hands, but by May 1824 he had come to regret it. He wrote a dispatch to Lord Bathurst full of complaints of Goulburn's disobedience and arbitrary behaviour: ". . . He obtained my leave about Twelve Months ago to insert a notice in The Sydney Gazette directing all letters, applications, &c. intended for me to be addressed to Him, with the view as he then stated of saving me trouble, and in order to enable Him to prepare Himself with the information relating to them, when they were submitted to me. . . ."[26] Goulburn used this power for his own ends, or rather for the ends of the party with which on arrival he had immediately allied himself, the exclusionists headed by John Macarthur. The Colonial Secretary suppressed some communications, others he answered without reference to the Governor. He failed to carry out Brisbane's instructions in "hundreds of instances". When the Governor remonstrated with him he replied, on 19th April 1824, in an insolent letter claiming that the Governor's proclamations and orders were invalid unless they went through his department.[27]

He established himself as a one-man bureaucracy and, what was even more serious, a highly partial one.

Brisbane continued to Bathurst in what one cannot but feel was a weak vein. "I consider it my duty not to conceal from Your Lordship that the Channel of direct application to The Secretary has long been considered the only sure means of obtaining the favor sought: Whereas a previous sanction even from me was as certain to defeat it, and this impression is very general through the Colony."[28] Brisbane then asked that Brigade-Major Ovens be appointed his private secretary so that he could at least send his dispatches home without the interference or cognisance of the Colonial Secretary. With the assistance of the Chief Justice, Brisbane had his way. Major Ovens was appointed as his private secretary at a salary of £200 a year. This was a colonial appointment and the Colonial Office could either disallow it altogether or send out its own appointee to replace the major. Goulburn was relieved of his office in December 1824, but had to wait until he was replaced. In 1825 he was still there, obstructing the course of the State's business as much as possible. Brisbane was unable to write because of rheumatism in his right arm, Goulburn would not write to dictation or co-operate in any way.[29]

One of Brisbane's difficulties was that now a civil service was taking shape he had no control over the appointments. A properly regulated service was at last possible because the colony had sufficient revenue to pay for one. Men were chosen in England for the various posts, Oxley as Surveyor-General, Captain F. Rossi as Chief of Police with a salary of £600 a year, James Bowman as Principal Surgeon (as distinct from the regimental surgeons) on £410 a year, Balcombe as Colonial Treasurer, Lithgow as Auditor, and so on. It was taken for granted that there would not be men on the spot with proper qualifications or that if there were they would be tied to one or the other faction. This meant that the Governor had his officials chosen for him and, far from keeping faction out of the public service, the oversea appointees, particularly Goulburn and Oxley, felt themselves superior to the inhabitants of a colony still largely penal and immediately allied themselves to the local "aristocrats", who made up the section of the community in which they naturally found their personal friends. The happy, wealthy, charming, and intensely English home of the Macarthurs was the natural recruiting ground for new-comers. Archdeacon Scott, the new leader of the Church in the colony, good man more intent on his spiritual duties than on party politics, nevertheless was instantly drawn into the exclusionist fold. Brisbane himself, looking into the mirror of English gentry, intended immediately to make John Macarthur a magistrate and only withdrew his intention, too late to keep the Macarthur friendship, when the judges waited on him to explain that Macarthur on the bench would mean endless quarrels with the other magistrates. Brisbane did not make the appointment allegedly because of Macarthur's participation in the Rum Rebellion and he was in due course reproved by Bathurst, who wrote tartly on 26th March 1823:

. . . I must acquaint you, that, considering the decided opinion pronounced by His Majesty's Government on the Transactions which led to the Arrest of Governor Bligh, and the length of time that has since elapsed, I am desirous to discontinue the revival of any discussion upon that subject; and as the conduct of Mr McArthur, since his return to the Colony, has been uniformly correct, and the pursuits in which he and his family are engaged have been of great advantage to the Colony, I should not have been disposed to object to his appointment to the Magistracy.[30]

It was a very chancy game for governors.

Surgeon Bowman married a daughter of the Macarthurs and soon, as a landed proprietor and grazier, far outdistanced his modest salary.

Discontent was generated in men on the spot who had looked for preferment, and the Governor was faced with intricate problems of precedence amongst government departmental heads.

When Brisbane did venture to make a local appointment it was very likely to be quashed. He wrote home in October 1824: "Having taken into my most serious consideration the languishing state of education in this Colony, I have been induced to appoint the Revd Thomas Reddall Director General of all the Government Public Schools of New South Wales, until the pleasure of His Majesty shall be made known to me."[31] He proposed a salary of £300 "to enable the nominee to bear up against the heavy expence of making continual tours of inspection". The appointment was disallowed.

During Brisbane's governorship he made an effort, on instructions from England, to iron out some of the curious twists in the colonial civil service. Special privileges were on the way out and their value or near value was being added to salaries. There was no longer a state of emergency, the common necessities of life could be bought. Except in out settlements it was not necessary for the Government to victual its servants. It was more economical to pay a little more in wages and salaries than to sustain an indirect and variable drain on its resources.

Officials were not to be allowed the use of government houses, except in very special circumstances, and the judge of such circumstances was to be Lord Bathurst and not the Governor. The former wrote in a dispatch dated 25th October 1824: ". . . you are most particularly instructed not to grant any house, where you have not been authorized to do so by my orders, without stating the special circumstances of the Case, and having recorded them in the Council Book, notifying the same to me, with the opinion of the Majority of the Council thereupon."[32] The Colonial

Treasurer was, Lord Bathurst ruled, to be allowed a house. Surgeons, with a remuneration of 7s. a day, were to be given an allowance for the keep of a horse.[33]

Brisbane was a little hurt when he found that he came under the pruning knife himself. He was no longer allowed the free use of government horses, or rather, he might use them, but if one died or became lame he must replace it at his own expense. His salary was, however, increased by £500 a year in lieu of fresh meat rations for his household. The Lieutenant-Governor received an additional £150 a year for the same reason and other officers in proportion. The feudal flavour of the early days was fast disappearing.

It was recognized that the payment or part payment of salaries by fees was undesirable and led to abuses. In future fees were to be paid into revenue and an increase in salary equal to part of their estimated value was paid to the officer instead.

No one was very pleased by these adjustments. Office was fast ceasing to be a gamble in which handsome prizes could be won and lost, as Captain Piper, the Naval Officer, found. Major Druitt, the Engineer Officer under Macquarie, who thought well of him, was another case in point. He was so poor when he arrived that he could not pay his mess bill in the ship, yet soon he was living in a handsome house and spending extravagantly. He was suspected of peculation but could not be court-martialled because every officer in his regiment hated him so openly that no impartial judgment could be expected. The case was referred to the Colonial Office and an investigation by the Chief Justice, Francis Forbes was ordered.

An inquiry had already been conducted in the colony by a committee consisting of the two judges and the Deputy Commissary-General and a report of 372 pages produced. Lord Bathurst was not satisfied with this, owing to the "respectability" of Druitt's character, his complaints and petitions, and the good offices of his friends.[34] Actually a cloud of doubt hangs over the whole affair, for many of the accusations rest upon the word of a convict lying in jail, who afterwards recanted.[35] Druitt was stripped of his land grants, but allowed to keep them until this action was ratified in England.

Land grants to civil officers were again frowned on, but still a man like Surgeon Bowman managed to acquire one to pasture his sheep and cattle, pleading that his predecessor, D'Arcy Wentworth, had become a rich landowner.

At the other end of the scale the little men, especially if they were honest, found the road very hard. The clergy was notoriously underpaid. Samuel Marsden, who was well able to take care of himself, received £350 rising to £400 a year, the Reverend Mr Cowper £260 to £300, the Reverend Mr Cartwright £240 to £300, the Reverend Mr Fulton £182 10s. to £250.

Cartwright in a memorial revealed his unhappy state. He had a large family, he had fallen inevitably into debt, he had housing difficulties and could not carry out his duties for lack of a horse, which he could not afford. He had been promised indulgences but had never received them. Lord Bathurst was moved to order that he be given £10 for every year he had served the Church in Australia, from 1818 to 1825. This was an isolated benefaction and did not cut at the root of the trouble.

More pitiful still was the story of James Mileham, assistant surgeon. He served in the colony nearly thirty years from 1796 until his death in 1824 without once going on leave ". . . and yet was in want. His latter years were pinched by penury; his declining health was alleviated by no comforts; and he terminated his mortal career after a lingering and distressing illness."[36] He had had a flash of hope, when D'Arcy Wentworth retired in 1818, that he would then be appointed Principal Surgeon, but he was too old and Dr Bowman was sent out from England to fill the post. Mileham struggled on, as his widow pointed out, on "a salary barely adequate to that mere respectability which his official situation made it incumbent on him to maintain", and "was utterly precluded from providing means for the future support of his family". So they were left destitute.[37]

In the lower ranks of the service an effort was made to replace convict clerks by the native-born, or cornstalks, who, it was remarked, sometimes with surprise, showed no signs of having inherited their parents' criminal tendencies. As a class, the cornstalks were not eager for clerical work. It was difficult to do without the convicts and, of course, the pay was so small that very few men were attracted from England.

Under Brisbane the executive side of the government seems to have been planned, but the Governor and the Colonial Secretary lacked between them the drive to make it a reality. What they and the Colonial Office achieved was a number of departmental heads, varying in ability, often warring with one another and with the Governor and ravaged by jealousy aroused by irregularities of salary and prestige. For instance, Balcombe, the Colonial Treasurer, it was discovered, was absent-mindedly being paid at the rate of £1200 a year and the indulgence of a rent-free government-owned house.[38] His salary was immediately reduced. Many of them, particularly such key men as the Colonial Secretary and Surveyor-General, took sides in the party cleavage within the colony. They often failed to support the Governor, not from any objection to his policy, but out of a self-interested partiality, as opposed to his conscientious impartiality.

When Sir Ralph Darling succeeded Brisbane as Governor he found the public service in a state of chaos. Frederick Goulburn had gone, but Major Ovens remained and had acquired much power. With him Darling began his reorganization. To Under-secretary Hay he wrote on 2nd February

1826: ". . . The Department of the Civil Engineer and the Private Secretaryship, united in the same person [Ovens], had become the grand Engine of the Government, and had engrossed the duties of all the other Departments; while, in fact, the unwieldly nature of the machine prevented its operation and caused a total stagnation in the Public Business."[39] And again:

> . . . every Department appeared to act for itself, without check or control, and indeed without any apparent responsibility. Money was drawn without any specific authority, and issued without any Regulation, or even a Voucher of any validity for its expenditure. Contracts were agreed upon without any written Document to render them binding; and purchases were made and supplies furnished without any representation of the necessity or Authority for the Expence. In short, the common routine and forms of Office were totally neglected.[40]

Some departments were overstaffed. Others were understaffed. For instance, the Office of the Naval Officer had only one clerk and customs revenue was being lost daily for lack of anyone to collect it. Salaries were madly disproportionate. The employees of the newer departments were paid much better than those in the longer established ones. The Surveyor-General received under Darling £362 a year whilst his assistants were being offered £500. The government service was maladjusted to the general economy of the colony. "What," asked Darling, "is to be expected of the Lower Classes, when they can get double and in some cases treble what they receive from Government?"[41]

In June 1826 Under-secretary Hay answered this dispatch. The Home Government was willing to co-operate with the Governor and proposed to establish in New South Wales a civil service like that in Ceylon and the Mauritius, sending out well-trained and efficient public servants, to be followed by young men as writers, who, under the tuition of their chiefs, could work their way up. Even a pensions scheme was outlined with benefits on retirement in proportion to contributions. Hitherto pensions, which often turned out to be blocks of land, had been matters for petition, solicitation and influence. Now this was to be regularized.[42]

Meanwhile Darling set to work in a business-like manner to straighten out the snarl on the spot. He introduced correct business methods. He asked for additional staff. He wished to set up "a proper Establishment of Customs", staffed from England, for he saw in it a legitimate profit for the Government. Trade was increasing and at times there had been as many as seven ships in port. "The Trade is increasing rapidly, and such an Establishment cannot any longer be dispensed with without serious injury to the Revenue. Smuggling, I understand, is carried on to a great extent, and there are no means at present of checking it."[43]

Darling turned his attention first to the Colonial Secretary's Office. McLeay, the new Colonial Secretary, was to have a chief clerk and eleven assistants, three of them muster clerks. "There are only two employed at present and both are incompetent Persons." Convict musters had not been sent to England for years. In future they would go forward yearly. The Chief Clerk was to have £360 a year and the lowliest assistant £52 a year. All fees were to go into revenue.[44]

Next came the Office of the Colonial Treasurer. Darling appointed a Board to inquire into its working. Balcombe, the Treasurer, had himself deposited a heavy security for his personal honesty and efficiency, but the arrangements for safeguarding public moneys were very insecure. He used his home as his office and kept the moneys in his bedroom. Darling proposed to open offices in the Barrack Square, which would be a financial centre, accommodating the Colonial Treasurer with his two clerks, the cash department of the Commissariat, and the Auditor's Office. "From the frequent attempts [at robbery], which have been made on the Commissariat, and the insecure state of the Treasury, the arrangement, which I have made for these Offices, is very desirable. . . ."[45]

Darling was still wrestling with the problem of convict clerks.

> It cannot be doubted that the employment of Convict Clerks has been a very serious evil. It degraded the offices, by placing individuals in them, who had forfeited every claim to character. Besides the smallness of their Salary, which seldom exceeded (£30) Thirty pound a Year, scarcely afforded the means of existence; and they are not a Class of Men, on whose resistance of temptation much dependence could be placed.[46]

If Under-secretary Hay's plans were carried out this evil would soon cease.

Whilst pleased with Hay's plan for an orthodox civil service, Darling immediately began to embroider it with embellishments of his own. He proposed an early retiring age as in the East Indies, but instead of returning to England civil servants would, if possible, be induced to settle, thus "increasing the respectable Class of Society". He asked for a "few well educated Young Gentlemen . . . to be employed as Writers". They would begin as junior clerks earning £200 or £250 a year and in four years would be senior clerks at £350 a year and have qualified to receive a free land grant of two square miles and £200 to stock it. "Thus would a foundation be laid, which the natural increase of Stock in this Country would rapidly extend, of obtaining an early independence, which would supersede the necessity of Pension; and the Govern't would reward its Servants at a very trifling Expence, and at the same time benefit the Colony in an important degree." After six years' service they would receive another square mile and after seven a fourth. They would then be expected to retire and make room for other young gentlemen, or, if not agriculturally minded, they could engage factors to run their properties and could continue in the service. This is the recurrent dream of the land, surprising to find in a man of Darling's prosaic nature. Needless to say, it came to nothing.[47]

The reform and tidying up of the administration was Darling's continuing interest and this work, though not completed, was his greatest contribution. In 1827 it was absorbing most of his energy and a note of disillusionment is struck.

> My hands have been more than full; the reform of every Office Department and Establishment, without one single exception of the whole Government in fact, has rendered it impossible to do what was required in every case. The machinery here is totally inedequate to such a Government as this, to which there is nothing similar under the Crown; and the exertion, which is consequently necessary, would exhaust the best energies of the most zealous. Besides, there is evidently an indisposition on the part of the Departments in general to conform to the Regulations laid down. They have been so long accustomed to act for themselves, without any attention or regard to unity of proceeding, that any attempt to establish system appears to be considered an unnecessary and burthensome restraint; and there is great difficulty in preventing the Regulations, which are made, from immediately becoming a dead letter.[48]

It is clear, too, that Hay's Model Civil Service was not eventuating. Any educated young gentlemen who came out as writers soon left the service. "The fact is the Mercantile Houses are so anxious to engage Young Men of integrity that they commonly give £200 and £250 a Year, so that the Public Offices find it impossible to retain the Clerks at the rate notified in my former Letter."[49]

Trouble over salaries continued. The Home Government did not understand how expensive living was in the colony or the corrosive effect of inequalities when a young clerk could earn £250 a year and a botanist, Fraser, who was Curator of the Botanic Gardens, received only 7s. a day and must pay his own travelling expenses when collecting specimens, or when Darling had to work hard to have the Colonial Auditor's salary raised to £600 a year, Brisbane having named £100 as suitable remuneration. Darling recognized that the reorganization of the civil service was more than a one-man job and appointed a Board of Inquiry, including Lithgow and two merchants. This was the nucleus of his later institution, the Board for General Purposes. It was like a smaller edition of the Executive Council with, as its main object, the reorganization of the Public Establishments. It consisted of the Lieutenant-Governor, the Colonial Secretary, the Chairman of Quarter Sessions, the Clerk of the Council, the Auditor, the Commissary, and a merchant representing the business world. These were all busy men, so the Board met usually at 6 a.m.

At the same time Bathurst was advising Darling to set up a Land Board to regulate land grants and sift applications. Administration through boards had begun in New South Wales.

The Lords of the Treasury did not make things any easier by imposing a new system of keeping accounts. Nor did the carking attitude of Viscount Goderich at the Colonial Office when he received from Darling a Blue Book giving, the Governor hoped, a full financial statement of the colony's affairs. He wrote:

> I have to request that, nothwithstanding the transmission of what has been called "the Blue Book" for the current year, you will be good enough to furnish me with a Debtor and Creditor Account of the whole Revenue and Expenditure of the Colony, under your Government for the last three years, specifying every variety of receipt from *whatever* source derived, as well as the nature of that source, whether from the Customs, Internal Duties, or any other mode of Taxation, with every detail relating thereto. I have also to request that you will transmit an equally minute statement of the appropriation of every item of Expenditure.[50]

It must have been exasperating for the stickler to find himself out-stickled.

The most hampering regulation of all was one laid down by Bathurst in October 1826.

> . . . no service shall be undertaken, which involves an expenditure above £200 Sterling without the sanction of His Majesty's Government being first obtained. . . . However desirable and important the objects may be in themselves, it never can be maintained that they are of that pressing and immediate urgency as to supersede the possibility of your sending home a Report, and affording His Majesty's Government time to give their consideration to the means, by which funds are to be raised for carrying similar undertakings into effect.[51]

This regulation remained in force and was a severe restriction on Governor after Governor. Two hundred pounds was a small sum in the growing economy and it could be a year before a dispatch was answered and in that time there could be a change of government in England and a right-angle turn in policy. Darling discovered that his power was anything but absolute.

Not only had he difficulties with his masters in Whitehall, but he had greater if imponderable difficulties with his subjects and officials. He was unpopular and so even his most reasonable and beneficent actions were suspect. He was the first Governor who had to face the barrage of a free Press. He was himself an inveterate organizer and he found opposition organized against him with an adroitness which he could not match. Most unfortunate of all, he quarrelled bitterly with the key man in his colonial world, Chief Justice Francis Forbes. He accused the judge of obstruction, of currying favour with the Press, with pusillanimity, with revealing matters that should have been confidential. Forbes's real sin was that he was too moderate, too tolerant, too liberal, not ready enough to waive the law, as he "interpreted" it, to please the Governor.[52]

From these ingredients many frustrations sprang, but perhaps too much stress has been laid on the obstacles and disappointments that Darling suffered in his efforts to form and reform the public service. There was much solid achievement to his credit. He cleared up the luxuriant confusion of the Naval Officer's Department. Captain John Piper was found to owe the Government £17,000. He paid £5000 and the balance was realized out of his estate. But was this all? "I fear, however," wrote Darling, "from the extreme negligence with which Captain Piper appears to have carried on the business of his Department, that the Duties have not been properly collected, and there are unluckily no means of ascertaining the extent of the deficiency."[53] Piper was very short of clerks, but he had a boat's crew skilled in the playing of musical instruments. At this crisis in his life he ordered the crew to row him outside the Heads of Port Jackson, then to ship their oars and take up their instruments. Under cover of the music he jumped overboard, but the crew shipped their instruments and saved him.

In place of the Naval Officer's Department Darling created a Customs Department on the English model under Captain Rossi, whose health had broken under the strain of his work as police chief. The bonded store, which had been ill run, was reorganized under new management. A Harbour Master was appointed.

Darling called for a report on the police by Captain Rossi and reorganized the force on his findings. As a social document Rossi's report is interesting and underlines the run-down state of the colony. Crime was increasing in Sydney, because with the discontinuance of the penal settlement at Port Macquarie and the concentration of convicts, both under sentence and time-expired, in the town it had become a depot for undesirables. Rossi recommended an augmentation of the force and better wages to raise the constables above temptation and to attract men of better character. For instance, constables on duty six hours a night had only been receiving £25 a year. Neither were pensions of one or two shillings a day after twenty-one years' service a sufficient inducement. Already, under Rossi, twenty-five constables had resigned because of the wretched pay and fifty-seven had been dismissed for misconduct. Sydney needed at least sixteen constables on duty every night, to whom could be added special constables, drawn from amongst the decent tradesmen and mechanics in each ward, properly sworn in but receiving no pay.

The system of offering rewards for the bringing in of bushrangers or other malefactors at large worked badly. The police would take no action till, with the increasing menace, the reward was raised. Better results would be achieved by decreasing the reward the longer the criminal was at large. As things stood, a reward of four dollars was paid for the capture of a runaway out for seven days and eight dollars when he had been missing thirty days. This was an open invitation to profitable negligence.

There were on the books certain "stationary police" who had no duties and should be struck off. Police were needed not only in the town but on the Parramatta Road, at Lane Cove and at Broken Bay. These should be "regular", not "honorary", constables.

Sydney was the natural centre for the police and the Superintendent should have sufficient men to be able to rush small detachments into the country as needed. At the time of writing the report (November 1826) town and country police were badly co-ordinated.

The Police Office was short of clerks and its work was in arrears. The building itself was so noisome that magistrates hesitated to enter it because of the "foul and confined air". It was in every way inconvenient and unsuited for use as a court.

The police were badly armed. They could only muster ten unserviceable muskets, eight swords, and four pairs of pistols. They had to borrow firearms from citizens.

Taking a wider view, Rossi advocated the appointment of police magistrates who would receive a salary, sit daily, and control the police in their districts. The honorary magistrates had given good service, but had not the necessary time to spare from their other occupations to be really effective.[54] This report was presented to the Executive Council, which approved it, and the Governor put it into execution. Two police magistrates had already been appointed by Brisbane at Parramatta and Newcastle at £300 a year, but the plan had been carried through so badly that Dr Macleod, the police magistrate at Parramatta, did not receive his salary for three years. Darling proposed to appoint them also for Liverpool, Bathurst, and Penrith. "These Duties are very Troublesome, and require constant attention," he wrote in a dispatch to Lord Bathurst. "I might add generally that the description of Persons, formerly employed in the different Situations of Government, were satisfied with small Salaries, being willing, as I presume, to take their chance of making their Employment answer their purpose; but Men of Character will not serve at present, unless properly remunerated."[55]

Darling thoroughly reorganized the Post Office after a Board of Inquiry consisting of the Colonial Secretary, the Auditor, and James Busby had looked into its working. This was a picturesque institution as Darling found it. The Governor issued a proclamation. The Postmaster at Sydney was to go aboard every incoming ship to collect the mail, to make out way-bills for all letters sent in bags, and induce masters of ships to hand over loose mail by paying them a penny for each letter and twopence for each parcel. The Postmaster was to keep a record book in which he must "regularly enter without erasure the Amount of Postage received daily" and must pay the total amount of postage to the Colonial Treasurer each month. An abstract was to be made up each quarter. When letters had lain unclaimed at the Post Office for three days the names of those to whom they were addressed were to be written on a notice-board. Only post-office officials were allowed behind the scenes at the office and the records were strictly confidential. For payment the Postmaster received ten per cent of the total amount of postage that passed through his hands. He was sworn into his office by the Judge of the Supreme Court or two Justices of the Peace, and he entered into a bond of £200 with two sureties to guard against misappropriation or carelessness. The Government Engineer supplied leather bags for the transport of internal mail and contracts to carry them were made with "gigs or other light vehicles" going inland. It cost 4d. to send a letter from Sydney to Parramatta or Port Macquarie, 6d. to Liverpool, 8d. to Windsor or Campbelltown, 1s. to Bathurst. Sea postage involved an extra 4d. Soldiers' mail was 1d. and all *bona fide* government mail, provided that the envelope was signed by one of the higher officials, a judge, or the Archdeacon, travelled free.[56]

We find that in 1826 the offices of Postmaster and Wharfinger were invested in the same person, who complained that the revenue of the Post Office was "so very small, so completely inadequate" that the appointment was worthless.[57] The Post Office and the Wharfinger's Office were for convenience one and the same, a room 9 feet 9 inches by 5 feet 8 inches. The expense of hiring this and a clerk swallowed up the fees.

Later that year Lord Bathurst waived the right of the Postmaster-General in England to regulate postal arrangements in New South Wales and left the matter to the Governor. Darling rationalized the postal system, putting the Postmaster and his staff on a fixed salary and making contracts for the delivery of inland mail.

He made plans for Sydney's first water supply as a government undertaking. James Busby was the engineer. The Tank Stream, together with numerous public and private wells, had long been inadequate, and in 1827 drought made the situation acute. The Lachlan Swamps, a chain of lagoons in what is now the Centennial Park area, was the nearest permanent supply. It was proposed to bring the water from there by pipe and tunnel to Hyde Park as a main distributing centre, then to the hospital and to various street corners where pumps would be set up. Fortunately it was not necessary to raise the water to the high ground on the north, the Rocks, as there was a sufficiency of springs there. Convict labour was to be used and the project was estimated to cost about £20,000. The money was to be raised by a loan paying four per cent, with a £700-a-year sinking fund towards its repayment. The citizens who benefited had to pay a water rate. "The Water Houses and Cisterns are Estimated without regard to their being made ornamental buildings, or embracing anything more than is absolutely necessary."[58] There were about 1053 private houses in Sydney which with an average rental of £30 a year should yield in water rates £1579 10s. a year.

The watering of ships would bring in another £400 and the Government would pay £350 into the fund for its establishments, giving a gross income of about £2329 with a management cost of only £700. Darling was confident that with the growth of the town the water supply could be paid for without hardship. This was the first government undertaking established on a proper business and financial footing.

The Botanic Gardens were made a government establishment. The Commissariat was reformed. In fact, the hand of the Governor was everywhere. His arrangements with regard to public moneys were particularly rigorous. Everything was to be accounted for and checked.

There was at last a standard of currency "conformable to that in England" . . . "public Accounts and pecuniary engagements and transactions of every description have been advantageously simplified, and the inconvenience and intricacies of the former system almost entirely done away".[59]

Government-owned houses, once allowed to senior officers as homes, were converted into government offices. Hours of work were from 9 a.m. to 6 p.m. Records were properly filed and safeguarded. Darling even devised uniforms for the higher civil officials, possibly to give them "face" beside their more ornate military brethren.[60]

Darling did not get all he wanted, for instance a Government Gazette, free of all connection with established papers, to be used solely for government proclamations, orders, advertisements etc.; nor could he get a sufficiency of trained staff to reorganize the Survey Department as he wished. Nor was he ever able to get government establishments running on oiled bearings. (Neither has any other administrator.) He rid the State of many inconveniences and individual officers of the opportunity of helping themselves to fortune by depriving them of fees and perquisites and establishing fixed salaries. To this there were only a few small exceptions. For example, superintendents of government farms were paid according to results and the farms became profitable. Coroners were still allowed the fees of office and so was the superintendent of Dawes Battery.

It was during Darling's governorship that administration was divided into two parts. In one were those departments handling convicts and their affairs; the other was the free or colonial establishment.

The Imperial Government paid the expenses of the former, those of the latter came out of colonial revenue.[61] It was fortunate that the colony had a man of Darling's practical and methodical mind to implement this change.

Sir Richard Bourke, Sir George Gipps, that admirable administrator, and Sir Charles FitzRoy carried on from where Darling left his project, still clearing up confusion, still plugging holes where revenue leaked away and incompetence made its entry, but now the task fell not so much on the Governor as on the Legislative Council.

A Police Act of 1833 reorganized the metropolitan force again, setting aside for the purpose an additional £1093 10s. a year to be paid out of the revenue from spirit licences. In 1838 and 1840 colonial Acts regulated the rural police. Darling's reforms had evidently come unstuck.

> The defective state of the Law as regarded the Police of this encreasing Town, the obvious inconvenience occasioned by the nuisances to be met with in its Streets, the danger of insalubriety if some of these nuisances were suffered to continue, and the innumerable disorders and indecencies which prevail in all populous places, when unchecked by the operation of penalties [have] . . . for some time past engaged my serious attention . . .[62]

wrote Bourke when transmitting the Act. It might have been Macquarie speaking.

In future the London model, set up by Sir Robert Peel, was followed in Australia. Water police as recommended by Captain Rossi, were established in 1846, the expense to be defrayed out of port dues.[63] In 1847 a Water Police Court was set up.[64] In 1834 the Police Department was taken off the estimates and paid for out of colonial revenue. This was a very unpopular arrangement, for it was a heavy burden on a young colony. In 1843 £16,004 13s. 8d. a year was spent for the protection of squatters and their flocks and herds in the bush and £2569 15s. 5d. a year on the water police of Sydney and Melbourne, in addition to the usual metropolitan expenses. The Home Government allowed the Colonial Government £433 8s. 8d. as a contribution to the Police Department. Both Bourke and Gipps, voicing popular sentiment, thought it should be at least £20,000 a year.

In 1847 once again new regulations were issued for the police. It was proposed to recruit men in England to serve for from seven to ten years and, as an inducement, they were to receive a bonus at the end of their service.[65]

Another Act, in November 1833, dealt with the water supply for Sydney and reconstituted it. It was now delivering six hundred "tuns" a month.[66] Busby superintended operations from 1827 to 1836, when "Busby's bore" ran two and a quarter miles from the source at Botany to Hyde Park. Bourke recommended that a company be formed to relieve the Government of the responsibility and to manage the supply on a business basis.

He envisaged something in the nature of a co-operative society in which those who used the water controlled it and paid for it.

In the period between Darling's governorship and the coming of responsible government the accent falls on the amenities, including education, and the efforts to introduce district councils or some other form of local government in the teeth of popular opposition.

Governor Bourke found, as was usual, that public buildings were falling into disrepair. He set up a Board to survey them.[67] He ran constantly into the difficulty of not being able to spend more than £200 on any one project without explicit permission from the Home Government. This galled him greatly and seriously hampered improvements. In renovating public buildings he tried the expedient, no new one, of calling for tenders and making contracts for all work, the Government supplying free convict labour.

The two major undertakings were a new Government House, paid for out of the sale of part of the Domain, long coveted by the commercial interests of Sydney,[68] and new barracks, removing the regiment from what is now Wynyard Square to suffer sandy blight on the outskirts of the town at Paddington.

The local government question was difficult and complex. It seemed only reasonable to the Home Government that in so scattered a settlement local councils should be set up to deal with wholly local matters. The idea had been included in the first edition of the New South Wales Act. The colonists would have none of it. Bourke favoured the idea as district councils would be valuable training grounds for self-government. His subjects did not see it in that light.

In 1840, under Gipps, a Bill to establish municipal councils was brought before the Legislative Council. Because it endowed the proposed corporations with taxing powers it met with a storm of opposition. The main aim, Gipps pointed out, was "to force the People of Sydney to take a proportion of these expenses on themselves". It appeared fair that those who had the benefits should pay for them. Even then Sydney was costly. In four years £54,997 had been spent out of colonial revenue on policing the city and £56,421 for general purposes such as paving, lighting, cleaning the streets and other amenities.[69]

The issue was joined and all the endemic quarrels in the colony were drawn into it. This was the city *versus* the bush; it infused new life into the old exclusionist-emancipist struggle, since in the Bill expirees of up to three years' standing were excluded; it involved the automatic opposition of all men of property to extra taxation; it raised the cry of "no taxation without representation" when it became clear that Gipps meant to keep the control of the police in his own hands even when their upkeep was paid for out of the rates, and, of course, the old bitterness over the Home

Government's control of land and over the unloading of the police establishment onto the colonial revenue was reawakened, if, indeed, it had ever dozed.

The moderate members of the Council were willing to agree to the Bill, provided the Corporation was endowed with land sufficient to supply it with funds, along the lines, one supposes, that the Church was endowed with land under the control of the Church and School Corporation. (Land was still the ready-made answer.) Others thought that the whole issue should be held over until the new Constitution was granted, when the colonial legislature could frame its own Bill. The purists declared the Bill, as a taxing Bill, was illegal. Gipps and his Council reached a deadlock. Gipps would not withdraw the Bill unless instructed to by the Imperial Government. Thoroughly soured, the Governor could only wish that local bodies had been set up by proclamation before the Council was given any powers.

The new Constitution was proclaimed in January 1843. District councils were included in the Act. To carry out the Act Gipps must set up the councils, but he could only do so through the newly constituted Legislative Council. A severe economic depression made the situation more difficult than ever. Gipps brought forward three Bills, one after the other, to constitute the district councils. They were all thrown out. The Council passed a motion:

> That in the opinion of the Council, the District Councils are totally unsuited to the circumstances of the Colony, the County Districts being unable to meet the additional taxation which would necessarily be required in carrying out the various objects contemplated by their institution, and the cost of the machinery requisite for bringing them into operation being of itself an obstacle fatal to their success.

This was straight from the shoulder and Gipps was asked to intercede with the Home Government to have clauses 41-50 of the new Constitution repealed. In December 1844 a Select Committee of the Legislative Council convened to report on "general grievances", declared the councils "unpalatable, odious and abhorrent to all classes". Gipps was bidden by his masters in England to force the councils upon the colonists. He could set them up by Letters Patent—that is, directly under Royal Authority—but only the Legislative Council could frame their *modus operandi.* Actually there was nothing he could do to force the unwilling colonists to accept institutions they disliked. The breach between Gipps and his Council was never closed. He remained undeservedly unpopular. His successor, Sir Charles FitzRoy, was equally helpless. Municipal and shire government did not become a reality in Australia until after responsible self-government had been established.

As for the public service, we glimpse it from time to time in the *Historical Records of Australia*, as in Gipps's "Report on the General State of the Colony", 1841.[70] The old difficulties are still apparent because they were inherent in the situation. Especially in the older departments, where salaries were lowest, the departmental heads were generally landowners as well and, since living in Sydney was so expensive, lived as much as possible on their properties. There was at least no fear of losing their services too soon. The well-educated young men brought out from England to fill government jobs were generally only using the appointment as a stopgap until they found something better paid or launched themselves as graziers. Nevertheless the over-all status of the service was gradually improving.

Yet confusion was still only just round the corner. Take the case of the surveyor's cows. George William Evans had come to the colony in 1802, had served as a surveyor and, crossing the Blue Mountains in the wake of Lawson, Blaxland and Wentworth, had explored the Promised Land and reported on it to Macquarie in fine, large, Biblical terms. He was rewarded with land and the loan of four cows and two oxen from the government herd. Thirty years later, in 1847, he was compelled to pay the Crown £336 for these animals and the cows' progeny. In vain he protested that he had returned them. It could not be proved that he had, for the government records had long ago, everyone thought, been lost or destroyed. Nor could it be proved that he had not. He was ruined. He could not leave it at that. He began a search for the missing records. They were found in the possession of W. C. Wentworth. The cows and oxen had been duly returned, but Evans had not demanded the return of his bond. The old man was pardoned, the money was returned, and the costs involved in clearing himself were paid.[71]

Students of Australian history must guard against the natural mistake of believing that reforms and panaceas outlined by governors and others came into operation as planned. The *Historical Records of Australia,* whilst probably the soundest source of information, still put a formal gloze on the situation that really existed. They are sometimes no more than a record of good intentions and rational thinking. The colony was not famous for its rationality. There were so many interested parties pulling in opposite directions, so much undisguised human nature and no very strong tradition. The over-all pattern tended to be chaotic.

"And so to bed."

REFERENCE NOTES

1 R. M. Crawford, *Australia,* p. 63.
2 See *Hist. Rec. Aust.*, ser. I, vol. v, for many specimens of Governor King's proclamations.
3 *Hist. Rec. Aust.*, ser. I, vol. ii, p. 235. 4 *Ibid.*, vol. xi, p. xxi (Introduction).

[5] *Ibid.*, vol. xii, pp. 144-7. [6] *Ibid.*, vol. xiv, pp. 265 *et seq.*
[7] *Ibid.*, vol. xiii, p. 99. [8] *Ibid.*, p. x (Introduction).
[9] *Ibid.*, p. 99. [10] *Ibid.*, p. 98. [11] *Ibid.*, p. 99.
[12] See Bourke Papers, vol. ii, Forbes to Bourke, 19th August 1836.
[13] R. M. Hartwell in *Australia: a Social and Political History* (ed. Greenwood), pp. 53-4.
[14] *Hist. Rec. Aust.*, ser. I, vol. xxii, p. vii (Introduction).
[15] *Ibid.*, p. 244. [16] *Ibid.*, vol. xix, pp. 719-24.
[17] *Ibid.*, vol. xxiii, p. 43. [18] *Ibid.*, vol. xxv, p. 607. [19] *Ibid.*, vol. xxvi, p. 529.
[20] *Ibid.*, vol. xi, p. 460.
[21] A very interesting account of the "Pioneer Surveyors of New South Wales" is given in a series of articles by John Weingarth in the journal, the *Surveyor*, vol. xxviii (19th February 1916), pp. 7 *et seq.*; vol. xxx, pp. 6 *et seq.*, 67 *et seq.*
[22] *Hist. Rec. Aust.*, ser. I, vol. x, p. 670.
[23] R. M. Hartwell in *Australia: a Social and Political History* (ed. Greenwood), p. 52.
[24] *Hist. Rec. Aust.*, ser. I, vol. x, p. 579.
[25] *Ibid.*, p. 665. [26] *Ibid.*, vol. xi, pp. 256-7. [27] *Ibid.*, p. 258.
[28] *Ibid.*, p. 256. [29] *Ibid.*, p. 556. [30] *Ibid.*, pp. 61-2.
[31] *Ibid.*, p. 380. [32] *Ibid.*, p. 381. [33] *Ibid.*, p. 102.
[34] *Ibid.*, vol. xi, pp. 108, 109, 213, 483-4; vol. xii, pp. 471, 473.
[35] *Ibid.*, vol. xii, pp. 475-8. [36] *Ibid.*, vol xi, p. 524. [37] *Ibid.*, p. 525.
[38] *Ibid.*, pp. 282, 493. [39] *Ibid.*, vol. xii, pp. 148-9. [40] *Ibid.*, p. 149.
[41] *Ibid.*, p. 150. [42] *Ibid.*, p. 344. [43] *Ibid.*, p. 151.
[44] *Ibid.*, pp. 368-9. [45] *Ibid.*, p. 371. [46] *Ibid.*, p. 367.
[47] *Ibid.*, vol. xiii, pp. 76-9 [48] *Ibid.*, p. 106. [49] *Ibid.*, p. 387.
[50] *Ibid.*, pp. 426-7. [51] *Ibid.*, vol. xii, pp. 607-8. [52] *Ibid.*, vol. xiii, pp. 692-4.
[53] *Ibid.*, p. 245.
[54] For Rossi's report see *Hist. Rec. Aust.*, ser. I, vol. xii, pp. 679-84.
[55] *Hist. Rec. Aust.*, ser. I, vol. xii, pp. 697-8. [56] *Ibid.*, pp. 91-5.
[57] *Ibid.*, p. 175. [58] *Ibid.*, vol. xiii, pp. 362-70.
[59] *Ibid.*, vol. xiv, p. 136. [60] *Ibid.*, vol. xiii, p. 584. [61] *Ibid.*, vol. xii, pp. 214-15.
[62] *Ibid.*, vol. xvii, p. 233. [63] *Ibid.*, vol. xxi, pp. 157-8. [64] *Ibid.*, vol. xxv, p. 613.
[65] *Ibid.*, vol. xxvi, p. 13. [66] *Ibid.*, vol. xvii, p. 269. [67] *Ibid.*, pp. 301-2.
[68] *Ibid.*, p. 753. [69] *Ibid.*, vol. xx, p. 777.
[70] *Ibid.*, vol. xxi, pp. 507 *et seq.*
[71] For the full intricacies of this story see *Hist. Rec. Aust.*, ser. I, vol. xxv, pp. 604-6.

CHAPTER XV

THE LAW AND THE PURSE

I. The Judiciary and the Courts

It must be clearly understood that from the time of the first British occupation of its shores Australia was never without law, the Civil Law of England. There was from the first no such thing as arbitrary or summary justice other than that which might be meted out for minor offences by a magistrate in England. The courts were civil courts, not courts martial, and the law they dispensed was the common law of England. These facts are masked by the appearance of the earliest courts of justice, for those who sat on the bench with the Judge-Advocate were inevitably naval or military officers. There was no body of civilians equal to the task. In fact, there were no civilians other than the prisoners and a scattering of servants. Trial by jury was impossible for lack of jurors, since under English law a man once condemned could not sit on a jury.

Judge-Advocate David Collins was a Captain of Marines on whom devolved this special duty. He had no training in the law, but he was equipped with a set of Statutes and was expected to apply the principles of English justice. The surviving records of his judgments show a greater mildness than those of magistrates like the Reverend Samuel Marsden some ten years later. His courts were conducted in a seemly manner, unlike those of Judge Jeffery Bent in the time of Governor Macquarie. Evidence was taken and every effort made to comb out the often tangled skein.

In such a society the cases themselves, though often criss-crossed by perjury and counter-perjury, were generally simple matters of discovering the true facts and did not involve the application of abstruse legal principles. There could not yet be litigation as there were but few civilians (and those humble men) and no property rights. The first courts were exclusively criminal courts. Troubles within the regiment—such nebulous charges as "conduct unbecoming to an officer and a gentleman"—were settled within the regiment by the ordinary procedures of courts martial.

The only really complex situation so far to arise was when a Court of Vice-Admiralty became necessary. This court tried cases of mutiny on the high seas, those involving prizes and the distribution of shares therein, and similar cases.[1] It was not often called together, but in 1799 Governor Hunter reported to the Duke of Portland that a Spanish ship had been captured off the coast of South America by two whalers and had been brought to Sydney as a prize. He convened a Court of Vice-Admiralty which condemned her and her cargo.[2]

Again in 1806 two Spanish ships were brought into Port Jackson and a Court of Vice-Admiralty declared that they were not prizes, on the grounds that England and Spain were not at war when they were seized. There were some shady dealings involved and the situation became very complex.[3]

The early governors were given the power to convene Courts of Vice-Admiralty, later it was vested in the Lieutenant-Governor, and at times there was confusion and delay because no one had the necessary power.

To return to the normal flow of justice, there was no conflict of power between the Governor and the Judge-Advocate, theirs was the relationship of Captain-General and subordinate officer. Conflict was only to arise when trained lawyers, first Richard Dore and then Ellis Bent, held the appointment. They brought with them not only the concept of the law's impartiality but also of its majesty.

The position of Judge-Advocate was a difficult and anomalous one. He not only convened and presided over the court, virtually a bench of magistrates, but he advised the prisoner, took minutes of proceedings, and kept the records.

The office was roughly modelled on that of the Chief Law Officer of the British Army, who bore the same title, but in Australia his duties were directed, not to the highly specialized requirements of the army, but to those of a young, growing, diverse colony. This is but another example of the Home Government's habit of adapting old procedures to new circumstances.

As the colony grew in population and complexity land became a source of wealth, and the two original classes of officers and prisoners were enlarged to include free immigrants, the native-born, emancipists, and expirees, the task of the Judge-Advocate became more and more difficult and finally impossible.

When the duty could be laid on an officer it was generally possible to find a suitable man. Lawyers and barristers of sufficient attainments and experience could hardly be induced to come so far for so small a salary (David Collins received 15s. a day for the dual appointment of Judge-Advocate and Governor's secretary), especially as it was unlikely to lead to anything better. When a lawyer was appointed he generally had some other end than advancement in view, such as health.

Dore, the first professional lawyer to hold office as Judge-Advocate, arrived in *Barwell* in May 1789. He was, one deduces, impecunious and sick. At first his relations with Hunter were amicable and when he asked for the additional position of Governor's private secretary Hunter appointed him. But, wrote Hunter:

> I . . . had very soon cause to observe that he was determin'd to be govern'd by his own views and interests in the line of his profession, and to follow, or rather to establish, such rules as best suited those objects, although not known in this settlement before his arrival, and which I thought ill-accorded with his situation here, either as an officer on public service, paid by the Crown, or the confidential situation in which he stood with me.

Hunter felt he had "great cause for being displeased with Mr Dore's manner of doing his duty, and for withdrawing that confidence I was dispos'd to have placed him".[4] Dore set aside the Civil Court twice in a manner that offended both the Governor and all "responsible men". He raised general ire by instituting high fees: "until Mr Dore's arrival, the inhabitants of the colony received justice in all their concerns without expence".[5] Of the fees for licences, ear-marked for the Orphan Fund, he claimed one third, an innovation which drew italics from Hunter. He imprisoned convicts for debt, thus defrauding the Government of their services and condoning their illegal trading and possession of property. As the Governor's secretary he inserted passages in dispatches to suit his own ends. He stirred up trouble and was a true precursor of the Bents. Dore did not trouble the Governor long, for he died insolvent in 1800 and was buried with whatever pomp was available, attended to his grave by the regiment, to whom Governor Hunter issued a feather for each man's hat for their "industry in forming the public parade".[6] It was a nice touch.

The colony was now without a legal officer and Richard Atkins, who had acted as Judge-Advocate between the departure of Collins and the arrival of Dore, was again pressed into service. He was a half-pay army officer who had arrived in the colony in 1792. One suspects that his aristocratic family off-loaded him. Coming to the colony free, he found his services in great demand. At Dore's death he was already acting as Registrar of the Court of Vice-Admiralty (a far from onerous job), magistrate at Parramatta, Inspector of Public Works in and about Parramatta and Toongabbie, and officer-in-charge of the shipping register. All these appointments were honorary. It need hardly be said that he had no knowledge of the law and history was to prove him pusillanimous. Everyone agreed that he was a drunkard.

Nevertheless he was *persona grata* in high places. Hunter put it on record that he gave "great assistance and satisfaction"[7] as a magistrate and "most perfect satisfaction"[8] in his other numerous duties.

Hunter and King may have been disposed in Atkins's favour because he was not only a man of birth but compliant. Macarthur was already, in

1796, Atkins's implacable enemy. He claimed that "Both by oral and written evidence will I prove that Mr Atkins is a public cheater, living in the most boundless dissipation, without any visible means of maintaining it than by imposture on unwary strangers whose business leads them to this settlement", and that "drunkenness and indecency are almost inseparable from him".[9] Somewhere between these extremes we may plot the character and history of that very small man. It is certain that he drank to excess and even more certain that he lacked the strength to swim in the very deep waters in which he presently found himself. He reflected neither dignity nor honour upon the position which he held. He was, also, to be involved in the struggle which led up to the rebellion of the New South Wales Corps against Governor Bligh. This, as Dr H. V. Evatt has expounded in his book *Rum Rebellion*, had many legal as well as illegal aspects. In them Macarthur showed himself a better lawyer than Atkins and a better tactician than Bligh. Yet the legal aspects of that notorious quarrel are rather a lawyer's museum piece than an integral part of this historical narrative. Both sides manoeuvred for place, or tried to save face. Bligh had poor support from Atkins, who was more of a liability than anything else. Had he been the cleverest lawyer in Christendom the result would have been the same. This, however, is a digression.

In a letter from Governor King to Lord Hobart dated 7th August 1803 we get a curious picture of the state of law in New South Wales. King was welcoming new Letters Patent for the regulation of the courts. He found them "excellent", but he pointed out that the trouble lay not in theory but in the people on whom the system had to rest. Civil cases were to be tried by three officers, of whom the Judge-Advocate was always one. The other two were a military officer plus a naval or civil officer. These men were sometimes drawn by lot. They had no knowledge of law and often found the duty of sitting in court an intolerable burden. In consequence, through indifference, they generally agreed with the Judge-Advocate. The litigants had little confidence in him, so that there was usually an appeal against every verdict to the Governor. The right of appeal could not be refused. "There is no want of litigation where law is cheap." The Judge-Advocate himself, because of his ignorance, was forced to rely on his clerk, the notorious Michael Robinson, who came out a prisoner in 1798, convicted of writing threatening letters. Convicted again of perjury in the colony, he was sentenced to secondary detention on Norfolk Island, but his sentence was deferred. Because he was a trained attorney "he still remains as an indispensable assistant to the Judge-Advocate, but Your Lordship will readily conceive the impropriety of the only Law Officer in this colony having so bad a character as an assistant. Perhaps such assistance would not be necessary for a professional man." The convict George Crossley was another blot on the judicial scene.

The Criminal Court consisted of the Judge-Advocate and six naval or military officers acting as judges and jury. King would have liked to see the panel enlarged to include merchants and other respectable citizens who came free into the country. Justice was too much in the hands of a small clique.

There had already been some grave miscarriages of justice. King cited an example. Surgeon Jamison, who was also a magistrate, was accused of assaulting one of his assistants. The assistant-surgeon asked for a court martial, but was refused. It was a matter for the Criminal Court. The case was postponed by interested parties until the King's ship *Glatton* had left port, which meant that the Judge-Advocate would be assisted by military officers only. When the case was tried it was found that the assistant-surgeon was the aggressor and that Jamison had acted in self-defence. He was formally acquitted, but was sentenced to find sureties that he would keep the peace for three years, or, in default, go to jail. By any standards this was very odd.[10]

The settlers were already asking for a system of trial by jury, but this was not yet feasible for the simple reason that there were not enough free persons to act as jurors.

In 1814 a Supreme Court was set up. The Judge-Advocate presided and was assisted by two local magistrates. From this court appeals went to the High Court or Governor's Court. There were now four courts, the two just mentioned, the Criminal Court, and the Court of Vice-Admiralty.

In the reconstruction that came with Macquarie a new Judge-Advocate was sent out. That a young and promising lawyer like Ellis Bent took the appointment was probably due to the weakness of his chest. He may have hoped that in a climate reported to be warm and healthy he would recover from his trouble. His brother, Jeffery Hart Bent, was appointed to the newly created post of Judge of the Supreme Court largely through Macquarie's good offices, and accepted it, one suspects, partly through affection for his brother and partly because his own peculiar temper made advancement in England difficult.

Had Ellis Bent been less tender in his professional pride, more tolerant, and if, above all, he had had a sense of humour, he could, I think, have kept Macquarie's good opinion and the new machinery of justice would have functioned. The ceaseless quarrels, already described, were to begin with trivial matters, but over them all hung the conflict of the Governor's absolute power in collision with the independence and impartiality of the judiciary. Unfortunately in politics the Bents showed no more impartiality than the Governor. Whilst Macquarie sought to build up an emancipist middle class as a buffer against exclusionist monopoly, the Bents, conceding nothing to circumstances, consistently played into the hands of the exclusionists, because of their legal horror of convicted men and also because the exclusionists, more nearly than any other group in the colony, reproduced the type of society that they were used to at Home. It is understandable, too, that after the manner in which Deputy Judge-Advocate Atkins had administered the law, and the scandal of Michael Robinson, they should wish to set their courts above all possible taint.

Owing to the clash between the Governor and the judges the new system could not, and did not, function. This was a fine example in a penal colony. The Governor's Court did not even open until after the recall of Jeffery Bent and the death of his brother. At the same time as the courts were reconstituted two barristers were sent out so that litigants would no longer have to rely on ex-convicts.

With the advent of property the work of the courts changed in kind and volume. By 1798 it was a commonplace, following the English custom, to imprison debtors, though how, being imprisoned, they could earn money to liquidate their debts is a puzzle. In that year Hunter, by proclamation, forbade the imprisonment of government servants for debt because of the damage to the service.[11] In 1799 he reported the prisons full of debtors. On his departure, as a final gesture of benevolence, he forgave all prisoners except such as were condemned to death, held for sedition, or imprisoned for debts.[12] On the Queen's birthday, 1803, Governor King also, to mark the happy day, released all prisoners, except debtors. Crimes against property were very seriously regarded.

Litigation was frequent and bitter. It was in the nature of a blood sport and relieved the tedium of that restricted society. The state of the Survey Department, always lagging far behind the opening up of land, and the informality of land titles, were calculated to increase it.

The courts were supplemented by magistrates as in England. These were the local gentry who could afford to give their time for nothing more than a few indulgences and the prestige of office. For a man of substance to be omitted from the Bench or the Commission of the Peace was somewhat conspicuous. This liberal use of magistrates was more dangerous in Australia than in England, where the tradition of service was longer, distances were shorter, and there was more leisure in well-to-do circles. The powers of magistrates were limited and just where the limitations lay was a matter of controversy. A test case, Burn *v.* Howe and Fletcher, arose in 1822 when the magistrate and his constable were sued successfully for exceeding their powers in a case concerning payment to a man named Dowse for making bricks.[13]

In and after 1798 Quarter Sessions were held regularly to settle civil disputes. All courts were adjourned at harvest-time because no one could then spare the time to attend them.

The judicial system that had worked so disastrously under Macquarie, because of the battle for power that it invoked, was given another trial under Brisbane with a new Judge-Advocate, John Wylde, and a new Judge of the Supreme Court, Barron Field. They were self-opinionated young men and soon fell foul of both the Governor and the magistracy.

On his arrival Brisbane found a curious state of affairs. On one side was the magistracy, bound in all its actions by the laws of England, and on the other his principal law officer, the Judge-Advocate, bound by his commission, as Brisbane read it, to the Governor alone. There were thus two bodies of law, English law and local law, the latter consisting of Government orders and proclamations, what you might call *ad hoc* law, as it arose out of special local circumstances and was designed to cope with situations and abuses peculiar to New South Wales.[14]

Wylde could not agree that he was subject to the Governor. He claimed that if the Governor's proclamations were contrary to English law they were illegal. He also claimed that the judgments of all magistrates in civil cases were subject to the Governor's Court, of which he was president. "It seems to me," he wrote, " . . . that the Jurisdiction of the Governor's Court can be questioned by no 'Authority', private or public, *here* or *elsewhere*, however *high* or Official. . . ."[15] This was aimed both at the Governor and the magistrates.

The magistrates met at the Court House at Parramatta on 25th March 1822 to consider their position.[16] The meeting drew up an address to Brisbane pointing out that if the Governor's Court could quash their verdicts their authority would be gone and every case would have to be tried in Sydney, as the disappointed party would appeal. This would be not only cumbersome and expensive but would lead to injustice. A magistrate living in the district or out-settlement would know the circumstances of the cases and the characters and histories of the litigants far better than any court in Sydney. The dispute centred on Master and Servant cases, under which Howe's case, already cited, came. Macquarie, in a proclamation of 21st November 1818, had given magistrates jurisdiction over disputes arising over wages. Wylde now argued that they had and could have no such jurisdiction.

Brisbane—throwing up his hands in exasperation, one imagines—laid the matter before the Colonial Office.

The answer to the problem was the setting up of a Court of Requests. Instructions were framed in England and transmitted to Brisbane by Lord Bathurst in January 1824.[17] There were to be five such courts at Sydney, Parramatta, Liverpool, Windsor, and Newcastle. They were to be convened frequently at the Governor's discretion. Thus would the magistrates be relieved of their civil law duties. It was not possible to find five men trained in law to preside at the courts, so Brisbane appointed one man, John Stephen, to go the rounds. Five separate commissions were made out to him and a salary of £600 a year out of colonial revenue allotted to him. Dr H. G. Douglass was named the Ambulatory Commissioner and was sent to England to be briefed. He was to receive £500 a year and his travelling expenses. This appointment, however, did not stand.

If this were a triumph for Wylde he did not remain in office to see it. From the first there was conflict between the Judge-Advocate and Sir Thomas Brisbane. Wylde took too much on himself. Wylde was an obstructionist. He refused to assist the Governor by giving him his legal opinion in writing.[18] Brisbane wished that his services could be dispensed with.

Wylde at least did something useful when in 1817 he assisted in the formation of the Bank of New South Wales,[19] and in 1821 made a digest of colonial regulations.

Judge Field was even more annoying to the Governor, who complained to Lord Bathurst that he had

> . . . embraced every opportunity of falsely and foully slandering me and my Government as Contemptible to various Individuals. I can ascribe no cause for His unwarrantable Conduct, as I had uniformly treated him with the utmost consideration; and never once used an expression to offend Him; I must therefore impute it to His having allowed Himself to become the head of a faction, with which He had been identified during the whole of this period, who seemed guided by no moral restraints in order to accomplish their ends. I wish I could allow myself to believe that the Court, over which he presided, had been free from this Spirit of Party.[20]

It was clear both in the colony and in England that a change in the judiciary of New South Wales was necessary. The plan was in preparation in England in 1823 and was included in the Imperial Statute 4 Geo. IV., c. 96: "An Act to provide, until the First Day of January, One thousand, eight hundred and twenty-seven, and until the End of the next Session of Parliament, for the better Administration of Justice in New South Wales and Van Diemen's Land, and for the more effectual Government thereof; and for other purposes relating thereto."

This Statute, as outlined earlier, set up a nominee Legislative Council. It also reformed the judiciary. The offices of Judge-Advocate and Judge of the Supreme Court were both abolished and with them went Wylde and Field. A Chief Justice was appointed. This was Francis Forbes.

Forbes was a party to the framing of the first New South Wales Act and was until his retirement in 1837 one of the strongest liberal influences in the colony. Of the first New South Wales Act (1823) he said that it was at first intended to be an Act for the reformation of the judiciary only. It

> . . . contained a whole code of laws, which were deemed so complex and unfit

for discussion in Parliament that it was suddenly determined to weave a legislative power into the body of the Act. . . . In consequence of the resolution thus suddenly adopted, many clauses were retained, which should have been expunged, such for example as the clauses relating to Courts of Sessions and Requests, the declaring of insolvencies, foreign attachments and other matters of purely local moment.[21]

This accounts for some peculiarities in the Act. On the judicial side it appointed a Chief Justice who was the colony's principal law officer, who sat *ex officio* on the new nominee Council, and to whom all the Council's legislation must be submitted so that he could certify that it was in keeping with the law of England and not repugnant to it. To him also the Governor must submit all his orders and proclamations so that from the point of view of the law they were valid. This removed a weakness and an ever open cause of uncertainty, particularly as the review was to be retrospective. Until this time the validity of local laws had been repeatedly questioned. They were now to be set on a proper legal basis. When the Chief Justice considered a proclamation to be of doubtful legality and authenticity it was to be referred to the Law Officers in England for a final verdict. Thus the past was to be consolidated. If the Governor and the Chief Justice disagreed as to the propriety and necessity of any regulation it was to be submitted to the Secretary of State for the Colonies. In time of emergency the Governor still had the right to act independently for the safety of the community. The Chief Justice was also named the Judge in the Court of Vice-Admiralty, thus settling that vexed question.

The Act set up a new Supreme Court, and recapitulated the sections establishing Courts of Requests and a Court of Appeal already described, and instituted Quarter Sessions. The two branches of the judicature, civil and criminal, were separated. The following law officers were appointed: an Attorney-General, a Solicitor-General, a Registrar of the Supreme Court, and a Sheriff to undertake the duties of the former Provost-Marshal. The first Attorney-General was Saxe Bannister, at a salary of £600 a year. Mr John Stephen was the first Solicitor-General and combined the appointment with that of judge in the Courts of Requests. The Supreme Court retained criminal jurisdiction and went on circuit annually in Van Diemen's Land.

The Courts of Requests relieved the magistrates of their duties in civil actions where a knowledge of the law was essential. They still tried minor criminal cases, but now they were responsible to the Chief Justice, not the Governor. Their position has regularized this side of human nature.

The Court of Appeals derived its constitution originally from Letters Patent, 1814, with the Judge-Advocate as its assessor, but only as regards points of law. The Governor was its key figure. "The proper function of a Court of Appeal is to review the decisions of the inferior Court, that is to say, to decide whether the judgment of that Court was right or wrong upon the facts in evidence before it. To admit new Evidence is to institute a new Trial, not to review a Trial already concluded."[22] This court was peculiar to Australia and had no counterpart in England.

The Governor's Court was superseded by Courts of General and Quarter Sessions. All sentences of death had to be ratified by the Governor and he must therefore have access to all court records, something that Wylde had wrongfully denied him.[23]

The judges were empowered to frame the rules of their courts. This regulation made impossible any impasse such as occurred between the Bents and Macquarie.

Most important of all, the Act provided for the rudimentary beginning of trial by jury. This was a modified version of the English practice. In criminal cases the jury consisted of seven officers, in civil actions of seven civilians. The jury of officers is a link with the constitution of the former Judge-Advocate's Court in which a panel of officers sat with him on the bench.

For civil jurors there was a property qualification of fifty acres of land or a house worth £300. At first juries were only used when both sides in a civil action requested one and were not often resorted to. Bathurst had suggested that the Executive Council consider the matter of trial by jury and make what recommendations it saw fit with the view of incorporating them in the New South Wales Act when it came up for revision. Brisbane had already, in October 1825, expressed his opinion.

> I could not fail to perceive that, by the Community at large, the mode of Trial by Jury was considered as a great improvement in the administration of Justice, and confident expectations were formed of its moralizing effect upon the people. Even among the few who were known to be unfavourable to the introduction of Trial by Jury, since the first shock of prejudice has been overcome, it has been silently gaining ground; and I verily believe at the present moment there are not a dozen Individuals in the whole Colony, who would openly come forward and oppose its being still further introduced.[24]

In August 1826 the Council deliberated. It recommended that all "crimes and misdemeanours" be tried by a jury of six officers or magistrates nominated and six inhabitants chosen by the Sheriff, as in England and that all civil cases be tried by a jury of twelve if one party wished it and the Court deemed it suitable. If neither party to a civil action wanted a jury the case was to be tried by Assessors, as used to be the custom. The choosing of jurors was a delicate matter. In England anyone who had been convicted but received a free pardon was eligible for jury service. In New South Wales it was thought best not to raise the issue.

Lists of all free citizens over twenty-one, of those pardoned, emancipated, or freed by servitude, of those who had already sat on juries, with, in every class, an estimate of their property, were compiled and then it was left to the Justices of the Sessions for the various districts tactfully to prepare jury lists. Grand jurors were chosen from amongst the "most respectable inhabitants: the power of prosecuting by information being continued in the Attorney General in all cases of felony where Grand Juries cannot conveniently be assembled".[25]

In January 1827 a public meeting drew up a petition to the King asking for a more liberal policy in choosing jurors. At present, the petitioners pointed out, four-fifths of the population were excluded from jury service. It was necessary "to revive among them [the Colonists] those English feelings and predilections, which a thirty nine years deprivation of it must according to the opinion of this party have so nearly extinguished". It speaks of "men, who though English by descent, may become Anti-English in heart by the force of a system, essentially Anti-English in its principles and operation".[26] This could be read as a thinly veiled threat.

When the revised New South Wales Act reached New South Wales in 1828 the scope of trial by jury had been widened but it was still hedged about. The Secretary of State, Sir George Murray, wrote to Governor Darling on 31st July 1828 that the decision whether or not a jury should sit in civil cases was a matter for the judge to decide: "That many cases will arise in which the application for a Jury ought to be refused is obvious" —that is, cases in which the parties are of different standing, in which public questions are involved, or which are too technical for a jury to understand. The main advance was that in future the development of the jury system would be in the hands of the Governor and his Council. Yet this, too, was only tentative. "For the present, I am not prepared to advise His Majesty in Council to impart to you and the Legislative Council of New South Wales the power of introducing Trial by Jury. This is a subject of such extreme importance that I have judged it more prudent to pause, until I can receive a full report upon the question in all its bearings."[27] Darling and each member of the Legislative Council were to report. The matter of choosing jurors was not overtly touched upon.

Other points in the new Act were that common law jurisdiction, like that of the Lord Chancellor in England, was to be vested in the Supreme Court; criminal informations could be filed now by any person, not only by the Attorney-General; circuit courts were instituted tentatively. By 1840 they were in common use. For the colonials none of these reforms went far enough. They claimed that they were none the less Englishmen because they lived beneath southern skies and that they should enjoy all the freedoms that Englishmen prided themselves on. They seemingly forgot that English liberties were still hedged about by property qualifications and privileges. The population of New South Wales was now about 55,000, of whom 35,000 were free. Amongst the technically free were counted emancipists and expirees. Those who clamoured for the full status of Englishmen were a relatively small body. The exclusionist, or "pure Merino" party was more interested in economics than politics. They were content to remain the ruling class in a penal settlement. They were, by and large, conservative not liberal. The military outlook prevailed amongst them, for many of them had been officers. They could look back to the "good old days" of monopoly and Tom Tiddler's ground. Amongst the emancipists there was a natural desire to rehabilitate themselves, and also in their ranks there were men who had been sent out for political "crimes", the Scottish Martyrs for instance, and they were anxious to continue the fight in the new world. They, too, wanted their share in what the colony had to offer for themselves and their children, and to have and to hold it they wanted recognition and security before the law. The spearhead of the militant Whigs were those who had come to the country free and were surprised and shocked to find that by conferring that favour on the new country they had lost their rights. They drew recruits from amongst the native-born—like Wentworth, who became their leader—the better placed emancipists, and a few of the open-minded exclusionists.

The Governors were so near to it all, were so deeply involved in work, personalities, problems, the home country of their prestige, that they saw mostly the failures of their predecessors and the intractability of their colonizing material. They may, half the time, have been as conscious of the lack of stationery as of the upsurge of a desire for liberties. It was for them to govern and it was not easy.

They had the practical problem of governing and it bred in them an autocratic temper. Darling wrote to Huskisson on 1st March 1829: "You may be assured that, composed as this Colony is, the Executive does not possess a particle too much power at present. The Laws of England were not made for Convicts; and a Convict Population requires more coercion than those Laws sanction, excited and supported too as these people have been."[28]

By the time Darling was at Government House the position had shrunk considerably in the eyes of the Colonial Office. Murray could write to Darling:

> To my surprise . . . I perceive that you are in the habit of issuing Orders or Proclamations expressive of your own opinions as to the merit or demerit of particular individuals and aiming at no immediate practical result. I am to desire that this practice be immediately discontinued. It cannot but be productive of many grave inconveniences, among which it is not the least that it involves a great sacrifice of the dignity of your Office, and invites the hostility of those with whom you condescend to enter into this unbecoming species of altercation.

In future it will be fit that every Government Order and Proclamation, which it may be absolutely necessary to promulgate, be framed in due legal form by the Attorney General of the Colony.[29]

The Governor was being metamorphosed from autocrat to figurehead even by the end of the 1820s.

The Home Government looked on from a distance.

The medallion painted in the South Seas had become recognizable as a colony. At first the Colonial Office had looked for efficiency and economy only. Take a strong man, give him absolute power, throw in a regiment and leave it to him, had been the recipe. It was valid only so long as the colony remained penal. With the growth of the wool industry, the influx of free settlers, and the evils of monopoly made overt, a change was obviously necessary. No man was strong enough—Bligh, for instance, or a sufficiently benevolent despot such as Macquarie—to hold the colony. The Home Government had to make concessions. It had learnt the necessity of being timely. It preferred the legal to the political approach. Trial by jury was a well-entrenched and delimited liberty. The body of English law could be entrusted to a Chief Justice like Forbes. An elected Assembly, for which the colonists were also asking at this time, was a very different matter. It could take the bit between its teeth and bolt even if its legislation were subjected to an Upper House of one, the Chief Justice, before it could become legal. The colonists had had no education in self-government, whereas the law could be applied by professional lawyers sent out from England. It is easy to see why, in the early days, the growing point was legal and not constitutional.

Once progress had begun it could not be halted, nor did the Home Government wish this to be done. It was simply cautious. A penal colony was a penal colony, and in the Rum Rebellion the rashness of allowing an oligarchy to gain power had been aptly illustrated. Yet in whom but another potential oligarchy could political liberties, if they were ceded, be vested? The fallacy that if a man had possessions he was above temptation was still current. So was the ideal of honorary service to the State, but New South Wales was more workaday than England. There was little inherited wealth and less leisure, and in consequence fewer men to give honorary service.

The Home Government by the 1820s was no longer looking only for efficiency and economy in government. It was giving its attention to the balance of power in the colony. The Governor's autocratic power had to be pruned back. It was seen now that the power of the judges, particularly the Chief Justice, might become too great. At first he had what was virtually a power of veto over all colonial legislation. He could declare any Act null and void on the grounds that it was repugnant to

English law and there was no one to say him nay. This power was taken from him and vested in the Supreme Court, later still (1847) every Colonial Act sent home for Royal assent went first to the Crown Law Officers, who could be counted on to be impartial, both uninfluenced by and ignorant of local pressures, for certification as to its conformity with English law.[30] The Chief Justice, too, was gradually relieved of his political functions. At first he sat *ex officio* in the Legislative Council, later he was debarred from presiding at the Council in the Governor's absence, and finally he was excused from attending the Council at all (1828).

The Secretary of State for the Colonies was anxious that the judiciary should not encroach on the prerogatives of the Crown.[31] The power of the Attorney-General was clipped when he ceased to be the only man in the colony who could bring a criminal indictment. Also, as the body of colonial legislation grew, regulating all spheres of activity, the power of individuals decreased and the power of the community as a whole was strengthened.

With the increase of a free civil population army officers became less important. With the restriction of the tour of duty of a regiment to three years they ceased to send down roots as the New South Wales Corps had done. The law-courts no longer had to rely on officers to sit on the bench. They had served their turn. In the early days they, and particularly the naval officers who would presently sail away, were more likely to be impartial than any other class in the small community; they, also, from sitting on courts martial, had some idea of judicial procedure. They had more leisure, since their military or naval duties were by no means as exacting as pioneering or the business of merchants. Gradually, however, the Government was able to dispense with their services in the dispensation of justice. They were replaced by civilians, first in the civil courts and later in the criminal courts. With the separation of convict and colonial establishments and the sending out from England of higher officials, such as the Colonial Secretary, they ceased to take much part in the state. In 1829 the control of roads and bridges passed to the Surveyor-General's Department. The Colonial Engineer was no longer chosen from the army officers available. The colony was fast losing its military appearance at the end of the 1820s and continued to do so until English regiments were finally withdrawn in 1870.

The power of magistrates was reduced and regularized. Too much authority had at first to be given to whoever was available. The settlement was scattered far and wide, the roads were bad or non-existent. It was difficult to bring cases for trial to Sydney. A heavy burden fell on the magistrates. There were inevitably scandals in which even well-known men like the Reverend Samuel Marsden and Dr Douglass were involved. In 1824 Archdeacon Scott was suggesting a "Police Magistrate with adequate

Salary and House who should *sit daily* and hear all causes of dispute in which *a convict* is concerned". And for cases involving the free and the emancipated a bench of magistrates should sit weekly.[32] This smacked of one law for the bond and one for the free. Only the first part of his recommendation was put into effect. Most of the cases in Parramatta and outlying settlements were master and servant disputes. The law was very strict for servants who left their work, failed to give satisfaction, or indulged in insolence. More rarely servants brought actions against their masters.

In 1824 the Attorney-General moved for the appointment of a stipendiary magistrate in each town and ruled that a magistrate sitting alone could not punish serious cases. They had to be held over for the Quarter Sessions, the accused being put on a bond.[33] This, together with the holding of petty sessions was confirmed by Lord Bathurst, 11th September 1825.[34]

An effort to keep down the expenses of the courts nearly wrecked the whole scheme. On 26th February 1827 William Carter, the chairman of Quarter Sessions, was writing to Governor Darling to complain that his salary of £200 a year was inadequate: ". . . the situation would not be worth holding, as no one could be expected to expose himself to the trouble and responsibility of the duties . . . and to the fatigue and in fact danger of travelling by land and sea . . . without something in addition to actual expenses". Carter was away from home about four months of the year, attended 16 sessions, and received only £50 for travelling expenses whereas it cost him £250. He had, too, been shipwrecked on one of his journeys north.[35]

Long before the coming of responsible self-government New South Wales had a complete judiciary on the English plan, the last military jury had been empanelled, rights and responsibilities had been allotted and, in outline at least, the system was complete. There were still some strains and stresses between the judicial and executive authorities. This was to be expected, since the tradition of power lay with the executive as personified by the Governor and the actuality was passing to the courts and the Legislative Council. Darling was in open conflict with his Chief Justice; Bourke, more liberal, still felt himself hampered. "I would just observe, however, that this very eminent Lawyer seems to entertain a very great jealousy of local authority, and to claim for his Court a total exemption from that subordination to the Executive, which the Constitution of England has wisely provided."[36] But he was also to praise him in the most generous terms: "I believe it would be difficult in the whole range of Colonial Courts to point out a Person on the Bench, who, from integrity and ability, legal knowledge and devotion to His Majesty's Service, is better entitled to the honour of Knighthood than Chief Justice

Forbes."[37] The shift of power may be said to have been accomplished under Governor Sir Richard Bourke.

Regarded as an evolution, the development of judicial power was rapid in New South Wales, and still more rapid in the other colonies, since the foundation colony acted as a spearhead. Once she won an advantage or reform there seemed no reason why the younger settlements should not enjoy it, too. Seen as a year-to-year struggle, progress was fitful and uneven. For instance, trial by jury was accomplished gradually, stage by stage, and met with opposition within the colony. This opposition was part of the fight that free inhabitants put up against the extension of civilian rights to emancipists and expirees. This was a constant leitmotiv in colonial society. In 1836 it was still a live issue and Bourke threw in his influence on the side of the emancipist. The need for circuit courts was long felt, it was granted in principle, but time passed and the Order in Council to bring them into being did not arrive. Lack of suitable personnel made it necessary to use military officers as jurors and civil servants as magistrates long after the desirability of doing so had ceased to be axiomatic. The former practice was finally discontinued in 1839.[38] Bourke, in a dispatch of 1st March 1836, analysed the situation. He had decided not to appoint any more civil officers to the Commission of the Peace. The situation was highlighted by the court of summary jurisdiction that sat at Hyde Park Barracks for the trial of convicts. The magistrates were honorary and, having their employment to attend to, were lax in their magisterial duties. Prisoners were often kept waiting for a long time in custody before they were brought to trial.

> There were . . . two classes of these official Justices, one which did no duty at all, another which did too much. Upon neither had the Government any well founded claim for the performance of this service. . . . The Surveyor General (one of the present subscribers who never attended himself) once complained to me that his Deputy was sitting on the Bench, whilst the Head of the Department was labouring at the Desk or on the Roads.[39]

Bourke reformed the Court by assigning the whole duty to the Principal Superintendent of Convicts and the Military Superintendent in Charge of Ironed Gangs in Sydney. They sat every morning and disposed of all the cases.

The Justices in Sydney were also expected to sit as assessors in the Supreme Court (an alternative to jurors). They were too busy with their official work to attend, so that court business would have been at a standstill had not the Registrar, himself a magistrate, been always at hand. Bourke, with the support of public opinion, decided to revise the magistracy, withdrawing all civil servants. It was part of a plan to insulate the public service from politics. This was approved by Secretary of State Lord Glenelg in August 1836. "I agree with you that the combination of subordinate employments in the Public Service with the very peculiar duties of a Magistrate in New South Wales is greatly to be deprecated; and I think that you acted with your wonted Judgement and decision in availing yourself of the first opportunity for bringing that system to a close."[40]

There was, too, the usual criss-cross of trial and error. Grand juries were set up, grand juries were considered unnecessary; a Solicitor-General was appointed, the office was discontinued. . . . In Governor Gipps's Report on the General State of the Colony in 1841 we get a clear picture of the judicature as it then stood. The Supreme Court handled every branch of the law and equity. Three judges were attached to it, the Chief Justice, a judge in equity, and one who handled bankruptcies. Circuit courts functioned at Bathurst, Berrima, and Maitland. There was a resident judge in the Port Phillip district. Quarter sessions were held in Sydney and at six country centres, their chairman, who was elected each year by the magistrates, was a salaried government officer. The jury laws were the same as in England, except that all convicts who came up for trial were tried without a jury and in the Supreme Court a judge and two assessors could act in lieu of a jury in civil cases. Grand juries had been abolished and criminal trials were on the information of the Attorney-General or the Crown Prosecutor. Courts of Requests in Sydney and country districts handled cases in which sums involved were under £10.

The magistracy was on the English pattern. The magistrates sat alone or in petty session. They had jurisdiction over convicts, but a single magistrate could not order more than fifty lashes or a petty session more than one hundred. Stipendiary or police magistrates acted as agents of the Government in various districts.

In the bush beyond the boundaries of location, Commissioners of Crown Lands, paid by the Government, kept order, settled disputes, and collected licence and other fees.

The structure was well articulated, it was in the English tradition, it was freed, as much as possible, from party politics, and it depended on salaried officials rather than on honorary service. On this foundation the later elaborations of the law are grounded.

II. Finance

1. *Currency*

Financially, as in so many other ways, the colony began at zero. All necessities were provided by the Government, there was nothing to buy and no money to buy it with. Everyone from the Governor downwards was fed by the Commissariat. Subsistence was only relieved by the shooting of game, the catching of fish, by private supplies brought out by officers or by thieving amongst the convicts and marines. Farming and fishing were carried on on a community basis.

Not until settlers were planted out on small farms could there be any surplus. For this there was a market in the Commissariat stores and receipts from the Commissary were the earliest form of currency. Hunter tried to disallow the use of receipts as money. He ruled that they should be presented to the Commissary in due course and notes received for them. The practice continued, however, for the farmers could not wait and private receipts and notes of hand began to circulate as well.

The matter of promissory notes was far from simple, as Frederick Watson pointed out:

> It had been the practice in giving promissory notes to express payment in some form of barter, owing to the lack of specie. Wheat notes were given as follows: the sterling value of the note was divided by the current selling price of a bushel of wheat, and the note made out for the corresponding number of bushels. The value of wheat naturally fluctuated. At the Hawkesbury it had been fixed at 9/3d. a bushel by general order in January 1806. Owing to the severe losses by floods in March 1806, the government price offered in the December following was 13/9d. In June 1807 private sales were transacted at 28s. Macarthur held a wheat note given by Andrew Thompson at prices current before the floods. On this note, Macarthur sued in the civil court for the specific performance of the contract on the basis of the bushels of wheat expressed. The court gave the decision that the note was an expression of value and not of quantity of produce. Against this verdict Macarthur appealed in July 1807, and Bligh dismissed the appeal without hearing the appellant. By this decision, Macarthur was compelled to accept a reduction in the number of bushels expressed in the note *pro rata* with the increased price of wheat between the dates on which the bill was drawn and on which it was liquidated.[41]

You see?

Barter also existed in the field of services. A convict gave services in return for lodging, assistance in harvesting was paid by a proportion of the crop, and so on. To take another example, when the first play was enacted in Sydney entrance was paid for in kind—wheat, butter, milk, etc.

A more fluid but always illegal medium of exchange was found in rum, the generic name for any spirituous liquor. In a life denuded of almost all normal pleasures and satisfactions, gambling and drinking became obsessions. They provided some sort of escape from the dreariness of it all. Services and commodities could be readily exchanged for spirits. It was those who should have been the guardians of law and order who fostered this traffic to their own enrichment. Officers were in the position to buy rum, soldiers received their time-honoured issue, and could, if they wished, exchange it advantageously. A raw spirit could be, and was, distilled from grain the colony needed for food. To say that rum was ever the currency of the colony is incorrect. In a general state of barter this was, by and large, the most desired article and exchanged to advantage. The giving of spirits to convicts was never officially allowed yet the practice was so widespread that even Chaplain Johnson exchanged rum for services in the building of his ill-fated church. The early governors naturally wanted a supply of specie to combat this evil, but the Home Government did not think it necessary.

Larger expenses of government, as when Phillip had to send to the Cape for supplies, were paid by notes on the Treasury.

Salaries were paid in England where, with few exceptions, the officers' dependants still were. It was usual for the officers to have agents who collected the money for them and distributed it or banked it according to instructions. This may have been all very well for the higher ranks, but for men on extremely small salaries it was a severe hardship. Grose wrote to Dundas on 30th May 1793:

> The superintendents and others in the employ of Government not being able to receive their salaries in this country has long been a subject of representation and complaint. I have therefore instructed the Commissary to appropriate to this purpose the money he has received on the sale of spirits purchased from the American ship *Hope*, and the which, immediately after the arrival of the *Bellona*, I desired might as expeditiously as possible be disposed amongst the military and civil officers.[42]

England was far away, and one can imagine that the clerks at the Treasury were sufficiently indifferent. Salaries and wages were often in arrears, sometimes they were not paid at all, at others irritating mistakes were repeated year after year and explanations and petitions from the Australian end were unavailing. For instance, Assistant Surgeon Thomas Jamison at Norfolk Island was confused with a superintendent of convicts of the same name and was given the same wage. He came out in *Sirius* as surgeon's mate in 1788. In 1791 he ranked as an assistant surgeon at £40 a year, but in emoluments found himself junior to his assistants. Hunter had personally tried to straighten out the unfortunate man's affairs when he returned to England, but unsuccessfully. Jamison wrote to Governor King:

> . . . the full salary of five shillings per day would not even procure the common necessaries of life, from the extravagant price we are obliged to pay for every comfort imported at this island, as the ships from Europe or India always stop at Port Jackson first, where their cargoes are disposed of, so that we are often necessitated to purchase them at second hand, sometimes at the enormous rate of five hundred per cent.; and we are obliged to pay ten per cent. for agency.

These are unavoidable expenses which are annexed to the assistant who resides here, without any additional emoluments whatever.[43]

The military were in a different position. Like any other regiment serving overseas they had their Military Chest, which was supplied with funds to pay the rank and file and such part of the officers' salaries as they wished to have in the colony. It was from the Chest that the ready money for "investments" came, that is, the buying of cargoes from such ships as visited the settlement with trade goods.

The Governor's instructions contained a clause expressly forbidding any trade or intercourse with foreign ships. The Navigation Acts prohibited such trade, and technically Australia was within the commercial sphere of the East India Company. It did not suit John Company to trade with so distant an outpost which had no profitable exports. East Indiamen were often employed to transport convicts; they then went on to China or India to pick up their ordinary cargoes of tea or other goods. The masters soon learnt that it would pay them to put in speculative cargoes to be disposed of in New South Wales. As the ships were chartered by the Government, Phillip doubted the honesty of the practice, but it was not stopped and the officers in the colony continued to buy up the cargoes and retail them again at a big profit. When permission to buy openly was refused the cargoes were smuggled ashore, a practice to which the lonely indented coast gave every assistance. The punishment for smuggling, if the smugglers were caught was, according to a Government Order of Hunter's dated 22nd March 1790, for the culprits to have their houses pulled down "and such other steps will be taken for their farther punishment as shall be judged necessary".[44]

By the time Macquarie was Governor twenty-three American ships, beginning with *Philadelphia* in November 1792, had come in to Port Jackson and had traded. Supplies had been bought from them on behalf of the Government. The plea of necessity was accepted by the Home Government for this irregularity.

There was no revenue, only expenses.

It was impossible even from the first to keep the colony within the narrow limits laid down for it. It had the will to live and progress. The expenses of the establishment were high, the endemic state of famine made it necessary to send ships for food to the Cape, to Batavia, to India, when no supplies came from England. The Duke of Portland nearly had a seizure when bills were drawn on the Treasury to the tune of £21,499 9s. 6d. and wrote to Governor Hunter that he could not "suffer the *Ganges* to depart without expressing my great disapprobation at the want of economy in the expenditure of public money".[45] Hunter, poor harassed man, was told he must economize.

It was the Commissariat that incurred the main expense. The hand of Governor after Governor was forced by the spectre of starvation. Money was spent and the necessity for the expenditure explained to the Home Government afterwards. The Home Government grumbled and paid.

Commissary Palmer complained bitterly of the work involved in keeping the colony's accounts when he had no reliable assistants. His instructions were to keep them as if the settlement were a King's ship. In 1796 there were approximately 10,000 inhabitants, which, he pointed out, would equal roughly the complement of twelve ships of the line, each of which would have had a purser. Now one man was expected to cope with the voluminous accounts. Palmer had been purser in *Sirius*, so he knew what was expected.

> I must beg leave to mention to your Excellency that I have been upwards of six years the Commissary, and have served in his Majesty's navy twenty-two years prior to my appointment here, and that I have no one emolument except that of my salary of ten shillings per diem, which in this country will go but a very little way in supporting me and my family. Situated as I am, I believe I may venture to say that no Commissary under the Crown, even where there is not anything like the duty to do, but has a greater salary, or some emoluments which makes the appointment better.[46]

Despite his poverty, Commissary Palmer managed to acquire a veritable hacienda at Woolloomooloo.

In 1799 the Home Government relented sufficiently to send out four tons of copper coins, value 1d. each or £550 gross, in the King's ship *Porpoise*, and the Duke of Portland smugly remarked: "The circulation of this coinage must very much add to the comfort and convenience of individuals, and greatly facilitate their dealings with each other."[47]

It did not, of course. There was too little of it and the denomination was too low. The same year *Kitty* brought out silver dollars to the value of £1000. This was more like it. The colony, where self-help predominated, soon acquired a heterogeneous currency of Spanish, Portuguese, English, Dutch, and Indian specie, in that order. This was supplemented by notes of hand or promissory notes for 3d. and upwards. Large sums could only be paid by the Commissary's notes, for these alone had credit behind them, and they had eventually to be redeemed by bills on the Treasury, a very slow process. Specie was constantly drained out of the country. Every time a ship came in with a cargo for sale it carried away all the money that the inhabitants could scrape together.[48]

The only remedy for this would be for the Home Government to send out goods over and above the bare necessities of life and allow the settlers to buy them. King tried to stop the drift by enacting that not more than £5 could be sent out of the country in any one vessel, penalty a fine of three times the amount involved and forfeiture of the original sum.

He also inflated the value of the copper coinage to 2d. in an effort to make it go further. Copper was legal tender up to £5. As each coin weighed an ounce even a modest sum would be a considerable weight to carry in the pocket. The proclamation was ineffective. "The inhabitants having been so long accustomed to the convenience of Government bills, and the worth of money so much depreciated that shillings and pence have never been considered of any value 'till lately, from these causes some difficulty has attended the copper coin being in general circulation."[49]

In 1803 King was still trying to manipulate the currency. He asked for more copper coins to be sent out, "as Government gains an advance of 100 p'r cent. on its issue, exclusive of its benefit as a circulating medium, which cannot be taken from hence on account of its increased value".[50]

Macquarie tried to take a short cut. He had the centres cut out of Spanish dollars, thus creating a new coin, familiarly called the "dump", and valued at 1s. 3d. The dollar thus clipped retained its value of 5s. sterling. This was another form of inflation. The peculiarities of the colonial financial system "terrified Traders, and prevented them from having any regular intercourse with Port Jackson".[51]

At the end of Macquarie's governorship "the circulating, remittable currency" was more than £200,000. An analysis of this was made up as follows:[52]

Drafts on British Treasury	£150,000
Store receipts for grain and meat	£20,000
Bearer notes issued by Commissary	£15,000
Notes of the Bank of New South Wales	£15,000
Notes of respectable private citizens	£10,000
	£210,000 stg.

Currency was still a source of trouble in 1822. The Directors of the Bank of New South Wales were writing a memorial about it:

The Spanish dollar has hitherto circulated at the nominal value of five shillings Sterling, being about 16 2/3rds Per Cent. above its real Sterling value as Bullion. When the Dollars were few in number and received indiscriminately with the stamped Government Five Shilling Token by the Commissary, who gave for the same Bills on the Treasury at their nominal and not real value, no injury or loss could be sustained by those Persons, who furnished the supplies required from Time to time by Government.

Within these last three Months, Dollars to a very alarming amount have been imported into the Colony, the Importers induced no doubt by the Knowledge that their Circulating value was greater here than in any other part of the World.[53]

The colony was now choked with dollars, all of which goes to show that it does not pay to fly in the face of economic laws.

> It was obvious that by such an influx of specie, the nominal value of the Spanish Dollar could not be maintained without a ruinous loss, and that the Dollar must revert to its intrinsic value as an exportable commodity, unless the Government declared them to be of that specific nominal value, and continued to make their sterling Payments in a Foreign Coin, thus rendered a legal tender.[54]

Settlers were being caught between nominal selling price and an actual buying price. For example, a merchant sold imported goods for dollars and when he sent the money to England in payment for further wares he lost 1s. 8d. in every dollar: "a depreciated *Currency* is made the medium of a *Sterling payment*".[55] Australia was already part of the world in her monetary transactions and could not with impunity remain isolated. A depression was precipitated.

The Governor might explain it all away.[56] But all the colonists could see was that they were being placed at a disadvantage. Their memorial, signed by 234 leading citizens, has a curiously modern ring:

> A rise in the price of necessaries will naturally induce a similar rise in the price of labour; and we respectfully submit to Your Excellency that it will be impossible, with our property and produce so greatly and so suddenly lowered, to continue to give those wages to our Convict Servants, which by the present ordinances of Government we are compelled to do. . . .[57]

In June 1825 Lord Bathurst set himself to unravel the financial tangle. The dollar was to be fixed at 4s. 4d., its intrinsic value. British copper and silver were to be supplied for small change, and £40,000 worth of silver was being sent out. Bathurst's objects were to drive out the Spanish dollar by robbing it of any advantage over British coins, to establish "an unobjectional and unvarying medium for the payment of the Troops" and "an uniform Currency in the whole of His Majesty's Foreign Possessions, founded upon and having reference to the currency of the United Kingdom".[58]

The Legislative Council passed an Act in 1826 establishing sterling as the only legal tender, repealing at the same time a former Act which had made Spanish dollars legal. The banks co-operated with the Government in making a successful change over.[59] Darling asked in that year for "a few thousand pounds in Sovereigns". The banks began to issue notes of small denomination, for 2s. 6d. and 5s., and later proposed to issue £1 notes which could be converted into Bills on the Treasury.[60] The Commissary's notes were to be called in as soon as there was a sufficiency of English coinage to cover them.

These changes were not made without inconveniencing merchants and traders, who complained through Edward Wollstonecraft, Chairman of the Chamber of Commerce, that in "the long interval, which has since elapsed without the substitution of any other perceptible currency, and the withdrawing all Dollar engagements", credit had dried up and there was a bank crisis:

. . . a Sum, little short of £200,000 Sterling in the shape of Promissory Notes in the hands of the Merchants and Banks of Sydney, is almost immediately beginning to fall due; and at the largest estimate, we are enabled to make of the Amount of British Sterling specie at the present moment in the whole Country, would very little exceed £10,000, or One Shilling in the Pound on this impending weight of engagements, falling due, exclusive of about £20,000 in Dollars at 4s. 4d. . . . If some money or representative of Money is not put immediately into circulation to supply the vacuum caused by the disappearance of the Spanish Dollars, and the Dollar Notes of the Banks, the difficulties of the Colony are only commencing, and it may take many years to restore the Public Credit.[61]

The Government was called on to back bank-notes. By the middle of 1827 sterling was firmly established and no effort had been neglected to rid the economy of Spanish dollars. There was by this time at least £30,000 in English currency in the Colony.[62]

2. *Revenue*

Revenue may be said to have come into existence during the tenure of Governor Hunter.[63] It arose out of the necessity for self-help. Hunter pointed out in an address to the settlers in 1799 that the Government had only provided public buildings hitherto because there had been no property in the colony. Now that there were the beginnings of wealth the colonists should take up the same responsibilities as men of substance shouldered in England. The immediate cause for raising money locally was the burning down of the jail in Sydney. To raise a new one would cost about £3954. This sum was in part provided for by a levy of 6d. a bushel on wheat, duties on spirits landed, and wharfage fees. The citizens of Sydney were also expected to subscribe money and labour.

The Jail Fund once begun was continued—a common habit with taxes. It was the first version of consolidated revenue and it was used not only for the building of jails but for other amenities, such as a bridge over the Tank Stream. A balance sheet for the year 1803 can be seen in the *Historical Records of Australia,* ser. I, vol. iv, p. 601. By this time hopes of voluntary contributions had faded and the fund was supported by dues and taxes.

Governor King, as one of his first acts, established a second, and one presumes more appealing public fund, since its object was charitable. This was the Orphan School Fund for the care of the many orphaned and deserted children in the colony and for those whose parents were too depraved to care for them properly.[64]

The Governor and his forceful lady pursued this worthy object with energy. The initial public subscription yielded £114 16s., nine pieces of chintz, two shawls, two pieces of white calico, three pieces of red gurrah, 35½ yards of print, six pieces of gingham, and 304 gallons of brandy (not necessarily for the consumption of the orphans). A further £196 was eventually subscribed. But this was not enough to house, clothe, feed, and educate 398 needy children. The first necessity was accommodation; a house was bought in Sydney and another built at Parramatta. By 1803, as the balance sheet shows,[65] Charity was nearly exhausted and taxation became the mainstay of this fund also.

The Orphan Fund persisted and increased its scope. Soon all revenue collected in the colony went either to the Jail (or Police) Fund or to the Orphan Fund. The former drew support from a tax on spirituous liquors. This began at a shilling a gallon and was raised from time to time. The trade could survive any tax laid upon it. However, smuggling was rife and a high proportion of the spirits landed escaped the tax. The Police Fund added maintenance to building of jails, supplied gratuities to soldiers, and pensions to retired public officers. It could also be applied to building and repairs quite unconnected with jails, even to the purchase of glass for the church windows at Parramatta. It was estimated that in the four years 1801 to 1805 £3493 3s. 2d. passed through the fund.

The Orphan Fund likewise drew money from a five per cent *ad valorem* duty on all imports from countries eastward of the Cape of Good Hope, from a tax of 1½ per cent on all goods sold at auction, from licence fees for the retailing of spirits, from port and wharfage dues, from the sale of water to ships, from fines levied in court and from profits made on selling government stores.[66] From these sources £3180 5s. 11d. was raised in four years, 1801-5. The amount seems very small, but then the colony was only in a small way, prices were low and revenue was at that time only in the nature of pocket money.

Even as early as 1802 there was a rudimentary Empire preference. Five per cent *ad valorem* duties were imposed on non-British goods. British goods were given preference over those from India and China and trading with the Americas was discouraged.[67]

The real spending was done by the Home Government for the upkeep of the convict establishment, the payment of salaries, the maintenance, intermittently, of a King's ship on the station and other expenses.

The net expenditure for one year, taken as a random example, under Governor King, who prided himself on his economy, was according to his reckoning £212,913 1s. 7½d. after he had deducted the alleged value of government stock and buildings.[68]

The cheese-paring Lord Hobart was not satisfied even with King's efforts.

> Altho' I do not wish you to conceive that I imagine there is any part of the expence incurred which has not been absolutely necessary, yet it is incumbent on me, in my official capacity, to point out to you the strict necessity of enforcing the most rigid economy in every branch of the public service under your management and control.[69]

Naturally, as the convict population increased the expense of the colony to the Mother Country rose, and with the influx of free settlers and growth of trade the revenue rose also. As revenue strengthened the Home Government unloaded more and more of its expenses on the local Government. For example, the colony was expected to pay Governor Phillip a pension of £500 a year and Governor Hunter one of £300 a year out of local revenue. In 1823 the Colonial Secretary and the surgeons, except those attached to the regiment, were paid out of the Police Fund.

Whilst the tax on spirits remained the chief money-spinner, revenue from customs was rising steadily. In 1821 it yielded £36,231; in 1831 it was £87,803 1s. 6d.; in 1841 it was £196,114 13s. 7d. Anyone particularly interested in the public finance of the early days should consult the Colonial Office's Financial Returns of the Colony of New South Wales. In these volumes, written in beautiful, official copperplate hand, complete figures covering all matters of revenue and expenditure can be perused. They may be seen in the Mitchell Library by grace of the Trustees.

Money from the sale of land went into a special fund. It was not colonial revenue, but, strictly speaking, belonged to the Crown, though it was spent on expenses incidental to the land, such as surveying, and on bringing out immigrants. Quit rents, when they were paid, were also due to the Crown and not the Colonial Treasurer.

The accounts for the convict establishment and the civil Colonial Government were separated under Governor Darling, the former was handled by the Commissary, the latter by the Colonial Treasurer.

By 1834 the colonial revenue was in such a healthy state that, much to the indignation of the colonists, the upkeep of police and jails was transferred entirely to the Treasury. It was not only the convicts and ex-convicts who made, as it was argued, a relatively large police force necessary. The scattering of settlements, the need to protect pioneers in the bush from the depredations of aborigines (a state of affairs often brought on by themselves or an inevitable result of taking the Dark People's sacred places and hunting grounds from them), and from bushrangers, and to carry law and order into the outback, were as cogent reasons for the maintenance of ordinary and Border police as the presence of known felons, but the free population could not forgive what they considered an insult as well as a burden.

In 1823 a Colonial Treasurer had been appointed and sent out from England. He took over control of finance from the Commissary, in civil concerns, from the Naval Officer, who had been an unsatisfactory mixture of harbour-master and collector of customs, and from the honorary treasurers of the Police and Orphan Funds. Governor Brisbane asked for an accountant. In 1824 William Lithgow, whose memorial is a name on the map, was appointed as the first auditor. Public finance was, in appearance at least, regularized.

Darling was heartily glad to be relieved of responsibility. "I have never for my own part considered that a discretionary power in the Expenditure or disposal of the public Money was at all desirable," he wrote.[70]

There was still no income-tax. The Treasury found money where it could, in customs duties, excise, licensing fees for the sale of spirits, wharfage and shipping dues, taxes on the proceeds of auction sales, on markets and fairs, tolls on roads and bridges, royalties on coal and timber, fines and fees. . . . One way and another, the citizen's hand must have been always in his pocket.[71]

The money came in in small amounts, revenue fluctuated and was expensive to collect. In 1826 the revenue was stated to be about £60,000.[72] Salaries were certainly small. In the 1830s, for instance, £33,000 covered the salaries of the Governor, the Superintendent at Port Phillip, the judges, and all expenses connected with the administration of justice, and an additional £18,600 covered the salaries of the Colonial Secretary, Treasurer, and Auditor, the expenses of their departments and of the Executive Council including pensions. Thirty thousand pounds was allotted to public worship.[73] These figures are given only by way of rough example and any effort to balance them would be futile.

Actually income-tax as we know it was not introduced in Australia until 1880, though it had been a commonplace in England since 1842. Tasmania had the initiative to move into the field first. It began with a tax on company dividends at source, and not until 1894 was it made applicable to individuals. In an article in the *Economic Record,* May 1928, W. F. Murphy gives a concise history of income-tax in Australia which can easily be followed up by those interested. In a table on page 72 he lists the "Income Tax Year" as applied to all citizens. It was introduced in South Australia in 1885; in Tasmania in 1894, although the idea had been pioneered in this colony; by an enabling Act in Victoria in 1895; in New South Wales in 1896; in Queensland in 1903; in Western Australia in 1908; by the Commonwealth in 1915 during the First World War. The youthfulness of a tax which is now so much a part of our lives often comes as a surprise to people not old enough to remember its inception. This is an aside which may be of some interest.

In 1841 the first public debt was incurred. It was a tentative and short-term measure entered into with trepidation and took the form of debentures to the value of £65,000 sold on the London market and secured on revenue from land. The money was needed for the purpose of bringing out immigrants. In 1842 the Colonial Government was issuing debentures at 8 per cent, redeemable in twelve months. But before the twelve months was up drought and depression had closed in on the colony, it could not redeem its debentures but renewed them instead. This was the beginning of the gigantic public debt which in 1954 stood at £3,606,803,000. It was not considered a Good Thing, for the current popular view was that a country or a colony was analogous to a person, for whom to be in debt was to be in danger. Opinion has since fluctuated; debt has in general come to be considered as not only inevitable but efficacious in a developing community, most particularly when the money can be raised within the country. That day, in 1841, was still distant. The debt provided a channel by which absentee English capital could flow into the country. It also tied Australia more tightly, for better or for worse, into the non-governmental financial system based on London.

The history of the public debt is immaterial here. Economics is dangerous ground for a historian to tread, but since nothing must be closed to him in pursuit of his general survey tread on it he must from time to time.

3. *Banks*

It was not enough that there should be a Colonial Treasurer (with public funds tucked away safely in his bedroom), nor was it enough that the British Treasury with its agent, the Commissary, should stand behind all colonial money dealings. The Home Government was slow to learn this, but Macquarie foresaw the settlement's need for an independent financial structure to grow up with and serve increasing private enterprise. In 1817 he founded the Bank of New South Wales by charter.[74] It was never a government bank. Its capital came from private subscribers. Nominally its capital was £20,000, but actually only £3625 of this was paid up when it opened its doors. All the Government did was to authorize its institution and to give it the formal support of a charter. The Home Government's reluctance to permit the founding of a bank probably arose from an *idée fixe* that New South Wales was a penal colony. It had already ceased to be one entirely and its landowners, traders, and merchants had the well-developed nineteenth-century attitude that they should be free to pursue their business interests and to use and enjoy their property without government interference. A bank was as necessary to them as a free Press was to become to their politically minded brethren.

The young Bank of New South Wales had many early difficulties, owing to the state of the currency and echoes of the oversea financial turmoil which followed the Napoleonic wars. In 1822 its Directors were asking, in a very modern manner, why war sacrifices should continue so long after the victory of Waterloo?

In July 1826 a second bank, the Bank of Australia was formed. This was the landowners' or exclusionists' bank. Macarthur supported it with his apparently limitless enthusiasm. Its capital of £100,000 was subscribed by a small clique in shares at £1000 par on which a first payment of ten pounds each was made—banking on a shoe string. Its first premises were a private house in Bligh Street, where it was run by a managing director, his deputy, two tellers, and a clerk.

Small as this enterprise sounds, it was sufficient to rock the ship. Most of the capital to found it was suddenly withdrawn from the Bank of New South Wales and with the money went a number of the bank's richest and most influential customers. The new bank also generously flooded the market with credit, offering ten times the amount of its capital. The Bank of New South Wales was so seriously embarrassed that its directors appealed to Governor Darling, assuring him of the bank's essential solvency, but pointing out the widespread ruin that would descend on the colony if, in this sudden emergency, it was forced to close its doors. Darling acted quickly. He appointed a committee to look into, virtually to audit, the bank's affairs and called together the Executive Council to consider what could be done.[75] The Bank of New South Wales was authorized to draw on the Government up to £20,000 sterling. This news was sufficient to re-establish its credit. The Treasury did not have to pay anything into its coffers. Treasurer Balcombe had also helped matters by paying large funds into the bank. When Darling reproved him for putting government money into jeopardy his defence was that the Commissariat stores had just been robbed, he had no money vault and only one sentry, and it was quite coincidental that his deposits had assisted the bank.[76]

In December 1826 Bathurst reviewed the bank situation as it affected the colonial treasury and laid down some rules.[77] The Colonial Government was to patronize both banks equally, but never to have more than £5000 on deposit in either. Revenue in excess of this was to be kept in a fire- and thief-proof vault to which there were to be three locks and three keys. When it was necessary to open the vault the Colonial Treasurer, the Auditor, and the other "appropriate person" were to meet, unlock the vault, and ceremonially deposit or draw out specie. Darling was not censured for saving the Bank of New South Wales but at the same time the Directors were warned that the bank's charter had never been ratified in England. It was null and void, but the bank might continue to operate if it did not look to the Government for help. Auditor Lithgow was directed to resign from the Board of Directors, because his presence there gave a false impression of government responsibility. When government money was in the bank the duty of inspecting its affairs was laid on the Auditor.

On the night of 15th September 1828 the Bank of Australia made the headlines with a sensational robbery. Building operations were in progress next door to the bank and thieves made their way through an uncovered drainpipe into the vaults and stole 2000 sovereigns, £750 in English silver, £2030 in Spanish dollars, and £14,500 in bank notes, a very bulky haul. Despite handsome rewards offered it was never recovered.

In July 1835 a third bank, the Bank of Australasia, was formed.[78] Times were good and competition between the banks was keen. Governor Bourke discovered in November 1837 that government officers received four per cent "interest" when they deposited public moneys. He reported this to Lord Glenelg and demanded that the "interest" be paid into the Treasury forthwith.[79]

In 1837 the Treasury was allowed to pay up to £124,000 into each of the three banks and store another £245,250 in its own vaults. Government money was a doubtful blessing to the banks now. They had to pay interest on it, and to equalize this they gave discount freely to their other customers, this in turn fostered speculation. Government money was liable to be withdrawn suddenly and in large sums for the financing of immigration schemes. In 1843, however, the banks seemed to be in a very strong position. Their total liabilities were reckoned at £1,076,319 and their assets at £2,718,507, with a reserve of some £380,000 in specie.[80]

But the testing time was at hand. The end of transportation deprived the colony of the large income that had flowed in from England to support the convict establishment. At the same time the labour supply was drying up and the Government was using its funds to bring out assisted immigrants. As the banks felt the pinch they reduced their credit. The land boom collapsed, the value of bank-notes fell by about thirty per cent. They became suspect. There was not enough specie for the needs of the community and some country districts were drained of it entirely and went back to a state of primitive barter.

The good years had brought in new capital, introduced through the establishment of new banks, for example, the Commercial Banking Company of Sydney and the Union Bank, financed from England and from which the shareholders expected to draw interest, and by the much more dangerous loan and trust companies. Gipps in a dispatch of July 1841 wrote, "A new era may, I think, however, be said to have recently commenced in the Colony by the arrival of the Agents of two extensive Companies, formed in England for the purpose of advancing money on Loans to persons in the Australian Provinces." This capital relieved the pressure on the money market and the companies spread a knowledge of Australia and its possibilities in England. But, the Governor added, "on the other hand, I cannot contemplate without alarm the ultimate consequence of the heedlessness, with which people are now mortgaging their Estates to these Companies; and the hazardous speculations to which they will be driven, in order to pay, or endeavour to pay, the annual interest on the sums they are now so improvidently borrowing".[81]

The Governor's fears were fully justified. The crash came and with it an estimated 1638 bankruptcies. The Bank of Australia was amongst them. Its assets, including its grand new premises, the Normal Institution, buildings, estates and blocks of land all over the colony, were unsaleable. The first public lottery was authorized to dispose of them. Each ticket cost £5 and there were as many prizes as tickets. This did little to liquidate the debt of £300,000. (There is a schedule of the Lots in the Plan of Partition, Bank of Australia, 1848.)

The Port Phillip Bank also suspended payment and a fine scandal blew up over the Sydney Bank.

> In the Sydney Bank, it is discovered that large sums of money have been applied by the Manager and Accountant to their own use; by the former it is said to the amount of £4,000, by the latter of £4,500; and also, that every Clerk in the establishment has been allowed, in a greater or less degree, to anticipate his Salary, or, in other words, to make use of the funds of the bank.[82]

In a general review of banking in the same dispatch of April 1843, it is pointed out that in 1834 there were two banks with a gross capital of £84,321 and that in 1843, just before the disaster, there were seven banks with a gross capital of £2,300,955. A number of them became victims to the over-speculation that they had encouraged. The Bank of New South Wales survived.

Many remedies were suggested for the black depression that had settled on the so recently prosperous colony. The Legislative Council went into committee, but little came of its deliberations. The experts were all for leaving the situation to be cured by time and laissez-faire. The trouble, they opined, was due to "an excessive disproportion between the profits of money and the profits of industry". They suggested mildly that banks and mortgage companies might *voluntarily* reduce their interest from 10 to 6 per cent and that public expenditure should be reduced. It was thought also that a system of protective tariffs might reduce imports and help the local producer. More daringly, the "Prussian system of pledge certificates" was suggested. This meant State loans to landowners to keep them in possession of their title and give them time to recover. A Land

Board would assess the value of a property and lend up to one half of it and it would issue "notes" that would become legal tender. This plan, which was not adopted, really meant that the Government should take over the role of the mortgage companies on a non-profit-making basis. A national bank, not unlike the Commonwealth Bank of today, was advocated by some.

The various factions could not come to an agreement on remedies. An Act was passed by the Legislative Council in November 1843 "to restore public Confidence and to provide for and regulate the issuing and lending of Land Board Notes and pledge certificates". Many considered this to be class legislation which would mortgage the whole community for the benefit of the graziers. It did not become law because Governor Gipps withheld Royal assent.

In September 1843 Wentworth got through the Council his Lien on Wool Bill, which enabled graziers to mortgage their clip and livestock without surrendering them. Two years later an Act in Council gave validity to this scheme.

There was much theory and little execution. Actually the crisis righted itself in time, with the help of the discovery that a fat sheep, boiled down, yielded 14s. worth of exportable tallow. Recovery was slow and many people suffered acute hardship. The weaker brethren, banks, businesses, individuals, fell by the financial wayside, the strong and the astute survived.

The discovery of gold brought in a new era in banking as in other spheres of life. Banks multiplied. In the land war of the 1860s they were in a position to stake the landholder. To buy his run or parts of it, to fence and put in other labour-saving devices, the squatter needed ready money. The selector had little in the way of security to offer. The banks, not unnaturally, preferred the established man, and so there began a new cycle of mortgages and bank loans.

To develop or even to keep his property the average squatter needed large sums of money. By good management and by grace of good seasons he could enhance the value of his run and then clear it of debt. In the 1850s he was hampered by lack of labour, in the 1860s he was reconstructing with the help of the banks. In the 1870s and early 1880s he had had years of prosperity to consolidate his position before a new crisis began to develop. Men who formerly had looked to the Government now looked to the banks. In the years of prosperity the State and the banks worked together to develop the country. The State built railways, for example, and taxed the community indirectly to do so; the banks lent money at interest. Australia in its vastness and in the generally difficult and unusual (that is, to settlers from England) character of the land could not be made to flourish without large capital expenditure, which only financial agencies and the State working in the name of the people as a whole could provide.

Although the country's wealth stemmed largely from grazing the majority of the inhabitants were city dwellers and the old exclusionist-emancipist quarrel lingered on as the city *versus* the bush and selector *versus* pastoralist. This chip on the shoulder of so many voters hampered the State in its legislation for the opening up of the bush and in financing long-distance projects. With time this attitude has been almost completely broken down, but in the last half of the nineteenth century it greatly strengthened the hands of the banks. The accent on laissez-faire, private enterprise, and competition made individual treaties between banks and pastoralists, merchants, or industrialists more acceptable than government planning. It took another major financial crisis and the advance of science slowly to instruct the people at large that the problems of the continent —transport, water, fire risk—were beyond the range of the banks and the mortgage and loan companies and that their solution was in the interests of all citizens.

The trend was always towards closer government control and supervision of banks in the general interest. It took two major depressions, however, that of the 1840s and that of the 1890s, to bring home the lesson that credit was primarily a public and not a private affair.

Alongside the trading banks there was another banking system which had peculiar application to Australia, the savings bank.

In theory at least, no convict might possess any money or object of value, but many of them brought with them their little hoards. These were often handed over to untrustworthy friends or associates and seen no more. From the first government officials were willing to take the money into safe keeping until the convict was freed or given a ticket of leave, but prisoners were more suspicious of this service than of their fellows.

In June 1819 the New South Wales Savings Bank was constituted at a meeting over which Governor Macquarie presided. Macquarie saw the necessity for a public institution which catered not only for convicts but for the thrifty poor as well.[83] He became the patron of the new bank, Judge Field its president. It had an office in George Street, Sydney and branches at Parramatta, Windsor, and Liverpool. The bank accepted deposits of from 2s. 6d. upwards and for every £1 left for a year it paid interest at 7½ per cent. The honorary bankers, all well-known citizens like Sir John Jamison, had to put up securities in land.

This bank grew out of one the merchant, Robert Campbell, set up, called the "Prisoners' Bank". From this, founded solely on his well-known probity, he drew some capital for his ventures and paid the depositors from $7\frac{1}{2}$ to 8 per cent on their money. Sound as Campbell was, this was a one-man affair and the need of the colony outgrew it as it did Mr Justice Field's well-meant efforts to safeguard convicts' money.

So closely was Robert Campbell connected with it that until 1833 the new bank was still popularly called "Campbell's Bank". In 1832 the first savings-bank legislation was passed and the Savings Bank of New South Wales replaced the New South Wales Savings Bank or "Campbell's Bank". This sounds more complex than it was. In Macquarie's day there was no such thing as a colonial Statute, only government orders. With the co-operation of leading citizens he founded his savings bank on a community basis, taking over the privately owned Campbell's Bank. In 1832 the bank was placed on a statutory basis and its name not so much altered as rearranged.

Savings banks developed in the other colonies to fulfil the same obvious need in much the same way. For instance, the Port Phillip Savings Bank was founded in 1841. It is only necessary, however, to follow the development in one colony.

The main difficulty was how to utilize the money deposited so that it could earn the interest promised and yet be at call at any time. In Governor Gipps's report on banking in 1842 we find that the Savings Bank was lending money on mortgage and discounting bills like any other bank. It was handling, not petty sums, but thousands. One convict, Henry Herring, had deposited as much as £500 in its early days. By Gipps's time the maximum deposit received from any one person was £200, interest had fallen to 5 per cent, and the management was vested in trustees appointed by the Governor.

The bank had grown and grown. In 1839 it was opening a hundred new accounts every month and in 1840 an average of a hundred and fifty and its deposits, not counting the money handed in by convicts, had reached £127,000. This favourable situation led the Governor to remark that there was "no Country, in which Labourers living in equal comfort can put by so large a portion of their Wages".[84]

In May 1843 there was a run on the Savings Bank and £20,000 was withdrawn in a panic lasting two days. A committee investigated the management of the bank and found everything in order, and it was able to ride out the storm.

In 1846 Governor FitzRoy reviewed the whole savings-bank situation, particularly with regard to the use of depositors' money. He thought investment should be limited to government debentures, that is, gilt-edged securities, and through this medium expended on public works. At this time nearly £5000 was pouring into the bank weekly.[85]

In 1847 it was proposed, with the approval of the Colonial Office, to invest the money with the Land Board, a government agency, with the one purpose of bringing out immigrants. There is a curious little quirk here, for the savings of the workers were in this way to be used to ease pressure on the labour market and so reduce wages!

The 1850s and 1860s were times of prosperity and expansion. In 1871 the Government Savings Bank of New South Wales began to operate in competition with the original bank. It had the great advantage of using post offices everywhere as its agencies. The earlier bank continued and was known, in Sydney at least, as the Barrack Street Savings Bank. Both survived the dark days of the early 1890s and two major "runs". They were finally merged in 1914.

In the meantime the Commonwealth had been established and all postal departments passed under federal control. The Government Savings Bank of New South Wales was undisturbed in its arrangements until 1912, when the Commonwealth Bank came into existence and the use of post offices was withdrawn from the Government Savings Bank of New South Wales. New centres had to be found and the branch banks were attached to State government offices, such as the Lands Office, wherever convenient.

In 1921 the Government Savings Bank of New South Wales threw out an important new shoot, the Rural Bank. Post-war conditions, a drought, and other factors made it necessary to assist primary industries with loans. There had been various schemes, such as the Advances to Settlers Board in 1898, none of them very satisfactory. Now a Bill was successfully carried through the State Parliament to create a branch of the Savings Bank to "grant overdrafts payable on demand to agricultural, pastoral, rural or primary producers, or to persons carrying on industries immediately associated with rural pursuits on the security of land, crops, wool, stock, plant, machinery, personal security, guarantees by co-operative credit associations, promissory notes, bills of exchange or any other security approved by the Commissioners". This was, and is, the Rural Bank.

Never did the Government Savings Bank of New South Wales seem so secure as when in 1928 it opened its handsome new head office in Martin Place. Yet in 1931, during the economic crisis, its credit being undermined by political causes, it was forced to close its doors. The Commonwealth eventually took over the bank's assets and paid depositors in full, and it resumed business as the Commonwealth Savings Bank, on, one believes, an unshakable foundation. The Rural Bank has continued a separate existence under State authority.

Post offices were again available as savings-bank branches. The Savings Bank, the little man's bank, continues to fill a need in the community and a large proportion of the citizens, great and small, avail themselves of it.[86]

4. *Trade and Commerce*

In an age when private enterprise was at a premium it was as severely handicapped as possible in the little settlement at what the world persisted in calling Botany Bay.

First there was distance, an important factor in planning the settlement, and then there was the very strict control that the Government exercised over it. Any possible exports or profits, flax or timber for instance, were earmarked for the Royal Navy. In theory at least, no ship and no individual sailed for New South Wales without permission from the Colonial Office. Trade with any foreign power was specifically forbidden in the Governor's instructions. The Honourable the East India Company had a monopoly of trade, if any, but showed no enthusiasm for developing it. This was natural. The Company's fleets traded with India and China. Its ships brought convicts and stores to Australia under contract and then went on to the East to pick up cargoes. They rarely, if ever, moved in reverse. Why bother with a barren land with no developed exports when they could get all their cargoes elsewhere? Again, the tonnage of vessels coming to Australia was strictly limited. The fear of mutiny was ever present and it was deemed unwise to carry too many convicts in one bottom. The building of ships of any size in Australia was also forbidden lest convicts escape in them.

The Home Government raised another barrier in that it was unwilling to set up the machinery of trade. There were currency difficulties for thirty years. The payment of salaries in England made it more difficult for civil and military officers to lay their hands on any capital locally. There was no trading bank until 1817. There were prohibitions on imports and duties on exports.

The Napoleonic wars made oversea trade more difficult still. They also distracted England's attention from her ugly duckling. The situation was this: no legal trade with England because the Government controlled the valves, no trade with Europe because of war and the Navigation Acts, no trade with the East because it could only be by grace of the East India Company, no trade with the Pacific from lack of shipping. No trade. It would appear that the colony at the end of the earth was hermetically sealed off, but the love of money can be guaranteed to find a way.

In January 1792 Governor Phillip established internal trade on a legal basis. He announced that private growers might bring their grain and other products to the Government Store for sale. This had previously been supplied entirely from government farms and by stores sent by the Home Government or, in an emergency, imported in one of the small King's ships on the station. In April of the same year Phillip set up a market at Parramatta and in June a similar one in Sydney. They were government controlled and on a barter basis. A clerk was appointed at each to record every sale. This, it was hoped, would suppress or diminish the black market already flourishing. This black market was supplied by stolen goods of all kinds, by the soldiers' rum ration or smuggled spirits, and even by aboriginal weapons and utensils which were stolen and sold as curiosities to ships' crews. When a road of sorts was opened between Sydney and Parramatta it was felt that the way of the wrongdoer was made easier. He could now pass from one settlement to the other in a night and dispose of the fruits of his thefts with less danger of being caught.

A private import trade began when ships' masters realized that there was a market in the hungry settlement and began to bring speculative cargoes. Some authorities attribute this perspicacity to the master of *Lady Juliana,* transport, which arrived on 3rd June 1790 with "an investment", others to the master of another transport, *Royal Admiral,* arriving in October 1792. The master of *Lady Juliana* did open a shop in the bake-house to sell groceries, glass, millinery, perfume, and stationery. But the venture was a failure. The stock was ill chosen and the prices too high. A *profitable* trade began with the advent of *Royal Admiral.* It was soon common practice, irregular, of course, but winked at. Shops were set up whilst the ships were in port and any unsold goods were generally left behind to be sold on commission by an agent. The laws of economics were the same then as now, and Phillip was angered to see ribbons and other luxuries being sold when the commonest necessities were so greatly needed. This trade sucked what little specie there was out of the country.

When the Marines were replaced by the New South Wales Corps the officers of the latter regiment were not slow to follow the lead of the ships' masters. They brought investments in their luggage and quickly realized that spirits were the most profitable.

Even before Phillip left his governorship these officers had formed a trading ring and had chartered *Britannia* to bring a cargo for sale from the Cape of Good Hope. We have already discussed the trading monopoly they built up during the interregnum between Phillip's departure and the advent of Hunter. Despite the apathetic disapproval of the Home Government and instructions without power to Governors to break it, this monopoly appeared waterproof; but nothing really is.

The discovery that the Merino sheep flourished in Australia at a time when there was a wool famine in England strengthened the hands of the officer class, but the processes of growth, helped by Macquarie, were to break their stranglehold.

These factors were the development of an unexpected staple in whale and seal fisheries, government enterprise, Macquarie's policy, and the infiltration of merchants and traders in competition with the would-be monopolists. These causes interlace, but can only be taken singly.

Amongst the ships of the Third Fleet there were five whalers, which, when they had delivered their convicts, were to go on to the coast of Brazil. It will be remembered that in those days ships sailed far south, rounded Van Diemen's Land, and so up the coast of New South Wales to Sydney. In this voyage of 1791 Captain Melville of *Britannia* was struck by the possibility of fishing off the South Coast. "I saw more whales at one time around my ship than in the whole of the six years which I have fished the coast of Brazil," he reported. He and other captains, as soon as their ships were cleared, set off to reap this sea harvest. They were not fortunate, for although *Britannia* killed seven whales she was unable to get them aboard and extract the oil because of storms.[87] This was only bad luck; the whales were there, and the English firm of Champion Brothers was soon interested and sent out their ship *Albion*. The wholesale slaughter of whales, seals, and sea elephants began.

By 1792 there was a whaling industry off the south coast of New Zealand. This was not very convenient, since there were no ports for refreshment and re-fitting. In 1797 both the Champions and the Enderbys were interested and were asking the Home Government for permission to use Australian ports, that is, Sydney and Hobart, more particularly Hobart. The whalers explored the coast as the graziers were later to explore the inland.

In 1798 *Nautilus,* Captain Bishop, was sealing off the coast of Van Diemen's Land and is reputed to have collected 9000 skins. Probably in the same year Captain Reed in his tiny ship *Martha,* about 30 tons burthen, discovered King Island in Bass Strait and came back to Sydney with 1300 seal skins and a great quantity of oil.

It was about 1800 that whaling and sealing in Bass Strait began in earnest and it was no uncommon sight to see fifty or sixty whales in the Derwent at one time. Sea elephants frequented King Island in great numbers and each one killed yielded half a ton of oil. In 1803 Surgeon Thomson reported that in four months 6000 sealskins and oil to the value of £67,500 were shipped from New South Wales in five ships and in 1804 that 270 men were employed in whaling and sealing from whom cargoes worth more than £121,000 were expected.

Governor King recognized that this uncontrolled slaughter would ruin the industry. In May 1803 he was writing to Nepean:

> Although a vast quantity of Sea Elephants and Seals have been taken and still abound about Hunters Island and Kings Island, yet from the different communications I have received I shall find it expedient to restrain Individuals from resorting there in too great numbers, and to fix certain Times for their visiting these places, to prevent the destruction of that Commercial advantage. Since I took Command 16,000 Gallns. of Oil and 27,846 Seal Skins have been imported from thence by Individuals, 1,063 Tuns of Spermaceti Oil have also been pro-

cured by the South Whalers, all which I need not point out as a rising Nursery for Seamen.[88]

His was a voice crying in the wilderness. He had no power to enforce his regulations and he had another worry. The profitable fisheries were attracting the Americans. They were not bound by the rules and regulations that cramped English and local whalers in the marketing of their product. They were often better organized than the British whalers and committed the grievous sin of being more successful, which led to bad blood.

The first American whaler, *General Boyd*, visited Sydney for "refreshment", which could not be denied, in June 1802. After that they came thick and fast, and in the November of that year King wrote to the Colonial Office for instructions as to policy. Not only were these interlopers scooping the trade, but they connived at the escape of convicts. Should their ship's company be short many masters made it up with runaways. In November 1805 King was writing home in a dispatch: ". . . I am sorry to say that if the most decided Checks are not given to the introduction of Americans and American vessels, any benefit this Colony may possess would become the property of Americans at the Expense of England."[89] War with Spain closed the Peruvian whaling fishery to England and made the new ones in the south more valuable.

King ineffectually forbade "foreigners", by which he meant Americans, to build ships on Australian territory. They did as they pleased. The American ship *Union* built a forty-ton schooner on Kangaroo Island where in 1803 her captain, Pendleton, had pioneered seal-fishing.

On the Tasmanian coast, in Bass Strait, and in isolated posts as far west on the mainland as Albany, whalers and sealers lived a wild, lawless, and piratical life. It was customary for each man to take to himself as many as five aboriginal "wives". Fat middle-aged women were much in demand because they were expert sealers. The technique was for the women, armed with clubs, to swim out quietly amongst the seals, who apparently mistook them for other seals, and then, when close to two seals, to club them suddenly. Maoris, too, were very much sought after as crew members, and King had to forbid that any who had come for one reason or another to Sydney should be lured into the whalers. A curious mixed population sprang up in the islands of Bass Strait, compounded of Europeans, Americans, Maoris, and aborigines from Van Diemen's Land and from the mainland, with perhaps a sprinkling of French blood.

The Governors in Sydney could do nothing about these highly irregular settlements, but they could and did follow another policy. They tried to strengthen the position of the English and colonial whalers. These laboured under serious disadvantages when it came to marketing their oil, bone, and skins. The East India Company stood in their path. The northern whale fisheries were subsidized by the Government; John Company, as it was called, had a monopoly in the south. It was illegal for independent ships to fish there and if they did bring their products into port they were subject to heavy duties. In 1797 the powerful owners, Champion and Enderby, supported by the Governor of New South Wales, made the first breach in this high wall of prohibition. They petitioned for the right for whalers to bring out trade goods to Australia. On the grounds, one suspects, of economy the Colonial Office took up the matter with the East India Company and permission was granted to carry goods for sale, provided that reasonable prices were charged for them.

Campbell's ship *Lady Barlow,* arriving in the Thames in 1805 with a full cargo of oil and skins, was seized as contraband and held for four months. She was then released, but only on condition that her cargo was sold on the foreign market. This forced sale was very unprofitable, it realized only about £700 and her owners suffered a heavy loss. It is not surprising that many cargoes were sent, not Home, but to China. It was easier to evade official attention there, but prices were not as good. A sealskin worth a guinea or more in London was apt to bring less than half that figure in the East.

In 1813 Lord Liverpool finally lifted the dead hand of the East India Company from Australian trade, and representations, particularly by influential wool-growers, led to a reduction of duties on Australian products.

Many of the by-products of the whaling and allied industries were very profitable to Sydney and Hobart. The whalers provided a market for foodstuffs, water, timber, and anything else there might be for sale, including sovereigns to make themselves ear-rings in true piratical style. They gave employment, particularly in Hobart Town, where a thriving ship-building and repairing business grew up. The early prosperity of the town stemmed largely from the whalers. During the wars, notably that with Spain, whaling captains were issued with letters of marque and brought Spanish prizes into Port Jackson. Most important, the whaling industry, in which local capitalists were soon taking part, helped to break down the trade monopoly of the Rum Corps.

About 1806 a profitable form of whaling was invented in Van Diemen's Land. Instead of ocean-going ships with costly equipment, which could be damaged or lost in bad weather, small boats went out when whales were sighted, harpooned them and towed them back to the shore where they could be cut up in safety and the oil extracted. This was called bay whaling and, according to Thomas Dunbabin, there were eight stations or plants in the vicinity of the Derwent, another on Maria Island and later a large installation at Twofold Bay on the mainland. This applied to black whales alone, since sperm whales are only found well out to sea. Sealers had a subsidiary industry in bartering seal meat to aborigines for kangaroo skins.

The stupid and wholesale slaughter of seals and sea elephants in Bass Strait destroyed the industry there, but whaling continued to be profitable until at least the 1840s and is now alive again in Western Australia on a controlled and scientific basis.

The *Australian Quarterly Journal*, first published in 1828, has an unsigned article,[90] possibly written by the editor, the Reverend Charles Wilton, a Cambridge graduate, extolling the Australian Sperm Whale Fishery.

> It has generally been remarked that, whilst Countries, exclusively Agricultural, have been immersed in poverty, those States, in which the public Spirit has been directed to Commercial persuits, have invariably become rich. . . . But in all Mercantile dealings there must be two parties, the buyer and seller. The thing bought must be paid for in some equivalent or other. The productions of the *Soil* of Australia are not sufficient at present to make such return to yield such payment. Where then is this equivalent to be sought for? Where should the child of England look but to the *sea*? The sea is our birthright and inheritance. Nature herself seems to point out to us our proper path and our real interests, by keeping us constantly in sight of the ocean. She presents an impenetrable barrier to our further inroads into the interior of the Country by an impassible morass; whilst she allures us to the almost interminable length of Coast swarming with Whales, and intersected by gulphs, creeks and harbours, without equals in the world, absolutely inviting us to make use of them. . . . All other ships of all other Nations have a voyage of 12000 miles to perform, to take up their fishing ground. We are here on the spot, in the very heart of the preserve. The London or Boston owner has from two to three years to wait for the return of his capital. Our ships would be filled in one third of the time. Merchants of Australia, open your eyes—use your reason.

After this clarion call the author comes down to tin tacks. He envisages a capital of £40,000 and a fleet of four ships. "In round numbers, therefore, four ships could be procured for £30,000 which would return oil to the value of £18,000 annually, exclusive of the share of the crew, which gives an interest of £45 per cent" and he goes on to explain the financial details, finally arriving at a profit of sixty per cent a year. He envisages a company subsidized by the Government—"and such a measure could not fail to endear the memory of GENERAL DARLING to the Colonists". A nice touch.

In that year, 1828, Sydney was setting itself up as an oil port. In response to pressure, land with a waterfront was made available for the whalers. It was called Mosman after Archibald Mosman, one of their number who took up four acres at the head of the bay. By 1835 he owned 38 acres there.

This was then a remote spot, and it needed to be, because of the smell. There were at this time at least twenty-one whalers based on Sydney.[91] In 1833 whale products made up half the exports from Australia.

Whaling persisted in Tasmania into the 1880s, and finally expired when *Helen* paid off her crew in 1893.

For a racy account, full of good stories, o' the whaling days I can recommend T. Dunbabin's "Whalers, Sealers and Buccaneers" in the Royal Australian Historical Society's *Journal and Proceedings,* vol. XI (1925).

In the early days both profit and succour came from the sea; it was the sheep that eventually turned men's eyes inland. In the meantime a race of sailors had grown up, aboriginal mingling with the free white man, and sea-going ships were being built in Hobart Town. By 1807 trade had begun in the Pacific, particularly in sandalwood for re-export to England. In 1813 nearly 700 tons of it, valued at from £50 to £70 a ton, were brought into Port Jackson.

With the curbing of the rum trade the exclusionist turned his attention more and more to wool, and independent traders were beginning to break down the monopoly. The first to become a resident merchant seems to have been Thomas Raby (or Reibey or Raibey or whatever spelling you fancy, for he was not particular himself). He was an officer in the mercantile marine and did some trading on his own account. It has been suggested that the goods he brought out in *Royal Admiral* in 1790 were intended for the Indian market, but the eagerness with which anything was bought in New South Wales led him to dispose of them here. This and the fortunate choice of a wife linked him with Australia and made him, with Robert Campbell a little later, one of the first free and independent merchants.

The wife was Mary Haydock, a young girl who was a convict but never a criminal. Raby, realizing that she had little in common with the other women, protected her during the voyage and saw to it that she was placed in a respectable home on landing. When she reached the age of seventeen he married her and she proved a sound partner in business as well as a good wife.

Raby left the sea, received a grant on the Hawkesbury, and went into business in Macquarie Place. He interested himself in timber and, with a fleet of two tiny ships, in whaling, and in the carrying trade to the Hawkesbury and Hunter Rivers. He died young and his wife, who had always had more acumen than he, continued a successful business career until she owned seven farms on the Hawkesbury, three shops and residences in Sydney, and a "country cottage" at Hunter's Hill. Amongst her ventures was the retailing of wines and spirits and a bakery. But this is looking ahead, for Mrs Raby lived and prospered until 1855. She was said to be worth £120,000, a sum equal to six times the capital on which the Bank of New South Wales was founded.

Robert Campbell, called the Father of Australian Commerce, cut a more important figure in early Sydney. Born in Scotland in 1769, he joined his elder brother, who was a merchant in Calcutta. He is alternatively represented as coming to New South Wales in 1796 and in 1798. It is probable that he arrived first in 1796 to inquire into the wreck of his company's ship *Sydney Cove,* for the Campbells were already trading with Australia. On his return to Calcutta he persuaded his brother that opportunities existed in New South Wales. In 1798 he was back again, asking the Governor's permission to set up as a merchant. Hunter thought it an excellent idea, since competition would help to break down the monopoly of the Corps, but the matter had to be referred to England. In the meantime Campbell was allowed to sell the goods he had brought with him, but only at a price permitted by the ring. Permission to trade arrived. Campbell bought three acres on the west side of Circular Quay where he built a house, warehouses, and a wharf, from which his family became known as the Campbells of the Wharf. He married the sister of Commissary Palmer and thus knitted himself into the commercial life of the community. Around his home he planted a garden and orchard which survived as a show place until 1855 when the land became too valuable for beauty. The Campbells must have been fond of gardens, for another that they planted beside their house in Bligh Street, later the Union Club, survived until 1958 and with its jacarandas was a solace in the hard city streets.

Robert Campbell traded with Calcutta and London; he took up contracts with the Government to bring in livestock and other commodities. He was interested in whaling, sealing, and trade in the Pacific and, as a corollary, he was a ship-owner. He became a grazier and pioneered the Canberra district, Yarralumla being one of his homesteads there. He prospered exceedingly and was respected as a fair and honest trader. The only thing that caused trouble betwixt him and the Governors was his propensity for bringing into the country more than the legal quantity of spirits. He took part in public life; he served for a time as Naval Officer, until Macquarie, who thought it improper for an interested party to hold such a position, tactfully persuaded him to resign; he served as a nominee on the Legislative Council, as his son did after him, and he was active in church and charitable organizations. He was also a director of the Bank of New South Wales. In fact, Robert Campbell's is a success story and he figured largely in the history of the colony until his death at the age of seventy-seven at his property, Duntroon, in 1846.

There were other merchants in the early years of the nineteenth century, not as correct or socially eligible as Campbell, but enterprising and prosperous. One of the best known was Simeon Lord. He had been a convict, but that did not damp him. He had many irons in the fire and axes on the grindstone. He practised as a customs agent, buying from ships and retailing to colonists and even to the Government; he was a licensed auctioneer in succession to Garnham Blaxcell; he was a shipbuilder and had interests in whaling and sealing; he set up woollen mills at Botany; he took as partners two first-fleeters, Henry Kable, a brewer amongst other avocations, and James Underwood, a shipbuilder and publican. Although a rough diamond, Lord was favoured by Macquarie, dined at Government House, and was made a magistrate, to the horror of free settlers.

Samuel Terry, another ex-convict, made a fortune trading at Parramatta, and many lesser men did well for themselves. The fishing was good in the troubled waters of the early days. The pattern was always the same: shipping (for communication was by water whenever possible), agencies for ships' cargoes, whaling and sealing, and above all the liquor trade. Trade was very flexible and all opportunities were seized, every one who had capital, credit, or inventiveness was eligible. The monopolists held their ground for a comparatively short time and when trade ceased to yield the 500 to 1000 per cent profit they had come to expect they turned their attention to wool-growing, a pursuit in which everyone in the upper crust, including the clergy—Marsden, for example—joined. In 1815 the *Sydney Gazette* announced that Australian wool had been sold on the London market at the unprecedented price of 5s. a pound.

Under Macquarie the emancipist class was encouraged in every way and so were the few men who belonged to neither group. For instance D'Arcy Wentworth, Garnham Blaxcell, and Alexander Riley were given a (far from watertight) liquor monopoly in return for building a hospital free of charge for the Government. They embarked gaily on this enterprise, without an architect, and the building is still standing and in use.

Besides encouraging merchants and traders not of the officer class, the Government itself made a brief excursion into trade in order to undersell and so break the vicious monopoly. The original idea was Hunter's, but King put it into execution. Cargoes of assorted necessities were sent out in transports, settlers chose representatives who, armed with shopping lists, bought direct from the ships at cost price, plus 50 per cent *ad valorem* to cover shipping, supervision and other out-of-pocket expenses. The expedient was not very successful, probably because those in charge had little knowledge of business. It withered away when *bona fide* traders, like Campbell, came on the scene.

Trade in the early days meant import and export. By 1794, barring accidents, the colony was self-supporting as far as grain and meat were concerned. Practically everything else had to be brought in and shipments from England were very irregular. After 1820 restraints on trade were lifted and the situation improved. Sugar, rice, tea, cotton, and muslins came from China and India, rum came from the Cape and from the United States. Practically everything else—including roofing slates, which came as ballast—was imported from England. After 1814 the Government made most of its purchases through Sydney merchants. In 1820 there were twelve importing firms in Sydney. Exports lagged far behind imports. In 1823 14,654 tons of goods in 55 vessels were received in Sydney, and 5500 tons, mostly whale-oil, sealskins, and wool, were exported in 16 vessels.[92] Tentative efforts were made to export wheat and coal to the Cape and India and horses to Batavia. Distances, lack of ships and of men to man them, convicts being ineligible, and uncertainty of markets made these lesser exports unprofitable.

Manufactures scarcely existed. Women and cripples wove blankets and a rough linen cloth at the Parramatta Female Factory, but not enough for the needs of the colony. In 1819 this industry was at its peak; 69,168½ yards of linen cloth was turned out as well as sailcloth and sacking. Hats, blankets, stockings, poor-quality clothing, unglazed pots, and short pipes called dudeens, were produced by private enterprise. In 1822 distilling began to use surplus wheat. Woollen mills were established at Botany and have been there ever since. A solicitor named Unwin began to refine sugar at Canterbury, but failed. With great difficulty the Government obtained the necessary plant for making salt from sea water and so was able to preserve meat. . . . It was a small beginning indeed.

It is interesting to note that enterprise preceded the mechanism of the business world. A Chamber of Commerce was set up in 1826 and approved by Governor Darling, but it was only a forerunner and did not last long. In 1837 there was a move to establish an Exchange; a committee was formed and enlisted government help, a site was provided, and the Royal Exchange Company was floated with a capital of £20,000. (This appears to have been the sum considered fitting for all public undertakings.) Delay followed delay and by 1850 the Exchange had still not come into being. The proposed site was continually changed and the requisite capital did not come in. When in 1851 a new and more stable Chamber of Commerce was formed fresh impetus was given to the project of a Royal Exchange. It was to be in Macquarie Place and the foundation stone was laid in August 1853. The discovery of gold and consequent shortage of labour delayed the opening of the building until 1857.

In January 1831 the first colonial insurance office, Australian Marine Assurance Company, opened its doors and was apparently the only one until 1836.

It is of little historical interest to continue the narrative of business in Australia, though it would yield some good stories, such as that of the office boy who habitually carried sums of up to £8000 in gold from one bank to another at the close of a day's trading and never was robbed. MacCavity *must* have been there.

It is sufficient to note at this stage that many elements that later were to figure so largely in the Australian story had already been sketched in. For example, reliance on, and control by the Government was already established in an age dominated by laissez-faire. This was due to the nature of the colony, and government responsibility was often denied by the Colonial Office, as when Governors were rebuked for helping, out of the public store, the victims of Hawkesbury floods. A spirit of independence was also, and not incongruously, present from the first. This spirit ran the gamut from uncontrollable lawlessness or the determination of the convict woman who declared that she would run away the moment she landed—and did so, into the hopeless silence of the bush, never to be found or heard of again—to the stiff-necked pride and acquisitiveness of the exclusionists and the uncontrollable freedom of the squatter in the vast interior. These things were inherent in the geography of the continent and the nature of the people who came to it.

Government trading was tried by Governor King, price-fixing was also implemented as government policy, not very successfully, by Macquarie and others. The pegging of wages and the adjustment of property to capital were tried early in the piece. Responsibility for banks, though disavowed, was intermittently taken in the interests of financial stability. State socialism, in fact if not in theory, analogous to present trends, existed in the early days and an attitude of mingled reliance on, and resentment of, the Government was built into the crescent national attitude.

The fever chart of boom and depression is one continuous graph from the first yesterday right through to tomorrow. The main reason for the zigzags has always been the dependence of Australia on a world many miles distant from her shores.

The earliest forms of depressions and booms were in the terms of near starvation and the full ration, and this depended on the arrival or non-arrival of supplies from England, as for instance the long perish between the arrival of the First and Second Fleets. As small areas came under cultivation there was the cross-pattern of good harvests and bad, floodings of the Hawkesbury or fertile years without floods. This pattern could work in reverse. A good harvest did not necessarily mean prosperity, though it might mean enough to eat. When the government store was full it closed its doors for sometimes as long as six months and farmers were left with practically no market for their abundant wheat, so they must feed it to the pigs, let it rot, or secretly turn it into a crude but still acceptable spirit which enjoyed the generic name of rum. There was even a plan, coinciding with the Government's efforts to break the rum traffic.

to set up government-controlled distilleries to provide a market for wheat, which could be shut down in times of scarcity, the distillery playing Box to the government store's Cox. Droughts played their part from the very beginning. In 1790 and 1791 heat and drought smote the little colony. Captain Tench wrote: "Cultivation on a public scale has for some time past been given up here, the crop last year being so miserable as to deter from further experiment, in consequence of which, the Government farm is abandoned, and the people who were fixed on it have been removed."[93]

At first the colony flickered quickly from bad to relatively good times. It was at the mercy of every circumstance, with no stamina of its own.

Drought and scarcity struck again in 1799 and between 1801 and 1803. In 1804 the Hawkesbury floods were more devastating than ever. The depression in England that followed the end in victory of the Napoleonic wars had its echoes in the colony, just as her absorption in war had adversely affected it by inevitable neglect. In 1826-7 drought and depression were back again and in 1831 no rain and bad times hit simultaneously. "Sudden depression in the Prices of Agricultural Produce and Stock greatly aggravated the embarrassment of the Settlers, which was occasioned by the long calamitous Drought," Governor Bourke reported.[94] This is a repetitive pattern to the present day.

Climatic reasons for depressions will remain until the progress of science leads to their control or the modification of their effects.

With the discovery of the means of wealth by the officers of the New South Wales Corps the prosperity of one section of the community often meant the ruin of another. Services and products of the soil were bought cheaply and often the payment was of dead-end value, such as rum, whilst all commodities were sold at high prices. Debt and ruin followed not only for the weak and unwary but for many of the most industrious small settlers, as Hunter's investigations revealed.

Whaling and sealing brought a boom of sorts, but, owing to the hazards of the sea, the uncertainty of markets, the uncontrolled and uneconomic plundering of the fishing grounds, the "poaching" of the Americans and the tariff barriers in the English market, it was an uncertain and doomed one.

Wool provided a more profitable staple, with a ready-made, hungry market, apparently inexhaustible grazing lands, and an animal to which the earth was peculiarly well suited, and whose life, not death, was a source of profit. The Colonial Office responded favourably to the new situation and prosperity was apparently assured. But there was a catch in it. Australia was now tied to world markets and world finance and their cycles and vibrations would affect her.

Tied in with wool and grazing generally was the land question. Land conditionally granted, sold at a fixed price or at auction, resold to the tune of ever changing values, became Australia's speculative trap. The possession of land always had a hypnotic influence. To possess was not enough, to play the land market was still better. There was so much land that the impression prevailed both locally and in England that land would pay for everything. It was the basic security for loans, the bait for investment. In good times the essential link between land and its productivity and between productivity and markets was often overlooked. With the increase of population and wealth, both local and available from overseas, speculative manias repeatedly overtook the community. The bubbles inevitably broke and reaction set in when adverse seasons, fall of prices overseas, or disturbance of credit took value out of the basic asset. The heavy depression of the early 1840s resulted from over-speculation and inflation. Complete recovery was assisted by the discovery of gold. The lesson was not learnt, it was to be repeated in the 1890s when the crisis, to be dealt with in the next chapter, was even more serious because land mania moved in from the bush to the cities, and because populations in all colonies were larger and so in bad times proved a greater burden to raise up out of their individual and collective slough.

Australia all through her history has been subject to a series of booms and depressions due to natural causes, to the overstepping of economic laws, or to world situations over which she had no control. The largeness of the continent, the sparseness of the population, and the necessity to learn from scratch how to adjust the crescent community to ever changing circumstances at home and abroad became a problem which was handled not by economists but by politicians answerable to public opinion.

REFERENCE NOTES

1 See *Hist. Rec. Aust.*, ser. I, vol. i, note 285. 2 *Ibid.*, vol. ii, pp. 355-6.
3 *Ibid.*, vol. v, pp. 740, 742, and see index.
4 *Ibid.*, vol. ii, pp. 244-5. 5 *Ibid.*, p. 246. 6 *Ibid.*, vol. iii, p. 42.
7 *Ibid.*, vol. i, p. 672. 8 *Ibid.*, vol. ii, p. 393. 9 *Ibid.*, p. 104.
10 *Ibid.*, vol. iv, pp. 350-5. 11 *Ibid.*, vol. ii, p. 358. 12 *Ibid.*, p. 621.
13 For the intricacies of this case, see *Hist. Rec. Aust.*, vol. x, pp. 639-48, and index.
14 *Hist. Rec. Aust.*, ser. I, vol. x, p. 633.
15 *Ibid.*, p. 647. 16 *Ibid.*, pp. 634-8. 17 *Ibid.*, vol. xi, p. 197.
18 *Ibid.*, vol. x, p. 633; vol. xi, p. 72.
19 *Ibid.*, vol. x, p. 676. 20 *Ibid.*, vol. xi, p. 199.
21 *Ibid.*, vol. xv, p. xii (Introduction).
22 *Ibid.*, vol. xi, p. 71 (Bathurst to Brisbane). 23 *Ibid.*, p. 72.
24 *Ibid.*, p. 893. 25 *Ibid.*, vol. xii, pp. 519-22. 26 *Ibid.*, vol. xiii, pp. 51-7.
27 *Ibid.*, vol. xiv, p. 263. 28 *Ibid.*, pp. 5-6. 29 *Ibid.*, p. 360.
30 *Ibid.*, vol. xxv, p. 774. 31 *Ibid.*, vol. xiv, pp. 7 *et seq.*
32 *Ibid.*, vol. xi, p. 412. 33 *Ibid.*, p. 477. 34 *Ibid.*, vol. xii, p. 59.
35 *Ibid.*, vol. xiii, pp. 134-5. 36 *Ibid.*, vol. xvi, pp. 516-17. 37 *Ibid.*, vol. xviii, p. 378.
38 *Ibid.*, vol. xx, pp. 306-7. 39 *Ibid.*, vol. xviii, p. 335. 40 *Ibid.*, p. 503.
41 *Ibid.*, vol. vi, pp. xvii-xviii (Introduction). 42 *Ibid.*, vol. i, p. 433.
43 *Ibid.*, p. 564. 44 *Ibid.*, pp. 690-1. 45 *Ibid.*, p. 649.
46 *Ibid.*, p. 651. 47 *Ibid.*, vol. ii, p. 341. 48 *Ibid.*, p. 437.
49 *Ibid.*, vol. iii, p. 151. 50 *Ibid.*, vol. iv, pp. 390-1. 51 *Ibid.*, vol. x, p. 676.
52 *Ibid.*, vol. xii, p. 508. 53 *Ibid.*, vol. x, p. 731. 54 *Ibid.*

[55] *Ibid.*, p. 732. [56] *Ibid.*, p. 733. [57] *Ibid.*, pp. 738-44.
[58] *Ibid.*, vol. xi, p. 636. [59] *Ibid.*, vol. xii, pp. 428-30. [60] *Ibid.*, p. 450.
[61] *Ibid.*, pp. 509-10. [62] *Ibid.*, vol. xiii, p. 183. [63] *Ibid.*, vol. ii, pp. 374-6.
[64] *Ibid.*, pp. 534-8. [65] *Ibid.*, vol. iv, p. 600.
[66] *Ibid.*, vol. v, p. xiii (Introduction). [67] *Ibid.*, vol. iii, p. 626.
[68] *Ibid.*, vol. v, p. xii (Introduction). [69] *Ibid.*, vol. iii, p. 575.
[70] *Ibid.*, vol. xiii, p. 123. [71] *Ibid.*, vol. xi, note 36. [72] *Ibid.*, vol. xiii, p. 54.
[73] *Ibid.*, vol. xix, p. vi (Introduction). [74] *Ibid.*, vol. x, p. 676.
[75] *Ibid.*, vol. xii, pp. 300-8. [76] *Ibid.*, pp. 336-8. [77] *Ibid.*, pp. 702-6.
[78] *Ibid.*, vol. xviii, pp. 9-11. [79] *Ibid.*, vol. xix, p. 187.
[80] *Ibid.*, vol. xx, p. viii (Introduction). [81] *Ibid.*, vol. xxi, p. 434.
[82] *Ibid.*, vol. xxii, p. 707.

[83] See *Hist. Rec. Aust.*, ser. I, vol. x, note 161, and for a report of the initial meeting, the *Sydney Gazette*, 19th June 1819.

[84] *Hist. Rec. Aust.*, ser. I, vol. xx, p. 800.

[85] *Ibid.*, vol. xxv, pp. 234-40.

[86] For those interested, Noel Griffiths's *A History of the Government Savings Bank of N.S.W.* fills in this story with many interesting details and exact information on banking Acts and statistics of growth. For a short but authoritative history of banking in New South Wales see *A Brief History of Australian Banking*, published by the Rural Bank of New South Wales in 1936. The Official Year Books of the States and of the Commonwealth are also mines of reliable information.

[87] *Hist. Rec. Aust.*, ser. I, vol. i, p. 307. [88] *Ibid.*, vol. iv, p. 249.
[89] *Ibid.*, vol. v, p. 602. [90] *Australian Quarterly Journal*, pp. 86-94.

[91] *Sydney Gazette*, 13th April 1830.

[92] My figures are from the *Australian Encyclopaedia.*

[93] W. Tench, *Complete Account of the Settlement at Port Jackson.*

[94] *Hist. Rec. Aust.*, ser. I, vol. xvi, p. 302.

CHAPTER XVI

THE NINETIES

Probably never before have people nursed such confident dreams that a perfect Commonwealth could be created in their own day.

—VANCE PALMER, The Legend of the Nineties.

And when hopes had collapsed, the immoderate ardour with which they had been entertained was matched by an equal intemperance with which the fretful victims faced the future.

—BRIAN FITZPATRICK, *The Australian People, 1788-1945.*

During the twenty years, 1880-1900, the Australian people became fully conscious of their nationhood.

—R. A. GOLLAN in *Australia: a Social and Political History* (Ed. G. Greenwood).

I. BACKGROUND OF PROGRESS

HISTORY CANNOT BE written, without confusion, in strict chronological order. It has a natural pattern of progress and pause, of change and absorption, of fact and myth. A legend may be more important in the long run than statistics as a source of action. Growth may be from without or from within and its realities are not always found where they are expected. The illogical must be allowed for as well as the evolutionary, because history is the long-term story of human beings in the endless struggle to build themselves a home. The historian, in his search for the modicum of truth allowed him by the circumstance of handling something in continual flux, must be given a certain latitude. Some threads of the narrative, as for instance the history of the savings-bank movement in Australia, are best followed from beginning to end at one time, other and larger phases must be followed through until they reach a natural pause, to be picked up again later in a different context. In a word, the historian must handle his material as he sees fit and that will rarely be arbitrarily.

The history of Australia has a clear beginning. Men of European stock came to make their home in a distant and practically untouched continent. A long period of adjustment followed. To begin with, adjustment was the most important problem. It measured the distance between survival and extinction. Adjustment is still going on, accumulating new factors, problems, and solutions. The discovery that the Merino sheep could flourish in Australia was one of the victories in the battle, but it also triggered off a new phase of evolution with enduring social and political consequences.

The discovery of gold was another turning-point. It broke into the pastoral pattern, changed the nature and direction of the population, and by its colour caught the imagination of men both inside and outside Australia, and that, too, is an ingredient of history. For two decades, the 1860s and 1870s, the effects of gold, social, political, and economic, were woven into the general adjustment.

The 1890s are generally accepted by Australians who think about it at all as another turning-point. It is more nebulous, more a matter of argument, than the earlier events just picked out of the historical basket for illustration. That the decade is chosen for highlighting is in itself significant. A legend was born, if not conceived, then and the legend has been potent.

The first thing to do is to describe briefly what actually happened in the 1890s, or such of the political, social, and economic events as seem cogent, and then to essay some evaluation of them. A strict date-line cannot be drawn round the period; it rarely can in history.

The situation that developed in the 1890s can only be seen, let alone explained, by the boom years of the seventies and eighties.

II. Finance and the Boom

Gold had given the Australian economy a great boost, and it had done more, it had induced a hopeful state of mind verging, it would seem in retrospect, on megalomania. Australia, after years in the barbarian wilderness, had discovered that she had the Midas touch. The unlocking of the lands in the 1860s, though the over-all effect was disappointing, added to the hopeful portrait. It was easy to become a landowner in this land of opportunity, the Government made it possible on generous hire-purchase conditions. The land, too, as time went on became more valuable and yielded more exportable products.

At first the very magnitude of the continent and the long sea miles that separated it from its natural markets left only one exportable commodity, wool. Neither long journeys over rough roads nor the sea passage to England could affect it. In the depression of the 1840s tallow was found to be another such export. In the 1850s gold became the export *par excellence,* much value in a small compass. Easily won alluvial gold gradually petered out in Victoria and the mining of reefs, demanding expensive crushing and other plants, fell into the hands of companies. The day of the fossicker was over, though many an old hand was still making his tucker at it, and with the invention of the cyanide process tailings of an early, more prodigal day, could be retreated with profit. In 1882 Mount Morgan in Queensland was discovered, a limited company with a capital of £800,000 was formed to mine it, and in fourteen years, 1886-1900, about two million ounces of gold, as well as copper, were taken out of it. In the next year, 1883, Broken Hill, where Sturt and his party had almost perished of heat and thirst in 1844, was discovered to have rich silver-lead deposits, and the Broken Hill Proprietary Company, with a capital of £400,000, was formed to exploit it in 1885. In 1898 thirteen years of working showed a profit of approximately £7,000,000. Such enterprises reinforced the legend of Australia's wealth and encouraged capital investment. They gave employment, thus adding to the general prosperity, but the profits did not go directly to the "diggers", as in what was already looked upon as the heyday of mining in the 1850s. The picture of the single adventurer or the group of mates with their gamblers' luck, and not the company of anonymous shareholders, was what appealed, and still appeals, to the average Australian as a self-portrait.

With the impartiality so often evident in the Australian story every colony in rotation was given its quota of mineral wealth. First came South Australia with copper strikes in the 1840s at Kapunda, Burra Burra, and Moonta. New South Wales and then Victoria found gold in the 1850s and 1860s. Tasmania and Queensland followed with tin, silver-lead, and copper discovered and worked respectively at Mount Bischoff, Mount Zeehan, and Mount Lyell. In the 1890s gold was found in Western Australia in the desert, Coolgardie, Kalgoorlie . . . and gold-rush fever possessed the land. In the first decade of the new century South Australia's turn came again when iron was found in fabulous quantities, two mountains of ore near Whyalla.

It was in the 1870s and 1880s that other sources of primary wealth began to be exploited. These were wheat, fruit, sugar, and dairy products. Before any of these could become profitable exports it was necessary to open up the country and to spend money on it in such a large way that only the Governments were strong enough to bear the expense.

This development consisted primarily in the building of railways, in the use of irrigation, of experiments in refrigeration, and the introduction of science to agriculture.

Transport had always been a problem, and with the ever wider scattering of settlement the problem became more and more acute. Roads had been the first answer. The distances were great, labour, even in convict days, inadequate and inexperienced, and the terrain, with a mountain barrier dividing the coastal plain from the interior, difficult. The climate, with its extremes of heat and cold, its unimpeded winds over the plains and its occasional very heavy rains, put more strain on the roads than the English ones, on which they were modelled, had to stand. They fell into disrepair faster than they could be repaired. The transport of goods was first by packhorse and then by the slow-moving but nearly indestructible bullock-wagon. Men went on horseback or walked.

The gold-rushes raised the density of population to a point where regular coach services became profitable. The first coaches were run by Emanuel King, a barber of Melbourne, and by James Watt, a publican of Bacchus Marsh. King carried passengers with "light swags only" to the Mount Alexander diggings, a journey of 74 miles, in a "two-wheeled spring van, driven by three horses", for £5, and Watt's service plied between Melbourne and Ballarat and charged 25s. single fare. The journeys were always exhausting and often hazardous.

It took an American, Freeman Cobb, and his three partners to see the possibilities of organized and reliable coach services. They imported their coaches—light vehicles suspended on leather straps which, though far from comfortable, could be relied on to travel any road, however rough—from America. They understood the benefits of advertisement, bought good horses, and with an obviously going concern were able to secure a contract for mails and a good subsidy from the Government.

In a "puff", the firm set out the delights of travel:

> There is something bracing, clear, and exhilarating in coach travelling, and it would be hard to beat the style of tonic one gets on a summer morn, seated behind a spanking team which bowls over roads and bush tracks beneath fragrant trees, giving their jolly jehu no trouble except to prevent them from pulling the pole clean out of the coach

There were nevertheless dangers from bushrangers, as well as from the many possible accidents of the road.

Freeman Cobb returned to America, but Cobb & Co. lived on and in 1858 became one of the multiple interests of another American, James Rutherford. As a dealer in horses he had travelled widely in Victoria, New South Wales, and Queensland, and had seen for himself the possibilities of improved coach services. Sometimes he had money to spare and sometimes he had none. With £500, the damages he received in an assault case, he bought into Cobb & Co. By amalgamation, purchase, and natural expansion Rutherford built up a large business. After 1862 his coach routes were spreading over New South Wales and by 1870 Queensland was included in the circuit. "The enormous proportions to which the business of Cobb & Co. had grown . . . may be estimated by the fact that by 1870 they were harnessing 6,000 horses per day, their coaches were travelling 28,000 miles per week, they were in receipt of £95,000 per annum in mail subsidies, and their pay sheet for wages exceeded £100,000 per annum."[1]

Cobb & Co. was not James Rutherford's only interest, big as it was with its allied undertakings of stores, factories, and inns, so that it was not unlike a horse-drawn precursor of Ansett's with its airlines, road-tourist trade, and hotel chain. Rutherford continued to deal in horses. He became a landowner and pastoralist. He was also Australia's first ironmaster at Lithgow. He was interested in the export of timber and for that purpose built sawmills in Western Australia in 1865, and in trade with New Zealand, but this last enterprise was short-lived.

Undismayed by the lengthening railways, Cobb & Co. moved its centre to Queensland and continued to serve the far outback until well into the twentieth century. Cobb & Co. was from first to last a purely private enterprise, the subsidies it received from the Government being merely in the nature of payment for carrying the mails. It could remain in the hands of a company because its expenses, although large in the aggregate, were well spread, it was fluid and flexible, new runs could be opened on demand and old ones discontinued if unprofitable. The risk was small. Certainly Cobb & Co. did much to open up the country by the freer circulation of people in it, but it was of little economic importance where the main problem was the bringing of primary products to the ports of export.

For this "unlocking of the export trade" railways were an essential. At first it was thought that, as in England and America, railways could be built by private enterprise with assistance, such as the free granting of land for track, marshalling yards, and station sites, by the Government. It was soon discovered that the initial expenses were too great for any organization less than the Government. Distances, cost, shortage of labour, and the necessity to import all material combined to hit up the capital outlay. The same sequence of events was rehearsed in all colonies.

The early story is full of colour and humour, as so many early stories are.

The first Australian railway was mooted in 1845 when a private Bill was passed in the House of Commons to authorize the building of forty miles of line connecting Sydney, Parramatta, Richmond, and Windsor at an estimated cost of £500,000. Railways were very much the vogue at this time in England, the modern age was typified by a locomotive. Little came of the project, but, hearing of it, the colonists were anxious to participate in the benefits of modern science. A public meeting was held in Sydney and in 1848 the Sydney Railway Company was formed and a project to connect Sydney and Goulburn by rail was initiated. The first sod for the first line was turned by Sir Charles FitzRoy's daughter on 3rd July 1850. Then came the gold discoveries. The workmen fled happily to the diggings. The Government brought in 500 navvies, they, too, disappeared in the same direction. Any labour that could be hired was extremely costly. The company borrowed from the Government until its debt was more than £150,000. Three locomotives were built in England by Robert Stephenson and Company of Newcastle for Australian use. This was going direct to the stable. The line was opened in September 1855. It was already, to all intents and purposes, a government line, for the Railway Act of 1854 had given the Government the right to take over existing lines and to build new ones and had set up a Commission of three to manage them.

Progress was slow. By 1865 there were 143 miles of line in the colony. The 1870s and 1880s were the railway age. Sir Hercules Robinson, the Governor, inaugurated an era of rapid expansion when in 1872 he preached "a vigorous policy of public works". In this he was not so much the initiator of a new policy as the prophet of one already desired and determined on. Australia could afford railways. She would have them and her difficulties would then be over. In 1885 there were 1732 miles of railway and in 1925 there were 5656 miles and construction still under way.

The story was much the same in Victoria. In June 1852 a deputation waited on La Trobe to ask for a loan, a grant of money to cover the expenses of survey and the free gift of all necessary land to build a railway from Melbourne to the diggings at Mount Alexander. It was well received and in February 1853 the Melbourne, Mount Alexander and Murray River Railway Company was established by an Act of the colonial legislature. Its aims were ambitious as the name suggests; its performance was not so good. In 1854 another company was in the field, the Melbourne and Hobson's Bay Railway Company, and it opened its line, the first steam railway actually to go into operation in Australia, in the September of the same year. The lines were ready, but, alas, the locomotives on order in England had not arrived. Nothing daunted, the company had an engine built locally. The train ran at fifteen miles an hour. After five days the engine gave up the ghost and its place was taken by a pile-driver mounted on a truck. The train moved again. In 1855 the locomotives arrived from England. Other rail companies sprang up and the Government tried to stimulate investment in them by guaranteeing interest to five per cent. They could not make their expenses and in 1860 all railways present and to come were taken over by the Government.

South Australia, with so many firsts to her credit, produced a phenomenon in 1851, the first government-planned railway in the British Empire. Adelaide City and Port Railway Company had been formed in London in the usual way, but it was soon clear that its shareholders were more interested in getting free land as a basis for speculation than in actually building a railway. The Government had the sense to see that the citizens had not the financial stamina to conduct a railway unaided and took over the project. The line was not opened until April 1856, having been delayed by the scarcity of labour.

In Western Australia the first railway, 1871, was privately owned by the Western Australian Timber Company and ran from Lockeville to Yoganup. After 1873 it and all others were government run.

In Queensland there was no dilly-dallying. The Government undertook to build railways for the common good from the first. It was a big colony, thinly populated, and in the interests of economy a gauge of 3 feet 6 inches was adopted.

The colonies were separated from one another by more than lines on a map. Each was jealously autonomous and between New South Wales and Victoria particularly there was a bitter rivalry. Railways were built, not with an eye to the natural formation of the land, or, indeed, on any particular principle except the determination to drain wealth towards the capital cities. No colony was yet rich enough to afford more than, at the most, two ports with all their costly installations. The capital and the chief port were one and the same and for economy all railway lines must converge on it. There was no other co-ordinating principle. Various interests lobbied for the railways that would best suit them. Members of Parliament promised their constituents railways and blindly fought to get them. There was no general plan even within a colony, and each colony existed as if in a vacuum. One result was patchy and uneconomic building, another was the break of gauge between the different colonies which has proved so harassing, particularly in war-time. New South Wales used the standard gauge of 4 feet 8½ inches, Victoria and South Australia the more comfortable one of 5 feet 3 inches, and Queensland a narrower one. As if this were not enough, subsidiary lines in the same systems had different gauges. At one time South Australia could boast six different gauges, Victoria and New South Wales four each, Queensland three and Tasmania two.

The chaos in Victoria became so bad that Richard Speight was brought from England as a Railway Commissioner to straighten it out and to curb rash and ill-judged spending. Speight and his colleagues, whilst instructed to clear up the mess, were not given a free hand. The public owned the railways and would tolerate no undemocratic interference with them. As Professor Shann so wittily puts it: "Log-rolling about new construction only shifted from the lobbies of Parliament House to the corridors of the Commissioners' Office at the opposite end of the city."[2] The uninstructed desire of the general public was that the railways should assist all producers with low freights and yet by showing a handsome surplus reinforce the idea of unsinkable prosperity.

Despite all this, the railways did serve the purpose for which they were constructed. They carried wool, wheat, coal, dairy produce, quickly, safely, and regularly to points of distribution and export. It was reckoned that whereas it cost 2s. a ton per mile to carry produce by road it could be done on the railways for sixpence.

This naturally gave a great impetus to wheat-growing. Between 1871 and 1875 £11,000,000 of loan money, most of it from England and at a high rate of interest, was spent on public works, railways absorbing the main part of it.

Naturally the problem did not end when products were brought to the ports of export. They still had to be shipped to their markets. Wool and wheat would carry, but there were other possibilities in meat, dairy produce, and fruit. To be successfully exported these required some method of refrigeration.

Here we come upon another man, Thomas Sutcliffe Mort, who, like James Rutherford, appeared to straddle his times. They took over in a more constructive and wholly respectable way the role of venturers like Ben Boyd. Mort was born in Lancashire in 1816 and came to Australia as a young man in 1838, presumably with his way to make, for we hear of him first as employed as a clerk and salesman. His light did not long remain under a bushel. In 1841 he was taking an interest in shipping and with others had formed the Hunter River Navigation Company. In 1843 he was also an auctioneer and wool-broker and his thoughts had begun to centre on ways and means of exporting meat. At first he worked on various curing processes, but these were not satisfactory. He and everyone else wanted something better than the salted meat on which the colony had been nurtured in the early days. In 1845 he founded Mort and Company, with its interests in ship-building and repair. Railways were in the air; he became a railway promoter in 1849 and, with the discovery of gold, he added that to his interests. His was the first Australian gold-mining company, the Great Nugget Vein Mining Company. From this he went on to other mining ventures, the Peak Downs Copper Mining Company in Queensland and the Waratah Coal Mining Company at Newcastle. Meanwhile in 1856 he had set up as a farmer at Bodalla where he had seventeen thousand acres of dairying country. Until recently his old home still stood there, derelict and empty. In one room, in a box or scattered over the floor, were family photographs, amongst them the picture of an English home of which "Bodalla" was the colonial copy.

Mort did not flit from one scheme to another. He added new interests whilst keeping the old ones. He constructed a dry-dock at Balmain, his shipyards built the largest ship yet to be launched in Australia, the *Governor Blackall*. He manufactured steam engines. He introduced a co-operative system by encouraging his workmen to take up shares in his enterprises. The whole of trade was his field, production, shipping, marketing, and ever his mind picked at the puzzle of how to send meat successfully to England. In 1870 he was making experiments in mechanical refrigeration. In 1875 he was ready for practical tests. He had slaughter-yards and freezing works at Lithgow and ice works at Darling Harbour. He sank £60,000 of his own money and £20,000 subscribed by squatters in a trial cargo of meat. Unfortunately the refrigerating machinery broke down at sea and the cargo was a total loss. He died at Bodalla in 1878, but in 1880 his dream came true, Australian frozen meat was on the English market. His work had made it possible. There have been improvements since, chilling instead of refrigeration, for instance, but the first step was the most important.

Not only meat could now be exported. The new technique applied to dairy produce and fruit. Tasmanian apples were to become the island's hope in the dark days that no one so far guessed would come.

Like dragon's teeth new problems were always arising. A way had been found to market Australia's primary produce. Now the earth was required to yield more and better commodities. The old hit-or-miss days were going. The great problem was rainfall. In a country of uncertain rainfall there was no certainty about crops and a drought could reduce flocks and herds by half. Science must be brought to the rescue if production were to increase. A real beginning was made in the 1870s and 1880s.

The problem of water could be solved in two ways, which have already been touched on in the chapter on Land. It could be spread through the dry lands by irrigation, provided there was a sufficient source, or the artesian water under the earth could be pumped up and used to water stock in their home paddocks or to keep them alive on the droving track. On the other hand, the problem could be met by adjusting crops so that they could live and thrive with a minimum of water.

Irrigation became practical politics in the 1880s. Edward Lascelles on his property, Lake Corrong, in the Victorian Wimmera gave a practical demonstration of results to be obtained from irrigation in conjunction with methods of dry farming.

Drought in the early 1880s turned men's minds to the possibilities of irrigation. It had been practised in other parts of the world, notably Egypt and India, from time immemorial, but the vastness of the Australian continent, the paucity of the permanent water supply, and private riparian rights, modelled on those of England, stood in the way of any organized or public irrigation scheme. In 1884, however, commissions were set up in both Victoria and New South Wales to inquire into possibilities. Alfred Deakin, for Victoria, visited India and the United States. His report was the basis for the Victorian Irrigation Act of 1886. This Act empowered the Government to name irrigation areas, on the advice of experts, to set up the necessary plants and to form trusts to manage, control, and distribute the water in the named districts. All riparian rights were declared a national asset. By comparison with the railways this was a well-thought-out and scientifically conceived scheme. The cost was to be covered by a levy on those who benefited to pay the interest on capital outlay and a sinking fund of 1½ per cent per annum. A beginning was made at Mildura on the Murray. George and William Chaffey, two Canadians, discovered and brought to Australia by Deakin, undertook to develop two 25,000-acre blocks at Mildura, in the heart of the dry country. Irrigation proved more difficult than expected, for the River Murray rose and fell rapidly. It became evident that it could only be successful in conjunction with water-conservation works. This entailed heavier expense and the trusts, with their limited money-raising powers, were soon in difficulties. By an Act of 1905 a Water Supply Commission was set up to manage irrigation as a government agency. The soil of the dry lands only needed water to make it fertile. After irrigation a fruit industry grew up beside the rivers.

New South Wales was slower off the mark and proceeded somewhat differently. In 1884 she set up a Royal Commission to consider the possibilities of irrigation. It sat for three years and it was not until the 1890s that any real progress was made. Trusts, analogous to County Councils, were founded at Wentworth, Hay, and Balranald with the task of pumping and distributing water. In 1896 all riparian rights were declared to be vested in the Government. In 1897 an expert from India was called in and in 1902 an Act of Parliament drew the whole sketchy structure together and voted £1,000,000 for irrigation purposes. In 1913 all irrigation work came under the control of a commission.

Other States followed much the same pattern, but with poorer facilities. Small-scale private irrigation schemes were encouraged so long as they did not conflict with government undertakings.

Dry farming is another matter altogether. It is the adjustment of agriculture to lower rainfall conditions. In the 1870s, wheat-farming having proved profitable, new land for its expansion was required. Victorians turned their eyes towards the Mallee. This is an area in the north-western part of the State which is dry and carries a thick belt of the dwarf eucalypts from which it takes its name. It was a pastoral district until the middle 1870s when the rabbit drove out the sheep. The growing of wheat there was made possible by the Mallee roller. This agricultural machine flattened and broke off the mallee scrub so that it could be burnt and the land brought under the plough. Lascelles showed what could be done here by clearing and irrigation and other wheat-farmers followed him. In New South Wales Farrer was working in the field on rust- and drought-resistant wheats which would also have improved milling qualities. He began his experiment in 1886 and twelve years later was appointed experimentalist in the Department of Agriculture. With improved facilities he produced his now famous Federation wheat. It was a dry crop resistant to rust. It appeared stunted in its growth, but this only meant that its vigour was not wasted on leaves and stems. It was not golden but bronze in colour. It had what was necessary for Australian conditions. By 1902 the Department of Agriculture was distributing seed in bulk and wheat-farmers were educated to the advantages of using pedigree and graded seed.

In South Australia Goyder's Line was crossed in 1874. Goyder was a government surveyor who plotted upon the map of the colony the boundaries of the area with an average rainfall of 14 inches a year. Beyond that line, he advised, it would be uneconomic to try to grow wheat. In an exceptionally good season all might be well, but the bad seasons would inevitably come. With drought-resistant seed and improved agricultural machinery the wheat-farmers crossed into the dry country and were sufficiently successful to stay there.

Despite increased acreage, the amount of wheat produced began to fall. Experiments at Roseworthy Agricultural College, South Australia, a government-run institution, discovered that the fault lay in the soil. The College began to preach the gospel of superphosphates. The farmers took little notice at first. After ten years of campaigning only 600 tons were being spread on the earth. A test case proved the value of the fertilizer; land dressed with it, even though there was a bad drought at the time, showed a .88 improvement of the wheat crop over the harvest for good years. Conviction spread and by 1902 24,000 tons were being used. The rot was stopped, wheat production began to increase again. The Wimmera (or Mallee) lands of Victoria were settled very largely from South Australia where many of the problems of farming dry country had been solved.

In 1885 Victoria had its Dookie Agricultural College. Science was moving slowly into the field of agriculture in particular and primary production in general.

These were the developing and developed natural resources of the country and they were the background for, and justification of, the phenomenal burst of confidence which characterized the 1870s and 1880s, the great boom period.

The most striking index of the boom lay in finance.

The English money market was under a cloud. Capital was looking for new outlets. Australia had hit the news with her gold and continued at intervals to produce mines of fabulous wealth. Everywhere was evidence of prosperity springing from a firm foundation in the land itself. In 1861 there were nearly 21,000,000 sheep in Australia. In 1891 there were more than 106,000,000 and the improved clip was seven times heavier than it had been thirty years before. The wheat lands had extended and new products were coming on the market. In twenty years the area under crop doubled and the quality of the products improved greatly. Prosperity was well entrenched and from England's point of view it was the right sort of prosperity. England herself was now primarily a manufacturer. Her strength lay in this and in her carrying trade. Australia appeared to be, not her rival, but her complement, a granary, a source of raw materials, an employer of ships.

Confidence was rooted in the soil, and what more fundamental basis could it have? In good times it is as difficult to imagine depression as it is to imagine cold during a heat-wave. Nobody wanted to doubt, either in Australia or in England. The boom suited them both. The evidence of good times, the expansion of railways for instance, or the 25,600 miles of telegraph line that existed in 1881, was taken as foundation for further confidence. The asset was increasing.

The machinery of finance now existed in Australia. The gold-rushes had acted as a forcing ground for the banks. They had expanded their businesses, new banks were founded. During the 1860s the banks had played an essential part in keeping the squatter on his run. They backed him against the selector, for he was the man with assets and, having sunk money in the land, the banks had to make good their alley by sinking more. Banks, despite warnings from England, were becoming speculative. The age of barter was not yet far distant in time, the land and its products looked solid and secure, the banks with their power to bind and loose could make them even more secure. The legislative power, which could have curbed the banks, had no wish to, for it was still in the hands of squatters and merchants and other solid citizens with a stake in prosperity and little or no financial training beyond that required to run a property or a mercantile house.

The transition from the conservative function of a bank to a more speculative and theoretically less sound one is set out with admirable clarity in the *Cambridge History of the British Empire*: "The steady use of land values in a young country offered, it was said, a sure margin of security in the long run; and the ease of transfer of land under the Torrens system made a clean certificate of title almost as negotiable a security as government stock or a first class trade bill. At the worst the land remained."[3]

Money for expansion was lent on land and from that it was a short step to loans on stock, plant, or wool, last season's or even next season's. This was not accepted without a rearguard action on the part of more conservative bankers and responsible government officials. But come it did and it had the blessing of the law. As a concession Australian banks carried a larger gold reserve than English banks and this was expected to trim the ship.

What nobody understood until after the event, when it is easy to be wise, was that, just as beauty is in the eye of the beholder, so value is not a solid substance but a conceit of confidence. Prosperity in Australia, stemming as it did from the land, appeared the most reliable and indestructible form of wealth. "At the worst the land remained."

Naturally the value of land rose. It was the source of wealth. Speculation in land was rife. It was bought, not for its produce, but to resell at a profit. In these circumstances land lost its reality and became a symbol of value, an entry in a ledger. Speculation left the bush and came into the cities. Here was the greatest density of population. Here was money and confidence. Speculation in subdivisions and land sales became a mania and even when the end of such a fever must have been clear to shrewd men they still hoped to make a fortune before the crash came.

John Haslam in his *A Glimpse of Australian Life,* published in 1890, gives a picture of the situation in its most elementary terms and he, grand moralist though he was, saw no harm in it.

> Soon after I got fairly settled to work, what is called a Land Boom set in. . . .
>
> In early days the Colonists who were shrewd and far-seeing bought up land in the cities and suburbs; each city investment of one acre carried with it a number of acres in the country free of cost.
>
> The prices paid for city and suburban lands in those days were trifling.
>
> In the boom mania a syndicate of six or more men purchases from the original proprietor for a term of years his section in the suburbs, at a price which gives a large margin of profit to the owner. Then this syndicate, having to make their profit, calls in a licensed surveyor, who makes his survey and cuts up the section into allotments of varying widths and depths.
>
> Large posters, attractive in appearance and often with a political meaning, are then placarded prominently about the city. Large and small advertisements are run in the different papers, and free tickets are available for anyone who wishes to go to the scene of action. Upon arrival a free lunch is spread, with beer, spirits, wines and champagne. When the populace have fared sumptuously the order is given to start the sale.
>
> Conditions differ in each colony, but usually ten per cent deposit and balance by bills in one, two or three years. These seem easy terms, and many a one who had no intention to buy land, starts bidding in the excitement and ultimately finds himself the possessor of one or more allotments.
>
> The documents are signed and a deposit paid, the bills are then sent him for acceptance and his difficulties as a land proprietor commence.
>
> In fifty out of every hundred cases only the first bill is met as a variety of circumstances arise that absolutely prevent the purchase being completed.
>
> Then the land becomes forfeited to the syndicate, and they resell it when a buyer comes forward. As the boom wanes these syndicates find they have too

much on their hands, then some of their number, through over speculation, become financially weak, and the onus of co-partnership falls on the strongest of them. But in cases where there is a total collapse, the owner gets back the land together with the syndicate's deposits. He holds on till there is another boom and sells again.[4]

This is symptomatic of the state into which the country was drifting, of the febrile excitement and unreal thinking that prevailed, but it represents only a local wave pattern, the writing on the sand. There was much more to the situation than that. Australia was a magnet for oversea capital. England was eager to invest in the land of opportunity. Australia never said no to money, even when the loans offered outstripped her capacity to absorb and utilize them. The more money that came to her the greater she felt her asset to be, the higher rose her confidence, for all the world as if she were a young debutante being showered with compliments.

Between 1876 and 1880 £22,000,000 came into the country on loan for public works and between £11,000,000 and £12,000,000 more were invested privately.

Between 1881 and 1885 £37,500,000 were borrowed by the four eastern colonies and another £30,000,000 or so were sunk in private undertakings. Between 1885 and 1890 £100,000,000 poured into the country. There was a general idea that round every corner there was a fairy godmother with gold or wool or some other pleasant surprise in her hands waiting to offer it to the lucky passer-by. It was said that in England highly placed men were touting for colonial loans and reaping a commission on the money that rewarded their go-getting tactics. To get money the colonies outbid the home market and one another, offering higher and higher interest. The money was siphoned in through the banks and through the less reputable land and finance companies which, with no gold reserve and no hampering rules and regulations, were cashing in on good times with easy credit. No one apparently remembered the early 1840s, when a similar situation had arisen.

In Victoria revenue was kept up by customs duties and in free-trade New South Wales by sales of Crown land. The customs were swelled by the widespread illusion of prosperity which egged men on to buy and buy, and Crown land as it was alienated became a diminishing asset. The rock of the State was crumbling.

Money came from more and more uncertain sources. Banks were lending money, which they had from England in the form of short-term fixed deposits at high interest, on the security of land and stock. That is, they were making long-term loans with short-term money, so the day of reckoning was bound to come. In 1891 Australian banks held nearly £40,000,000 on fixed deposit for from one to three years.

New South Wales and South Australia heard the warning bell, Victoria did not heed it. The two former colonies had visible proof in a crippling drought that the golden days of prosperity could not go on for ever. In 1886 the Commercial Bank of South Australia closed its doors. Ominously the price of wool fell on the oversea market. "Incipient land booms in Adelaide and Sydney died of fright,"[5] as Professor Shann put it.

As yet Melbourne had no doubts. She was the financial centre of Australia, she was booming. Building societies followed the land and finance companies, the latter now, since the brakes were taken off, calling themselves banks. The building societies had plenty of English money to invest and, since every family wanted to own or build a house, they lent money not on their clients' present but on their future prospects.

Up and up rose the spiral. An artificial situation existed and that is always dangerous. More money had been poured into Australia than she had the population to use. At this time there were only about a million people in the whole of Victoria (to be exact 1,140,088), and the population for Australia in 1891 is assessed at 3,177,823.[6] Although the potentialities were there they were often long-distance ones, whilst the money that fed them had to pay interest from the first and was often due for repayment long before the schemes it had been used for came to fruition. Speculation is the get-rich-quick method and speculation is barren. Men's faces were turned from the realities of development to speculation in the cities. The whole population, it would seem, had turned gambler and shared the feeling that they could not go wrong. The deteriorating state of affairs was masked by an outward seeming of prosperity and by the buoyancy of revenue which arose not directly out of permanent values, but, as we have seen already, from customs and Crown land sales, both of which would dry up once the cold wind began to blow in earnest. The banks, which might have been a brake on the situation, only increased the danger. In 1887 the Victorian Banking Act of 1864 had been amended so that "any incorporated banking company" could lend on a wide range of securities formerly considered doubtful, on city land, houses, ships, merchandise of all sorts, and on products whether harvested or only in expectation. Bankers could use their own discretion in taking advantage of this. It was legal. Old and well-established banks were chary of such unconventional policy, but many of the loan and finance companies, by a stroke of the pen, turned themselves into banks and the world was theirs.

This financial juggling was not restricted to the world of big business. It seeped right down to the little man. Wages were high and, with all the public works and private building under way, labour was short. Full employment gave a sense of security. The employee as well as the employer looked forward to owning his own house and garden. One of the beauties of living in the new world, where social distinctions were not as rigid as in the old, where the cities were not so large and where there was land in plenty, was that no one need despair of owning a block of it and enjoying the privacy and privileges of a householder. Even with a good wage coming in regularly few had the capital to put down for a home. The building societies, of which there were now a number, came to their aid. Either by balloting, so that members in turn had the use of the combined capital, or by loans these societies financed home-building. It was a variant of the time-purchase system, and right and left the future was mortgaged for immediate benefit. Things reached a pass when practically everyone was living beyond his means and the public and private interest bill was rising. Trading banks, in order to get money to pay interest on their commitments, were offering 5 per cent interest on deposits.

III. The Crisis

The situation was over-ripe. When in December 1889 the Premier Permanent Building Association of Melbourne went into liquidation confidence was shaken. This might have been an isolated incident, but it was not. Much more serious was waning confidence overseas.

Argentina, which had been enjoying a boom similar to Australia, found herself in difficulties and oversea investors drew an analogy. Then the London firm of William Westgarth and Company failed. They had held a great quantity of colonial stock and this was suddenly thrown on the market. In 1891 the Australian colonies found that they could float no more loans in London. It came as a shock. Fortunatus's purse had shut with a snap.

The world parity of wool fell from 12¼d. a pound in 1884 to 7d. a pound in 1893. The price of metals fell sharply and so did that of wheat. Most serious of all, confidence failed. The English investors wanted their money back. They brought pressure to bear on the banks and other agencies, which in turn tried to draw in the moneys owed to them. Many squatters were in the hands of the banks, for they had needed ready money for fencing and other improvements. As the price of wool fell they aimed at greater production to make up the leeway and this led to overstocking. Their only hope of raising money was to sell stock, their only economy was to cut the labour employed to the minimum and to reduce wages. The home market was glutted with men and beasts.

Since Australia depended almost entirely on her primary products any fall in prices there echoed through the whole economy. Almost everyone was dependent directly or indirectly on wool, wheat, or metals. It profited no one that the seasons were good. The small man in the suburbs who was buying his home on time payment through a building society was as badly stung as the erstwhile wealthy grazier whose land and flocks were mortgaged to the bank. The banks and finance companies, caught between customers who could not pay and creditors who demanded their money, found themselves in desperate straits.

There was no machinery to deal with a crisis. The economy in general was embarrassed because almost everything Australia needed had to be imported. To pay for her imports she had to export. With the bottom out of the export market the balance of trade was against her and she could be paralysed for lack of the commonest necessities other than foodstuffs. That was the Government's worry. Revenue fell away sharply. Victoria tried the expedient of raising her customs duties; this discouraged trade still further and revenue fell lower. The mainstay of revenue in New South Wales had been land sales; now no one wanted land. It was there, as substantial as ever, but the value had gone out of it.

When the crack began to widen there was about £275,000,000 of oversea capital invested in Australia. To pay the interest on this and to keep public works going the various Governments were raising loans. These swelled the interest commitments and made further loans necessary, since exports could not foot the bill. When there was no more capital offering for loans public works stopped and serious unemployment ensued. What had happened on a national scale now happened in the domestic field.

Private enterprise was still the watchword. The Government had done nothing to curb the prosperity of the banks and finance companies in the boom years and now it did nothing to save or help them in the moment of crisis. Nor did they stand together. In Melbourne, during the financial year 1891-2, twenty-one building societies and loan companies failed and in Sydney another twenty went into liquidation. In March 1892 the Mercantile Bank of Victoria closed its doors and in January 1893 the Federal Bank, a bank of issue, also failed. Eleven other banks failed and the misery spread. The Bank of South Australia was tottering on the brink of ruin when a timely merger with the Union Bank saved it. In 1891 the Bank of Van Diemen's Land failed and the little island at the world's end was fortunate to find a new asset in the export of apples. Bank reserves of gold were fast draining out of the country to meet oversea commitments.

As an emergency measure the Government in Victoria proclaimed a five-day bank holiday. This precipitated a panic. Some of the older and stronger banks wisely kept open and weathered the storm, but six more banks were amongst the casualties. In all, twenty-two banks in Australia suspended payment and only ten came through unscathed, amongst them the Bank of New South Wales and the Union Bank. Shareholders were deemed personally liable for their bank's debts. Many private bankruptcies, involving money to the grand total of about £132,000,000, also occurred. The whole fabric was in ruins and hardly a household in Australia did not feel in one way or another the effects of the collapse.

IV. The Labour Movement

There was another factor which, whilst apparently adding to the general distress at the time, was to have far-reaching consequences in the future.

It has often been pointed out that hard times alone do not produce revolutions. It is the alternation of good with bad times that works up the necessary head of steam. There was no revolution, in the terms of, say, the French or Russian revolutions, in Australia during the 1880s and 1890s, but there was a reshaping of political thought and the emergence of a new social attitude.

The trade-union movement, of course, was not an Australian invention. It had had its rise in the craft guilds of the Middle Ages. During the Industrial Revolution in England a new spirit had begun to move within the old shell. Agitation amongst workers for better conditions and a greater share of profits had been harshly repressed. The Tolpuddle Martyrs and the Dorchester Labourers had been transported as convicts to Australia for no greater crimes. They and others like them had brought a new militant attitude with them.

The situation in the new world differed widely from that in the old. On the one hand, the feudal past did not exist in Australia. Society from the first was more fluid. A shrewd and energetic man could work his way from the bottom to the top of the ladder, given reasonable luck. There was no class of hereditary landowners, no leisured class. Amongst the successful the self-made man prevailed. It was a frontier society and the physical circumstances of life in the bush begot a certain equality. You have only to read *Settlers and Convicts*, written by Alexander Harris, an English artisan, to realize the solidarity and natural socialism of the free itinerant bush worker. The bushranger was the folk hero, not because he stole but because he defied authority. His exploits were the epics of the bush as the stamina and performance of the grass-fed horses were its *fabulae*.

On the other hand, the convict beginnings of the colony and the assigned-servant system put the workers at a severe disadvantage from the first. Alexander Harris points out that from a practical point of view there was no very clear line of demarcation between the ex-convict, ticket-of-leave man, and the free worker. The harsh Master and Servant Act (1828) took up where the convict system ended. Under it a man could be jailed for leaving his employment or even for failing to give satisfaction in the performance of his work.

Mateship existed before it became a word to conjure with, and so did a general background of oppression and of freedom and equality, with a picturesque slant.

The first trade union existed as early as 1840. It was the Australian Society of Compositors, founded in Sydney. It, and a similar organization of carpenters and joiners in Melbourne, faced two ways. They hoped by combination to obtain better wages and working conditions from their employers and also to keep the unskilled worker from poaching on their preserves. They wanted not only a shorter working day and a higher wage but also to regulate the number of apprentices any one employer could take on and the standard of training they should receive.

These early craft unions had no political significance. They were described by H. T. Donaldson as "partly religious, partly social and partly industrial".[7] They were not unlike friendly societies with an industrial bent. They assisted unemployed members or, if one of the brethren died, helped his widow and children. After the coming of self-government there was a little lobbying and in general the eight-hour day was the rallying cry. Strikes were not unknown. Donaldson obligingly lists them for us. The first occurred in November 1829 when the compositors struck, holding up the publication of the *Australian*.

In March 1837 the *Sydney Gazette* reported a conflict between seamen and ship-owners over wages. The daily wage was at that time 3s. The men demanded 4s. The owners met and issued a statement in which they said "the demand for increase of wages does not arise from the scarcity of seamen or labourers or from inadequacy of wages . . . [but was made by] a systematic, organized body, whose intentions are not yet fully developed, but whose object, if accomplished, would materially retard the progressive advancement of our colonial marine".[8] Employers and employees were in collision for the first time as organized bodies. Strikes remained rare until the 1850s.

With the discovery of gold and consequent shortage of labour the craftsman found himself in a very strong position. He could demand a high wage—that is, high for those days—and his services had a scarcity value. With the fear of unemployment banished, the unions began to assert themselves. In 1855 employees of the Australian Agricultural Company struck at Newcastle and next year the stonemasons, who had combined in 1852, struck for an eight-hour day. This ended in compromise; working hours were reduced, but so was payment, from 15s. to 12s. 6d. a day. The compositors struck in 1858 and there were mining strikes in the same year and in 1861. During the latter strike non-union labour, in this instance sailors, was called in and there was rioting. In 1873 the iron trades were "out" in Sydney for four months and won an eight-hour day. In 1874 Sydney cabmen struck and in 1875 the militant compositors staged their third strike. In 1877 the stonemasons used the strike weapon to obtain an extra shilling a day. In 1878 it was the seamen's turn, and this time the grievance was the employment of Chinese sailors. An attitude was taking shape. Donaldson continues:

During the erection of the Exhibition Building in the Domain the carpenters engaged there struck for an additional payment of 2/- per day, on account of the extra danger that was incurred through working in the lofty tower that was being erected; the men, however, after being out only four days, returned to their work at the former scale. The strike of the Wharf Labourers occurred in 1882. During its continuance the whole of the shipping trade of Sydney was injuriously affected. In 1888 we had the Bricklayers' strike and that of the Hunter River Miners. By the latter all trade at Newcastle was paralysed, and all industries in which coal was required were seriously interfered with. Had the Mountain and South Coast Miners joined issue with their Northern brethren, the results would have been most disastrous; as it was, fears were entertained that the gas supply of Sydney would have to be discontinued, and in consequence of the experience of this Strike the Australian Gaslight Company altered its form of contract so as to be relieved from the obligation to supply gas during the continuance of any strike in the coal trade. It is hoped that the appointment of the Hon. E. Barton, Q.C. as arbitrator will render future strikes unnecessary.[9]

Such was the prelude to the Labour resurgence in the 1890s. According to Donaldson there were at the turn of the century about 25,000 unionists in New South Wales in seventy-six "societies". Unions were, he opined, a Good Thing.

We . . . have sufficient faith in them to believe that they will not in the future abuse their strength any more than in the past, but will continue to discharge their duties not only honestly, but legally, legitimately and peacefully, and thus will help to solve the most crucial question of our day—the reconciliation of Capital and Labour—

And build the road for the bannered march of Crowned Humanity.

These were the days of hope and confidence when prosperity was strong enough to raise all classes above want so that there was little or no social acrimony. Trade unions were like any other mutual benefit societies and the law did not trouble itself with them. The only statute applying to them in New South Wales was the Trade Union Act (1881) which made registration voluntary and protected the funds of the union; Victoria passed a similar act in 1884. The other colonies followed.

As early as 1879 a conference of trade-unionists had been held. It transcended colonial boundaries. The second congress in 1884 was more political in tone and advocated payment of members of Parliament, the first step towards Labour representation in Parliament. There was still no Labour Party. It is true that in 1875 the trade-union vote had elected a member to Parliament in New South Wales and soon after members loosely bound to the cause of trade-unionism were elected in Victoria, South Australia and Queensland.

The trade-union movement in Australia stemmed from England and was organized, not by the native-born, but by men from the British Isles who brought with them both theory and experience. For the average Australian the issue was an academic one so long as the good times lasted. He was more interested in working as his own master, particularly in the itinerant bush crafts, than in combining with fellow workers. He was too much a Jack of all trades to throw in his allegiance with any one group. The age of subsistence, barter, and reliance on the government store was still recent. An indigenous independence made him reluctant to combine.

The growth of cities and the psychology they bred, the expansion of the building trades following the influx of population in the golden fifties, both prepared the ground for trade-unionism. The boom years in which wages were high and the standard of living rose created confidence. Three crucial issues took shape; they were wages, hours, and conditions of labour, and with them a passionate resentment against cheap labour, particularly the Chinese, who might undersell the Australian workman and reduce his standard of living.

The building trade won an eight-hour day quite early in the piece, in 1855 in New South Wales, in 1856 in Victoria, and in 1858 in Queensland. South Australia followed in 1873, Tasmania in 1874, and Western Australia in 1896. Everywhere this signal victory, which at first applied to only a few trades, was celebrated annually in a public demonstration.

The Labour movement simmered in the decades between 1850 and 1890, inhibited now by patches of unemployment, now by good times which made agitation appear unnecessary. After the building trade unions came the mining unions, then the seamen organized themselves in 1874. In 1871 in Sydney a Trades Council bound the unions together and in 1879 a similar rallying point came into existence in Melbourne, and in that year an all-Australia congress was convened by the Trades and Labour Council of New South Wales in Sydney.

By 1885 fissures began to open in Australian prosperity and wages, which had been buoyant, began to fall. This threat infused new life into the Labour movement and added another facet to the impending crisis. To falling prices and financial entanglement were added labour troubles and unrest culminating in strikes and a bitterness hitherto unknown. Both employers and employees slowly realized that they would have to fight for existence and, unhappily, they did not realize that they were both falling into the same chasm of depression. Each hoped to survive at the expense of the other. Both had learnt to organize, both had built up an embattled philosophy. Internecine strife was added to the troubles Australia had to face.

The London Dock Strike was an object lesson to the Australian workers. They contributed £30,000 to the victory of their fellows overseas. (Later when the Maritime Strike was raging in Australia a contribution of between £3000 and £4000 came from England.) This was a magnificent gesture and was an index of the generous and idealistic spirit that was abroad. Although precipitated by economic circumstances the Labour movement of the 1890s was idealistic and romantic. It synchronized with a burgeoning of national culture which, because of its use of the vernacular, its earthiness, its homespun humour and its accent on the common lot of the common man, in reaction against the polite polish of the imported article, seemed to be the preserve of the little man, the worker, the potential unionist rather than of the better educated but equally Australian capitalist. A proletarian and picaresque literature in which the underdog was hero grew up. It was romantic at core rather than realistic. It gave the new and enthusiastic Labour movement an emotional background. The concept of mateship raised the struggle above a crude and simple desire for more money and shorter working hours and turned the battle into a crusade. It had, as Vance Palmer has pointed out, "less root in definite quarrels over work and wages than in the fundamental principle of unionism".

Beside the emotional impetus there was a philosophy, and imported philosophy. Henry George's *Progress and Poverty*, published in his native land, America, in 1879, hit the Australian consciousness like a thunderbolt ten years later. The theme of the book was a single tax imposed on the unearned increment of land. Nothing could have appealed more to the landless working man. Eternal prosperity could be financed, but not out of his pocket. The spell of landed prosperity was on him, but it was inverted. Those who owned land should and could foot the bill for progress. In providing labour the worker had made his contribution. When Henry George visited Australia in 1890 he received a tumultuous reception. The fourth Trade Union Congress, to which representatives came from all over Australia, espoused the Georgian doctrine to the limit. It passed a resolution: "That a simple yet sovereign remedy, which will raise wages, increase and give remunerative employment, abolish poverty, extirpate pauperism, lessen crime, elevate moral tastes and intelligence, purify government and carry civilization to a yet nobler height, is to abolish all taxation save that on land values."[10] The Single Tax programme attracted, for a time at least, many of the best brains in the country who were ready to believe in a panacea. Single Tax Leagues sprang up throughout the country.

Another book by another American, Edward Bellamy, ran like wildfire through bush and suburb alike. *Looking Backward* preached socialism and the coming of a workers' millennium. Bellamy Clubs rivalled Single Tax Leagues and both were equally indices of the optimism that informed all walks of society. The moneyed had their speculations, the workers had their ideas and ideals, the others had their new-found patriotism.

Prophets were not lacking at home. The *Bulletin,* a weekly paper founded in 1880, provided an outlet for the new awareness, the Australian way of life. It brought together and made vocal those who were reaching out towards a practical patriotism and who looked to the world about them for their inspiration and allegiance. The *Bulletin* sponsored George's economic philosophy at first, though with many others it was later to discard it.

In 1890 an outright workers' paper (which the *Bulletin* never was) was founded, the *Australian Worker,* and it was delivered automatically to every unionist, carrying argument and slogan into the home and the workshop.

More influential were two fighting journalist-agitators, William Lane and W. G. Spence. Lane was born in Bristol in 1861 of mixed English and Irish blood and, after experience in Canada and the United States as compositor and journalist, came to Australia in 1885. The new environment suited him to perfection. He was both leader and led. As a free-lance journalist he was able to tell the people exactly what they wanted to hear. He had the Irish gift of words and the energy to hurl himself whole-heartedly into a cause. Politically and philosophically he was an all-rounder, believing equally in the teachings of Bellamy, George, Marx, and Belfort Bax. Above all he believed in State socialism and set out to educate the worker through his newspaper articles, pamphlets, speeches, and debating clubs. His slogan, in tune with the prevailing optimism, was "Socialism in our time". His personal influence was very great. In 1890 he founded his own paper, the *Boomerang,* and later the *Worker* in Queensland; the latter was financed through the unions so that he was independent of advertisers. In 1889 he established the Australian Labour Federation and was leader and organizer in the strikes of 1890 and 1891.

His subsequent history is interesting. After the apparent collapse of the Labour movement in Australia he lost heart, scrapped the labour of years, and transferred his energy to a new Utopia of his own dreaming. He wrote off Australia. What he wanted was a *tabula rasa.* He found it in Paraguay where the Government, seeking population, was willing to give him a free grant of 450,000 acres with no strings to it. He formed the New Australia Co-operative Colonization Society on highly idealistic lines. Some 240 pilgrims joined him to found a new State in virgin country. They were pledged to pool their resources and live in communal equality. All children were to be wards of the state and their parents were to be their guardians. Religious differences and strong drink were alike taboo. A sum of £30,000, of which Lane himself contributed £1000, was raised, and a small ship, the *Royal Tar,* was taken up and manned by members of the society. It sailed for Paraguay on 17th July 1893. The voyage to Montevideo took three months and there was still another 1200 miles to be travelled up the River Plate to their garden of Eden. This was not accomplished without hardship and grumbling. To keep his settlement together Lane was forced to take a strong line at variance with his creed. He soon had the name of a despot. Three months had not passed before serious trouble began. Three men, bored by it all, went for a jaunt to a neighbouring village and broke their vow of total abstinence. In a word, they came home drunk. Lane took a serious and humourless view of this and expelled them from the society. This caused a rift and to carry out their expulsion he had to bring in Paraguayan soldiers. The murmurings grew louder.

In March 1894 more settlers arrived, led by Gilbert Casey. He and Lane disagreed, and all the disaffected gathered under the leadership of Casey. True to type, Lane decided on a fresh beginning and with forty-five followers and their children he set out into the wilderness to found another Utopia. The Paraguayan Government was at first unwilling to help him, but finally agreed to the new settlement, provided it contained at least seventy-two families.

Eighty-five of the original settlers had already thrown themselves on the mercy of the British Consul in Montevideo, who reluctantly repatriated them. Nobody was pleased with Lane; his ideas were troublesome and expensive. The new settlement, which he called Cosme, would have died at birth had not one of his loyal supporters, a cousin of Robert Louis Stevenson, come into a small legacy which he gave to the cause.

Cosme had its troubles. Lane went to England to recruit settlers and in his absence quarrels broke out. When he returned with a few converts he found the place almost deserted. He could not fulfil his contract with the Paraguayan Government. Hardships and the disparity in the number of the sexes discouraged even the most faithful.

In 1900 Lane himself departed, leaving his brother John in charge. The two settlements, though they persisted in a small way, lost much of their original character. Lane went to New Zealand where for a few months he earned his living as a journalist. He then returned to Sydney and founded the *Worker* newspaper. Australia was by this time involved in the Boer War and Lane's imperialist sentiments gave offence to his comrades. He returned to New Zealand and worked on a conservative paper. He had a wife and seven children to support, yet he strained every nerve to repay the money his followers had sunk in Paraguay. His story illustrates the high-flown and, alas, impracticable idealism of the early Labour movement.

William Guthrie Spence, another leader of the period, was a very different man. He was able, well-balanced, and above all practical, a robust man where Lane had been delicate, hail-fellow-well-met where Lane had exercised charm. Less showy and evangelical than Lane, his work as a union leader and politician was more enduring. He was born in the Orkneys in 1846 and came to Australia as a boy. From the age of twelve he was earning his living, mostly in the mines of Victoria. He remembered the Eureka Stockade, and with his own eyes had seen the soldiers march out against the insurgent miners. This may have brought the realities of the situation home to him, but it did not turn him into a fanatic.

Spence, from his own experience, knew the hardships of a miner's life, its dangers, its uncertainty, its poor reward. He saw that the Master and Servant Act, as it was amended in 1846, ranged the State on the side of the employer. A born fighter, he tackled the problem with his mind rather than his emotions.

In 1874 an Amalgamated Miners' Association had been formed in Victoria and three years later the Mines and Machinery Act in the same colony had regulated conditions in deep-level mines and removed many of the dangers. Times were good and with this achievement many miners felt that they no longer needed to unite. Not so Spence. He took a long view. He saw that the miners in New South Wales had been easily defeated by the introduction of non-union labour when they protested against a fall in wages. Recessions would always bring an increase in unemployment as well as a reduction in the standard of living, so that employers could be sure of a labour pool on which to draw. A strong nation-wide organization was the only protection.

In 1878 he threw himself heart and soul into the task of extending the Amalgamated Miners' Association to all the colonies and to all types of mining, whether for metal or coal. He was soon a marked man. No one would employ him, and so he became the first professional union organizer and agitator. He was remarkably successful, though he had to struggle against the innate conservatism of the miners as well as the entrenched hostility of the employers. His influence spread as far afield as New Zealand.

By 1886 he realized that his work could not stop with the mines. Many miners were also shearers, or perhaps one should say that many shearers were also miners, for shearing was a seasonal occupation. As miners they had learnt the value of unity, as shearers they became intensely critical of the bad working conditions that prevailed and the arbitrary power of the grazier.

Living conditions for shearers on the stations were often squalid and typhoid fever a very real danger. Provisions could only be bought from the station store at an enhanced price. Before he began work a shearer must sign an agreement which set out two prices. If one sheep in a pen were badly shorn or injured in any way the second, lower, price was paid on all the sheep in that pen, and the grazier or his overseer was the sole judge of bad shearing. On this clause earnings were cut to a minimum.

On 3rd June 1886 Spence formally inaugurated the Amalgamated Shearers' Union and within six months it had 9000 members. It had always been difficult to organize the nomadic, independent bush workers, but now, with falling prices, it had become a matter of urgency. There was, too, a stiffening of experienced unionists in the miner-shearers and a powerful organizer in Billy Spence.

As Professor Shann puts it: "Under Spence's leading the union, while providing 'benefits', relied rather on the power of ideas than of money, and spent freely on the education of its members in 'union principles'."[11]

These union principles included insistence on a contract drawn up, not by the employer, but by the union, and also on an iron rule of solidarity, or "mateship" as the shearers preferred to call it. Scab is a revolting disease in sheep and it was the name given to any man who took work in a shearing shed without joining the shearers' union. He was apt to receive the same treatment as the afflicted sheep. He was dipped and, worse still, he was ostracized. Such a strong public opinion was built up within the union against non-union labour that fear of their fellows became stronger than fear of unemployment. Mateship was a genuine ideal, almost a religion in the outback, but it also, in the early days of unionism, had a background of coercion. (Randolph Bedford, politician and writer, wrote a pamphlet *The Story of Mateship,* which although not published until much later gives a good but strongly partisan picture of union ethics in the 1890s.)

The solidarity that was essential to the trade-union movement coalesced with that older, deeper, natural mateship that had grown up in a hard land where to meet and yarn with a fellow human being on the track or beside the waterholes was an event of importance. The common factor that bound these two different versions of mateship together was the folk literature that was just emerging into print.

Of this time Vance Palmer writes:

> During the next few years the gospel of unionism swept like wildfire throughout the back country, carried by crusaders who were often filled with religious passion. They preached a doctrine of brotherhood among the faithful and punishment for the heretic and the scab. Soon they developed a technique of persuasion that was extraordinarily effective. Guerrillas would ride up to a shed where non-union men were working and pitch a camp just outside the station boundaries: from this emissaries sallied out at night to carry out their duties of conversion. Often it was merely a matter of talking over men who had come from the agricultural districts and knew nothing about unionism: sometimes pressure was applied by threats and violence. The organizers of those days had no doubts about the end justifying the means. They believed that refusal to join a union was treachery to the cause of the workers, and they carried an olive-leaf in one hand and a bludgeon in the other or perhaps it would be better to say a union-ticket and—whatever weapon was most effective. Spence himself was

an amiable peace-loving man and a strong believer in tact, besides as president, treasurer, and general director of the movement he could not afford to advocate violence of any kind. His plan was to conciliate the squatters in each district by posting them circulars and copies of the union rules and trying to arrange a conference, as for the refractory ones among the men he felt it was only a matter of finding the right argument or the right time. Yet he had a secret belief in the occasional usefulness of the water-cure and could tell with a chuckle of men who had become firm believers in unionism after a second ducking in the creek.[12]

In one respect the shearers were in a stronger position than the miners. Coal and ore stayed quietly in the earth whilst disputes wound to a slow settlement, but sheep had to be shorn at the proper time or crippling losses were incurred. In good times a station-owner was willing to meet the shearers rather than have his sheds idle. The union contract was accepted, but with tacit reservations. The victory of the men was a little too easy to be natural, but they did not realize that at first. The real testing time was to come in the early 1890s.

The stage was set. The bush workers were organized, they were made confident by their successes, and they had a simple, fervid philosophy. In the cities the various small separate unions were bound into a whole by the Trades Hall councils, and in Sydney after 1884 there was a strong maritime council which linked in brotherhood seamen and waterside workers. The unions and their organizers were intent on their own affairs, few of them were interested in the general financial pattern. There was a boom. Good. The worker must have his share. He wrested his prosperity from unwilling employers and he did not see why, when the bankers and financiers were caught by the ebb tide, he should give up his hardly gotten gains. Both sides were myopic.

It was only when wool prices fell seriously and signs of financial collapse began to appear that the squatters, taking a leaf from the unionists' book, united. A pastoralists' union was formed in Queensland and, still following the same pattern, linked up with other groups in a Federated Employers' Union. The members believed in their own survival as ardently as any unionist, they believed also in the importance of their contribution to national wealth. They were a compact body, they still commanded money, and since the legislators and the magistrates were largely drawn from their ranks they had not only tradition behind them but the power of the State.

The financial crisis precipitated an industrial crisis and they twined together to make ruin doubly black.

The clash was bound to come. It came from an unexpected quarter. The Marine Officers' Association had for months been asking for a conference with ship-owners to discuss their grievances. At last, their patience exhausted, they sought to affiliate their union with the Trades Hall Council. The ship-owners were profoundly shocked that men who were virtually professional officers should throw in their lot with the workers. Discipline at sea would suffer, they said. The quarrel was past repair. The officers walked off their ships in every Australian port. It was a test case and recognized as such. The Amalgamated Miners' Association struck in sympathy and the shearers, who had grievances of their own, also ceased work in September 1890. Unionists not actually on strike refused to handle "black" wool and "black" coal.

It was very nearly a general strike. Business was brought to a standstill. The real issue behind it all was the right of workers to combine in their own interest. This was legal, but it was so hedged about with restrictions as to be ineffective.

Public opinion was divided on the issue. The Chief Justice of Victoria, George Higinbotham, thought that the strikers had right on their side and gave practical expression of his opinion by making a substantial contribution to union funds. Sir Charles Lilley, Chief Justice of Queensland, agreed with him, Cardinal Moran also threw in his considerable influence on the side of the strikers on grounds of abstract justice. The general public, inconvenienced by the stoppages, on the whole blamed the men. The Governments in all colonies were unreservedly on the side of the employers. In the interests of law and order police and even the military were sent against the strikers. This was something that the men would not forget in a hurry.

Inevitably there were incidents. The strikers had their Defence Committee, the employers called a Pan-Australian Conference in Sydney. Both sides were intransigent.

The unions asked for a conference, it was refused whilst the strike continued. They offered to recruit special constables for the maintenance of order. Sir Henry Parkes, then Premier of New South Wales, refused this offer. Special constables were enrolled, but it was claimed, and generally believed, that they were drawn from a section of the community hostile to the strikers.

On 19th September 1890 the Riot Act was read at Circular Quay, Sydney, and mounted troopers charged a crowd which had collected to watch and threaten a band of owners and their supporters who "in top hats and lemon-coloured gloves" were bringing their wool, under the protection of armed special constables, to load it onto ships there. The gesture was overtly provocative and the crowd, many of them unemployed and under pressure, not unnaturally took a poor view of it. Bullets answered stones. No one was killed, but a number were injured and the situation was worsened. In Melbourne, too, troops were called out to disperse a meeting of strikers and Colonel Tom Price was reputed to have given his men the order, "Aim low, boys, and lay 'em out."

Incidents such as these, which everyone understood and which had a dramatic value, did more to create bad blood than the divergence of principle on which the trouble was founded.

In the bush shearers formed strike camps. These assemblies of men without women, many of them armed with kangaroo rifles, most of them mounted, were bodies to be reckoned with. Actually little violence took place. A few sheds were burnt; a few small communities went in fear of guerrilla bands. That was all.

The Maritime Strike, so called from its origin, raged for about three months. Some 50,000 men were directly involved, 16,000 of them shearers. Unionists in employment and outside supporters raised a fighting fund of £50,000. But the strike was doomed to failure. Spence himself recognized this. No general strike could succeed because funds would inevitably run out. To call out the shearers when they were earning good money at the height of the season was a tactical error. The dramatic gesture defeated the general object. In employment and contributing to union funds they would have been far more useful than in their picturesque strike camps, which were the Australian equivalent of the Parisian barricades.

The men could not hold out. They had wives and children to support, few had any substantial savings. Mateship was all very well, but men had to eat. It was not only Maltese labourers who were willing to work under police protection for whatever their services would bring in.

The first to strike, the marine officers, caved in and went back to work on the owners' terms. The other unions followed suit. The shearers, who had imposed union labour and the union contract on at least ninety per cent of the stations, found themselves back where they started, working once more under terms dictated by the pastoralists. Everyone was poorer and angrier. Trouble smouldered on in western Queensland, a democratic colony which had preferred to run its own unions. At Clermont and Barcaldine strike camps persisted after the movement in the south had collapsed. Ten thousand men continued their own private resistance. It was a colourful moment in history, little more. They boasted of their invincibility. They were implacable and if they chose to ride south they could take Australia and set up a republic. They flew the flag of Eureka and beneath it built a little world of their own. The Government of Queensland would not tolerate this secession. It sent soldiers and police to keep the peace and to protect non-union labour recruited in the south for the shearing. The movement collapsed. Its leaders were arrested, tried, and condemned to prison with the help of archaic statutes. The militants, like William Lane, dreamt of new beginnings under a new sky, of self-governing co-operative states in South America or Western Australia, the Golden West. Instead, the majority drifted back to work, took to droving, and scattered through the great uncaring Never Never, a legend to themselves.

V. Recovery and Adjustment

Now came the time of reconstruction and recovery. The financial depression, the bank smashes, the loss of trade and clip when most needed, the loss of wages, had brought desolation into almost every home. The bubble had burst, the fine romantic illusions of perpetual prosperity and triumphant mateship had proved delusions. The economy had to be rebuilt.

The experts were called in. Their smooth advice was to let things run their course. Time would cure all. These things ran in cycles. This was not very comforting advice.

The crisis was actually short-lived, but the following depression lingered on. Each colony had to tackle the situation in its own way. Victoria had suffered more severely than New South Wales. Her remarkable prosperity had made her the financial centre of Australia; in Melbourne hope and speculation had spiralled higher than anywhere else. She had further to fall. Her policy of protection had fostered industry whilst free-trade New South Wales was still relying almost entirely on her primary products. As the world market revived the primary producer did better than the manufacturer with his limited market. An extra dose of protection only resulted in a further slump in the Victorian revenue.

David Syme, the apostle of protection, had in the boom years become one of the most powerful men in Melbourne. He had disseminated his ideas through his paper, the *Age*. Now everyone looked to him for a solution, but all he could do was to produce a scapegoat. He picked on the Railway Commissioners, with Richard Speight, the expert from England, at their head. They were the guilty men who had caused the inflation, and inflation, by giving men false values, had led to all the other troubles, including the industrial disputes. He loosed his wrath against them in the columns of his paper, dubbing them incompetents and traitors and calling for their dismissal.

Not unnaturally, Speight brought an action for libel against Syme. It dragged on for three years and in the end he was awarded a farthing damages. This may have been profitable for the lawyers and entertaining for the public, but it did not help the cause of reconstruction.

The hour did not produce a financial or political genius, but it did produce a steady, sober, hard-working Premier, George Turner, who set to work to reconstruct the colony very much as if it had been a run-down trading company. Economy and retrenchment were his watchwords, to balance the budget his first concern. Victoria must pay off her oversea loans and live on her own income. All must make sacrifices. In 1894 he put a Bill through Parliament empowering the State to collect income-tax, a small one by present standards. By 1897 he could show a surplus, but the colony was stagnating and population was drifting away. Seventy-five thousand, it was estimated, had left Victoria, most of them for the goldfields of Western

Australia. Time, as the experts had prophesied, gradually brought back prosperity. Relations between New South Wales and Victoria, never cordial, were not improved by the set-back Victoria had received and the rather better conditions prevailing in New South Wales.

The Premier of New South Wales, Sir George Dibbs, took strong and purposeful action as soon as the financial crisis developed. He saw that the best remedy was to strengthen the banks and so avoid panic. He rushed three measures through Parliament. Firstly, he made good bank-notes by making them the first charge on the banks' assets. That is, he put local credit before the repayment of oversea loans. Secondly, the Governor in Council was empowered to make bank-notes, instead of gold, legal tender if any bank asked for this assistance. In this way he put the resources of the State behind the banks. Thirdly, the Treasury was empowered to lend money to the banks up to half the amount of the sums deposited with them in current accounts.

So strongly entrenched was the idea of private enterprise that one bank closed its doors rather than accept government help. After that the banks were forced to fall into line with government policy. Confidence returned and Sydney banks were soon transferring some of their gold reserves to Melbourne to stabilize the economy there. The world began to realize that Australia was not bankrupt after all. Cecil Rhodes, the far-seeing Premier of South Africa, led the return of capital by offering to invest his country's surplus in Australia. Of all the money, estimated at between £35,000,000 and £36,000,000, invested by England in Australia during the boom only about £3,000,000 was lost, the rest was repaid.

Sir George Dibbs by prompt action had re-established stability in New South Wales. After him came Sir George Reid, a lawyer, a *bon viveur,* a wit, who overhauled and rationalized the financial structure of the colony. It was he who established the annual budget. Money was voted by Parliament to cover the expenses of each year, that is, estimates were drawn up and provided for, and at the end of the financial year the books were closed, any unexpended money went back into consolidated revenue, and any debits were dealt with in a supplementary budget. There was no carry-over from year to year, for this had been found in the past to cause chaos and to complicate national book-keeping. The financial machinery set up by Reid was claimed to be the simplest and most effective in the world at that time.

Like Turner in Victoria, Reid resolutely refused to borrow money from overseas. For revenue he continued to sell Crown land, to collect excise on liquor, and levy a tax on narcotic drugs, such as opium. This last was instituted to control a dangerous traffic rather than to bring in revenue. Apart from this excise and duty Reid was a staunch free-trader. In this respect he followed English practice. He believed that New South Wales would attract customers for her primary products by allowing their manufactured goods to enter duty free. He believed that the home population was still too small to support industry except in a very small way. It was therefore better to concentrate the colony's energies on producing wool, wheat, and meat and to take what was needed in the way of manufactured articles in exchange from countries, particularly England, which could manufacture them far more cheaply. It is always true that commodities produced in large numbers (or mass produced) are cheaper than those turned out by expensive machinery in small numbers.

Adam Smith laid it down in his political philosophy, outlined in his book *The Wealth of Nations,* that each country should specialize in whatever it could produce best and most cheaply, the guiding principles being geographical position, climate, soil, natural resources. According to this theory, Australia, on account of her size and her distance from European markets, was a natural source of raw materials for the industrialized countries. Reid's faith in free trade, whatever its philosophy, bore fruit. New South Wales recovered quickly and became both the financial and distributing centre for Australia.

In Victoria, largely through the influence of David Syme, a different and equally defensible hypothesis was current. It behoved a country at the end of the world to be self-sufficient. Her lines of communication could so easily be cut by war or for some other reason. Victoria, compared with New South Wales, was relatively small, the volume of her primary products would not, in the nature of things, be as great. She had a large urban population and the gold-rushes had brought out men of all trades and professions. Was it not sensible then to encourage industry to supply home needs, to give employment for the great number of citizens unsuited to the bush and, indeed, not wanted there? To begin with at least, manufactures could only flourish if they were protected by a tariff from the cheaper imported article. New South Wales was a devout free-trader, Victoria a devout protectionist. If Victoria was to make her tariff wall unscalable she had to exclude goods from her sister colony as well as from overseas, and this led to further ill-feeling between the two colonies, betwixt whom jealousy and irritation had always existed.

The other colonies also effected a reconstruction, each in her own way. In Western Australia it was gold and the forward policy of John Forrest, her Premier. In Tasmania it was the export of fruit and the development of her mines, in Queensland it was cattle, and in South Australia, that most progressive little colony, it was a blend of farming and a tenacious will to work and grow.

The Labour movement had to reconstruct, too. In the early nineties the unions had been badly beaten, but something had been saved. An attitude of mind had been created and survived. A slogan was born: "mateship". Most important, within the movement there had dawned a recognition of the importance of the unskilled worker. At first the unions or craft guilds had looked on him as an enemy. Now, because of the numerical strength of the unskilled and the threat they might become to the movement if unorganized and unindoctrinated, they were received into the brotherhood of Labour.

The unionists had learnt several valuable lessons. Strike tactics could be two-edged, hurting the men more than the employer. Many turned from the drama of direct action to an agitation for arbitration, wages boards, and similar methods of righting their grievances. The bitter knowledge that the State had ranged itself on the side of the employers also seeped into their leaders' minds. The inevitable answer to this was for Labour to form a political party and fight its battles with constitutional weapons in Parliament.

Defeat was turned by the apologists into a crown of laurel. George Black, in his pamphlet *The Origin and Growth of the Labour Movement in New South Wales,* published in 1915 to mark the twenty-fifth anniversary of the formation of the political Labour Party, declaimed:

> The strike as a strike, failed, it really was a victory. The magnificent loyalty of the strikers . . . and the splendid self-denial of their martyred wives were equal in heroism to the undying deeds which are blazoned in the glowing pages of history. Out of this industrial conflict's dying embers sprang the never-since-extinguished flame of the Labor political crusade—a new fire which reached from earth almost to heaven, to re-kindle in the veins of an old and cold world the warm glow of a rejuvenated humanitarianism.[13]

That is, of course, a matter of opinion, but these are not cynical words. Men believed them, and that in itself was an important factor. The early spirit of idealism is well portrayed in William Morris Hughes's *Crusts and Crusades*, which tells with humour the story of campaigning on a shoe-string.

The idea of a Parliamentary Labour Party did not come as a thunder-clap of inspiration when direct action failed in 1890. It had been in the air for some time, but it was not feasible until the electoral basis was widened and members of Parliament were paid. In 1889 Dan O'Connor had introduced a Payment of Members Act in the New South Wales Legislature and it had become law under Parkes. In October 1890 a union leader, Robert Harris, presented the Trades and Labour Council with a definite plan. He moved two resolutions. Firstly, "That, with a view to securing the better representation of Labour in Parliament and to organize effectually all favourable to the said object, the Council deems it advisable to establish Labour Electoral Leagues in every electorate where practicable throughout the colony", and secondly, "That the Parliamentary Committees be instructed to prepare a scheme for the organization and government of the same."

These resolutions were passed and were submitted to the rank and file of the party in March 1891. They were accepted. The Labour Leagues came into existence with an annual subscription of 2s. Each league was autonomous, paying only 6d. out of every subscription to the central body to form a fighting fund.

The platform worked out for the new party is most revealing. Its first plank was manhood suffrage, without even the six months' residence condition and the abolition of plural voting. (Men with property in various districts had voted in each, thus strengthening the landed interest generally.) Next came free compulsory education, and Parkes was their man for that. Then the eight-hour day for all trades; factory legislation to ensure safety and prevent sweating; inspectors to be appointed by the unions; a group of reforms applying particularly to mining; the repeal of that old snag, the Master and Servant Act, with amendments to the Trades Union Act; the establishment of a Government Department of Labour and of a National Bank; the vigorous prosecution of irrigation and water conservation schemes; the setting up of local governments and a general decentralization policy. Well down the list came "Federation of the Australian Colonies on a National as opposed to an Imperial basis" and a voluntary defence force. The thirteenth plank was reminiscent of Henry George:

> The recognition in legislative enactments of the natural and unalienable rights of the whole community to the land upon which all must live and from which, by Labour, all wealth is produced, by the taxation of that value which accrues to land from the presence and needs of the community, irrespective of improvement effected by human exertion; and the absolute and indefeasible right to property on the part of all Crown tenants in improvements effected on their holdings.

There was an isolationist touch in the claim that all government contracts must be executed in the colony and a glance at the Chinese question in the demand that all goods made in China should be clearly labelled as such.

It was a very practical policy, for the unionist was at heart no doctrinaire, despite his flirtations with Bellamy and George. There was no declaration of the rights of man, neither was there any pronouncement on free trade and protection or any other fiscal matter. The prevailing influence was Chartist. Parkes had been a Chartist, so had David Syme, Graham Berry, and many another man making his mark in Australia. It was a class rather than a national platform and therein lay its weakness.

Curiously, in its chagrin and resentful militancy, the Labour movement chose Sir George Grey, sometime Governor of South Australia and of New Zealand, as its hero. He was a nineteenth-century liberal if ever there was one. John FitzGerald writes as an eye witness of the impact of this old and steadfast man:

The Commanding figure of Sir George Grey loomed up in this Convention [the Federal Convention of 1891]. His bold and advanced Democracy, though it was coldly received in the Convention, was hailed as a Labor evangel outside. . . . I shall never forget the scene in the Town Hall, Sydney, early in 1891, when Grey addressed an immense audience, which filled the hall and galleries and spread away into the remotest corridors and out into the adjacent streets. He was over eighty years of age then, and very feeble, so that his voice could not be heard further than a few yards from the platform, but not a soul of that great audience stirred, not a man left; they stood watching with rapt attention the frail figure and the white bearded face, knowing as they did that Grey was advocating the foundation principle of Australian Democracy—that principle which made the fortune of the Labor Party afterwards—manhood suffrage, knowing that the great aristocrat and pro-consul was the friend of Democracy. During the election, which followed soon after, the name of Grey was constantly invoked, and received always with enthusiastic cheers; while at that meeting this phrase —"They say we are leaderless, but we shall never want a leader while Grey lives"—evoked a storm of applause.[14]

In 1891 the Parkes Government fell and in the general election, vastly to their own surprise, Labour elected thirty-five candidates. At that time 144 members sat in the New South Wales Parliament.

The Parliamentary Labour Party was launched and Caucus, the power behind the party, was immediately inaugurated. It sought to strengthen the party by imposing a pledge that members would vote as a block. Issues would be threshed out outside Parliament, a vote taken, and members must bind themselves, whatever their personal opinions, to abide by the decision of the majority. This was something new. The Labour Party was out to win, it had been tempered in fire and behind it there was a strong emotional impetus. John FitzGerald, the barrister-at-law quoted earlier, writing long afterwards from the personal experiences of his youth as a compositor, speaks of "much brutal and assertive bossism which made men writhe. I have experienced it myself, and I can still feel the pang of resentment—and this resentment of the mass meant much for Unionism."[15]

Caucus was bitterly criticized, it was unparliamentary, issues were decided on a "ticket" and not on their worth as expounded in legitimate debate from both or all sides in the House. That policy had been and was being framed in private houses or clubs was not considered at all the same thing. It is doubtful if members of Parliament, except perhaps in non-party measures such as those, shall we say, dealing with cruelty to animals, have ever been won over by eloquence in the House. Debates educate the public and satisfy or dissatisfy the constituencies, but they do not suddenly change the allegiance of members on either side of the House. Nevertheless the general theory was that a member of Parliament owed his first and strongest allegiance to the voters who had elected him and in all honesty must honour the promises he had made to them. The Labour Party was revolutionary in openly claiming that members must follow the party line, no matter what their constituents thought. The answer given to this was that the party line was in the best interest of the majority.

Not all members elected in the Labour interest were willing to accept the rulings of Caucus and in its infancy a split occurred in Labour ranks. In its history there were to be many such splits.

The Parliament into which the thirty-five Labour members erupted differed considerably from any House that exists in Australia today. The party system barely existed. There were roughly two parties, the Free-traders and the Protectionists. However bitterly they might oppose one another on that issue, the members of each were drawn very much from the same propertied class. In a relatively small community personalities were important. Men were popular or unpopular because their constituents knew them and liked or disliked them for reasons quite remote from policy. The personal victory is not unknown today; in the 1890s it was far more common.

The whole structure of Parliament was precarious. There was really no immediate need to restrict the life of Parliament to three years, for its average term was no more than eighteen months. There was a perpetual political flicker, almost, you might say, a St Vitus's dance. Between 1856 and 1901 New South Wales saw thirty governments come and go. Victoria, nearly as inconsequential, had twenty-nine. South Australia indulged in forty-two, Tasmania, apparently the most stable, had only twenty, and Queensland from her separation in 1859 till 1901 had twenty-two. You can count them up for yourself in the *Australian Encyclopaedia* or in the various Government Year Books. Brian Fitzpatrick characterizes the legislation of the period as "hasty, inconclusive, *ad hoc,* amateurish".[16] The art of government had to be learnt, and with an ever-changing personnel and a somewhat capricious electorate the process was slow. As far as my knowledge goes it has never been completely mastered anywhere by any body of men, so a little uncertainty in the young Australia can be forgiven.

The Labour members entered Parliament with a more definite programme of social reform than the legislature had ever heard of before. They also had a greater measure of solidarity. But, although they had learnt to debate in their unions and Electoral Leagues, they were amateurs in all else. Above all, they calmly wiped as unimportant the question of free trade or protection. They were quite frank about it.

> Poverty, misery of every kind, lack of employment and sweating exist in both free-trade and protection countries. If that be so, how can it make any difference to the great mass of labour which fiscal policy is uppermost? Neither policy means a greater share or a fairer share of the wealth locally created or im-

ported to the hands who work for the country or a greater opportunity of access to the sources of wealth. We have come into this house to make and unmake social conditions.

So spoke one of their leaders, quoted by V. S. Clark in his *The Labour Movement in Australasia.*[17]

George Black put it even more flatly:

We have not come into Parliament for the £300 a year, but because of the £300. We are pledged not to regard in any way the fiscal questions, because those who returned us think there is no health in a merely fiscal system for those who labour either with hand or with head. The Labour Party has come into politics neither to support Free Trade nor Protection, but that Ministry that will give us what we want. . . . We expect something more than promises. The motto of the Labour Party is Support in return for Concessions. If you give us our concessions, then our votes shall circulate on the Treasury benches; if you do not, then we shall withdraw our support. But we have not come into this House to make and unmake Ministries. We have come here to make and unmake social conditions.

This manifesto well illustrates the blending of romanticism and hard-headedness which characterized the movement in its early days. Labour was to learn that money was not only the concern of those who had it, but that a fiscal policy was of prime concern to all citizens.

The Labour members and their supporters were only mildly socialistic. They were democratic and practical. The State Parliaments they entered were, by certain oversea standards, democratic also. There was no hereditary aristocracy with entrenched privileges. There were rich men eager to safeguard their interests, but the majority of them were self-made. Society was more homogeneous than in England in the nineteenth century. There were many non-unionists who were just as anxious to remedy injustice and secure fair working conditions as any labour demagogue. Professor Portus points out in his sober way: "To the existence of this block of opinion, Labour in Australia owes far more than its leaders generally acknowledge. . . . For forty years conditions were preparing in Australia which made possible the advent of Labour on the political stage."[18]

The "conditions" referred to, to quote an impeccable authority, can be summarized:

Manhood suffrage was introduced in South Australia (1855), Victoria (1857) and New South Wales (1858). Voting by ballot was established in Victoria (1856), South Australia (1856), Tasmania and New South Wales (1858) and Queensland (1859). Triennial Parliaments were instituted in South Australia (1856) and Victoria (1859). By 1890 the major portion of the Chartist programme had been embodied in the constitutions of the Australian Colonies.[19]

From 1882 Factory Acts regulating and inspecting conditions of work had been passed and in 1895 public opinion in general had been so shocked by "sweating", or unfair pressure brought to bear on piece workers, that in Victoria, where industry showed the greatest development, the matter had been taken up by the Legislative Council. As for federation, the movement was under way in the 1880s and it was, as Labour leaders insisted it should be, a domestic matter not imposed or guided by the Colonial Office. Payment of members was first enacted in Victoria in 1878 and the other colonies followed suit. Chinese immigration was restricted in the eastern colonies from 1881. Compulsory education became law in all colonies between 1873 and 1880. It is obvious then that democratic reform was well on its way before the first Labour member sat in Parliament and that many of the planks of their programme referred to a continuation, not an initiation, of these reforms.

It was thirteen years before Labour became His Majesty's Opposition, but in that time they acquired considerable power as the party of balance, giving support in return for social legislation. Their first term in Parliament was disappointing. The Labour members achieved nothing except some electoral reforms. They discovered that nothing was as easy as they had expected and that the Upper as well as the Lower House needed the education that they were so willing to give. Their second general election in 1894 found two Labour parties in the field, one willing to pledge its members to Caucus, one intent on preserving independence. The result was, naturally, a loss of power. The number of members had by now been reduced to 125 and consisted of 58 Free-traders, 40 Protectionists, 15 "Solidarity" Labour members, and 12 independent Labour members. Sir George Reid, as the leader of the Free-trade Party, was ready to treat with Labour and form a government. In the election of 1898 Labour split again, this time on the federation question, but showed an increase of seats in a smaller house. To this day many of Labour's planks have been nailed into the Statute Book by non-Labour governments.

This brief outline of the formation of the parliamentary Labour Party has been restricted to New South Wales. One test case seems sufficient, since the story repeats itself in different colonies. In Victoria the Labour Party was slower in its rise to power, yet paradoxically achieved more results in Parliament by bargaining. In South Australia the cleavage between Labour and "liberal" or "conservative" parties has always been less, and in Queensland more pronounced. In Western Australia, probably because of the miners' vote, the party has been strong from its inception, whilst Tasmania has been in the main conservative. All States have made roughly equal democratic progress.

VI. A Many-sided Decade

Life in Australia burgeoned in the 1890s. It was a time of struggle, of defeat, and of victory snatched from defeat. It had many aspects. It was a time of precipitation. Much that had been slowly evolving in the life of Australia was brought to its climax. Cleavages and unities were both strengthened in the paradoxical way of history. Brotherhood was discovered in struggle. The Labour movement brought bush and city together. In an atmosphere of conflict a federation of the colonies was worked out. A national literature, small, compact, earthy, was born. Fifty years had passed since the end of transportation. More than thirty years of self-government had begun to educate a people in the science of governing. There was confidence and there had been some very instructive failures. The curious amalgam was beginning to take shape to itself.

To many of those living at the time, and still living, none of these things were apparent. Some, like John Haslam, who wrote his *A Glimpse of Australian Life* in 1890, wrapped themselves in a cocoon of conventional morality. His chapter headings have a charming inconsequence, for example: "Political life—Railways and Road; Irrigation and Sanitation; Inter-colonial steamers—Education etc; Liquor trade—Tea Rooms etc; Wealth and its duties—Poverty etc." In the last named chapter he remarks:

> Poverty as well as wealth is found amongst us due undoubtedly to a great variety of causes; but the cases of true poverty in these colonies never shew themselves in demonstration. It quietly bears its sad lot with resignation, and many a noble man and woman have been starved out and died in these lands because they were too proud to steal and to beg they were ashamed.[20]

"And very right and proper," we can hear him say as he settled down to his enormous Sunday dinner.

He was not a hard man: "A certain amount of the prosperity some men have ought to be set apart for moral and religious duties. These are the foundation of our happiness, the moral governor of our social well being. . . . Hospitals should be supported but only for the *worthy* poor. . . ."

His financial stance, which he evidently thought very progressive, is interesting, too.

> . . . we want to dismiss the parochial notion about the national debt being wiped out by the existing generation. If we keep the interest paid on loans, touching which the security is the wealthiest place in the world, we can trust in a manly way those who will follow us to combat with the splendid heritage passed on to them, and meet the engagements of their forefathers with the wealth it will be theirs to control.[21]

It is unlikely that Mr Haslam was singular. He represented a great body of opinion against which the new life stirring in the continent had to join issue. He was worthy, satisfied, and successful, he had no taste for change and loaded all his opinions with moral sanctions. The Haslams have to be taken into account as well as the William Lanes and the W. G. Spences.

Another old-timer, E. H. Collis, in his very pleasant book *Lost Years* looks back on the 1890s as a halcyon time.

"The golden age of the middle class in Australia," he writes, "may be put roughly as between 1880 and 1910, and the nineties—despite the bank smashes of 1893—were the high noon of that day. Everything was cheap, good and plentiful, so that the cost of living was low. People whose incomes ranged from £300 to £600 a year could lead dignified lives."[22]

"We were a simple community," he sums up happily.

To anyone who is interested in an over-all picture of the 1890s in Australia I heartily recommend Vance Palmer's *Legend of the Nineties,* which is of literary as well as historical interest.

REFERENCE NOTES

1 W. Lees, *Coaching in Australia,* p. 29.
2 E. O. G. Shann, *An Economic History of Australia,* pp. 306-7.
3 *Cambridge History of the British Empire,* vol. vii, part 1, p. 367.
4 J. Haslam, *A Glimpse of Australian Life,* pp. 11-12.
5 E. O. G. Shann, in *Cambridge History of the British Empire,* vol. vii, part 1, p. 369.
6 Again, for authentic figures, see the New South Wales and Commonwealth Year Books.
7 *Sydney Quarterly Magazine,* 1889, p. 269.
8 Quoted by G. Lightfoot and J. T. Sutcliffe in *Trade Unionism in Australia* (ed. M. Atkinson), p. 49.
9 *Sydney Quarterly Magazine,* 1889, p. 274.
10 Quoted, V. Palmer, *The Legend of the Nineties,* p. 76.
11 E. O. G. Shann, *An Economic History of Australia,* p. 319.
12 V. Palmer, *National Portraits,* pp. 125-6.
13 G. Black, *The Origin and Growth of the Labour Movement,* p. 15.
14 J. FitzGerald, *The Rise of the Australian Labor Party,* pp. 14-15.
15 *Ibid.,* pp. 6-7.
16 B. Fitzpatrick, *The Australian People, 1788-1945,* p. 204.
17 V. S. Clark, *The Labour Movement in Australasia,* pp. 75-6.
18 G. V. Portus in *Australia: Economic and Political Studies* (ed. M. Atkinson), p. 165.
19 *Cambridge History of the British Empire,* vol. vii, part 1, p. 259.
20 J. Haslam, *A Glimpse of Australian Life,* pp. 120-1.
21 *Ibid.,* p. 130.
22 E. H. Collis, *Lost Years,* p. 114.

CHAPTER XVII

FEDERATION: "ONE PEOPLE, ONE DESTINY"

I. Early Proposals

The Australian colonies had always been individualists. Their origins were diverse, their capitals were widely separated from one another, and the outlook of their people, we may as well acknowledge it at once, was parochial in the extreme. The Imperial view that they were analogous to English counties found no favour locally. They were not in the least like English counties. Attempts to introduce local government bodies were long resisted with that hostility which resides in the pocket. Local government would have to be financed and it was a rare citizen who felt that it would be worth the cost. Local government could have been a first step towards union or federation, but the wish to federate grew slowly.

As early as 1847 Earl Grey, at that time Secretary of State for the Colonies, suggested federation. To his impartial gaze it must have seemed foolish and wasteful that six colonies, all situated on one island continent, racially homogeneous, all following the same course of development, all with similar interests, should not combine for the better regulation of mutual interests. At the lowest level it would mean less paper work for the Colonial Office. From the Australian point of view it would mean greater efficiency and economy.

In July 1848 Grey was writing to Governor FitzRoy in all sweet reasonableness:

> . . . the communication by land between the Districts of New South Wales and Port Phillip is already completely established; that of the latter with South Australia is becoming not inconsiderable, and, in the rapid progress of events in these advancing communities, the intercourse between them will yearly become more and more intimate and frequent. If, therefore, these three portions of the mainland of Australia should be placed under distinct and altogether independent Legislatures, each exerting absolute authority as to the imposition of duties on goods imported, the almost inevitable results will be that such differences will grow up between the Tariffs of the several Colonies as will render it necessary to establish lines of internal Custom houses on the frontiers of each. The extreme inconvenience and loss, which each community would sustain from such measures, needs no explanation; it will therefore be absolutely necessary to adopt some means of providing for that uniformity in their commercial policy

which is necessary in order to give free scope for the development of their great natural resources and for the increase of their Trade.[1]

Even this very thin end of the federal wedge was rejected. It is true that New South Wales, Victoria, and South Australia made a three-year trade treaty, but it broke down almost immediately.

Transportation had ended seven years before, the Imperial Government had it in mind to give the Australian colonies a greater measure of self-government and to lead them on to independent nationhood. The time seemed ripe to Earl Grey to outline a plan of union together with the other reconstructions; to quote his own words:

Some method will also be devised for enabling the various Legislatures of the several Australian Colonies to co-operate with each other in the enactment of such laws as may be necessary for regulating the interests common to those possessions collectively—such for example are the imposition of duties of import and export, the conveyance of letters, and the formation of roads, railways, or other internal communications traversing any two or more of such Colonies.[2]

These were very moderate and practical suggestions, but they were not welcomed. The elevation of the Governor of New South Wales as Governor-General of Australia with power to call together a House of Delegates, whose members would be elected by the various legislatures and whose expenses would be paid by a levy, on a percentage basis, on the revenue of each colony to implement these ideas, was even more distasteful.

The Committee of the Privy Council on Trade and Plantations in 1840 discussed the proposal and believed that it would help the free flow of trade. The Committee could only advise, it had no power to implement its suggestions. The idea of a loosely federated Australia had taken hold in England and in 1850 a Bill to give effect to it was sponsored by Earl Grey and was passed in the House of Commons.

It remained a dead letter. None of the colonies liked the idea and England had no intention of forcing it on them. Sir Charles FitzRoy, it is true, received a commission naming him Governor-General, together with a warning not to interfere with the domestic affairs of any of the colonies. The proposed House of Delegates was never called together. On one solitary occasion the Governor-General, at that time Sir William Denison, tried to use his influence to smooth out a tariff dispute. In 1861 the office was abolished as it was obviously a sinecure.

In Australia itself William Charles Wentworth was one of the few men with whom the idea of federation found favour. In the Select Committee of the Legislative Council of New South Wales appointed in 1853 to frame a constitution he advocated a General Assembly to handle inter-colonial matters and a proposal setting out the powers and duties of such a body was included in the Committee's recommendations. A similar Committee in Victoria made a vague gesture in the same direction.

Getting little support at home, Wentworth went to England and lobbied industriously for what was now one of his pet schemes. He worked upon the General Association for the Australian Colonies to petition the Colonial Office to bring up the federal issue again in the House of Commons and in 1857 he was instrumental in having a Bill drafted. Had it been passed it would have been no more than an enabling Act under which the colonies could band together voluntarily to handle matters of common concern. Wentworth knew his Australia, and in this Bill insisted that all members, great or small, should have an equal voice. The Colonial Office, where Labouchere now sat in Grey's place, received the suggestion coldly and nothing came of it.

In 1852 that stormy petrel, the Presbyterian divine, John Dunmore Lang, had published in London a pamphlet entitled *Freedom and Independence for the Golden Lands of Australia,* in which he outlined a Utopian United States of Australia, on the American model but much improved. Beyond a few newspaper articles it aroused no interest.

The idea of union, however, never quite died. In the mid 1850s there was a flicker of interest both in New South Wales and in Victoria. They both set up Select Committees to debate concerted action. In New South Wales a programme was drawn up and successfully presented to the Legislative Council, largely by the efforts of Edward Deas Thomson. The Victorian Committee, in which Charles Gavan Duffy was the moving spirit, recommended an intercolonial conference. This, in the vernacular, was passing the buck. No one was interested in what had been virtually a two-man movement and the leaders found that they were wasting their breath.

For the next twenty years little or no general interest was taken in any federal scheme, though in 1867 Henry Parkes was predicting "a more permanent federal understanding" than the occasional conferences forced on the colonies by practical issues.

II. The Case Against Federation

It is easy to see why the Australian colonies at that time had no stomach for union.

To begin with, they were not drawn together by the fear of any external danger or enemy.

The British Navy was supreme. No European power would dare touch one of her possessions. There had, it is true, been little flutters of alarm over the French or the Russians or the Dutch or the Spaniards, but no one feared anything more serious than a raid in war-time or an attempt to plant a colony on some uninhabited part of the long coastline. The East had not yet awakened from its long doze and no hostile action was expected from the near north.

Defence hardly existed as a motive for federation, and even if it had unity would not have made much difference in the face of a determined enemy. To this day Australia, with her long coastline, her small scattered population, and the concentration of her life in a few vulnerable cities, is indefensible. Her battles have been fought elsewhere.

Geography and history were also inimical to federation. The capitals of the various colonies were widely spaced from one another. There were physical difficulties in the path of union, well illustrated in the days when the Port Phillip district was part of New South Wales. The Government in Sydney did not understand the needs of a settlement at a different stage of development, five hundred miles distant. The coming of a measure of self-government made things worse, not better. The Port Phillip district had the right to send representatives to the Legislative Council in Sydney, but where could it find men willing and able to set aside their professions and work or leave their properties for months at a time to attend the Council's sittings in Sydney? And if men did make the sacrifice it was ineffective, because they were in a hopeless minority. The citizens of Melbourne were forced to elect men resident in Sydney to represent them.

Van Diemen's Land, too, from very early times was virtually independent, though nominally attached to New South Wales. The sea passage to the island was slow and dangerous. There was a shortage of ships. Urgent matters could not wait until they were decided in Sydney. The Lieutenant-Governor was practically a free agent from the beginning.

South Australia and Western Australia differed in their origins from the eastern colonies and looked directly to England. They were impossibly distant from Sydney. Sea routes were hazardous, overland routes were slow. There was no common centre where representatives of all colonies could gather conveniently. If any federation came into existence it must have its meeting place in one or other of the capital cities, or move from one to another in rotation.

Again, the different colonies were in different stages of development. New South Wales and Victoria were the strongest and most populous and for that reason were feared by the others. Tasmania was a pocket paradise and ranked second in seniority to New South Wales, but she was too often the forgotten island. She was loaded down with convicts, often of the worst type. Many of her most energetic sons left for the mainland as soon as they could. The horrors of the convict system and the terrors of bushranging were greater in Van Diemen's Land than on the mainland because a sturdy and prosperous middle class was slower to develop there and a state of secrecy through neglect existed.

South Australia, bounded to the north by barren lands, was agricultural rather than pastoral and differed considerably in temper from her sisters to the east. With a doctrinaire beginning, she suffered many early hardships, had a greater infusion of foreign blood, mostly from Germans in search of religious liberty, ran to small holdings instead of big ones, and was progressive but poor.

Western Australia was so very distant, so large, so thinly populated, so far behind the other colonies in development, that she hardly seemed to belong to the family at all.

Victoria and New South Wales had most in common, but they were divided by jealousy, envy, and general bad feeling, to which history continually added more fuel. To begin with, the settlement at Port Phillip was disallowed by the Government in Sydney and then, since it was a *fait accompli,* it was grudgingly accepted and constituted. It was inconvenient and against current policy to have so distant and independent a daughter. The relationship irked the future Victorians from the beginning. Her citizens had one desire, to be free of the Government in Sydney and to manage their own affairs. The phenomenal prosperity of the new settlement aroused feelings of envy in the older one. The Victorians were not only proud of their prosperity, they considered themselves superior to New South Welshmen because no convicts had ever been sent to Port Phillip. True, some ex-convicts had seeped in from Van Diemen's Land and the labour problem had been relieved by "exiles" from England, but they did not count. The Port Phillip district was pure and the rest of New South Wales was not. In 1850 the colony of Victoria was established, but the hatchet was not buried. Victorian goldfields were superior to those in New South Wales. Prosperity made the southern colony the financial centre of Australia. The policies of the two Governments not only differed, they were in conflict. When New South Wales was a free-trader Victoria had a protectionist policy and treated New South Wales like a foreigner. Victoria was chagrined by her financial collapse in the 1890s, which was more serious and handled more badly than the troubles in New South Wales. Envy changed hands. The bad feeling between the two expressed itself in many ways that today seem childish. One of its fruits was the broken gauge in the two railway systems, which was to cause so much inconvenience and expense.

All the colonies, whether or not they felt any particular rancour against one another, were very much taken up with their own domestic affairs and progress. They had little energy, money, or personnel to devote to wider schemes. They had fought to be separate. They saw little to gain from unity. They were united under the Crown, that was enough.

There was, too, a philosophy of isolation. Australia as a whole and each colony in particular wanted to work out its destiny in its own way.

They thought in terms of a new beginning. There was always the fear that "the West in halcyon calm" might "rebuild her fatal nest" on the virgin Australian soil. There was also the fear that the sometime convict colonies would contaminate those born free or that the older settlements would communicate their mistakes to the newer ones. The belief that an entirely new beginning was possible was idealistic and, in communities just coming of age, very potent.

How much better it would have been, however, if Earl Grey's proposals had been accepted or if the colonies had hearkened to W. C. Wentworth, whose scheme of federation tactfully gave equal rights to all States, great or small. But if "ifs" and "ands" were pots and pans, what would become of the tinkers?

III. The Case for Federation

A genuine indigenous move towards federation began in the 1880s, and slowly ripened in the 1890s. The *volte face* takes some explaining.

It was, of course, inevitable that some day the Australian colonies would unite. To begin with, by the 1880s communications had improved. Railways, roads, and telegraph lines had brought the capital centres closer together. There was no longer the excuse of long delays. There was increasing intercourse.

The cities were compact units, but the bush knew no boundaries. Itinerant bush workers followed their crafts wherever they took them; drovers overlanding cattle and sheep followed the seasons, seeking grass, water and markets without reference to boundaries. They carried their folklore with them. Both grazing and wheat-growing were spreading farther and farther afield. Sheep from New South Wales were feeding in Australia Felix, South Australian farmers were pioneering the Wimmera, Tasmanians, as their island reached saturation were migrating to the mainland. Gold in Western Australia drew diggers from all over Australia, as a generation earlier Victorian gold had drained population from the other colonies. The continent was losing its patchiness and being laced into a whole.

There were other more sharply outlined reasons for unity. The Labour movement was one of the harbingers of federation. In the 1880s it became clear to union leaders that victory in one colony was not enough. Longer hours or lower wages on the other side of an imaginary line would be a menace. Affiliations of unions, intercolonial conferences, a common fear of cheap imported labour and a common creed of mateship made the movement Australia wide. If one section of the community could achieve federation so could another. Employers followed their interests and united. Industrial unity preceded political unity. The latter was the more difficult, for the old jealousies remained, the lesson of give-and-take had to be learnt and there was little fervour.

There were now two powerful issues that drew Australians together. One was defence, the other was immigration.

The British Navy was as strong as ever, but the Imperial Government did not see eye to eye with the Australian Governments. The eastern colonies, most particularly Queensland, began to observe with anxiety the growing interest of European powers in the Pacific. In 1884 the Germans annexed part of New Guinea, and the French had already established themselves in New Caledonia in 1853 and were sending habitual criminals there, a matter about which Australians were not unnaturally touchy. England was interested in Europe and the balance of power. Australia was interested in the Pacific and wanted to see a stronger Imperial policy there. There were rich islands either uninhabited or peopled by black men who, whether gentle and peaceable or warlike, were equally unable to defend their land against any European power that coveted it. Australians, for reasons of defence and trade, wanted England to move into the Pacific before other nations realized its possibilities. England was reluctant to take on any more commitments. In 1874 the flag had followed trade in Fiji and a High Commissioner of the Western Pacific was appointed. His role was rather to protect the native races than to further national aims.

In 1875, under the influence of Sir Henry Parkes, the New South Wales Cabinet proposed a very definite scheme of expansion which included the taking by England

> . . . not only of the magnificent island of New Guinea, but of the islands of New Britain, New Ireland and the chain of islands to the north-east and east of New Guinea from Bougainville Island and San Christobal, the south-easternmost of the Solomon group, the New Hebrides, including Espiritu Santo, Mallicolo and Sandwich, with smaller adjoining islands, and the Marshall, Gilbert and Ellice Islands, to all of which the traffic from the port of Sydney extends.[3]

This memorandum was brushed aside by Lord Carnarvon. He saw no danger, nor did he see why England should spend money and incur risks for the sole benefit of colonies that had asked for and been given self-government.

Parkes proposed a chartered company, on the lines, one supposes, of the East India Company, to govern and exploit the territory without involving the Imperial power. It was too late in the day for this expedient. A New Guinea Colonizing Association, inspired from Australia, was formed in London, but was not strong enough to change government policy.

Australia was dissatisfied. The danger was nebulous, but it was there. Isolation was simultaneously a treasured creed and a national danger. This is not as contradictory as it sounds. What all Australians wanted was to be left alone to work out their own salvation in their own way. They would brook no interference in their domestic affairs, but they looked to England to preserve them from all threat of foreign invasion or interference. The empty Pacific was a potential danger. If only it could be turned into a vast British lake all would be well. Under the protection of the Union Jack Australian trade would flourish and the might of Her Majesty's Navy would frighten off any powers that showed signs of poaching on what Australians felt was their geographical preserve. It seemed so simple to Australians, who were on the spot, but not nearly so simple to the distant English taxpayer.

When McIlwraith, the Premier of Queensland, took the law into his own hands in 1883 and annexed part of New Guinea to save it for the Empire, all the Australian colonies applauded, but Lord Derby refused Imperial consent. The danger of German annexation and the effect it might have on the trade route through Torres Strait he declared "altogether indefinite and unfounded". Queensland, he pointed out, as the employer of kanaka labour and the focus of some very unsavoury scandals, was not the best guardian for native peoples.

In 1884, however, England moved. A slice of New Guinea centring on Port Moresby was declared a British Protectorate. Within ten days Germany was ready with her answer. Bismarck proclaimed a German Protectorate over the north coast and neighbouring archipelago, where German trade interests were entrenched. Alarm flared up throughout Australia.

Victoria, New South Wales, Queensland, and New Zealand all separately urged on the British Government a Pacific policy of annexation. United, they might have carried more weight, but as separate small voices they were, in the sweep of colonial policy, negligible.

A feeling of impotence mixed with vague alarm did much to draw the colonies together. They might not like one another, but in the Pacific they had common interests and those interests, they felt, were being disregarded.

Australia felt herself to be unique; to the British Government she was part of the Empire and came under an over-all policy. She was not a favourite child, but a headstrong one who might, through her ignorance of world politics and her ill-considered, independent action, prove a danger.

The defence of Australia was not neglected. It was considered as an integral part of Empire defence and not according to the Australian's own, naturally biased, desires. As early as 1860 Gladstone set up a Royal Commission to look into colonial defence. Another such Royal Commission sat in 1880. The general policy that emerged from these investigations and from the working of public opinion both in Australia and in England was that the Navy undertook to maintain the freedom of the seas and would be at call in the unlikely event of invasion, but that the colonies should maintain and pay for internal order and the defence of their ports. British regiments were withdrawn in 1870 and were replaced by militia.

In 1887 the first Colonial Conference was called in London and defence was one of the principal subjects for discussion. That the Conference was called at all was an important step towards co-operation between the Imperial Government and its self-governing colonies, and it did much to improve relations. At last the Australian delegates were given the over-all picture and the colonies were invited to come in as partners—junior partners, of course, but still partners. An agreement on naval defence was reached. The six Australian colonies and New Zealand agreed between them to contribute £126,000 a year for naval protection. This money was to be used to set up a squadron of five cruisers and two torpedo boats to be stationed in Australasian waters. It was part of the Royal Navy, but could not be withdrawn without the consent of the seven colonial Governments. The colonies also undertook to erect at their own expense such fortifications as an army expert from England might advise. Major General Bevan Edwards was sent out to make a strategic survey of the continent. It was clear to him, as to all succeeding experts, that so large a land mass could not be satisfactorily fortified by the small population that inhabited it and the comparatively meagre funds at their disposal. His report did little to comfort the Antipodeans. They still could not make the Mother Country see that what they feared was not immediate danger of invasion but the setting up of foreign bases within striking distance of the vulnerable Australian coast.

It was at this conference that the New Guinea question was settled by a compromise. Between them the Australian colonies were to pay £15,000 a year and Queensland, as the colony most affected through proximity, was to control but not appoint the Administrator of British New Guinea.

Australia's position in the Empire and her situation as regards defence were now clarified. The colonies knew how much and how little they could expect in the way of aid. Their relative unimportance in the general scheme had struck home. It was quite plain that for their own good they must stick together. An occasional intercolonial congress was not enough. However independent they were in domestic matters, they must present a united front to the world. The world consisted of England, whose benevolent gaze was only too likely to be directed elsewhere; the Pacific Ocean which England did not want and which was too large for the Australian colonies to exploit and too rich to go for ever unregarded; all the nations of Europe, any of whom, in the kaleidoscope of international affairs over which Australia had no control, might become an enemy, and who if they had *pieds-à-terre* in the Pacific could swoop down on

Australia or effectively cut her trade routes; and lastly Asia, whose ever increasing millions could so easily swamp the small, isolated white settlements.

Defence, then, was one strong motive for federation. Another was connected partly with defence and partly with the Labour movement. It was the question of the immigration into Australia of cheap labour. Really cheap labour was generally coloured—brown, black, or yellow.

There were some who wanted to keep Australia white for eugenic reasons, some who feared the growth of racial problems as exemplified in America and South Africa, but the main objection to the infiltration of Chinese, coolies from India, and other dark peoples, was the threat they offered to the Australian standard of living. The free artisan had experienced the competition of convict labour. That had been bad enough. It had passed, but it had alerted workers to the dangers. Coolies would be infinitely worse than convicts, for, expecting little of life, they were content to work for the lowest wages and to live and breed on the breadline.

The founders of Australia had taken it for granted that the disproportion of the sexes would be redressed by the importation of Island women. One of the advantages that Sir Joseph Banks saw in Botany Bay was "the certainty of being able to obtain abundant, cheap labour" from Asia. But the hungry years made it impossible to bring in more people from the Islands or Asia. Wool-growing required little labour, and that was supplied by convicts. Agriculture became the province of the small man, often the ex-convict, and he and his family worked the farm. There was no industry, like cotton-growing in the southern States of America, that needed much unskilled labour. More by good luck than through policy Australia was kept white in her early days.

Later, when convicts were no longer available, there were various schemes, often favoured by the squatters, to bring in Indian or Chinese coolies. Labour was almost perpetually scarce. Employers used to assigned servants felt it a great hardship to have to pay wages higher than those current in agricultural England, especially since much of the work required little skill. Railways could have been built more cheaply with Chinese labour. Aborigines, though they made fine stockmen, could not be looked upon as a reliable labour pool. Much of Australia was hot and dry—not, it was thought, a white man's country.

But public opinion was in general against such schemes. Those agitating for self-government felt that an influx of ignorant and servile labour would postpone the happy day. Those who had fought for the abolition of transportation were ready to fight a new invasion for the same reasons. The Colonial Office, which favoured emigration from England to relieve agricultural distress and unload paupers, vetoed proposals of this nature.

The man in the street did not like the idea for a complex of inarticulate reasons in which patriotism, insularity, fear for his job and his wages, and distaste for working side by side with members of races he looked on as inferior, were inextricably mixed. India proudly refused to let any of her people go to be servants in a foreign land. Theoretically China did not export labour either, but a little bribery and manipulation could overcome that obstacle.

It was not until gold was discovered in Australia that Asiatics were attracted in any numbers. Then they came in hordes. Some of them were adventurers in their own right, but the majority were servants sent by Chinese capitalists to mine for their masters in return for a very small wage. They were soon extremely unpopular on the goldfields, for reasons already canvassed. From the point of view of the Government the Chinese miners were unprofitable. They drained wealth out of the country whilst making no contribution to its development. Between July 1856 and June 1857 it is estimated that 116,903 ounces of gold worth over £500,000, was exported to Canton. There was no export duty on gold, so this was a dead loss.

In seven years between fifty and sixty thousand Chinese arrived. They could never be counted as citizens. There was, in any case, no machinery for naturalizing Chinese. They returned to China with the gold they won, except for a few who stayed on to become market gardeners or station cooks.

In 1853 there were two thousand Chinese in Victoria. The first anti-Chinese riot occurred at Bendigo in July 1854; by 1855 the number had increased to ten thousand. A Royal Commission on Gold Fields that year recommended a restriction on immigration. No ship might carry more than one Chinese for every ton burthen, and a poll tax of £10 was extracted on landing. They had also to pay a tax for every year they stayed in the country.

It was difficult to implement these clauses. When Victoria tried to control their entry the Chinese disembarked in Sydney and border-hopped. In one year, 1857, nearly fifteen thousand landed in South Australia and from there made their way to the goldfields.

There were more anti-Chinese riots. In 1855 the Chinese were driven off the Buckland River goldfield, robbed of all they had, and their tents burnt. From then on the trouble was endemic. Protectors were appointed to shield the Chinese from the ill-will of the white diggers, but it is doubtful if they brought much enthusiasm to their unpopular task.

It was obvious that Victoria alone could not control Chinese immigration. In 1857 South Australia passed a restrictive Act similar to the Victorian one and in 1858 New South Wales tried to do likewise, but the Act failed to pass the Upper House. Discouraged from staying in Victoria,

Chinese began to pour into New South Wales. In 1861 there were 21,000 of them, or one in sixteen of the population, on the New South Wales goldfields, and rioting took place at Lambing Flat. In the November of that year the Chinese Immigration Restriction Act was passed and the influx stopped. In 1863 only sixty-three Chinese arrived.

These restriction acts embarrassed England, who at the time was making a treaty of friendship with China. It was against Imperial policy to discriminate against any particular nation. The danger being past, the three colonies repealed their legislation. But when gold was discovered in Queensland was more alarming than it had been in the south because By 1877 there were 17,000 Chinese on the Palmer goldfield. The situation in Queensland was more alarming than it had been in the south because the white population was smaller. The Chinese population reached the ratio of one in ten. The ten included women and children, whilst the Chinese were all adult males.

Queensland tried in 1876 to put through a Gold Fields Act which was in reality an Act restricting Chinese immigration, though to soften the blow "African aliens" were included. It was a ticklish moment. The Convention of Peking was sitting and the Act was most distasteful to the Home Government. Royal assent was refused. Queenslanders were furious. The Secretary of State for the Colonies tried to be soothing. He pointed out that the Chinese could be very useful in tropical agriculture. "Penal legislation," he pointed out, was hurtful to African and Asiatic subjects of the Empire. Their immigration might be regulated, it must not be prohibited.

In the face of such interference with her domestic affairs Queensland appealed to the other colonies for support, talking of "the community of Australian interests". Victoria rallied to her side, New South Wales expostulated with the Imperial Government but was ignored, South Australia was content to sympathize only.

The Bill was re-presented in 1877 with "any person" substituted for "Asiatic and African aliens", but including the same heavy taxes on Chinese. A clause by which the entrance tax was refunded on departure was included as an inducement to go home. This Bill became law and the numbers of Chinese began to fall. Between 1877 and 1888 only five hundred Chinese entered Queensland. It was not until 1880 that the Home Government agreed to treat immigration as a local matter for the colonies.

The flood had subsided, but the trouble was not over. In 1878 the Australasian Steam Navigation Company began to employ Chinese crews. They paid each man £2 15s. a month instead of the £8 they had to pay a white seaman. The Chinese crew members were brought to Sydney for use in the Queensland coastal trade. This was too much. Australians refused to work with the underpaid Chinese. Seventeen ships were tied up. Coal-miners refused to supply fuel for ships with Oriental crews. Support came from the workers in all colonies; a strike fund was opened and generously supported. Fifteen thousand people signed a petition to the Queensland Government asking it to withdraw its subsidy to the steamship company. There was no doubt that Labour throughout the continent stood firm on this issue. The last Chinese crew was discharged in 1882, a slow-motion result, but a victory just the same.

The first Intercolonial Trades Union Congress was held in 1879, in the heat generated by the strike. If the defence issue smouldered, the Chinese issue flared. It must always be remembered that the strong feeling engendered was not racial, it was primarily against the underselling of labour and the threat to standards of living.

In the early 1880s the influx of Chinese again caused alarm, and not only in Labour circles. Outbreaks of smallpox and leprosy frightened the general public. Statistics showed that more and more Chinese were arriving. In the census of 1871 there were 7200 Chinese in New South Wales, or 1 in 70 of the population. In 1880 of every 55 people one was a Chinese. In 1881 in all Australia it was 1 in 50, or 50,000 adult male Chinese in a mixed population of two and a half million. One of the reasons for the rising numbers was that the United States and British Columbia were now restricting their intake of Chinese. It was rumoured, truly or falsely I do not know, that China was quietly transporting her felons to Australia.

At the end of 1880 Sir Henry Parkes called an intercolonial conference to discuss the danger. As a result every colony except Western Australia agreed on a common policy. New Acts restricting immigration on the old lines were enacted by each legislature. Queensland's was the most stringent Act. Ships were allowed to bring in only one Chinese for every 50 tons burthen and a poll tax of £30 was extracted from every would-be migrant on landing. This colony was particularly nervous because the ban did not apply to the Northern Territory, where the labour situation was such that Chinese and other Asiatic workers had to be admitted. True, they were prohibited from leaving the Territory, but some were sure to drift east or south.

By 1886 Western Australia thought better of her policy and came into line. She saw Chinese flocking to her goldfields and establishing monopolies in her pearling industry.

For the moment the Home Government took no notice, though the restrictions applied to Chinese who were British subjects as well as to others.

In the late 1880s the situation worsened. "Australia for the Australians" had become a popular slogan and people began to talk about "the yellow peril". Policy went beyond restriction of immigration; many wanted Chinese excluded altogether. All eyes were turned resentfully to the Northern Territory. Thousands of Chinese migrants flocked thither, ostensibly to work on the railway but more often to fossick for gold or for rubies in the MacDonnell Ranges. There were at that time only about seven hundred white men in the Territory. They panicked. Vessels from China were quarantined and Chinese residents were restricted to a radius of twenty miles round Darwin so that officialdom could keep track of them. Finally Darwin was closed to new arrivals and those already on the sea were diverted to Queensland ports.

There were rumours of a conspiracy, sponsored by the Chinese Government, to infiltrate her nationals into Australia and swamp the white population. Numerous cases of illegal entry were discovered, stowaways, forged papers, or the use of one genuine certificate by tens or even hundreds of compatriots.

To Australia's fear that her standard of living would be lowered was added fear of extermination or worse.

A good deal of this was "paper talk", but the alarm it aroused was genuine. It was not only Labour supporters now who feared the Chinese, it was that powerful, anonymous person, the man in the street.

An international situation was working up over the ever more stringent action to exclude Chinese. China resented what she felt to be, not unnaturally, an insulting discrimination against her nationals. In May 1887 a Commission was sent to Australia to investigate the position of Chinese there. Its findings were not as lurid as they might have been, but the Chinese Ambassador in London made a formal protest, pointing out that a poll tax on one set of migrants was contrary to international law and that Great Britain, through the action of Australia, was breaking her treaty obligations.

A harassed Secretary of State for the Colonies, Lord Knutsford, asked Australia to be at least a little more tactful and suggested limitations on migrants from all foreign countries with a clause attached giving discretionary power to suspend them. The Australian Governments pointed out that European migrants were not only welcome, they were necessary for the survival of the vast but still thinly populated continent. Such legislation would frighten them away. A quota system was repugnant to public opinion also, for it would mean a regular intake of unwanted Orientals. Besides, few Australians felt any desire to placate China. Had not the Chinese taken advantage of the simple Australian and by every wile and trick abused the country's hospitality, shipped away her wealth, and foisted on her clean population filthy Oriental diseases? There was considerable anger against the mother country because she appeared to favour aliens above her own flesh and blood, because she gave no support to a policy on which Australia's very existence now seemed to depend. The best they could hope from her was that she would take no notice.

Angry public meetings, deputations to Parliament, and Press campaigns both expressed and whipped up public opinion. In New South Wales the Lower House passed a Bill excluding all Chinese. The Council hesitated to ratify it, the Supreme Court declared it illegal, but an appeal to the Privy Council brought the welcome assurance that Australian citizens had the right to admit or debar whomever they chose.

In June 1888 another Intercolonial Conference was called to consider the danger. The Home Government was invited to send delegates, but in its maddening way refused to do so. The colonies decided on uniform legislation. The moderates secured the dropping of the poll tax, but only one Chinese for every 500 tons burthen was allowed to enter the country in any ship. This was virtually exclusion. It was also made an offence for a Chinese to move from one colony to another. The Home Government was asked to take up the matter diplomatically with China and try to win a voluntary undertaking to forbid emigration to Australia except for students, merchants, travellers, and officials, all of whom would be birds of passage; also that Crown Colonies, such as Hong Kong, should be forbidden to sanction Chinese emigration to Australia.

Diplomatic negotiations were opened, but in Australia public opinion was out of control. Even while the talks were proceeding new measures were taken against the Chinese, and the Chinese Government refused to come to terms.

The day was saved by the shipping companies. Their object was profit and they found that bringing Chinese immigrants to Australia landed them in endless trouble and frequent loss. Regulations were always being changed. They might set out in good faith with a cargo of migrants only to find it illegal to disembark them. They gave up. The yellow tide began to recede once more. In 1888 there were nearly 50,000 Chinese in Australia, in 1901 they had dwindled to about 32,000.

Nevertheless a White Australia Policy was to be one of the main planks of federal policy when at last the Commonwealth came into being. Its history has been told at some length here, rather than in the chapter on immigration, because it was this issue that fused the separatist and jealous colonies into a whole. It began as a party issue, it became a national one. It had a bread-and-butter basis, it acquired an emotional content. Wrath against England for her half-hearted support was nearly as great as wrath against the Chinese who were stealing the Australian heritage. Fear and anger were greater than petty jealousies. It was obvious to all that six colonies acting as one were stronger than six guarding their independence of action. The very fear that one colony might let down the rest drove them towards unity.

Although public opinion as a whole was in favour of excluding Chinese immigrants, there were always sections of the community who, for economic reasons, wanted some form of cheap labour. The growing of sugar in Queensland, experimentally from 1843 and on a commercial basis from 1862, required more labour than the cattle industry. Cane-cutting was not considered a white man's job. The planters were willing to employ coolies, especially Indians. In 1862 an Act was passed in the Queensland legislature permitting the entry of Indians under the system of controls demanded by India. The scheme did not prove workable and kanakas from the Islands were employed instead. They were indentured labour, to be employed for a certain time only and then repatriated. Their recruiting was often not of the gentlest and some very damaging scandals reached the outside world. In 1884 the kanaka system collapsed and a fresh bid was made to bring in labour. The unions had something to say about it, and the Queensland Government refused permission to planters to import their labour "privately". The planters then agitated for separation. It is symptomatic of the greater sense of unity abroad that no one outside Queensland would tolerate the idea. It was undemocratic, and a planter State was almost sure to be a good imitation of a slave State, or so the majority of Australians felt. The plan, though taken out and dusted now and again, has not made much headway.

The Northern Territory was also considered too hot for the white manual worker. For many years Chinese, Japanese, and Malays infiltrated into the Territory, and up to 1890 various efforts were made to bring in Indians. This failed because India insisted on safeguards and the planters wanted the Government to shoulder the expense and the risk of admitting the coolies. In fact the Government—the Government of South Australia at that time—was expected to maintain a labour pool from which the planters could draw and to which they could return the workers when no longer needed.

Western Australia, by reason of its size and its late start, was in perpetual need of labour for development. It tried convicts after transportation to the rest of Australia had ceased. It found itself unpopular with the other colonies. It admitted Chinese coolies in small numbers and again the timing was wrong. Too many Chinese came; Western Australia took fright and joined in the move for exclusion.

During the 1890s the battle to keep Australia white continued. It had become a habit. By 1893 all the stragglers amongst the colonies had been converted. In March 1896 there was yet another Intercolonial Conference on the subject. The Japanese had now become a source of anxiety, especially in the north, and the Anglo-Japanese Commercial treaty of 1894 made action against them unpopular with the Imperial Government. The size and variety of the Empire was in itself an embarrassment. It was most unfortunate that throughout the long immigration dispute the accent was laid on colour. Restriction and Regulation Bills could not fail to antagonize India and other British possessions and to harass Secretaries of State who were endeavouring to weld the Empire into a whole.

Without the White Australia Policy Australia must some day have federated. It was logical, it was inevitable, but there had to be some one issue that appealed to the average citizen in all colonies to bring it about. The actual framing of federation proved a very ticklish business, for each colony wanted to keep her cake and eat it.

IV. Conventions and Referendums

The story of the manoeuvres that actually led up to the establishment of the Commonwealth is not a very exciting one. It tells of a series of conferences and conventions, of wrangles, public and in camera, over State rights, of elder statesmen expressing fine sentiments and each in turn claiming to be the only begetter of the federation.

The movement that led on to victory began perhaps in 1870, when the Victorian statesman Charles Gavan Duffy called together a Royal Commission to consider some sort of federal union. Some platitudes were uttered and it was generally agreed that union was desirable, preferably a voluntary one of two or more of the colonies. Nothing definite proceeded from the Royal Commission.

The real trouble, apart from apathy, was the wide divergence of the fiscal policy of the two leading colonies. New South Wales stood for free trade, Victoria for protection. The smaller colonies ranged themselves more or less behind Victoria. A few feeble attempts at customs unions fell through. Downing Street was raising its hands in despair over those troublesome children "down under" who complicated Imperial policy and international trade by their whims and fancies. The cleavage was very real in Australia.

Ten years drifted by and Sir Henry Parkes took a hand. At a conference in 1880 on the evergreen problem of intercolonial customs duties he proposed the establishment of a Federal Council. This was to be a "non-party measure". It was to deal with certain matters of common interest, but above all it was to educate the people at large in the theory of federation. To use the idiom of another age, it had no "oomph", it was attached to no burning cause, it was not linked to any issue of national importance. The Federal Council came lazily into the world; a Bill was framed in 1881, it was amended at another conference in 1883, and finally in 1885 the Federal Council Act was passed by the Imperial Parliament. The mountain had brought forth a particularly timid little mouse. It had no powers, legislative or executive, it could only squeak its advice. No one took much notice and New Zealand turned her back on the scheme altogether.

The Naval Agreement of 1887 in which all the colonies joined, seemed to bring federation a step nearer, and Sir Henry Parkes, taking advantage of the rapprochement, made his famous after-dinner speech at Tenterfield on

24th October 1889. His commonsense attempt at federation in 1880 had been a failure, now he appealed to emotion and to the growing sentiment of patriotism. He did not mention fiscal policy, but he touched on defence and the unification of the railways.

> Believing as he did that it was essential to preserve the security and integrity of these Colonies that the whole of their forces should be amalgamated into one great federal army, whenever necessary,—feeling this, and seeing no other means of attaining the end, it seemed to him that the time was close at hand when they ought to set about creating this great national government of all Australia. . . . As to the steps which should be taken to bring this about, a conference of the Governments had been pointed to, but they must take broader views in the initiation of the movement than had been taken hitherto; they must appoint a convention of leading men from all the colonies, delegates appointed by the authority of Parliament, who would fully represent the opinion of the different Parliaments of the colonies. This Convention would have to devise the constitution which would be necessary for bringing into existence a federal government with a Federal Parliament for the conduct of national business. . . . He believed that the time had come . . . and they would have an uprising in this fair land of a goodly fabric of Free Government, and all great national questions of magnitude affecting the welfare of the colonies would be disposed of by a fully authorised constitutional authority, which would be the only one which could give satisfaction to the people represented. This meant a distinct executive and a distinct parliamentary power, a government for the whole of Australia, and it meant a Parliament of two Houses, a house of Commons and a Senate, which would legislate on all great subjects. The Government and Parliament of New South Wales would be just as effective as now in all local matters, and so would be the Government and Parliament of Queensland. All great questions would be dealt with in a broad light and with a view to the interests of the whole country.[4]

It is difficult to recapture now the electric effect of these words. It seemed that Athene had sprung fully armed from the head of Zeus.

In November of the same year Parkes was making another spirited speech, this time at St Leonards.

> He proposed no makeshift measure—no initial step, but he said, in the face of all these Australian colonies, in the face of England and the world, that the time had come when Australia would gather herself together as one great commonwealth, under one flag and one Government. (Loud applause) He proposed to establish the machinery for the perfect government of Australia. Were they prepared for it? . . . Were they not prepared, with this enormous line of coast, this magnificent territory, and this brilliant number of intelligent men and women and fast-growing children. (Loud applause) Not prepared! They were prepared for any emergency which could arise. There was nothing in the shape of national life for which they were not prepared, and, as their objects were of a peaceful and law-abiding nature, and in harmony with the civilisation, the progress, and the intelligence of the world, what had they to be

afraid of? And what was there which could induce them to hesitate and hold their breath whilst they were on this grand road to nationality? (Cheers) He said nothing about their great cities, but was it not the case that every visitor who came to these shores, however intelligent and acquainted with the civilized world, was simply amazed at the splendour of Melbourne, Sydney, Adelaide or Brisbane. These were cities which could bear a high place in any civilized country of Europe, or in any State of the American Republic. These cities were an evidence of the hardihood, the enterprise, and the intelligent energy for progress of our people. Were not their young men equal to the young men of any country in the world? (Applause) . . . He said that the time was not only near, but the time had come. The scheme which he proposed was, as he had just said, a complete system of Federal government. It must be founded in the light of the teaching of Canada and the United States (Applause). There was no doubt whatever that the great founders of the Constitution of the United States copied its principles from the British Constitution, and there was no doubt whatever that the very able men who engaged in the federation of the North American colonies had before them constantly the example of the United States and the example of England.[5]

The veteran statesman knew how to touch the springs of pride and emulation. Behind the scenes the mood was not as high-pitched and amongst the people the effect of oratory was evanescent.

A Premiers' conference did meet the following February in Melbourne to discuss the substance of Parkes's plan. It was an anticlimax. Vance Palmer has described it:

. . . it was in an atmosphere of strain, with employers and unionists making ready to try their strength, that the representatives of seven colonies (including New Zealand) met for a Federal Conference in Melbourne during the hot February of 1890. There was an element of unreality about the gathering. Nothing seemed further from the minds of the elderly politicians involved than the subterranean conflict that was going on in the community. They held their inaugural banquet, which was garnished with the usual flowers of oratory; their debates were reported at great length in the press; concern was felt about the health of Sir Henry Parkes, the lion of the occasion, who had to spend a good deal of time on his back at Menzies Hotel. At the week-end they repaired to the Dandenongs, where they could find some relief from the Melbourne heat in the tree-fern gullies.

But in spite of the vast publicity given to the Conference, its proceedings left a sense of emptiness. The public mind just then was concerned with other things than federation.

"The cautious and measured enthusiasm at first created," said the *Bulletin*, "has been replaced by an indifference too intense even to be critical, and in spite of the frenzied efforts of political boomsters no new interest can be evoked."[6]

Of Parkes, the *Bulletin* wrote:

The old man doesn't feel well. He knows how meaningless is ninety-nine per cent of the talk in which he must feign an absorbed interest. Sometimes he relaxes his cramped hand by pottering to the table and pretending to hunt for papers in a red-covered box. He has put no papers in the box and he takes none out of it. Emblematic of the conference is that red-covered illusion. Quite empty.[7]

The time had not come and would not come for another ten years.

Another conference was called for 1891. It was described by Parkes as "memorable" and "the most august assembly which Australia has ever seen". It drew up definite proposals for federation and presented them to the colonial Parliaments. They pleased no one, least of all Sir Henry Parkes, still Premier of New South Wales at the age of seventy-six.

The proposals laid down by the 1891 Conference were mild and tentative. Defence, of course, should be a federal matter. Few would disagree with that. There should be free trade between the colonies, and the new government, if formed, should control customs duties. That could be construed as both a victory and a defeat for protectionist Victoria. It would mean that New South Wales must abandon, or lie in danger of abandoning, her free-trade policy, and it also meant that dutiable goods might seep free of charge into Victoria from the other colonies. Above all the conference emphasized that the sovereign rights of the colonies should remain intact.

Two types of federation, or union, were open: one in which the States delegated certain definite functions to a central body, the other in which the power rested with the Commonwealth and duties were delegated to the States. There was no doubt which model Australia, like the United States before her, would choose.

The actual form of the government-to-be was dictated by precedent and tradition. It should be bicameral, a House of Representatives, elected on a population basis and a Senate, also elected, but in which each State was equally represented. So far, so good.

Outside the Parliaments there were some enthusiasts. New South Wales had its Federation Leagues and in Victoria the Australian Natives' Association campaigned for federation.

Conferences had become a habit. The one held at Corowa in 1893 produced a new approach. It was decided there that the parliament of each colony should be asked to pass an enabling Act to set up yet another conference, composed this time of elected representatives. This convention would then try its hand at framing a federal constitution, such constitution to be submitted to the people at a referendum. This proposal did much to conciliate the Labour vote, hitherto suspicious that something was going to be "put over" under the cloak of federation. Any constitution that emerged from this plan would be truly democratic.

Parkes had lost the centre of the stage; his quarrel with Edmund Barton as to which of them had done most for federation detracted from the fine sentiments he expressed on the platform. In Victoria Alfred Deakin had become the chief advocate and his work eclipsed anything done in New South Wales.

Parkes had been a man of the people, an ex-Chartist who had come to Australia in 1839, tried various trades ranging from toy-making to journalism, and had entered politics through the anti-transportation movement and the influence of Robert Lowe. Alfred Deakin was born in Melbourne in 1856 and, though a barrister by profession, had turned first journalist and then politician. He became known as the sponsor of irrigation schemes. Patriot and idealist, he threw himself whole-heartedly into the cause of federation. Far less the demagogue than Parkes, Deakin had a more abiding influence, for his honesty and sincerity were never questioned and he did not embroil himself in quarrels arising out of jealousy. His most important work was done after the establishment of the Commonwealth up to his death in 1919.

Another leader of the federal movement was Edmund Barton, born in Sydney in 1849, trained to the Bar but seconded to politics. His distrust of Parkes drove him into the opposition led by Sir George Dibbs. Like Deakin he was present at the 1891 conference and was one of the architects of the abortive constitution which arose out of it. He is said to have made three hundred public speeches in three years in support of federation. He was a little too academic to appeal to popular audiences, but he did inspire a number of disciples in the universities. Like Deakin, he was above reproach, his enthusiasm was genuine and his contributions as a lawyer to the Constitution, when it was actually framed, were invaluable.

Parkes has had his say in *Fifty Years in the Making of Australian History* (1892) and Deakin in *The Federal Story, 1880-1900* (1944), both of which are well worth reading. Barton is represented mainly by reports of his public addresses. George Reid was a late recruit to the movement, but a weighty one!

The names of Samuel Griffith of Queensland and Charles Cameron Kingston of South Australia should also be honourably remembered.

The financial collapse of 1893 had convinced many people, in a painful way, that the colonies were not as strong as they thought they were. Federation might give greater stability. The idea was seeping into public consciousness from many directions.

At a conference in Hobart in 1895 it was George Reid, one-time enemy of federation, who gave the keynote: "that this conference regards federation as the great and pressing question of Australian politics". The conference went on to adopt the proposals of the Corowa conference of which Dr Quick of Bendigo had been the moving spirit. (It is interesting to remember that this conference at Corowa had not been a meeting of politicians but of representative citizens eager for action.) An enabling Bill was framed and submitted to each of the colonial Parliaments. After delays caused by the greater urgency of local issues New South Wales, Victoria, South Australia, and Tasmania passed the enabling Acts. Western Australia wanted to be different, but eventually drew up her own enabling Act. Queensland alone stood out and the other colonies at last decided to proceed without her.

The elected representatives met in March 1897 in Adelaide. The electors showed their approval of federation by sending to the convention men, like Barton, who had been its strong and consistent advocates. Kingston was elected president and Barton leader of the convention. The blue-print of 1891 was in the main accepted, but there were still many points to be hammered out. The main division was between the strong colonies and the weak ones—that is, from the point of view of population. Equal representation of all States in the Senate was all right, but how much power would the Senate have? If both Houses were equal the new Australia could look forward to a series of deadlocks. Tradition founded on the House of Commons gave the power in all Bills involving appropriations and taxation to the House of Representatives. A compromise was reached and the Convention divided into three committees to prepare the Bill which would be submitted to the electors before being sent to the Imperial Parliament for ratification. To the layman all this may seem slow and cumbersome, but the issue of federation was of the utmost importance. The united nation must be built to last. Many of the delegates were constitutional lawyers, only too aware of the pitfalls of a constitution hastily thrown together. Everything had to be thought of and a workable compromise arrived at that would satisfy the highly individual and suspicious members.

The Convention had consisted of ten delegates, a workable number, and the most important committee, the constitutional committee, of three. On 22nd April the Convention adjourned whilst the Bill was submitted to the various Parliaments. Storms followed. There were differences of principle, disagreements on points of law, and the old latent jealousies.

It was not until January 1898 that the draft with its criticisms and amendments went back to the Convention. After two months of hard work the Bill was ready for the referendums.[8]

The referendum in New South Wales was a very real hurdle. Here, but not in the other colonies, a majority of 80,000 was required before the referendum could be deemed to have passed. The Premier, Sir George Reid, was lukewarm. He did not give the people a lead. He himself said publicly that he would vote "yes", but there were "serious blots" on the Bill and all voters should settle the matter for themselves. It was from this advice that he earned the sobriquet, "Yes-No" Reid. He well knew that there was a strong opposition to federation in the mother colony and he did not want to lose votes.

The vote was taken in June 1898. Victoria, South Australia, and Tasmania accepted the draft Constitution. In New South Wales there was a majority in favour, but not a sufficient majority. In every colony a great many citizens were too apathetic to vote at all. In the general elections in New South Wales in that year federation was the burning question. Reid went to the polls as the Liberal Federal Party, and the Opposition, led by Barton, called itself the National Federal Party. There was a wide gulf between them.

Reid scraped home, called another convention, and secured some amendments to the draft Constitution.

This necessitated new referendums (federation was proving expensive). On this occasion, in 1899, all the colonies including Queensland but excepting Western Australia, approved the Constitution.

It had now to be submitted to the Imperial Parliament, and a delegation, headed by Barton, carried it to England. The Secretary of State for the Colonies, Joseph Chamberlain, was not wholly enamoured of it. To him the Empire came first and it appeared that Australia reserved too much to herself, thus impinging on the Queen's prerogative. He asked for five amendments, amongst them one which made the Crown the final arbiter of legislation in the Commonwealth as it had been in the colonies. In conference both sides were stubborn. The Australian Premiers, appealed to by Chamberlain, said in effect that the Constitution was no affair of theirs, it was the expressed will of the majority of the people.

By this time Western Australia was willing to join the movement, with certain reservations, and New Zealand asked leave to come in as an original member at some unspecified future date.

The Australians received unexpected support from the House of Commons when the Bill was presented, rather reluctantly, by Chamberlain. It passed both the Commons and the Lords with the minimum of amendment and received Royal assent on 9th July 1900. The Queen bestowed the pen, ink-stand, and table used on this occasion as mementoes to the Commonwealth.

V. The Federal Constitution

The Imperial Act which gave birth to a united Australia was called simply "An Act to Constitute the Commonwealth of Australia". It was proclaimed on 17th September 1900.

It provided for a Governor-General, appointed in England, to represent the Queen and to give, in her name, the Royal assent to the Acts of the Federal Parliament; for a Senate in which each State was equally represented by elected members; for a House of Representatives whose numbers, elected on a population basis, would always be adjusted to equal double the number of senators (this was to prevent it from becoming too large with increasing population and therefore unwieldy); and a High Court.

The Governor-General is the head of the executive power of the Commonwealth. He opens, prorogues, and dissolves parliaments, gives the Royal assent or, if he thinks fit, may reserve legislation for ratification in England. Like the Queen, he acts on the advice of his Ministers, and instances of independent action in what he conceived to be the interests of the people at large, the mother country, or the Empire, have been few. His social influence as head of the State is great.

Under the Governor-General comes the Cabinet, which originally consisted of the Prime Minister, Treasurer, Attorney-General, Postmaster-General, Vice-President of the Executive Council, Ministers of the Interior, Defence, Public Works and Railways, Trade and Customs, etc., and generally two Ministers without portfolio. Under the Ministers and responsible, through their under-secretaries, to them are the various government departments. The executive power carries out the enactments of the legislature.

In the *Official Year Book of the Commonwealth of Australia*, No. 37 (pp. 76-86) there is given a complete list of Commonwealth Government departments, their functions and the Acts they administer.

The legislature, as we have seen before, is bicameral. The Senate is composed of six representatives from each State. For the election of senators each State is regarded as a constituency. They are elected for six years. Every three years half of them retire, but may offer themselves for re-election. This device was to ensure a certain continuity of policy. The Senate cannot be arbitrarily flooded by additional members as a nominee Upper House can, and, for that matter, as the House of Lords can by the creation of new peers. Every enactment of the House of Representatives must go on to the Senate and does not become law until it is passed there. This guards the interests of the smaller States. They can band together in the Senate and throw out any legislation which they think is directed against their interests. Actually the Senate votes on party rather than provincial lines, but at the framing of the Constitution this was not clearly foreseen.

The House of Representatives is elected for three years by manhood (and womanhood) suffrage. There is no property qualification for candidates, as in the old Legislative Councils. Any elector has the right to present himself for election if he so wishes, but, to stop cranks or purely frivolous candidatures, the would-be member must put down a money deposit which is refunded to him if he is elected or if he polls more than a certain proportion of the votes. In practice few men offer themselves for election unless backed by a party, but the independent member is not unknown. He may be elected on grounds of personal popularity, or out of distaste for other candidates, or for other reasons. Unless he is a man of outstanding quality the independent member is unlikely to exercise much influence. From the beginning all federal members have been paid for their services.

The connecting link between the legislative and executive branches is the Cabinet and, in a formal and titular sense, the Governor-General.

All money Bills must be initiated in the House of Representatives. The Senate has the right to reject but not to amend them, unless by negotiation in some minor way. A distinction is drawn between such adjustments and what is termed "hostile amendments", that is, amendments that alter the nature and purpose of the Bill.

When a deadlock occurs between the House of Representatives and the Senate (and money Bills are the most fruitful source of such disagreements) the procedure is for the House of Representatives to reconsider and repass the Bill in question. If the Senate is still obdurate the Governor-General may dissolve both Houses, unless a general election is due in less than six months.

The Bill then comes up again before the two new Houses. If the Senate throws it out a third time a joint sitting of both the Representatives and the Senators is called and a vote taken. This generally ends the matter, since the House of Representatives has a numerical superiority.

The judiciary consists of the High Court of Australia with a Chief Justice and a number of puisne judges. This is a court of appeal from the Supreme Courts of the various States and from verdicts of its various members sitting alone. It has original or primary jurisdiction in cases involving two or more States or their citizens, in matters relating to federal powers (such as cases arising out of treaties, etc.) or affecting the diplomatic corps. The most important function of the High Court is that it decides constitutional issues. Laws duly passed by both the House of Representatives and the Senate may be declared invalid by the High Court. From this power it gets its title of "guardian of the Constitution". Needless to say the appointment of judges is, in theory, non-political and for life. The verdicts of the High Court are final except in a few cases when appeal to the Privy Council in England is permitted.

The High Court is the supreme constitutional authority. Using the Constitution of the Commonwealth as its touchstone it decides the validity of Acts when called upon to do so. It does not have to vouch for all Acts in the way the Judge-Advocate and later the Chief Justice was expected to do in earlier times. The High Court only takes cognisance when an Act is challenged and a test case brought before it.

The Commonwealth Constitution is a written constitution of the rigid variety, unlike the British Constitution which is unwritten and flexible. The details of the Australian Constitution were all contained in the Act of the Imperial Parliament which set it up. Its powers were exactly those powers which the States in their common interest were willing to allow it. Most of them are uncontroversial. In the matter of power, the States, not the Commonwealth, may be regarded as the residuary legatees.

In 1900 no one knew that Australia was to be faced in the not so distant future by two wars, and that to cope with them as a nation the Commonwealth would need more than the power to organize defence. Means were provided for amending the Constitution, but they made it as difficult as possible. First, any amendment made must be passed by an absolute majority in both Houses or one House must pass the Bill twice. Then, at least two months after but in less than six months, the Act must be presented to the electors for ratification in a referendum. It is supposed that during its passage through Parliament and in the two months after the people will have been put in possession of all the facts and educated by the Press and propaganda from both sides. The referendum is only successful if a majority of all the electors are in favour and if a majority of the States, taken as units, approve. If an amendment affects one State in particular that State must show a majority in favour of it before it becomes law. This is another device to protect the smaller States from being swamped by the larger vote of the more populous ones.

Electors have shown themselves very chary of voting "yes". It has been said that if a referendum were brought forward to abolish referendums the vote would automatically be "no". Up to 1956 there had been twenty-four referendums concerning constitutional amendment and in only four of them had the proposals been accepted.[9] These related to the election of Senators, State debts, and social services. Efforts to give the Commonwealth wider powers are almost inevitably turned down.

For a concise account of the Constitution and its scope no one could do better than consult the *Official Year Book of the Commonwealth of Australia*. The information is repeated in each issue. In No. 42 it is set out on pages 6-26. The full text of the Act is given and all the powers allotted to the Federal Parliament are listed. They cover defence, foreign affairs, including treaty-making (but the Department of External Affairs was not set up in its present form until 1936), external and interstate trade and commerce, posts, telegraphs, and telephone services, fisheries, currency and legal tender, banking "other than state banking", insurance "other than state insurance", weights and measures, copyrights, patents, and trade-marks, naturalization and aliens, foreign corporations, "conciliation and arbitration for the prevention and settlement of industrial disputes extending beyond the limits of any one state", lighthouses . . . and so on through thirty-nine articles.

Chapter IV of the Constitution, Section 101 states: "There shall be an Inter-State Commission, with such powers of adjudication and administration as the Parliament deems necessary for the execution and maintenance, within the Commonwealth, of the provisions of this Constitution, relating to trade and commerce and all laws made thereunder."

Trade and commerce was likely to be a vexed question, considering the different views of the component States. The Commission, however, was not called into being until 1913, after the passing of the Interstate Commission Act 1912. It consisted of three men, with A. B. Piddington, K.C., as chairman, and had a tenure of seven years. Its first investigation was into the tariff system, concerning which it issued seventy reports. It subsequently reported on such subjects as new industries, trade in the South Pacific, and charges for the carrying of mails.

The Commission was, to begin with, purely an advisory body. Deakin called it "the eyes and ears of the Commonwealth Government". In 1915, following a test case in the High Court, the Interstate Commission lost some of its powers and became a sort of permanent Royal Commission. In 1920 the members had served for seven years; for the Commission to continue they had either to be re-appointed or other men nominated to replace them. The Government did nothing. The Commission passed away painlessly. It had not been a success. The chief aim in introducing this body had been to make the Constitution more flexible and to inquire expertly into such questions as riparian rights and tariffs, so that when Parliament came to formulate Acts it would have data to work on.

Obviously to carry out its functions the Commonwealth needed money. It was given taxing powers and after 1915 citizens found themselves compelled to make out two taxation returns, one for the State in which they lived, the other for the Commonwealth.

To begin with, the Commonwealth had a surplus from customs duties and excise and from profit-making concerns such as the post office. The 1914-18 War altered that.

With the foundation of the Commonwealth the cause of free trade was lost. Australia became a protectionist country, but the former protectionist States lost a large slice of their incomes. Of all the moneys collected the Commonwealth was not expected to retain for its own use more than a quarter, the remainder was to be distributed amongst the States. This was the Braddon Clause; (in New South Wales, where it was unpopular, called the "Braddon blot"), because it had been introduced by Sir Edward Braddon and passed by the Convention of 1898 during an all-night sitting.

In 1910 a more definite arrangement was made. The Commonwealth gave the states 25s. per capita of population. In 1942 the clumsy dual income-tax arrangements were abolished, the Commonwealth alone collected taxes and out of them financed the States. This arrangement cannot be said to have worked smoothly, though it is more economical and in the interest of the individual taxpayer.

Money is naturally always a sore point, and so was the location of the Federal Capital. It was generally felt that the capital of Australia should not be fixed in any of its existing large cities and that it would be most inconvenient to have a perambulating capital. Like Washington, D.C., it should be removed from the business centres and their alleged lobbying—though with swift modern transport the insulating value of a few miles is questionable. It was not until 1908 that Canberra was fixed on as the site of the Australian capital. It was within New South Wales, but more than a hundred miles from Sydney. Nine hundred and thirty-nine square miles of idyllic pastoral land was ceded to the Commonwealth and there a city was planned and slowly, very slowly, came into existence. Whilst waiting for Canberra to be habitable, Melbourne remained the provisional capital. Each State had its sop and remained, one guesses, unsatisfied.

In the early conventions and deliberations leading up to the Commonwealth New Zealand had taken a half-hearted part. She was isolated unless she threw in her lot with her more populous neighbour, yet there were many reasons why union with Australia would be to her disadvantage. Captain W. R. Russell in a speech at the 1890 Conference made these clear. He said:

> There are very many points in which the colony which I represent would be glad to join in happy concord with the continental colonies, but to say absolutely that that colony would be prepared, at any rate for the next few years, to merge its young manhood in the more mature life of the Australian colonies would be to lead the Conference to believe what I cannot hope. We have many interests in common, but it is probable we should not at once submit ourselves to a Government in which we should have so unimportant a part. Mr Clark, the Attorney-General for Tasmania, remarked when addressing the Conference to-day, that with every district's physical environment there comes a distinct national type. With a population of 700,000 people in New Zealand, dwelling in an island where the climate is dissimilar to a very great extent from that of Australia, which has been colonized in an entirely different manner, and speaking colloquially, having had a very much rougher time than the Colonies of Australia, we are likely to develop a very complete individuality—a distinct national type. We have had to struggle against not only a more boisterous climate than Australia, but against a dense vegetation; and we have had to carve our homes out of the wilderness, which, though marvellously prolific and fertile, nevertheless masks a country in which self-denial has had to be practised by its settlers to an extent of which the people of the Australian continent have no conception. . . .[10]

Captain Russell did not mention the stormy Tasman sea, which at the end of the nineteenth century would have proved a serious obstacle to rapid and frequent communication. It was for the general reasons he outlined, and in particular on account of the New Zealand Maori policy, of which they were justly proud and which they were unwilling to hand over "to an elective body, mostly Australians, that cares nothing and knows nothing about native administration", that New Zealand finally decided not to throw in her lot with Australia. There is much in this speech that makes it obvious that New Zealand would have made an uneasy partner. There is no reason to believe that New Zealand ever regretted her withdrawal. Western Australia felt much the same, and in the end had to be practically coerced into the scheme.

Perhaps too much weight has been given to the jealousies of the States forming the federation, their natural divergences, the compromises that went into the framing of the Constitution. They were all there, but there was also genuine democracy and idealism.

The Commonwealth Constitution embodied practically the whole Chartist programme, once thought so revolutionary and dangerous. It provided for manhood suffrage, payment of members, triennial parliaments. . . . It was, in fact, the very mirror of progressive nineteenth-century liberal thought. All proceedings of its Houses were public and were published in Hansard. In the Press every citizen could read the gist of what had occurred in the House. Public opinion could express itself not only at the polls but by the right of public meeting, petition, and delegation. If citizens were too lazy to take up their rights and defend their convictions it was not the fault of the Constitution.

It was explicitly stated in the preamble to the Adelaide convention of 1897 that the object of federation was "to enlarge the powers of self-government of the people of Australia". On which Sir Robert Garran comments:

> The intention was to direct the attention of opponents and luke warm supporters to the fact that, though federation involved the surrender by the Governments of the several colonies of certain rights and powers, yet as regards each individual citizen there was no surrender, but only a transfer of those rights and powers to a plane on which they could be more effectively exercised.[11]

By making it "rigid" those men who drew up the Constitution strove to keep it intact against the onslaughts of particular interests. They were not to know that war and change would so soon strain to breaking-point the careful restrictions of power, the nice balance, that they had evolved. They set down a good foundation of hardwood.

For the idealists a new star had risen in the firmament: "One people, one destiny", "A Continent for a Nation and a Nation for a Continent". The ties with the mother country were not broken; they now rested on sentiment rather than on law; they were voluntary instead of compulsory.

A nation, men felt, had been born and unity had come about not under duress but through the will of the people, exercised in long and careful deliberation during peace-time.

VI. The Years 1901-14

The great task was only just begun.

The opening of the first Commonwealth Parliament in Melbourne by the Duke of York on 9th May 1901 gave the Press every opportunity to express its fervid optimism in the garlanded phrases of the day.

The Melbourne *Argus* reported the great occasion:

> By the hand of royalty, in the presence of the greatest concourse of people that Australia has seen in one building, and with splendid pomp and ceremonial, the legislative machinery of the Commonwealth was yesterday set in motion. The day was full of smiles and tears, the smiles predominating. Rising gloomily the dispersing clouds allowed the bright sun to peep through, and when the great ceremony was in progress in the Exhibition-building, the atmosphere was radiant, and illuminated the vast spaces of the building and the great sea of faces with a bright Australian glow.
>
> A sight never to be forgotten was the assemblage which, in perfect order, but with exalted feeling, awaited the arrival of the Duke and Duchess in the great avenues which branch out from beneath the vast Dome of the Exhibition-building. We have not in Australia any sense of the historical prestige which attaches itself to a royal opening of the British Parliament. There the stately function is magnificent in its setting and pregnant in its associations, but it is in scarcely any sense of the word a people's function.
>
> Here, by a happy inspiration, the function was made to the fullest extent a popular one. Twelve thousand seated in a vast amphitheatre—free people, hopeful people, courageous people,—entrusted with the working out of their own destiny, and rejoicing in their liberty, must be impressive by reason of their numbers alone.
>
> But there was not wanting the splendour of accessories. The mighty arches of the dome, the spread of the great transepts, the grace of the decorations, were in themselves inspiring. . . .

And so the superlatives unwound.

The Old Hundredth was sung, prayers were offered up by Lord Hopetoun "setting aside all complicated questions of religious procedure", the Duke made his speech (and how many, I wonder, were able to hear it?). Science was not forgotten. "The Duchess touched an electric button which gave the signal outside for the hoisting of the Union Jack on all the State schools of the Colony and for the sending of a message to England declaring the object of the journey of the Royal envoys accomplished." Then the trumpets rang out and the cannon fired a royal salute. (It will be noticed that the flag hoisted was the Union Jack and not the Blue Ensign with its Southern Cross and one large star, which later became the national flag of Australia.)

And so to business. Before elections were held a Cabinet was nominated by the Governor-General. The first Prime Minister was Edmund Barton, "Australia's noblest son", in default of W. J. Lyne, who had been, as Premier of New South Wales, asked to form the first ministry and had failed to do so. Barton was the more suitable man in that he had always been an ardent advocate of federation, whereas Lyne had opposed it. It was a ministry of all the talents, including Deakin from Victoria, Kingston from South Australia, and Forrest from Western Australia.

The elections were held, the two Houses assembled. An enormous programme was outlined. All the machinery of a new national government had to be set up and legislation on those matters to which the Commonwealth in a large degree owed its being, such as a White Australia policy and a uniform tariff system, was popularly demanded.

It took ten years to get the Commonwealth under way. At its inception 1910 was already a marked year because it was then that the Braddon Clause, regulating the financial relations of Commonwealth and States, ran out. In its original form it had been conceived as perpetual. George Reid, after a vigorous campaign, had caused it to be restricted to ten years.

The early Federal Parliaments were not very well organized. The party system existed, but in an inchoate way. The main divisions were the old ones of free-traders and protectionists. The Ministry was protectionist, the Opposition free trade. These divisions did not hold on other questions. In short, party division was fiscal. It was not founded on general political philosophies or on divergence of class. Only the Labour Party, which had twenty-four members in the first Commonwealth Parliament, was well organized, prepared to vote as a bloc (except on the fiscal issue, wherein the other two parties were united within themselves), and to fight first and foremost for improved conditions and standards for their constituents, not considered geographically, but as all the workers of Australia. The Labour members sat on the cross benches and gave their support to which ever side was most willing to bring forward social legislation.

The early years of the Commonwealth are often referred to as the "bookkeeping period". The necessary departments and services, such as Post and Telegraphs, had to be set up and made to function. State models and personnel were available and these routine matters did not take up so very much of the Houses' time. Other matters laid down in the Constitution took longer. The High Court was not inaugurated until 1903 and the Interstate Commission was not formed until 1913. Not until 1908 was the site for the Federal Capital chosen and the land it was to stand on was not formally ceded to the Commonwealth until 1911. Canberra was opened in 1927.

By and large four questions monopolized most of the attention of the Federal Parliaments up to 1914. They were (i) the White Australia policy, (ii) the delicate and difficult business of tariffs, (iii) the even more pressing matter of defence and (iv) what might broadly be called labour legislation.

1. *The White Australia Policy*

In 1901 Barton brought forward an Immigration Restriction Bill. As we have seen, the desire for a "White Australia", which had been brewing since 1841, was not a matter of party. All sections of the community, except a few planters who wanted cheap labour above all else, desired it. The means of bringing about the end were open to discussion. The States had been working independently and in alliance on the vexed question. Tactless restrictions had embarrassed the Imperial Government. The Commonwealth was looking for a new formula. One had been suggested by that earnest imperialist Joseph Chamberlain. This was the so-called Natal method of restriction which, aimed as it was against Asiatics, named no names and mentioned no pigmentation. The Government there proposed an "education" test with which it was highly unlikely that any coolie could comply.

The Australian Act required a dictation test. The die-hards did not like it. They thought it an evasion beneath the dignity of a true-born Australian. On the other hand, it was acceptable because it saved face. A dictation test in English was discussed and abandoned because it might keep out desirable immigrants. A test "in any European language" was substituted. In 1905 "prescribed language" was substituted for "European language". The choice of the language was left to the customs officials and on at least one occasion was stretched rather far when Gaelic was nominated.

H. G. Turner in his book *The First Decade of the Australian Commonwealth* quotes an arbitrary use of the regulation.

> In November, 1903, the second mate of a German sailing ship, who had been punished for smuggling in New South Wales, was called upon to undergo the language test. He had received a University education in Germany, and spoke English, German, and French. But in view of his conviction, the Custom House officer considered him an undesirable immigrant, and gave him a test in Greek. Failing in this, he was charged with being a prohibited immigrant found within the Commonwealth, and sentenced to six months' imprisonment.[12]

The difficulty with such an Act, as with book censorship, is that it is by its nature too often administered by tactless, ignorant, or biased under-officials.

Southern Europeans, particularly Italians, were not welcomed by some Australians. Feeling on this issue ran so high that a Commission was appointed to look into the part played by Italians in Western Australia. It found them to be in general good citizens, co-operative, and healthy; that they were not underselling Australian labour and were as willing as the next man to join a trade union.

The Act made no attempt to exclude Europeans unless they were criminals, diseased, or coming in as indented cheap labour. Japan, who herself had a restrictive immigration policy, was willing to come to a mutual arrangement with the Commonwealth. The Act, however, made no exceptions, and Japanese feelings were deeply wounded.

The Labour members took a particular interest in the Bill, for they wished to see excluded not only Asiatics but any "foreign" labour, even skilled men from England. In 1903 Labour attempted to force an issue when twelve English boilermakers landed in Fremantle to work for the Western Australian railways and again when six hatters came to Sydney. These serio-comic incidents brought Australia into disrepute and had nothing to do with the main aim of the Immigration Restriction Act, which proved a successful and not too insulting method of control.

Critics facetiously pointed to large blank areas on the map and asked if that was what was meant by a "White Australia". It was generally accepted that restriction should have its complement in the encouragement of the right type of immigrant.

In all logic Asiatics could not be barred from Australia whilst Pacific Islanders, the kanakas, were being brought into and employed in Queensland for cane-cutting. So in the same year as the Immigration Restriction Act was passed, Barton also sponsored a Pacific Islands' Labourers' Act.

Trouble over the kanaka question in the years preceding federation has already been briefly outlined; it is necessary to consider it in more detail here.

In the 1860s the growing of sugar-cane on the Queensland coast had begun in earnest. Towards the end of the decade Louis Hope had five thousand acres under sugar. In 1872 a very respectable export trade in sugar, and its by-product, rum, had grown up, and was worth more than £36,000 annually. In 1877 the figure had risen to over £180,000 and in 1880 to over £280,000. Research had evolved a type of cane resistant to disease; a central mill, or co-operative, system had cut down production expenses, and the industry was booming. It was a formidable vested interest and it rested on cheap labour. In 1863 Captain Robert Towns had brought in, privately, sixty-seven South Sea Islanders with the idea of growing cotton. The cotton did not grow, but the kanaka idea did.

Queensland was tropical, there was a widespread belief that her lands could not be worked by white men, or at any rate free white men. A desire for convicts had been scotched; plans to bring in Chinese or Indian coolies had been vetoed. In the kanakas the planters saw their salvation.

The number of Pacific Islanders imported grew rapidly. Democratic feeling was outraged. Was not this a form of slavery and would it not lower the standard of living? The strongest feeling was in the south. The planters of North Queensland began to agitate for separation. They wanted their own State in which they could pursue wealth in their own way. They had good geographical arguments, but behind it all lay the kanaka question. A compromise was reached. Kanaka labour might continue, but recruitment and treatment of the workers must be strictly supervised and after a certain time they must be returned to their homes.

Samuel Griffith crusaded for the exclusion of kanakas and got an Act through Parliament in Brisbane in 1883 forbidding their employment after 1890. The secession movement made no progress because a new colony could not be formed without the consent of the Imperial Parliament and it would only act on a recommendation from a colonial legislature. Brisbane was unlikely to petition Whitehall to subdivide Queensland. English capital was invested in Queensland, and were the colony to be divided its security would be lessened. That, too, was taken into consideration.

Griffith believed that white labour could work in the canefields, and so, as things turned out, it could. His policy helped to bring about an economic change. The Government subsidized the setting up of crushing mills with modern scientific equipment. This encouraged the small holder who, though he must pay higher wages for cutting, received a better price for his product which was more economically processed.

Nevertheless the kanakas lingered on and the Commonwealth Government resolved to end the matter for ever. Its Pacific Islands' Labourers' Act provided for the deportation of all kanakas. It was argued in the Houses for six months. The planters of Queensland had no chance against the representatives of Australia as a whole, however piteously they moaned that they would be ruined. It was prophesied that twenty thousand white men would be thrown out of work if the sugar industry failed.

The Bill became law on 12th December 1901. Many planters stopped planting in protest and in 1903 the Sugar Bounties Act was passed. This amounted to about 40s. a ton, provided the cane was cut by white labour. By 1909 it was costing the country £1,800,000. The industry revived and the Islanders were sent home at government expense.

Except for the nor'-west and the Northern Territory, Australia was white in practice and theory and nothing short of invasion seemed likely to upset the will of the people at last speaking with one voice. A White Australia (so unhappily named) became to Australia what the Monroe doctrine is to the United States. The end is not yet. What, thoughtful people are saying, will the end results of such a policy be in the face of an overcrowded, resurgent, and adjacent East whilst so many areas on the Australian map remain empty and white?

2. *Tariffs*

As might be expected, the tariff question caused more opposition. The majority of States favoured protection and it was incorporated in the Constitution. The Commonwealth was to collect all customs duties and excise and from these moneys to reimburse the States to the tune of at least £8,000,000. New South Wales, under Sir George Reid, went down fighting. If tariff there had to be she would like to have seen one for revenue-raising purposes only and not for protection. Hers was a lone voice, she was facing a *fait accompli*. The Governor-General in his speech to Parliament, analogous to the speech from the Throne, said:

> Revenue must, of course, be the first consideration; but existing tariffs have in all States given rise to industries, many of which are so substantial that my advisers consider that any policy tending to destroy them is inadmissible. A tariff which gives fair consideration to these factors must necessarily operate protectively, as well as for the production of revenue.

In 1901 interstate free trade was established. There could be little argument about that, it was one of the foundation policies of the Commonwealth.

The real battle was joined when, on 18th April 1901, C. C. Kingston of South Australia introduced a Customs Tariff Bill, a Distillation Bill, and an Excise Bill. Already in October 1901, when Turner brought down his first budget, some tariff resolutions had been submitted. The debate on these lasted for six months. It was pursued with great acrimony and drew down on the Government a vote of censure. This, of course, was the work of Sir George Reid. The text of his censure ran:

> That this House cannot accept the financial and tariff proposals of the Government.
>
> (a) Because they would place the finances of the Commonwealth and the States upon an unsound and extravagant basis.
>
> (b) Because they fail to adjust the burdens of taxation and the advantages of the free list in an equitable manner, revealing a marked tendency which this House regrets to observe to press upon necessaries of life, and appliances used in our farming, mining and pastoral industries, more heavily than they do on many articles of luxury.
>
> (c) And because they would, in their operation, destroy the stability of the revenue by making imposts for national purposes a source of undue profit to a few individuals and a few favoured industries, at the expense of the whole community.

This was a clever indictment and it provided the House with argument for three weeks. When at last the vote was taken the Government won by fourteen votes. Protection had come to stay.

This was the prelude to the Customs Tariff Bill, which took a further hammering for six months. It ended in a compromise, but one that satisfied no one. A very moderate tariff ranging from 5 to 25 per cent *ad valorem* duties was finally passed. Both sides were exhausted. In all, twenty-one months had been spent by what was probably the wordiest Parliament in our history on the tariff question.

In 1908 the tariff came up for revision. Sir William Lyne, then Treasurer, dubbed the original tariff "wishy-washy" and proceeded to outline the "New Protection". This was to give much higher, and it was hoped, more effective protection to manufacturers. There was immediately a great outcry. The cost of living rose and the consumer felt himself penalized in the interests of the few. Protectionists tried to lay the blame on traders who raised their prices out of all proportion to the new duties. If consumers had to pay more for commodities they wanted to pay less in wages. Wages actually did fall, by from 3s. to 5s. a week, as the cost of living rose. An appeal by public servants for higher salaries to meet their increased expenses was refused on the grounds that they, like everyone else, would profit by the growing prosperity of the country as a whole.

Whilst the Bill was under discussion lobbying rose to an unprecedented intensity. Practically every manufacturer in the country besieged the House, pressing the claim of his product for protection.

The truth seems to have been that Australia was not yet sufficiently self-supporting to stand a high tariff. So many essential commodities had to be imported, because they could not be produced in sufficient quantity locally to supply the market, that the consumer was seriously penalized. The Government was forced to recognize this and tried to patch the situation by setting up a Board of Trade, consisting of three impartial men, insulated from political influence, to adjust wages to the new fiscal conditions, to supervise the tariff and report on hardship and anomaly. The Board was also, in a vague way, to protect the consumer.

A Tariff Commission was busy sorting out the industries that needed protection from those that did not. The Labour Party and Mr Justice Higgins, pioneer of industrial arbitration and the minimum wage, also took a hand. If industries received protection they must pass on some of the benefits to their employees. Unless they could show that they were paying a "fair" wage, they would be charged excise. The manufacturer who co-operated was entitled to use a Commonwealth Trade Mark.

The situation was hopelessly complicated, the machinery improvised to safeguard and please everyone, and in particular to retain the support of the Labour Party, was inexpressibly clumsy. The High Court cleared the air by declaring the Excise Bill unconstitutional. With it the Board of Trade fell through.

The tariff of 1908 (sometimes referred to as the 1907 tariff as it was conceived in that year) almost doubled the duties on imported goods as laid down in 1902; it also included Imperial preference, that is, it allowed a rebate of 5 per cent on some three hundred commodities imported from the United Kingdom. The high tariff had to be bolstered up by bounties. Industries paying a fair wage but serving a small market were got on their feet and kept there by means of money grants from the Government. Bounties were, and continue to be, the price Australian citizens pay for their high standard of living. Besides the sugar bounty, to encourage the employment of white labour in preference to coloured, the system was gradually extended to tobacco, rice, rubber, iron and steel products, kerosene, and various other commodities. The idea was born; it was later to be used to trim the Australian market in competition with the world market and to be applied to dairy products, dried fruits, and various other primary, as distinguished from secondary, industries.

In 1914 the tariff was again revised and still with an upward trend. By this time Australians were more used to the idea and there was not the same outcry. The world, after all, had not come to an end in 1908.

Reviewing the whole situation in 1913, the Interstate Commission found that local manufactures had increased by 62 per cent and imports by only 52 per cent, factories had increased by 21 per cent, and 57 per cent more people were employed in them. The cities were growing larger whilst population in the bush was almost stationary. The Commission went on to point out that these figures did not necessarily indicate progress since the high tariff was keeping alive industries so ill-run and "archaic" that they would not survive in open competition.

The country was now so geared to protection that no change was likely or even possible. The Labour Party had decided to espouse the protectionist cause, for a return to free trade would, they believed, spell unemployment and lower wages. So many considerations were involved that a reversal of policy was now impossible. A greater element of artificiality had entered the Australian economy than ever before.

3. *Defence*

Defence was another of the foundation stones of the Commonwealth. With the granting of self-government to the Australian colonies it had been generally felt in England that they should make some contribution to their own defence. The colonies were quite happy to go on as they were and were untroubled by the withdrawal of British regiments in 1870. They had every confidence in the Navy. Several unfounded war scares and an increasing awareness of the Pacific's potential, however, made them more conscious of their helplessness. In 1889 Major-General Bevan Edwards was sent out from England to report on the possible military defence of Australia. He recommended a co-ordinated plan under a single authority and named a sum of money, running into millions, which was necessary for adequate fortification but which in those days appeared staggering and far beyond the financial ability of any colony.

In 1901 the Commonwealth set up a Ministry of Defence. Sir Edward Hutton was named Commander-in-Chief and undertook the task of amalgamating the militias and volunteer forces of the various States into one force.

A Colonial Conference was held in England in 1902 under the presidency of Joseph Chamberlain, and one of the subjects discussed was defence.

Barton, representing Australia, undertook to pay £240,000 a year for naval protection. The Secretary of State for War proposed that each colony should train a small army, the cost of which the United Kingdom would share. These men would be available for service wherever and whenever the Empire required them. The cost to Australia of such a scheme would be about £180,000. It was not the money but his knowledge of the Australian outlook that deterred Barton from agreeing. The Naval Agreement was not popular in Australia and the military arrangement could not have been carried through. In 1903 and 1904 Defence Acts set up a peace-time volunteer force and empowered the Governor-General to conscript all men between the ages of 18 and 60 for service *in Australia* in war-time. Garrison and cadet corps were also raised on a voluntary basis. Military districts along State lines were mapped out and in 1905 a Council of Defence was formed to deal with policy and a Board of Administration set up. Certain powers, such as control of the railways for troop movements, would automatically come into force in war-time. From the point of view of the British Army it was all most unprofessional.

Compulsory military training had been suggested by William Morris Hughes in Parliament in 1902, but he received little support. The idea did not quite die away and in 1905 the Australian National Defence League began to agitate for it. In 1907 Deakin proposed it again in Parliament. His scheme was the slightest of sketches. Young men between the ages of 18 and 20 were to be required to spend 46 days in camp over a period of three years, and a military college was to be established as the nucleus of an officers' corps. In 1909 an amended Act was passed.

In 1910 the Commonwealth invited Lord Kitchener to come to Australia and report on defence. In his opinion not less than 80,000 trained men would be needed to defend Australia. He drew up a detailed plan along the lines of the one already in operation, but with wider scope. Training could begin in schools with boys of twelve and compulsory camps should be held for young adult males. The latter would be paid for the time lost from their jobs.

Kitchener also recommended the establishment of a military college. "Australia," he said, "could only expect to produce officers of the type required by the establishment of a Military College, similar in ideals, if not altogether in practice, to the Military College of West Point in America."

This advice was acted on at once and Colonel Bridges was sent on a tour of the famous military colleges of the English-speaking world. The Royal Australian Military College came into being, at least as a plan, in 1911, and Ian Hamilton declared: "We have been lucky enough to go one better at Duntroon than the United States at West Point or England herself at Sandhurst."

The "one better" was perhaps the democratic nature of the College. Boys were accepted entirely on their merits by competitive examination, they were charged no fees, even their uniforms were provided. Places were allotted to all States ranging, at its inception, from twelve cadets from New South Wales to one from Tasmania. Under these circumstances no military caste could grow up and the best available material, without considerations of family or influence, could be utilized.

The College may be said to have sprung out of the old Australia. The site chosen, necessarily in the Federal Territory, was Duntroon, a property with homestead, belonging, like Yarralumla, the Governor-General's residence in Canberra, to the Campbell family. Old Robert Campbell had pioneered the district about 1825 and had built there a veritable manor house, which is still standing and part of the College. The Commonwealth Government bought it from his descendant, Colonel John Campbell, with 370 acres of land. Duntroon is two miles from Canberra and the first cadets were enrolled on 27th June 1911, just in time to provide young officers for Gallipoli. Ten New Zealanders are admitted annually. Colonel J. E. Lee has written a very readable history of Duntroon from 1911 to 1946, from which the earnest student may gain a wealth of information.

Defence provided the Commonwealth Parliament with ten years of dickering. In 1911 the plan took definite shape. Compulsory military training and a military college had been established. Australia was represented on the Imperial General Staff at its headquarters in London. An arrangement with England, embodied in the Defence Act of that year, had also been made for an Australian Navy. There had been various schemes and proposals. Australia had contributed to a British Squadron; Prime Minister Andrew Fisher had planned a "mosquito" fleet of about fifty small, fast ships. Australia was to have her own navy in part subsidized by England . . . now all these schemes were scrapped. Australia would have a navy consisting of one cruiser, two auxiliary cruisers, six destroyers, and three submarines. The whole expense would be borne by Australia and the ships manned by Australians. It was not adequate, but it would be her own, and it was a Welshman, William Morris Hughes, who pressed home the decision.

It is true that Australians had gone to fight in Sudan and in the Boer War, but these had been decisions made by individual colonies. Australia as a whole was now looking to her defence. If she had a White Australia Policy, she must have a defence policy. Danger was not overt, but it had been envisaged.

4. *Labour Legislation*

The social legislation passed by the Federal Parliament in the first fourteen years of its life is best treated elsewhere (see Chapter XXII "Results in the Making") as it is a continuous story which could only suffer from being presented piecemeal. It should be kept in mind, however, that social legislation was from the first one of the major considerations of the new Commonwealth. The record would be lopsided if such a claim were not pegged out here.

5. *Other Problems*

Beside the questions listed many others came up in the first fourteen years of federation.

The Commonwealth expanded. In 1902 Queensland relinquished its interest in the territory of Papua to the Commonwealth. The first importance of Papua lay in its function as a buffer state to the north. If the primary importance of Papua were defence, then it was logical that the Commonwealth should control it. Papua was treated as a Crown colony and, having the great good fortune to have administrators of the calibre of William MacGregor and Hubert Murray, a just and wise rule was built up there. Curiously, when you consider the colour of the inhabitants, the White Australia policy was extended to cover this Crown Colony. The result was that Papua was kept for the Papuans, instead of being overrun by more wily races as Malaya has been. Another form of protection was given to the indigenous inhabitants by the land laws. Planters there certainly were, but they held their land only on lease from the Government, which gave the Administrator greater powers of control. Murray set the moral tone. White men came into Papua as "trustees", not as exploiters. The Commonwealth did not look on Papua as a source of wealth but rather as a responsibility, a policy that was to pay good dividends long after when Australian soldiers followed the Kokoda Trail.

In 1909 South Australia handed over the Northern Territory to the Commonwealth for much the same reason. It was the open door to the north both as regards defence and the infiltration of Asiatics. South Australia had made a valiant attempt to develop the huge and climatically and geographically difficult area. (The wets are so wet, the drys so dry, and the distances before the advent of aeroplanes were so great.)

In 1863 the Colonial Office, finding the north of Australia somewhat of a problem, had regularized the situation. A large slab had been added to Queensland and South Australia undertook the 523,620 square miles that neither Queensland nor any other colony wanted. The politicians in Adelaide little knew what they were undertaking. They embarked on a land-development scheme with sales at fixed prices and underwriting companies in London. An Administrator and staff were sent north and a settlement made at Escape Cliffs, a most unsuitable spot. Disease and then mutiny destroyed it. A more sensible attempt was made in 1868 when G. W. Goyder, a surveyor, was sent with a large staff to select and lay out another site. He chose Palmerston, the Darwin of today. This was better, but not good enough. Goyder's task was greater than anyone expected. The survey took so long that intending landowners were discouraged and backed out. This cost the South Australian Government £73,000.

Undaunted, South Australia undertook in 1871 the mammoth project of building the Overland Telegraph. Labour troubles, climate and termites were sent to try the organizers. Rumours of gold unsettled the workers. In 1874 Chinese coolies were brought in to do the work. Often they preferred to do something else, to fish, to grow peanuts, to fossick. More than £500,000 went down the drain but the telegraph line was completed in just under two years, largely owing to the energy of the Postmaster-General, Charles Todd (after whose wife Alice Springs was named).

The next project was a railway to connect north and south, begun in 1886. Building began from both ends, but the ends never met. A line extended from Darwin to Pine Creek and from Adelaide to Oodnadatta. Between the two there is a gap of 1100 miles. There was no more money. The scheme came to a standstill. The railway was later extended to Alice Springs. (If you are interested in a witty and personal description of the northern section read Xavier Herbert's *Capricornia,* of which the railway may be said to be the hero.)

The Northern Territory was the locale of many unrealized dreams—and may continue to be. Agriculture, gold, precious stones, Vesteys, Air Beef . . . one dream has succeeded another.

In any case, with the coming of federation South Australia was willing enough to give up the Territory. She would divest herself of continual expense and she would not be haunted by the fear of another power or another State pressing down on her from the north. The transfer took time. The South Australian legislature had to pass a surrender Act and the Commonwealth Parliament had to pass an acceptance Act. There were monetary adjustments. The Commonwealth reimbursed South Australia for the £2,748,000 she had spent on the Territory. The Commonwealth also undertook to complete the railway line, which was not as simple as it sounds, for an argument arose as to whether the line should run due south to Adelaide or take an easterly bend for the benefit of western Queensland. All these negotiations took from 1906 to 1911, and then the Commonwealth had to set about reorganizing the administration, the land policy, and almost everything else, and dovetailing the two systems into one another. The Northern Territory is still the land of hope and mirage, the unknown quantity, though since World War II the Government has undertaken a scientific survey of its resources.

In 1914 the Commonwealth took over Norfolk Island. Australia and its environs were tidied up in the first fourteen years of federation.

These years, to the outbreak of war, were the prentice years. Much that was chaotic, ill-judged, and even comic happened. There were brilliant men, sound men, men experienced in the colonial legislatures, but the over-all impression left by the early years of the Commonwealth is one of ineptitude. There were endless debates, much bickering, many abortive Bills, a general (one feels) lack of direction. The party system had not taken firm shape, the issue of protection or free trade lived on as a confusing cross-current. Only the Labour Party had a definite all-Australia objective, and it was subject from the first to schisms. There was no hereditary ruling class versed in politics, as in England. The general temper of the people was not socialistic but it was egalitarian, which meant that for politics and government no particular skills were required.

From 1901 to 1914 there were nine ministries, three of them in the Labour interest, the others a little difficult to classify but in general termed liberal, when they were not coalitions, like the "Fusion Ministry" of 1909.

This state of affairs might have gone on indefinitely had not the war of 1914-18 acted as a catalyst.

REFERENCE NOTES

[1] *Hist. Rec. Aust.*, ser. I, vol. xxvi, pp. 531-2.

[2] *Ibid.*, vol. xxv, p. 702.

[3] *British Parliamentary Papers, Accounts and Papers* (1876), vol. liv, p. 814.

[4] *The Federal Government of Australia: Speeches delivered on various occasions, November 1889-May 1890*, pp. 4-6.

[5] *Ibid.*, pp. 19-21.

[6] V. Palmer, *The Legend of the Nineties*, pp. 132-3.

[7] F. Fisher, "The Federation Conference: a peep at the third day's business", *Bulletin*, 22nd February 1890, p. 5. The whole commentary makes good, if facetious, reading, and illuminates the contemporary scene.

[8] For those who wish to study in more detail the workings of this most important conference, printed records of the debates of the three sessions, *Official Report of the National Australasian Convention Debates* (Adelaide, 1897), *Official Record of the Debates of the Australasian Federal Convention* (Melbourne, 1898), and *Official Record of the Debates of the Australasian Federal Convention* (Sydney, 1897), may be consulted in leading public libraries or purchased (probably) from the Government Printers of the three States concerned.

[9] See *Commonwealth Year Book, 1956*, p. 73.

[10] Quoted in C. M. H. Clark's *Select Documents in Australian History*, [vol. ii] *1851-1900*, p. 477. It may not be out of place here to remind students that Clark's compilations provide a valuable and convenient means of approaching original sources.

[11] *Cambridge History of the British Empire*, vol. vii, part 1, p. 445.

[12] H. G. Turner, *The First Decade of the Australian Commonwealth*, p. 29.

CHAPTER XVIII

WAR

They were . . . the finest body of young men ever brought together in modern times. For physical beauty and nobility of bearing they surpassed any men I have ever seen, they walked and looked like the kings in old poems. . . . As their officers put it, "they were in the pink of condition and didn't care a damn for anybody".

—JOHN MASEFIELD, *Gallipoli.*

What had they done during this last and culminating period of their history? The efficient soldier who was their leader sets it out as he would in a statistical fashion. From 8th August, the day, in Ludendorff's own testimony, called "Germany's Black Day", to 5th October, the five divisions, weak to start, and becoming weaker from losses, which there was no flow of reinforcements to replenish, until at last they were almost skeletons, captured 116 towns and villages, as well as hamlets, farms, brickfields, factories, sugar refineries and similar groups of fortified buildings. One division had taken the impregnable Mont St. Quentin from the Prussian Guards, another the renowned fortress of Péronne held by the picked volunteers of an Army, and yet another the ridge of Bouchevesnes. They had thrust the enemy back from the outer defences of the Hindenburg Line and pierced through the line itself, after first meeting an unexpected and dangerous position in which two remnants of divisions had rescued two full American divisions from the completion of a great disaster. During that period they had ejected the enemy from 394 square miles of French territory, and, during the process, the Five had engaged 39 separate divisions—20 once, 12 twice, 6 three times, and 1 four times—each engagement representing a distinct period of line duty for the hostile division. Of these divisions, at least 16 had, by the time of the Armistice, to be disbanded on account of their losses. From 27th March, when their sangfroid and determination had saved Amiens, to 5th October, the prisoners they had taken numbered 29,144, and the guns 338, apart from innumerable machine guns and mortars. In March the five divisions had represented nine and a half per cent of the whole of the other 53 British divisions on the Western Front. Their captures, by the same comparison, were as follows:—Prisoners 23 per cent; guns 23½ per cent; territory 21½ per cent of the whole of the British Army. They had been the spearhead of the attack—the central attack which shattered the German arms and inspired the others to north and south. Thus was written the last page of a record which commenced with Gallipoli.

And so the infantry of the A.I.F. laid aside their armour and became, what remains of them, just the sort of fellows you know—or so they seem.

—Leonard Mann, *Flesh in Armour.*

The war was, no doubt . . . the forcing house which hastened our development, but the present position of Australia, its relation to world politics and to other nations, is due to conditions arising out of modern methods of production and in particular to improved means of communication.

—William Morris Hughes, before the Royal Australian Historical Society, 23rd February 1926.

I. A Bolt from the Western World

Colonization had been thrust upon a quiescent, if not acquiescent, continent. Many ideological fairies had gathered round the baptized but still unregenerate child, and its highly experimental education began. Only in this last, long overlooked island could laboratory conditions so nearly perfect be obtained. There was much theory and little science, it is true. Experimentation could be carried on because distance and the Royal Navy gave Australia a measure of security that no longer exists in the world, except perhaps in the Arctic or Antarctic wastes. That security lasted for more than a hundred and twenty years, though the imagination had discovered a few small rifts.

Everything effective, including ideas, was imported. Four of the colonies were conceived in England without relation to the soil on which they were to grow. The other two, Victoria and Queensland, were the result of an overflow of population from Van Diemen's Land and New South Wales respectively. Distance and the differences inherent in distance, coupled with difficulties of communication, caused them to be divided from New South Wales and erected into separate colonies.

Not only the initial ideas and the population but the means of livelihood and development were imported into Australia. The continent did not initiate, it accepted or rejected. Except for timber everything that was grown for use or profit was brought into the country. Sheep and cattle and poultry were brought in. Skills were brought in.

The ingress of ideas, people, commodities, usages, could be and was, by and large, regulated and controlled. The source was almost inevitably in the United Kingdom or one of her dependencies, such as South Africa or India. The Colonial Office was not the only valve. There was a more practical one, a virtual monopoly in the carrying trade, bolstered by the Navigation Acts.

When gold was discovered an overwhelming majority of those who flocked to dig it were from Great Britain. Their advent set in motion a chain of reactions, just as the advent of the first settlers had, as the Merino had for that matter. The active principle had the same source.

Constant renewal from the British Isles seems to have acted as a catalyst. Ideas and ideals rejected at home found space in the traditionless bush.

Adjustment of man to earth was the growing point of a "new" people but the impulse to move forward, to shape and reshape the still pliable life of the colony, came again and again and again from men born in Great Britain.

The continent hung on a long pendulum. It had an outline of its own, its own problems and necessities, but the silver cord was not broken yet. Australia's destiny was being shaped, as usual, in the northern hemisphere.

These are truisms but they cannot be iterated and reiterated too often. Despite self-government, despite a great many other factors, Australia's motive force remained outside herself. This is no talk of "shackles". That would be absurd. It is the logic of fact. A homogeneous people, no "melting pot" as the United States was to proclaim itself to be, with one main source of man-power, ideas, means of development and security, Australia in its Pacific and Asian context remained Anglo-Saxon to the core. A secret, but not incompatible, life was welling up. A nation might be forming within a nation, but it had neither the wish nor the ability to separate itself. Even the elements that were from time to time referred to as seditious were inherited rather than indigenous. They were, for example, usually Irish in origin and sprang from grievances that had nothing to do with Australia or her history.

An allegiance that went deeper than will or knowledge bound Australia to Great Britain; no other power made any bid for her allegiance. She was, as she wished to be, isolated from Asia. In moments of restiveness flickering glances were cast at the United States of America, as the elder sister who had left home. The American idea had certainly entered into the Australian Constitution, but America was not a counter influence. It was the only possible one, but it did not exist in any concrete way. Between Australia and European powers there was the language barrier that distance made impossibly high. Australia desired isolation in which to become herself. That self was, by a saturation of influence, predominantly British.

In the matter of war Australia knew very little. Except for the Boer War, the Sudan, and some frontier fighting, the United Kingdom had been at peace since the Crimea. There had been no "total war" since the fall of Napoleon in the early days of Australia's existence.

Except for the Boer War veterans, many of whom were very much alive in 1914, no one knew of the horrors of war, whilst many at school and in their general reading had imbibed the current highly romantic version—the Sir Henry Newbolt tradition, one might call it, or equally the Henley tradition, of "England, my England". War was something rather splendid that did not happen.

Interest in foreign affairs and world politics ran very low. Australia was connected with the outside world by cable, but as yet there was no radio set in every home. Diplomacy was still secret. Tension was increasing in Europe, but Australians were happily unconscious of it. They did not seek to know. There was a Defence Act, and in 1907 lines of co-operation with the Imperial Government had been laid down to cover the eventuality of war, but the only danger of which most citizens were even remotely aware was one that might arise from foreign ambition in the Pacific.

News of the assassination at Sarajevo duly reached Australia on 30th July 1914. It was politely deplored in the newspapers, but Australia had other things on her mind, including a general election and a drought.

War came as a bolt from the blue. Sir Edward Grey's efforts to preserve peace were as little known as the complicated network of treaties brought into action by Austria's determination to seek reprisal against Serbia. Germany backed up Austria while Russia sided with Serbia. France was tied to Russia and Britain to France by defence treaties, both were pledged to maintain Belgian neutrality. It probably seemed far-fetched twelve thousand miles away, but the frontiers of Europe were bristling and the resentments of a decade were finding an outlet.

The whole affair, it would seem, had little to do with Australia. Her interests were not directly involved nor was her security threatened, for Japan, the only naval power in the Pacific to be reckoned with at that time, was bound to Britain also by a defence treaty.

As arranged, an alert was sent out in code to the Empire, including, of course, Australia, on 29th July. It read: "See preface defence scheme. Adopt precautionary stage. Names of powers will be communicated later if necessary." It was at first wrongly decoded and the Minister for Defence could make nothing of it. The truth seeped in through the naval stations in China and New Zealand. The Navy was put on a war footing, but not the Army. The Minister for Defence, Senator Millen, was unwilling to act without the Prime Minister, who was absent from Melbourne campaigning for the forthcoming election. Mr Cook received urgent messages in cipher, but as he did not have the key with him they meant nothing. The Governor-General, Sir Ronald Munro-Ferguson, was in Sydney. The parts of the puzzle were scattered, the habit of secrecy was defeating itself. London pressed the Governor-General to find out what Australia was doing. Sir Ronald at least understood the seriousness of the situation, if no one else did. It was not until 1st August that the Prime Minister was illuminated and called the Cabinet together, but its members were scattered over the continent nursing their constituencies. The Minister for Defence was in Sydney, but went with the Governor-General to Melbourne. On 2nd August Australia came to the ready.[1]

It was the eleventh hour. Belgium was invaded and war was a certainty.

The Australian delay had simply been one of bewilderment. The response when it came was full and adequate. A cablegram was sent to the Colonial Office:

> The Government is prepared to place the vessels of the Australian Navy under the Control of the Admiralty. The Government is further prepared to despatch an expeditionary force of 20,000 men of any suggested composition to any destination desired by the Home Government. Force to be at complete disposal of Home Government. Cost of despatch and maintenance will be borne by this Government. . . .[2]

The offer was accepted after an almost imperceptible hesitation.

There is no doubt that Cook expressed not only the willingness of the Cabinet but of the Australian people. To the people Joseph Cook said with emotion: "Whatever happens, Australia is part of the Empire right to the full. When the Empire is at war so is Australia at war. All our resources are in the Empire and for the preservation and security of the Empire."[3]

Andrew Fisher, the leader of the Labour opposition, contributed his famous phrase: "Should the worst happen, after everything has been done that honour will permit, Australia will stand behind the mother country to help and defend her to our last man and our last shilling."

There are here overtones of evident but sincere romanticism. In a similar vein William Morris Hughes proposed that in the crisis the election be dropped, that the Cook Government return to power and, in the common cause that united all parties, its stultifying majority of one should no longer be allowed to hamper action.

The majority felt that it would be better to carry through the election, which was already under way, and so to get a clear verdict from the people. The war and its prosecution was now the main issue and both sides competed in their eagerness. The result was a Labour victory with forty-two out of seventy-two seats in the House of Representatives and thirty-one out of a possible thirty-six in the Senate.

Australia was committed to a war she had not made. Talk of "over before Christmas" was in the air, but to the thoughtful it was obvious that a long and bitter conflict lay ahead. How did Australia stand?

II. Australia at the Outbreak of War

The total population of Australia, aborigines excepted, was in 1914 almost five million. The country was prosperous, the temper of the people was hopeful. The depression of the 1890s was forgotten and the people as a whole were marching forward confidently. As regards the outside world, the majority were ill-informed, but not, of course, as ill-informed as the outside world was concerning Australia. That remains, there is evidence to prove, an all-time low. From lack of travel (so far, so expensive), from an innate idealism and romanticism—not incompatible with a sardonic humour and a practical, down-to-earth stance so visible in known circumstances and domestic politics—they were willing to take the old world from which they had sprung at face value. It was a time of idealism at home with a new Commonwealth and a young Labour Party, and Australians were willing to believe in idealism and purity of motive in their own kin.

After protracted periods of peace wars are apt to be received with popular enthusiasm, as witness the, looked at from today, hysterical jingoism with which the Boer War was received in England by a large section of the population. Lord Tennyson could cry out upon the "piping times of peace", the "cheat and be cheated and die" routine, elevating the "clean" death on the battlefield. Many other poets and leader-writers had much the same attitude. *Dulce et decorum est pro patria mori.* Patriotism and war were, singularly, yoked together. Drama is always exciting, and in prospect and retrospect war is dramatic. Whilst praising themselves for the peaceful, civilized manner in which they had achieved federation by conference, convention, compromise, referendums, and Act of Parliament, many Australians yet felt a hidden discontent with the absence of battle honours, a false concept that manhood and nationhood must be proved by deeds of valour. History is the story of human beings, and they, Heaven knows, are curious creatures.

The causes of the war—beyond simple concepts like honour, treaty obligations, and Brave Little Belgium—were so much Greek to the average Australian. When an eminent cleric referred to the struggle as "a trade war" everyone was shocked—nearly everyone. The nobility of sacrifice, the heroic image, the high platitudes of politician and journalist, were sweet in the ears. This attitude was completely sincere. There was a true willingness for sacrifice and a proud generosity. The pledges made were honoured. But as the years went on there was, as we shall see, a reversion to type.

Australia was then psychologically, if not intellectually or materially, prepared for war. The Commonwealth spoke as one man. For the time being all differences were sunk and to give aid to the uttermost capacity of the State and the individual was the overriding intention. The giving was without fear because the seat of war was far distant. It did not touch Australian soil and there was confidence in Britain and France, especially Britain of course, to settle the whole presumptuous affair quickly and completely. Without hesitation, in that confidence Australia was ready to denude herself of her Navy and her fighting men. The mood was high, heroic, and selfless.

Later it was borne in on men's minds that this was no simple and easy conflict between right and wrong, that Britain, and all she stood for as mother and defender, was seriously threatened and that the Empire of which Australia was part and, with the exception of New Zealand, the last outpost, was in great danger. With that realization, and only then, a motive of self-interest may be said to have entered into the struggle.

Quite apart from the will to fight, a great deal of organization would have to go into the preparation of an effective fighting force. Fourteen years earlier, even nine or ten years earlier, Australia would not have had even the makings.

There was little warlike history, no navy or army families with a long tradition of service, but there was, in a small way still, a defence organization.

To begin with, the colonies had federated. There was a central Government with the weight of the whole population behind it. It had a blue-print for defence. (It had always been "defence", never "expansion" or "aggression".) Duntroon Royal Military College was functioning. It had begun to turn out the right sort of officer material. The Navy was small, but it existed. It was manned by Australians trained on the British pattern. It could become an indivisible part of the Royal Navy at a moment's notice. Compulsory training of schoolboy cadets and young adults had been in force for several years. Almost at the moment war was declared the Melbourne *Age* was complaining that the system was both unnecessary and costly and should be cut down to cadet corps. The small amount of training given under the compulsory system did not create an army or even sketch out a fighting force, but it had instilled some rudiments and created an attitude of mind. It was a beginning.

To stiffen the trainees there was a body of Boer War veterans, still of fighting age, who had seen service, in a very different war it is true, but then every war begins where the last one left off and the men behind it have to learn new lessons and techniques.

Australia had a reservoir of horsemen, bred to the saddle, used to rough going and skilled in improvisation. She had the horses, too, the famous "waler" breed. She had men of initiative and independence. And they were the greatest asset.

There were leaders ready and waiting for the hour. Sir John Monash and Sir Harry Chauvel on the military side, and on the political side the dynamic Welshman, William Morris Hughes. Happy is the country that can throw up leaders when it needs them most. In August 1914 they still had to be discovered.

On the home front Australia had at least the beginning of a financial system, based on the Commonwealth Bank, which could be used and expanded to handle the financial side of the war effort.

III. "With Lips that Burn . . ."

In the perspective of time the military aspect of the war is probably the least important. The battle honours are not forgotten, but their lasting importance lies in the impact they had on the Australian imagination, and their contribution to the Australian legend. Two chapters of that myth had already been created and absorbed, the bush and its peculiar people, mateship and the religion of mateship. Now came the legend of the soldier. When I write the words "legend" and "myth" I use them in their real sense and *not* as synonyms for something untrue or imagined. The legend, the myth, of a nation is its psyche or, if you will admit the word, its soul.

Battle honours meant something else. They meant that a small population lost 60,000 young men killed in action or died of wounds or sickness, and suffered a total casualty list of about 320,000. No exact figure could be fixed for that, for war has its secret as well as its open ravages, and the loss goes beyond the individual; it includes his children who would never now be born. Australia was trying to build up her population; she could not afford 60,000 dead, all men in the pride of life. But that was how it was. Australian casualties were very high. She lost more men than the American Army, a direct loss, not a loss in proportion to population. Hers was the highest casualty rate in the Empire.

The story of the campaigns can be told in outline only. To begin with, twenty thousand men were promised and they were put unreservedly at the service of the High Command, as all Australian fighting men and arms were to be until the end of the war.

The first shot in the war, that is the first shot fired by the Empire, rang out in Australia. A single shot and the only one with hostile intent to be heard in Australia. Just before war was declared the German ship *Pfalz,* lying at Victoria Docks, Melbourne, decided to make a break for it. The usual formalities were completed, a pilot came aboard to take her out, then came news of the declaration and the officer commanding the batteries at Queenscliff was ordered to stop her. She did not obey his signals. He fired across her bows. The captain of *Pfalz* was for going on, he and the pilot fought on the bridge. The next shot would have taken her amidships. It was not fired. Reason and the pilot prevailed. *Pfalz* stopped and was interned. This is only a curiosity of history.

The first Australian campaign was on Gallipoli. In January 1915 it was decided to seize the narrow isthmus of Gallipoli, guarding the Dardanelles straits, the Hellespont of the ancient world, and held by the Turks.

The importance of the Dardanelles can be seen by looking at the map. It is the entrance, the only one, to the Black Sea into which four of the great rivers of Europe, including the Danube, flow. These rivers are highways into Europe. Whoever controls the Dardanelles controls the Black Sea ports.

The object of this thrust was to break through to Constantinople, the Istanbul of today. This, it was hoped, would knock Turkey out of the war, impress the Balkan States, make available the granaries of Odessa, cut the enemy's lines of communication, and relieve Turkish pressure on Russia in the Caucasus. The scheme was well imagined, but, on the highest levels, badly carried out.

The general in command was Sir Ian Hamilton and the force was composed of British, French, Indian, Australian, and New Zealand troops, the last two acting in concert, with the support of the Royal Navy.

In this plan the Australians and New Zealanders (the Anzacs) were allotted a section in the Narrows. The landing was to be at dawn on 25th April 1915. Things did not go well. The Turks knew all about the invasion, the preparations had been too obvious.

In the darkness and with the drifting tide the rowing boats in which the men were taken ashore made their landfall about a mile north of the arranged spot. Here, instead of fairly level country, the Anzacs were faced by a steep rugged terrain with the Turks entrenched on the ridge above them. The casualties at the landing were heavy. The first ridge was taken under fire and again the losses were great. Plans were out of gear, communications bad, the advance irregular. It was what is called a "soldiers' battle", depending for what success there was—and, amazingly, three ridges were captured—on individual initiative. That suited the Anzacs.

John Masefield, the poet, has described the terrain:

> Viewed from the sea, the Peninsula is singularly beautiful. It rises and falls in gentle and stately hills between four hundred and eleven hundred feet high, the highest being at about the centre. . . .
>
> In the brief spring the open ground is covered with flowers, but there is not much open ground. In the Cape Helles district it is mainly poor land growing heather and thyme; farther north there is abundant scrub, low shrubs and brushwood, from two to four feet high, frequently very thick. The trees are mostly stunted firs, not very numerous in the south, where the fighting was, but more frequent north of Suvla. . . . In reality the suave and graceful hills are exceedingly steep, much broken and roughly indented with gullies, clefts, and narrow irregular valleys. The soil is something between a sand and a marl, loose and apt to blow about in dry weather . . . but sticky when wet.[4]

It was not unlike Australia, "twenty miles of any rough and steep sea coast". It was hot and dry in summer and bitterly cold in winter. It gave nothing but resistance, and everything that was needed had to be brought ashore. The Allies could only be reinforced and victualled with difficulty, for the Turks it was much easier. It was said, by the Germans, that the landing could not be made. It was made. The Allies were outnumbered two to one. They not only landed but they held on, entrenching themselves.

On 2nd May the Australians were withdrawn, having lost half their number. Three days later they were detailed to join the English and French in another attack. It, too, petered out with heavy losses, 1100 of them Australian.

In August they participated in the combined attack at Suvla Bay, penetrating to the Turkish trenches on Lone Pine Ridge. These were covered with blinds or palings and sometimes two feet of earth. They had to be forced open or taken from the rear. It was, Ian Hamilton said, "a desperate fine feat", but it was unavailing.

The campaign was too costly, it was not showing results, and the High Command decided to evacuate the peninsula. This was carried out between 18th and 20th December 1915, in freezing weather. So great was the secrecy that the men were got off with only two casualties.

The decision was reached after much hesitation. Hamilton had been recalled and replaced by Monro, who reported unfavourably. He had, in any case, always doubted the advisability of this expensive second front. The Admiralty was anxious to force the Straits. Eventually Kitchener himself came out to evaluate the situation.

Far from achieving the results hoped for, the Dardanelles campaign had drawn the attention of Germany to the Balkans, and with the support of Bulgaria she was preparing an offensive against Serbia and Greece. The Prime Minister of Greece, Venizelos, who favoured the Allies, while the Greek King, Constantine, did not, appealed to England for help. This would mean pouring troops into Salonica. It would not be possible at that stage of the conflict to send an army to Salonica and reinforce Gallipoli in a big way. The damage to prestige had already been done. After much argument in the Commons, the Lords, the Admiralty, and Military Headquarters, it was decided to cut the losses and pull out men and ships from Gallipoli. Warfare had reached a fairly static stage of trenches and mines and the soldiers had no idea that the game was up.

In January 1916 the Australians were back in the training camps in Egypt, destination France. Recruiting had been stepped up by the heavy casualty lists and the knowledge that the war was far more serious than had been at first believed.

In April 1916 the Anzacs were thrown into the defence of Armentières. In July they were ordered to the Somme, where after weeks of bitter fighting they captured and held Pozières at a heavy price. Twenty-one thousand men were lost in nine weeks of battle. They were withdrawn to Ypres for a "rest cure", but in October 1916 were back on the Somme attacking Butte de Warlecourt in "flood, mud, frost and snow".

In 1917 the Germans were retreating, but the heaviest fighting of all was ahead. Bullecourt, Messines Ridge, Hill 60, Polygon Wood, Zonnebeke, Ypres, Passchendaele. . . . The soldiers had to face not only the enemy but the unaccustomed severity of winter and a constant shortage of ammunition.

They were tempered like a Toledo blade in fire and water. Passchendaele cost them about 30,000 men. Reinforcements were not coming forward as liberally as necessary.

Even at the beginning of 1918 the war was still going badly. Following the revolution, Russia had dropped out, the Italians were more a responsibility than an assistance. Germany was able to concentrate her full might on the western front. In March 1918 the Australians who were being "spelled" were rushed into the line to help in the defence of Amiens. It was the great spring offensive—"the rites of spring". On 5th April they were fighting before Villers-Bretonneux and around Dernancourt and Albert. Later in the month they were stemming the German offensive before Hazebrouck. On 23rd April the Germans broke through at Villers-Bretonneux, but by a pincer movement were cut off and exterminated by British and Australian troops acting in concert; "an enterprise of great daring", the Commander-in-Chief, Lord Haig, who was chary of praise, called it.

In July, after the capture of Hamel, the Australians and Canadians, supported by British armour, broke through the German line and advanced for nearly eight miles. This was the turning-point of the war.

The Australian battalions, depleted as they were, were now accepted as shock troops of the finest metal. To them fell the assault on Mont St Quentin, which was considered almost impregnable. When it was taken, "one of the finest feats of arms in the whole war", to quote H. S. Gullett, Germany was thrown back on the defensive. The next attack must be on the Hindenburg Line itself, the main German fortification.

The Americans, at full strength and with every gimmick known to the army, but inexperienced in actual warfare, were sent against it, with the Australians, now at quarter strength, in reserve. The Americans fell back in confusion and the Australians went forward to take the objectives. They had no artillery, only their rifles, machine-guns and hand grenades. They broke through the Hindenburg Line and captured Montbrehain beyond. It was their swan-song in France. They had been in battle almost without relief for two months and had suffered 21,000 casualties. They had taken 29,000 prisoners and about 340 guns. Their deeds outshone the actions on Gallipoli, and yet it is the heroic defeat that has always eclipsed the heroic victory.

This brief account of the Australians in France is not satisfactory. It cannot be, for it is impossible to disentangle the Australian story from the general story of the war. The Commonwealth troops were used by the High Command where and when it thought fit, they were a part of the general pattern. No action was theirs alone. They may have been the spearhead, but British, French, and other Dominion troops, far more numerous, bore the brunt of many an action.

The five Australian infantry divisions were from time to time remodelled and reconstituted; they were separated from the New Zealanders; different brigades were given different objectives; the command passed from General Birdwood to Sir John Monash. It has not been possible here to follow all the permutations and combinations.

For a detailed and authentic account it would be well to go to the *Official History of Australia in the War, 1914-1918*, or to Dr Bean's resumé, *Anzac to Amiens.*

It was only the infantry that went to France. The Light Horse, called the Anzac Mounted Division, commanded by Sir Harry Chauvel, remained in the Middle East, where they could be used to the best advantage because the fighting was highly mobile. These men, mostly from the bush, had been dismounted and had fought on Gallipoli. Chauvel's command came under that of the English army officer, General Murray, a man whose mind was as mobile as the task he had undertaken and who valued his unconventional Australians in a way that was not universal in the regular army. He said of them, "These Anzac troops are the keystone of the defence of Egypt", and again, "I rely entirely on my Anzac Mounted Division", and "any work entrusted to these excellent troops is invariably well executed".

Their first task was to guard the Suez Canal, but it became obvious that offensive rather than defensive tactics were necessary. Chauvel led his force over the Canal and into Sinai. They were supported by British artillery.

Desert warfare entailed many things other than fighting. The knack of improvisation learnt in the bush was very handy. The search for water and its utilization to the best advantage was no new thing for the Australian. Care of the horses under desert conditions was a major work in itself.

The force camped at Romani in the hope that the Turks would attack. They gained experience, much of it painful, in raids. By emptying and sealing wells the Turkish approach was canalized.

Romani proved a trap and the Turks walked into it, to be defeated after hard fighting. This ended any fear of a Turkish invasion of Egypt with the capture of the Canal as its climax.

Chauvel moved on to El Arish, which had been deserted by the Turks, and made it a centre for raids. Following his progress, Egyptian labour was building a railway and a water pipe-line. Water was the first necessity and the campaign could not be carried on without ammunition and food. The railway was a slow but vital part of manoeuvres.

Gradually the Sinai peninsula was cleared of the enemy. The next objective was Palestine. The re-formed Turkish line ran from Gaza to Beersheba. The first move was to encircle Gaza. A lightning attack was made and it seemed as if victory was certain when the troops, a mixed force of Australians, New Zealanders, and English, were, to their acute disappointment, told to retreat.

It was the old question of water, and Turkish reinforcements were approaching. On other occasions orders to retreat had been disregarded, but this was too large an operation for independent action. The first battle of Gaza was a stalemate.

A second attempt on 19th April failed, the Turkish were stronger, the plan of campaign less subtle. General Murray was recalled as a consequence and General Allenby took his place. Allenby was at once immensely popular.

Allenby attacked the other end of the Turkish line at Beersheba, using the Light Horse as his spearhead. It was a classic cavalry action, though the Light Horse had only bayonets, not yet the swords to which they were promoted later. The immediate prize was water, the wells of Beersheba. The oasis was taken in a charge, the horses jumping the Turkish trenches, their riders dismounting for hand-to-hand fighting. The end came so quickly that the Turks had no time to destroy the wells.

> The day was gone. The moon looked down on the still and silent field. In the town, men laboured. The smell of water, cold and sweet, was released in the dusty air. Standing, weary and patient, out among the ridges, the horses smelled it, and a whinny ran from line to line.
>
> Throughout the night the streets of the town were loud with the clatter of hooves walking. Brigade after brigade, the horses were led in, light horse and gunner, to drink with slackened girths and bitless mouths at the wells of Beersheba.[5]

Gaza was taken and Allenby's force drove deep into Palestine, being everywhere welcomed by the Jews. Jerusalem was captured on 9th December 1917, the 10th Light Horse, recruited in Western Australia, being part of the attacking force.

In January 1918 the Australian Division, now equipped with swords like the cavalrymen, occupied Jericho and raided the country east of the River Jordan. A new enemy was malaria, and sickness ravaged the army.

The Turks, good soldiers themselves, were now stiffened by German leadership and German troops. The Arabs, thanks to Colonel Lawrence, had joined the Allies. Allenby's real offensive was along the coast. Tiberias was taken and Damascus was evacuated. The army, cavalry and infantry, swept up the coast to Beirut and Tripoli. The Turkish army was beaten and on 31st October 1918 Turkey signed an armistice.

This hard, successful action was by no means an Australian preserve, but the Light Horse, or some sections of them, were in every action. The Australians had proved themselves first-class desert fighters. And so had their horses, none of whom could be brought home because of the Eastern diseases they might carry, but as a last act had to be destroyed.

As for the Australian Navy, it became on the outbreak of war part of the Royal Navy and saw service in the North Sea and the Atlantic. But first there were jobs to do nearer home.

There was escort duty; there was the threat of German New Guinea and the more active threat of the *Emden,* which was raiding in the Indian Ocean, and the *Scharnhorst* and *Gneisenau* doing likewise in the eastern Pacific.

Because of *Emden* and other possible raiders it was unwise to send out thirty-eight transports laden with troops without a proper escort. A British battle-cruiser *Minotaur,* the Japanese *Ibuki,* and the light cruisers *Sydney* and *Melbourne* were given the duty. On 9th November 1914, while on convoy duty, the cruiser *Sydney* fell in with *Emden* off the Cocos Islands and in a gun duel damaged *Emden* so badly that her crew had to beach her, a total wreck. *Sydney* picked up and took prisoner a number of the crew swimming in the rough sea or cast up on the beach. In Captain Glossop's words:

> A whole day was occupied in getting the Germans on board the *Sydney*. Some of them including a doctor had reached the beach by swimming. The German doctor broke one of his legs, and, having drunk a large quantity of salt water, died in delirium. Nearly all the men picked up were suffering from shock. Besides 80 wounded Germans, the *Sydney* took away 200 prisoners when it left for Colombo. . . . The whole of the upper deck had to be used for the accommodation of Germans. . . .[6]

Emden had accounted for a number of British freighters and her elimination was a very heartening episode.

Melbourne and *Sydney* also played their part in rounding up the other two raiders. It was the Australian Navy with a volunteer expeditionary force that, immediately on the outbreak of war descended on German New Guinea, interned those of its white population who could prove dangerous, and eliminated the possible threat from the north.

To complete the picture, Australia supported half a wing of the Air Force operating in Mesopotamia. Australians fought on every front, on land, sea, and in the air. Numerically in the great mass of men and armament thrown into the war by the Allies her contribution was small, some 329,000 men sent overseas, of whom 60,000 did not return. It was the only entirely volunteer army in the field.

IV. Organization for War

Details of the organization behind a war long since fought and won are not very inspiring and would not be touched on here, except that this was Australia's first war and many complex problems had to be worked out to get an army into the field and quickly.

It does not take much imagination to realize how gigantic a task it was to get twenty thousand men overseas between August and Christmas 1914.

The men had to be enlisted, put into uniform, equipped, and transported twelve thousand miles. Training camps, medical, dental and hospital services, food supplies, including forage for horses, had to be organized. So had a pay branch, a mail service, chaplains for every faith, recreational facilities, care for dependants and a thousand other necessary objectives.

Australia was not geared for any of this, and improvisation on a vast scale had to be undertaken practically without notice. It is true that the general defence scheme drawn up after Lord Kitchener's visit had allowed for the setting up of four factories, one for small arms, one for explosives, one for uniforms and clothing generally, and one for harness. The mere planning of these factories had raised a storm. Government enterprise was rank socialism, what was the matter with private enterprise? The clothing trade boycotted one factory by out-bidding the Government for skilled labour.

At the outbreak of war the small arms factory at Lithgow could turn out fifty rifles a day, the explosives factory was not much past the sample stage, and the Geelong woollen mills did not begin until 1915 to make khaki cloth, blankets, and flannel.

On top of all its other difficulties, Australia wished to manufacture shells for heavy artillery. One of the spurs was distance and the real danger of isolation. The Prime Minister, Andrew Fisher, preached a doctrine of self-sufficiency. Australia must be "self-contained" because she could no longer trust to vital supplies manufactured twelve thousand miles away. Even leaving enemy action out of consideration, there was a major transport problem arising from lack of shipping. To produce shells meant re-tooling, metallurgical research, and close liaison with England so that the products should meet the changing requirements of the war. In its early stages England was known to be short of munitions and the Commonwealth was eager to help. The Sunshine Harvester works, railway workshops, and non-profit making combines of engineering firms, such as the Barrier Munitions Company Pty Ltd, were prepared to undertake the manufacture of heavy shells under the Federal Munitions Committee. The scheme was not feasible. England could not spare experts and was naturally chary of sending secret blue-prints and formulae across the world. Australia could not keep up with the rapid development forced on the armament business by the war. A compromise was reached. Australia sent steel and munition workers to England, where the infinitely greater industrial potential was better able to handle the situation. Australia was, if anything, too willing. She was eager for full partnership in every field and to pay her way as well.

Following through the process of creating an army, any fluent speaker was good for recruiting, and any old soldier serviceable for enlisting the volunteers. Training camps were set up on racecourses and any other convenient locations. There were problems of discipline and hygiene—trouble, for instance, about putting hotels out of bounds. Chaplains, doctors, nurses, medical orderlies, stretcher-bearers, were all enlisted in the same way as the fighting men and were imbued with the same spirit.

It soon became evident that the distances separating the various capital cities made it difficult to implement a general uniform training scheme. Nor were there sufficient experienced instructors. It was decided that all but preliminary training should be given in Egypt and later, to some extent, in England. This shared training had a unifying effect on men drawn from different States and different walks of life.

The soldiers were put into uniforms. Their clothing was made by contract or in government factories. It differed from the standard English pattern; it was less formal, more comfortable; there were no traditions behind it, only an idea of serviceability. This was a small matter, perhaps, but it gave the Australian soldier a sense of individuality. He could feel, if he wanted to or thought about it that way, that his uniform typified his way of life, practical and free.

"The conveyance of an army of 20,000 men, with horses, baggage, equipment, forage, stores and all medical and other requirements on a 12,000 mile voyage, raised problems of no little magnitude," the *Official History* remarks sedately.[7] The Government owned no ships. It had to requisition them. A committee was appointed to survey all ships that lay in Australian ports and decide on their suitability as transports. When the ships were taken up they had to be made over and this was done at high speed. To give an idea of how quickly the work was done, *Demosthenes* was prepared for 1500 troops in 60 hours, and the *Palermo* was fitted to carry 400 horses and 100 men in 53 hours.[8] For the first contingent twenty-eight ships were selected; another ten from New Zealand joined them.

At first the troopships sailed with the maximum of public demonstration. This was morale-building, but hardly safe. Later the men were often embarked in the early hours of the morning before daylight, but the soldier was never denied the right of being accompanied by his family to the wharf, and the pathetic, unmilitary sight of men carrying their children or walking with their wives or mothers up to the gang-plank was the usual thing. And it did not lower morale. It wasn't that sort of morale.

The danger of sending crowded troopships on such long journeys and the possible danger created by the 34,000 (approximately) Germans resident in Australia led on to a strict censorship of newspapers, mails, cables, films, foreign books and pamphlets, even phonograph records. The War Precautions Act of 1914 was an enabling Act, and from it sprang three volumes of regulations. It empowered the Commonwealth Government to take any action it thought necessary for safety during the war. There was the usual hysteria, whales were mistaken for submarines, birds for aeroplanes, and harmless individuals for Schmidt the spy. Potentially dangerous Germans or Australian-born citizens of foreign blood were placed in internment camps, where they were well treated and the obligations of international law observed. Prisoners of war from Singapore, Ceylon, Siam, and the Straits Settlement were also sent to Australia for safe keeping. Officialdom kept its head, and it is improbable that many loyal or innocent individuals were penalized for the accident of foreign birth. After 1916 all aliens, whether enemy or not, were required to report weekly to the police. There were no proven instances of enemy spying. As an instance of hysteria, forty-two place names were changed in South Australia alone because they had a German flavour, and German music was almost universally banned.

Used to a free Press and open debate, the Australian people did not take kindly to censorship, especially as a feeling grew that "things were being done behind their back". Much the same sort of hysteria arose over censorship as over enemy plots, except that it was milder in its incidence. The restlessness under restraint reached a climax in May 1918 when the Labour Party made an official protest to the Prime Minister. No clear line was drawn in the public mind between necessary precautions and official interference for the sake of interference. There was an ingredient of war psychosis in it all.

We now come to what is really the crux, viewed historically, of Australia's organization for war. With extraordinary energy an army had been raised, equipped, and dispatched to the other side of the world. Both on Gallipoli and in France the Australian divisions suffered severe casualties. They had to be reinforced regularly and amply.

It was a volunteer army. The first enthusiasm, subsequent reverses, and the steady pressure of public opinion brought plenty of recruits. Men who were willing to go to fight were accepted. There was hardly such a thing as a reserved occupation unless it had directly to do with the war effort, such as ammunition work. It was an unplanned enlistment and an improvised economy.

As the number of men eligible and willing to serve dropped, recruiting campaigns became more and more fantastic. Under the volunteer system it was impossible to regulate the flow of men into the army. It was apt to be a spate or a trickle. The system was a matter of pride, but it did not work evenly.

William Morris Hughes, the "strong" (and eloquent) man of the war years, was at first in favour of a voluntarily enlisted army. There was no shortage of men, the problem was rather to equip and embark them. In 1916, however, recruitment was not so healthy. People, especially those with sons or brothers overseas, began to murmur that "shirkers" were letting the side down. Early in that year Hughes went to England, where he was lionized and invited to attend cabinet meetings. Incidentally, he saw the working of conscription in England and learnt that it was to be enforced in Canada. On his return he found a fairly strong conscriptionist party. There were Universal Service Leagues advocating it at the top of their voices. The newspapers supported the idea, the trade unions, which had supplied as many volunteers as any other section of the community, were against it. Labour politicians were divided. W. A. Holman, the brilliant Labour Premier of New South Wales, favoured conscription. Andrew Fisher had baulked the issue by surrendering the Prime Ministership in favour of the post of Australian High Commissioner in London.

Hughes knew that he was putting his hand into a wasp's nest when in September 1916 he called together a secret session of both Houses of Parliament. The result of that session was a Military Service Referendum Bill. Hughes was dramatically expelled from the Labour Party, twenty-four members of the New South Wales Political Labour League followed him out. Holman was also ejected from the party. It was split from top to bottom. The Bill aroused all the latent animosities in the community. The Irish, always a strong minority, under Archbishop Mannix, who openly said that Australia had already done her share and more than her share of the war effort, were violently anti-conscriptionist. It was not a religious issue; Archbishop Kelly in Sydney strongly advised his flock to vote in favour of conscription. Other men high in the Roman Catholic hierarchy declared it a secular matter about which every voter must make up his own mind.

Hughes, knowing the opposition there would be, and, since he once shared it, understanding the depth of feeling involved, did not try to force a Universal Service Act through Parliament. The Defence Act had established compulsory military service within Australia, but made no provision for an expeditionary force. For these reasons Hughes appealed directly to the people.

An enabling Act was passed and the first conscription referendum was held throughout Australia and wherever Australian troops were located, on 28th October 1916. The question could have been more temptingly phrased. It read: "Are you in favour of the Government's having, in this great emergency, the same compulsory powers over citizens in regard to military service for the term of this War, outside the Commonwealth, as it now has in regard to Military Service within the Commonwealth?"

It was lost by a narrow margin. There were 1,087,557 votes cast for conscription and 1,160,033 against. Victoria, the stronghold of Archbishop Mannix, had a majority in favour; New South Wales, Queensland, and South Australia were against it. Of the soldiers, 77,399 voted for it, 58,894 against.

This was a body blow to the Prime Minister. He handed in his resignation on 17th February 1917, but asked the Governor-General to re-commission him. He was now leader of a new party, the Nationalist Party, and formed a coalition ministry with five former Labour members and six from the erstwhile opposition. When he went to the country after a double dissolution in March 1917 he was returned with a strong majority. He won every seat in the Senate, which had formerly been strongly Labour. In the House of Representatives he had a good working majority.

The main issue of the election had been conscription. It would appear that Hughes had a mandate from the people, but he had pledged himself not to bring in conscription without another referendum.

The second conscription referendum was held on 20th December 1917. This time the question read: "Are you in favour of the proposal of the Commonwealth Government for reinforcing the Australian Imperial Forces overseas?" Once more it was lost, with four States against.

Hughes took this as a vote of no confidence and resigned. There was no one else who could govern. The Labour Party had committed suicide, the Nationalist Party was the popular choice. On 10th January 1918 the Governor-General asked Hughes to form a government. He went back with the same Cabinet as before.

In April Sir Ronald Munro-Ferguson tried to infuse new life into the recruiting campaign. He called together a conference of forty leaders drawn from all sections of the community and addressed them. It was what, in the vernacular of today, would be called a pep talk.

> It may be said . . . that the Empire, or rather the Anglo-Saxon race, had unanimously determined to make whatever sacrifice may be necessary to make good this determination [to win the war]. Australia is, I am convinced, equally certain of her cause, equally convinced of the necessity to overthrow German militarism. But there is at present a discrepancy between her will power and her man power. This meeting is . . . to consider how the two can be brought into harmony.

Even this flagellation in high places only brought a slight improvement in enlistment figures. No one knew then how near the conflict was to its end.

Professor Scott rather grandiloquently referred to the conscription campaigns as "the crest of the political watershed during the war".[9] It is an illogical but very human story. Looking back it is doubtful if, had conscription been carried, very many more effective fighting men could have been wrung out of a small population. Australia had other roles to fulfil. She was also a granary.

V. Production

Despite protective tariffs Australia was in 1914, first and last, a primary producer. Manufactures only accounted for about twenty-seven per cent of her wealth. These manufactures, the greater part of which centred on Melbourne, were almost entirely for the home market. Australia could not compete on the world market with manufactured commodities, because with a relatively high standard of living and a small population she could not produce commodities as cheaply as countries where wages were lower and the home market so large that economical methods of mass production could be employed.

With the coming of war the whole of Australia's economic pattern was upset and she was presented with a three-way problem: how to market her products under war conditions; how to make them a part of her war effort by supplying England with foodstuffs, wool, and metals; how to adapt and enlarge her manufactures so that she could produce the materials of war and satisfy the home market which could no longer be so easily supplied from the United Kingdom as in times of peace, both because industry in England was turning over to war production and because of an acute lack of shipping.

1. *Primary Production*

The days of laissez-faire and "Leave it to private enterprise" were over, at least for a time. "Business as usual" was the popular slogan, but business could not go on as usual. Only the Commonwealth Government could tackle so large a problem as re-channelling it. It had power to do so, if not from the Constitution, then from the War Precautions Act.

Before the war Australia had sold where she found her markets. Germany, after the United Kingdom and France, had been the largest purchaser of Australian wool. Australia had also imported goods heavily from Germany. In 1914 a Trading with the Enemy Act put an end to that. Various amendments up to 1916 stopped the leaks in the original Act. Trade could only be allowed with the United Kingdom, her allies, and certain favoured neutrals like the United States. It would be all too easy for some neutral countries to pass goods on to Germany or Austria. The Commonwealth Government virtually took over control of the export of primary products.

War stepped up the need for wool, particularly for uniforms, blankets, and knitting yarn. Australia needed vast quantities of khaki woollen cloth to equip the A.I.F. England and France needed it, too, against the coming of the northern winter. Until November 1916, subject to the provisions of the Trading with the Enemy Act, wool sales continued as usual. In that month the British Government and the Commonwealth came to an agreement. The needs of the home market were to be met and then the Imperial Government undertook to buy the surplus at a fixed price of 15½d. a pound. This was an increase of 55 per cent on the pre-war price. Most important, England undertook to come and get it; she found the ships to pick it up. A Central Wool Committee was set up with a government-nominated chairman and members representing the growers, brokers, buyers, and manufacturers. This impartial and representative committee created machinery for appraising the wool, allotting the local market its quota, and releasing the balance. This method of disposal involved new financial arrangements. The grower knew what price he would get, and since the scheme was backed by the Government itself he could have no doubt, even in the turbulence of war, that he would receive it. In order to enable him to carry on, 90 per cent of the price of the wool was advanced to the grazier within a fortnight of its disposal. The other 10 per cent was paid later. The chances of the auction room were eliminated, all wool of the same grade was paid for at the same price wherever it was grown in Australia. There was provision for distributing amongst the growers any extra profits that might be made.

The Central Wool Committee functioned until 1921 to steer the industry back to normal after the war. The clause covering the distribution of excess profits became important when in 1919 the price of wool sky-rocketed. The British Government had made similar arrangements to buy New Zealand wool and practically cornered Empire wool, that grown in South Africa excepted. It was called the Imperial Wool and Sheepskin contract. France was allotted a quota.

B.A.W.R.A. (British-Australian Wool Realization Association Limited) took over the functions of the Central Committee to deal with "carry-over wool" that is, the large stocks of wool on hand when the war ended. The Australian Wool Council was the intermediate body. It was not, as the Central Committee had been, a government body, but one representing buyers and sellers. B.A.W.R.A. was a limited company, like any other, registered in Melbourne in 1921. It acted as agent for both the British Government and the Commonwealth. Growers held preferential shares in it in proportion to the wool they had in the carry-over pool. The company's asset was wool already appraised but not sold in 1921. In 1926 it went into liquidation, its task accomplished. There was talk of keeping B.A.W.R.A. as a permanent body, but at a meeting of shareholders this was rejected and auction sales began again.

Wheat set a more difficult problem. At the beginning of the war there was a serious shortage owing to drought. In any case, wheat was not as necessary to the United Kingdom as wool was, she had other more accessible markets. Steps had to be taken to protect the wheat farmer, often a little man, rather than as with wool, to ensure a supply to England. As Professor Scott puts it:

> . . . when news began to come over the cables of the destructive activity of the German U-boats, and the consequent shortage in marine tonnage, the wheat farmers of the Mallee and Riverina, the South Australian plains, and the arable belts of Western Australia, realised that they, as well as shipping in the

North Sea, the Atlantic and the Mediterranean, were in a certain sense being torpedoed.[10]

Wheat was more perishable and less valuable than wool. For example, when, during the war, a ton of wool was worth £144, a ton of wheat was worth only £9. Again, as the *Official History* points out: "To carry 500,000 tons of Australian wheat to Great Britain engaged 100 ships for six months, the voyage being more than three times as long as that from Canada."[11]

It was providential for Australia that when, after the poor 1914-15 harvest, the 1915-16 harvest proved a bumper, disease and adverse conditions had produced a scarcity in North and South America. There was now a market for wheat, but between Admiralty requisitions and sinkings there was inadequate shipping.

The Commonwealth Government put forward a wheat-pooling scheme for the whole of Australia and set up a Wheat Board consisting of the Prime Minister (Chairman), the Ministers for Agriculture in each State and representatives of the four biggest wheat-handling firms, the latter forming an Advisory Board. Boards were also set up in each State. The Board undertook to sell the wheat, find transport, and make advances to the farmers. The ready money needed for this scheme, some £15,000,000, was put up by the banks at the moderate interest of five per cent. The Wheat Board did effect the sale of the accumulated wheat, with the purchaser finding the shipping, but not before mice and weevils had seriously damaged the stacks. The mouse plague was most spectacular and ruinous. To give an idea of its magnitude it is only necessary to quote the Victorian Vermin Destruction Department, which reported that in three days thirteen tons of mice were destroyed at three railway stations where wheat was stacked. They were thwarted by an improved type of silo made of galvanized iron sheets with the tops flanged outward so that mice could not get in. After mice came weevils. This plague was conquered by sterilization of the ground around wheat stacks, and much grain which had been attacked was saved by heating.

To take care of the London end of the marketing a Wheat Committee, consisting of the High Commissioner and the Agents-General of the various States, was set up. Farmers were assured of 4s. a bushel for their wheat. It sold in London for 5s. a bushel, the extra shilling covering freight, handling, and loss. Although this appears an advantageous arrangement for the grower, the farmer, with his usual conservatism, regarded it with suspicion and complained, without taking geography into account, that Canadian wheat was fetching a higher price than Australian. He was fortunate to sell it at all and would not have done so without government aid. The Wheat Pool continued to function until 1921 when the market had regained its natural equilibrium. The farmers by this time were so accustomed to it that they wanted it retained. In default they set up their own co-operative bodies.

Similar arrangements were entered into for the marketing of dairy products and meat. The United Kingdom undertook to take the surplus at a guaranteed price and to find the bottoms.

Always the trouble was shipping. In 1917 a Commonwealth Shipping Board was set up to control all shipping, both overseas and interstate, so that it should be used to the best advantage and to secure priorities for the most urgent cargoes. The Board had two sub-committees, the Overseas Central Committee sitting in Sydney and the Interstate Central Committee in Melbourne.

In 1916 when Hughes was in England he had bought fifteen ships of various size and pedigree to be owned and run by the Commonwealth. He paid £2,000,000 for them. After two years, charging only moderate freights, they had paid for themselves. Hughes also planned to end the shipping deadlock by building at least forty-six vessels in Australia. The war ended before this project could be carried out and it was dropped. The Prime Minister's persuasiveness also secured a greater allotment of ships for Australia from the Imperial Government than might have been expected.

Australia was a useful granary, despite her distance from the battle fronts. Her products helped to win the war, for England's large population was unable to feed itself or to supply the necessary raw materials for survival and the war efforts.

In her marketing controls and pools the people of Australia learnt valuable lessons in co-operation. It was co-operation and not dictation. The interests concerned were always represented and consulted. The Commonwealth also learnt the habit of command.

Metals were on a somewhat different footing from other primary products. Australia's principal metal market had been in Germany. The whole structure of marketing had to be destroyed. The German-controlled Lead Convention and Zinc Combine were liquidated. The deeply entrenched German interests in copper, molybdenite, wolfram, and other metals were rooted out. In war-time metals are a first necessity for ammunition and armament. Australia's metals were saved for Imperial use.

In September 1915 the Commonwealth Government established an Australian Metal Exchange. Its prime object was to prevent metals reaching enemy countries by roundabout routes. Those who sat on this committee were carefully screened. No one of foreign birth, even if naturalized, was admitted. A strict check was kept on the export of all metals. A cargo could not be cleared without the consent of the Minister for Customs. Zinc and copper were sold only to the United Kingdom.

It was also part of government policy to encourage the smelting and processing of metals in Australia as part of the war effort. In 1915 the Broken

Hill Associated Smelters Proprietary, a Zinc Association, and a Copper Association were sponsored by the Government. They had the form of companies, and their Boards of Directors consisted entirely of government officials. Works at Broken Hill were far removed from any possible enemy action, and those at Newcastle accessible to shipping. Their ingots and shell-cases, sent to England, were pronounced highly satisfactory.

2. *Secondary Production*

With drastic cuts in her imports, Australia was thrown back on her own resources to fill her needs. The creation of smelting works, just referred to, is a case in point. The textile industry was encouraged by the war, the coal industry depressed. To meet current needs many small or "back-yard" industries sprang up. But the over-all increase in factory workers was not very great. In 1913 there were 337,000, in 1918 376,000. It has been computed that 400 additional articles were added to Australian manufactures.[12]

In 1917 a Luxuries Board forbade the importation of unessential goods and this stimulated local ingenuity.

Inevitably Australia remained a primary producer. Any large-scale change-over to industry in the midst of a world war was impossible. There was the question of skilled men; in fact, there was the whole question of labour, for many men had left their jobs for the Army. There was the question of tooling up, even of making tools to make the tools required in any industry. A certain amount of assistance could be had from the United States prior to her entry into the war, and if the enterprise had a direct bearing on the war England made an effort, hard pressed as she was, to supply vital parts or even on occasion key men.

It was no time to start industries, but shortages created by war underlined the necessity for Australia to be more self-supporting. A definite impetus was given to industry, even if there were not much immediate visible result. Australia's role was still that of granary and she did not have the surplus energy and manpower to change it.

Australia came out of the war with a changed economic pattern. She had formed new habits. Exports to the United Kingdom had risen, imports had fallen by the end of the war from 60 per cent to 41 per cent. Imports from the United States had risen from 11 per cent to 25 per cent of the total. New export markets had been found in Italy and Japan, and Japanese goods were being accepted, though with reluctance.

Australia learnt much from the war, more on the home front than on the battle-fields. She learnt techniques, and from the use of these techniques has sprung much of her subsequent development. She also learnt to think in a large way.

VI. Financial Adjustments

War and reconstruction cost money. To find money, practically overnight, a small economy had to be expanded. Ways and means had to be found and they were found.

Until 1914 the Commonwealth had always had a handsome surplus, which was divided amongst the States. It had sources of revenue in customs duties and in the post and telegraph services. Its expenses were relatively small. Now they became enormous. Sir Joseph Cook, Prime Minister at the outbreak of war, declared that Australia had never been "in a stronger financial position than now". This was probably true. There was high potential wealth, but it had to be tapped.

For expansion and development Australia had relied in the immediate past on loans raised in England. British capital was willing enough to put money into what looked like a good investment. A glut of loan money in the early 1890s had been one of the factors in a severe depression. Investors had for a time been frightened off, but they had come back, and with the country itself as security money was readily obtainable.

One of the first effects of the war was to make it much more difficult to negotiate loans overseas. Capital looked inwards. The United Kingdom had to finance the war and expand her resources. Australia could not look to oversea loans to raise money. It is true that a special war loan was raised in London immediately after the outbreak of war. This was more in the nature of financial assistance from the Imperial Government than the ordinary investment loans that preceded it. While the war lasted private investment could not be expected.

Trade fell away, markets disappeared, the shipping bottle-neck became apparent almost at once. In that first month, August 1914, exports fell in value by more than £1,500,000. It was only after the Commonwealth Government had taken measures to regulate exports and had made arrangements with the United Kingdom to buy and carry surpluses that the export trade got on its feet again. It was clear that the Commonwealth Government could not rely on customs duties for an increase of revenue. They decreased.

In the first shock of war everything appeared, from a financial angle, worse than it was. Unemployment increased, many private enterprises were severely shaken. What Australians did not realize at first was that primary products would be as necessary to the prosecution of the war as fighting men. Adjustment was necessary; only a central power could swing the unwieldy mass of six separate economies into unity. By the War Precautions Act of 29th October 1914 the Commonwealth took to itself the right to control trade in relation to the war effort, that is, to control trade. The States, particularly New South Wales, used to independence, did not accept this very gracefully. To finance the war the Commonwealth had to have economic control.

So far the Commonwealth had not collected income-tax. It was unwilling to embark on anything so unpopular immediately. It decided on two other policies, on inflation and on loans.

It was not called inflation, but that was what it was. To raise funds at short notice the Commonwealth increased the note issue. It had the legal power to do so. Under the Australian Notes Act (Amendment) 1911 the Treasurer was empowered to issue notes against a gold reserve valued at a quarter of the issue. To amass the necessary reserve the Government borrowed £18,000,000 from the Imperial Government, £10,000,000 worth of gold from the banks, and forbade the export of gold. Against the £10,000,000 worth of gold the Commonwealth could legally issue notes to the value of £32,000,000 and this is what it did in June 1915. The Commonwealth Bank and all the trading banks gave the maximum of co-operation. They went off the gold standard in favour of the Commonwealth and made all adjustments between themselves by cheque instead of by transfer of gold as formerly. The Commonwealth cornered gold in order to back its notes. There was no financial panic, the issues were backed by the country itself and had the consent and assistance of organized finance. Stock exchanges closed for about a month after war began, then they re-opened. It was obvious that the financial bottom had not fallen out of the country.

The other main means of raising money was through loans. Up to June 1918 the Commonwealth had borrowed £49,000,000 from the Imperial Government. This was a small sum compared with the produce of local loans. These added up to £188,465,000 by June 1919. As time went on and the need for money became greater these local loans came perilously near being forced loans. Those who could subscribe and did not were called on to explain. Capital was forced into the loans because other means of investment were blocked. Unnecessary capital expenditure was forbidden, that is, businesses could not expand unless by so doing they helped the war effort. One way or another every industry and every individual was canalized towards the one object. Conscription for military service failed, but financial conscription succeeded. Even the smallest sums invested in war loans were acceptable. It was a genuine community effort. The flotation of the local loans, because so much service by the banks and other institutions was given free, cost remarkably little, something in the region of £500,000. It is claimed by some economists, Professor Copland amongst them, that these war loans were of the greatest benefit to the Australian people in the long run. They were a form of compulsory saving and investment and they supplied the stock exchanges with a huge block of gilt-edged securities such as they had never had before. This could not fail to have a stabilizing effect on the financial structure.

Even so, not enough money flowed in for the vast expense of waging war, which meant not only the upkeep of a fighting force but many new civil undertakings, such as marketing schemes, which all cost money. The Commonwealth was forced to have recourse to direct taxation. To quote Professor Copland:

> Whilst the Commonwealth relied upon loans to finance the war, it was obliged to raise increasing funds from taxation. In 1914-15, war expenditure from revenue amounted to £640,218 as compared with £14,500,000 from loans. In the following year, the figures were £3,800,000 and £37,400,000 respectively, in 1916-17 £11,800,000 and £53,100,000, in 1917-18 £11,900,000 and £55,000,000, and in the last war year, 1918-19, £21,200,000 and £62,200,000.[13]

These figures, from an authoritative source, speak for themselves. Money from taxation rose higher and higher. Existing taxes, such as the land tax, were increased and new ones continually added. In 1914 it was a succession tax or probate, in 1915 income-tax began in a modest way. In 1917 it was a heavy war-time profits tax. This served a social as well as a financial purpose, because there was murmuring and discontent over rumours that war profiteers were making immense fortunes. Very well, said the Commonwealth Government in effect, if they are we'll take their excess profits from them and dig them back into the war effort. An entertainment tax was also introduced in 1917. Attempts to increase revenue through tariffs were unproductive.

To realize the burden the people were carrying it must be remembered that these Commonwealth taxes were in addition to State taxation. All money earned, except excess profit, was taxed twice, and as time went on this was not very cheerfully borne.

As a result of inflation, controls, and shortages the cost of living rose sharply and inevitably. Professor Copland in the volume already quoted gives some data. Over the war period, 1914-18, the cost of building materials rose by 144 per cent, coal and metals by 119 per cent, textiles by 131 per cent, meat by 47 per cent, groceries 37 per cent, agricultural produce 35 per cent, dairy produce 21 per cent. . . . By his reckoning the over-all rise in the cost of living was 46.6 per cent, or if two items, fresh food and groceries, were isolated it rose 71 per cent. Increased prices came right into the home and sat down at the dinner-table. Rents went up, too.

So did wages, but irregularly and not in proportion. Professor Scott estimates that men's wages rose about £1 a week and women's about 10s., averaged over the four war years.[14]

The rise in the cost of living was not unexpected. It was discussed at the Conference of State and Federal Ministers called by Cook at the beginning of the war. On 31st August 1914 a Royal Commission was appointed to analyse the foodstuff situation, to determine what would be needed for home consumption and what would be available for export, the Government Statistician, G. H. Knibbs, being one of the three commissioners. The work of the Commission was purely exploratory. It could not *do* anything, it could only make recommendations. The Fisher Government eased it out of existence.

In March 1916, after a wrangle over legality which Hughes easily sliced through, the Commonwealth, under the powers of the War Precautions Act, established a Prices Adjustment Board. This strongly resembled another Royal Commission. It could recommend, and on its recommendations the Governor-General was empowered to take action in "proclaimed" areas and in regard to certain commodities. It was all very tentative and not very effective.

The States came into the arena. Each State undertook to introduce uniform price fixing legislation. In practice their action was not uniform but tangential and the bills withered away. The whole thorny subject was handed back to the Commonwealth.

The Prices Adjustment Board functioned from March to August 1916. The Commonwealth then appointed another body, the Necessary Commodities Commission, and the Board resigned. The Commission appointed a Prices Commissioner for each state and the Northern Territory. When the legality of price-fixing was questioned the High Court ruled that any legislation of the Commonwealth Government that contributed directly or indirectly to the war effort was legal under the War Precautions Act. This Commission was very active, fixing prices right and left, but they continued to rise just the same. The Commissioners recommended prosecutions for overcharges of ½d. Shopkeepers complained that they would be ruined, since the fixed prices did not leave them a sufficient margin of profit to remain in business. In the view of the Minister for Trade and Customs the real function of price-fixing was to prevent profiteering. Economic conditions were forcing prices up. The most the Government could do was to put on a reasonable brake. The Commissioner also had some control over wages and the duty of advising the Minister of dangerous scarcities so that action could be taken. The shortage of cornsacks in 1918 was a case in point. The Government bought up all supplies and resold them equitably to the farmers.

Use was also made of the Interstate Commission which had been set up under the Constitution in 1913, but it ran aground on legal difficulties.

The States went merrily on making their own arrangements, the whole question of price-fixing becoming more entangled and more controversial. The man in the street looked to the Government to stop profiteering, the man in business clamoured for his just margin, the Interstate Commission was mildly of the opinion that there was little profiteering, that the rise in prices was in the nature of things, sometimes helped on by government controls and that nothing could be done about it.

Government intervention in the economic field was made inevitable by war conditions, to maintain equilibrium, to raise the essential money. But one patch generally requires another.

VII. The Reverse of the Bright Medal

As the war progressed there was a change in the temper of the people. Although they were far from the firing line, strains, stresses, and anxieties left their mark. History made hay of Andrew Fisher's fine words. The "last man" was answered decisively in two conscription campaigns, the "last shilling" became a bitter haggling over profits, the witch-hunt for the profiteer. In the almost universal, sincere fervour of the early days of the war all cleavages in society seemed to be healed. Australia went to war as an undivided nation. Later the old rifts reappeared, exacerbated by war conditions. The Labour Party provided the cockpit.

The A.I.F. was a good cross cut of the community. The *Official History of Australia in the War of 1914-1918* gives a table,[15] compiled from military sources, of the occupations of the enlisted men. It reads:

Professional	15,719
Clerical	24,346
Tradesmen	112,452
Labourers	99,252
Country callings	57,430
Seafaring	6,562
Miscellaneous	14,122

and the Commonwealth Statistician, analysing the first spate of enlistments totalling 53,000 men, states that 43.2 per cent of them were registered trade-unionists. There is then no question, despite the bitterness which developed, but that one section of the community was as brave and willing as another.

The schism between Labour and anti-Labour parties began with the first conscription referendum. It is generally agreed that it was lost on the trade-union vote. There were other sections of the community that opposed it, many landowners, for instance, feared to lose the small labour force they had gathered together to run their properties, many women for purely personal reasons, many hardy democrats who hated compulsion for whatever reason or purpose, and on the lowest rung there was the tendency of the man in the street, when in doubt to say no. There was also a section of the Irish vote that was opposed not only to conscription but to the war, the reason lying in antipathies engendered in their past history. Then, too, a number of Labour politicians, with William Morris Hughes and W. A. Holman at their head, left, or were expelled from, the Labour Party on the conscription issue.

The basic truth probably lies in economics. With inflation and the rising cost of living many a working man whose wages had not risen in proportion, and who saw, or thought he saw, "the boss" making a very good thing out of the war, was touched in his pride. A soldier's pay was not good, though the Australian soldier received more than his English or French brother, and dependants had a fairly thin time with rising costs and shortages and many inevitable inconveniences. These things created a revulsion against the war, an unwillingness to be forced into action or to force other men to make the sacrifice. There was also a shamefaced feeling amongst many non-combatants, old men, women, or the physically unfit, that they had not the right to decide the conscription issue. No other nation was put to the acid test of deciding for or against conscription by referendum. It was a difficult and often cruel decision for the individual. A substantial minority of the soldiers themselves were against it out of pride, or perhaps out of fear that their ranks would be watered down by unwilling conscripts.

Paradoxically, the nation, having refused conscription, voted to power the man who had most passionately urged it upon them. If the trade-unionist vote lost the referendum the Labour Party also lost its supremacy. The electorate turned it down flatly and gave the Nationalist, or Coalition Party, a mandate to prosecute the war with vigour. The failure of the second conscription referendum was in no wise a vote of no confidence in Hughes. Born in Wales and nurtured in the Labour Party, he was both convinced democrat and fiery nationalist. He was the man chosen without a shadow of doubt by the majority to lead them.

The sound beating at the polls did little to sweeten the temper of the trade-unionist or to brush the chip from his shoulder. Throughout the war years the number of registered unionists grew steadily. In 1916 and 1917 there was a spate of industrial disputes, more particularly in New South Wales.

War or no war, the trade-unionist had never given up his free-born right to protest when he thought himself unjustly treated. In 1914 there had been 337 disputes leading to strikes in the Commonwealth and over a million working days were lost. In 1915 there were 358 strikes, but most of them only chicken-feed. In 1916 the flare-up really began, there were 508 strikes involving over 170 thousand men and more than a million and a half working days lost.[16] It must be remembered that, owing to labour shortages incident on recruitment, many men were overworked, particularly older men who stayed on in their jobs because of the war, and this made them in some instances cantankerous. Of sedition it is safe to say there was very little indeed. Most of the causes of dispute were the old ones, pay, hours of work, conditions, victimization, real or suspected. Occasionally they arose out of a refusal to work with Germans, even if naturalized and considered by the authorities too harmless and well intentioned to intern. This sort of thing is an index of the spy hysteria that cropped up in all walks of society. Men in mines not unnaturally felt that they were part of the war effort, as indeed they were, but they were not going to be put upon because their work was essential. To lay disproportionate blame on them, as some were very ready to do, is simply another variant of the "profiteering" outcry. There were two elements in the population, as there had always been, and each suspected the other.

In November 1916 coal-miners, most of them in New South Wales, struck for what was really a reduction of working hours. They would work eight hours a day, but it must be reckoned from "bank to bank", that is, their day's work would begin when they entered the mine and end when they left it, though it took them sometimes quite a considerable time to get to the seam on which they were working. Coal was vital. The Prime Minister intervened, setting up a tribunal which considered the men's log of grievances and ruled in their favour. The Commonwealth Arbitration Court, presided over by Henry Bournes Higgins, would not arbitrate because the strike weapon was used whilst the matter was *sub judice*. It was blackmail. Mr Justice Higgins declared that "apparently the men are neither loyal to the public nor to their own union", and that they "were refusing to supply coal the country wanted in time of war, when it was actually required for transports". Such words gave a lead to public opinion.

In 1917 the number of disputes resulting in strikes was lower, 444, but the disputes were more serious, more men were involved and 4,600,000 working days were lost, worth over £2,000,000 in wages. The trouble began with the waterside workers in May 1917. At the beginning of the war they had agreed to an award which was to last five years. At that time 1s. 9d. an hour for ordinary cargoes and 2s. an hour for dangerous or unpleasant ones had seemed satisfactory. By 1917 the cost of living had risen steeply and they asked, not unnaturally, for 2s. 6d. and 2s. 9d. an hour. The matter went to Arbitration and the wheels of the law ground slowly through it. The waterside workers became impatient. At Rockhampton they refused work on the award wages on which the ship-owners were standing pat. Mr Justice Higgins, that good friend of the wage-earner, again commented "These men deserve to be pilloried in the circumstances for refusing to work these ships unless they get more money." Public hackles were rising and the unions were losing faith in the Arbitration Court. Nothing increases bad feeling like bad feeling. A first-class industrial dispute was obviously ripening. In August 1917 railway workers in New South Wales came out on strike against the "time card system", a piece of scientific management that it was hoped would increase the efficiency of the railways by supplying data as to exactly how much labour was needed, where and when. It was not directed against the employees and from a distance appears a flimsy and futile excuse for direct action.

The waterside workers, still angry over their own grievances, and coal-miners, a section of the community whose segregation and hazardous employment make them particularly susceptible to persecution mania, struck in sympathy. All eastern Australian ports were paralysed and the whole transport system was brought to a standstill. Industry was crippled by the lack of fuel. More than twenty unions were involved. It was a general strike. Seventy-nine disputes grew out of the original one.

The time for a general strike was ill-chosen. In August, before harvest, there was plenty of labour available. The general public was unsympathetic and the Commonwealth Government, armed with its War Precautions Act, was in no mood to stand any nonsense. The Government seized the means of transport right down to horse-drawn vehicles, set up a Volunteer Service Bureau for enlisting labour to replace the strikers, made it a penal offence, under that most useful enabling Act, for anyone to interfere with the loading of ships, and applied to the Arbitration Court to have the waterside workers' union deregistered. This act of excommunication, which Mr Justice Higgins refused, would have robbed the union of the benefit of awards. There was a little violence and much angry argument. On 19th September the railway strike collapsed. Its members had rushed into it with insufficient funds to wage a long battle. Other unions were not in a position to help them. The Government held out an olive-branch. The "time card system" should be tried for three months and then investigated by a commission. If it were proved a source of injustice and hardship it would be abandoned. Trouble smouldered on the coalfields. The uselessness of a general strike, that dramatic gesture, was fully proved. In 1918 a Board of Trade was set up in New South Wales as a supplementary arbitration and conciliation body. It may have been hoped that the Board by timely action could stop strikes spreading from New South Wales, where most of them had their origin.

In 1917 the situation probably seemed more inflammable than it was. Compromise was not dead, men like Higgins, who might castigate strikers, were still intent on seeing justice done. The general strike was a flash in the pan, not a symptom of civil war or a concerted attack on the war effort. The presence of a small group of malcontents, the I.W.W. (Industrial Workers of the World, otherwise translated as "I Won't Work") with ideas and bushels of subversive pamphlets imported from America, created a stir and focused more attention on themselves than they warranted. Twelve members were tried and convicted in Sydney in 1916 for conspiracy and sedition. Before the law they were no more than common criminals who had engaged in sabotage. Curiously they were transformed into martyrs. The *Worker,* edited by H. E. Boote, began agitating for the release of one of the men, Donald Grant, whom he claimed had committed no crime and was a staunch Labour man. Boote so wrought upon public opinion that the New South Wales Parliament appointed Mr Justice Street as Royal Commissioner to re-investigate the case. Apart from the unearthing of a few minor flaws he did not discover any injustice. The matter did not rest there, five judges of the Supreme Court of New South Wales were called on to investigate. They supported the sentences. In 1920 Boote was still flogging his hobby-horse and the Premier, John Storey, called in Mr Justice Ewing of Tasmania to make another impartial inquiry. Ewing found that some of the witnesses for the prosecution were "liars and forgers" and that some of the evidence against some of the men could have been misinterpreted. Ten of the prisoners were released and were given a reception in the Sydney Town Hall with banners reading: "Welcome to the Martyrs."

Nine I.W.W. supporters were also tried in Perth, where Mr Justice Burnside treated them like naughty little boys to be let off with a caution. Read in the cool light of another day their slogans and pratings of revolution and sabotage sound like the tough talk of juvenile delinquents.

Many unionists, particularly those, mostly rural workers, organized in the Australian Workers' Union, proved themselves invariably calm and co-operative throughout the war.

Labour unrest was a part, but a vocal part, of widespread war weariness and strain. The response of the "other side" to it, and the heresy hunt for the profiteer, were part of the same thing. Practically the whole population was overworked. A small nation had taken on an uncommonly big task. Many were also emotionally overwrought as a result of the heavy casualty lists. The obverse and reverse of the medal were made of the same metal.

VIII. Australia and the Peace

When the war was won the peace had still to be won. Australia's contribution to the war was a communal one, her share in the peace treaty pivoted on one man, the Prime Minister, William Morris Hughes.

Socialist, ex-trade-union secretary, Labour politician, lawyer, Hughes was also an ardent nationalist and imperialist.

"Without the Empire," he told the Royal Australian Historical Society, "we should be tossed like a cork in the cross currents of world politics. It is at once our sword and our shield."[17]

He was by nature a great fighter. Like Churchill, he found his apotheosis in leading his country to victory. He was quite fearless and never overawed by great names or great occasions. He was eloquent. He was a lawyer versed in special pleading, he had also been an itinerant bush worker. He had the proper passports. He was shrewd, tough, an exhibitionist and a romantic. He was, in fact, just what Australia needed. He was convinced of Australia's importance and incipient greatness.

He has documented his career well in three readable books: *Crusts and Crusades: Tales of Bygone Days* (1947), which covers in a series of humorous sketches his career from work in a Queensland railway construction gang to Prime Minister of Australia and Vice-President of the Reparations Commission; *The Splendid Adventure: A Review of Empire Relations Within and Without the Commonwealth of Britannic Nations* (1929) and *Policies and Potentates* (1950), a survey in sketch form of the war and the peace.

Hughes went to England in 1916 for consultation with the Imperial Government. He made quite a hit. Asquith invited him to attend Cabinet meetings, as a guest and spectator, of course. That was not what Hughes wanted. He had come not to consult but to insist. Australian soldiers had fought on Gallipoli and had suffered a defeat. The defect lay not in the courage or endurance of the men but in "inchoate plans" and bad leadership. "There Australia had been in the vanguard, but was told nothing before the landing and nothing about the evacuation; although we were told that the evacuation had been decided upon beforehand, we had not been given an opportunity of expressing an opinion about an operation which we had been warned might involve forty per cent casualties."[18]

This infuriated the democratic soul of Mr Hughes. He meant to place an Australian in the councils of the War Office. No one else had ever thought of such a thing. Hughes crashed the War Office. Kitchener passed him on to Sir William Robertson, who heard him out and asked if he had a nominee. He had. Robert Anderson. The story should be told in Hughes's own words.

While we sat there awaiting the coming of Mr Anderson . . . the General asked me about him.

"What is he—is he a soldier?"

I replied that he was a major or something in the Militia. This was too much for the General.

"Militia! Militia!" he shouted. "We'll have no blasted Militia here."

"Oh," said I, "very well, he can come as a civilian."

This was even worse. "Civilian!" he barked, in his best barrack square voice. "We can't have any blanky civilians in the War Office."

The very suggestion shook him to his foundations. At my off-handed reference to the Militia he had started from his chair and waved his arms about, but at the suggestion that our representative could be a civilian he slumped down heavily on his seat, and after his first outburst sat there shaking his head. . . . He had delivered an ultimatum—he had dug himself in, and from him there was no appeal.

Kitchener would, I knew, be most sympathetic, he would deplore Sir William's narrow-minded outlook. But that was as far as he would go. As for the Prime Minister and the rest of the Government I knew only too well that it would be waste of time to approach them. But I was quite determined to have a representative in the War Office, and since a frontal attack was ruled out, a flank movement was indicated.

"Yes, yes, General," I said quietly, "I quite see the force of your objection to the Militia. . . . I shall not press it further. But I confess that I was a little upset at your reception of my alternative suggestion that he should come as a civilian. I had thought that would have got over your difficulty about having a Militia man in the office. However, having heard your views I see I was mistaken and realize that a civilian in the War Office—in a highly confidential position—is out of the question. Well, General, this talk has been most helpful. Australia wants a representative in the War Office. He must be a man acceptable to you personally, and hold suitable military rank in the Australian Military Forces. Very well," I went on, "I am satisfied that you will approve Mr Anderson personally. He is a man of fine character, and as for the rest, I will make him a General."

"What! What!" said Sir William. "You'll make him a General!"

He passed his hand over his eyes, like a man just coming out of an anaesthetic. His lips moved, although I couldn't catch a sound. He looked at me with an expression bordering on awe. "You'll make him a General!!" It was a staggerer. He couldn't believe it. . . .

"Yes sir. It's a bit late for tomorrow, but he'll be a General by ten o'clock English time on Wednesday morning."

The General of course knew exactly what this meant. Kings in the brave days of old made knights on the field of battle, and Colonels had been made Generals for conspicuous bravery in some sanguinary engagement. But this was in a class by itself—a civilian who had never heard a shot fired in anger made into a General in twenty-four hours by a little man—a civilian *in excelsis*—sitting in a chair in his office. The General sat there silent and motionless. He felt that he was confronted with a situation in which neither words nor action counted for anything. It was time to close the session. . . .

. . . Brigadier-General Anderson proved a great success.[19]

That is Hughes's own account. Whether or not a little colour has been added I would not like to say. The desired result was obtained. Hughes had taken the first step in Australia's peace campaign. He was getting her a hearing.

Lloyd George succeeded Asquith as Prime Minister of England, another Welshman, look you. Asquith had been a fine gentleman, but he lacked a strong fighting spirit. His motto had been "wait and see". His gesture in calling Dominion Prime Ministers to attend a conference and Cabinet meetings had been merely formal. Only one had attended, W. M. Hughes, but he had been enough to make it, in his own words, an "unfortunate experiment" from the point of view of Asquith. Much against the Prime Minister's grain, or better judgment, Hughes had succeeded in having himself sent as one of the British representatives to the Economic Conference in Paris, held between 14th and 17th June 1916. The little man was a gadfly. He had spoken his mind at the Economic Conference, unhampered by anyone's policy or lack of it. So greatly was his independence feared by Asquith that a move was even made to postpone the Conference until he should have gone home.

The French newspaper *L'Illustration* reported not only Hughes but his impact:

He is a little man of frail appearance, narrow shouldered, rather stooped. His long face, seamed with lines, reminds one of some of our Breton peasants. We expected to see one of those powerful Australians who look capable of carrying the world on their shoulders. . . . But he has only to speak to reveal in an instant the tremendous force that is embodied in that debilitated frame. One has to hear him in council. At first he sits doubled up and lets others do the talking. The partial deafness from which he suffers and which would have discouraged any less energetic spirit, compels him to make a prodigious effort of his whole being to follow the thread of the discourse. Already he has been forgotten by the other speakers. But suddenly he straightens out, darts forward his thin arms and the double trident of his extended fingers, and projects into the centre of the flabby discussion an incisive remark. It is not only his face that carries—a distinct face, a metallic face, that cuts across all the others. His first words convince you that he is determined to push his thrust home, and that no obstacle will stop his indomitable will. One understands at once the ascendency which this little Welshman—who resembles a black spider—has been able to obtain not only over audiences in Australia and England but over the oldest parliamentary hands in Europe.[20]

The Paris resolutions which arose out of the conference were mainly concerned with the transition from war to peace and the protection of the Allies' natural resources and their commerce from such evils as dumping.

Hughes stood for "an aggressive post war commercial policy". (The full official story of the Conference may be read in British Parliamentary Papers, 1916.)

Hughes returned to Australia. The first conscription campaign was ahead of him. But he had left his impress behind him. Lloyd George in March 1917 summoned the first Imperial War Cabinet. The Dominions were being taken into partnership. Except when military secrecy forbade, all meetings were open to the Press in true democratic style. An Imperial Conference sat at the same time with the function of bringing recommendations and suggestions before the Cabinet. Australia alone was not represented, but maybe a small, belligerent ghost sat in on the sessions.

These Cabinet and Conference meetings were planned as annual events extending beyond the end of the war. Having obtained the right to take part in Imperial deliberations at the highest level, a right visibly founded on war co-operation in arms and men, the Dominions were henceforth accepted as partners. Of this I do not think that it is too much to claim that Australia, through her Prime Minister, was the pathfinder.

The first Imperial or War Cabinet was, in the nature of things, experimental. In 1918 and 1919 it was a tempered instrument.

In 1918 Hughes was back in England for the War Cabinet and Imperial Conference meetings. It was during this session that the war ended. The meetings had begun in the black days of the German spring offensive. Casualties were high, reinforcements running low. The United States wanted another eighteen months to two years to get ready the hundred divisions she had promised. None of the experts believed that the war could end before 1920. A war-weary world found scapegoats, rightly or wrongly, in the military high command. The War Cabinet passed censures and made recommendations. There was still the will to fight and an unshakable belief in final victory, but a new fear was beginning to move in men's minds. Would the United Kingdom, with her gutted resources and manpower thinned out to danger point, have the strength to win the peace? In this there was the tacit knowledge that she needed her Dominions gathered about her to support her at the Peace Conference when it came.

Hughes was in no doubt about Australia's role. It was to attend the Peace Conference with full right to speak and to sign the treaty when it was made. It was not only a matter of prestige and justice, though those came into it, there were also questions coming up at the Peace Conference that touched Australia vitally.

The war ended on 11th November 1918 with a provisional armistice. While the terms of the armistice were still being discussed the Germans were pressing for the inclusion of President Woodrow Wilson's Fourteen Points. On this occasion the United Kingdom Government had a relapse, not unnoticed by Hughes. The Dominions were neither consulted nor informed.

Hughes was an imperialist, he may have been a romantic, an idealist he was not, and the Fourteen Points, coming from the United States which had suffered so little on its home front, seemed to him not only removed from reality but positively dangerous. They would cast away the fruits of victory before they were even tasted. If German colonies should be returned New Guinea would once more become a danger; if the freedom of the seas were conceded, what of the defence of Australia? If the racial equality clause went through the Covenant of the League of Nations it would skittle the White Australia Policy. Why should Germany inflict so much damage and not pay for it after? He believed in victory with reparations and his countrymen were with him, and so was the man in the street in all the Allied Nations.

As a preliminary to attaining his object of a seat for Australia at the Peace Conference Hughes began a vigorous advertising campaign. He saw to it that everyone knew the part Australian soldiers had played in the various campaigns. He was also at pains to enlist French sympathy and support.

The British Cabinet was not entirely in favour of Dominion representation at the conference, though aware of its advantages. (Could they have feared that Mr Hughes would throw a spanner into the delicate mechanism?) The other Allies, more particularly the United States, were not anxious to see the United Kingdom's power and influence extended by the presence of a family party.

In 1919 the Peace Conference itself opened. Hughes and Cook represented Australia. It was apparently the most lively Peace Conference in the annals of Western history, or perhaps that was only because the world was allowed to know more about what went on. Personalities bulked large.

Hughes and President Wilson were from the first mutually antipathetic. Major-General Seely of the British Air Ministry remarked:

> Among the many misadventures that befell President Wilson, not the least disconcerting was the presence of Mr Hughes, Prime Minister of Australia, at the Conference. This strange man had the knack, possessed by none other, of knocking the President completely off his balance. As a natural consequence the President tended more and more to view any proposal from Australia with a somewhat unfriendly eye.[21]

Hughes in retrospect applied the sharpness of his pen to Wilson:

> "He was an idealist, but his ideals had feet of clay! His notes about peace based upon justice and right were beautiful to read, but justice and right counted for nothing with him, when force, strongly arrayed, threatened them. He was bold, but not too bold; his word was his bond, but when his personal interests were involved he abandoned those who, relying upon his support, had committed themselves to a policy which he himself had suggested.[22]

And he asks, "Was he then a lath painted to look like iron?"

The President lost three of his points: "Freedom of the Seas", "No Indemnities", and "No Annexations". On the last Hughes joined issue with the great man and had a partial victory. It had been taken for granted that Germany's former colonial possessions would be handed over to the victor nations most interested in them, thus German New Guinea would go to Australia, Samoa to New Zealand, South West Africa to South Africa. . . .

Then the Conference ran into the "No Annexations" clause. A formula was sought. It was found in mandates. This meant neither the annexation nor the giving up of the territories in question. The mandatory nation was a guardian who governed for her own safety and the good of the mandate, which did not make it an integral part of her territory.

President Wilson set his face against German New Guinea becoming an Australian mandate, we are led to believe through hostility to Hughes, who had touched him on the raw more than once by pointing out that Australia had more war casualities than the United States and similar jabs at God's own country. Hughes was out to win. New Guinea was Australia's bulwark. He argued eloquently and effectually. The President in retreat suggested, idiotically, that a referendum be taken amongst the natives of New Guinea. When that was vetoed the President sulked. If a mandate were given to Australia, Wilson threatened to leave the conference. Most delegates were alarmed, and Lloyd George tried to soothe and even coerce Hughes. If he persisted in his policy of holding on to New Guinea he was not to count on the British Navy.

Hughes's reactions, as recounted by himself, are too good to miss.

> Then, turning to Lloyd George, I said, "As to what you have said, sir, about the British Navy's not being available to support Australia in the event of her continuing to hold possession of New Guinea, despite President Wilson's opposition, you and I will go to England, and ask the people who own the Navy what they have to say about the matter."
>
> I followed this up with some burning words about men who, forgetful of the dignity of their high office, the great traditions of the British people and their heroic valour and immense sacrifices in the war, prostrated themselves in meek subservience before the representative of America—for whose people he was no longer entitled to speak. And then having exhausted my stock of vituperative English I fell back upon Welsh—the ideal language for giving full expression to the emotions and passions. And believe me . . . I said "a mouthful". My words poured out in a foaming cataract: they were highly personal, the kind of words even the most conventional of men would on occasions dearly love to use, but for what the prim and proper people all round them would think. To the members of the Cabinet staring at me open mouthed, they were words full of sound and fury without any definite meaning, but they hit Lloyd George between wind and water. He knew what they meant all right; but he had not heard anything like them since he was a boy![23]

All this was very human—and probably lost nothing in the telling—but was lacking in that dignity to which Hughes had appealed.

Hughes won his point at the Conference. He was not satisfied with an ordinary mandate, however. New Guinea came into a special class, mandate class C. Australia was to have the same authority over New Guinea as over the mainland, "differing from full sovereign control as a nine hundred and ninety-nine years' lease differs from a fee simple".

The Conference voted for reparations and Hughes was appointed Vice-Chairman on the Reparations Commission upholding the claim for £25,000,000,000 to be divided amongst the nations that had suffered.

Soon Hughes was clashing with President Wilson again. Wilson was chairman of the Covenant Committee, which was drawing up the Covenant of the League of Nations. Hughes was a staunch believer in the League, but the proposed Racial Equality Clause wouldn't do at all. Passed, it would have destroyed the White Australia Policy and ended controlled immigration. It ran counter to one of the President's own Fourteen Points, that every nation should be free to govern its own domestic policy. Would Australia be free, would she long remain free, if she gave up all control over immigration? On this issue Hughes saw himself being outvoted. His eloquence was in vain. He employed other tactics. He appealed to American newspapers on the Pacific Coast where the fear of infiltration, particularly by the Japanese, was already strong. They protested so vigorously to the President that he had to let the issue drop. That day Australia made an enemy of Japan.

Hughes signed the Treaty of Peace in Australia's name, but his consent was not valid until it was ratified by the Commonwealth Parliament.

The matter was urgent; the Imperial Government cabled the Governor-General repeatedly to inquire if Parliament had ratified the Treaty. The House would not be hurried. It was not until 10th September that Hughes moved a resolution of assent. It was argued for four days and then passed unanimously. There remained in the minds of the Opposition at least a lurking resentment that the Japanese had been allowed to take possession as mandatories of the Marshalls, the Carolines, and other islands in the North Pacific.

REFERENCE NOTES

1 The full story of this seriocomic incident may be read in the *Official History of Australia in the War of 1914-1918*, vol. xi, pp. 6-11.
2 Quoted, *ibid.*, p. 11.
3 *Argus*, 1st August 1914.
4 John Masefield, *Gallipoli*, pp. 5-6.
5 F. D. Davison, *The Wells of Beersheba*, pp. 76-7.
6 Quoted, *Daily Telegraph*, 28th June 1917.
7 *Official History of Australia in the War of 1914-1918*, vol. xi, p. 220.
8 *Ibid.*, p. 222.
9 *Cambridge History of the British Empire*, vol. vii, part 1, p. 575.
10 *Official History of Australia in the War of 1914-1918*, vol. xi, p. 583.
11 *Ibid.*
12 *Ibid.*, p. 549.
13 *Cambridge History of the British Empire*, vol. vii, part 1, p. 592.
14 *Official History of Australia in the War of 1914-1918*, vol. xi, p. 634.
15 *Ibid.*, p. 660.
16 *Ibid.*, p. 665.
17 *J. Roy. Aust. Hist. Soc.*, vol. xii, p. 196.
18 W. M. Hughes, *Policies and Potentates*, p. 156.
19 *Ibid.*, pp. 160-2.
20 Quoted, *Official History of Australia in the War of 1914-1918*, vol. xi, pp. 331-2.
21 Quoted, *ibid.*, p. 758.
22 W. M. Hughes, *Policies and Potentates*, pp. 242-3.
23 *Ibid.*, pp. 237-8.

CHAPTER XIX

DEPRESSION AND SOCIAL EXPERIMENT

The 1920s began a new phase of Australian development. If the portents of coming change were less startling than those which disturbed the ancients they were there for the discerning; few Australians, however, read the signs aright and most assumed that the post-war years would reproduce the familiar pattern of the pre-war period. The break, of course, was not sharp, the more important developments being extensions from earlier movements, but the change in outlook, emphasis and actual policy gave a newly minted character to the coinage of Australian values.

—GORDON GREENWOOD, in *Australia: a Social and Political History.*

THE YEARS BETWEEN the wars were uneasy ones. Although the war brought development in many fields it left, like a receding tide, the flotsam and jetsam of many problems. It was over, but the fruits of victory, as always, were disappointing, and the casualties, the great effort, the improvisations which had forcibly extended a small community, left their mark. A new effort, the rehabilitation of the returning soldiers, had to be made immediately. The 1920s were prosperous but feverish, the 1930s were clouded by depression, and when it lifted the fear of another war took its place.

I. REPATRIATION

The repatriation problem did not begin at the war's end. From the days of the landing at Gallipoli men were being invalided home and the community was pledged to give them every care and, when they left the military hospitals, to re-establish them in civil life. Some, of course, went back to their peace-time jobs which old men, women, and the medically unfit had held for them, others were so changed and unsettled by their experiences that they could no longer fit into the old pattern. Others, enlisting straight from school, had no skills or professions. By 1917 a network of committees had been set up and Acts passed by the Commonwealth Parliament to deal with the question. But the real problem began with the ending of hostilities. Before that only wounded, mutilated, and sick men had returned, and their first need was medical care. Minor injuries were treated in England and it was only the incapacitated who were sent home.

After November 1918 an army, most of them fit and anxious to take up their lives again, had to be brought back. This was not simple. Shipping was scarce and in great demand. There were prisoners of war to be repatriated. Canada, India, South Africa, New Zealand were all clamouring for transport. Armies had to be re-embarked from the various fronts. Foodstuffs and other necessities had to be brought in as usual. The problem was so acute that the Prime Minister himself took a hand. The Australian soldier was in no mood to be kept waiting. Except for those who had had two months' Anzac Leave, none of them had seen home since they were embarked because of the long voyage entailed. They had enlisted voluntarily and were by no means meek. Whilst waiting to return they were given educational opportunities as a first step towards rehabilitation.

The return of the Australian soldiers was a masterly manoeuvre and was executed not only with the maximum expedition but with a consideration that cut through red tape. It would have been simpler to send them back unit by unit, but less just. Those who had served longest came home first, the married men before the bachelors, those with jobs waiting in advance of those who had to be trained and placed.

To repatriate the Australians required 137 ships making 176 voyages. All these ships had to be chartered in a competitive market. Some authorities thought this would take eighteen months. Actually, the last transport sailed on 23rd December 1919. In addition, the Light Horse had to be brought back from the Middle East. The same tactics were employed.

Actually the time-lag made repatriation a little easier. The market was not suddenly flooded with men seeking jobs. There were thorns enough. To begin with, there was difficulty between the Commonwealth and the States. The Army was a Federal matter and the States were content to let the Commonwealth bear the expense of repatriation. But when it came to soldier settlements the States owned Crown land and were jealous and tenacious of their rights. More than thirty-five thousand servicemen, when in February 1916 a questionnaire was circulated, elected to go on the land. Some of these, of course, changed their minds or had them changed by circumstance, but in any case the issue was too vast for the States to handle. They needed Commonwealth help, but were unwilling to give up control.

The repatriation question inevitably resolved itself into a network of committees. The average Australian is cynical about committees, boards, and commissions, but his country's whole history is littered with them and the Commonwealth in particular has leant heavily upon them. The thoughtful will realize that this is an attempt to use the expert to best advantage. The expert is not infallible; he is, like anyone else, a man of his time; he follows fashions and is hypnotized by shibboleths, but he is, or should be, more useful than the layman. It is part of the egalitarian outlook of the Australian that he tends to trust the man in the street before the expert, the demagogue rather than the statesman, to find the patent remedy more efficacious than the scientific conclusion. This is democracy carried to the nth. By and large, the States have shown themselves empirical and the Commonwealth has striven after the scientific approach.

To begin with, each State had its repatriation programme. War Service Committees were set up in each local government, council, or shire area. They were answerable to a State War Council. They were financed out of patriotic funds, that is, donations from the public to assist the war effort. A special drive was also made to raise money for the Australian Soldiers' Repatriation Fund. This was to tide men over the gap between demobilization and settling into a job or business, or, if the soldier elected to settle on the land, to provide him with seed, stock, and plant. The Commonwealth donated £250,000 to the fund, but the public held back. The war was not yet won. They had little confidence in the committees. In Victoria alone nine authorities were involved. An effort to raise a loan of £10,000,000 failed. There was too much competition.

In 1917 repatriation was handed over to Senator Millen for complete reorganization. He defined the question:

> We mean by repatriation an organised effort on the part of the community to look after those who have suffered either from wounds or illness as the result of the war and who stand in need of such care and attention. We mean that there should be a sympathetic effort to reinstate in civil life all those who are capable of such reinstatement.

An Australian Soldiers' Repatriation Bill was passed by the Federal Parliament and a Repatriation Department under an honorary commission was set up. Six State Boards under Deputy Controllers were responsible to the Commission.

This again was not a success. Ninety-eight per cent of the staff of the Repatriation Department were returned men. This was considered fit and proper, but it did not get round the difficulty that many of them had had no experience in administration. The honorary principle was generous but unworkable.

As time went on the whole question became more and more complex and more and more money was needed. To begin with, medical treatment was the most important factor. When discharged from hospital many men, wishing to be their own bosses, elected to operate small businesses. The Repatriation Department set them up, but too often, lacking training and having war scarcities to combat, they failed.

The Department undertook to finance returned soldiers, at the rate of £2 2s. a week for single men and £3 6s. for married men, until they were settled (this appears penurious today, but money had a higher purchasing value then); to make grants to cover any emergency; to pay for training in a profession or trade and for the necessary instruments or tools of trade; to supply free transport anywhere in Australia, provision for dependants and assistance to them (including training in any vocation elected), pensions for war widows, passage money to bring to Australia the wives of men who had married overseas or their fiancées (14,000 women took advantage of this, but if the soldiers failed to marry the girls within a month of their arrival they were expected to refund the fare to the Government), a grant of £35 to buy furniture for those setting up a new home. . . .

In 1914 a scheme for war pensions had been initiated and in 1920 this came under the Repatriation Department. These applied to the incapacitated soldier, his wife, and his children under sixteen. The amount required for pensions snowballed until 1931, when the Government paid out £7,774,806; after that it began to decrease.

With so many men returning and wishing to marry and make a home, there was an acute housing shortage. They looked to the Government. The need was met in New South Wales, to take one State as an example, by the War Service Homes Act, 1918. This set up a War Service Homes Commission which considered applications. It lent £700, and later £800, to the soldier applicant to build his home, requiring no deposit and charging an interest rate of only 5 per cent. Under the same Act, mortgages were taken over by the Government at a very reduced interest. There were 11,373 applicants for loans by 1920 and 2630 mortgages had been taken over. Voluntary effort also played its part. Neighbours rallied round and in working bees ran up simple homes. Altogether more than 36,000 homes were built in one State alone.

This was improvisation, or spade-work. The main work of rehabilitation was to settle soldiers on the land. It was the traditional answer and, in the main, the traditional technique was followed. Of those who elected to settle some twenty thousand had had experience, the balance craved an open-air, "free" life. To find land for all was a tall order. There was Crown land, but the best of that had long since been taken up. The States would have to buy back or resume properties. Commonwealth and State officers met in conference and wrangled over expense. The States wanted to keep control while the Commonwealth found the money. They came to a half-and-half agreement. The Commonwealth put up £500, later £625, for each settler and also contributed to the resumption of estates and the opening up of the country by roads, bores, and similar means.

With the best will in the world, the soldier settlements were, on the whole, a sad failure. The land, often badly selected, was bought at the top of the market. The holdings were too small to support a family. Interest charged was low at first, but as the value of the land dropped it became a burden. Bad seasons snatched away the scanty margin of profit.

Most serious of all, settlers not already accustomed to the land received little or no training. By 1929 the situation was so bad that in New South Wales Mr Justice Pike was appointed to investigate. He brought all the faults to light and reported that there had been a gross loss of £23,525,522. Many settlers had given up in despair. In 1940 only 26,591 of them, out of 336,310, remained on the land. The largest and most successful soldier settlement was at Griffith in the Irrigation Area, where 700 had been planted out. On the whole, the difficulties of the land had been underestimated and optimism allowed to have its head. The ex-soldiers themselves put a tremendous amount of labour into their rehabilitation.

By 1933 the Commonwealth Government alone had spent £238,000,000 on repatriation and there were other sources of help as well from the States. Every soldier on his return home was given a gratuity. This was in the form of bonds. It was hoped that this money would be used to set him up in business. An outstanding example was when 400 returned soldiers pooled their gratuities to found the Returned Sailors' and Soldiers' Woollen and Worsted Co-operative Manufacturing Company at Geelong; £60,000 in bonds was put into the undertaking and the Commonwealth lent another £50,000. The venture was an outstanding success.

The State made itself responsible for the education of the soldier's children and, in the event of his death, the care of dependants. There were, at the peak, 450,000 of them. Profits from the Army Canteens, which, while keeping prices down, had been run on sound business principles, were devoted to the education of soldiers' children, and Sir Samuel McCaughey, the millionaire bachelor pastoralist, left a large slice of his fortune for their technical and professional training.

Another advantage granted by law was preference to returned soldiers. Any ex-soldier applying for a job received preference. Except in unusual circumstances, in which rare skills were called for, he must be appointed even if civilians had far better qualifications. Selection committees could only pass over an ex-soldier if it could be proved beyond a shadow of doubt that he was unable to fulfil the position for which he had applied.

Returned Soldiers' and Sailors' Leagues became powerful pressure groups whilst keeping alive a sense of comradeship and disseminating advice and assistance. It looked as if the "returned men" were forming a State within a State.

It was claimed that Australia's treatment of her fighting men was the "most liberal in the world". Its failures were due to lack of judgment rather than of goodwill.

The economy had to absorb them, but it must be remembered that their return created a greater demand for commodities and services, and therefore more employment.

II. Boom: The Pattern of the 1920s

The years following the war are generally referred to as a boom period, but, looked at closely, they were a chaotic and uneasy time. The change-over to peace was nearly as difficult as the change-over to war, and it lacked the emotional impetus. There was a reaction against war measures and war-time leaders, notably William Morris Hughes, who no longer appeared a saviour, but, to some people, very like a dictator.

The Commonwealth had acquired enlarged powers during the war, and the inadequacy of the Constitution, particularly in time of crisis, had been proved but not accepted.

New economic techniques had been improvised and producers were unwilling to give up State help.

Australia had new responsibilities, particularly in her New Guinea mandate, which came into force in 1921, and had to learn to shoulder them. She also had a greater place in the world forced upon her.

All these matters were controversial. There was progress, but dissension went side by side with it. The economy looked good, but was it sound? That question was to be answered within a decade.

Lastly, Australia, having fought her first war, tasted her first victory and, being inexperienced, expected too much of it.

The political situation was tetchy. The Labour Party had split on the conscription issue and it continued to have trouble within its ranks. It fell into two halves. One was the political Labour Party, moderate in outlook. It had to be moderate to survive and to function. I am not suggesting that this moderation was in any way insincere. Men with practical experience in Parliament and in their electorates knew that if they advocated violent change they would effect nothing. The other was industrial Labour, which, the Australian Workers' Union excluded, adopted a more radical attitude. Bitter feeling aroused by a not ill-founded suspicion that the workers had come badly out of the war converted many of the unions to socialism, and after 1920, when the Australian Communist Party came into existence, to Marxism. Nominal wages had risen, but not "real" wages, that is, wages in relation to the cost of living. The war, agitators told the men, had been used as an excuse to break strikes. They had been "got at" and they resented it. Whether this were true or not made little difference. A state of mind was produced. The year 1919 was clouded with industrial unrest. There was a dispute at Broken Hill which lasted eighteen months. In February 1919 seamen struck in Queensland and the trouble spread to other states. Waterside workers also struck on the job-control issue. This was a very real grievance and is by no means dead. At the pick-up for work on the wharves some men were victimized, others favoured. It was an internecine struggle. It was well illustrated in its human terms by the

American film *On the Waterfront,* released as late as 1956. In December 1919 a Marine Engineers' dispute came to a head. These strikes perhaps sound worse on paper than they were in reality. Australia's prosperity was not greatly affected by them. She was still able to market her products overseas.

Despite strikes, which, even when just, irritate the general public, Labour was regaining its power. Its organization was improving and there was a move towards unification. Labour was thinking in Federal terms, and at the 1921 interstate conference held in Melbourne one big union embracing all Australian workers was advocated. Six years later the Australian Council of Trade Unions came into being. Six years may seem a long time, but jealousies and suspicions between States had to be overcome and the idea had to sink into the mind of the rank and file. The A.C.T.U. was in effect an all-Australian trades union.

A distinction must be drawn between the A.C.T.U. and the Federal Labour Party. The former was a combination of State Labour Parties and its aims and objects were distinct from the Federal Labour Party. It was more radical, it sought oversea affiliations, as with the Pan-Pacific Trade Union Movement, but was in all other matters "isolationist". It was pacifist, opposed to immigration on the grounds that Australian jobs should be the preserve of Australian workmen, and believed, not in co-operation, but in the class war as the means of attaining its objectives. The main objective was, of course, a bigger share for the employee in the profits of industry, primary and secondary, and a strengthening of government control. There appears to have been some confused thinking, for the White Australia Policy, to which Labour clung for the same reason that it disliked immigration, matched ill with the Pan-Pacific Trade Union Movement. There were revolutionary mutterings, but no revolution. Whilst complaining of being downtrodden, any self-respecting unionist would have been mortally offended had it been suggested that he had a slave mentality. As an Irishman will hark back to persecutions that he never personally suffered, though they were very real, so a trade-unionist looked back to the horrors of the Industrial Revolution and made them his own. There were doctrines and slogans, but when things came to the sticking-point the Australian nation showed itself remarkably homogeneous.

The 1921 Conference had made a gesture towards socialism, the 1927 Conference revoked it. In effect, it agreed that socialism would be ideal, but the time was not ripe for it. The people must be educated, and on that pious thought the issue was, for the time being at least, shelved. Scullin had subscribed to the tenets of the 1921 Conference, but when he became Prime Minister he realized that a middle course was the only practicable one.

On the whole Labour favoured government control and State enterprise. The Commonwealth Shipping Line, the Commonwealth Trading and Savings Banks, had been conspicuous successes. It was taken for granted for geographical reasons that the State Governments should own transport. In the twenties, particularly in Queensland, State enterprise went much further. There were government-owned and operated mines, smelting and coke works, a produce agency, sheep stations, butchers' shops, fisheries and canneries, even a State-run hotel. Some were a success, some were not. The depression and a revulsion of feeling had swept most of them away by 1930.

In New South Wales the State brickworks, Monier pipe-works, and metal quarries were profitable and well run, the New South Wales trawling industry was not. When the Liberals came to power, with Bertram Stevens as Premier, they were discontinued whether successful or not. He represented private enterprise, which looked on government shows as anathema.

There was also within the Labour movement a distrust of the bicameral system. The party wished to dispense with Upper Houses as undemocratic, and in Queensland they succeeded in abolishing it in 1922. Upper Houses, it is true, are not as responsive to public opinion as the Lower Houses, because in normal times their components change more slowly. This, however, has proved as favourable to the Labour Party as to any other. One suspects that opposition to them was automatic, due to an unconstitutional confusion between Australian Upper Houses and the House of Lords. In the absence of a hereditary ruling class a Senate could be just as much a brake on reactionary as on revolutionary legislation.

Unlike similar parties overseas, the Australian Labour Party has been singularly devoid of intellectuals. There were the Utopians of the 1890s, but they were discredited by events. Tags have been from time to time imported, like the so-called "Red objective" of 1921 with its slogan, "Socialization of industry, production, distribution and exchange", but on the whole immediate practical gains have been preferred to doctrinaire aspirations, and a man of the people, like Chifley, more readily trusted than a proselyte from another stratum of society.

State Labour began to win back the electorates. Probably its isolationist policy was its trump card. The electors had had enough of war; they wanted Australia to live to herself, developing her resources, which many considered boundless, and steering clear of European entanglements.

With the increase of industry there was, of course, a greater number of electors likely to vote Labour. The steady increase of trade-unionism during the war had also spread political consciousness. Often a trade-unionist would vote Labour out of solidarity, even if in his heart of hearts he disagreed with the platform. In the 1920 elections Holman fell from power in New South Wales and a Labour Government came in. The other States, Victoria excepted, followed suit.

The Commonwealth was different. The party was more moderate, the gap between the Liberals, or Nationalist Party, and the Labour Party was smaller, the issues were greater. The same electors might vote Labour in a State election and Liberal in a Federal election. Your average Australian is not doctrinaire.

There was ferment in the Liberal Party, too. In 1919, after the manner of woman being formed from Adam's rib, the Country Party came into existence. It gave form to the old division between the city and the bush. Australia's was (and is) an urban civilization, but her wealth comes from the country. Up till the 1850s the squatters had been the ruling class. With increasing democracy setting a premium on numbers, they lost ground; they were few, the city dwellers many. A sense of injustice arose. "We produce the wealth, yet we are politically impotent." This deep-rooted feeling found expression in a new party led by a country doctor, Earle Page. The Country Party stood for decentralization, the formation of new States and, at first, for free trade. The success of B.A.W.R.A. modified the last plank. The Country Party soon came to favour protection and government assistance for the primary producer. The Country Party has always been conservative in outlook.

Many shook their heads over the appearance of a third party and saw Australia falling into the difficulties inherent in a multiple party system, the sort of impasse that was later to befall France and Indonesia. They need not have worried. The Country Party has always been in alliance with the Liberals. There is still virtually a two-party system, with the Country Party as the right wing of the Liberals, paying especial attention to the problems and aspirations of the bush, and the Communist Party the small left wing of Labour.

In the general elections of 1922 the Country Party won fourteen seats, which gave it the balance of power in the House of Representatives.

Supreme as a leader in war-time, with the peace Hughes began to run into shoals. His work at the Peace Conference did not please everyone. He was an imperialist and he also wanted to see Australia a nation in her own right. Despite her willingness to enter the war, Australia still hankered after isolation. She fought for the mother country, not for her own safety. The war over, she wanted to return to her domestic concerns and give them her whole attention. She did not seek responsibility. Even the New Guinea mandate for which Hughes fought so staunchly was unpopular. It would be an expensive nuisance. There were some, not a few, who did not even desire to see Australia represented at the Peace Conference.

Then, too, there were many who felt that Hughes had too much power, that he was developing into a dictator, and they had a healthy distaste for such. The Country Party disliked him heartily and worked for his downfall. When in 1922 they held the balance of power Earle Page agreed to support the Nationalist Party, provided it dropped Hughes. Hughes resigned in February 1923 and advised the Governor-General to call upon Stanley Melbourne Bruce to form a ministry. And so the Bruce-Page Government came into power. The Cabinet was composed of six Liberals and five Country Party members.

Bruce was a great contrast to Hughes. He was a dyed-in-the-wool Liberal, a Cambridge man with an Australian accent, an athlete, a returned soldier and a business man. His apprenticeship to politics had been short, which meant perhaps that he had fewer enemies. He inherited a lot of problems but kept his feet until 1929.

One of the principal difficulties bound to face any Prime Minister was the relationship of the Commonwealth to the States. The Constitution had safeguarded the rights of the States. The war had expanded the powers of the Commonwealth. The War Precautions Act gave the Federal Cabinet and Parliament legal right to override the States; also, to prosecute the war, the Commonwealth moved into the loan and taxation field. It acquired a wider financial experience than had been envisaged when the Constitution was drawn up. Hughes was in no hurry to repeal the War Precautions Act, and with a heavy war debt and the responsibilities of the repatriation scheme the Commonwealth could not retire and live on customs dues. The power of the purse had come to stay.

There is a story of a house that collapsed because the builder made the fatal mistake of taking the scaffolding down before he put the wallpaper up. Hughes did not want to relinquish the War Precautions Act before the Constitution was amended. A referendum to extend the Commonwealth's powers to deal with monopolies, a tentative nationalization programme, was defeated in December 1919. Three States were in favour of the change, three against. It was, as usual, a stalemate.

The main point at issue between the States and the Commonwealth was money. Since the Surplus Revenue Act of 1910 the Commonwealth had been distributing money to the States on a *per capita* basis. The war had increased the Commonwealth's commitments. The public at large felt that double taxation was an intolerable burden. The Federal Government was dissatisfied with the whole arrangement. William Watt, the Deputy Prime Minister, put forward a scheme. Under it, *per capita* payments to the States would cease, and the Commonwealth would relinquish the right to tax incomes under £2000 a year. This would compensate the States and abolish double taxation except in the higher income brackets. At this time, 1919, it must be remembered that £2000 a year was a much more sumptuous income than it is today. The States, however, were so hostile to this suggestion that it was not worth while putting it to the vote.

The dispute seemed as endless as it was blind. In 1923 the States and the Commonwealth met in conference to discuss taxation, but it was not until 1926 that the States Grants Bill virtually abolished the *per capita* payments. The States had refused a Royal Commission to inquire into finance, so Bruce decided to force the issue. The Act allowed the States one more year of the old arrangement. After that the Commonwealth would take over the States' debts, paying 2s. 6d. a year for every £100 of debt and the States 5s., the money to go into a sinking fund which, it was hoped, would extinguish all debts in about fifty-eight years.

The Loan Council, set up on a proper legal basis, would in future control all borrowings and conversions. All the States, except New South Wales, agreed and the way was open for the taking of a referendum to make the necessary constitutional changes. The referendum was held on 17th November 1928, and was accepted by all States. This was almost a miracle. Two referendums had been lost during 1926, one concerned with industry and commerce and the other with the maintenance of essential services. It looked as if the negative habit were deeply embedded, but everyone, the Premier of New South Wales excepted, was heartily tired of the long financial dispute and glad to have it settled. The taking over of State debts by the Commonwealth had first been mooted at a joint Federal and State conference in Hobart in 1905 and pressed in 1909 by the Prime Minister, Andrew Fisher. Thereafter the issue continually recurred. It was at last consummated.

Borrowings for development had rocketed between 1918 and 1921 from £14,000,000 to over £40,000,000 a year. It was becoming fantastic. The Loan Council, which consisted of the Commonwealth Treasurer and the Treasurer of each State, was to be a brake on it or at least to rationalize it.

The debts transferred to the Commonwealth amounted to £672,120,415. The Commonwealth would pay about £7,500,000 towards the interest each year, besides contributing one-third of the sinking fund. The weak financial positions of Tasmania and Western Australia were acknowledged by special grants of £378,000 and £380,000 respectively for a limited period. The contestants, if not satisfied, were exhausted.

Australia had acted as a nation during the war, now in peace-time she gave, reluctantly it is true, proof that she could achieve financial solidarity. It was just as well, for within a year a depression was to test her strength.

It is particularly difficult in Australian history to separate political and economic issues. George Elton Mayo puts his finger on the reason in his *Democracy and Freedom* (1919), a doctrinaire pamphlet of considerable, if dated, interest.

. . . in Australia . . . the social function of the more important occupations having been obscured, an attempt has been made to solve the resulting problem by political means. . . . The process is more complete in Australia than in other countries; industrial grievances have been generalised into a political party issue. . . . The fact that economic problems require economic solutions is disregarded; the political and economic activities of society are hopelessly confused. . . . Every economic difficulty is immediately generalised as a political issue, the public takes sides, and thereafter public discussion implies emphasis of one aspect and suppression of other, equally vital, aspects of the problem.[1]

One does not have to go all the way with Professor Mayo to see that there is a seed of truth in this. It applies more to the States than to the Commonwealth. The Commonwealth has made a consistent and repeated attempt to consult the experts. Commissions, boards, and panels have not always been popular with the electors. This can be put down to a number of causes, to the pocket consciousness of the taxpayer, to the natural parochialism of a small people, and to a deeply inbred egalitarianism. The experts are rarely as encouraging as the politicians. Taking sides is an old habit, and impartiality, though intellectually approved, has a damping effect. Besides, certain sections of the community found it hard to believe in the impartiality of the university-bred economist or scientist. The same attitude works also in reverse. A distinguished professor of moral philosophy, at the end of a lecture in which he had put the case for socialism with great eloquence, saw fit to add, "But I, I vote with my class." A strong sense of class distinction, rooted in history, has quite naturally given rise to an aggressive egalitarianism and a painful suspicion of the expert or the foreigner.

The Commonwealth Government, with a wider outlook than that of the States, has a readier acceptance of non-party issues and in times of crisis accepts coalitions. The war of 1914-18 imposed a training on the Comwealth whilst it was still in the experimental stage and malleable. The military expert took over, he was followed by the economist and the financier.

From then on it was a short step to the scientist. In 1920 the Commonwealth set up the Institute of Science and Industry. It tackled, in a small way to begin with, the problems of primary and secondary production. In 1926 the Science and Industry Research Act was passed and the more powerful Council for Scientific and Industrial Research came into being. The Government had now undertaken the sponsorship of a wide research programme. It was a form of development that paid high dividends in the Second World War. Research on a scale beyond the capacity of any university, company, firm, or association was undertaken and co-ordinated. Pure and applied science alike came within its scope, anything from astrophysics to the calibration of instruments. The findings of the research teams, duly copyrighted or patented, belong to the people of Australia and, when used abroad, become a source of income. The Council was financed out of revenue and by contributions from industry. Overlapping and trade secrets were alike eliminated. In 1949 the Council, widened again, became the Commonwealth Scientific and Industrial Research Organization. It has its own Minister in the Cabinet, but is free of political control.

C.S.I.R.O., pioneer and adviser, has proved a more effective and stable influence on production and development than the ephemeral State enterprises already mentioned, because assistance is substituted for competition.

The Council for Scientific and Industrial Research began with an income of about £250,000 a year, the Organization which grew out of it was to spend more than £4,000,000 annually. A shortage of scientific personnel was one of the initial difficulties and a Science and Industry Endowment Act put up £100,000 for the training of research men.

This form of government "interference" in the economic structure of the country has been highly successful. The subject of tariffs, controls, and subsidies was much more thorny.

Protection, it will be remembered, was one of the original planks of the Commonwealth Constitution. Manufacturers desired it, the Labour Party supported it in the expectation of increased employment, isolationists and those who thought nationally hoped that through protection Australia could become self-contained and redress the balance of geography. Finally the new Government looked to tariffs as a painless way of providing itself with revenue. To pay its way and reimburse the States for their loss of revenue, the Commonwealth required a levy of about 18 per cent on imports. In the first Commonwealth Tariff (1903) some goods, especially those required for development, were admitted free, and the revenue lost on them had to be made up on other commodities, particularly luxuries. The tariff was reviewed in 1908 when preference to imports from the United Kingdom was incorporated, and again in 1914. The trend was ever upward. Even if revenue was the first consideration, the effect of raising the tariff was to give more protection to home industries. The whole subject was controversial. The opponents of the tariff claimed that it kept alive uneconomic industries and penalized the consumer. The Government appointed a Royal Commission to look into the rights and wrongs of the tariffs. Its chairman was Sir John Quick, but the Commission deliberated from 1905 to 1907 nevertheless. The 1908 tariff embodied its recommendations. Some bounties on rice, tobacco, cotton, iron, and steel were included, for these industries needed government help over and above protection to get onto their feet.

The 1914 tariff brought forward by Fisher's Labour Government introduced no new principles, only raised the duties.

During the war revenue from tariffs fell away, but war conditions, by cutting down oversea supplies to bare essentials, acted as a protection to home industry. The effect of this was reduced by lack of labour owing to enlistment.

In 1920 a new tariff was prepared. It is described as a "three-decker tariff", but bears no relation to the sandwich. It increased preference to the United Kingdom. This was a natural carry-over from the war-time contracts by which Great Britain had undertaken to buy Australian surpluses. This mutually profitable arrangement had strengthened the commercial bond. It gave higher protection, and in this there was a new twist. English capital was flowing into Australia to found new enterprises. Protection was one way of encouraging these welcome investors. The intention was made clear in outlining the protection that would be given to industries not yet founded. The preference idea was extended to other favoured countries by an intermediate tariff schedule. So you have your three decks: a general tariff, a considerable preference to goods of English origin, and a smaller preference to the commodities of nations with whom trade treaties or arrangements had been made. The 1920 tariff was considered necessary, not only to foster industry but to prevent "dumping", or the unloading of goods at a cut price, by countries where means of production, especially labour, was cheap. Japan, for instance, was in a very advantageous position to flood the Australian market with cheap goods. That she was prevented from doing so by customs barriers led to ill-feeling and Japan refused to buy anything from Australia except wool and flour.

In 1921 a Tariff Board was created to look after the practical details of the tariff; these included the classification of goods into one or other class, consideration of special cases for increase or reduction of duties, and a watching brief for the consumer to restrain manufacturers from exploiting him under cover of the tariff. It was an advisory body, empowered to hold inquiries and collect evidence.

On the advice of the Board a new tariff schedule was issued in 1925. It was an adjustment. Forty-seven items paid less duty, fifty-three paid more. The over-all revenue and protection were increased rather than reduced, but it was hoped the changes would prove more equitable. In 1925 special duties were promulgated to give additional protection to the iron and steel industry.

So matters rested for the moment. The next set of import duties arose out of and are part of the story of the depression which hit Australia at the end of the 1920s.

Professor L. F. Giblin in his *Economic Survey of Australia* has estimated the value of protection to Australian industries in a table which he warns us is only an approximation.[2]

	1902	1928-29
Value of production	£32 million	£177 million
Value per head of population	£8.3	£28
Value per head of population at 1902 prices	£8.3	£14
Value of production per head	£100	£168

It is naturally very difficult, even with the statistical material available, to estimate how much of this progress was due to protection and how much to other causes.

The simple basic idea of charging customs duties on imports grew into something much more complex. The 1914-18 war upset the Australian economy. The Government had to intervene to adjust marketing to the war effort and stabilize prices through controls. Certain advantages were obvious. Controls could not be taken off too suddenly when the war ended. The Country Party was formed in the rural interest. It was at first anti-protectionist, but on second thoughts advocated protection if it were applied to primary production. These were Australia's *exports*. Protection now came to include bounties and subsidies to assist exporters as well as duties levied on imports, that is, "all-round protection".

Professor Copland had described the protection of primary products as "a series of accidents". With all due respect I should myself call it a series of improvisations that were later elevated into a policy.

"Protection" was tied to politics through the Country Party and into the economic set-up through the holy and sacred standard of living. Wool excepted, Australian goods were too expensive for the world market. The expense arose out of relatively high wages and long-distance freights. If surplus was to be exported, government manipulation must make it possible or the home market bear the cost.

Sugar is the classic example. At first it was grown on the northern rivers of New South Wales and in Queensland, particularly the latter, with cheap kanaka labour. This was contrary to the White Australia Policy and the social conscience. It was discovered that white men were able to work in the sub-tropical sugar climate, but, of course, their services were much more expensive. The Government, provided only white labour was used, gave Australian sugar a monopoly of the market at a fixed price. The industry prospered, the home market was fully supplied, and there was about forty per cent of the crop available for export. Sugar is usually produced in countries where labour is cheap, and Australian sugar could not hope to fetch more than £10 a ton in the raw state. In Australia it was worth nearly £20 a ton to the growers. To enable them to export forty per cent of their produce at the end of the 1920s the home price had to be raised to £26 a ton. This, with preference to England, where sugar is not grown, kept the industry on its feet. The cost of protecting sugar was, in 1931, about £5,000,000 a year.

The consumer had to bear the burden. Here it is as well to quote the analysis of a top-ranking economist:

> Wages, skilled and unskilled, in Australia are for the most part determined automatically on a cost-of-living index, based on the prices of the simple foods and housing. Food and housing cost about 60 per cent. of the wage, so that if the cost of sugar to the average wage earner goes up 1/- per week, wages go up two-thirds as much again, or 1/8d. per week. The result is, therefore, an increase in *real* wages. With 78 per cent. of wage earners in the working population for every £100 added to the price of sugar, £78 falls on the wage earners, and two-thirds as much again or about £130, is added to the costs of the employer. If the employer is in any sort of sheltered industry, he will be able to raise prices and pass on such increase in costs, because all sheltered industries are similarly situated and there is little elasticity of demand for export commodities. . . . The industries competing with imports are practically all protected and so are some of the export industries.[3]

It was hardly to be expected that sugar could long remain teacher's pet. Other primary industries demanded the same preferential treatment. There were dairy products, for instance. As long as only enough butter was produced to supply the home market all was well, but the policy of settling soldiers on the land meant more dairy farms and a surplus of butter. Butter was needed in the world, but the Australian price was too high for world parity. To meet the difficulty the Paterson Stabilization Scheme came into existence. From 1926 butter factories paid 1½d. a pound into a sinking fund which distributed a bounty of 3d. a pound on all butter exported. This 3d. was added to the local price. New Zealand could do better than that and could land butter in Australia at a lower price than it could be produced locally. Sixpence a pound duty was declared on butter coming into the country. The Australian dairy farmer acquired a monopoly and the bounty rose to 4½d. a pound. Giblin's remarks on sugar apply equally to butter. In 1931 the consumer put £4,000,000 towards his standard of living into the butter dish.

The same story can be told of dried fruits and other products. A habit has been formed of bridging the difference between Australian production costs and world parity by raising the price on the home market.

The economic structure was becoming more and more artificial, or, if you look at it from another angle, more scientific. Australia is far distant from her markets. She has always been dependent on primary products which fluctuate from season to season and are influenced by a variety of factors beyond the grower's control. Laissez-faire could only be a success where Australia had a virtual monopoly, as in fine wools. With other products Australia is at a disadvantage, particularly when she insists on maintaining a certain standard of living. The gap between production costs and world parity has to be met. It could be patched by borrowing, but a safer and more reasonable method was the planned economy.

In 1925 the Commonwealth set up a Department of Markets. The Minister-in-Charge, the Honourable T. Paterson, stated its functions:

(a) The supervision over and control of the grade and quality of goods exported;

(b) the organization of oversea marketing and the control of trade publicity abroad; and

(c) the collection and dissemination of commercial information.[4]

The 1914-18 war had taught Australia to act as a whole, the Department of Markets gave that lesson form. It was an essay in co-operation. Professor Copland might have been commenting on the new department and its overt policy when he wrote:

> The fundamental condition of stabilization is an accurate estimate of demand and a production according to the quantity that will be absorbed at the price fixed. Such estimates are accompanied by carefully devised advertising campaigns, and a systematic effort to foretell the short and long period trend of general business conditions and of prosperity in the special business concerned.[5]

Stabilization, he further pointed out, could never be complete because "supply is never completely elastic".

In Australia marketing control meant stabilization, which included price-fixing, adjustment of production to meet the expected demands of the market, and an endeavour to establish standards that would beat competition. This was necessarily experimental and fallible. There could not, in the circumstances, be any exact science of marketing. Australia could not swing the world markets, she could only adapt herself as nearly as possible to the forecasts of experts. The economist and the scientist were in the good days of the 1920s replacing the politicians and the individual capitalist in the marketing field.

III. Depression and Recovery

Since the crash of the 1890s much had been done, or attempted, to underpin the economic structure. The banking system had been strengthened, especially in the creation of a central bank, marketing had been rationalized according to current economic doctrines, a Loan Council endeavoured to regulate public finance, and apparent wealth had grown, but the depression which began in 1929 skittled all precautions and theories.

The greater complexity of the economic structure led not to strength but to weakness. As Professor Copland puts it: "The more complicated the industrial structure, the more pronounced and disturbing will the fluctuations be."[6] Or, as W. R. Maclaurin said, "so much rigidity had been introduced into the Australian economy that the price structure rapidly became distorted".[7]

In 1920-1 there had been a recession, but the economy had made a quick and apparently complete recovery. As someone has pointed out, a recession occurs when your neighbour is unemployed. It is a depression when you yourself are jobless.

In 1929 there could be no doubt that the economic situation was serious. The causes lay outside Australia. Prices were falling on the world market, confidence was going out like a tide. Australia was particularly vulnerable to this trend because she was dependent on the sale of her wool, wheat and metals, and because in the falsely good years after the war she had borrowed very heavily overseas.

The depression of the early 1930s closely resembled that of the early 1890s, a period of boom, borrowing, speculation and expansion, followed by a collapse which had its origin overseas. This time Australia had further to fall.

Australia was one of the first countries to succumb to the depression and one of the first to emerge from it. Almost overnight she found herself with a diminished and diminishing income from her exports whilst the interest bills on her loans remained high. She was committed to £27,000,000 in interest annually payable overseas. From 1919 to 1929 borrowings had increased rapidly. Maclaurin estimates the amount borrowed in these ten years as £225,000,000, 70 per cent of it for development of the country. This was, of course, desirable and desired, but it was not financially sound, because money borrowed at high interest was used for long-range projects which brought no quick returns. There had to be a wide margin of prosperity to make this not only profitable but possible. From 1923 to 1928 Australia had more money than she could absorb. The money had to be paid for, of course. Investors in England and the United States were anxious to lend, but they expected a good return. Loans were contracts that were binding in bad times as well as in good.

The Government had also to find money to pay interest on the large loans raised internally during the war and after, and it must honour commitments to returned soldiers and their dependants, which increased in bad times, since many of those set up in businesses or planted on the land failed. As in earlier land-grant times, the Government could not collect its debts. Under self-government, the loss had to be spread over the taxpayers.

State and Federal Governments were also the custodians of the standard of living. A people always critical of authority looked inevitably to it to initiate large-scale development and sustain standards. Public works, such as railways, roads, irrigation, electricity, have always been looked on as the natural function of the Government. This is not to detract from the large part played by private enterprise or by non-governmental co-operative movements. The fact remains that most development projects have been too large for any body except the Government to undertake, and the Government has also had its finger in some of the larger public companies, such as the Colonial Sugar Refining Company.

As the Federal Government entered the domain of public works and development there was inevitable conflict and overlapping between State and Commonwealth schemes. The Prime Minister, S. M. Bruce, who succeeded W. M. Hughes, was acutely aware of this wasteful lack of co-ordination. In 1926 he established a Development and Migration Commission with the object of mapping out the field of development and inducing (he could not force) the States to submit their plans to a central body for round-table discussion.

In 1927 he campaigned for the Loan Council. It had existed since 1924 as an advisory body. He wished to see it given legal status and power to integrate State and Commonwealth finance, particularly in the sphere of loans. The Premiers' Conference of that year endorsed the plan and in 1928 the Constitution was amended by agreement of all the States, without referendum. In 1929 the Financial Agreement Act passed all the legislatures. It was most important that a centralized control was established before the depression.

This machinery could be utilized in dealing with the depression, but could not avert it. From as long ago as 1922 imports had exceeded exports. This unfavourable balance of trade had been masked by general optimism and by the increased revenue which came from customs and bore the complexion of prosperity. In 1927 there was a surplus in the Commonwealth Treasury, but thereafter all the treasuries began to show deficits.

For the great majority of citizens the depression meant unemployment. When unemployment rises above ten per cent of the wage-earners the situation is critical. In Australia it rose to thirty per cent and that figure only covered registered workers; there must have been many more, not members of trade unions, who were thrown out of work, or, leaving school, could not find employment, or whose businesses or undertakings crumbled to nothing because of the unemployment of others.

Many said, "This is worse than the war." There was no one to give commands and in place of brotherhood there was the bitterest competition.

Men of action, to many of whom war had been an adventure with which they had felt quite capable of coping, now found themselves helpless and ashamed. The whole community seemed to shrink. Where there had been a shortage of houses there was now a surplus. Families lived together to save rent. Landlords dependent on rents could not extract them and suffered the pinch. Everywhere the misfortune of one pulled down others. Marriages broke under the strain, but juvenile delinquency is said to have decreased because fathers had more time, if less money, to give to their children. Anxiety gripped those in jobs for fear of losing them and the jobless because they did not know where to turn. Each feared the other. Bitterness grew and there were murmurings of revolt, but these had little meaning and were scarcely more than explosions of nerves. A change of government, however radical, was unlikely to bring alleviation.

In the 1890s bimetallism had been preached as a panacea, now the cry was Douglas Credit. The resources of the country, believed by many in the 1920s to be inexhaustible, were still intact. They were the property of the people and should be treated like assets in a bank on which all could draw. It was a chimera, but provided for many that modicum of hope without which life cannot be sustained.

The Governments, Federal and State, took action that was at first only palliative. In the 1929 elections the Labour Party, led by Scullin, came to power after a long sojourn on the Opposition benches. Few of the members of the new Government had had much administrative experience. It was faced with serious and urgent problems and was handicapped both by a minority in the Senate—it held only seven of the thirty-six seats—and by its own platform. The Labour Party had always set its face against any lowering of the standard of living. It was now caught between its deficits and its policy. The situation appeared to call for retrenchment on a grand scale. The Government was unwilling and unable to do this, arguing, not unreasonably, that any sudden cessation of government expenditure would only cause more unemployment. Scullin made some economies, but only along the lines of Labour policy. Migration was cut to the bone and national military training was abolished.

In the financial sphere something had, obviously, to be done. During the war Australia had gone off the gold standard and had only returned to it in 1925. Now, in 1929, she was forced to abandon it again. To honour debts in London the Commonwealth needed gold. A law was passed permitting the Commonwealth Bank to take over the gold reserves of the trading banks. This eased the situation, gold was shipped overseas, and the banks were backed by government credit. The value of gold rose and mining, which had retrogressed, took on a new lease of life.

To redress the balance of trade a new high tariff was promulgated and some articles, particularly luxuries, were prohibited. A complementary effort was made to stimulate export. A Wheat Marketing Bill, which guaranteed a fixed price to the grower, was lost in the Senate.

None of these measures did much good. The depression deepened whilst the Government was only tinkering with it. Australia was no longer popular on the London money market. J. T. Lang, the Labour leader of New South Wales, did not improve matters by his claim that the depression was a capitalist conspiracy against the workers, his avowed intention of repudiating debts, and his unorthodox policy of inflation. The British Government suggested that a representative of the Bank of England should visit Australia to confer with the Prime Minister and Premiers. It was a suggestion that could hardly be declined. In June 1930 Sir Otto Niemeyer arrived, some felt in the role of a bailiff.

His advice was cold and stern. Australia must retrench and economize to the uttermost. Tariffs should be reduced and borrowing should stop. Not unnaturally, he considered only the financial aspects of the dilemma. Although the Premiers' Conference agreed with him and in theory implemented his advice in the "Melbourne Agreement", William Morris Hughes was infuriated and sprang to the rebuttal with all his old verve. Many agreed with him and Lang carried opposition to the point of absurdity by an appeal not to reason but to emotion and class prejudice.

P. H. Partridge outlines the clash between Federal and New South Wales State Labour succinctly:

> The personalities of the two leading antagonists contrasted strangely. The Prime Minister was physically not robust, mild in manner, sincere and responsible, hesitating, cautious, fundamentally orthodox. . . .
>
> Although it was intellectually incoherent, Lang's policy was well calculated to appeal to the prejudices of large sections of the Labour Movement. . . . Lang promised that when he was restored to office he would increase wages and return to the shorter working week. In the course of 1930 . . . he began to direct his fire against Australia's creditors abroad. The Australian worker was being sacrificed for the English bondholder, and Niemeyer had come to prepare the sacrifice; his real mission was to force the Australian Governments to cut wages and social services. Australia's financial difficulties were due wholly to the burden of war debts, which Australia had in any case incurred to save Britain during the first world war; the British Government had failed to honour her own debt to the United States, but refused Australia a similar relief. The Scullin Government was allowing the banks and "financial interests" to govern in its stead. . . . Opposition to retrenchment was certainly spreading rapidly in Labour circles in New South Wales, and support for the repudiation or postponement of interest payments; at the same time, the Scullin Government was moving slowly and fearfully in the opposite direction.[8]

The schism within the Labour Party and the shock of Niemeyer's authoritative advice did much to delay even palliative action. The "Lang

Plan", with its accelerated government expenditure balanced by repudiation of interest commitments, was in conflict with the "Theodore Plan" and both fell by the way. E. G. Theodore was the Commonwealth Treasurer and generally believed to be the ablest man in the cabinet. Unfortunately his probity had come into question and had been the subject of a Royal Commission. His plan lacked the colour and dash of Lang's and was beyond the understanding of many electors. It was a financial arrangement which promised "blood, sweat and tears" rather than immediate improvement. In essence, it seems to me, it owed something to Douglas Credit and was founded on a "fiduciary note" issue based on the country's resources and disseminated by the central bank.

The Commonwealth Bank, without whose agency it could not be put into effect, rejected it on the grounds of unorthodoxy. Some of its other provisions, such as the reduction of interest rates and devaluation of the pound Australian, were to recur in later schemes. Theodore, despite the Bank's opposition, pushed his banking bills through the House of Representatives to lose them in the Senate.

The Lang Plan, though it had a demagogic appeal, blew itself out. The majority of the electors were too sane to believe in miracles by manipulation and too orthodox at heart to be happy with a policy which, if applied in private life, they would acknowledge to be dishonourable. The relief was general when on 11th June 1932 the Governor, Sir Philip Game, dismissed Lang for breaches of the law. He went to the country and the country rejected him and his plan. An ugly situation simmered down. How near the State was to civil war it is difficult to say. There was much sound and fury and the anti-Labour (or anti-Lang) sections of the community raised a quasi-military private army under the name of the New Guard. There was little secrecy about it and no State control. Whether it approximated more to an insurgent force or to the boy scout movement it is now impossible to say. When its *raison d'être* was gone it withered away.

The party split and its own diffidence had wrecked the Commonwealth Labour Government. The answer was the same as before, a break-away under a former Labour member, Joseph Lyons, who formed the United Australia Party. This party was successful at the polls in 1931. It was not so much a coalition as the old Liberal Party renamed. Under it enough unanimity was achieved to carry through remedial measures already planned.

In the meantime the States had, with Commonwealth help, given some rough first aid to the unemployed. The dole, whether in money or food coupons, kept them from starving. Relief works were begun and those employed received the full wage, but they were usually rostered to work, say, one week in three. By this hair-splitting the standard of living was kept inviolate. The public works run for relief were often intentionally rarified.

Men were, for instance, put to building scenic roads rather than to repairing roads already in existence on the theory that relief workers should not compete with or take work from men already in employment on necessary work. I do not say that this was the invariable rule, far from it, but it was a trend.

Money for relief was raised of necessity by increased taxation, a 15 per cent levy on incomes over £500 a year, a companies tax of 11 per cent, a sales tax which began at 2½ per cent but which, like the duty on spirits in the early days, was found so useful that it was raised repeatedly.

It was in mid 1931, when the depression was showing the first faint signs of lifting, that a definite policy was formulated and followed with good results. It is probably true, as Partridge points out, that the other abortive schemes—Theodore's Plan, the Gibbons resolution, the communication from the Economics Division of the Australasian Association for the Advancement of Science, the experts' memorandum to the Treasurer (the experts were Giblin, Copland, and Dyason), even Lang's Plan—did something to educate the public and their legislators to accept what came to be called the Premiers' Plan because, evolved by experts, it was accepted by the Prime Minister and the Premiers of all States in conference.

The move began in the Loan Council and was, of course, sponsored at one remove by the Commonwealth Government. The Loan Council appointed a sub-committee, which co-opted a number of leading economists, to survey the whole situation and advise on measures to cope with it. This committee is often referred to as the Copland Committee from its chairman. It produced "A Plan for Economic Readjustment".

The main heads of the plan were:

(*i*) Reduction of government expenditure by 20 per cent.

(*ii*) A reduction of "real" wages by 10 per cent. This would apply to the Public Service and all wages fixed by award and generally by internal arrangement in large private enterprises or public companies. Smaller concerns had often already reduced wages not covered by awards or even, secretly, those that were. Pensioners also suffered a cut.

(*iii*) Increase of taxation including a graduated supertax. The Commonwealth and the States both raised ordinary income-tax, sales tax went up to 6 per cent and primage to 10 per cent.

(*iv*) A reduction of the interest rate on internal public debts by 22½ per cent. This was in effect compulsory conversion of government stock, though called voluntary, with a penalty for non-compliance. Amongst the most trenchant critics of this measure was R. G. Menzies, who said, "Does it make a theft respectable by instituting domestic economies at the same time . . . ? This is the Lang Plan plus hypocrisy, plus a pretence that under the stress of the moment and in the emergency of the country, we feel compelled to do what otherwise we would not do."[9]

(*v*) Reduction of interest on bank deposits and on overdrafts.

(*vi*) "Relief in respect to private mortgages", which apparently meant a quasi-moratorium. Banks were encouraged to continue to lend money on good security.

(*vii*) The devaluation of the Australian pound as against sterling by not less than 20 per cent. This had already happened and even highly respectable institutions, such as the Bank of New South Wales, had been dealing in what was technically black-market exchange; devaluation was tantamount to paying exporters a bonus of not less than 20 per cent.

(*viii*) The use of Treasury bills to finance public works, etc.

The catch-cry that went with this reorganization was "spreading the sacrifice" or "equality of sacrifice". It was an effort to reduce the unhealthy swelling and bring the economy back to normal on a lower level. It was also a more subtle attempt, which could only be partial, to carry out the spirit of one of the often heard demands: "Put *everyone* on £5 a week."

It was not an orthodox, certainly not a doctrinaire, solution. It attacked the economic problem from two opposite directions, by deflation in the reduction of wages, salaries and interest, by inflation in the use of Treasury bills (as against notes issued by a bank founded on its gold reserves) and in depreciation of the currency. It was hoped to balance reduction of spending power by a decrease in the cost of production, so that even though less money came into a home the same amount of goods could be purchased.

Complete equality of sacrifice could not be achieved, but some alleviation was offered to every class affected by the depression and something was demanded from those not directly impoverished. At either end of the scale there were cries of "Woe! Woe!"—from Lang Labour and from high finance. But the plan worked. It could not have worked without fairly general co-operation. Everyone was heartily sick of the depression. No one believed that "prosperity was round the corner". So a willingness to try a remedy, however unpleasant, was engendered.

All the States, except New South Wales, followed the Premiers' Plan faithfully, and that most difficult State came into line after the eclipse of Lang. In the Commonwealth Lyons came to power in a more hopeful atmosphere than Scullin had ever breathed, though unemployment was still high and the disaster of the failure of the Government Savings Bank of New South Wales after a run, was still to come. The Commonwealth Savings Bank escaped the same fate when its alarmed depositors were reassured by the Treasurer that it would be backed to the full amount of the deposits.

Slowly the submerged world swung back into the light. The price of wool improved and the devalued pound made it still better. It is true that the rest of the community was paying for the devaluation as it paid for bounties and market stabilization schemes, but the prosperity of primary industry was still Australia's prosperity. Seasons were good, the flow had begun again.

Australia paid her annual £27,000,000 interest bill overseas, the price of her earlier optimism, and this went a long way towards re-establishing her credit. She was able by 1934 to convert most of her high interest bearing stock to 4 per cent.

An investigation carried out in 1932 showed that although unemployment was still acute the share market was rallying, government stock was rising, the banks were more confident, and their deposits were swelling. There was much still to do, but the economy was adjusting itself. There were those ready to say that this would have happened, Premiers' Plan or no plan.

IV. Looking Outward

Between the two wars internal problems consumed most of Australia's energy. Hughes had fought with every weapon in his considerable armoury to obtain a place for Australia amongst the nations of the world and to secure her power in the Pacific. His fellow countrymen were not particularly grateful. Nationhood as a sentiment was all very well, as a responsibility it was not so good. The country was still obstinately isolationist and the habit of dependence on the Royal Navy for defence and, for foreign affairs, on British statesmanship, was deeply ingrained. To be separate, to work out a peculiar destiny founded on social rather than political ideals, was a creed. She needed time and security and, like a trusting child, expected the old world to give them to her. She had been in leading-strings and only found them irksome when they meant interference in her domestic policies.

World War I, which did not touch her own soil, did little to educate Australians. It was the United Kingdom that, from the value of the Australian soldier and the impact of Hughes, learnt to think of her erstwhile colony as a nation.

In 1911 Prime Minister Asquith had declared: "The authority of the United Kingdom in such grave matters as the conduct of foreign policy, the conclusion of treaties, the declaration or maintenance of peace or the declaration of war, cannot be shared." War was declared in 1914 without consulting the Commonwealth and practically everyone considered that right and proper.

During the war the co-operation of the Dominions was sought, they sat as separate entities at the Peace Conference and signed the peace. Out of this emerged something new. The Empire had become the Commonwealth of Nations. This was not accomplished suddenly, it was an evolution which in the 1950s was still going on.

When in 1931 the Statute of Westminster was passed by the Imperial Parliament, it gave legal form to the Balfour Declaration of 1926. In this Balfour had declared that the Dominions were "autonomous communities within the British Empire, equal in status, in no way subordinate one to another in any aspect of their domestic or external affairs, though united by a common allegiance to the Crown and freely associated as members of the British Commonwealth of Nations".

Although a general announcement of policy coming from a high place, this declaration could have been easily rescinded under a change of government. The Statute fixed the policy. It only expressed something that was already *in esse*. By it, Australia, with the other self-governing Dominions, was given the right to speak for herself in the world, to make war or refrain from war, to enter into treaties, appoint ambassadors and consuls, and generally to pursue her own course.

The Commonwealth was so little interested that it did not even proclaim the Statute until Curtin did so during another war. A High Commissioner in London and a few strategically placed trade commissioners fulfilled her modest needs. The bonds of sentiment and commerce with the United Kingdom had been strengthened, not weakened, by the war.

Prime Ministers attended Imperial Conferences in London and were more or less (often less) taken into the confidence of the Government as regards foreign policy. When Australia was not, no offence was taken. She was willing to follow where England led. In 1922, in the trouble with Turkey known as the Chanak incident, Australia immediately offered to send a contingent but it did not come to that.

If Australia was indifferent to foreign policy she was strongly Imperialist. Hughes had given the lead. Bruce had followed it and they had only made articulate an old habit. Her place was in the Commonwealth of Nations, it was her world. She gave Imperial preference and sought it, not always successfully. Although she was anxious to be bound to England, England was equally anxious to buy in the best market, and Australia's geographical position militated against her.

The reasons behind the United Kingdom's change of front are not far to seek. Although victorious in the 1914-18 war, she had received a body blow that reparations could not heal. The world was more complex and dangerous than it had been in the golden days of Queen Victoria. Shipping losses and the growing power of rivals had reduced her carrying trade. She no longer had a near-monopoly of the results of the Industrial Revolution. The strain of protecting her grown-up children was too great. She had given them self-government and now she was ready to release them into the world. Self-governing Dominions were not profitable in the manner of

Crown Colonies. If they could fight as partners in a major war they could take care of themselves. To hold them by statute was neither necessary nor possible.

When in 1935 Western Australia, labouring under a sense of wrong because her economic development was being hampered by dumping from the eastern States, appealed to the Imperial Government to back her move for secession from the Commonwealth, she was refused. Such interference was "beyond the jurisdiction claimed by the Parliament of the United Kingdom".

Australia was free, quite free, except for financial and commercial dependence.

The League of Nations was a rather different matter. The idealism behind it appealed to a large section of the Australian community and she was proud to be a faithful member, taking her share of responsibilities. Here, too, she followed England's lead. In 1935 she proclaimed sanctions against Italy in the Abyssinian affair and sent H.M.A.S. *Sydney* to Gibraltar for service in the international force. The League of Nations was looked on almost as if it were an extension of the Commonwealth of Nations. What criticism there was came mostly from the Labour Party, where isolationism was strongest and all foreign entanglements were regarded with suspicion.

To come nearer home, there was Australia's policy in the Pacific, which could hardly be called foreign. By fits and starts Australia, particularly the State of Queensland, had been aware of danger from the occupation of islands in the Pacific, and on her near north especially, by foreign powers. At the Peace Conference Hughes had secured a C class mandate over German New Guinea, but had had to agree to Japanese mandates over islands north of the equator. The little man would have preferred outright annexation in New Guinea, but the United States stood in his way. A C class mandate was the next best thing as it conferred virtual sovereignty.

The taxpayers were not particularly pleased and foresaw a burden of responsibility and expense. British New Guinea, or Papua, had not been a source of profit. Great Britain had annexed the territory in the 1880s and the administration had been delegated to the Commonwealth in due course.

Papua, and Australia herself for that matter, was fortunate in having a first-class administrator in Sir Hubert Murray, who opened up the country and not only protected the natives from exploitation but improved their living conditions. The Native Plantations Ordinance of 1918 preserved the land to their use. As they became prosperous the natives were taxed on a *per capita* basis not less than 5s. and not more than £1 a year, the money to be used for their betterment in scientific research, medicine, village improvement, education, child care. . . . The policy was expensive and only paid its way whilst the prices of rubber and copra were high. They fell, and services could only be maintained by the Australian taxpayer. The

Navigation Acts prohibiting the use of coloured labour in ships channelled the export of Papuan products through Australian ports, particularly Sydney, which added to the expense of marketing.

When the New Guinea Mandate came into force in 1919 a Royal Commission, with Murray as Chairman, considered whether it should be administered with Papua. They found against and a separate administration was set up in 1921. The two years cost Australia over £1,000,000, and when the civil government was established it was beset with so many difficulties, including a shortage of trained personnel, that many wished that they had never been saddled with the mandate. It is easy to see why Murray was unwilling to merge the two territories, which were at different stages of development. His trained staff would have run so thin as to be ineffective.

Fortunately, the opinions of the over-thrifty and the indifferent had no effect on government policy. An efficient administration was built up and an island cover to the north of Australia maintained. This in some measure counterbalanced the other effect of the Treaty of Versailles which gave Japan bases, secret in their isolation, in the North Pacific.

V. And Life Went On

The twenty years between the wars had been a feverish time. None of it conformed to what people had been accustomed to look on as normal life. First there had been a boom, then a depression, and finally the long, slow, agonizing approach of another war. Despite the unevenness of the times, there had been much visible, even spectacular, development.

Partly as a result of the war communication had improved vastly. Air travel and wireless telegraphy, now in universal use, had shrunk the world.

Because of her great distances the use of the aeroplane meant more to Australia perhaps than to any other country. It was not distance alone that affected her, but distance from her natural point of attachment in Europe. Australians very rapidly became air-minded in the two decades of peace.

The story had begun before the war, as long ago as 1894, when Lawrence Hargrave had experimented, flying box-kites at Stanwell Park, on the South Coast of New South Wales. He had lifted a weight exceeding 200 pounds sixteen feet into the air. It was at that time a remarkable achievement. His kites can still be seen in the Museum of Applied Arts and Sciences, Sydney, labelled, with an outline of his exploits.

It was not until 1909 that Australia came into the picture again when G. A. Taylor made an experimental flight in a motorless biplane at Narrabeen. In the next year Duigan was flying his home-made aeroplane at Mia Mia in Victoria, and the well-known illusionist Houdini was sporting a French Voisin at Diggers' Rest. The first Australian aeronautic display was given in Perth in 1911 by Hammond, using a Bristol, and in the same year

W. E. Hart flew from Penrith via Parramatta to Sydney, the first cross-country flight. On the eve of the war Guillaux initiated an air mail, flying from Melbourne to Sydney.

This is a slender story, its events little more than curiosities or nine days' wonders.

Australians were flying in Mesopotamia during the war, and, as soon as it was over, the strides that aviation had made became apparent. In 1919 Wrigley and Murphy made the first transcontinental flight, Point Cook to Darwin, and A. L. Long in a 46-hour flight crossed Bass Strait from Victoria to Tasmania. We are amongst the great pioneers in the same year, with Ross and Keith Smith making the first flight from England to Australia. The next year Parer and McIntosh, though dogged by misfortune, repeated the feat and won the Commonwealth prize of £10,000. Two years later the first regular passenger service was inaugurated by the Queensland and Northern Territory Aerial Service (Q.A.N.T.A.S.). In 1924 two flights round Australia, a distance of more than 8000 miles, were accomplished, one of them in 90 hours' flying time.

In 1926 Cobham and his crew in a seaplane made the England to Melbourne flight and return. The year 1928 was a great one, though it began with the loss of Hood and Moncrieff in a first attempt to cross the stormy Tasman. H. J. L. Hinkler, who was later to crash in the Apennines and be buried in Florence, made the first solo flight from England in a light plane. "Hinkle, Hinkle, little star, fourteen days and here you are."

It was in this year that Kingsford Smith in his famous "bus", the *Southern Cross,* first came into the picture, crossing the Pacific from the United States to Australia. Later in the year, with the same partner, Charles Ulm, he flew non-stop from Point Cook to Perth and made the first successful crossing of the Tasman, both ways. They were emboldened to begin a passenger service serving Brisbane, Sydney, Melbourne, and Tasmania, which operated until 1931 when one of their planes, *Southern Cloud,* was lost without trace till its wreck was found in the Alps in 1958, twenty-seven years later. This was such a blow to the confidence of air travellers and such a heavy financial loss to the company that it went out of business. A freighter service to England had meanwhile been initiated.

The battle of the records was now on. Amy Johnson, the girl from Hull, was the first woman to fly solo from England in a tiny Puss-Moth plane, armed with hope and a knife to fight sharks should she come down in the sea. That was in 1930. In the same year Kingsford Smith set up a record for a solo flight, England to Darwin. In 1931 C. W. A. Scott cut flying time from England to Darwin down to nine days four hours eleven minutes, and J. A. Mollison, who later married Amy Johnson, flew from Wyndham to England in 8 days 19 hours 25 minutes. In 1933 Kingsford Smith had whittled it down to 7 days 4 hours 44 minutes and Ulm, Allan, and Taylor in their plane *Faith in Australia* (formerly the *Southern Moon* of the wrecked air service) did it in 6 days 17 hours 56 minutes, and for H. Broadbent it was 6 days 21 hours 15 minutes' solo flying. In 1934 C. W. A. Scott won the Melbourne Centenary air race from England to Melbourne in 2 days 23 hours 18 seconds. The whole nation followed the race on its wireless receivers to the exciting finish.

Progress was in every direction. "Smithy", with Captain P. G. Taylor as his partner, was flying to New Zealand and west-east across the Pacific to America. It was in 1935, when flying with Smith and Stannage, that Captain Taylor performed the heroic feat of crawling out on a wing of the plane in motion to feed oil to a failing engine, for which he was awarded the George Cross. A modest account of the flight may be read in his book, *Call to the Winds*. Ulm had by now opened an official air-mail service to New Zealand and to New Guinea. The Queensland and Northern Territory Aerial Service had taken a new name, Qantas Empire Airways Limited, and was carrying mail to England via Singapore.

When in 1935 Kingsford Smith and J. T. Pethybridge were lost on a flight from England to Singapore the age of the pioneers may be said to have ended. "Smithy" had had much fame, he had been a national figure and a pathfinder, but, in money values, the return for his work had been inadequate. His last expedition was ill-found and he was already beyond the optimum age for flying. The air claimed as victims most of those who pioneered it.

The following year, 1936, Australian National Airways was registered as a limited company. Air mails and air travel became ordinary amenities of life. A.N.A. was soon joined by other lines, Trans-Australia Airlines, Ansett, Butler, East-West Airlines. . . . Oversea flights were handled by Qantas and B.O.A.C., linking with the great airlines of the world, and air travel grew ever faster and smoother until England could be reached in two days.

The aeroplane made all the difference to the bush. It meant not only fast transport, but bushfire spotting, broadcasting of seed and fertilizers, more controversially, seeding of clouds to bring rain . . . but that development was in the future.

The aeroplane was tied into an enterprise which had begun in 1912. The Reverend John Flynn, a Presbyterian minister travelling through the Northern Territory, had seen the need of the lonely, scattered population for help in sickness as well as for spiritual comfort. The Australian Inland Mission was founded not only to spread the gospel but to set up bush hospitals in remote places, disseminate literature, and help in the education of bush children. Patrol padres moved about their huge parishes by pack horse or camel buggy and later in trucks. The first hospitals were at Oodnadatta and Port Hedland. The movement progressed even during the war, but distances were so great and the centres only pin-points of light. In emergencies help was often too late. The answer was a combination of two-way radios and the Flying Doctor Service in 1928. Small pedal wireless sets, or transceivers, were installed on the stations, at first in the Gulf country and then all over the inland. A doctor and his plane were centred on Cloncurry. He could be reached by wireless, could give advice and, if necessary, visit the patient and bring him into the nearest bush hospital. The idea grew and spread, more doctors and more planes were brought into service. Much of the sting was taken out of the loneliness of the bush, in sickness or accident help would come quickly and the pedal wireless could also be used for communication and gossip, much as the telephone can be used nearer in.

Another community effort peculiar to Australia which, though it had its birth early, showed the greatest development during this period, was the Surf Life Saving Clubs.

In 1906 Lyster Ormsby, a resident of Bondi, was instrumental in calling a conference of the various clubs that practised on Sydney beaches and evolving a standard technique of rescue and resuscitation. By 1910 life-savers, all voluntary, were required to pass an entrance examination in first aid and resuscitation methods. Drills and parades fostered the team spirit and competitions kept up enthusiasm. Gear, such as the reel, was evolved for team rescues. Rosters were worked out so that the bathing public would have constant protection at week-ends and on holidays.

During the first war the clubs faded away as practically all their members enlisted. In 1920 they revived and have continued to flourish. Surf-boats, watch-towers for sharks, and a patrolling plane have been added to the gear where possible, and club-houses built on the beaches. By 1930 there were seventy-two clubs in New South Wales, seven in Queensland, four in Western Australia, and one in Tasmania. The idea has even been adopted here and there overseas.

On the cultural front there had been two marked advances, both stemming from the Commonwealth Government. In 1932 the Australian Broadcasting Commission was founded as a government agency. It draws its income from listeners' licence fees. It has set up stations in all capital cities and many country towns so that most of the continent has access to its programmes. It has stimulated music by building up orchestras and bringing out from Europe and the United States artists and guest conductors. Symphony concerts and youth concerts at a reasonable price cater for those who prefer personal attendance to listening-in. A percentage of all broadcasts must be local in origin, and thus a hearing is secured for Australian composers, musicians, playwrights, and writers and speakers of all descriptions. The Commission is willing to absorb as much talent as offers and by its competitions, particularly in music, to give young artists a chance to prove themselves.

The Commonwealth Literary Fund, set up at the instigation of the Fellowship of Australian Writers in the 1930s, sponsors courses in Australian literature at the universities, finances writers, guarantees publication and awards honourable pensions to those who, having given their lives to letters, find themselves unprovided for at the end of their active life. The most important aspect of the Commonwealth Literary Fund is the public assertion that the writer is of value to the community.

These are only a spot check on developments between the wars, they are representative, not definitive. The 1920s were a period of over-all progress. New buildings changed the faces of cities. Canberra at last came slowly to life. Manufactures increased in numbers and variety, the drift to the cities continued, and there were those that lamented the passing of "the old Australia".

REFERENCE NOTES

1 G. E. Mayo, *Democracy and Freedom*, pp. 42-3.
2 L. F. Giblin, *Economic Survey of Australia, 1931* (ed. Copland), p. 122.
3 *Ibid.*, p. 124.
4 *Economic Record*, vol. iv (February 1928), p. 124.
5 *Ibid.*, p. 8.
6 See his article in *Problems of Industrial Administration in Australia* (ed. G. L. Wood), p. 814.
7 W. R. Maclaurin, *Economic Planning in Australia, 1929-1936*, p. 18.
8 P. H. Partridge in *Australia: a Social and Political History* (ed. Greenwood), pp. 352-3.
9 Quoted, W. R. Maclaurin, *Economic Planning in Australia, 1929-1936*, p. 83.

CHAPTER XX

WAR AGAIN

This was but the classic pattern of the defence of freedom by freemen; the pattern that is the special possession of no one nation, but is the final proof of achievement for all.

—G. L. Wood, *Australia.*

I. Prelude to a War

The depression was over. It had left many scars and taught, presumably, some lessons. Budgets were balanced again, the tide of prosperity was coming in, but times were not normal. The fear of a new war in Europe was spreading like a dark cloud over the sky. From 1933 onward the figure of fun, Adolf Hitler, became a real danger to peace. His coup in Munich and the widespread hysteria of the German people showed that there was substance behind the extravagant plans so openly outlined in his book, *Mein Kampf.* The purges, the persecution of the Jews, the domestic espionage, the too healthy strength-through-joy and the blatant Aryan myth were unfolded before the startled eyes of the English-speaking people. The French built the Maginot Line.

The dictatorship of Mussolini was scrutinized more closely. Behind the regular train services, the slum clearances, and the suppression of begging, torture by castor oil and other ugly symptoms of absolute power came to light.

Over a large part of Europe the light of democratic government was being snuffed out. The League of Nations, losing ground all the time, abided strictly by its rules. What happened in Germany and Italy was domestic, the League could not interfere. In the Abyssinian war it applied sanctions against Italy, the aggressor, but they were ineffective.

The rift between the ideologies of the dictator and democratic States widened. The dictators dared not stand still. They must provide their peoples with circuses if not bread. A scapegoat, or enemy, was essential to keep their minds off the internal situation and to build up their pride. Therein lay the great danger to peace. Never was a situation so well documented. The Left Book Club, a democratic, not a Communist body, to name only one agency, kept the world well informed of what was happening inside Europe.

THE LIGHT HORSE SERGEANT

From the painting by G. W. Lambert, A.R.A., in the possession of the National Art Gallery of Victoria

CAROLINE CHISHOLM

In the 1920s there had been a big peace offensive expressing itself in the Kellogg Mission, in "non-violence" protests, in disarmament. In the blaze of idealism there was also an element of economy. Now a cold trickle of fear began in men's hearts.

Australia was affected by the new situation. She had indulged in pacifism and had abandoned national military service. She was now bombarded by propaganda literature and films which revealed the worsening situation in Europe. The first wave of refugees was arriving, they were for the most part the prudent ones who had seen the writing on the wall and had got out of Europe in time with enough money to finance the long journey to Australia and there begin a new life. Many of them were Jewish. They brought new skills and a new attitude to life.

The Civil War in Spain loomed up as a portent. Constitutional government was defeated in Spain and another area in Europe fell under a dictatorship. To thinking people it was evident that sooner or later there would be war in Europe. A Pacific war was not yet envisaged, though since 1931 the Chinese "incident", to wit, Japan's invasion of North China, had been in full swing and in 1933 Japan, as well as Germany, resigned from the League of Nations and the year after withdrew from the London Naval Treaty.

The majority took it for granted that if Britain were at war Australia would be, too, though she was no longer technically bound to follow in the mother country's footsteps. Even those who did not feel impelled to declare war in a quarrel not their own knew that war in Europe would rob them of the defence on which they had always counted and cut vital lines of communication.

The Lyons Government was in power during the 1930s. It will be remembered that Joseph Lyons, a Tasmanian, had begun his political career as a Labour man. By a truly Australian metamorphosis he had become the head of a Liberal, or United Australia, Party Government. His policy was naturally of the middle-of-the-road type and he himself, a man of integrity but no great brilliance, was the sort of leader most sympathetic to the electorate, a safe man, an ordinary man well calculated to represent the man in the street. In 1933 he had begun to rearm Australia with the accent on the Air Force. In 1928 Sir John Salmond of the Royal Air Force had been invited to inspect and advise upon the then rudimentary Australian Air Force. He had recommended a root-and-branch reorganization costing about £2,000,000 for equipment alone, and a nine-year training plan. With the fall of the Bruce-Page Government and the onset of the depression this was scrapped. The Government built up its naval strength rather than the Army or Air Force. In the years that followed depression, idealism and the Labour Party's policy had reduced defence to vanishing point. To quote the Hon. Paul Hasluck:

By the beginning of 1933 the Australian defence system had reached its lowest point for twenty years. The training strength of the military forces was below 28,000. The commissioned strength of the navy was two cruisers, one destroyer, a depot ship, a sloop and a motor-boat, and the sea-going personnel numbered 3122. The air force had an approved establishment of less than 1000 officers and men plus a Citizen Air Force of 300, and its handful of aircraft were primitive. Senator Hardy said its twenty-eight front-line machines would be "about as effective as a box of crazy kites bought in a toy shop". The annual defence expenditure had been halved. The achievements of the Bruce-Page five-year programme, moderate as they may have been, had been dissipated. In 1933 Australian defence had to start again to build up the severely-reduced services. The chief disability was not that services had been truncated and weakened and had lost good men, but that for three years of depression the political discussion of defence matters had been almost solely along the lines of who should or should not be retrenched.[1]

Time was running out. In the new Government of 1933 a veteran of the 1914-18 war, Senator Pearce, was Minister for Defence and Hughes was back in the cabinet, albeit as Minister for Health. Between them they ensured that something was done and above all rallied public opinion. Hughes, with all his old sparkle, declared that "the Dove of Peace has fled to regions unknown. Mars once again in the ascendant smiles sardonically at Geneva. Yet Australia in an armed world is almost defenceless."[2]

A Citizens' National Defence Committee sprang up in Sydney, the Press became vocal, the Salmond plan was revived. Rearmament was a live issue once more.

The Department of External Affairs—still very young, for it had come into being in 1935—was by 1937 shaping a foreign policy. It recognized and publicized the danger from Japan, but had nothing better to suggest than a treaty with her, an equivalent of appeasement. The actual shape the war was to take was even outlined as the maximum danger ahead—war with Germany in Europe, with Japan in the Pacific, and a third enemy, such as Italy, astride the lines of communication.

The problem of the war was posed, only the solution was lacking. As late as March 1939 the Lyons Government initiated a new three-year defence plan. The Air Force was growing both in numbers and efficiency and, as a supplement to the Army, Hughes sponsored a militia which by 1939 was 35,000 strong.

The difficulties of Australian defence must not be underrated. It was not only a matter of a small people defending a vast coastline, but it was also a problem in co-ordination. Since Australia was a member of the British Commonwealth of Nations, her defence plans were, in theory at least, part of a general scheme which was discussed but ineffectually, at the annual

Imperial Conferences. Geography, unless complete control of the seas could be postulated, made co-ordination very difficult to realize. Danger threatened from at least two opposite directions. The Dominions differed in outlook and vulnerability. Actually by 1939 Australia was spending more *per capita* on defence than any of the other members, except the United Kingdom, and with New Zealand she was the most vulnerable. The British base at Singapore was her bulwark, ironically comparable to the Maginot Line for France.

The crux of the matter really was that the initiative lay with the enemy elect. Hitler's megalomania, which he had imparted all too readily to the German people, made them completely ruthless and reckless. Japan, disappointed in the spoils of one war, affronted by the White Australia Policy and feeling her way to leadership in the Far East, was also consumed by a daemonic pride. Both peoples were militaristic and proud of it. When bluff failed they were ready to fight. The prevailing attitude in the United Kingdom and the Commonwealth of Nations was completely different. Peace was almost universally desired. A rational and tolerant democracy led to the ill-starred policy of appeasement and the tragicomic capitulation of Chamberlain at Munich, which condoned the absorption of Czechoslovakia and Austria into the German bloc. A moral problem existed, while on the other side there was no problem. There is the shape of Greek tragedy in the bitter consequences of the ideals of peace, non-interference and non-aggression which disarmed the former protector of small nations in the face of militant dictatorships and its result in the sacrifice of Spain and Czechoslovakia. Rearmament became an obvious necessity, but it was for defence and not offence, and was in the spirit of an age already gone, if it ever existed.

Anthony Eden, then Secretary of State for Foreign Affairs, summed up British policy in a speech delivered in November 1936:

> These arms will never be used in a war of aggression. They will never be used for a purpose inconsistent with the Covenant of the League [of Nations] or the Pact of Paris. They may, and if the occasion arose they would, be used in our own defence and in defence of the territories of the British Commonwealth of Nations. They may, and if the occasion arose they would, be used in the defence of France and Belgium against unprovoked aggression in accordance with our existing obligations. They may, and if a new Western European settlement can be reached, they would be used in defence of Germany were she the victim of unprovoked aggression by any of the other signatories of such a settlement. I use the word "may" deliberately, since in such an instance there is no automatic obligation to take military action. It is, moreover, right that this should be so, for nations cannot be expected to incur automatic military obligations save for areas where their vital interests are concerned.[3]

This might seem outside the range of Australian history proper, but it was part of the involvement.

As war drew closer with slow fatality there was nothing that Australia could do about it except what she had always done, trust to British diplomacy and follow her lead. Despite Hughes, the Balfour Declaration, and the Statute of Westminster, she was not consulted much more fully in matters of foreign policy than before the First World War. Her Government accepted the policy of appeasement apparently without serious criticism and rejoiced automatically and short-sightedly over the Munich fiasco. The community as a whole took it for granted that if the United Kingdom were forced into war Australia would be there.

Politically this was an easy decision for the Liberal, or United Australia, Party; to follow had always been its policy. For the Labour Party it was not so simple. Its interest in foreign policy had always been slight, crowded off the platform by more pressing and immediate domestic problems. It was inherently isolationist. Australia should mind her own business and develop her own way of life, Australia for the Australians and no enthusiasm for immigrants who might compete on the employment market. Money would be better spent on improving conditions than on armaments. The Labour Party had even greeted coldly proposals for closer co-operation with the United Kingdom on defence because it feared that Australia would be drawn into purely European conflict. The left wing of the Party confused the issue with imported talk of capitalist and imperial wars waged for the benefit of the arms and munition industries and with the intention of distracting the worker from his "proper study", and in the name of national emergency depriving him of his rights. These opinions did not go very deep but they were expressed. The Labour Party sat uncomfortably on the fence. Its considered pronouncement in conference in May 1939 was: "We maintain that Australia will adequately play its part in imperial defence by the maintenance of the inviolability of the Commonwealth of Australia." These were curiously empty words and could only suggest neutrality. How neutrality was to be maintained was not even suggested.

Another shade of opinion within the Labour Party separated the threat from Japan from the European conflict. The one was of vital importance to Australia, the other was not. At Port Kembla waterside workers struck rather than load *Dalfram* with scrap metal for Japan, believing, and rightly, that it would be hurled back at them as munitions of war. There was in the one party a great variance of opinion and much confusion. But this painful state was not by any means restricted to the ranks of the Labour Party, though it was more candidly expressed there than anywhere else. The more thoughtful the citizen, the more difficult it was for him to decide what attitude to adopt. There was fear on the threshold, there was traditional allegiance, there was the impossibility of foreknowing when and how the enemy would strike. Australia was unprepared, but her potential was far greater than it had been in 1914. Industry had made strides and she was in a much better position to arm herself. The depression had taught her to organize and to act in concert, her militia was seasoned by veterans. Anzac was still alive, classless and uncomplex.

II. Pattern of War

The pattern of this war was truly a world-wide one and to disentangle the part of one nation would be to throw it out of proportion. A record of events without comment, it seems to me, would form a useful background to the final section of this chapter.

On 1st September 1939 Hitler invaded Poland and the United Kingdom reached her sticking-point. She declared war. She had the blue-print of a defence, but she was not prepared, except as regards the Navy, for large-scale offence. The situation in Europe was as unpropitious as it could be. At the end of August Russia and Germany had signed a non-aggression pact. Austria and Czechoslovakia, with its valuable munitions plant at Skoda, were now extensions of Germany. Italy under Mussolini was naturally allied to Germany and, although not formidable in a military sense, was geographically important on account of her position in the Mediterranean. Spain under Franco owed a debt to Hitler and even in neutrality the Iberian peninsula was a stopper in the mouth of the Mediterranean. The United States was entrenched in benevolent neutrality and was unprepared for war.

Britain was powerless to aid Poland, which was quickly overrun. Germany, busy with this assignment, was in no hurry to commence hostilities. The so-called "phony war" lasted from September 1939 to April 1940. Both sides prepared for action, one with a sure knowledge of its objectives, the other defensive and waiting on the event.

On 30th November Russia invaded Finland. Again Britain was unable to help the smaller nation, though public opinion set hard against Russia. The Russo-Finnish War in perspective appears like a dress rehearsal. For what, was not then clear, but Russia was trying out her armaments as Hitler had already done in Spain and Italy in Abyssinia. In less than four months it was all over and a peace had been signed in Moscow. In the meantime, Russia had moved west to participate with Germany in a partition of Poland.

Nineteen-forty was the year of catastrophe. In the spring Germany moved west, invading Denmark and then Norway. The courage and friendship of the Norwegian people and access to her shores by the Royal Navy offered a brief hope that this time Germany had overreached herself. Norway was conquered, but remained a thorny prize, Sweden escaped occupation by co-operation and with her iron proved a valuable asset. The flat lands of Denmark were quickly overrun.

On 10th May—a cloudless May—Hitler invaded Holland, Belgium, and Luxembourg in one great forward thrust. On the same day Winston Churchill became Prime Minister of Britain.

Within five days the Dutch Army capitulated and on the heels of this inevitable defeat the King of the Belgians ordered his soldiers to lay down their arms. The British Expeditionary Force in the Lowlands was caught between a wave of fire and the sea. It was obvious that France was crumbling. On 28th May Britain began to evacuate her army at Dunkirk. This was disaster, but heroic disaster. Under heavy gunfire and air attack the Navy, with old men and boys using any craft that would float, brought home their men, wounded, shattered, without equipment.

The defeat of Dunkirk was the spiritual, if not the material, turning-point of the war. There were black days ahead, but the spirit of a people had been aroused and Churchill was there, its very embodiment, to see that it did not sleep again.

In June Italy declared war and France fell. The unthinkable had happened. In a last-minute effort to avert the collapse of her ally Britain offered France union. It must have seemed a shadowy and impracticable suggestion in a situation already so far gone. France was partitioned and lived on in a quasi-freedom under the puppet Government of Petain, the hero of Verdun, a battle twenty years away.

Germany, with a consolidated Europe behind her, now had bases within sight of England. The war at sea, by raider and submarine, intensified, a war of attrition, and extended even to the Tasman Sea.

On 10th July 1940 the Battle of Britain began from the air and by September the blitz on London was in full swing. The courage of the people was tempered again in fire, this time in their homes and familiar streets. Churchill promised them "blood, sweat and tears". As a token of the new offensive spirit, British bombers were over Berlin for the first time on the night of 25th-26th August.

The United States remained neutral, but President Roosevelt was staunchly pro-British. He realized that the time would come when America would be at war, too. But she was not ready. Meanwhile she gave help, both voluntary and official, within the bounds of her neutrality, destroyers in return for bases to relieve the drain on shipping and, early in 1941, the Lend-Lease Agreement was signed by which the States were willing to supply Britain's needs at a price and on condition that British ships came for the goods. All holdings of American securities in private hands as well as gold reserves were organized to pay the bill.

In September 1940 Italy had invaded Egypt with the intention of cutting communication lines. A new front was opened in North Africa and between January and March 1941 Wavell, with Australian divisions amongst his troops, successfully swept the coast from Bardia to Tobruk. As a diversion Italy invaded Greece and divisions, including again Australians, were drawn off from North Africa to her aid. This was disastrous. A German army under Rommel gathered in the desert and took back Wavell's gains from the weakened army, all except Tobruk, which, held by the Australian 9th Division, came under siege in April 1941 and remained cut off, except from the sea, for the next eight months. Meanwhile the Germans had come down in force into Greece and Yugoslavia, had driven out the Allies and followed them into Crete, whence they had to be withdrawn on 1st June 1941 with considerable loss.

Australian troops were next employed on a successful six weeks' campaign in Syria to prevent the Germans from getting a foothold there and threatening Egypt. This operation, a chancy one, made in Churchill's phrase "with such forces as we can find", the degree of opposition being an unknown quantity, was decided on without consulting Australia. As all went well this was not made an issue. It rankled more that the failures, disastrous operations in Greece and Crete, had also been undertaken without Australia's consent.

The increasing danger in Australia's near north now altered the focus of the war for her. In September 1940 Japan had ranged herself openly with Germany and Italy in a Tripartite Pact. She was also increasing her aggression in China and moving south. There was no open declaration of war, but it was clear that, using the European war as an umbrella, Japan meant to step up her plans for conquest in Asia. In July 1941 they were in south Indo-China. The Soviet was not likely to interfere with her plans as Germany, with what now appears incredible folly, had invaded Russia on 22nd June 1941, and the two nations were locked in a deadly struggle. (Russia had become automatically an ally and the dangerous task of supplying her with munitions of war through Murmansk lay ahead.)

After Indo-China there seemed no reason why the Japanese should not turn their attention to Thailand, Malaya, and the Netherlands East Indies. The Colonial Dutch were alarmed and sought British aid, there being no hope of help from their own homeland, which was now under German control. Australia was anxious to know what British policy would be in the event of further Japanese aggression. The answer was, by and large, "Singapore", and this was not wholly satisfactory. The base was not fully equipped and, although it was expected to hold out for six months until the Navy could send capital ships to relieve it, the situation from Australia's point of view was shaky. America's attitude was the greatest puzzle. She had interests in China and by policy supported Chiang Kai-shek, who addressed his appeals for help to her. But in her security would it be worth her while to give up her neutrality for any reason outside her own boundaries? For Australia it was obvious that there could be no security without the United States. Yet she could rely only on herself. Hasluck puts the situation succinctly:

The essential quality of the decision [that is, to send Australian troops overseas] at the time it was made is to be found in the fact that Germany and Italy were the actual and existent enemies; to resist them and to retain the possibility of victory against them it was thought essential to hold the Middle East gateway as well as the Atlantic gateways to Central Europe and to maintain Allied oil supplies. For this immediate end the Australian Government took a chance in respect of the prospective enemity of Japan, inasmuch as it neither reinforced Singapore nor greatly strengthened its home defence forces.

In reaching this decision the Government had not been neglectful of the possible aid that diplomacy might give in the Far East, nor of the importance of trying to ensure the goodwill and aid of both the Netherlands and the United States of America and to ameliorate relations with Japan. By reason of the events in Europe the Netherlands was now an ally and thus one obstacle to closer cooperation had been partly overcome, but the United States was still a neutral and her policy in the Far East was cautious, self-dependent and sometimes puzzling. The opinion of the Australian Department of External Affairs in a submission of 9th July was that every indication pointed to the conclusion that the United States would not come into war if Japan attacked Australia.[4]

Cordell Hull for the United States, seconded by the Commonwealth Government, continued to have diplomatic exchanges with Japan up to the last minute in the hope of extracting some promise to halt aggression. On 30th November 1941 a Japanese fleet was reported to be moving south from British North Borneo. It was clear that diplomacy had been another screen behind which the Japanese had moved forward.

Dramatically, on the night of 7th-8th December, Japan struck in three places—in Thailand, in Malaya, and at the American base at Pearl Harbour. The base was caught unprepared and sustained considerable damage. It probably satisfied Japanese pride to score off so powerful a potential enemy. It was bad tactics, of course, for the blow to American pride was irreparable. She declared war at once on all the Axis powers. Australia had an ally with untapped potentials and the greatest standing resources in men and *matériel* in the world.

The Australian Prime Minister, John Curtin, made his famous appeal:

Without any inhibitions of any kind, I make it quite clear that Australia looks to America, free of any pangs as to our traditional links of kinship with the United Kingdom. We know the problems that the United Kingdom faces. We know the constant threat of invasion. We know the dangers of dispersal of strength. But we know, too, that Australia can go and Britain still hold on. We are therefore determined that Australia shall not go, and we shall exert all our energies towards the shaping of a plan, with the United States as its keystone, which will give to our country some confidence of being able to hold out until the tide of battle swings against the enemy.

This was frank and realistic. It gave offence to some, amongst them R. G. Menzies, past and future Prime Minister. The appeal to the United States was not one-sided. In an authoritative article written before hostilities began John Gunther had said that should America go to war with Japan Australia was the only possible base from which operations could be pursued. It was not out of altruism that General MacArthur, escaping from Bataan, came to Australia to organize and lead a great American offensive.

Nor was Australia unable to make a worthy contribution to the Pacific War now beginning. She had raised four divisions, the 6th, 7th, 8th, and 9th. The 6th, 7th, and 9th had seen service in the Middle East and were battle-hardened veterans. It had been a risk to send them away, but their value was more than doubled by their experience. The 8th Division the Commonwealth had insisted on sending to Malaya for her own defence. The 9th she had already called back home from the siege of Tobruk. These divisions, like the first A.I.F., were composed entirely of volunteers. The Royal Australian Navy had served in the Atlantic and Mediterranean and was now coming home. Two ships had been lost off Tobruk and H.M.A.S. *Sydney* had been sunk on convoy duty in the Indian Ocean by the raider *Kormoran,* but not before she had sunk the Italian cruiser *Bartolomeo Colleoni* in an earlier engagement.

To quote official figures:

The total strength of the A.I.F. on 2nd December 1941 was 151,240, of whom 120,569 were overseas actively engaged in the war against Germany and Italy. In addition about 211,000 men had been trained for home defence in the Citizen Military Forces and 132,000 of them were in camp or on full-time duty in Australia. A Volunteer Defence Corps of 50,000 had been formed. The Royal Australian Air Force had a total strength of close on 60,000, of whom 49,000 were serving in Australia and 11,000 overseas. Out of the total enlistments since the beginning of war, about 14,000 were aircrew trainees for the Empire Air Training Scheme. The Navy, with a total strength over 20,000, had over 13,000 men serving afloat. . . .

Before Japan attacked, Australia had been afforded time greatly to expand her munitions, aircraft and shipbuilding industries. Since the outbreak of war approximately 35 new government munitions factories and 77 munitions annexes had been built or commenced in Australia. It was estimated that, on the second anniversary of the outbreak of war about 50,000 workers were directly engaged in munitions manufacture and about 150,000 were indirectly engaged.[5]

For Australia the war had now fallen into two parts and it was in the Pacific that her destiny lay. In Europe the tide turned, the great R.A.F.

offensive was pressed home against Germany; Allied armies pierced what was elegantly called "the soft under-belly of Europe" to liberate the Italians, who wisely changed sides; the second front was opened through Brittany and fierce fighting led on to victory. V.E. day came at last with the surrender of Germany on 8th May 1945, but, unlike the 1914-18 war, Australians took no part in the final offensive, they were fighting beside the Americans in the other great arena.

The Pacific War had some general resemblance to the European War. The United States and Australia were unprepared for the attack on Pearl Harbour and its immediate military consequences. They had underestimated the Japanese war potential, thinking of them as an impoverished and somewhat backward people, even though history had supplied a sample of their prowess in the Russo-Japanese War. The victory of Japan then had been attributed in the main to the weakness of an effete Russia. History teaches so little that Japan was allowed to repeat the coup of Port Arthur at Pearl Harbour. In the same way, the world at large did not expect Hitler to carry out the plans for conquest that he had published in *Mein Kampf*. The writing was on the wall, the readers were asleep.

As in the European War, the enemy took all the tricks to begin with and it was only slowly that confusion was orientated into a steady advance which ended, with the aid of science, in a victory which came like a clap of thunder. The catastrophes of 1940 were equalled by the catastrophic advance of the Japanese between December 1941 and April 1942, Pearl Harbour to the Battle of the Coral Sea.

In one night the American fleet in the Pacific was practically eliminated and vital shore depots were destroyed or damaged over a wide area. In the same month Japan subjugated Thailand after a brief resistance and persuaded or forced the Siamese to declare war on their side; they occupied the northern Gilbert Islands and landed in the Philippines; on 10th December, that black day, they sank the British capital ships *Prince of Wales* and *Repulse* and landed on Guam. The Royal Navy was now as impotent in the Pacific as the American. The whole vast area was wide open to attack. Already in early December Hong Kong was under fire by land and air and was captured on 25th December. Still in the same month the Japanese were in Sarawak, North Borneo, and far-away Wake Island. They continued to "mop up" the Philippines, entering Manila, the capital, on 2nd January 1942. They were simultaneously raiding Burma, penetrating the Netherlands East Indies, and threatening Malaya. War was coming very near to Australia. Kuala Lumpur fell on 11th January, and on the sixteenth Rabaul was bombed. The Japanese were penetrating our near north and the "screen of islands" looked flimsy indeed. So did Singapore. It was not only Europe that had a soft under-belly, Singapore had one, too. Her defences looked to the sea, danger was coming swiftly by land from the north and already in early January Japan had air bases within striking distance of the once vaunted fortress.

Before the defence of the Netherlands East Indies could be organized they were lost. On 24th January Lae, capital of New Guinea, fell and on 3rd February Port Moresby, capital of Papua, Australian territory, was being bombed.

Their conquests, particularly in the Indies, had the very practical advantage of supplying the Japanese with as much oil as they needed.

It was clear that Singapore, manned by British, Indian, and Australian troops, was doomed. It capitulated on 15th February and some 15,000 Australians of the 8th Division were taken prisoner to suffer in the next three years incredible hardship and brutality.

For the first time in history enemy action penetrated to the Australian mainland when heavy raids on Darwin began on 19th February. In March it was the turn of Broome and Wyndham, with the Japanese in complete possession of the Indies. The battle of the Java Sea had gone badly for the Allies in February when they lost five cruisers and six destroyers. In the spirit of singeing the King of Spain's beard, Japanese submarines had raided the coast of California on 23rd February and bombers were over Colombo and Madras in the following April. The advantage seemed entirely with the enemy. Well might Ian Morrison, correspondent for *The Times* in the Pacific theatre of war, exclaim:

> In six months she had seized the richest colonial area in the world and had secured untrammelled access to the sources of supply of those raw materials which had been the chief weakness of her economy. What a time it must have been in Japan! Victory after victory, Pearl Harbour, the sinking of the *Prince of Wales* and *Repulse*, the fall of Hong Kong, of Manila, of Singapore, of Rangoon, of Batavia! Can any country in the world's history ever have known such a marvellous succession of victories in such a short space of time?[6]

It was staying power that triumphed in the end and the United States had it. Already in March 1942 American bombers had had their first substantial success when they broke up a Japanese concentration of warships and transports off Lae. In the same month General MacArthur escaped in an open boat from besieged Bataan, one of America's last outposts in the Philippines, arriving in Australia on 18th March to take command of the gathering American forces. Bataan fell three weeks later, on 9th April 1942, and its name was written on the General's heart as surely as Calais was on Queen Mary's.

Slowly America was achieving air and sea superiority. In April she raided the Philippines and—great boost to her damaged morale—bombed Tokyo and other Japanese cities on 18th and 19th April.

On 4th May the American Navy broke up another Japanese concentration, evidently an invasion force coming south, in the Solomon Islands. The turning-point as far as Australia was concerned came in the Battle of the Coral Sea (4th-8th May 1942). Japan lost two aircraft carriers and it is estimated eleven other Japanese ships were sunk and seven damaged. The Americans did not go unscathed, losing the aircraft carrier *Lexington*.

Japan might continue to be victorious in China and elsewhere, but a full-scale invasion of Australia was no longer likely. In June another beard-singeing operation was carried out when three midget submarines penetrated the defences of Sydney Harbour. They were sunk without attaining their objective, the destruction of American ships in port, especially the *Chicago*.

Between 3rd and 6th June the Japanese suffered a major defeat in the Battle of Midway. It was American air power against Japanese naval strength and, like the Battle of the Coral Sea, it was in the modern style. The naval units involved never saw one another.

In August there began the Battle of the Solomons, a long sporadic engagement reaching its peak in the naval battle of 13th-15th November, when the Japanese sustained heavy losses. By 1st February 1943 it was over; the enemy withdrew from Guadalcanal.

The situation was at last in hand. The advance of the Japanese was stopped, it remained to throw them back from their entrenched positions. On 13th February MacArthur sent thirty bombers against Rabaul, which the Japanese had built up into their main base or jumping-off place. It is said that fifty tons of bombs and 3500 incendiaries were dropped that night. The Japanese then made Lae their headquarters, or would have done if the Battle of the Bismarck Sea, in which the Royal Australian Air Force co-operated, had not sunk, damaged, or dispersed the convoy on its way there.

In November 1942 the Australians began the most difficult campaign of their military history, hard going as it had often been. They, with their American Allies, had the task of retaking New Guinea. The Japanese had landed on the north coast and, against all expectation because the terrain was considered impossible, they had crossed the Owen Stanley Range. In what is often called the Papuan campaign the Australians drove them back over the Kokoda Trail. At first the citizen force, the Militia, was sent. How badly led and poorly supplied they were has since been revealed. They had courage but little else, no air cover, not sufficient food, and, most serious of all, no experience in the difficult jungle fighting. Later the hardened divisions trained in the African desert were thrown in. The Kokoda Trail is their epic.

Morrison, as an eye-witness, writes of the jungle warfare:

Not only was the actual fighting hard, but all fighting in the jungle imposes a great psychological strain on soldiers. They are fighting blind most of the time. The enemy may be at your side, and, if he remains still, you will not know that he is there. He may be at the top of the tree at whose base you are resting. . . . Our men fought and lived, therefore, in a permanent state of nervous tension, perhaps largely unconscious, engendered by their never being quite sure where the enemy was, where he might be. In addition to a strong heart and a strong body, jungle warfare demands the strongest nerves.

The hard fighting was accentuated by the hardness of the conditions of living. In the Owen Stanleys it would begin to rain regularly about three o'clock in the afternoon. Rain would pour down, most of the evening, much of the night. Our men would be on groundsheets with gas-capes stretched above them to keep the rain from beating directly on their bodies. But these did not keep them dry. The men who were holding positions in the front line could not even put up gas-capes. They just had to lie in the pouring rain.[7]

There was the tropical heat of the day, the biting cold of the night, the long supply lines that made food short, the wetness that prevented the lighting of fires to warm it, even if it had been safe to do so; there was sickness and exhaustion; above all, there was isolation. It was not possible to give the men frequent periods out of the line as it had been in Europe or even in the desert. It was a non-stop war. There was no chivalry against such an enemy, no civilized approach, no prisoners, for they were too difficult to guard and feed. The Japanese made this simple by not surrendering. They fought a valiant rearguard action, whatever else might be said of them.

Milne Bay, on the malarial coast, was the Allied depot for supplying the troops in the Owen Stanleys. Here construction battalions worked on the making of air-strips and the creation of other necessary installations. They were subject not only to disease but to constant enemy attack. The first Japanese air-raid came on 4th August 1942. They increased in intensity and at the end of the month the Japanese, supported by naval vessels, landed more than 2000 men. After heavy fighting in the worst possible conditions, they were defeated and withdrawn.

The long pull of the Kokoda Trail went on. On 23rd September General Blamey arrived to take command. On 2nd November the Australians took the village of Kokoda, valuable because it had an air-strip. By the end of the month the campaign ended in victory. The three-pronged assault on Gona, Buna, and Sanananda on the Papuan coast then began and was carried on by Australian and American troops. After hard fighting the Japanese were forced to evacuate the region.

The early mistakes in New Guinea and Papua were being remedied. The Australians learnt the art of jungle warfare, the supply system was improved, liaison between the services and between Australian and American commands ran more smoothly. In 1943 the tide of war had turned. On 15th September of that year Lae was retaken.

In 1944 the Australian Army advanced in northern New Guinea and landed on New Britain where Japan had her headquarters at Rabaul. As the Americans advanced in the Pacific the Australians took over Bougainville in the Solomons and conducted mopping-up operations. By January 1945 the Americans were back in the Philippines with the R.A.A.F. in support, the Netherlands East Indies were being won back, American headquarters were moved from Brisbane to Hollandia, Japan itself was being raided. From the end of November 1944 super-fortresses were attacking Tokyo from a base in the Marianas, with Guam, Tinian, and Saipan built up as supply centres. This was effective up to a point, but the distance was too great. The base was 1500 miles from the target. Admiral Nimitz was instructed to capture Iwo Jima in the island bridge between Tokyo and the Marianas. Gilbert Cant has described the island as "Hell's Acre".

> Iwo is five miles long and a fraction under three miles across at its widest point, and embraces eight square miles. For so small a fly speck, it has been compared with an extraordinary catalogue of shapes: a pear, an otter, a mutton chop, a sea monster, a gourd, a leg of mutton, a miniature South America and a mis-shapen dumbbell.[8]

To mix the metaphors a little more, it was a very tough nut to crack. It was cracked eventually at great cost. It was 660 miles from Tokyo, but that was not all. In Japanese hands it had been a strong point with radar and anti-aircraft installations and fighter aircraft in the path of bomber raids on Tokyo. It had to be eliminated.

The next step forward was to Okinawa. It took from 1st April to 22nd June 1945 to subdue the island. "After Okinawa everything that happened was in the nature of anti-climax."[9] It was like that. The engagement had lasted for three months of bloody, desperate fighting. In the meantime, Manila had been recaptured and Australian and Dutch forces were gathering in the East Indies.

On 14th July 1945 the American Navy moved in to bombard the Japanese coast. Defeat was obvious, but the end came suddenly. On 6th August the first atomic bomb was dropped on Hiroshima and its blast shook the world. It is believed that one bomb killed about 80,000 people. Two days later Russia was actively at war with Japan. On 9th August the second bomb fell on Nagasaki. It was the end. In five days Japan surrendered. On 2nd September terms were signed in Tokyo Bay.

The long struggle was over. The victors had suffered such losses that rejoicing was damped by shock. The problems of peace were ahead. Australia participated in the occupation of Japan and the effort to remedy the unchangeable by an infusion of democracy. Soon a schism opened in the national consciousness, markets versus the memory of 15,000 prisoners of war.

III. The Home Front

1. *Political Adjustments*

The war found Australia in a state of political crisis. There was nothing new in that. Lyons, the Prime Minister in the United Australia Party Government, had died in office in early 1939. The succession was not clear. His party had been disintegrating in internecine quarrels. Page, the leader of the Country Party, had not sufficient support to carry the Prime Ministership. Menzies had resigned as deputy leader and retired to the back benches because he felt that the party's and his own personal integrity were involved when the National Insurance plan, pledged at the polls, was dropped. Page attempted to form a Ministry, but could not reconcile the factions within the party. S. M. Bruce, High Commissioner in London, was asked to return to politics and accept the leadership of the United Australia Party. The terms did not satisfy him, and without much enthusiasm Menzies, who has never suffered fools gladly, was elected. On 26th April 1939 he took office as Prime Minister. It fell to him to declare war on 3rd September 1939. With him it was axiomatic that if the United Kingdom went to war Australia went with her. "The peace of Great Britain is precious to us, because her peace is ours; if she is at war, we are at war," he had said. He was untroubled by doubts on that point at least, and his Ministers prepared for war in a more logical and thorough manner than ever before in peace-time. He did not invent the concept of "national planning" for war, he inherited it and carried it through.

The work was unspectacular and few of the electors were aware of it. It covered much more than the defence scheme. It was a blue-print for the mobilization of the whole nation for war and, as Hasluck points out, it was as much the work of permanent heads of government departments and of expert advisers as of the Cabinet and Parliament.

It had its legal basis in two acts, the Supply and Development Act, which had to do with the production of munitions, the training of scientific and technical staff for that purpose, stock-piling, and the change-over of peace-time to war-time production, and the National Registration Act, whose object was to collect data on the skills of all citizens in order that they could be used to the best advantage for the war effort. An Advisory Panel on Industrial Organization consisting of leading industrialists was set up to smooth the path of the mobilization of secondary industry. There were also other Panels and Committees, such as the Accountancy Advisory Panel. The Liberal Government, true to its policy, was seeking the co-operation of private enterprise and non-governmental authorities. These had the great advantage of being *in esse.*

Meanwhile the Defence Department was compiling a War Book for which no legislation was required. The idea was not original, but followed the lines of a similar compilation in the United Kingdom, as recommended by the Imperial Conference of 1930. It was comprehensive and covered co-operation with Great Britain, between the States and Commonwealth, and between the armed services. Military, economic, and industrial aspects were all surveyed, new instrumentalities outlined, and plans to lay before Cabinet immediately on the outbreak of war were prepared. It fell into two main parts: preparatory measures before the declaration of war, and action to follow the declaration, not forgetting civil defence. It was completed before hostilities began and in effect put all Australian resources, whether of manpower or material, in the hands of the Defence Department, together with a detailed plan of liaison. It included a draft of the National Security Bill, which was to be the enabling Act supplying the constitutional power necessary for putting its scheme into effect. As much was foreseen and done in advance as the murky and uncertain situation admitted. All this was very different from the state of unpreparedness that existed in 1914. But something of the "fine careless rapture" was missing.

Finance had to be left to Parliament, but the Defence vote had been steadily stepped up. When the States boggled over co-operation, as they did before the war, it was usually on the money issue. As part of the machinery of co-operation the Loan Council gave birth to another committee consisting of Federal Ministers and State Premiers to deliberate on the subject and submit proposals to the Loan Council, which had come to personify the Purse.

When war came the National Security Act was passed and many of the plans outlined in the War Book came into force. The main trouble was that the war, though it was now a fact, remained as enigmatic as ever. During the phony war period no one knew which way the cat would jump. Confusion due to this uncertainty was blamed on the Government. It was only human that so many and so detailed paper plans in the face of a situation that failed to crystallize led to some stultification. To take a very minor example, air-raid shelters were prepared in the cities and then securely locked up to prevent vandalism.

This did not help the insecure United Australia Party Government. At the elections in 1940 it lost ground. Menzies scraped back to power, but was dependent for his majority on the votes of two independent members. Under Curtin the Labour Party had consolidated itself into a powerful opposition. Menzies, in the patriotic interest, suggested a coalition and even offered to surrender the Prime Ministership to Curtin. The proposal was rejected. This should not be looked upon as any coldness towards the war effort, the Curtin Government was to disprove that. It is probable that the Labour leader refused because he did not think a coalition Government could succeed. It would not be united. He would inherit all the internal bickering and the popular distrust expressed in the elections, and the necessary strength for total war could not accrue.

Menzies, losing the support of the independents and much harassed by dissension in his party, resigned in August 1941. Arthur Fadden (Country Party) made an abortive attempt to form an administration which foundered on the budget two months later. The Governor-General called upon Curtin, who carried on with the existing House until 1943, when his party had a marked success at the elections.

A War Advisory Council, which was non-party, had robbed Curtin's reluctance to join with the United Australia Party of its sting. As far as prosecution of the war went, Australia was united in effort.

Curtin was no sooner in office than he had to face war in the Pacific. Speaking to the people he said:

> This is the gravest hour of our history. We have a heavy responsibility. I ask every Australian, man and woman, to go about their allotted task with full vigour and courage. We Australians have imperishable traditions. We shall maintain them. We shall vindicate them. We shall hold this country and keep it as a citadel for the British-speaking race and as a place where civilization will persist.

Brave words, but lacking the Churchillian touch.

In one way his task was easier than Menzies's had ever been. The disasters of 1940 and the knowledge that her men were in battle had certainly hardened Australian morale, but the war was still distant. After Dunkirk all available rifles and other equipment were shipped to England. The response was emotional.

Now the appearance of an enemy on the very threshold had an astringent effect. Party and personal differences were sunk at last. The blue-prints came to life, manpower regulations really meant something. There could be no more groping. It was action stations for all.

The tormenting issue of conscription did not arise. The Second A.I.F. was entirely volunteer. The Citizen Military Forces, the "Chocos" as they were called, were conscripted for service within Australia. No referendum was needed to send them to New Guinea when the crisis arose. The Defence Act was amended in 1943 with support from both sides of the House. The events of 7th-8th December 1941 doubled the enlistments of the previous months (4702 to 10,669). Very soon every able-bodied man and woman had his or her logical place in the war machine.

New Commonwealth departments and instrumentalities were set up to meet the growing complexity of the war effort. The first was the Department of Information in September 1939, followed by a reorganization in November of the same year of the Department of Defence into four departments, Defence Co-ordination, Navy, Army, and Air. In 1940 came the Departments of Munitions and of Labour and National Service, which included Rehabilitation. In 1941 the Departments of Aircraft Production (English experts had said that it was impossible for Australia to produce aircraft of a type and in sufficient numbers to benefit defence, yet it was done), of External Territories, Home Security, Transport, and War Organization of Industry were created. In 1942 there were changes, but only one new Department, Post-War Reconstruction, separated out from Labour and Industry. After the war most of these new departments withered away. The list is an indication of how much of the economic life of the country the Government took over to fit its war plans.

All was not accomplished without friction. There was endemic trouble between the States and the Commonwealth. In war-time it was necessary that the Commonwealth should have dictatorial powers. These had been sought through the co-operation of the States and made legal by a short term National Security Act. The States nevertheless resented the assumption of power by the Commonwealth, particularly in its financial aspects. In 1942, to achieve equality of taxation amongst other things, the Commonwealth assumed the sole right to collect income-tax, making the States annual grants in compensation—a compensation which was never deemed adequate.

For Australia, war-time expenditure was astronomical. In the financial year 1942-3 it rose to £562,664,000. The necessary money was raised, in the main, internally by taxation, by loans, by war savings certificates, and by voluntary non-interest bearing loans. As there was full employment and many were earning more than ever before in their lives, the returns from income-tax and indirect taxes were swollen in proportion. There was not the same anxiety over finance as there had been during the 1914-18 war. It was taken for granted that the necessary money would be found and it was. Australia was richer and she was totally involved. The coming of American troops in great numbers, their victualling and their spending, also helped the economy.

A further source of trouble was the Communist Party, always numerically small, about five thousand known members, but very vocal and always in opposition to all other parties. The most irritating feature of this gadfly in war-time was its overriding allegiance to Russia. Communist literature and slogans were calculated to create or increase war hysteria and to spread scepticism of the Allied cause, of the Home Government, of the motives and performance of all bodies and organizations that could not be labelled unmistakably "proletarian". Fascism and Nazism they could hardly condone, but they could and did attribute the same qualities to the Allied cause. The illogicality of many of their arguments and the parrot-like quality of their "dialectic" were often masked by the emotion and confusion of the times.

Until Russia was attacked the war was attributed to "imperialist gangsters" and the always effective cry of profiteering was raised. That Communist sabotage of the war effort was going on was freely believed. Under National Security Regulations censorship shut down firmly on Communist publications and the movement went underground more or less effectively. On 15th June 1940 the Communist Party was declared illegal. This step was only taken after careful thought and much hesitation. The Government in its war against Fascism was little anxious to attack free speech or any other liberty of the people. There were a few raids to seize subversive literature, a few prosecutions, but on the whole the ban was interpreted very mildly and in December 1942 was lifted as the result of an undertaking by the party that it would co-operate in the war effort.

There were other disturbing influences of a general nature.

> Chronic lack of trust seemed to be one of the most marked characteristics of Australian politics, as of Australian social life, in the early years of war. Some of this lack of trust was due to experiences in the period between the two wars; some was due to deep differences in outlook and theory; some was the fruit of sectional greed, for any person or group which has not learnt to make concessions or sacrifices itself cannot believe that the action of other persons or groups is anything else but mean. Perhaps other and more deeply involuted reasons for distrust could be found in the course of a more far-reaching exploration of the historical, social and physical influences that had shaped the character of the nation.[10]

These seem more like the common characteristics of people under pressure of anxiety than a peculiarly Australian trait. When the anxiety was realized, as it was in England, though to a less degree, much of the carping and self-seeking disappeared.

2. *Social Adjustments*

The war penetrated into the life of nearly every citizen. Like it or not, he was organized for the war effort. In theory at least every physically and mentally fit adult up to forty-five years of age had to register and work in some capacity. Mothers of families and others irreplaceable in the home were, of course, exempted. *That* was their essential war work. Many over forty-five took jobs or engaged in voluntary work with one of the numerous patriotic organizations. Many men and women who reached retiring age during the war worked on. Their experience was valuable. Women entered fields where they had never been seen before in munitions works, aircraft factories, and the like. Under the Manpower Committee and

Director of Manpower Priorities no one might leave his or her job without permission and might be "directed" (a euphemism for "compelled") to undertake any task in any part of Australia. These regulations were actually applied with toleration and the mobilization, complete on paper, was not put into effect.

Whilst enemy aliens were interned, neutral aliens were for the most part drafted into the Civil Construction Corps to work on roads, air-strips, and other such projects of military value. The annual report of their activities was on the "Most Secret" list. This was consonant with the employment of aliens. The labourer never saw the whole of the plan.

Enlistment was regulated. Men in reserved occupations were not accepted as volunteers because their specialized knowledge and skills were more valuable on the home front than in the fighting line. This by-passed much of the bitterness that existed in the First World War against those who did not offer. If a man were not in khaki, it was for some good and sufficient reason beyond his control.

Australia's role was very different in the 1939-45 war. Her prime function was not to supply fighting men, though her fighting services in ratio to population did not fall far behind her allies. After listing the numbers in the services, Hasluck writes:

> In proportion to total population, this was equivalent to a mobilisation of 3,000,000 British under arms or 9,500,000 Americans under arms. The actual figure for Great Britain in the middle of 1941 was 3,800,000 under arms and for the United States in the middle of 1943, 9,200,000 under arms.[11]

The magnitude of the war effort can only be realized when to the armed services all the other activities directly or indirectly bearing on the war are added. Every type of munitions, except tanks, was produced in Australia. New factories were built and existing plants taken over and converted. Conversion generally meant re-tooling, and labour, often highly skilled, was needed to manufacture the tools to build the machines which finally did the work. To acquire enough skilled men, training courses were speeded up and the trade unions accepted dilution, that is, they allowed many more apprentices and trainees to be taken on than would be economic in peacetime. Much of the work, optical munitions for instance, had never before been done in Australia, and workshops were in effect laboratories under the control of scientists. It was also very difficult to assess the cost of producing something never before manufactured in Australia. Companies or privately owned factories could not be expected to enter into contracts blindfold. The solution was the controversial "cost plus" arrangement, the "plus" indicating an agreed percentage of profit. On these terms the manufacturer could afford to compete in the labour market to the profit of his employees. The scheme was open to malpractice, but it is difficult to see how pioneering industry could be carried through in any other way. Good profits were made, high wages paid and the Government won back a good percentage in taxation. Money flowed through the hands of the people as never before, but there was less to spend it on as the Government, in the interests of manpower, had shut down all luxury trades.

There was also rationing. The first item to be rationed was petrol, in 1939. As all petrol had to be imported, as large quantities were needed for military purposes, and as shipping was growing scarcer this was only to be expected. Nevertheless it raised a storm of protest and caused a good deal of hardship to the private motorist. It cramped spending and knocked the bottom out of the motor trade. Various expedients such as producer-gas attachments like glorified bath-heaters, or balloon-like supplies of coal gas, were harnessed to motor vehicles, and they at least moved, making the air horrible with their fumes.

From 1942 onwards clothing and a number of basic foods, such as butter, meat, and tea, were rationed by means of coupons. The housewife was often inconvenienced, but she was in a fortunate position in comparison with her sister in England. The health of children and expectant mothers was safeguarded, but many tired middle-aged people resulted from short commons in essential foods. Inevitably a black market grew up with its twin, panic buying. Building, other than for war purposes, was forbidden, and with the boom in war-time marriages another acute housing shortage developed.

The times were feverish. A large proportion of the population was overworking, many homes were ravaged by anxiety for husbands and sons fighting overseas. Life was full of inconveniences and prohibitions, none the less galling for being reasonable. Fear stirred and flared. Rumours proliferated, nerves were strung to breaking-point.

The national broadcasting stations battered listeners continually with propaganda. The broadcast news sessions and commentaries were a centre of interest in most homes. Efforts to explain away defeats and failures and to condition the people to a new way of life were often unsuccessful, producing suspicion rather than calm. Uncertainty reigned. Some fled from the coast, others received English children, refugees from the blitz, into their homes, others again regaled themselves with spy mania. Most worked until they were too tired to think.

Into this atmosphere came the American soldier. He was welcomed as a saviour, but he also whipped up hostility by being better paid and found than our own men, by acquiring all the acquirable girls, all the remaining taxis, and scooping up the few luxuries still available. The Americans were well-behaved and generous, if occasionally patronizing to the natives. Malicious stories pursued them and there were some brawls with Australian soldiers who felt themselves dispossessed. American Headquarters moved to Brisbane and the northern capital was swollen beyond its normal capacity. It was the day of the serviceman, the expert, and the organizer. The man in the street went to the wall and that was against the Australian grain.

The American Army had to be fed. This taxed the land and its resources. While importers had withered, exporters who at the beginning of the war saw their markets disappearing were fully extended in providing for two armies as well as the civilian population.

The year 1942 marked the peak of effort; in 1943 American victories in the South-west Pacific and the throwing back of the Japanese in New Guinea eased the pressure. By that time also, although there was war-weariness, most people had adjusted themselves to a different sort of life. It was one of the ironies of history that it fell to Curtin's Labour Government to impose, though not to create, most of the controls and to conscript labour within Australia and fighting men for the Pacific and New Guinea, policies to which the Labour Party had always been inherently opposed. In the final event Australian politics have generally been realistic and one party has implemented the policy of the other when necessary. At first sight, and before the event, John Curtin might not have appeared a likely national leader in wartime. He rose to the crisis, not with the *élan* of a Hughes but with dogged determination, with a co-operativeness that made the Australian-American relationship, which could have bristled with difficulties, workable, with moderation in the use of his great powers, with selflessness and with the retention of the common touch always so valuable to an Australian politician. In general the people of Australia followed in his footsteps.

The seasons wheeled overhead and in 1944 and 1945 there was a severe drought.

3. *The Role of Science*

In no other war had the scientist played so big a part. The Battle of Britain was won by the Spitfire and Hurricane fighter pilots, "the few", and they were enabled, with excellent but numerically insufficient aircraft, to win it by the help of a scientific invention that was the result of an accident. I refer to radar, the war's top secret.

When war appeared inevitable a committee of eminent scientists was formed, under Tizard, to consider ways and means of defence. What was required was an early-warning device that would signal the approach of enemy aircraft in time for fighters to assemble against them, preferably before they reached the coast. All scientists of any standing were circularized for an answer to this riddle. It came from Dunton Watts, who remembered that the Postmaster-General's Department, when making some experiments, had achieved unexpected and, apparently, freak results. Wireless long waves projected into the atmosphere had picked up echoes, or images, of bodies that crossed their path. It was considered an interesting but quite useless phenomenon. Imagination connected this with the detection of approaching aircraft. A group of scientists bound to the uttermost secrecy worked on the practical application of the idea on a small desert island off the coast of Norfolk, and achieved results.

Crudely put, radar is the sending out of electrical impulses into the atmosphere; when they reach the ionosphere, one of the outer layers of the atmosphere, they are deflected back to earth. Any object caught in their path is reflected as a white pip on a cathode-ray oscilloscope. From this rudimentary form radar was developed by the use of short, or centimetric, waves to reflect objects at sea level, such as the periscopes of submarines, to give longer coverage and to produce not only pips but detailed and, even to the lay eye, easily recognizable pictures as clear in the night as in daytime. Radar towers were built round the coast of England and supplied information to the fighter squadrons. With the men and machines available, it would have been impossible to keep aircraft in the air all the time.

England shared the secret of radar with the United States and asked each of the Dominions to send a physicist to England to receive special information. Dr D. F. Martyn went from Australia and brought back the basic information on which the Division of Radiophysics, within the Council for Scientific and Industrial Research, was founded. A group of young scientists had to be gathered together with a team of select instrument-makers and other technicians. Australian scientists participated in the experimental stages, one of them, for instance, being responsible for the important development which made it possible to transmit and receive with the same piece of apparatus. There seemed nothing to stop the Japanese from following up their advantage when Darwin was raided from the air, and teams of scientists with their "bread-board sets" were flown there and gave a practical demonstration of the uses of radar. It halted the raids. They became too costly for the attackers.

Later in the Pacific War Australia was able to supply radar sets to the American forces as well as to her own. They proved in many instances more serviceable in the field, because more rugged, than the highly evolved and finished American installations.

Radar proved to have many uses in the detection of submarines and surface craft as well as aircraft, in meteorological forecasting for the benefit of the R.A.A.F. and in navigation of both ships and aircraft in fog or other adverse conditions.

Germany had arrived at the general principles of radar by independent research, but was so confident in the strength of her armies, as well she might be in 1940, that she did not expend the necessary time and money in developing it. She remained quite ignorant of centimetric radar until a plane carrying it was brought down at Rotterdam. The invention of this more subtle instrument had been considered so important that for a long time it was not entrusted to planes. The obvious advantage of its use from the air finally overbore the restriction.

The reaction of Japan to radar was interesting. As Germany's ally the principles had no doubt been communicated to her. Her scientists were able to reconstruct centimetric radar from a newspaper report of the plane in Rotterdam. They thought it was a German invention. On the other hand, they showed a curious denseness. The only protection against radar was to scatter small strips of silvered cardboard over the target by the ton. This could be used to protect aircraft from ground radar; it confused, or "jammed", the image. The Japanese knew of this, but instead of dropping tons of "ribbon", they dropped it by the handful.

Modern naval battles could be fought without the combatants seeing one another, using their radar eyes. The difficulty of mistaking friendly ships or aircraft for those of the enemy was got over by a special signal, I.F.F., sent out continuously.

Science had many other applications in Australia, as elsewhere. The scientist was probably of more importance in Australia, as more pioneering had to be done, in such fields as optical munitions, dark adaptation for aviators, the thousand and one problems turned up in the establishment of new industries connected with munitions and new techniques in the fighting services. All the sciences were involved, physics perhaps most vitally, chemistry, metallurgy, botany (particularly in the acclimatization of drug plants when oversea supplies were cut off), and medicine. The war also made urgent matters of standardization, interchangeability of parts, calibration of instruments, and the whole field of precision engineering.

The main government undertaking in the scientific field was the Council for Scientific and Industrial Research, which expanded enormously during the war and entered new fields in pure and applied science. Scientists were also employed in munitions factories and laboratories attached to most big undertakings. Their work, since trained manpower could not be wasted, was co-ordinated, generally through the C.S.I.R. It was the day of the "backroom boys".

4. *Debit and Credit*

In that she suffered some 79,000 casualties in the war, Australia was seriously weakened. For the second time in twenty-five years, reckoned a generation, she lost a great swathe of her physically fit young men. That the population loss was more than made up by the immigration of British and foreign men and women either anxious for a new start in life under better conditions, or forced out of their own countries, was not quite the same thing. Many of those who survived unmaimed, particularly the men of the 8th Division, trapped in Malaya and held prisoners by the Japanese under unspeakable conditions, brought back an ineradicable strain. Many lingered on in hospitals, deprived of normal life and its happiness.

Having learnt from the mistakes of an earlier war, the authorities carried out the rehabilitation of ex-servicemen more successfully this time. The accent was on training undertaken by the Commonwealth Reconstruction Training Scheme, familiarly known as C.R.T.S. Every man who wished to and had the necessary mental qualifications could attend the universities and train for a profession at the public expense, including a living allowance. Technical and trade courses were also available on the same terms. If a man elected to go on the land and had no previous knowledge he was schooled in the type of farming or animal husbandry he intended to take up and kept informed of the best methods and procedures by Departments of Agriculture. The land made available, generally through the resumption of large properties, was better chosen than in 1919 and the years following, and more care was taken in adjusting the size of the blocks to the nature of the soil, the rainfall, and the other characteristics of the land. Rehabilitation and reconstruction had been in preparation from the beginning of the war and some first-class administrators had been employed. Former jobs, of course, remained open to returning soldiers and preference to them when applying for other positions was rigidly enforced.

One result of the war and its aftermath was that the number of trained personnel in Australia was enormously increased. Boys had been encouraged to study the sciences, they had been trained and drilled in all the skills required in the making of munitions and other war activities, including many never before open to them in Australia. Perhaps as important, they had acquired a habit of hard work and of sticking perforce to their jobs. In the Navy and in the R.A.A.F. particularly, they had learnt trades. C.R.T.S. gave training in many fields to those who had missed it through being on active service. It must be admitted that the habit of unremitting work suffered a diminution once the crisis was over.

The nation was equipped with skilled men and modern plants ready for the change-over to peace. Many men and women had exceptional opportunities. They had full employment and the chance to learn and qualify. Women, in particular, gained a greater degree of emancipation than in the First World War. They found that they had a wage-earning capacity that after the war they were very often unwilling to give up. Whether a more efficient attack on life and the insurance of a means of livelihood, if they were forced back on their own resources, made for happier marriages or not will always be a moot point. Working girls received less training in the domestic arts and the power of the family over its womenfolk was lessened by financial independence. The emancipation of women has always boiled down to their financial independence.

Australia, then, at the end of the war, was ready to go forward, for she had the men and the machines as well as the wool and the wheat. As the world at large continued to be troubled and had suffered, except in the United States, great war damage, Australia by its isolation became attractive again to oversea capital. She was economically in a good position.

In the political arena there were both gains and losses. The power of the Commonwealth had been strengthened. There were, and are, some who did not look on this as a "Good Thing". But if Australia was to be a united nation and to develop her standing in the world it was necessary. Others again felt, and feel, that it is wasteful and extravagant for a small people to support seven governments and that the movement towards one government with sovereign powers is healthy.

After 1945 the Commonwealth had to give up many of its war-time powers and retire from price and other controls, but a residuum of power remained in its hands and the habit of looking to the Federal Government had been formed in the citizens' minds. Did not Canberra control the purse-strings?

The art of government had progressed. The simplicities of an earlier day were outmoded. The demagogue continued to exist as a front, but government had become more and more an intricate affair of high finance and economics, of experts and bureaucrats.

As always in war-time, democracy suffered. For survival, conscription of labour as well as of soldiers, and controls in many fields, had to be imposed. Censorship clamped down on free speech. A political party had for a time been banned. Things which men had said "would never happen here" had happened and had been accepted. For the good or protection of all the economy had been planned down to the last detail to stop waste and the leakage of man-hours. Parliament enacted. To carry out the Acts and spawning regulations, new government departments and hosts of public servants, not to mention endless forms in triplicate, were necessary. The bureaucrat, unimportant in himself, in the mass came near to ruling the country.

The depression of the early thirties prepared the way for national planning just before and during the war. The war again, with government intervention in every sphere of life, prepared the way for the Welfare State.

Although since the passing of the Statute of Westminster Australia had had the right to control her own foreign relations, she had little interest in doing so until the war taught her that she must fend for herself. The fending consisted mainly in turning to the United States for a help that it fortunately suited that great country to give. No statute could alter the geographical position of Australia, the size of her continent, the paucity of her population, or make her overnight a great nation. She could, and henceforth did, range herself with the small nations. She planted out diplomatic posts and brought her mind to bear more than ever before on the Pacific and the Near North, the Far East of the Western world.

The Minister for External Affairs, Herbert Vere Evatt, who represented Australia at the creation of the United Nations Organization, realized well enough that it was to Australia's advantage to range herself with the other small nations of the world, in the hope, vain it would seem, that collectively they would amount to a great power, as well as taking her place in that scattered constellation, the British Commonwealth of Nations. Like Hughes before him, but less successfully, he strove to make Australia heard, he fought unavailingly, together with other small nations, against the veto clause which would give to great signatories the power of halting action. He also strove to preserve all domestic questions from international interference. The difficulty here was the White Australia Policy. Australia meant to retain it. It was a corner-stone of her economy. Could it be considered entirely domestic?

Australia's policy in the Pacific and Near North settled into two principles: (*i*) a screen of islands for defence which makes it imperative that she should control New Guinea as possession or mandate, and the other small islands in her vicinity; (*ii*) friendship with the emergent Asiatic nations to the north. The chief contribution to this has been a leading part in the Colombo Plan designed, by offering educational facilities, to help backward nations to help themselves. So far so good, but the White Australia Policy is a grave impediment to friendship. Indonesia's pretension to Netherlands New Guinea cannot be tolerated if the island screen is to be kept intact. The march of Communism presents still another difficulty, and the United States policy of building up Japan as a base against and counterbalance to Communist China at the same time strengthens Australia's greatest potential enemy. There is no hereditary or cultural tie of friendship and interest with the Near North and, except with Japan, little trade, for the good reason that the peoples neither want nor can pay for our wool and other products. Isolation recoils on our own heads.

The most definite and hopeful move has been the pact signed by Australia, New Zealand, and the United States (A.N.Z.U.S.) in 1951, with its aim of keeping the peace in the Pacific. Great Britain was denied membership. How far the pact will hold is yet to be tested. The United States is as naturally isolationist as she is self-contained.

Australia is more aware of the world about her, more developed, better able to supply her own needs, but, if anything, less secure.

Little nation, what now?

REFERENCE NOTES

[1] P. Hasluck, *The Government and the People, 1939-1941*, pp. 40-1.
[2] W. M. Hughes, *Australia and War To-day*, pp. 155-6.
[3] Quoted, P. Hasluck, *The Government and the People, 1939-1941*, p. 54.
[4] *Ibid.*, p. 226.
[5] *Ibid.*, pp. 559-60.
[6] I. Morrison, *This War Against Japan*, p. 58.
[7] *Ibid.*, pp. 71-2.
[8] G. Cant, *The Great Pacific Victory*, pp. 337-8.
[9] F. O. Hough, *The Island War*, p. 387.
[10] P. Hasluck, *The Government and the People, 1939-1941*, pp. 565-6.
[11] *Ibid.*, p. 559.

CHAPTER XXI

IMMIGRATION: "POPULATE OR PERISH"

THE HISTORY OF Australia is almost the history of immigration, for every white inhabitant is an immigrant or the descendant of one. The aborigines were themselves immigrants in pre-history. Also, immigration is closely bound up with defence and the supply of labour, with cultural advancement and increasing amenities.

The first unwilling migrants were the convicts. They were expected to supply all the labour necessary for the foundation of the colony, but Governor Phillip was soon asking that some free labourers, preferably family men, be sent out to give a stiffening of respectability to the struggling settlement. It does not take much imagination to see that there was little inducement to anyone to come to Australia in the early days. It was distant and had a bad name. Only depressed conditions at home and the promise of land grants could induce anyone to come voluntarily. To begin with, the country was used as a dumping ground for free emigrants, paupers, malcontents and, more respectably, veterans of the Napoleonic Wars who could not be fitted in at home and could be cheaply recompensed with land in the colonies.

Phillip had no success, but in 1793 *Bellona* brought out some free settlers who were given land grants at Liberty Plains (the Strathfield-Homebush district). Grose complained of them, particularly of the millwright.

> I am sorry to observe I do not expect much benefit from this man; he is by no means so expert as he pretends to be, and he has unluckily been on board the hulks as a convict. He is recollected by a number of his old associates, and, from some dirty tricks he has already attempted, I fear he has not forgotten all he learned when in that situation.[1]

The millwright was evidently one of those that his country could well spare.

Governor Hunter in his instructions was bidden to encourage free settlers "without subjecting the public to expense", they were to be given larger land grants than the emancipists and as much convict labour as they wanted. Hunter saw clearly that free immigrants would not come to the country whilst the needs of the colony were supplied from government farms.

> . . . if it is the wish or intention of Government to have this colony increase to a state of respectability, some encouragement must be held out to respectable

settlers and industrious people of all descriptions. This can never be the case if it be the intention of Government to cultivate land enough for the maintenance of all the convicts sent here. The farmer will be labouring for a mere subsistence; he can never cloath himself and family if he has no market for his surplus corn, and if Government does not become his purchaser he can have no market.[2]

Government did intend just this, of course. It wanted things both ways. The convict was to earn his keep and the free settler was to be satisfied with land and subsistence and the privilege of taking convicts off the store. Hunter, too, came to the conclusion that "very few of those sent out by permission of Government are likely to benefit the settlement". Immigration at that stage was a stalemate.

Another type of immigrant was the Anglo-Indian who, having reached retiring age or being invalided out, felt that the Australian climate would be more beneficial to him than the English. In July 1799 at least three families approached the Home Government for permission to settle. They asked for free transport for themselves and their effects and livestock, land and the right to bring in Bengal rum.[3] This proved a blind alley, probably because neither the Home Government nor Hunter would approve the rum.

In 1801 Governor King, writing to the Duke of Portland, raised the question of family immigration but not very hopefully. To bring out a large family would cost £150 and another £250 to keep them until they were established, "and it often happens that period discovers their total incapacity and idleness, and that being continued to be fed at the public expense is the only means of saving them from perishing".[4] The Governor urged the Home Government to select immigrants with care.

In 1802 we know that free settlers arrived in *Perseus* and *Coromandel*, twenty-eight of them in one group alone. More came in the King's ship *Glatton* in August of that year, amongst them a Mr Bedell who was "represented to have a perfect knowledge of Agriculture, having held a very considerable farm in his own hands, but which through Youthful Indiscretion he has found it necessary to relinquish". The Governor was instructed to "place him above the common class of settlers".[5] Even this desirable gentleman was more anxious to leave home than to arrive. The *Glatton* settlers were sent to the Nepean, where on the whole they were mostly "going on with great spirit and well applied industry".

Here and there we catch a glimpse of these settlers. There was Bridget Heath, for instance, who was supposed to be coming out "to her brother". Her real name was Edwards and the brother was her lover, who found on second glance that he did not want her and left her destitute. The Government, Governor King remarked, "was much imposed on".

In his report to Lord Hobart in March 1894, King claims that there are now 543 settlers supporting 351 wives and 589 children and employing 463 labourers. It is not clear that these were all free immigrants, the numbers probably include emancipists.

Further free settlers came out in *William Pitt* in 1805 and from the cargo in the ship it is plain that the colony was growing in sophistication and wealth, for it included 50 Gentleman's hats, 6 pieces of Superfine cloth, linen drapery and horse medicines.[6]

Land and subsistence had now given place to a new lure. Macarthur had demonstrated that there was money in fine wool. This attracted a different class of settler, men of property. The Blaxlands, John and Gregory, were the vanguard. John Blaxland chartered his own ship, *The Brothers,* to bring out his family, a wife and five children, his bailiff and servants, his livestock, rations for the voyage, and fifteen tons of effects. His ready capital was rated at £6000. Gregory Blaxland sailed in *William Pitt*. They were more interested in arriving than departing, and were treated as assets of value. The Governor received special instructions. They were to be allowed 8000 acres of land of their own choosing and the services of one convict for every hundred acres for eighteen months at the store's expense. This advent suggested to the Government that New South Wales could be something more than a dumping ground. The Blaxlands immediately joined forces with the officer class and in that category were from time to time troublesome to the Governor.

In 1806 a further refinement in the person of "Mrs Chapman, a widow lady" arrived as "Governess and Teacher", and Bligh was directed to "afford her due Encouragement and assistance".

Governor Macquarie discouraged free immigration. So many convicts were sent out during his governorship that, far from there being a shortage of labour, settlers could not absorb them, and to keep them employed more and more public works had to be undertaken. Artisans and farmers he did not need, reinforcements of the *ancien régime* he did not want. How difficult men of capital, or alleged capital, could be was illustrated soon after Macquarie's departure by Lieutenant Vickers Jacobs, an officer of the East India Company and a friend of Commissioner Bigge, who brought, he said, £10,000 and an "unblemished reputation and purity of private life . . . hitherto little known in any class of society" in Australia, and in return made exorbitant demands for privileges and became most vocal in his complaints of delay and frustration. Lord Bathurst himself was drawn into the conflict and Brisbane reluctantly gave Jacobs a licence to occupy 2000 acres of land and an allotment in Newcastle. "I did not see how I could do less after Your Lordship's letter . . . and after the correspondence which had passed between this and the Indian Government, I did not know that I could do more."[7] Jacobs had turned out to be in bad odour in India, boycotted by his brother officers and on the point of dismissal from the service. He was little more than an adventurer, a bird of passage, who eventually disappeared from the records in what he picturesquely described as "atmospheric spleen". Only distance made his deception possible.

Brisbane, unlike Macquarie, held no brief for the emancipist and hoped to see the colony develop and expand through the immigration of free men. In particular he wanted mechanics. Employers preferred them as more reliable than convicts, and the convicts themselves had more chance of reform away from the temptations of towns. The exaggerated value attached to a convict mechanic in the absence of a free man to do the work robbed his punishment of its sting. The ill effects of monopoly were illustrated by the presence of two hundred convict mechanics undergoing secondary punishment, for felonies committed in the colony, at Port Macquarie.

There was already an agitation in the colony for the free institutions, particularly trial by jury, of the mother land, but how could these aspirations be satisfied unless there were a sufficiency of reputable citizens who had come to the country free, to sit on juries and fill the necessary offices? It was clear to Brisbane that progress could only come by the dilution of the convict population.

The setting up of the Australian Agricultural Company in 1823 brought a small spate of immigrants as servants of the company and did much to advertise its existence in England.

Meanwhile Lord Bathurst had had a bright idea, to be followed up by Lord Goderich. Times were bad in England, there was much unemployment and paupers were becoming a serious charge on the parishes. To send them to Australia would relieve the situation both locally and in the colony. Women were sent from the Foundling Home in Cork. They were redundant in Ireland, but in New South Wales there was a constant disproportion of the sexes and a scarcity of reliable female servants. Unemployed agricultural labourers were also shipped out with, it was hoped, mutual benefit. It was an unorganized arrangement, for Lord Bathurst in a dispatch of 31st March 1827 expressed himself as unwilling to sponsor any free emigration scheme. It would be too difficult. Anyone willing to pay his own passage, or whose prospective employer would pay it for him, would be permitted to come out in a transport, and if employment were awaiting him he might travel free.[8]

The granting or sale of land (it had become practically the same thing) was for a time a patronage enjoyed by the Secretary of State for the Colonies. As it was a matter of grace and favour it gave the Colonial Office control over this type of immigrant.

If immigration through government channels was in the early days of the catch-as-catch-can variety, the Reverend John Dunmore Lang, a Presbyterian minister and public figure, evolved and carried out a plan for family immigration. Respectable tradesmen with the skills most in

HENRY LAWSON

From the portrait by Sir John Longstaff in the possession of the National Gallery of New South Wales

AN ABORIGINAL

From Elkin, *The Australian Aborigines*

demand in the colony were chosen in the United Kingdom and brought to Australia in a chartered vessel. *Stirling Castle* arrived at Sydney on 3rd October 1831, with a hundred mechanics and their families. The initial expense was met by a loan of £1500 from the Government on the understanding that the immigrants would pay back their passage money in instalments from the wages they earned. Lang claimed that he could bring out a family for as little as £50.

Three factors precipitated a definite immigration policy: bad times in England, shortages of skilled labour and of women in the colony, and, finally, the cessation of the assignment system in 1839.

In January 1831 Goderich was writing to Governor Darling propounding an immigration scheme. Unemployed agricultural labourers should be sent to Australia at the joint expense of the Home and colonial Governments. Money could be raised at the Australian end by a tax on assigned labour of, say, 10s. a year for every convict and another small tax to be extracted from those employing the superior free labour. The Colonial Secretary hoped that this arrangement would reduce the competition between free and convict labour by making the latter more expensive. In return for their free passages the immigrants should pay something back to the Government as they earned. As an additional inducement and to stabilize the scheme he further suggested that the immigrants enter into indentures with their new masters for not more than seven years' service.[9] This was tentative.

Settlers were also to be encouraged to nominate and bring to Australia the servants they required. If they did this the Government would forego the quit rent due on their lands. As quit rents were rarely paid in any case, and as they amounted to so little that it was not worth the Government's while to prosecute, the concession was almost meaningless.

To clarify matters a Commission on Emigration was set up in England to select and dispatch agricultural labourers and an officer was appointed locally to receive, superintend, and place them. It damps one's enthusiasm for the scheme to learn that the superintendent who assigned convicts was deemed the most suitable person for this duty.[10] Settlers were asked to state how much labour they required, of what kind, and what wages they would pay. Preference to unmarried men was suggested or a mixed cargo of thirty families and fifty single men.

The plan to tax employers of assigned convict labour was deemed impracticable and would have, in any case, lapsed when assignment was abolished. As there were 13,400 convicts in 1831, the tax that could have been collected would have been a substantial sum. There was chronic difficulty in collecting taxes or any other moneys, however. It was decided that the colonial Government should pay £20 towards the passage money of each immigrant family out of general revenue and recover it, if possible, after landing. It rarely was possible. No one was very pleased with these arrangements, least of all the immigrants, who found themselves competing with cheap labour and dragged down to the social level of the emancipists or the time-expired convicts. The women were more fortunate. At home they had had little to look forward to, in the colony it was a truly ill-favoured and cross-grained lass who could not marry. They had a scarcity if no other value. The Commission made careful rules to safeguard their morals and plant them out in suitable situations, but, no doubt, once landed they found their own level, whatever it might be.

Red Rover arrived in 1832 with 202 women aboard. Their passages had cost £15 a head, not £8 as Governor Bourke had expected. They were immediately

> . . . placed under proper care in the old Lumber Yard, and, with the advice and Assistance of Some of the Ladies of Sydney, they engaged themselves as Servants as opportunities offered . . . their number was at first very rapidly reduced; but the demand in Sydney became slack, and the disinclination of the Women to go far into the Country occasioned Some delay in disposing of the least promising among them.[11]

Fourteen were left in the Lumber Yard and gravitated to the Female Factory, there being nowhere else for them to go. Servants received from £9 to £11 a year in wages and their keep.

It was under Governor Bourke, with Lord Goderich at the Colonial Office, that a systematic immigration scheme was at last worked out. It was in two parts. Bounty immigrants were sponsored by colonists and assured employment on arrival. The sponsors received a bounty on every approved man and woman they brought out. The Government had its own scheme, by which it took up immigrants in England and paid £12 towards their passage money of £17. The immigrant was expected to find the other £5, for which promissory notes were accepted. Unfortunately the Commission was dissolved in 1832 and a committee of gentlemen was persuaded to undertake, on an honorary basis, the selection of applicants. Actually the task was usually left to the ships' masters, with the result that very poor material, particularly women of bad character, was brought out. They were expected to produce a certificate of respectability signed by a clergyman, but these were often either forged or given on hearsay without investigation. A committee of officials and ladies met them on arrival and undertook to place them, but after *Bussorah Merchant* landed a cargo of undesirables in 1833 the ladies withdrew in horror. An Emigrants' (*sic*) Friendly Society also existed in Sydney to help and protect them.

In three years, 1833-5, £2075 was advanced to ship out single women and £7670 for agricultural labourers and mechanics. Of this money only £167 3s. 2d. was recovered from the men and nothing from the women. They had scattered and "it was found impossible to prove the handwriting on notes in any case", probably owing to illiteracy. The Secretary of State gave up the struggle in 1835, thereafter passages were free. In September 1831 Lord Glenelg discontinued special immigration projects for women. He included them in the bounty system. Settlers were granted £30 for each married couple, £5 for every child between two and seven years, £10 each if between seven and fifteen, £15 for unmarried daughters between 15 and 30 years of age or for unmarried girls under 30 coming out chaperoned by a married woman and as part of her family group. It was hoped in this way to make sure of the respectability of the migrants. On Bourke's suggestion, a panel of naval surgeons replaced the honorary committee of gentlemen in selecting immigrants. As it was made part of their regular duty it was hoped that they would have a more responsible attitude.

In March 1837 Glenelg regularized the financial side. Revenue from land in Australia, which was still the property of the Crown, not of the colonial administration, was allocated to immigration. Two thirds of it was spent on the bounty system and one-third kept for the government scheme. The rates of bounties were raised. To quote the figures given in the Introduction to volume xvii of the *Historical Records of Australia,* Series I, between 1832 and 1836 2052 single women and 1778 persons in family groups arrived under bounty and fifty were brought out by the Government. In addition 5422 unassisted immigrants arrived. The average age of the women was a little under 21 years. The cost was paid out of land revenue.

In 1837 the panel of naval surgeons was replaced by a Chief Agent employed full time on a salary of £1000 a year. Two-thirds of the land revenue was now sent to England to defray expenses at that end and one-third held to pay bounties on arrival. A naval surgeon travelled in every ship to control discipline as well as health. The scheme was restricted to citizens of British birth, with the exception of a few vine-dressers. John Macarthur had imported some German viticulturists, and the indomitable Dr Lang argued that since New South Wales had a climate like the Mediterranean, farm labourers from Italy would understand its soils and products better than those from England.

On the whole the system worked fairly well. The worst abuses were weeded out, though the chaperonage of a married woman over young girls was often more nominal than real. Masters of ships were restrained from abusing their charges by the presence of naval surgeons, by being required to enter into bonds for the safe conduct of the immigrants, and by receiving gratuities when they landed them in good health and the naval surgeon aboard gave a certificate of correct conduct during the voyage. There were unfortunate episodes, such as that of *Lady McNaghten*, which not only had too large a quota of immigrants but was laden with cargo as well. The doctor in charge was inexperienced and when fever broke out fourteen adults and fifty-three children died of it.[12] This story could be balanced by that of the *Augusta Jessie* which carried a cow that the children might have fresh milk. Of the migrants in her, Bourke wrote: ". . . their general appearance is that of rude health, the bloom of their English complexion being hardly impaired by the voyage."[13]

The migrants themselves were often disgruntled because they believed they were coming out to free land grants. That was not the idea at all, they were to be servants and to form a layer of free and honest workers between the convicts, ex-convicts and emancipists, and the settlers. There was no land for them unless they could afford to buy it. In 1836 a group of them petitioned Glenelg asking for compensation because they had been misled by a too rosy picture of life and opportunity in Australia. Many of them, however, did well. Bourke reported in 1836 that

> . . . wages . . . now earned by Mechanics of various descriptions, would be thought extravagantly high in England. Many Journeymen Artizans, who arrived a few years ago, have in fact assumed the station of Master Tradesmen and are erecting some of the public works under contracts with the Government.[14]

Single women and girls were the most difficult to handle. When a matron was appointed to look after them and handicrafts supplied to occupy them on the voyage they fared best. Like Phillip, Bourke assumed personal responsibility for them when they landed.

The dual system of migration reached its peak in the late 1830s. It was a time of prosperity in the colony and the revenue from land was high. Governor Gipps was an excellent administrator. Plenty of immigrants were offering and the country could absorb them. The Legislative Council formed a special committee on migration and advised that bounties should be increased. The bounty system was more popular, especially with landholders, than the government scheme, but Gipps argued that it alone could not bring out enough people.

The bounty system was about 21 per cent cheaper than the government system,

> . . . reckoning men, women, and children all alike, and making no difference for the quality of the Emigrants; but, if this difference be taken into consideration, and especially the smaller proportion of children introduced by the Bounty system, the advantage of that system must be estimated considerably higher; and I am inclined to think with the Committee that 200 Government Emigrants cost as much as 300 Bounty ones of equal value to the colony.[15]

But then the bounty system was likely to become more expensive as higher bounties were paid, and, worse still, to attract adventurers if they smelled a profit, which would not accrue from the government scheme.

It was obvious that transportation would not continue much longer and there was a general fear of a labour shortage. Neither Gipps nor Glenelg would agree to the importation of indentured Indian coolies. When towards the end of the decade a fierce drought smote the country and revenue fell sharply, Gipps made the revolutionary suggestion of raising a short-term loan to keep up the flow of immigrants. The scheme was ingenious. In 1839 there was £180,000 in the Colonial Treasury and an expected revenue of £400,000 a year. This was not enough. Gipps asked that a loan be floated in England and guaranteed by the Home Government. The usual procedure was for the Colonial Office to pay the expenses of immigration, except for the bounty moneys due on the landing of the migrants. The Colonial Treasury cleared its debt not by sending money to England but by paying it into the Military Chest, where it was offset against England's colonial expenses. Gipps now asked permission to draw on the Military Chest for advances up to £100,000 a year. "Such an arrangement," the Governor pointed out, "would in effect be the same as if the Lords of the Treasury were to advance to us the first instalment of the Loan, and not bring us into the money market until after such instalment should be exhausted." He required in all a loan of £1,000,000. As soon as the first instalment was exhausted the Loan would be floated and the amount gathered in paid to the Home Government in liquidation of the advance. This, of course, would ensure the interest of the authorities in making the loan a success, and by advancing the money give investors a lead in confidence.

England had an interest in immigration over and above the welfare of the colony. She still wanted to export her paupers and her unemployed. This is illustrated by the swindle perpetrated by Colonel Wyndham of Lissafin on his tenants. Rather than renew their leases, he persuaded them to accept free transport to South Australia, where he assured them they would quickly make their fortunes. That his sister was Mrs Gawler, the Governor's wife, lent colour to the tale. They sailed, to be dumped in Sydney with no provision for their future.

Edward Macarthur held out as one of the advantages of his plan for opening up the country by the use of steam packets that land would thus be made available for thousands of indigent English families.

The trouble was that Australia was not only suffering the temporary inconvenience of a drought. She was in for a depression. In 1841 there were bounty "orders" to be fulfilled within two years involving £979,562, which the colonial Government was quite unable to pay. Lord John Russell at the Colonial Office gave Governor Gipps a sharp rap.

> A multitude of persons acting independently of each other are simultaneously making Contracts with Mechanics, Artizans, Husbandmen and others for their removal to New South Wales. On the faith of these Contracts, men abandon their trade and their Houses, sell their property, and purchase outfits as Emigrants. In some cases they even contract marriages in reliance on the

promises made to them in your Name. . . . If such Orders are not acknowledged as valid, by reason of the lapse of time, the Emigrants are deeply injured.[16]

They would have to be honoured even up to a million pounds. In future the Governor must not allow more bounty orders to be issued than the land revenue would cover. In rebuttal Gipps complained that the bounty system had caused the depression and not *vice versa.*

Later in the same year Lord Stanley, Russell's successor, overhauled the immigration question and he, too, blamed Gipps, particularly for not sending estimates of expenditure home each year, so that the deficit burst on the Colonial Office like a bombshell. He summed up:

Upon the recommendation of the Committee of Legislative Council, the Scale of Bounties was increased, and they were made as nearly as possible equal to the actual Passage Money. Proprietors and Settlers, moreover, did not nominate and select the Emigrants, but the real practice soon became that the Correspondent of some extensive Ship-Owner in England applied at Sydney for large Orders without any particular proprietor requiring the labour, and the Ship-Owner then sent out the numbers sanctioned, trusting to the general fitness of the people for enabling him to obtain the Bounty.[17]

There follows an analysis of the two immigration schemes for the years 1837-1839:

	Government Scheme		Bounty Scheme	
Year	*No. of Emigrants*	*Cost*	*No. of Emigrants*	*Cost*
1837	2,688	£43,341	742	£8,585
1838	6,463	£122,318	1,622	£22,398
1839	4,096	£89,414	2,814	£43,020

After 1839, with a falling economic barometer, the numbers of bounty immigrants had risen, the usual consequence of a boom. It had fallen away from its original purpose into the hands of speculators. The Home Government took it over and all applications had to be routed through the Board of Emigration, which reviewed candidates for fitness and made itself responsible for conditions on the voyage.

Stanley added:

. . . I cannot take upon myself absolutely to sanction the validity of Orders issued prior to January, 1841, and not yet presented to the Land and Emigration Commissrs. . . . I shall hold you personally responsible for any issue of money in virtue of any such Order. It is also my intention to give public notice that no Emigration on Bounty Orders will be sanctioned by Her Majesty's Government previous to the 1st of August next.[18]

This was virtually the end of the Bounty System and all assisted immigration. The Australian economy could not absorb more people unless they brought their own resources. The effects, however, were not over. Immigrants continued to arrive and there were no jobs for them. Most pitiful was the plight of many young girls, ignorant and helpless, who could not afford to wait even a week for employment because they had nothing. A very remarkable woman, Caroline Chisholm, herself the mother of a large family, came to their rescue. She petitioned the Governor and received from him the use of some derelict premises. Here she sheltered the girls, living with them for their protection, and feeding them as best she could. Where possible she placed them in situations through her friends. She knew that although the city was barren the girls would be welcomed in the bush, and could there earn their keep and probably marry. The distances and the strangeness of it all baffled them. They had no opportunity to find jobs for themselves outside the town. Mrs Chisholm made sorties into the country with drayloads of her protégées, finding them work on farms and runs where there was a married woman, generally a harassed mother only too glad to have the services of a free immigrant girl.

Caroline Chisholm could not handle the whole problem, but she did much to help the stranded immigrants. The crisis passed, but her interest in immigration continued and she campaigned for the bringing out of family groups as the only humane way of increasing the population of the strange new land, and the most likely to succeed.

Even through and after the depression the legend of a "land of opportunity" lingered on and men of some substance or their younger sons continued to arrive in small numbers at their own expense. One such was Alfred Joyce, referred to before. The story of his voyage to Australia, in one of his father's ships, as told by himself, affords an interesting comparison with the tales of other voyages that I have from time to time related.

The ship, the *London,* 350 tons, took a hundred and eleven days on the voyage without making a landfall between England and Melbourne. Young Joyce was, of course, a cabin passenger and dined in the cuddy not too badly. A sheep was killed each week and eaten from head to trotters. Occasionally there was fresh pork or poultry. In between times it was salt beef and pork, porpoise liver when one was harpooned, curry and salt fish. "The latter often made into what was called 'twice-laid', that is served up a second time mixed with potatoes and fried. Potatoes were the only vegetable we had." These viands were washed down with "plenty of cheap sherry" and at dinner, "after the ladies left the claret past round exactly twice, always beginning and ending with the captain; when it reached him the second time he rose up and the rest of us followed". There was a light lunch at 11 a.m. of ale, biscuits and cheese. Dinner was at 2 p.m. Fresh water was scarce, a gallon a day per person for drinking and washing, and so foul-tasting and smelling that it was hung out on the poop rails in buckets "to purify". Amusements were somewhat limited. There was a pianoforte on which everyone tried their luck with "varying success".

> A cornopeon, operated upon by a somewhat indifferent performer did not altogether give complete satisfaction and roused a somewhat strong remonstrance from a fellow passenger, which led to serious altercation and threats of violence; but a large and superior musical box gave general satisfaction, as it tinkled out its pretty melodies over the calm waters on the warm tropical evenings. The clear notes of a feathered songster on board a passing ship drew the rapt attention of all on board, reviving, as it did, the recollection of the land we had left behind us.[19]

In addition there were, I suppose, books, conversation, quarrels, and baths taken in tubs on the deck or under the spray of the ship's pump. The intermediate and steerage passengers fared worse. This was not an "emigrant ship".

The first phase of assisted immigration was over. It had consisted of the flow of convicts up till 1840 and, in the early days, the comparatively few men who came as soldiers or officials and stayed to graze, to farm and to trade. The idea, if it ever existed, of a purely penal settlement soon broke down. The Government went through a period of indecision. Should it encourage men of capital by land grants, primarily for the prosecution of the wool industry, with convicts and ex-convicts as the work force? Should it extend the convict idea by including paupers, foundlings, the depressed and the unemployed who were a charge on the community at home? Should it build up a pool of free mechanics, artisans, and agricultural labourers? All policies were followed with varying degrees of insistence. Systematic assisted immigration canalized into bounty orders and a government-run scheme. These reached and passed their peak of usefulness. New abuses arose even as the old ones were rooted out. The economic depression of the early 1840s destroyed the whole fabric by making assisted immigration redundant.

Almost before the country was on its feet again the great gold discoveries began. There was no need to assist immigrants, they came in their thousands. It took the country another twenty years to absorb those who had come to stay. Out of the gold-rushes came what might be called the reverse, or negative, side of a national immigration policy, the prohibition of Chinese and other Oriental and dark-skinned migrants, known as the White Australia Policy.

The society that arose out of the decades of gold and reconstruction was very different in its complexion from the old Australia. The urban element was stronger, democracy was more vociferous, the worker more class-conscious. The trade-union movement was under way and was becoming a social and political force. The trade unions not only upheld the White

Australia Policy but were suspicious of any form of assisted immigration. The fear of unemployment made competition unwelcome. The depression of the early 1890s made that fear a reality. Once again Australia was not in a position to absorb more population. For forty years following the spate in the 1850s there was a fairly steady flow of new colonists, mostly from the United Kingdom, but they came at their own expense and for private reasons.

With the turn of the century and the establishment of the Commonwealth there was a new national awareness of the size of the continent and the scantiness of the population. The States, uniting to reinforce the White Australia Policy, became more alert to the necessity, for reasons of defence and development, of attracting people of their own race to settle. One after another the States produced policies for assisting British migrants. These schemes were not wildly popular or of very wide scope. Parochialism was strongly mixed into growing Australian nationalism. Even people of their own stock were potential strangers, and the still young country was sensitive to their criticisms and occasional patronage. Another inhibiting factor was the jealousy the States felt towards Commonwealth powers. The Commonwealth, on which all matters of defence devolved, was more enthusiastic than any of the States in encouraging immigrants "of the right sort", but the States looked on immigration policy, the White Australia Policy excepted, as a domestic matter, and Alfred Deakin, the Prime Minister, had to step delicately when he urged a uniform and vigorous policy to attract immigrants. Even his proposal in 1904 to establish an office in London at Commonwealth expense to advertise the opportunities Australia offered and to select the most suitable men and women from those offering, was greeted coldly. The States preferred to act separately through their agents-general.

By 1906 an immigration policy, virtually the same in each State, was in being. Its aim was primarily to develop the land and raise up a sturdy class of small holders. It was Phillip's idea and Macquarie's idea all over again. It was imported from England, where the yeoman farmer was sometimes described as the salt of the earth. It was not only that. To establish agricultural settlements and assist farmers to come out and work them would not bring the Government into conflict with the trade unions and Labour Party. They were very tetchy about the importation of workmen, skilled or otherwise, and had shown a lack of any sense of proportion and of humour on two fairly recent occasions when they had opposed, and even invoked the law against the importation of indentured labour, to keep out six hatters and a bunch of boilermakers come to work for the railways. Again, the spread of cultivation would do more to fill in the emptiness of the map than the swelling of already large town populations. The plans were too often unrealistic. Only certain areas in Australia lend themselves to small farms for reasons of climate, rainfall, fertility and access to markets.

Conditions were so different from those prevailing in England that many of the techniques of farming would have to be relearnt, and there was no training scheme as a prelude to the planting out of settlers. In some ways the immigration policy of the 1900s was less practical than the bounty scheme, which at its best was adjusted to the exact needs of the community for certain types of labour.

By 1912 the Premiers' Conference was willing to accept Commonwealth co-operation. It asked the Federal Government to pay for 25,000 assisted passages every year. After some negotiations the Prime Minister, Joseph Cook, agreed to subsidize State schemes to the extent of £150,000 a year. Between 1911 and 1913 about 230,000 immigrants came to, and stayed in, Australia. The Commonwealth now had its office in London, not primarily for immigration purposes, whence it disseminated literature on and information about Australia. The genial and witty Sir George Reid was the first Australian High Commissioner in London and worked to stimulate immigration both from the British Isles and Europe.

All too soon war swept across the world. The machinery remained, but could not be used. After the war the first assisted immigrants might be said to be the wives and fiancées, married or betrothed overseas, of the returned soldiers.

In 1922 the subject of migration was raised again on the basis of "populate or perish". This time it was taken for granted that the Commonwealth would be the prime mover, though the States, as owners of the land, were taken into close co-operation through the annual Premiers' Conferences. Although most thinking Australians realized the necessity for increasing the population at a faster rate than could be hoped for from natural increase, the new policy was not initiated until the Imperial Conference of 1921. Here problems of population were discussed on a wide basis as they affected the British Commonwealth of Nations and most particularly the United Kingdom, where in some ways population had reached saturation point, and it would be profitable for men and women to seek new homes within the Empire. W. M. Hughes, at that time Prime Minister, felt strongly that Australia should take advantage of any such folk movement and immediately brought forward an Immigration Loan Bill. Its immediate aim was to bring 8000 British migrants to Australia, 600 of them for Western Australia where the spaces were widest and emptiest, and 2000 for Victoria where closer settlement of the land would be easiest. This was a special project. The pre-war arrangements for bringing out immigrants and helping them to settle on the land were also to come back into action. Land settlement was still a State matter, but the Commonwealth acted as middleman, negotiating with the United Kingdom, raising loans, handling the financial arrangements, and generally channelling the new citizens to the States as and how they were ready to absorb them.

The Labour Party, even in the good days of the 1920s when there was little unemployment, showed a distaste for schemes which sank large sums of money for, they obstinately believed, the good of the new-comers. The party felt there was much to be done to help Australians before anyone else was brought out to share the profits and pleasures of their land. H. S. Gullett, the Minister for Trade and Customs in the Bruce-Page Government did everything in his power to put the issue on a non-party basis. He wanted the support and advice of the trade unions as much as that of other interests concerned. In 1926 the Liberal Government in power succeeded in establishing the Development and Migration Commission, an advisory body of four expert members. Its function was to investigate, with the impartiality of a Royal Commission, the needs of the country for manpower, the pattern of development and the way in which immigration could be used to fill these needs and further these schemes. It was to act as a liaison body between Commonwealth and States and it was hoped that it would lift immigration out of the sphere of party politics and emotions and make of it a tool for a general, planned development. The power that the Commission developed, analogous in its way to that of the Loan Council, despite its tentative and purely advisory origin, is most aptly described by Greenwood.

The Commission came to be placed in a position where, within the limits of political willingness to accept its decisions, it was largely in control of the direction of development within the country. The trend was for the Commonwealth, through its agency and through its financial superiority, to assume responsibility for general planning, while the States, again with certain qualifications, were becoming the administrative agents for implementing national plans. The form of agreement between the Commonwealth and State Governments under the £34 million agreement laid down that any State Governments desiring to participate in any settlement or public works scheme must submit its proposals for approval by the Commonwealth, which in practice meant by the Commission. Not only did the general scheme have to be submitted, but estimates of costs and a good range of details under a list of classified heads. Furthermore, Commonwealth representatives had the right of investigating the progress which had actually been made. The States do not appear to have offered any serious objection to this procedure and, indeed, from time to time they were anxious to avail themselves of the investigating facilities of the Commission on questions of State policy. If this trend involved some increase in Commonwealth authority and some corresponding diminution of State power, only the Federal purist would object on that account; under a governmental system which was moving towards quasi-federalism, there was much to be said, both on the grounds of co-operation and efficiency, for the Commonwealth's assuming more and more a general planning function, with the States contributing to the plan and implementing agreed decisions.[20]

As Professor Greenwood has not failed to point out, the accent was on development rather than on immigration. It might be supposed that this logical approach and insistence on a lasting value to the community at large would draw the Opposition's sting. But the electorate often reacts against logic and the impartiality of the expert. It could be argued that an increased population engaged in productive work would make more employment for all, but by the end of the 1920s it was obvious that there was not more employment but less and less. That this was not the result of any immigration scheme was hard to explain to dispossessed people in search of a scapegoat. A great deal of organization had, after all, yielded only a relatively small increase of population. Only something over 212,000 assisted migrants came into the country between 1921 and 1929 and the £34,000,000 drive of 1925 only produced about 31,000 in 1926, the "best" year, a figure substantially below the pre-war quota.

Black depression settled not only on Australia but on the Western world and America. Assisted immigration ceased. Since the 1840s there had been no long period, interrupted by neither wars nor depressions, in which to try out immigration schemes. History was broken by too many shoals.

In the troubled 1930s there was a fairly large influx of Continentals fleeing before persecution. They were not government-assisted, they either paid their own passages and brought money into the country to equip themselves for a new life, or they were assisted by national or religious groups already in Australia. They were for the most part city dwellers and introduced new ideas in the community, most particularly, perhaps, in food.

There was some popular hostility towards these unhappy people. They were "different", they naturally clung together in groups, there were language difficulties, and when they succeeded in business or in the competition for housing there was jealousy. Folk-lore is always with us, and legends of their anti-social behaviour, their predatoriness, their unbearable condescension, even their dirtiness, were passed from mouth to mouth, related over back fences and in chain-stores. Owners of flats and residentials were proud to inform their Australian tenants that "you won't find any reffos in this building". It was difficult for them to re-enter the professions in which some of them had excelled. The British Medical Association was loth to register foreign doctors unless they took an Australian degree. This was hard, and yet there were some grounds for suspicion. There was no means of checking qualifications and experience and the plausible charlatan was not unknown. The engineering profession appointed a panel to investigate the claims of engineers and, if convinced of their authenticity, they were hallmarked as eligible for employment.

The new-comers themselves had often suffered and were embittered. It was hard to have to begin life anew, in a country they would never normally have considered settling in. They thought they should receive more sympathy and interest. Everything was strange. The older people looked back instead of forward. Of course, the situation was difficult.

Ill feeling rarely extended to the children, who, attending Australian schools, quickly learnt to speak, think, and behave like the other children and were accepted on their own merits. As time went on, so were their fathers and mothers if they were willing to come half-way.

There is no doubt that Australia benefited in many ways by the arrival of these people with their new skills and from the impact and stimulation of new ideas and a different way of life. Given a generation or two, by intermarriage and adjustment, they are likely to sink into the population with barely a trace of foreign origin, even their names weathered to more easily pronounced variants.

These refugees were the vanguard. At the end of World War II it was obvious that there would have to be a redistribution of population between the old world and the new. Australia was one of the obvious destinations for people uprooted or displaced by war or anxious to leave the scene of so much sorrow and desolation and to bring up their children where there was at least the illusion of safety. Australia was at last ready to receive them. As the Hon. H. E. Holt wrote:

> The ill-wind of the Second World War served one useful purpose for Australia. It dispelled the fog which had obscured more widespread recognition of our urgent need for a rapid increase in population. The danger of invasion by a determined, well-equipped enemy, so clearly disclosed and so narrowly averted, did more than all the political oratory and journalism of the preceding fifty years to convince the great mass of Australians that they must either populate and develop their vast continent or accept the probability of having it taken from them.[21]

Perhaps what Mr Holt meant was that the Labour opposition had at last seen the light. It was the Curtin Labour Government during the war that envisaged a new and much more ambitious immigration policy than Australia had ever known. Curtin appointed a finding Committee, not of economists, but, more characteristically, of senior public servants who might be termed experts in administration, to advise the Government as to post-war immigration. The Committee's report was tabled in 1944 and a Ministerial Department of Immigration was planned. It fell to Curtin's successor, Chifley, to implement the policy. A. A. Calwell, Deputy Leader of the House, was appointed the first Minister and built up a large department with ramifications not only in the Australian capitals but in the United Kingdom and most European countries. In four and a half years, and the figures are Calwell's, a staff of about 24 had increased to 5000 and 700,000 immigrants had been brought out. This was mass migration. The gross increase in population was not great because large numbers of evacuees and refugees were returning home. From 1948 onwards there was a definite gain.

There were many problems to be faced in getting mass immigration under way. The plan was born under and initiated by Labour Governments, but there was still the difficulty of getting the rank and file, slower to move, less well informed, more obstinate in their beliefs, to "think migration". It was not easy. Times were good, jobs easy to get, there was much more work than workers. That made a difference. It is easy to forecast that in a depression the New Australians would be the first to lose their jobs. Fortunately the trade-unionists' insistence on the maintenance of a certain standard of living has ensured to the new-comers award rates of pay, except perhaps when employed on undisclosed conditions by their own nationals. For mass migration to succeed, there had to be some revolutionary thinking. The trade unions appear to have been more receptive than the professional classes. The achievement of receptivity in the Australian population was the first hurdle.

A matter of careful forethought and arrangement was the channel through which the migrants were to come and their selection. The approach has been from a number of angles and through various agreements made overseas. The most important has been the United Kingdom Free and Assisted Passage Scheme, worked out between the British and Australian Governments. For this the British Ministry of Labour and National Service received all applications and, jointly with Commonwealth representatives, interviewed those seeking entry to Australia, determined their general suitability, investigated their qualifications if they were tradesmen or technicians, and finally subjected them to a thorough medical examination. No one suffering from tuberculosis or any other disabling disease was eligible.

This was relatively straightforward. There were subsidiary schemes for British nationals such as the Empire and Allied Ex-Servicemen's Scheme, in which the Returned Soldiers' League and similar bodies have taken a particular interest, the Irish Scheme, and the Malta Agreement.

In the Displaced Persons Scheme and the subsequent Dutch, Italian, and German agreements, the utmost care had to be taken in screening applicants for security and health reasons, most particularly the displaced persons coming from camps where illness bred of malnutrition was rife and where antecedents and political colour were difficult to determine, resting generally only on the applicant's own statements. There has always been the fear that Nazi agents or other persons with a subversive outlook would make their way into the country under cover of being displaced persons. The majority of these unhappy and ill-used people had no desire to come to Australia, whereas it was the British migrants' free choice. They would for the most part have preferred to go to the United States, but that country's quota system of immigration stood in their way. Only the most eligible made the grade. The chance that they already had friends or relations in Australia was remote. By reason of their experiences and consequent psychological factors the difficulties attending their absorption were great. Their immigration somewhere was compulsory as they no longer dared to return to their original homes or had any place or status in the world.

Agreements to receive Dutch and Italian immigrants were signed in 1951 and a German Agreement in 1952. These nationals were recruited from those willing to come on an occupational basis, to provide workers of a type scarce in Australia. Much of the preliminary work of selection fell to the authorities in their own countries.

Immigrants from all sources, displaced persons excepted, fell roughly into three classes:

(*i*) Those nominated by relations, friends, or public-spirited citizens who had some personal knowledge of them through mutual friends and were willing to guarantee them housing and employment on arrival. A great proportion of the British migrants fell into this category. This a little resembles the bounty system, without the bounty, of course. It is an elastic method of fitting new citizens into the community.

(*ii*) Those selected from applicants by Commonwealth officers. They were housed at Commonwealth expense on arrival, too often, unfortunately, for lack of anything else, in camps, hostels or improvised housing settlements, until they could be placed in living-in jobs or better housing found for them. This class of immigrant was expected to work wherever directed, generally at labouring jobs or on the domestic staff of institutions such as hospitals, for two years, in return for their passage money. This often inflicted hardship on the not-so-young, as they had been trained to and had qualified for quite different work and were acclimatized to a different social standing. It did not help them to take up in society the work they were most fitted to do at the end of the two years. For the young it was not so difficult. There were men and women of all ages also who did not think it too high a price to pay for the re-attainment of security. Displaced persons came as unskilled labour; if they could make their way out of that category it was thanks to their own energy and character.

(*iii*) "Special Projects" workers. These were mostly skilled workers in trades in which Australia was weak, brought out to work on developmental schemes like that of the Snowy Mountains Hydro-Electric Authority. These were generally single men, including a number of Norwegians who were especially adapted for work in the snow country.

Each of these groups presented difficulties, some, of course, more than others. Where difference of language was the main trouble the Commonwealth conducted classes at the camps and hostels and besides this tried to give all migrants not going immediately to friends or relations a rudimentary knowledge of the country they had come to.

Evening classes were provided for migrants already working. Some 18,000 were taking advantage of them voluntarily in 1953. For those out of town there were correspondence classes of which 9500 availed themselves in the same year. The Australian Broadcasting Commission also assisted by special sessions in English for New Australians, and by the issue of booklets reinforcing the lessons.

It has been government policy to prevent migrants as far as possible from clinging together in national groups and forming small States within the State, as happened in the United States. Geography and the scattering through schools and industries have so far prevented this type of coagulation to any great extent. It exists more nearly amongst the German settlers of South Australia, products of an earlier migration, who live in communities and, at home and in church at least, speak their mother tongue.

Shipping to transport immigrants to Australia was one of the bottlenecks that had to be broken. There was a world shortage of shipping owing to war-time sinkings, the repatriation of soldiers after the war, and reawakening commerce. From 1951 onwards this was facilitated by a body which became known as the Inter-governmental Committee for European Migration. It was backed by seventeen countries, was non-profit-making, and intended to carry migrants from Europe to countries like Australia willing to receive them, using the fleet of ships that had once belonged to the International Refugee Organization.

The price of bringing immigrants into the country has naturally been very heavy. There do not seem to be any exact figures as to the *per capita* cost but it has been assessed at between £1000 and £2000, taking into account the overhead expenses, 5000 salaries, travel allowances, conveyance of the migrant, his housing, interstate travel, education and the numerous forms of assistance he has the right to expect. That may be the capital cost, but it is not the real cost to the community. A large population earning and spending money, engaged in developmental work which will enrich the future, is profitable to the nation as a whole. Most migrants eventually become taxpayers and make their contribution to Consolidated Revenue, from which the money was drawn to bring them to the country. The value of individual migrants naturally varies, some are an excellent bargain, others leave the country again as soon as they are able, or become a permanent charge on the taxpayer.

Post-war migration schemes differ from earlier ones in that they are not a purely Australian effort but they tie in with international organizations. Also, although the most desired immigrants are still those of British stock, the net is cast more widely and people of practically every free European nation are brought in. We are, like America before us but on a smaller scale, a "melting-pot". Variety has been the very essence of it. Political or social changes and the disruption of war precipitated a large-scale folk movement which has fanned out as far as Australia.

Another point: land settlement and immigration have practically parted company. With returned servicemen to be catered for and many other Australians, particularly young men brought up to the land, so land-hungry that Crown land and resumed estates opened up for settlement are balloted for, there is little to offer the New Australian. With the mechanization of farms and the streamlining of grazing properties there are not many jobs awaiting rural workers. The New Australian may go into partnership with a fellow countryman, settled earlier on the land, or he may, when he has enough capital, buy a farm or an orchard in the open market like anyone else. He has little chance of being settled on it by the Government.

The migrant is wanted primarily for big schemes like the water conservation network in Victoria or the Snowy Mountains Hydro-Electric Authority, which require labour of all grades of skill or no skill. He is used primarily for development and, during his first two years, for dead-end jobs.

He is helping in the expansion of the country, but is he, critics ask, filling the great open spaces? When he works for an irrigation project he helps to bring more land under cultivation, but that is not what is generally meant. He congregates in the cities, where he is usually more at home, or in gangs and messes. He is not expected to be a small farmer or individualist. His contribution to defence is indirect, for on the whole the Army, the Air Force, and the Navy do not want him, for security reasons. The State that is the most open, spacious, and vulnerable, Western Australia, has complained that it receives the smallest quota of immigrants.

The last question is, naturally, how many immigrants have come to Australia in the post-war drive. To quote the figures supplied by the Commonwealth Department of Immigration for the period January 1947 to September 1952, the Australian population increased by approximately 1,182,600, of which net migration contributed 555,000 or 47 per cent. The actual percentage increase in the population over this period was 15.7 per cent, of which net migration contributed 6.1 per cent. During 1949 and 1950, when migration reached its highest level, the average annual rate of population increase was 3.24 per cent.

Migrants who were financially assisted by the Commonwealth and other Governments to settle in Australia during the period January 1947 to September 1952 numbered 388,400 or 57.5 per cent of the estimated gross permanent intake of 675,450. They included 170,200 displaced persons resettled under the Mass Resettlement Scheme and 170,000 British migrants under the United Kingdom Free and Assisted Passage Scheme. Arrivals under minor assisted schemes include 17,480 Empire and Allied Ex-servicemen, 11,730 Maltese, 6950 Dutch, 1450 Irish and 9050 Italians.

Unassisted migrants over the same period included 146,300 British, 46,500 Italian, 18,695 Dutch, 10,774 Greek, 6200 Polish.[22]

The *Year Book of the Commonwealth of Australia*, No. 43 (1957), gives some interesting figures. At the end of June 1954, 95.5 per cent of the Australian population was British (85.7 per cent Australian born, 9.8 per cent migrants) compared with 99.5 per cent in 1947 of whom 90.2 per cent were born in Australia. Of foreign elements in the population the most numerous were Italian (90,018), Dutch (53,458), Polish (49,746), German (31,448), Yugoslav (18,124), Greek (17,843), Ukrainian (17,239), and Latvian (17,225). The 1954 census revealed that there were less than 6000 Americans in Australia and 38,949 persons who were still stateless (pp. 567-8). On page 572 an interesting table showing population movements by immigration and emigration, 1901-56, appears. Exact figures for assisted and unassisted migration between 1926 and 1956 are also given.

The "departures", so often ignored in any discussion of immigration, are shown as uniformly high. There is no better source of information, laconic though it be, than this *Year Book*.

Happy migrants encourage more migrants. They bring out their relations and friends under the sponsoring system. If they are successful they inspire their fellow countrymen to try their luck in Australia also. They warm a new hearth overseas. For reasons of climate Mediterranean peoples are naturally drawn to Australia.

By the census of 1961 Australia's population had reached the 10,000,000 mark. She has more sons and daughters to call on in need and that is more important than filling the white and often barren places on the map with agricultural settlements doomed to failure.

Quality of population is more important than numbers. The United Kingdom herself was a little nation, and so was the Greece of Pericles.

REFERENCE NOTES

1 *Hist Rec. Aust.*, ser. I, vol. i, p. 416.
2 *Ibid.*, p. 559.
3 *Ibid.*, vol. ii, p. 479.
4 *Ibid.*, vol. iii, p. 330.
5 *Ibid.*, p. 533.
6 *Ibid.*, vol. v, p. 487.
7 *Ibid.*, vol. xi, p. 123.
8 *Ibid.*, vol. xiii, p. 213.
9 *Ibid.*, vol. xvi, pp. 36 *et seq.*
10 *Ibid.*, p. 297.
11 *Ibid.*, pp. 757-8.
12 *Ibid.*, vol. xviii, p. 726.
13 *Ibid.*, vol. xix, p. 129.
14 *Ibid.*, vol. xviii, p. 514.
15 *Ibid.*, vol. xx, p. 412.
16 *Ibid.*, vol. xxi, p. 431.
17 *Ibid.*, pp. 543-5.
18 *Ibid.*, p. 549.
19 A. Joyce, *A Homestead History.*
20 *Australia: a Social and Political History* (ed. Greenwood), p. 317.
21 H. E. Holt, and others, *Australia and the Migrant,* p. 1.
22 *Ibid.*, Appendix A, pp. 165 *et seq.*

CHAPTER XXII

RESULTS IN THE MAKING

If I were a young man, with all the world in front of me, I would want to be in Australia at the beginning of what will be its most wonderful period of development. The overall picture in Australia to-day is one of the most stimulating things anywhere in the world.

—R. G. Menzies, quoted, *Sydney Morning Herald*, Supplement, 30th June, 1958.

The politics of the future are social politics, and the problem is still how to secure the greatest happiness of the greatest number and especially of those whom all previous legislation and reform seem to have left very much where they were before.

—Joseph Chamberlain.

I. Standard of Living

The only firm basis for any standard of living is security, and the economic security of a community is best achieved by ensuring to the breadwinner a fair share of profits earned in industry, primary and secondary. The economy of Australia is mixed, resting partly on planning, originating in and administered by the Government, and partly on free enterprise bound only by the law of the land. The Government could protect, and has protected, the wage-earner by legislation and the establishment of Wages Boards and Arbitration Courts. The man working for himself or receiving his income in the form of dividends from a company does not receive the same direct protection. He does receive it indirectly in that the Arbitration Courts are also courts of conciliation and as such do all in their power to avert strikes and industrial upheavals. If he is a manufacturer or shopkeeper the greater and steadier the spread of income through the population the more business he is likely to do. Tariffs protect him and his employees jointly. He and his family share in many of the social services and benefits and, should he fail, he has the assurance of subsistence. He is by the exercise of his talents and acumen liable to make more money and perhaps attain a higher standing in the community than any wage-earner or salaried officer as such.

The blending of private enterprise and State planning makes for elasticity and marks the difference between a socialist and a Welfare State.

Trade unions began early in New South Wales, but were, to begin with, more akin to Friendly Societies than to the modern organizations bearing their name. In the late 1870s and early 1880s workers began to band together in their own interests. In 1879 there was an Intercolonial Trades Union Congress and from 1884 such meetings became more regular and effective. The first hurdle was to have unions legally recognized. They disclaimed all interest in politics and were interested only in the maintenance of wages and the improvement of working conditions. Most of their members had come from the United Kingdom and harked back to the bad conditions of the Industrial Revolution, much as the Irish kept alive in a new land the memory of persecutions and famines in the old world. There were vested interests in Australia certainly, but they were not of the magnitude or so well entrenched as in industrial England. Outside the towns the bush was a great leveller in the early days. The convict tradition set labour back, but, on the other hand, many successful and well-to-do citizens had worked their way up from nothing and there were in consequence fewer hard and fast social differences. The militant democracy brought into the country by the gold-rushes expunged most of the old master-and-servant relationship, just as the influx of population diluted the convict inheritance.

In 1883 a Royal Commission was appointed by the Victorian Parliament to investigate sweated labour. Its findings aroused public opinion and strengthened the hands of the trade unions. Sweating was more than the hard lot of those involved, it was recognized as something that undermined the position of labour as a whole. A conception of the Australian standard of living was already born, though still an infant.

Labourers in cities and in the mines were more ready to organize than rural workers. It was, like love, a matter of propinquity. An eight-hour day and health and safety regulations in factories and mines were the first objectives.

Falling standards in the 1890s precipitated strikes which showed that unionists were ready to stand together and to fight for their standard of living. When direct action failed, as it was bound to do in a time of depression, the Australian Labour Party was formed to fight its battles constitutionally. The two sections of the Labour movement, the political and the industrial, have always remained separate, though allied. The industrial, as the less responsible, has always been more open to outside influences, more socialistic or even extremist. The Australian Labour Party, especially when in office, has shown itself realistic, and again and again on matters of conscience, such as the conscription issue, its leaders have crossed the floor of the House. Although Liberal members have rarely been converted to Labour, it is no new thing for a Liberal Government to introduce measures advocated by their opponents. Although not as closely resembling one another as, to the uninitiated eye, Republicans and Democrats appear to do in the United States, they have much in common and the electorate turns from one to the other to get what it wants. The majority of the electors stand midway between. They want fair play and they like a change now and then. Both parties have thrown up occasional great men.

It was a Liberal Government that in 1896 set up in Victoria the first Wages Board with the purpose of adjudicating in industrial disputes and by an impartial survey of circumstances to fix a "fair" wage. In 1901 New South Wales established an Arbitration Court, a similar institution with a different name. The other States followed suit with their Wages Boards (Tasmania) or Arbitration Courts (South Australia, Queensland, Western Australia).

More indicative still of public opinion was the Arbitration and Conciliation Court built into the Commonwealth Constitution. Both parties were agreed on it, one because it promised industrial peace, the other because it promised to provide a bulwark for the standard of living.

The Court was constituted in 1905 by the Liberal Deakin Government. It was revolutionary. It acknowledged the trade unions as equal parties in a dispute with the employers. The trade unions were recognized as "natural and legitimate associations performing a necessary function in the economic system".[1] Deakin approached it in a spirit of idealism:

> Such legislation multiplies the opportunities of the masses for obtaining those reasonable concessions which hitherto too often required to be wrung from reluctant hands under the pressure of storm and stress and devastation. On the other hand it enables employers to settle many minor difficulties which might become magnified into great causes of disturbance and dispute, and to dispose piecemeal of causes of irritation which, if allowed to accumulate, would break out into social festers, requiring more radical, if not surgical, treatment.[2]

He was looking back to the turmoil of the early 1890s and he had a touching belief in sweet reasonableness.

Mr Justice Henry Bournes Higgins was appointed to the new court and approached his task in a liberal and creative spirit. His Harvester judgment of 1907 introduced a new humanitarianism into legal judgments and was the real starting-point of the basic-wage system as we know it today. He thought in terms of "needs" rather than of economic values. He proclaimed a "fair" wage based on "the normal needs of the average employee regarded as a human being in a civilized community". His average employee had a wife and three children. The minimum wage for an unskilled worker arrived at by this reasoning was two guineas a week. Small as this appears, it was an advance of about twenty-five per cent on current rates and, better still, it was a certainty. Over and above the basic wage there were margins for skills which varied.

Up to 1947 the basic wage as laid down by Mr Justice Higgins was only altered four times. It was adjusted, generally upwards, to keep pace with the cost of living, but not altered until 1921, when Mr Justice Powers, inquiring into the wage, which was felt to be out of date, recommended a rise of 3s. a week and quarterly automatic adjustments to the cost of living. His recommendation was accepted. The automatic adjustments were in accordance with an index of prices for all necessary commodities and expenses such as foodstuffs, clothing, and rent, and for a few luxuries, such as tobacco, which have become necessities for the majority of people. This index was kept up to date and the basic wage revised every quarter in relation to it.

The compilation of the index was, to begin with, difficult, since the Government Statistician had first to collect reliable data on prices, there being none in stock, so to speak, and these had to be kept up to date by reference to the constant variations of market prices, from which an average had to be struck every three months. It took more than two years to compile an index for food and rent alone. It was only after 1921 that adjustment of wages became quarterly and automatic, based on an improved and completed index. This method of adjustment, though it appears fair, has one serious drawback. The worker has no incentive to decrease the cost of living by greater output. It would only mean that there was less in his pay envelope.

A bare list of prices was not enough, they had to be related to family needs and circumstances. To this end it was usual to take evidence from housewives as to the incidence of expense on their family budgets.

The second alteration was in 1931 when, as part of the deflationary policy for dealing with the depression, the basic wage, like every other controllable payment, was reduced by ten per cent. In 1934 the third alteration occurred when the ten per cent was restored. In this juggling the Powers judgment was dropped and the Harvester judgment was once again the rock-bottom foundation.

The fourth change came in 1937 when the basic wage was raised by a "prosperity loading". A new steering idea was at this time introduced, that is, industry's "capacity to pay". The prosperity loading amounted to 6s. a week in New South Wales, Victoria, and Queensland, and 4s. a week in Western Australia and Tasmania.

The basic-wage policy, though generally considered a useful and progressive piece of social legislation, has its critics, who point out that a minimum wage automatically becomes a maximum wage, that the courts only concern themselves with the minimum wage and working conditions and the maximum working hours, thus actually slowing down the progress of the worker towards a higher standard of living. Critics have also pointed out that there was a serious brake on the adjustment of the basic wage to the cost of living. For instance, rising prices in the 1920s reduced the real value, or spending power, of the basic wage to between 15 and 20 per cent below its value in 1911. In 1936 it was only 7 per cent above the 1911 mark. Whilst productivity had risen 60 per cent, wages rose only 20 per cent. This, I may suggest, does not show the whole picture. It presupposes that the great body of workers remained on the minimum wage, which is not true. For those who did other factors, such as social services and educational opportunities, improved the position. The 20 per cent increase in wages is net, whilst the 60 per cent increase in productivity is gross. But that subject could be argued to eternity.

The history of arbitration and conciliation, basic wages and awards, is a complex one. The Harvester judgment established a basic or minimum wage which was generally acceptable. It was only the beginning. It drew a line below which the standard of living might not sink. The court did not take into consideration conditions of work or its hazards, the theory being that these should be eliminated or minimized by Factory Acts insisting on safeguards to health from fumes, dust, effluents, or other harmful substances involved in manufactures or mining, protection of machinery to prevent accidents, protective clothing or goggles where necessary, and all the other guards found to be necessary in the safe carrying out of various occupations. Dirty or dangerous work not covered by Factory Acts remained a matter of bargaining between employer and employee. In the event of accident or the contraction of an industrial disease, such as miner's phthisis or lead poisoning, workers' compensation came into action.

Certain classes of workers did not profit fully from the basic wage. The largest class was women, who at first received only 54 per cent of the male basic wage; the percentage, however, has risen until equal pay for equal work has become more than an aspiration. The theory behind the lower wage for women was that whilst a man had to provide for a family a woman had only herself to care for, an arrangement that worked in favour of bachelors and to the disadvantage of widows with children, daughters supporting parents, or other women with dependants. Aged or very slow workers could also be legally paid less.

A man with more than three children was at a disadvantage, which child endowment was intended to redress.

Conciliation and arbitration were embraced with such enthusiasm that Australia boasts seven different courts. The most important, and of increasing importance, is the Commonwealth Court. In its constitution the accent was on conciliation. Its aims were to promote goodwill in the industrial field, to encourage round-table conferences between representatives of employers and employees when, disputes having arisen and spread to two or more States, the disputants appealed to the Court. When essential services or key industries are involved arbitration can be declared compulsory. Usually the Court only takes action when asked to arbitrate, but once the Court has been called in its ruling must be accepted. Any union with interstate membership may submit its log of grievances to the Commonwealth Court. When all circumstances have been impartially considered the judgment is given in the form of an award binding on the whole industry which has come up for review.

Each State has its own court on similar lines. All workers, industrial or rural, are covered by awards either Commonwealth or State. These awards are a superstructure built over, but unconnected with, the basic wage. It can easily happen in a large organization that some employees work under a Commonwealth, others under a State, award, a circumstance which leads to discontent when one award is more generous than the other. Awards cover the whole field of industrial life: wages, conditions, holidays, hours of labour.

The unions were, and are, the accredited representatives of the workers, but the privileges they have won in the courts have always applied to non-unionist workers as well as to unionists. In the interests of solidarity and in order to have, through the dues of members, sufficient fighting funds, the unions have made a drive for membership. They won, first, preference to unionists, a policy which employers usually endorsed because it lessened friction, and, finally, compulsory unionism in New South Wales. This last Act, forced on political Labour by industrial Labour, caused heart-burnings, for some felt it to be an infringement of the individual's liberty. It was not really revolutionary or new, professional unions having led the way. Objections were *au fond* generally political. Conservatives, in the sacred name of liberty, disapproved of joining unions even if they were organized in their interests. In this context, it could be argued that the inclusion within unions of numbers of Liberal voters could, if they exercised their rights in shaping union policy, do much to modify the stance of industrial Labour.

Arbitration achieved a place in the public mind only second to the White Australia Policy. In time employers came to favour it even more than employees, although it is clear that it ensured to the latter substantial gains in a constitutional manner. By bargaining the unions might have achieved much, but bad times would have reversed the deals. There was a lot to be said for having the government stamp on awards. Progress was put on the Statute Book. When the Bruce-Page Government sought to alter the arbitration system in 1929 it created a furore and broke its own back. In 1927 the Government had determined to reform arbitration and in 1928 brought forward its Conciliation and Arbitration Act. It was obvious in the Prime Minister's introduction to the debate that he was dissatisfied with the working of arbitration. He said:

> A system of compulsory arbitration can be continued only if both sides obey the law, which must bind and be observed by both parties, otherwise the system must go. This bill is an attempt to ensure that compulsory arbitration shall continue, and that both sides shall observe it. I suggest that it is

essential for this country that the system shall continue, and that the great experiment in which we have indulged shall not be jettisoned.[3]

The words "experiment" and "indulged" strike a warning note. Professor Greenwood sums up the Act:

> The Government . . . endeavoured in one clause after another to sheet home responsibility to the unions and union leaders for the observance of awards and the prevention of disputes while the Court was actually considering the matter. Finally the attempt was made to deal with the crucial economic problem of continuous interruption to industry and the progressive upward movement of wage rates. It took its stand upon the interests of the community in general and upon the capacity of the economy to bear an expanded wages bill. In future the Court was to consider not only the social question of a reasonable standard of living, but the economic question of the capacity of a particular industry to pay.[4]

The snag about this was, who could determine how much an industry could afford for its wages bill? Judges are not economists. Statistics, as surely as cameras, can lie. The conciliation side of the Arbitration Court, from which so much had been hoped, had not come up to expectations. If awards did not satisfy the unions there was generally trouble. The Court was impartial as far as it is within the compass of human beings to be impartial. Both sides were myopic. It looked sometimes as if the unions were attempting to blackmail the Court by the use of the strike weapon. They did not always suspend direct action whilst their log of claims was *sub judice*, which is the common rule in all litigation. Union leaders were in the position of politicians who had to please a large and, in the nature of things, self-centred electorate. Minor incidents often caused disproportionate irritation. Industrial Labour has always been more leftist than political Labour. It was easier for the Court to find a more responsible attitude amongst the comparatively few employers, who, moreover, feared strikes and the disruption they caused. It has always been easier to exact penalties from the employers for non-compliance than from the unions. Fines, or at worst deregistration of the latter, have been ineffective and have made bad blood. The Prime Minister was closely allied with business interests. There were times when arbitration jogged along like a cart with square wheels. It was not clear, however, what should be put in its place to attain a greater measure of success.

There were defects in the system that could not be foreseen at its initiation. Firstly, there was the conflict between Commonwealth and State awards. This was settled by the High Court, which ruled that the Commonwealth Court should overrule the State courts. It was unfortunate that the Court could only act when there was a dispute. A revision of wages in all industries in times of industrial peace might have been more successful.

When tempers were roused on both sides one or the other was sure to resent the judgment and to be uncooperative. The courts moved slowly, and this was a grievance. For this reason, in war-time, when delay was most serious, Hughes took crucial issues out of the hands of the Court and appointed special tribunals to adjudicate.

At first firms or industries begun after the foundation of the Court were not amenable to its jurisdiction and their employees did not profit by awards. This was circumvented by citing employers who did not conform to the ruling rates before the Court.

Politics and obstructionism unfortunately were introduced into a field in which impartiality was most important. The Communist Party, always strongest in industrial Labour, was automatically opposed to the arbitration system and set many adherents or fellow travellers against it. Some unionists, particularly coal-miners, who live in quasi-closed communities and through their work are the more subject to accident and sickness, have proved uncooperative. Every flouting of the Court has weakened its power. The Court must carry strong powers of conciliation indeed to heal a breach which has existed in one form or another between two sections of the community since the foundation of the colony.

The Conciliation and Arbitration Act of 1928 raised a storm of protest, penalties for non-compliance were resented, and the direction to unions to hold secret ballots was resented even more. The general tone of the Act aroused hostility throughout the Labour movement. It did not bring about better relations. They worsened.

The following year the Bruce-Page Government decided to withdraw the Commonwealth from arbitration and leave it to the States to handle. This had been precipitated by conflicting legislation in the States and the obvious entanglement of seven arbitration systems, together with a tendency artificially to foment disputes interstate in order to bring them to the Commonwealth Court.

The new proposals were included in the Maritime Industries Bill. They raised a storm of protest, led by the veteran W. M. Hughes. The Bill was defeated in the House, which was tantamount to a vote of no confidence, and when the Government went to the polls there was a landslide in favour of Labour. The Prime Minister himself lost his seat, an unprecedented event.

The Australian people had a sentimental attachment to their arbitration system—even if it did not work smoothly. It was one of the most valued exhibits in the shop window.

There have been factors other than the basic wage and the Arbitration Court that have pegged or improved the standard of living. In the 1880s Victoria had passed several somewhat ineffective Factory Acts regulating certain types of labour—for example, employment of women and children

—and in 1885 the Factories and Shops Act fixed closing hours. For shops this was 7 p.m. on week-days and 10 p.m. on Saturdays. A maximum working week for minors of 56 hours was set up. Factory Acts were passed in New South Wales, Victoria, and Queensland in 1896 and the other States soon came into line. Later Acts were directed to stamping out the worst evils of sweated labour, the regulation of apprenticeship and of child labour. As early as 1873 in Victoria, no woman (housewives and mothers excepted) was allowed by law to work for more than eight hours a day. In New South Wales new ground was broken by the Employers' Liability Act of 1897, which followed an English model and made the employer liable for injuries sustained by his employees whilst at work. Compulsory insurance was not brought in until after the turn of the century. These Acts and others showed a growing consciousness of public responsibility. As time went on the Government took more and more responsibility for conditions of work until, during and immediately after World War II, the Commonwealth Department of Labour and National Service was setting standards for conditions of work and staff amenities down to the last detail.

From the beginning of trade-unionism the battle cry had been "an eight-hour working day". The building trades were the first to get it, notably a group of stonemasons at Parramatta in 1855, but it was not enough to attain it piecemeal and by grace. The unions wanted to see it on the Statute Book or written into awards. Mr Justice Higgins in the Commonwealth Arbitration Court began to award a 44-hour working week in 1920. It was already a practice in some industries.

In 1939 the average working week, taking Australia as a whole, was 44.29 hours, the shortest working week being in Queensland, 43.46 hours, the longest in Tasmania, 45.33 hours.

By 1946 the Australian average was 39.95 hours, the shortest week being in Western Australia, 39.51 hours, the longest in Tasmania and South Australia, 40 hours. These figures, taken from the *Official Year Book of the Commonwealth of Australia*, refer to male workers and are only an average. In many industries men were working longer and receiving overtime pay.

After World War II Saturday work was largely discontinued. Shift work, taking into account work done at night or on holidays, equated working time with wages. After the war Commonwealth public servants on an average worked 36½ hours a week. The annual Labour celebration and public holiday with street processions, long known as Eight-hour Day, has become Six-hour Day, when not called Labour Day.

The tariff was used by Prime Minister Deakin to improve labour conditions. His "new protection" was framed not only to help the manufacturer but also to spread its benefits to his employees and to the primary producer. Only those manufacturers who paid "fair and reasonable" wages were to benefit. This was difficult to implement and proved untenable, but it had converted the Labour Party to protection. It opened new vistas of progress, for, as the Labour leader Fisher said, "The Parliament which has the power to impose Customs and Excise duties is the only effective body to determine what shall be the wage conditions in the industries to which those duties apply."[5] Similarly, it is presumed, a Parliament which voted bounties on primary products could dictate conditions for rural workers.

The most interesting experiment in industrial peace has been successfully put into action in Broken Hill and is now in its third decade. As might be expected from its isolation and the components of its population, the frontier city had been a cauldron of industrial unrest, but this has changed since the Barrier Industrial Council began to function. This body co-ordinates all the unions and treats with the employers. As the price of industrial peace it won a "lead bonus" for every employee, including typists and stenographers, adjusted to the world parity of silver-lead, and additional to award rates. This keeps everyone happy. The name of the bonus is misleading; it has nothing to do with the risk of lead-poisoning. It is, in effect, a profit-sharing scheme. The "lead bonus" is not a principle that could be applied to industry throughout Australia. It is the exceptional richness of the Barrier lode and the financial power of the big companies working it that make it possible. Moreover, economists tell us that wages can be too high as well as too low for the health of the community. Very high wages lead to inflation. In Australia, though they may seem good, they are in fact reduced by taxation, direct and indirect, and by counter-inflation or government schemes of credit expansion.

I have not meant to suggest that the high standard of living which is part of Australia's gospel is restricted to wages and working conditions. It applies to the whole community. Secondary industry is protected, primary industry is helped by bounties, marketing schemes and the freely distributed results of government-sponsored scientific research. For those in need and for the public in general there are the social services. The standard of living in all its ramifications, from free education to the Arbitration Court, is financed out of revenue raised by taxation, customs duties, and fees. Australia pays for her fancy.

II. Social Services

Australia, as a community of white men, began its existence as a Welfare State—welfare of a rough and ready kind, certainly. The Government made itself responsible for the food, clothing, medical attention, education, if any, and spiritual care of the whole community. This was not a policy, it was a necessity arising out of the circumstances of the settlement. Self-help became the rule as soon as feasible. Governors were rapped over the knuckles for helping, out of the public store, farmers ruined by floods. Maintenance by the Government had a slur on it because it was the lot of the convict.

Governor King and his lady set up the Orphan School Fund, which drew the necessary finance from the limited colonial revenue but was administered on a voluntary basis. It was primarily for the housing, clothing, feeding, and education of orphaned or deserted children who would otherwise have starved or slipped into crime and immorality. The accent was on charity. Macquarie founded the Benevolent Society to care for the sick, the aged, the destitute. The Sydney Dispensary was another early charitable institution for distributing free medical care to the poor. Those who could not afford treatment in their homes were, as a matter of grace, taken into hospitals maintained for convicts.

Charity waxed and waned and generally went hand in hand with religion. The ruling doctrine was laissez-faire and the comfortable assumption was that if men were willing to work they could look after themselves. If they did not work, they were worthless. This was a not unnatural assumption in a country one of whose main troubles had been shortage of labour. The well-intentioned helped, spasmodically, the old, the sick, and the orphaned. Public opinion allowed children to go to work very early in their lives. All this was the very negation of the Welfare State as we define it. In it assistance is, or should be, given to those who need it as a right and accepted with the natural dignity of a sundowner taking his hand-out at a station. The Welfare State provides a basic security as well as a basic wage. Its citizens assume responsibility for the weaker brethren. There are, of course, disadvantages, but not as great as those of insecurity. Benefits, like rain, fall on the heads of the worthy and the unworthy alike, and, short of indictable offences, it is not the business of the bureaucrat or anyone else to sit in judgment.

Except for free compulsory education, which came in the 1860s, and an old-age pension scheme for "deserving persons" passed in New South Wales in 1900 and shortly afterwards in other States, there were few social services until 1929. How people weathered the depressions of the early 1840s and early 1890s it is difficult to say. The population was smaller, the ties of family stronger, neighbourliness greater, and families managed, somehow or other, to turn the difficult corner. The magnitude of the disaster of the 1929-33 depression made government action essential. Queensland alone of the States had an unemployment insurance scheme with small, limited benefits. Immediate help for the unemployed had to be improvised. It took the form of doles and public works on which the jobless were rostered.

A. Campbell Garnett in his *Freedom and Planning in Australia* makes an analysis of the situation in 1933 when, although the depression was receding, insecurity was still the rule. At that time 31.6 per cent of the country's breadwinners were earning less than £1 a week, 47.4 per cent less than £2, 59.9 per cent less than £3, 72.4 per cent less than £4, and 83 per cent less than £5, from which he deduces half of the family units in the population were in acute want.

During the depression those still in employment or enjoying reasonable incomes were taxed to provide the dole. Times improved, but the levy remained as a social services tax.

G. V. Portus finds the roots of the Welfare State, or the Social Service State as he calls it, in "humanitarianism, the desire for social efficiency, and the fear of the consequences of discontent".[6]

Humanitarianism in the 1890s resulted in State aid for the aged. It bore fruit in 1900 in New South Wales when an old-age pension of 10s. a week was paid to men over 65 and women over 60. There was a means test and applicants had also to produce references as to character; Victoria quickly followed with a similar scheme. The Commonwealth was empowered by the Constitution to enter this field. In 1905 it appointed a Royal Commission to consider ways and means. Its findings resulted in legislation. The Old Age Pension Act, which included invalid pensions payable to adults of any age incapacitated by illness or accident, was passed in 1908. In 1912 the means test was relaxed to the extent of allowing the pensioner to own a home and to receive in addition small allowances from relations or to earn similar amounts. In 1925 the amount of the pension was raised and the means test again liberalized by the Bruce-Page Government. It has continued to rise (but so has the cost of living) and carries concessions like free medical and hospital treatment, reduced fares on public transport, and funeral benefits up to £70. With a home and the statutory amount of additional income it is possible for elderly people on the pension, particularly in a group of two or more, to live a modestly happy and comfortable life. For those who are alone, with no additions to the pension and no relations to care for them, life can be lonely and grim, especially if complicated by ill health. Clubs for "Over 60s", charitable organizations like "Meals on Wheels", try to soften their lot, but cannot cope with the needs of more than a small percentage of the poor and lonely. Churches and other organizations provide homes, generally small cottages for two, three, or four persons so that there is company without the institutional touch, but they are dependent on donations. For the destitute sick the Government supplies hospitalization as far as accommodation will stretch.

Most public servants are covered by a superannuation scheme, which they have contributed to whilst in employment and which is guaranteed to them for as long as they shall live whether or not their contribution is exhausted. More and more large firms and organizations provide insurance schemes to which both they and their employees contribute to ensure security in old age and also to retain the services of their employees up to retiring age. More and more people are being covered and stabilized. No moss for the rolling stone.

As early as 1910 both the Liberal and Labour Parties were urging a national insurance scheme covering pensions, sickness, and unemployment benefits to which all citizens would contribute according to their means and from which all would benefit. It was to be, could only be, on an actuarial basis. It raised a good many complex problems with the future as an unknown factor.

The Bruce-Page Liberal Government in the 1920s had as part of its platform a National Insurance Scheme to make provision for "casual sickness, permanent invalidity, old age and unemployment". A Royal Commission was appointed to consider what was virtually a codification of social services and recommended in favour of such a scheme exclusive of unemployment insurance. For this they recommended the appointment of a Council representing the Government, employers, and trade unions, which would get men back into employment by equating supply with need and, if necessary, re-training them. A National Insurance Bill was prepared, but got only as far as its first reading when the Government fell on the arbitration issue. (For a survey of the scope of, and difficulties confronting, a national insurance scheme, see Dr Ronald Walker's article in *Social Services in Australia* edited by W. G. K. Duncan.) New Zealand has established a compulsory contributory national insurance scheme already under way with bonuses distributed to all citizens without a means test. Australia has chosen to tackle her problems piecemeal.

In 1912 the Fisher Labour Government passed an Act granting every mother (not father) a £5 allowance on the birth of a child. This is often referred to colloquially as the "baby bonus". It was designed to tide families over the extra expense incurred at such a time and so ensure that mother and child received proper attention. With rising costs the bonus was increased. It was, and is, non-contributory and available to all mothers without a means test.

The Child Endowment Act of 1941 passed by the Menzies Government made national a scheme which had originated in New South Wales in the 1920s under the Lang Labour Government. The rate under the State scheme, whose wings had been clipped in the hostile Legislative Council, was 5s. a week for each child after the first. Under the superseding Commonwealth plan which extended it to the whole of Australia, it became 5s. a week for the first child and 10s. for every other child.[7]

Widows' pensions "for preserving the family against disintegration" were also on the New South Wales Statute Book in the 1920s. They applied to widows over fifty years of age without dependent children, when presumably it would be more difficult for them to learn a skill or find employment, and to widows of any age with children under fourteen years of age.

A pound a week was paid to the mother, plus 10s. a week for each child. The age to which the child received the benefit could be extended to sixteen if he were either physically handicapped or particularly gifted and therefore able to profit by the extra two years' schooling which would bring him to apprenticeship age. These pensions came under Commonwealth control in June 1942. The pensions were raised to £4 5s. and £3 7s. 6d. respectively a week, and a benefit was allowed to childless widows under fifty to help them over the period of readjustment. The maximum period for this is 26 weeks.

In regard to health, authority had imposed quarantine regulations spasmodically from the earliest days. This naturally became a function of the Commonwealth in protecting Australians from diseases brought in from overseas. It took over control of interstate quarantine in 1909 and enlarged its powers in 1913 following an outbreak of smallpox in New South Wales.

Invalid pensions were legislated for at the same time as old-age pensions. Public Health was entirely a State matter until the mid 1920s. The Government subsidized public hospitals, provided asylums for the insane, and contributed to institutions supported by public subscription for the blind, the deaf, and the dumb.

The First World War and the severe influenza epidemic that followed it focused more attention on public health than ever before. It had been an axiom that the Australian climate was so good, the air and soil so untainted with infections, that public health was a subject with only limited application. The Commonwealth now became aware that the over-all situation left much to be desired, that services were patchy and diverged from State to State. In 1921 the Commonwealth undertook some phases of medical research and education. This was followed up by the appointment of a Royal Commission. Its findings in 1925 led the Bruce-Page Government to establish a Federal Health Council. It advised and co-ordinated. In ten years' time it was replaced by the National Health and Research Council. Meanwhile in 1927 the Commonwealth Department of Health was created. It set up serum and other laboratories and conducted researches, notably in industrial hygiene and tropical diseases. It sponsored the 1928 Cancer Research Conference.

Eventually the Commonwealth and the States between them provided services covering the whole field of medicine from education to research, from baby health centres to campaigns against cancer, tuberculosis and polio, from the free medical and dental care of schoolchildren to the education of their parents in hygiene. Public hospitals received financial help from the Commonwealth on condition that they opened their doors to all patients without a means test. This was necessary because they had equipment not to be found in any other institutions and could give treatment not obtainable for money elsewhere. Free medical examinations and diagnosis by specialists are available to all citizens who ask for them at a public hospital without their necessarily being admitted to the hospital. The Hospital Benefits Scheme was launched in 1944, a voluntary contributory arrangement which entitled members to treatment in hospital at reduced fees. This was an insurance policy sponsored and contributed to by the Commonwealth Government. This was followed by a similar Medical Benefits Scheme, which at first met with opposition from the medical profession but has since proved of value to both doctor and patient. The deduction of medical expenses from income-tax is another means by which the Government encourages its people to maintain their health by lightening the financial burden of consultation and treatment.

State Governments have interested themselves in housing, even to the extent, in New South Wales, of adding a portfolio to the Cabinet. They have also put into force policies of slum clearance, the largest and most successful being in Victoria.

In many other ways citizens in need can receive free assistance. For instance, legal advice is dispensed gratis to those who need it but cannot pay a lawyer's fees. Many people do not take up their rights or even know that they exist.

The most difficult problem in a Welfare State is unemployment. How can security be extended to relieve workers of the fear of unemployment and to give them at least subsistence should it overtake them through no fault of their own? In good times the problem is easy to solve. In times of recession or depression, when unemployment is highest, the community is least able to carry it. An unemployment insurance scheme would need a long period of prosperity to begin with so that it could build up a sinking fund from contributions, individual and government, sufficient to meet the shock of a heavy drain upon it without laying too great a load on the depressed economy. It is difficult to get the elector to believe in depressions and unemployment when times are booming. When the first puff of cold air comes it is already too late. By 1958 no unemployment insurance act was on the Statute Book, except Theodore's Unemployed Workers' Insurance Act passed in Queensland in 1923, which had proved an insufficient bulwark to stem the flood of unemployment six years later.

The trend has been to dodge the issue, to mend the situation by bringing unemployed men and empty jobs together through Government Labour Exchanges, transferring where necessary city workers to the country or drafting them into new industries. Government touting overseas for new investments, especially in the form of factories, has at least one eye on the employment situation. No election plank is more popular than "full employment". Increasing population makes larger and more varied manufacturing programmes possible. The comparative tranquillity of Australia looks goods to foreign capital. So does an abundance of certain raw materials.

The economy must continually expand if full employment is to be maintained.

A pattern is discernible in the growth of the Welfare State. A precedent was laid down in the earliest days of the settlement of looking to authority. This to some extent continued so long as Australia remained a penal settlement. The Labour Party from its inception fought for the amelioration of the workers' lot by government action. The Government was organized society helping itself with no taint of charity. Through it citizens attained rights. Self-government had not proved a cure-all, but it could be used for social legislation.

The 1860s saw the coming of compulsory, free education under Sir Henry Parkes. In the period between the foundation of the Commonwealth and the outbreak of war in 1914, some basic social legislation was passed particularly, in the Federal sphere, by the Deakin Government.

In the 1920s the States, most particularly New South Wales under Labour, were active in social experiment and the Commonwealth Liberal Bruce-Page Government had a programme of reform. In the 1940s and 1950s the pattern was filled out.

The Welfare State is continually under fire. The chief criticism is that its citizens are governed by bureaucrats. In social services the administration eclipses the original legislation. Parliament lays down a principle, government departments and hosts of public servants are necessary to implement it. Regulations, by-laws, forms in triplicate multiply at public expense, a paper jungle grows up. There are delays and irritations. Social legislation must always be guarded against those who would, if they could, impose upon it. More paper, more red tape. This is a problem in administration. It is not insoluble. Changes have come so fast that the administrative machine has not had time to adjust itself. Discontent with the present administrative machinery is the first step towards more streamlined methods. . . .

Again, it is said that the Welfare State takes away the freedom and initiative of the individual. This might be true if the complete Welfare State were ever achieved, a place for everyone and everyone in his place. But the Australian economy is mixed and likely to remain so. There are prizes beyond the bounds of basic security. Also, there is a freedom that can only exist when there is security. The older pieces of social legislation are the more acceptable. Few people, for instance, would rather see the aged herded in workhouses than leading lives which can be free and happy, helped by a subsidy from the taxpayer.

Ideally, freedom from want for all is one of the great desiderata of human society. Like everything else it has to be paid for. For the reverse of the picture the curious reader could not do better than to read Morris West's *Children of the Sun.*

III. Religion, Education and the Press

These three are linked in a history of toleration and freedom—high-lighted, of course, in the breach. In such a settlement as the early Australia, the church, the school, and the newspapers represent authority's public relations policy.

Religion

The Church was represented in the First Fleet rather perfunctorily by one chaplain, Richard Johnson, who was treated perfunctorily, particularly by the officers of the regiment. He was in the position of an army chaplain, responsible in the last resort to the Commander-in-Chief. He was the Established Church in Australia. Whatever their faith, or lack of it, the convicts must receive from him "with humility" the crumbs, scattered thinly amongst so many, of religious instruction and consolation. He built a church, it was promptly burnt down by members of the congregation. The Established Church was not, and was not allowed to be an ameliorating influence.

No other religion was at first tolerated. Two Catholic priests had been willing to sail with the First Fleet, sharing the convicts' lot and expecting no payment or support, but they had been forbidden. In 1803 Governor King emancipated a Catholic priest, Dixon, and allowed him to hold services at Sydney, Parramatta and the Hawkesbury in rotation. He was hedged about by restrictions and police attended his services.[8] The experiment was a success, the behaviour of the Irish convicts improved and King attributed it to "their being indulged in their religion".[9] Dixon was allowed a salary of £60 a year.

It must be remembered that Catholics were still restricted in England, that the bulk of them in New South Wales were Irish convicts, many of them on political offences, so that a flavour of sedition clung to their religion. King's "indulgence", small though it was, was humane and tolerant.

Macquarie went further. He gave government consent and help to the building of a chapel, the first St Mary's, in Sydney and himself laid the foundation stone. Governor Brisbane wrote frankly to Lord Bathurst on 28th October 1824:

> Altho' I am no advocate for the tenets or doctrines of the Church of Rome, still I consider that, in proportion as Roman Catholics increase, Priests should be sent for their spiritual instruction, as it is a remarkable fact, of which perhaps Your Lordship cannot be aware, that every Murder or diabolical Crime, which has been committed in the Colony since my arrival, has been perpetrated by Roman Catholics.
>
> And this I ascribe entirely to their barbarous ignorance and total want of education, the invariable companions of bigotry and Cruelty, as well as the parent of Crime.

One priest, Brisbane believed, could not bring religion to a tithe of them.

> Thus these unfortunate People are left destitute of every blessing resulting from education, or its application to the Culture of devotion . . . thus benighted and bereft of every advantage that can adorn the mind of Man, or characterize the European from the Aboriginese, there will soon remain nothing but the shade to distinguish them.[10]

The Governor suggested that as a practical beginning he should make available money to roof, floor, and put in the windows of the chapel on which the faithful, although the poorest section of the community, had already spent £3000 and the Government granted £452. The building was, he thought, "too ornate", and the Colonial Secretary, Goulburn, described it sourly as a "religious, political and elegant undertaking".

Brisbane's plan to give pound for pound of government money for each further subscription raised voluntarily virtually established the Catholic Church as under government protection.

In 1824 the Presbyterians were asking the Governor for a subsidy towards building a Scots Church in Sydney and for a salary for their minister, the Reverend John Dunmore Lang. The memorial was signed by thirty-two free settlers headed by Antill and Piper. Brisbane refused; these men were rich enough to build their own church. He was reprimanded by Bathurst and told to pay a third of the cost of Scots Church. By 1827 Wesleyan missionaries were also being subsidized.

Whilst the Church of England remained for the time being the Established Church, the Government had become the patron of religion as such.

In the Quarterly Return of convicts for 1st April 1827 there is an analysis of their religious grouping. There were one pagan, 46 Jews, 174 Presbyterians, 1746 Catholics, 2199 Anglicans. The pagan was no doubt well catered for.

In November 1835, on the urgent recommendation of Governor Bourke, the Secretary of State for the Colonies formally approved of State aid for all religions. In 1830 all disabilities had been removed from Catholics and a state of religious toleration was established which Bourke hoped to see reflected in the colony.

An established church as such was unpopular in New South Wales. Bourke advocated government grants to all religious organizations, including synagogues, on a pound for pound basis, which would put a premium on self-help, the erection of churches, rectories, parsonages, manses, the payment of stipends, ranging from £300 to £1000 according to church attendance. He felt that in the past the distribution of government aid had been unfair. In 1834, for instance, the Colonial Treasury had spent £11,542 10s. on the Church of England, £600 on the Presbyterian Church, and £1500 on the Catholics. It was estimated that the last-named denomination amounted to one-fifth of the entire population.

In July 1836 the Legislative Council passed an Act embodying Bourke's proposals. It was a "pacification" that was to last until 1863 and was virtually the end of the Established Church in Australia.

To return to the vicissitudes of the Church of England: in October 1834, New South Wales was proclaimed an Archdeaconry by Letters Patent, and the Reverend Thomas Hobbes Scott, who had been Commissioner Bigge's secretary was named the first Archdeacon with a salary of £2000. His parish was enormous, including as it did, Van Diemen's Land, and it was part of his duty to visit all schools.

The question of the financial support of the Church had to be reviewed. From the beginning the Chaplain or chaplains had received a grant of land as a glebe. But conditions were very different from England, and unless he farmed it himself, as both Johnson and Marsden did, it was unproductive. Whenever Macquarie set up a new township he marked out land in it for the support of church and school. Now a new and ambitious scheme was afoot, still founded on land. One-seventh of the land in each county in a continuous block, of "average fertility and equal share of water and communication", to be called "clergy and school estates", was to be secured by grant to a Corporation of which the Governor, Lieutenant-Governor, Chief Justice, the Archdeacon, the Colonial Secretary, the Attorney-General, the Solicitor-General, and all the members of the Legislative Council were members. A charter was issued to the Corporation. As new counties were opened up the allotment of lands to the Corporation was to be the first consideration; private grants would then be made. If suitable land was not available in the counties already settled the Church was to be compensated by land elsewhere. The Church thus became at the stroke of a pen the largest landowner in the colony. It is easy to see that Lord Bathurst was more zealous for the Church than Lord Sydney had been. It was hoped that these great estates would not only support the dignity of the Church but provide sufficient income for the salaries of the clergy, for church buildings and for the maintenance of schools. The Archdeacon, even more zealous than Bathurst, asked that in addition all government reserves be added to the church lands. It would appear that ample provision had been made. But the result was disappointing. Even when the Church was given good land cleared by government labour it could not realize more than about 5s. a year for an acre on long lease.[11] It was not practicable for the Church to utilize the land itself for grazing or farming. The Church, like any other landowner, suffered from the delays of the Survey Department. It was difficult for the Colonial Office to understand all this. It thought persistently in terms of English land values and was encouraged to do so by the claims of successful men like Macarthur.

Funds from the Corporation proved inadequate. In 1827 the Church was claiming one-eighth of customs revenue on the grounds that Macquarie had set it aside for orphan schools. It also expected to receive the 13,000 acres he had granted the Orphan School for Boys, since it was now the official guardian of education. Governor Darling did "not presume to judge" whether he should hand over £6000 and upwards every year from customs. He awaited instruction from Home. Nor was he willing, on the ground that it was not within his power, to lend money to the Corporation except to pay the stipends of the clergy. In due course Lord Goderich ordered Darling to give the one-eighth to the Church and to further meet its needs until the estates brought in sufficient income.

In 1827 the Archdeacon was complaining of the inadequate provision for the Church and clergy; £250 a year was "totally inadequate to maintain a respectable Station in Society". He proposed a beginning salary of £400 a year plus a personal land grant of 1280 acres. There were other grievances. Clergymen came to the colony expecting good conditions and concessions which they never received. They could no longer bring out their effects free of charge in convict ships. The cost of living was high, "middle men" robbed them. Everyone was out to make money but the clergy, who, since they must be "spotless", could not take up the opportunities for profit. By falling into debt "they placed themselves under obligations to Persons, whom they ought to keep at a distance".[12]

Darling agreed with most of this and made his own more moderate recommendations to Lord Goderich, a commencing salary of £400 a year, an increase of £100 a year after seven years' service, a good house to live in and the use of twenty acres as near as possible to the church; sons on reaching the age of nineteen to be granted three square miles on condition they remained in the colony, and daughters two square miles at the age of eighteen; widows, a pension of £100 a year; none of the concessions to be deducted from the Church's one-seventh part of each county.

By 1828 the glebe lands at Sydney, Parramatta, and Liverpool were being sold by auction and £100 a year granted to each of the incumbents in lieu of the land. It is not surprising that in February 1833 an Order in Council dissolved the Church and School Corporation. It had been a failure. The Order in Council did not propose any alternative plan. The lands already granted were sold for what they would fetch and the money applied to the maintenance of the Church. It was clear that the expense would devolve, as it always had done, on colonial revenue, until parishioners were able to support their churches and clergy. Bourke's plan, already referred to, of supporting all denominations in ratio to their adherents came into operation.

Bourke had also recommended at the same time that Australia be made a bishopric, attached not to Calcutta as formerly but to Canterbury. At the same time the Catholics should be allowed to appoint a Vicar-General and the Presbyterians a Presbytery. This was acted on. Bishop Broughton became the first Bishop of Australia. He did not sit on the Legislative Council as the Archdeacon had, and the Church was thus removed from the political conflict. In 1847 he was named Bishop of Sydney and new bishoprics were created at Melbourne and Newcastle.

Bourke welcomed the new era:

> I cannot conclude . . . without expressing a hope, amounting to some degree of confidence, that, in laying the foundations of the Christian Religion in this young and rising Colony by equal encouragement held out to its Professors in their Several Churches, the people of these different persuasions will be united together in one bond of peace, and taught to look up to the Government as their common protector and friend, and that thus there will be secured to the State good subjects and to Society good men.[13]

And so peace might have reigned had it not been for the question of education, which was from the first closely interwoven with religion.

Education

At the foundation of the colony an educational system was not envisaged, unless a collection of religious tracts for distribution could be ranged under that heading. In 1793 it was the Chaplain, the Reverend Richard Johnson, who founded the first three schools acting for the Society for the Propagation of the Gospel. They were small and limited in scope, and the attendance was ragged. The regiment ran its own school for the education of soldiers' children. In 1801 an Orphan School for Girls was founded to preserve them from delinquency and give them enough practical education to train them as servants and enough religion to keep them, it was hoped, on the straight and narrow path of virtue. In 1819 a somewhat similar institution was set up for boys. Both were financed by the Government out of such dues and fines as were available, supplemented by charitable contributions.

Early in the century the Hawkesbury provided an instance of self-help. There were about 380 children in the farming districts and their parents subscribed in kind to build a schoolhouse. Governor King donated bricks from the Brickfields and sent convict labour to help with the building. A two-storeyed building 100 feet long by 24 feet wide, described as "lofty", was erected. It was to be a combined church and school. "A person of the Missionary Society" fulfilled the function of clergyman and schoolteacher. He was given his rations from the store in return for conducting Divine Service, and was paid as a teacher by a yearly levy of 2d. an acre on the farms. That, at least, was the theory of it. It is doubtful if it proceeded in the orderly way laid down. Enterprises so rarely did.[14]

The earliest schools were government rather than church schools, though clergymen or missionaries were usually the only people with enough time and the minimum of education to teach the children. In 1820 there were about 30 schools, most of them ephemeral, and an estimated 844 pupils receiving instruction, or, as Dr Crowley points out, one child in seven.

Macquarie was anxious to promote education, but was hampered by a lack of teachers. He was also, though perhaps he did not realize it, hampered by the fact that land grants—and they were practically all he had to offer except rations—were not, in the colony's state of development, sufficient to maintain the simplest system of education.

The establishment of the Church and Schools Corporation placed education definitely in the hands of the Church of England. Education that was not religious education was barely conceivable, especially in such a colony, certainly not to Lord Bathurst. Land, of course, was to provide the necessary money. It was to be leased or rented and, after the current expenses of religion and education were paid, the "overplus" was to be put into a sinking fund to meet future capital expense. Brisbane was instructed as to the schools.

> The nature and character of the Schools to be instituted must necessarily be regulated by the nature of the population for which they are intended. The first point will be to secure to every Child the means of acquiring a good practical English Education; and on that basis it will be easy to establish, progressively, such improvements and refinements as the progressive State of Society may render necessary. But the extent of the School Reserves must be calculated, not merely with reference to the Institution of Primary Schools of a simple Nature, but of Schools of a higher Order and ultimately of an Establishment of the nature of an University.[15]

No one could say that Bathurst lacked breadth of vision. This was the first time a university was mentioned. Hope was to be consummated in the 1850s.

Education did not prosper. Brisbane endeavoured to co-ordinate the haphazard system existing.

> Having taken into my most serious consideration the languishing state of education in this Colony, I have been induced to appoint the Revd. Thomas Reddall Director General of all the Government Public Schools of New South Wales, until the pleasure of His Majesty shall be made known to me.

He suggested a salary of £300 a year, "to enable the nominee to bear up against the heavy expence of making continual tours of inspection to all the straggling schools of this extended territory". Reddall was a chaplain who had run a small private school at Macquarie Plains, a "dominie school", since 1820, using Dr Bell's educational method.[16]

It was not His Majesty's pleasure that Reddall should be Director-General of Education. The position was redundant. The Archdeacon, who was Official Visitor, would do what co-ordinating was necessary.

In 1826 the Archdeacon reported on education, prefacing his remarks with a statistical outline of the growth of education. (He had not much faith in the reliability of his statistics, having seen the manner in which a census was conducted.) According to him, in 1810 there were 2304 children in the colony, of whom 440 were receiving education at four Crown schools and one private school; in 1813, out of 3000 children, 600 attended either the two Crown schools or 15 private schools; in 1820, of 5688 children, 844 received tuition at 19 Crown and 11 private schools; in 1824 826 of the 5042 children attended 15 Crown schools and 991 the five private schools, that is, a total of 1817 were receiving education of some sort, exclusive of those in the Orphan Schools, which had fallen into decay and gave little tuition and that of a low grade; in 1825 there were 4724 children, 802 at 18 Crown and 980 at five private schools, leaving nearly 3000 children without any tuition at all. The next year, 1826, saw an improvement, 1035 children were attending 20 Crown schools and about 990 were in private schools.[17]

It is interesting to note how the numbers of schools waxed and waned and the distribution of pupils between types of schools varied from year to year. Many schools were short-lived and were of the "dame" or "dominie" type, varying in usefulness according to the person in charge. On the whole, the teaching was poor in the extreme. Archdeacon Scott conducted classes for teachers lasting three months. "I do not hold out any very sanguine hopes [of them]," he wrote, "but, situated as we are, these are the best materials we have to work with. . . . The Persons who offer themselves for Schoolmasters cannot pursue any other object, and they are consequently compelled to pay the price demanded, at which provisions are retailed out"—that is, the exorbitant price of meat and bread at 7d. and 4d. a pound. Where there were no shops the schoolmasters were dependent on the generosity of the farmers—the first Parents' and Citizens' Association.

The Crown Parochial Schools, as the Archdeacon always calls them, stressing their position in relation to the Church, offered only elementary education; the private schools, often in charge of a clergyman with a dual-purpose church hall and schoolhouse, sometimes took the pupils further along the road to learning.

Sydney's most amazing schoolmaster was Dr Halloran, an ex-convict and not a reformed one at that, who from 1819 onward conducted a school in Sydney to which many of the best families sent their sons. Even from jail he petitioned Governor Darling for a land grant to assist him to open "a free grammar school".

> Your memorialist has . . . engaged and has determined to throw open Mr Lord's capacious Rooms in Macquarie Place for the reception of "One hundred Youths", to be instructed in Commercial, Mathematical and Classical learning, on conditions adapted to the respective circumstances of the several Applicants for Admission.[18]

The request was refused. The Governor was proof against the Doctor's persuasiveness.

Of a different calibre was W. T. Cape, whom Brisbane had appointed headmaster of the Sydney Public School. There was no taint upon him, he was "a Freeman and Livery man of the City of London". He, with the assistance of three sons and a daughter, drawn from his family of ten, taught 320 pupils "to read, write and cypher" for a salary of £100 a year and free housing.

There were various academies of doubtful scholastic value for young ladies, where the arts and graces of society were taught to raw colonial maidens.

Methods of education differed. Archdeacon Scott evidently preferred the Madras system, but only one school used it, and only one teacher, "a young colonial boy", knew anything about it.

The cost of education was high by the standards of the day, £1 8s. 2d. a head as against 5s. in England. This was due to the scattered population and the high cost of living.

The system of education under the Church and School Corporation was not a success. Attendances were sketchy. Neither the Catholics nor the dissenters liked the rule of the Church of England and often boycotted the schools. There were also many like Solomon Wiseman (of Wiseman's Ferry) who boasted cheerfully that he had seven sons and none of them had ruined his brain by learning to read and write. Or else the children had too far to go to school, or their services were too useful on the farm or in the home.

There were signs that the situation was improving. Saxe Bannister, the Attorney-General, had exerted himself to establish the first Infant School in Sydney and it drew the gratifying attendance of between sixty and seventy children a day. Technical education had made its début in a School of Industry, suggested in the first place by Mrs Darling and encouraged by her patronage. It took twenty girls under fourteen and "bids fair to rear a class of persons hitherto much wanted in the Colony". It did what the Orphan School had failed to do. It was run on a charitable basis by public subscription.

The Archdeacon envisaged public schools on the English plan and Brisbane thought about founding a university.

In 1827 there existed a chain of "Parochial Schools" giving free education to the age of ten years, after that it cost the parents 3d. a week if they could afford it. There was the Sydney Free School for "higher education", that is, English grammar, the more advanced branches of arithmetic, and Latin. Despite its name the pupils paid 15s. to £1 a quarter "according to their progress in the class"; 1245 pupils enrolled, about 860 actually attended regularly.

Two King's Schools were founded, one at Sydney that withered away, and one at Parramatta that prospered. They were on an English model and took both day boys and boarders. In 1833 there were 54 boarders and 15 day scholars, the former paying £28 a year, the latter £6 to £10. The Presbyterians moved into the field of education in the early 1830s, founding Scots College with the aid of a government loan secured by a mortgage. The Government voted the Catholics £800 for schools in 1834.

Something had been done, but not nearly enough. Bourke, that liberal-minded Governor, reviewed the situation and decided that the bitterness over education which had grown up between the different denominations was incurable, that the Government should withdraw its help from church schools and create national schools, Christian in character but not tied to any particular sect. Religious instruction should be limited to the daily reading of passages from the Bible without commentary. "Liberal" salaries should be paid to teachers, say £100 to £150 a year, and any fees collected from parents should be used for equipment and repairs to school buildings. He hoped that children of all creeds could then study harmoniously together. It was not economic for the State to support a multiplicity of schools founded on religious differences. His opinion was strengthened by the poor quality of the "parochial schools".

I am inclined to think [he wrote to the Secretary of State for the Colonies] that Schools for the general education of the Colonial Youth, supported by the Government and regulated after the manner of the Irish Schools, which since the year 1831 received aid from Public Funds, would be well suited to the circumstances of this Country.[19]

The church school would not be shut down nor would government support be withdrawn until there was a national school in the district. After that they might continue at their own expense.

Bishop Broughton was aroused to fury by this display of religious toleration. "A Protestant cannot subscribe to the erection of a Place of Worship for Roman Catholics without guilt," he stormed.[20]

Lord Glenelg, at the Colonial Office, supported Bourke, beginning with a pious preamble:

. . . In no part of the world is the general Education of the People a more sacred and necessary duty of the Government than in New South Wales. With a view not only to higher interests, but also to the good order and social improvement of the Colony, too great a value can scarcely be set upon the promotion, by all due means, of those habits and principles, which tend so eminently to elevate the human character, and to oppose the firmest obstacle to crime and immorality.[21]

Becoming more practical, His Lordship ruled that the subject of education be handed over to the Governor and the Legislative Council, who, being on the spot, would understand best the needs of the colony. He strengthened Bourke's hand by approving his tolerance. "To none of the numerous Christians of those persuasions should opportunities be refused for Worship and Education on principles which they approve." [22] He thought that the State should continue to subsidize all church schools, but only in proportion to subscriptions from their supporters. He agreed to non-denominational schools on the Irish plan, to be supervised by a Board of Education, composed of representatives of the different religious denominations. The schools themselves would not give religious teaching, but time would be set aside during which the clergy and pastors of the different faiths might come and instruct their adherents. He wanted education to be "in a true sense national", excluding no one. He called in the British and Foreign School Society, which had its own educational system, for advice.

With this strong lead from the Secretary of State and from the Governor, the Legislative Council agreed to the establishment of national schools. There was, however, much opposition to what would seem an eminently fair and rational scheme. Anti-national-school meetings were held and a petition to stay the Government's hand was drawn up and carried 1300 signatures. Instead of allaying sectarian bitterness the project increased it. A meeting in the district of Illawarra was the first to vote in its favour. Gradually other sections of the community, as they came to understand what was intended, supported the national schools.

The educational task was enormous. Not even the towns were adequately served by schools and many country districts had no facilities at all. There were insufficient funds, not enough teachers, obstruction on religious grounds, and it was not yet compulsory for parents to send their children to schools where they were available. The Irish method had to be abandoned because only teachers trained by the British and Foreign School Society were sent out from England. Governor Gipps had little choice but to change over to this method. The clear lines of Bourke's plan were being blurred. The dual method of supporting church schools and supplying national schools was expensive and ineffective. Catholics refused to allow their children to attend schools with Protestants. Gipps proposed that schools for Protestants of all shades should be set up and assistance given to Catholic schools. This might have simplified matters, but the Legislative Council voted against it.

Education just drifted on by a series of compromises which pleased no one. There were: (*i*) Church of England Orphan Schools for boys and girls supported by the Government at an annual cost of £6000; (*ii*) Catholic Orphan Schools assisted by the Government to the tune of about £1500 a year; (*iii*) Parochial Schools established before 1836, now given a fixed subsidy of £2950 a year; (*iv*) Catholic schools of the same type on a subsidy of £720. Other church schools received £1 from the Government for every £1 subscribed, which meant that those needing most help received least. In 1840 a grand total of £14,700 was being spent on education and there was very little to show for it. Gipps would have liked to see a clean sweep of existing schools and the foundation of purely undenominational ones, reverting to Bourke's plan. That Bourke's national schools were ineffective was, at least in part, due to Lord Glenelg's attitude. That well-meaning man read tolerance as pleasing everyone rather than as actively seeking their co-operation in a plan designed to be fair to everyone. He wished to see assistance still given to denominational schools, and this he weighted heavily on the side of the Church of England by the pound-for-pound scheme because the adherents of the Church of England were the most numerous and richest section of the community. He drew a red herring across the trail by calling in the British and Foreign School Society after the Irish plan had been decided upon.

Gipps was as surely doomed to failure as Bourke had been. He was caught between the Legislative Council, which did not agree with the idea of non-denominational schools, and Lord John Russell at the Colonial Office, who thought he had acted weakly in changing to the British and Foreign School Society plan, and who had ideas of his own. He thought that State aid should be reduced by a quarter or half and that the rest of the money needed should be made up out of local rates and contributions from parents.

Gipps wrote a series of minutes to the Legislative Council logically pointing out the costliness and uselessness of the present plan (or lack of it). Logic did not have the last word. Wollongong provided a sad commentary. In this district there was no history of sectarian bitterness and at a public meeting it had expressed itself in favour of national schools. Gipps thought it would be an excellent plan to try the experiment of an undenominational school. No sooner was it built than the Church of England erected a school there, too, the Catholics began one, and the Presbyterians proposed one. The district became a hotbed of strife.

In 1844 the Legislative Council appointed a Select Committee to look into education. It found that out of 25,676 children between four and fourteen years only 13,000 were receiving any education. In its report, delivered in August of the same year, it recommended the national school system controlled by a Board (to remove them from political and, if possible, religious control) and the foundation of a teachers' training college in Sydney. When the report was put to the vote in the Council it was passed by a majority of one.

The fat was in the fire. Fifty petitions against national schools, with an aggregate of 15,118 signatures, and twenty-four petitions, with 2100 signatures, in favour, were presented. The will of the people was clear; they preferred to muddle along. Moreover, the Treasury was empty. Gipps gave up.

Governor FitzRoy set up two Boards of Education, one for national schools and the other for denominational schools, hoping to run the two systems in double harness. This state of affairs lasted until 1866. There was some tinkering with it, such as the inquiry of 1855, when the laxity and inefficiency of, and poor attendance at, the schools generally was revealed, but nothing radical was done in New South Wales until 1866, when Sir Henry Parkes brought in a Public Schools Act. It set up a single Council of Education in place of the two Boards, and although government subsidies were still given to church schools in existence before that date, new ones were not to receive any help. This brought the power of the State down heavily on the side of the national schools. Public opinion had been modified, though the churches protested. The national schools were generally welcomed, only the Catholics refusing as a body to co-operate. The Irish system was reinstated. In 1880 a new Act in New South Wales withdrew all help from denominational schools, dissolved the Council of Education, and set up the Department of Public Instruction. Aid to other than State schools finally ceased in December 1882. The modern educational programme was launched. It has since been expanded to include infant schools, high schools, domestic science and technical schools, agricultural high schools, special schools for the mentally retarded and opportunity schools for the brightest children, correspondence courses for bush children beyond the reach of schools, library services, health services, and many other refinements. Universities, adult education schemes, the Workers' Educational Association, technical colleges, extension lectures, and teachers' training colleges have built up a system of tertiary education to which all, according to their needs and abilities, should have access. Parkes set the standard which has been adhered to, that education should be free, compulsory, and secular.

The other States trod much the same road. South Australia, where religious liberty had always been highly valued and which was preponderantly nonconformist, led the way in abolishing State aid to denominational schools in 1851, or as soon as she was allowed a measure of self-government, and concentrated on a system catering for all. Tasmania followed suit in 1859, Queensland in 1862 when she became a separate colony, Victoria in 1870, and Western Australia in 1895.

The universities from 1850 onwards have escaped trouble by being resolutely secular, the first in the Empire to separate religious and secular studies. The churches conduct their own theological colleges and seminaries. Western Australia broke new ground by establishing the first free university, to which merit is the only passport.

Education is a State matter, but during World War II the Commonwealth opened an Office of Education. Its primary function was to handle the Commonwealth Reconstruction Training Scheme (C.R.T.S.) for the returning servicemen. It has remained as a liaison body organizing Australia's share of the Colombo plan, working in with the United Nations and in general attending to all educational matters with an international or interstate slant. It subsidizes State universities and awards scholarships liberally. Most important, perhaps, it has founded the Australian National University at Canberra, a research, not a teaching, body, which attracts post-graduate students from all over the world and has brought home some of Australia's more famous sons.

In this short account only the historical aspects of education have been explored, the rest belongs to a history of education as such.

The Press

The First Fleet brought a number of unexpected things, amongst them a hand printing press. It was used occasionally to print government orders and proclamations for which purpose it was operated by George Hughes. He never had the name of government printer, it was probably just an odd chore for him. In 1803 it was put into regular operation to bring out the first Australian newspaper, the *Sydney Gazette and New South Wales Advertiser*. The first issue saw the light on 5th March. The printer and publisher was George Howe, and, after his death in 1821, his son Robert. The paper was a private venture, but the Governors used it for communicating their orders to their more literate subjects. Beside government orders, it printed items of local news, titbits from overseas when ships came in, and advertisements. Its circulation was small. It was not remunerative, but that it existed at all was remarkable. Each issue before publication was submitted to the Governor's secretary and later to the Colonial Secretary, who initialled it as approved. That it should be censored was taken for granted and raised no protest.

In 1824, when Brisbane was Governor, a second newspaper, founded by William Charles Wentworth and another barrister, Robert Wardell (1794-1834), and called the *Australian* came into existence. The Governor's permission had not been asked and the news sheet was not submitted for censorship. This aroused Robert Howe, who asked that his paper should be "removed from restraint". Brisbane was quite willing and the censorship was lifted on 15th October 1824. Australia had a free Press.

Since the *Sydney Gazette* was dependent on government notices it was not likely to offend its patron. The *Australian* reserved to itself the right of criticism and looked for its sales amongst those who had grievances. The young colony was finding both its feet and its voice. When Lord Bathurst received the first batch of copies, he raised his eyebrows and opined "That the entire exemption of the publishers from all restraint of the local government must be highly dangerous to a society of so peculiar a description". Brisbane does not seem to have resented a little free speech, though some sections of the community were subjecting him personally as well as his administration to criticism. The *Australian* went on its way unchecked. "The Freedom," remarks Frederick Watson in his Introduction to volume xiii of the *Historical Records of Australia*, "was . . . inopportune, as it coincided with the beginning of political agitation in the colony."[23] That, of course, is a matter of opinion.

In May 1826 a third newspaper, the *Monitor* (whose name suggests a watching brief), was founded by Edward Smith Hall, an able man who felt himself ill used by the Government in his efforts to obtain land and seek an appointment. In the following April the irrepressible Dr Halloran also brought out a newspaper, the *Gleaner,* but it was short-lived because it lacked financial backing, and was of little importance.

The *Australian* and the *Monitor* teamed up against Governor Darling, who had brought out instructions from Lord Bathurst not to censor them but to curb them. In accordance with these instructions, he required all newspapers to be registered and their editors or owners to enter into a bond with two sureties to make provision for the payment of any fines they might incur on conviction for blasphemous or seditious libel. It was Bathurst and not Darling who suggested a further safeguard, that newspapers should carry a licence as well as registration, which could be revoked by the Governor with the concurrence of the Legislative Council at any time, and that each issue pay stamp duty, the revenue brought in by this means to go towards defraying printing costs for government orders, proclamations, notices and the like.

Through no fault of his own Darling made a bad beginning with the Press. It is on record that he was loth to use his powers to obtain an "insignificant tax". He made a conciliatory gesture towards the other newspapers by deleting "Published by Authority" from the front page of the *Sydney Gazette*, a description that had never had a secure foundation.

The attack on Darling began with pinpricks. Edward Smith Hall was the first editor to fall foul of the Governor and to be prosecuted. The matter was dropped when Hall piped down. But the war was on. Wentworth and Wardell were campaigning for a greater measure of self-government and, like Macquarie, they turned to the large emancipist class. Its destiny and future lay within the colony, it was more inflammable than the "pure Merinos", who, after all, had what they wanted. The emancipists were the target for agitation and the way to make them conscious of political injustice was to play upon their grievances, real or imagined. Attacks on the Governor and his administration may have been purely tactical to begin with, but tempers on both sides were soon aroused and an element of personal vindictiveness entered the conflict.

Frederick Watson sums up in his Introduction to volume xiii of the *Historical Records of Australia*:

Darling, the figurehead, was unfortunate in being the victim of circumstance, but Darling, the individual, does not merit three-fourths of the odium cast on his administration, although he was responsible for an increased vindictiveness, caused by his somewhat narrow disposition and the adulation of his supporters, which he must have tolerated, in the *Sydney Gazette*.[24]

The unfortunate affair of Sudds and Thompson gave the newspapers an opportunity to attack the Governor as a tyrant. Not only the Governor was involved, the Archdeacon and the Attorney-General, Saxe Bannister, considered themselves libelled. Darling took advantage of the powers given him by Lord Bathurst and brought two Bills before the Legislative Council, the first to license newspapers and resume the licence at will, the second to impose a stamp duty. They passed the Legislative Council, but Chief Justice Forbes disallowed part of the first Bill as repugnant to the law of England. The second he accepted but the amount of the stamp duty was left blank. Fourpence an issue was considered. In the absence of Forbes it was set at 6d. on Archdeacon Scott's suggestion. On 4th May 1827 the new Acts were published in the *Sydney Gazette*. The same stamp duty was charged in England, but there circulations were large. Here even the *Sydney Gazette,* with a subscription list of 2000, declared that it could not meet the tax. The *Australian* had a circulation of 1200, the *Monitor* of 1000, and the *Gleaner* 200. The tax would put them all out of business. This was attributed to the Governor for malice, yet he was only carrying out instructions and the Acts had been passed in a regular and legal manner.

Forbes now disallowed the stamp duty Act on the grounds that when he had agreed to it he had believed the amount of the tax was to be 4d. When raised to 6d. it was obvious that the Act had an intention beyond what was set out in its preamble. This caused a serious rift between the Governor and his Chief Justice. The judiciary now appeared to take sides against the Governor, particularly Judge Stephen, who allowed Wardell to call Darling a "tyrant", a "scoundrel", and a "monster" in court. Darling brought libel suits right and left, but in the end got no satisfaction. His law officers advised him to let the matter drop.

Under the popular and liberal Governor Bourke temperatures returned to normal. The freedom of the Press, subject to the law of libel, was assured. In Van Diemen's Land Governor Arthur's attempt to control the Press was abortive. It had gained too strong a hold and the tendency in Australia, as in England, was towards free speech.

The Press has remained an important ingredient in Australian life, the three most influential publications being the *Sydney Morning Herald*, first published in 1831, the *Age*, first published in Melbourne in 1860 by David Syme, a Scot, a radical, and the apostle of protection in Australia, and the *Bulletin,* which came out in Sydney in 1888 and gave expression to the new nationalist impulse of the 1890s. Syme, particularly, was more than an editor, he was a power in the land, and through his paper and his sponsorship of Alfred Deakin exerted a great political influence. He advocated, besides protection, manhood suffrage, closer settlement of land, and the reduction of the powers of the Legislative Council, in favour of the Lower House. His battle for protection began in 1860 when his was a lone voice. He was full of fight. When advertisers boycotted the *Age* he reduced its price from a shilling to a penny. Not only did the sales skyrocket, but he reached the mass of readers who could not have afforded a shilling. He won over his readers; advertisers who could not afford to ignore a paper with so large a circulation, pocketed their principles and came back. In four years the State of Victoria was converted to Syme's way of thinking. When he died in 1908 King David, as he was called, had seen most of his projects fulfilled.

All three papers continue to flourish and to mould, more or less, the minds of their readers.

IV. Development

This is a subject that the wary historian approaches with caution. It would be so easy, and with the best will in the world, to write advertising copy, to point to successes and ignore failures and muddles. There have been plenty of all three. Also, its subject-matter lies outside the field of history proper.

Firstly, before indulging in too much pride, it must be remembered that much Australian development stems from work done overseas, in England, in the United States and elsewhere, and has been adapted to Australian needs and conditions, also that many of the men whose work is subject for pride, like that of William James Farrer, were not Australian-born and often had to battle against inertia or even downright hostility.

This was inevitable. For most of its history a small population in a large continent lacked the funds and the personnel for the long slow research that must be the prelude to original or revolutionary development schemes in any field. Bread and butter came first. On a population basis Australia has probably produced as many distinguished and brilliant men and women as any other country, but, lacking opportunity at home, many of them have left the country to seek their fortunes overseas. We have exported brains to an alarming extent. Now, with a fuller life open to them, a research organization of world standing and a greater recognition of the value in fame and money that they should command, some are returning home and some scholars, scientists, and artists are being attracted hither from other countries, either to live permanently or under contract for a certain time. Others, driven out of Europe by persecution or the effects of war, have found asylum here, but many of them, alas on account of parochial jealousy, have not been allowed to give of their best.

Development in Australia falls roughly into three parts, the bringing of Australia into line with the Western world, from which her population sprang, by the creation of the basic amenities, such as communication; secondly, the mastery of the difficult and delicate land, with its individual problems of climate, rainfall, and soil deficiencies, and its disabilities of soil erosion, deforestation, and pests, for which our own ignorance and carelessness are to blame; and, thirdly, a development in industry roughly parallel to that taking place overseas.

It would be quite impossible, and pointless as well, to tell the full story of progress in the amenities. A spot check will be enough.

With the vastness of the continent and the scattering of the inhabitants incidental on land grants, government reserves, the patchiness of the soil and the scarcity of water for stock, transport and communications have always been of the first importance. To begin with, the human foot was the only means of transport. Men walked. Stores from ships, bricks from the brickfields, timber from the bush, were moved from place to place by teams of men. Horses were imported for officers and carriages for their ladies, everyone else continued to walk, except that the journey to Parramatta was made by water, in a slow colonial boat called (but not officially) "The Lump". It took two days, tying up for the night. The streets of Sydney until the time of Macquarie were full of stumps, ruts, and refuse. The first road joined Sydney to Parramatta, sixteen miles of it.

As pioneering began, supplies were carried into the bush by packhorse. Roads there were none, although they were envisaged. When land grants were made a provision was added for roads. The Government reserved the right to resume without compensation any land required for them. In some instances the grantee undertook to make roads at his own expense. Occasionally in the towns residents banded together to pay for their own roads in what were to become the suburbs. The Old South Head Road, Sydney, was originally made by the rank and file of the current regiment (who actually had very little to do in the way of military duties) and paid for by the residents.

Even town roads and main roads, paid for by tolls and allegedly kept in order by convict labour, were in a chronic state of disrepair. Wood passes on the folk-tale: "A bullock once sank out of sight in the main street of a Victorian village, and a horse which passed soon afterwards staked itself on the bullock's horns."[25]

Packhorses, except for the solitary traveller, were replaced by the bullock-wagon. It was slow travelling, but the great-hearted beasts could be relied on to surmount all obstacles and the bullocky's verbal encouragement was proverbially lurid.

Government policy as to roads varied from Governor to Governor and was generally an improvisation. Sometimes it was the Surveyor-General who was in charge of road-making, sometimes an engineer, Major Druitt for instance, Macquarie's appointee. At one stage Corps troops were sent from England but were later withdrawn. The scattering of population over great areas made road-building a major problem. The most famous road was the one Paymaster Cox built over the Blue Mountains in record time and without the loss of a life, in Macquarie's time.

Along the coast sea transport was preferable and easier than land routes, but it was hazardous enough and tiny ships without sufficient water and frequently without even the common comfort of a compass often came to grief.

In the 1850s the buggy had arrived from America and remained standard family transport in the bush until well into the twentieth century, when the Model T Ford began to take its place.

The gold-rushes revolutionized transport. In 1853 Cobb and Co. coaches began to run from Melbourne to Bendigo. They, too, were of American origin, which was natural, as the frontier conditions there were more akin to Australia's than anything in England. With large wheels and light but wiry bodies they could bump gaily in and out of ruts and no damage done. Soon they were running to all the diggings. By 1861 they were on the New South Wales roads and in 1865 the network had spread to Queensland.

Railways began in the 1850s. The first from Melbourne to Port Melbourne was opened in 1854. In New South Wales construction languished for lack of labour. Everyone had left for the goldfields. The initial cost was so great that a private company could not even complete the rail from Sydney to Parramatta. All over Australia railways became government projects. The 1860s to 1880s was the great railway age. They opened up the country, bringing new lands into production because now there was a means of getting products to market quickly. Railways did not supersede the other means of transport, they were rigid and needed feeder services.

Australian railways have not been a success story. State jealousies, the short-sighted, criminal folly of broken gauges, political chicanery, vote-wooing, deficits, and plain muddle have scarred their history. It has not been the whole story, of course. Railways have made a great difference to national development, especially to the wheat-farmer and for the carriage of all perishable products.

Railways have been in part responsible for the centralization of the nation's commercial life in the capital cities. They have drained the country towards the few ports. To duplicate railways and port installations would have been more expense than a small population could bear. Cross-country lines, taking the shortest routes but ignoring State boundaries, would have been unthinkable. Two wars high-lighted the inconvenience of the broken gauges, but the expense of standardizing was so great that even in the 1950s it was being postponed. In 1935 the estimated cost was £57,000,000 and prices have been rising ever since.

The advent of the motor-car brought further changes. It did not really make itself felt until after the First World War. The accent was on roads again. Transport became faster and more mobile. The loneliness of the bush shrank. So did railway revenue. Road hauling is by private enterprise, the railways are State-run, the maintenance of the roads necessary for haulage is another government matter. In 1925 in New South Wales a Main Roads Board was set up to control and maintain the more important roads, leaving only the lesser ones to municipal or shire authorities. Registration fees, or part thereof, on motor vehicles were to provide the finance. This was really another form of toll. The Board later became the Department of Main Roads. Other States set up agencies or departments with similar functions but different names.

The motor-car has streamlined daily life, adding to its speed, hazards, and happiness. Australia by reason of her distances became as automobile-conscious as any other part of the world.

Australia, for the same reason, is now said to be the most air-minded country in the world. The aeroplane has shrunk the loneliness of the bush once again and has brought Australia within two days' flying time of England.

The manufacture of rolling stock, motor-cars, and aeroplanes have all become Australian industries. They have developed the country and are part of the development.

The lines of communication with the outside world have shortened. In the beginning, a voyage to Australia by sailing ship could take anything from four to nine months or even longer, and the return trip, being, except in unusual circumstances, circuitous, *via* China or India, could well take a year. Wool was responsible for a fast direct service from 1843 onwards; the wool clippers raced for England with the season's clip. They were fast sailing ships and could still compete with steam. The voyage averaged three months.

The first steamship, *Sophia Jane,* worked by paddles, arrived in 1831. In 1869 the Suez Canal sliced a fortnight off the voyage. In 1852 the Pacific and Oriental Steamship Company began regular sailings and by 1900, wonder of wonders, the voyage could be made in six weeks. This affected not only the transport of passengers and freight but the purveyance of newspapers, books, periodicals, fashions, and gossip.

Communications is more than the transfer of bodies and goods. It covers the written and spoken word. In the first years of the settlement the conveyance of letters was a matter of grace. Captains of ships would carry them as a favour, friends going Home would take them. The first post office was opened in Sydney in 1809. It was what would today be called an agency. Letters brought by ship were listed outside the post office or advertised in the *Gazette* and could be claimed on payment of a shilling. Deliveries began at Parramatta, the carrier getting a penny for each letter. This was payment by results, or piece-work, for he had no other wage. In the bush policemen on their rounds carried the letters. In 1828 a letter weighing ¼ ounce cost 3d., more if it had to be taken inland. It was always the recipient who paid up till 1838. The high cost of sending letters to and from England or into the bush accounts for the habit of "crossing" or writing lengthways on the page as well as across till the letter had a checked appearance, difficult to read. (But there was reputedly more time in those days of large families and everything made-in-the-home.)

After 1834 letters were delivered by contract and in the 1850s Cobb & Co. became the Royal Mail. As early as 1838 stamped sheets of paper had been sold at the post office at 1s. 3d. a dozen, reduced in 1841 to a penny each. By 1850 postage stamps were in general use. The invention of the postage stamp was one of Australia's offerings to the world. It led to a hobby that almost ranks as an industry. One by one the States adopted penny postage.

At its inception the Commonwealth took over all postal business and by 1911 the rate for a ½-ounce letter was a penny to any place in Australia. In 1934 it rose to a minimum rate of twopence for an ounce, and it has been rising ever since. In 1901 the Post Office handled 220,000,000 letters; in 1931 it was up to 761,000,000 and in 1956 more than 1,700,000,000 letters and packets were handled. The General Post Office in Sydney does a larger volume of business than any other in the Southern Hemisphere. This is more a matter of universal literacy than of population figures.

The year 1854 seems to have been a turning-point, for it was then that the first telegram was sent in Australia, all the way from Melbourne to Williamstown. South Australia came next with a telegraph system in 1856, followed by Tasmania in 1857. In 1858 New South Welshmen were not only sending telegrams internally but had links with Melbourne and Adelaide. Perth came into the picture in 1869 and achieved telegraphic communication with the eastern States in 1877. In 1869 a cable was laid from the mainland to Tasmania.

The most ambitious programme, of course, was the telegraph from Adelaide to Darwin, which there connected with a cable and brought Australia into instantaneous touch with the world. The small colony of South Australia undertook the project and in two years carried it through almost impossible country, roughly following McDouall Stuart's overland route. The drive of Adelaide's Postmaster-General was largely responsible for its success. The estimated cost of the telegraph was £120,000, the actual cost £420,000. It was completed in 1872 and the price of a telegram to England was £9 for 20 words; by 1934 it had dropped to 10s. for 20 words. In 1950 it cost 1s. 3d. a word, in 1958 10d. a word. In 1876 Sydney was linked to New Zealand by cable and in the first two years of this century Perth was connected with Durban in South Africa and Brisbane with Canada.

The telephone arrived in the 1890s. It was urban, cheap, and of no great use to the average citizen because there were so few subscribers. By many it was approached with fear and trembling, and only at times of dire necessity. In 1951 there were 79,239 subscribers throughout Australia and it was possible to hold a telephone conversation with practically any part of the civilized world.

Dates and figures make bony reading, but here they give perspective, particularly as many of the amenities have been referred to, in passing, elsewhere.

Lord Sydney, and two men who should have known better, Sir Joseph Banks and Matra, who actually visited the place, had exorbitant expectations of the Australian earth. Because the climate on the east coast was good and much of the country thickly timbered, they expected it to produce everything—wheat, fruit, flax, tobacco, cotton—with tropical abandon. It was hoped that the convicts could live, economically, off the country. It was soon discovered that they could not. The aborigines alone knew the secret and nobody asked their advice, nor would their nomadic way of life have been feasible. Provided the seed had not heated on the voyage, first crops on land where the timber had been burnt and the ashes dug into the soil were fairly good, but the earth was soon exhausted and farming, except on the rich river flats of the Hawkesbury, was peripatetic; when one patch became infertile there was always another, though clearing was a major effort. Droughts and floods recurred. Because eucalyptus flourished in the sandstone country it did not follow that other crops would. There were exceptions like Captain Kemp's famous garden and orchard at what is now the corner of King and George streets, Commissary Palmer's hacienda at Woolloomooloo, the Reverend Mr Johnson's cabbages and oranges, Campbell's orchard on the west side of Circular Quay, and Macarthur's bountiful orchard at Camden. On the other hand the government farm on the site of the present Botanic Gardens languished, and to get settlers on the land, even in a very small way, needed government help. They had to be provisioned for a couple of years, assisted with free labour and, of course, supplied with seed and such rudimentary agricultural implements as were available in the Commissariat store. Governor Brisbane put gangs of convicts onto clearing land to prepare it for farmers. None of these things solved the problems which were inherent in the earth. S. M. Wadham has summed up the early years:

> The usual devices were tried by various Governors—storage of surplus grain, alternative uses e.g. distillery, guaranteed prices for part of the produce and assistance to the settlers. They were quite unavailing, the new colony made little progress until the development of the production and export of wool gave it a new life and a new hope about 1820.[26]

Government help to the man on the land has been no modern innovation, it has been in the nature of things.

Closer settlement and the yeoman farmer have been a recurrent dream which the country has pushed aside. In despite of politicians and democratic theories, Australia is best suited to large properties. Government schemes for planting men on the land have almost invariably erred on the side of subdividing the land into blocks too small to sustain a family. One of the reasons for this has been labour shortage, increased, particularly in the bush, by the desire of every man to be his own master. For this reason it is desirable to have farms of such a size that a man and his family can work them. A hundred and sixty acres may be large enough to work, but not large enough to be profitable except in special circumstances. The idea of group settlements, too, presupposes relatively small blocks, otherwise distance makes co-operation impracticable.

The difficulties of marketing produce, either on the restricted home market or getting it to the capital cities for export, have made small properties uneconomic. Railways helped, refrigerated trucks, cold storage and freezer cargoes made it possible to carry and export perishable commodities, dairy products, fruits and the like. Unlike wheat and wool, these could be produced profitably on small farms.

But there were still two big problems, soil deficiencies and lack of water.

Roseworthy Agricultural College in South Australia preached the use of superphosphates. Farmers were slow to respond. When they did a revolution in agriculture began. There followed soil surveys which revealed with scientific exactness what constituents the soils lacked to make them fertile. When these were added—and sometimes only a trace was required—areas considered barren came into production. By and large there is a phosphate deficiency in Australian soils. In parts of South and Western Australia dressings with copper salt have shown a profit. The planting of subterranean clover has improved soils by introducing nitrogen. Scientific pasture improvement, though expensive, has added greatly to the carrying capacity of grazing lands.

More important than soil constituents is water. Most of Australia, about two-thirds of the continent or over 3,000,000 square miles, has a rainfall of less than twenty inches a year; some parts of the continent have a very low rainfall indeed.

The problem is a teasing one. Where rainfall is high, as in the north where there is a wet season, the soils are poor because the goodness has been leached out of them. Some of the best soils, as in the Wimmera, are dry. The problem is to bring water to the good soils.

Apart from coastal rivers, there is only one large river system in Australia, the Murray-Darling-Murrumbidgee and its tributaries. This system and the snows of the Alps are the only large water supplies that can be tapped for irrigation schemes. (There are, it is true, some smaller ones.)

Irrigation and water conservation are of first importance, but there must be water to begin with. In dry spells many Australian rivers west of the Great Divide run dry or go underground. In drought even the Darling is salty from minerals in the banks.

Victoria pioneered irrigation and water conservation. Severe droughts in 1877 and 1881 proved that development was being blocked by lack of water. The 1880s saw the beginning of irrigation on a large scale. In 1882 Echuca and Waranga Shires combined to set up the Goulburn-Waranga Irrigation Scheme, which eventually built 2400 miles of irrigation channels to water one-third of a million acres. All riparian rights belonged to the Government, so it was natural that the Government or government agencies should control irrigation. In 1886 trusts were established in Victoria and government loans made to them for irrigation works. Weirs were built on the Goulburn and Loddon rivers and water distributed from them. The brothers Chaffey, who had had experience with irrigation in the United States, tapped the Murray and the irrigation areas of Renmark and Mildura came into being. Land that had been so dry that it "wouldn't even support a kangaroo" became the centre of the dried-fruit production area. By 1944 it was yielding 104,000 tons of fruit, mostly for export, worth some £6,000,000 a year. In 1958 Australia was producing about 13 per cent of the world's currants and raisins.

In 1906 a State Rivers and Water Supply Commission inherited the trusts and from them about ninety water schemes were established in the one State of Victoria. Already that State had been able to meet the great drought of 1902 with a water storage of 172,000 acre-feet.[27]

The scheme grew and grew. New South Wales and Victoria shared the largest project, the Hume Reservoir, which from the air looks like a great lake, and feeds 5000 miles of irrigation channels to Victoria alone, watering 2,000,000 acres. Red Cliffs, Mildura, Merbein, Leeton, and Griffith came into existence with their vineyards, orangeries, orchards, and rice paddies. The Wimmera-Mallee system and many smaller ones followed. They are interlocked so that in drought water can be pumped to wherever it is needed most. There is a limit to development, however, because the water supply is limited.

When the lands were "unlocked" by legislation in the 1860s every selector was required to dig a dam to supply his stock with water. Flying across country you can still see these little rectangles of water near lonely homesteads. This idea was incorporated in the irrigation scheme. Farmers were required to dig large dams which were filled each winter from water conservation. This reduced evaporation, always high in the hot inland climate. By 1947 approximately a quarter of Victoria was supplied with "organized water" for crops, stock, and domestic use.

Before the Snowy Mountains Authority came into being the most ambitious water conservation scheme was Burrinjuck Dam on the Murrumbidgee. The main canal carries water for 90 miles to irrigate some 70,000 acres of rice paddies, orchards, and fodder crops. Thanks to this, Australia can supply her home market with rice and during World War II was able to victual the troops in the South-west Pacific arena.

The greatest scheme of all comes under the Snowy Mountains Authority. It is a long-range project with a dual purpose. It will irrigate, using the waters of the Snowy River and the snows of the upland regions around its source, and it will provide electricity for farms and towns and such industries as may spring up, over a wide area. The water, carried through 80 miles of tunnels and 300 miles of aqueducts, falls 2000 feet and this veritable Niagara is used for the generating of electricity. It meshes with the Murray Valley irrigation scheme and adds, it is estimated, £30,000,000 worth of water to it every year. The Snowy Mountains Authority is financed by the Commonwealth Government and may cost £422,000,000, but it is so planned that as each section is completed it comes into operation. The map is being changed, artificial lakes created, towns moved, mountains pierced. It has become a major tourist attraction. The work has an international quality, with French and American contractors and technicians and workmen from all over Europe, including many Norwegians. New South Wales and Victoria will be the main beneficiaries.

South Australia has its Todd River Scheme and more than 40,000 acres irrigated from the Murray for orchards and vineyards.

Queensland, with less water, has little irrigation, but cashes in on artesian water. Western Australia has an irrigation area south of Perth which makes the State self-supporting in dairy products. A giant scheme is to trap the flood waters of the Ord River, which flows at the rate of 1,640,000,000 cubic feet of water a second into the sea. This, distributed over dry Kimberley country, should make a great difference to its productivity.

Water engineering, because of scarcity, has had especial significance in Australia. In 1906 water was carried 550 miles from Mundaring Reservoir outside Perth to the goldfields in Kalgoorlie, through a steel pipe 30 inches in diameter. Eight pumping stations send 5,000,000 gallons of water a day across the desert to make the once disease-ridden town not only habitable but thriving. Some of this water is used to irrigate wheat and grazing lands adjacent. There is another scheme to carry water by pipe line from the Murray at Morgan to Whyalla, the iron port on Spencer's Gulf, and from Menindee on the Darling to Broken Hill. There is the vast Warragamba Dam which supplies Sydney with water. . . .

Artesian water is another matter again. The Great Artesian Basin underlies about one-fifth of the continent, an area of 600,000 miles. Most of it is in Queensland, 118,002 square miles in South Australia, 80,000 in New South Wales, 25,000 in the Northern Territory. It is tapped by bores, drawn up by windmills, and either stored in tanks or allowed to run in channels through the paddocks so that stock does not have to be moved for watering. It is generally mineralized and sometimes comes hot from the ground, but it is wholesome for stock and in some districts can be used for all homestead purposes. This is water collected from rain or river seepage in porous strata at varying depths under the earth's surface. Besides the Great Basin there are lesser ones: the Desert Basins in Western Australia, one at Eucla in otherwise waterless country near the Great Australian Bight, the Murray River Basin. . . . The supply, though constantly renewed, is not unlimited and shows signs of diminution. It has been the saving of large areas where without it stock could not have been run.

There are other ways in which the dryness of the continent can be circumvented, dry farming, the breeding of drought-resistant wheats, fodder conservation to make good years carry droughty ones, reafforestation to conserve moisture.

The Commonwealth Department of National Development takes a hopeful view of the water situation. F. L. McCay, the Department's Assistant Secretary, writes:

> The percentage of rainfall used in the United States and Great Britain, which means the percentage collected or stored for city, industrial, irrigation, stock and farm usage, is about the same—5 to 6 per cent.
>
> The Australian figures of .019 per cent, by contrast, indicate the disproportion between rainfall and its effective utilisation in this country.
>
> It is obvious therefore that there is plenty of rainfall yet to be utilised if it can be conserved for use. What is needed is more research and an accurate survey.
>
> We need accurate recordings of rainfall, snowfall, snow melting rates and courses, stream discharge measurements in low and flood conditions, evaporation rate, percolation and absorption rates, catchment capacities and so on.[28]

There are scientific means of reducing evaporation, the great thief of water, by the Mansfield process for instance. There is rain-making, not yet of great practical value, but who knows whither the research will lead?

There are many possibilities, but the problem is still there. No one, seeing the vastness of the land and reading the rainfall figures, can doubt it.

As Mr McCay says: "The pattern of Australian development . . . has always been greatly influenced by water availability and will continue to be so."

The control of floods is one more water project for Australia.

There are other problems, an infinity of them, resulting from an ignorant interference with the delicate balance of the continent, from carelessness, and from ruthlessness.

There was so much land, beyond their wildest dreams, that the pioneers felt no need to conserve it. The trees were their enemies. They deforested large areas, laying them open to wind and rain erosion, and this resulted in dust bowls and loss of fertility. They overstocked on the get-rich-quick principle so that native grasses were eaten out, and, in times of drought, the very roots were dug out by the starving sheep. They cropped the land mercilessly till it could produce no more. They were careless of fire and took no precaution against flood. These censures do not apply to all, but to a fair proportion. They racked the land, thinking that because it was wide it was indestructible.

Science has since taken a hand to repair the damage, a long, slow process. Eroded land can be rehabilitated by reafforestation, by contour ploughing, and by other means. The lost grasses can be replaced and pasture improvement brings the country into better heart than ever before. The bush is more fire-conscious. To fight a bushfire is a community job. Fire-breaks, equipment, regulations that compel property owners to keep down dangerous undergrowth in dry seasons, warning systems and education of the public have done something, but a dry year after a series of good years generally means trouble and a bushfire that has a good hold on a wide front can rarely be halted until the wind changes.

Research bodies, the State Departments of Agriculture, the agricultural colleges and high schools, the Young Farmer Clubs, are educating the man on the land in the best use of his property to maintain and improve its fertility, to plant to the best advantage, to save trees for windbreaks and to hold moisture, and grasses to hold the soil. . . .

Australia in her virgin state had no pests and no predatory animals except the dingo, which was an immigrant with the aborigines aeons ago, the fruit-eating flying fox, the bandicoots with a taste for potatoes, and a few such others. The kangaroo tribe, because herbivorous, could take the sheep's grass, though some might say the boot was on the other foot. It was the white settlers who brought in the most serious pests.

Unthinkingly they introduced the rabbit as another food supply, as a pet. The rabbit found the Australian terrain as much to its liking as the

Merino had. It multiplied, it spread, it competed with the sheep for pastures, it cost the farmer, the grazier, and the taxpayer millions to control. A fence was not enough, it had to be a fence sunk so deeply into the ground that the rabbit could not burrow under it. Rabbiters with their dogs and ferrets were employed on every station. Poison baits were laid. At harvest rabbits were rounded up in the last of the standing wheat and there was a mass slaughter. But still they proliferated. It was an offence even in the cities to keep two rabbits of different sex. Droughts reduced the rabbit population as they decimated the sheep, but in good seasons back they came. To restrict their spread a rabbit-proof fence was built across the continent. Nothing availed until the introduction of myxomatosis, a virus disease, innocuous to human beings but death to rabbits, a lingering painful death, unfortunately. Rabbits are infected and let loose, the disease spreads and spreads. Is the rabbit menace at an end or will the survivors develop an immunity? There is already reason to believe that immunity will win the battle.

Of the sparrow, brought from England and sold to homesick settlers in the towns, it is said that a farmer from the old country wept with sentiment the first time he saw one and wept with rage a year later. The bulbul, another new-comer, is a plague to orchardists. Animals and birds imported into a country where their hereditary enemies do not exist to keep their numbers down may cause serious loss. It is even feared that pet goldfish, if accidentally released into creeks or waterholes, will do great damage.

With no quarantine regulations pests like the fruit fly entered the country to cause untold loss. Amongst plants it was equally bad, if not worse. Prickly pear arrived as an ornament and stayed to overwhelm and render useless great areas of once productive country until its antidote, an insect called the cactoblastis, was introduced to destroy it. It did.

The whole litany of noxious weeds from St John's wort to skeleton weed entered the country, generally in seeds clinging to imported plants or fruits, and an attempt to eradicate them has employed an army of inspectors, raised the sale of weed-killers and sprays, absorbed endless man-hours and incurred great loss. There is now a strict plant quarantine, but the slip-rails have been put up after the brumby got into the pasture.

This is only a token story of development in the primary field. It does not, for instance, touch on the vital field of wool research to keep the product on which, in the last resort, prosperity depends, more than a match for cheaper substitutes. Nor does it outline the work of the Commonwealth Scientific and Industrial Research Organization on behalf of all primary industries. It has only been my intention to take instances in order to mark out a zone. A more detailed account would belong to another kind of history.

Secondary industry is in the nature of things more derivative. If Australia had followed the theories of Adam Smith she would have remained a primary-producing country and would possibly have been the happier and more tranquil for it. The world situation made this impossible. Whilst Britannia ruled the waves her remote colony could safely develop along natural lines. Two world wars endangered communications and the impossibility of importing supplies from England when she needed all her manpower for her war effort forced Australia to supply her own needs as far as possible, in manufactured goods, and to contribute matériel, especially in World War II.

Another factor which made Australia an industrial country was pressure of population. Wool-growing at any time gives comparatively little employment, so does farming as it becomes increasingly mechanized. Mining has waned. To talk of pressure of population in a country which in parts, the Northern Territory for instance, rates one person to every 263 square miles, sounds curious, but the cities are large. Many of those who came to dig for gold were city born and bred, and so were later waves of migrants, most particularly the New Australians. As I have stressed before, the country is unsuited to small holdings. This leaves us with a large margin of population for industrial undertakings, both operatives and consumers. Full employment is the desideratum. For economic reasons and to absorb her urban populations into employment, Australia has to industrialize.

Again, her remoteness from the cockpit of Europe, her supplies of coal and mineral wealth, have attracted manufacturers from overseas. A population reaching the 10,000,000 mark in 1959 and likely to continue expanding offers a market worth considering. High tariffs make it more economic to manufacture in Australia or to allow Australians to manufacture under licence than to send goods in. The Australian technician and workman, despite an unfortunate reputation for "near enough good enough", is on the whole intelligent and capable of extending himself. Despite high wages, with a basic wage hovering round £15 a week, he is still considered better value for manufacturing processes and machine-shop work than the cheap labour of countries with low standards of living. There are industrial disputes, but, except in peak years, many who live close to them are surprised to learn that they are not as serious or as frequent as in the United States or even in the United Kingdom.

Particularly since the war there has been a closer tie with the United States. In 1958 approximately 400 factories were working under licence from the United States and 185 firms registered in Australia were subsidiaries of their big brothers in America. They often carry Australian names—for example, Australian Oil Refining Proprietary Limited of Kurnell, Sydney—employ Australians, conform to Australian conditions, but draw their capital from America and send home the profits or "royalties". Abrasives, motor-cars, oil-refining, rubber, copper, and pharmaceuticals are all heavily sponsored in Australia by America. This is not philanthropy. American capital comes here because it is worth while.

> The United States Department of Commerce figures record the written down book value of United States investment in Australia at the end of 1956 as £245 million of which £118 million was in manufacturing (probably excluding petroleum refining from the definition). . . . Gross fixed private investment in Australian manufacturing was running in 1956-57 at about £200 million a year.[29]

This is big, but the investment from the United Kingdom is bigger, it is estimated at two-thirds of the total oversea investment in Australia since the end of World War II. Add to this industries with their roots in England already established, and it is impressive. British interests are strong in engineering projects, building materials, radio and TV, textiles (particularly wool, nylon and cotton), processed foods, heavy industrial equipment, paints and non-ferrous metals.[30] The in-flow of British capital (although Canada and not Australia is the favourite child) has risen steadily.

The past has shown that there are perils in the influx of oversea capital, though manufactories are more stable and less dangerous than loans. They are eagerly welcomed by politicians, who have an eye always fixed on employment, that barometer of well-being. A little over 1,000,000 people, or a third of the breadwinners, were in 1958 engaged in manufacturing projects of one kind or another in over 50,000 factories.

The educational value of new industries cannot be overlooked. The Australian workman learns new skills and has opened to him a greater diversity of employment and opportunity.

To dwell upon oversea investment in Australia is not to minimize the local effort, which has been outstanding, particularly in the production of agricultural machinery and of steel. Australian steel is reputed the cheapest in the world. In the ten years 1946-56 its production increased 120 per cent and the works reached the position of supplying all domestic needs.

In a lifetime "Made in Australia" has ceased to be a warning of inferior quality. World contacts and immigration have something to do with this. There is also a general demand for better quality goods.

From Aspros to farm tractors Australian secondary products go forth into the world. Sydney's Ready Mixed Concrete Limited has the largest spread of all, having plants in England, Germany, Singapore, and Brazil.

Reading brochures, studying statistics, one is liable to get a somewhat inflated view of Australian development. We are still a small people in a small way of business by world standards. But we are growing, and to be going somewhere is often more exciting than to arrive, if one may paraphrase a famous quotation.

REFERENCE NOTES

[1] Isles and Williams in *Australia* (ed. G. L. Wood), p. 236.
[2] *Commonwealth Parliamentary Debates*, vol. xv, p. 2867.
[3] *Ibid.*, vol. cxviii, p. 5008.
[4] *Australia: a Social and Political History* (ed. Greenwood), p. 327.
[5] Quoted, *ibid.*, p. 218.
[6] G. V. Portus in *Social Services in Australia* (ed. W. G. K. Duncan), p. 18.
[7] *Commonwealth Year Book*, No. 43, p. 531.
[8] *Hist. Rec. Aust.*, ser. I, vol. iv, pp. 104-5.
[9] *Ibid.*, p. 394a. [10] *Ibid.*, vol. xi, pp. 382-3. [11] *Ibid.*, vol. xii, p. 393.
[12] *Ibid.*, vol. xiii, pp. 774-8.
[13] *Ibid.*, vol. xvii, pp. 229-30.
[14] *Ibid.*, vol. v, p. 11. [15] *Ibid.*, vol. xi, p. 140. [16] *Ibid.*, p. 380.
[17] *Ibid.*, vol. xii, pp. 313 *et seq.* [18] *Ibid.*, vol. xiii, p. 71.
[19] *Ibid.*, vol. xvii, p. 231. [20] *Ibid.*, p. 232. [21] *Ibid.*, vol. xviii, p. 202.
[22] *Ibid.*, p. 203. [23] *Ibid.*, vol. xiii, p. vii. [24] *Ibid.*, p. ix.
[25] F. L. W. Wood, *Concise History of Australia*, p. 245.
[26] S. M. Wadham in *Australia* (ed. G. L. Wood), p. 141.
[27] See L. R. East, "Water Conservation and Irrigation" in *Australia* (ed. G. L. Wood), pp. 166 *et seq.*
[28] F. L. McCay in "Australia Unlimited", Supplement to the *Sydney Morning Herald*, 30th June 1958. [29] Quoted, *ibid.*
[30] See *British Manufacturers in Australia*, published by the Commonwealth Department of Trade, Industries Division.

CHAPTER XXIII

THE DARK PEOPLE

. . . its only inhabitants before 1788 were Stone Age people, said to be the only race which could serve as a common ancestor for all mankind.

—A. G. L. Shaw, *The Story of Australia.*

I have never, anywhere in the world, seen people who have such an air of having no connection with the society on whose fringes they live. They are Outsiders indeed—so much so that they would appear to be, for the most part, beyond even resenting their wretched circumstances.

—Malcolm Muggeridge, *Sydney Morning Herald*, 4th June 1958.

I. Origin and Evolution to 1788

To discuss the aborigines in the last chapter of this history may appear at first glance to be a reversal of the proper order of things, but history has made of them a codicil to the Australia story. By using the word "codicil" I do not intend to be derogatory. As things stand, the nature and history of this ancient and different people is an appendage to the success-and-failure story of the white man in their traditional home. To bring the two together as one people should be, and I hope will be, one of the advances of the future.

It is generally accepted by anthropologists that aborigines are of Dravidian origin, that they came from as far away as the Caucasus or Northern India, that their root stock was not so different from our own. The pigmentation of their skin comes from the sun and not from the blood (an unscientific statement, I know). This theory of origin depends on hair structure, the fairness of the new-born aboriginal child, and most important, the complete blending over several generations of aboriginal and white without the throw-backs that occur from an admixture of Negro blood.

The aborigines were Australia's first migrants. In some prehistoric folk movement they were driven from their original home by stronger and more warlike tribes. When this happened and how long the trek took can only be matters for surmise. All that is certain is that it was very long ago indeed, probably before the world had settled into its present geographical shape, when the islands between Australia and Malaya were more nearly a land bridge than they are today. The straits between them were negotiable by primitive craft, and Tasmania was still part of the mainland. Only the imagination can suggest over how many decades or centuries the "invasion" lasted or what proportion of the migrants survived the journey and acclimatized themselves to the harsh new land. They found another, more primitive, nomadic people in possession and as they moved south they, in turn, drove these people before them. In 1788 a remnant, perhaps as many as 2000, lived in Tasmania, protected by Bass Strait, to be exterminated directly and indirectly by the coming of the white man. Called Tasmanians, they differed in type from the aborigines of the mainland, being negroid in their physical characteristics.

Through millions of years the aborigines adapted themselves to the continent of their adoption as surely and as perfectly as the eucalypts. Except in the far north, where they may have had some contact with Papuans and Malays, no outside influence worked upon them. Naked they came into the world. Of the lares and penates they may have had in their original home they brought none with them. The dangerous voyage in dug-out or canoe made that nearly impossible, or, if they originally had any chattels, it was quite impossible to replace them. Only the dingo came, too.

What the aborigines did bring to Australia was an adaptability which spelt survival and the spiritual inheritance of a dream. It is usual to refer to these people as Stone Age men of the present. This does not mean that they lacked the intelligence to progress, to till the soil, to acquire goods, to build a civilization as we use the term. It only means that they had no opportunities, because the land offered them nothing but subsistence.

To adapt themselves was, when you come to think of it, a greater achievement than to build up a new world by bringing in, and having continuous access to, the products and techniques of an established civilization overseas. We honour our pioneers for going out into the bush, enduring, learning, and making a new life there. The aborigines had a far harder task, for they had nothing behind them either in knowledge or material possessions. (It could be argued that they were nearer to the earth than nineteenth century man, with less to unlearn.) What it cost them will never be known. The fittest survived.

They accepted the terms of the continent and imposed none on it. Their life was nomadic because they must follow the food supplies from place to place and season to season. Agriculture and the fixation of life it brings was impossible because there were no plants suitable for cultivation and the food supplies of any one district would be exhausted if they took from it more than a margin of increase. For the same reason they kept their numbers small by postponing the marriage of young men until they had completed long and intricate initiations. During the years of his initiation it was death for a man to touch a woman. Families were restricted, children likely to be a burden on the tribe were not allowed to live, and young wives were given to old men to balance the search for food.

After centuries of wandering the aborigines left hardly a mark upon the continent, a midden of oyster shells and bones, a few flimsy dams of stones for the trapping of fish, carvings on flat rocks or in caves, that was about all. Their mia-mias or gunyahs of bark or boughs soon went back to the earth they grew from. In the temperate climate their hardy bodies needed no clothes; for ever on the move, possessions would have been an embarrassment and they had none except such as were essential, bark canoes, wooden spears and boomerangs, throwing sticks, a few household vessels of wood or bark, and, for their dream life, the sacred tjuringa, bull-roarers, stone knives. . . . Their art, their history, their recreation were summed up in the evanescent corroborees which ceased to exist outside memory when the dancers' feet were still, and in their rock and totemic carvings. They lived with skill and laughter, and they had their dream world so old that even the wisest could no longer more than half understand it. They had their code of laws, blindly obeyed, which were no gibberish but directed to survival. For instance, their marriage taboos made inbreeding and degeneration impossible. They had no written language, though some anthropologists see in the message-sticks the vestiges of a long-forgotten script. But for that reason they do not lack quick long-distance communication, which is made through smoke signals. They can read the earth. Their tribal battles were and are more ritualistic than real. Survival is more important than bloodshed, manhood is gauged by wisdom, age, and prowess in hunting.

When A. G. L. Shaw speaks of them as "the only race which could serve as a common ancestor for all mankind" he follows in the footsteps of modern anthropological research. The Australian aboriginal, isolated, disciplined, stripped of inessentials, is a most curious palimpsest of history. In his pantheism and belief in place spirits he resembles the ancient Greeks; he follows ancestor worship in common with China; totemism is also indigenous to Mexico; his closely patterned life has something of ancient Egypt in it (or modern protocol); corroboree harks back to the religious, symbolic chronicle and mime dances of prehistory everywhere, surviving into historic times most particularly amongst Spaniards; descent through the female lines is matriarchy once again; something similar to his fertility rites, applied in Australia to plants and animals, for food sources, can be found in Frazer's *The Golden Bough*; the communal sharing of possessions, in this instance food, is no new or regional thing, for it had its ideal in the Golden Age of Saturn; group responsibility for the acts of the individual was common in Western Europe in the Middle Ages and lives on today, debased, in the persecution of the Jews and in the vendetta; J. B. R. Love in his most sympathetic book, *Stone Age Bushmen of Today*, claims to find rudimentary traces of Christian ethic and ritual, inherited, of course, from some far distant common source, for the aborigines were cut off in Australia long before the birth of Christ; the tribal system itself belongs to the common dawn of time.

The aboriginal has never been that figment "the noble savage", but he has been, is, and can be a full human being with, as a people, a most rare and highly developed gift for adaptation. He let the continent frame his daily life in that long pause between his migration and the coming of the white man. His spiritual or dream life is an older inheritance still from remotest prehistory, retained in cipher because in Australia until 1788 there was no influence to destroy it or drive it out.

It is interesting to note that although the white man, unless a most exceptional character, would not have dreamed of taking advice from the poor naked savage, his ways, particularly in the early days, fell into a rough copy of the aboriginal way of life. He became a nomad. Farming was peripatetic, the squatter ranged the interior, moving on and on in search of grass and water. The free bush workers were, on the whole, nomadic. They were no man's servants. They moved from job to job, shearing, dipping, fencing, horse-breaking, droving, under contract: since bush work is seasonal much of this remains, though the runs are fenced and the homesteads fixed. Bush conditions begot sharing, communal living in bark hut or camp, mutual help against the titanic disasters of flood or fire, mateship without questions. Bushmen learnt to steer by the stars, to find water in arid land, never quite to live off the country, but by initiative and improvisation to survive.

The white man with his possessions and his ignorance erupted into the close-knit pattern of the last waste and isolated continent in 1788. They had a great deal to learn, but they did not realize that. They believed that they came bearing gifts; in reality, as they adapted themselves, they were to receive.

II. Good Intentions and Bad Practice

To the aborigines the coming of the white man was a nine days' wonder. He was a joke to them, as they were to him. At first the new-comers took only a small fraction of the coast. They made little difference to tribal life. The aborigines were friendly, but, from the First-fleeters' point of view, uncertain in temper. Trade goods handed out so bountifully pleased them for a moment and were then cast aside. They had no place in their immemorial design of life. The black man understood hunger and thirst, but the white man had no conception of his taboos, his pattern of life. It did not enter his blond head that his dark brother would not consider him a superman and would not desire or benefit by what he had to give.

The aboriginal had a property sense only as regards his tribe. When his spears were taken from him, his land occupied, his sacred places unregarded, fish caught but not shared, he was angry. He made reprisals. If he suffered a wrong and speared a white man, he made no distinction between the innocent and the guilty. The group, not the individual, was responsible.

Phillip received instructions to treat the aborigines with kindness. He understood well enough that when there were clashes it was almost invariably the fault of the convicts. They were the aggressors. He did make a couple of mild punitive expeditions against the aborigines after there had been killings. It was the inherent belief in the prestige of the white man and the knowledge that inoffensive men would suffer for guilty men that moved him to do this. His own relationships with the aborigines were good. His courage never wavered and when he was wounded by one of them he recognized it as an act of fear. Reserved and nervous with his own officers, he was genial in his contacts with the aborigines and honestly believed that he would do them a great service by spreading civilized habits amongst them. As they would not come willingly to live in the white man's camp Phillip sought to do good by force. He kidnapped young men, held them virtual prisoners whilst he taught them cleanliness and the use of the knife and fork. His plan was then to liberate them to be, he hoped, ambassadors to their tribes and spread the light. Not unnaturally the plan failed. The gentle Arabanoo died of smallpox, Colbee escaped, and the wily Bennelong became a cheerful cadger when in the mood for it. The tribes vanished like shadows into the bush.

There was no native policy, just a vague benevolence. A paragraph in Phillip's instructions read:

> You are to endeavour by every possible means to open an intercourse with the natives, and to conciliate their affections, enjoining all our subjects to live in amity and kindness with them. And if any of our subjects shall wantonly destroy them or give them any unnecessary interruption in the exercise of their several occupations it is our will and pleasure that you do cause such offenders to be brought to punishment according to the degree of the offence. You will endeavour to procure an account of the numbers inhabiting the neighbourhood of the intended settlement, and report your opinion to one of our Secretaries of State in what manner our intercourse with these people may be turned to the advantage of this colony.[1]

Phillip soon found that no advantage was to be reaped from the aboriginal except occasional succour when white men lost themselves in the bush, nor could he estimate their numbers with any accuracy. Current theories placed the population of the continent at anything from 150,000 to 300,000 in 1788, and Phillip opined that between Broken Bay and Botany Bay there were about 1500 aborigines.[2] He carried out the policy of conciliation in so far as they were receptive and his subjects controllable. He wrote of the aborigines in a dispatch:

. . . every precaution that was possible has been taken to prevent their receiving any insults, and when I shall have time to mix more with them every means shall be used to reconcile them to live amongst us, and to teach them the advantage they will reap from cultivating land.[3]

That was in the early days of his governorship.

Phillip's officers co-operated with him and, indeed, took a great interest in the aborigines, who provided almost the only source of entertainment open to them. Captain Watkin Tench, in particular, is full of anecdotes and evidently did his best to see the aboriginal as the noble savage of the Rousseau tradition. The convicts and soldiery were less tender. Eighteenth-century Englishmen were very sure of the perfection of their own brand of civilization and the anthropological approach to native peoples had not yet dawned.

Whilst the settlement was small and under the eye of the Governor treatment of the aborigines could be fairly well controlled, particularly as the tribes soon withdrew to a safe distance and came no more to Sydney Cove. As settlement fanned out and distances defeated supervision the situation worsened.

The aborigines saw no harm in plundering crops on the Hawkesbury River in 1795. There were "several accidents". Five white men were killed and several wounded. Colonel Paterson, then Acting Governor (on the wrong side of the blanket), saw the danger of supplying the settlers with firearms, and such a state of panic worked up that there was talk of abandoning the most fertile area in the settlement. Two subalterns and sixty privates were sent to protect the four hundred settlers on thirty miles of river frontage.[4]

Paterson took hostages, one man and four women, and:

I mean to keep them until they can be made to understand that it is not their interest to do us injuries, and that we are readier to be friends than enemies; but that we cannot suffer our people to be inhumanly butchered, and their labour rendered useless by their depredations, with impunity.[5]

In the next year, 1796, Governor Hunter was asking for "a few stands of firearms" to be issued to settlers for their defence against the aborigines in the same dispatch that he lamented: "All the arms which had formerly been sent out had been issued to different people long before my arrival, and I fear that many of them have fallen into the hands of worthless characters."[6] The Governor was arming the settlers while he was advising them "that they do not wantonly fire at or take the lives of any of the natives, as such an act would be considered a deliberate murder, and subject the offender to such punishment as (if proved) the law might direct to be inflicted".[7] Hunter also warned settlers not to encourage the aborigines to "lurk about" their properties.

The pattern was set. When the Blue Mountains were crossed authority in Sydney had even less control. Incidents at Bathurst caused Brisbane to declare martial law "over the mountains". This proved ineffective. The aboriginal was not warlike in the manner of the Red Indian, and in this the settlers were fortunate, but he did resent the taking of his land and could not understand why he might spear kangaroos but not cattle or sheep. Reprisals begot reprisals in the usual human way. Good or bad relations depended on circumstances and the character of the individual settlers. The Church does not appear, in the early days, to have been interested in saving black souls. The Reverend Samuel Marsden, who showed such missionary zeal in New Zealand, was apparently indifferent to the aboriginal or wrote him off as too primitive to receive the Gospel. The authorities continued to preach conciliation and to make sporadic attempts to civilize aborigines. Macquarie founded his school for aboriginal children at Parramatta and deeply offended the Reverend Mr Marsden in the process by not asking his advice or even inviting him to visit it. At first the Governor was most sanguine, but the enterprise faded away. The pupils went on walkabout. Their adaptability led them to accept the Governor's good intentions with pleasure. They were quite able to learn and for a little while were delighted to do so, but they had no conception that school was something that went on and on. They probably looked on it as a white man's corroboree and a play corroboree at that.

Little is to be gained by recounting all the recorded black and white incidents. The relationship of the two peoples was incidental. Authority had no policy except a general humanitarian gesture, the aborigines put up no organized opposition. The Church took little interest until 1825, when the Church Missionary Society asked for 10,000 acres of land as an aboriginal reserve. It was granted to them at Tuggerah, then called Yawanba or Reid's Mistake. Other than missionaries (there was one to begin with), no white man might enter it. A Board of Trustees was appointed and the land subdivided into thirty-acre blocks which the aborigines were expected to cultivate. The mission was to draw its funds from the timber on the land, felled by the grateful aboriginal.[8] The scheme was doomed to failure, just as a later reserve and mission at Wellington Valley was.

By 1826 the position was recognized as most unsatisfactory. Archdeacon Scott reported: ". . . as our Interests advance, their Misery and extinction are most positive, and that, unless some immediate steps be taken to relieve them, extinction will take place in the course of the next 30 Years." He concludes "that, unless the Government are prepared to go to the length of feeding and clothing the whole of them (4500) at an immense Expense, and that constantly, not the least progress will be made either as to Civilization or Conversion".[9]

R. Sadleir, reporting from the field, had a more ambitious project. It was that the Government should employ all the aborigines, feeding and clothing them in compensation for services and "good conduct"; that a Resident Magistrate be appointed to mediate between the aborigines and the white settlers; that missionaries be encouraged (there were now two in the field), and that a chain of stations be set up throughout the country at a cost of £500 a year each, on each of which six black families would be settled.[10] This was ambitious, humanitarian—and unworkable. The aborigines did not want to be settled or pinned down. It went against the grain of centuries.

Everyone agreed that in contact with white men the aborigines deteriorated morally and physically. They must be segregated in their own interest as far as possible. Civilization could not be applied like an ointment, nor could the centuries be bridged in a few decades.

Wilberforce's anti-slavery campaign had a profound effect in England and it coloured opinion in Australia, too. After the achievement of his object in 1833 there is discernible a new interest in, and sympathy for, the dark people. The Myall Creek murders in 1837, when twenty-eight aborigines, both men and women, were killed on what turned out to be a trumped-up charge of outrages, aroused public opinion to fever-pitch and seven white settlers were hanged for the crime. Their plea, "We were not aware that in killing the blacks we were violating the law . . . as it has been so frequently done before", is very revealing. In the safe isolation of the bush, aborigines had been shot, their waterholes poisoned, and hand-outs of flour laced with arsenic, and no more punishment had been meted out than if the victims had been dingoes. Their immemorial life was shattered and they were punished for they knew not what. In 1833 something approaching a pitched battle was fought by moonlight at Pinjarra in Western Australia, and drew down the official disapproval of the Colonial Office. Some settlers, Angus McMillan for instance, were on very good terms with the aborigines of their districts and there was no trouble.

In 1836 a Select Committee of the House of Commons sat to consider the status of the aborigines, "to secure them the due observance of justice and the protection of their rites, to promote and spread Christianity among them and to lead them to the peaceful and voluntary reception of the Christian religion . . .".

The dispatch from Lord Glenelg acquainting the Governor of the findings of the Committee reads:

Your Commission as Governor of N. S. Wales asserts H.M.'s sovereignty over every part of the Continent of New Holland. . . . Hence I conceive it follows that all the natives inhabiting those Territories must be considered as Subjects of the Queen, and as within H.M.'s Allegiance. To regard them as Aliens with whom a War can exist, and against whom H.M.'s Troops may exercise belligerent right, is to deny that protection to which they derive the highest possible claim from the Sovereignty which has been assumed over the whole of their Ancient Possessions. . . . If the rights of the Aborigines as British Subjects be fully acknowledged, it will follow that, when any of them comes to his death by the hands of the Queen's Officers, or of persons acting under their Command, an Inquest should be held to ascertain the cause which lead to the Death of the deceased. Such a proceeding is important not only as a direct protection to Society at large against lawless Outrage, but as it impresses on the Public a just estimate of the value of Human Life.[11]

Nothing could be clearer than this statement of the intentions of the Imperial Government and yet in Australia a flaw was quickly found. The aborigines were not Christians, they did not understand the nature of an oath, and for that reason their evidence could not be accepted in any court of law. The treatment of the aborigines remained a matter of grace rather than of justice.

The inquiry did not stop at pious generalizations. The Select Committee elaborated a scheme. A Chief Protector with a salary of £500 a year and four assistant protectors at £250 a year were to be appointed. The protectors must live with the aborigines, learn their languages, and go on walkabout with them, conciliating them and winning their confidence by every possible means. They must defend their rights, protect their property, and report regularly on their condition and needs to the Chief Protector. They must encourage agriculture and, if possible, persuade each tribe to settle in one district. They must educate the children, spread Christianity, control and issue the "moderate" supplies of food and clothing supplied by the Government for the use of the aborigines and, lastly, they were expected to collect scientific data.[12]

The scheme did not work, mainly because it was not adjusted to the tribal organization of the aborigines. It expected too much of them and of the protectors. For this work it was difficult to find suitable men. George Augustus Robinson, a bricklayer of Hobart, who had "pacified" the Tasmanian aborigines and was looked on as an authority, was appointed Chief Protector and proved unequal to the work. Commissioners of Crown lands were also appointed protectors, but had little time for the work and could not fulfil all the duties. Many settlers were uncooperative. They considered the findings of the Select Committee of the House of Commons as so much sentimental nonsense. Incidents continued. Major Nunn, with a posse of police, fell in with a tribe in lands beyond location; one trooper was speared and several aborigines were killed. Three white men were killed on a journey north, and eight of the eighteen men in Faithfull's party were speared on the way to Port Phillip. Many settlers thought that aborigines should be controlled and disciplined rather than protected, and the Protectors were apt to feel and act with their own kind rather than with their charges.

Border Police were maintained out of the money collected from grazing licences to protect white lives and property. The bush was so vast that it could not be adequately policed. Authority at Sydney took the attitude that if settlers penetrated into the distant bush they did so at their own risk and advised those travelling or droving to form parties large enough to protect themselves. Military posts were established at wide intervals, only on the so-called roads.

Governor Gipps took his cue from Whitehall, but he realized how difficult it would be to enforce any regulations. "All we can now do is to raise, in the name of Justice and humanity, a voice in favor of our poor savage fellow creatures, too feeble to be heard at such a distance."[13] He held inquests as directed, but it was impossible to get evidence as the settlers stood together, distance reduced fact to rumour, and the aborigines were inarticulate or their evidence was unacceptable. Glenelg was not satisfied. He did not think that the Governor took a strong enough line. He suggested prompt and severe action against white settlers who killed aborigines, "not in self defence but wantonly", and advised the taking of hostages from the tribes to ensure good behaviour. He did not understand the difficulties of getting evidence or the futility of taking hostages.

In or about 1839 an Aborigines' Protection Society was formed with, as its first objective, the acceptance of aboriginal evidence in court. Without that there could be no justice.

The situation remained unresolved. J. H. Wedge, a surveyor who had played a large part in settling the Port Phillip district, had a new idea. The civilization of the aborigines should be put on such a footing as would make it

> . . . *to the interest of the Settlers* to join with the Government in bringing about and establishing a permanent friendly feeling, not only as far as the interests of the Colony are concerned, but also as an act of humanity and justice due to the Natives, upon whose territory, as Colonization advances, successive encroachments will be made.[14]

The sentiments were unexceptionable but vague.

By 1840 aboriginal reserves were delimited and an inspector appointed. The most important of these reserves was the Wellington Valley, where a mission had been established. Except the missionaries and government officials no white men, "particularly stockmen", might enter the territory. The trouble was that the aborigines, being nomadic, did not stay on the reserves. They attended the schools for a little while, then melted away. There was no real analogy between the Australian aborigines and the

African tribes, though Lord John Russell seems to have thought that what would suit one would suit the other.

Governor Gipps interested himself in the aborigines and there is no doubt that he did the best he could for them, but it was uphill work. He visited the Wellington Valley Mission and found the two missionaries stationed there at loggerheads. (They were probably suffering from isolation and barrack-room fever.) He adjudicated and dismissed one of them, who departed, taking all the children from the school and some of the adult adherents with him, thus rendering null and void the Governor's offer of prizes for reading and the "useful arts".

Gipps not unnaturally felt that responsibility for aborigines was a government, not a church matter, and that if the Church Missionary Society wished to carry on the work of conversion to Christianity it should make some monetary contribution to the support of mission stations. As only 50 acres out of 7000 in the Wellington Valley had been cultivated, Gipps did not recommend further grants. It might be better, he thought, to raise money by selling part of the land He was not a man to suffer inefficiency with equanimity. He was just, but not sentimental.

> . . . the language now held by this Government is that the Aborigines are Her Majesty's subjects; and that, whilst they are entitled in every respect to the benefit and protection of English Law, they are amenable also to the penalties which are imposed on infractions of the Law, whether the offence be committed against one of themselves or against White Men.[15]

To this he added a rider that the Law must sometimes be modified for them because of their lack of understanding. The Legislative Council was in favour of taking their evidence in court, though they did not understand the nature of an oath. Gipps thought this unnecessary as the Crown assigned them counsel for defence and in any case they were nearly always acquitted. This is an index of the good feeling towards the aborigines in the towns, where there was no conflict. They were not, Gipps asserted in a dispatch of 24th July 1842, a conquered people and the Government did not treat them as such.

Then comes a truly period touch. Gipps felt that, after religion, the most civilizing influence would be the possession of money. They should be taught to work for wages and he even considered offering a bounty to anyone who would employ them. A £5 fine was imposed on anyone who gave or sold liquor to an aboriginal. The same restriction applied to firearms. A bill to protect aboriginal women came before the Legislative Council. As usual, intentions were good, but it remained very difficult to enforce the law in the bush. Even while Gipps was framing his aboriginal policy, twenty-eight of them were murdered in the Liverpool Plains district.

By 1844 it was evident that plans for converting and civilizing the aborigines were a failure. By that time the missions had faded away and the protectorates were being clipped. In March 1844 the Governor was writing home: "I have not thought it right . . . entirely to break up the Establishments of Protectors of Aborigines in the Port Phillip District; but I have made arrangements with Mr La Trobe to keep the expenses of them . . . within the sum of £3000. . . ."[16] There was an economic depression and philanthropy was somewhat damped.

In 1842 a corps of native police had been formed in the Port Phillip District under the command of an Englishman named Dana, and in the bush they were found to be much more efficient than white men. The services of trackers had been enlisted much earlier in New South Wales.

Year by year the official reports on the aborigines became more despondent. It was impossible to educate them; they were indolent and unreliable, though, if well treated, they would defend a station against strange tribes. The protectors on the whole took their duties seriously, but had little success.[17] About this time, 1845, half-castes began to present a serious problem.

In 1843 the Imperial Government had again intervened on the side of the aborigines. It felt that they suffered injustice by being debarred from giving evidence in court. An Act was therefore passed admitting unsworn evidence providing that the colonial legislatures ratified it. For the rest, Governors were enjoined to use "care and vigilance" to give the aborigines a fair deal. This is vague, but then so many patent schemes had proved unworkable from lack of knowledge and understanding rather than from negligence, that in general the Government was in retreat from its native problem.

South Australia, under Governor Grey, devised the most successful policy. The office of Protector was abolished. Reserves were much reduced, but the right of aborigines to move freely over pastoral land was asserted. Small settlements were established for them and supplied with government-owned flocks and herds. The aboriginal, it was discovered, took much more kindly to pastoral pursuits than to agriculture. They fitted in better with his nomadic way of life. The Government supplied rations to the tribes at the time of year when food was scarce, otherwise they were left to follow their own customs. This helped without debasing them. Grey set out the rights of the aborigines in a Public Declaration and, in a smaller State, he had more opportunity to enforce it.

For roughly forty more years incidents occurred sporadically in the bush. The atrocities were not one-sided. For instance, on 17th October 1861 nineteen white men, women, and children were surprised and massacred at Cullin-la-Ringo Station in Queensland. The aborigines were undoubtedly ill-treated, their numbers diminished, and even where there were the best intentions contact with the white man and his ways undermined their tribal customs without giving them anything they could believe deeply in their place. They were confused, and an unhappy people does not increase. Many died of a spiritual malaise or as the result of well-meant mistakes, as when, for their own protection, they were confined on islands off the Western Australian coast or in Bass Strait, or, when ill, taken into the alien world of a hospital.

The aborigines were never a very serious menace to the white man and by about 1880, by reason of discouragement and falling numbers, they ceased to be a menace at all. When the white man had finally and unmistakably won the land his attitude to the aboriginal changed. He was a useful stockman, a curiosity, a subject of scientific interest.

The Tasmanian story stands a little apart. The aborigines there were negroid, less intelligent, less adaptable, and met with even harsher treatment. At first they showed themselves friendly, but as early as May 1804 the so-called Black War had begun. Lieutenant Moore and a posse of soldiers fell in with a band of aborigines armed for hunting. Thinking them hostile, the lieutenant ordered his men to open fire. There were many casualties. The next year was one of scarcity. White man and black man were both short of food and competing for the game on the island. The Tasmanians' eyes were opened. Their land was being taken from them, the interlopers with their firearms were more successful in the chase. Friendliness was replaced by resentment. The more brutal amongst the convicts were generally shipped to Van Diemen's Land, the sealers were equally tough, control from Hobart was vestigial. When in 1830 Governor Arthur called together a committee to look into the aboriginal question a horrifying story of atrocities and the inevitable reprisals was revealed. The Governor decided to prevent further trouble by confining the natives to one part of the island. He had first to catch them. Employing 2000 men for seven weeks at a cost of £35,000 he tried to round up the Tasmanians and imprison them behind an arbitrarily drawn "Black Line". The expedition was a complete failure. The Tasmanians melted like shadows into the bush and the soldiers clumped unsuccessfully after them. They did succeed in capturing one woman and one boy. The costly attempt was given up.

G. A. Robinson, a Methodist lay preacher, offered his services to bring the Tasmanians in by persuasion. Between 1831 and 1835 he persuaded two hundred to give themselves up voluntarily. This feat is often praised and Robinson spoken of as an apostle to the Tasmanians. In reality, though he was probably quite unaware of this himself, his conciliation had a Judas touch. The unfortunate natives were segregated on Flinders Island in Bass Strait with Robinson as their guardian. They pined and died. The last male Tasmanian died in 1869. Truganini, one of the more persistent sex, died in Hobart, aged 73, in 1876. It was thought that she was the last Tasmanian, but one more, also a woman, was discovered on Kangaroo Island. When she died in 1888 the race was extinct. Some mixed-bloods still survive, particularly in the Bass Strait area.

The Port Phillip district provided the most colourful story. The approach of the Port Phillip Association led by Batman was, in 1835, quite different from that of the pioneers in any other colony. As the settlement was unauthorized by the Home Government, the Association sought title and goodwill by "buying" the land they wanted from the native "chiefs" and by paying them an annual tribute. Batman was quite unaware that the aborigines had no conception of buying and selling and that there were no chiefs in the accepted sense. John Pascoe Fawkner described the transaction in his acid style:

> Batman fell in with the blacks, and gave them some small presents and got them ignorantly to sign a deed conveying to the Company about half a million [acres?]. . . . The Company bought, or pretended to buy and sell to one another, their shares of the land they pretended to have bought off the aborigines until they found that the Home Government would not tolerate such a glorious piece of humbug.[18]

The Association came in for some bitter criticism for their "grotesque trickery, fantastic and absurd". It was evidently considered more worthy, certainly more conventional, to take the hunting-grounds of the aboriginal without recompense.

The Association proclaimed its intention to civilize the aborigines and set up a board consisting of Batman, Simpson, and Wedge to protect and conciliate them. In William Buckley, a member of David Collins's abortive settlement in 1803, who had not followed him to Van Diemen's Land but had preferred to go native, they found a liaison officer, not a very good one as it turned out, for he could not speak the language.

What followed is in the best musical-comedy vein. In 1836 Captain Lonsdale was appointed as magistrate in charge of the settlement and brought with him detailed instructions to settle aborigines in villages, get them to work in return for food, restrain them gently from insolence and dishonesty, and conciliate them with presents. He was issued with 250 blankets, 200 check shirts and 500 red nightcaps for this purpose by the Ordnance Department in Sydney.[19] The aboriginal reserves were to be managed along the lines of Owen's socialist community in Lanark, Scotland.

Mr Justice Burton in Sydney enjoyed some doctrinaire musings on the subject. First the aborigines were to be induced to give up their nomadic life and settle, then they were to be introduced to the joys of civilization, and, finally, it was to be broken to them that they could only receive these benefits if they worked. The joys would consist of presents, rations, huts to live in, and education. Burton seems to have doubted whether adult aborigines would appreciate education, but infant schools would catch, tame and detribalize the children at an early age.

A missionary, Langhorne, was sent out from England, arriving in January 1837 armed with instructions which he soon found fitted the circumstances very ill.

Whilst New South Wales had had, to begin with, no native policy, Port Phillip had a superfluity, a hotchpotch of Christian doctrine, Lonsdale's instructions, and Burton's theories. Governor Bourke saw nothing incongruous about it all. When he visited Melbourne in March 1837 he inspected the proposed aboriginal reserve on the Yarra, distributed clothing to the assembled aborigines, presented Mr Langhorne to them and exhorted them to be loyal. It is unlikely that they understood a word he said.

Langhorne was the only man with doubts. The more he studied the aborigines the more doubtful he became, until at last he came to the conclusion that, far from bettering the aborigines, his mission was harmful to them, and he resigned. The whole fabric collapsed.

Another experiment took its place. A Native Police Corps would be formed and the primitive character developed by responsibility. Captain Maconochie, whose theories for the reformation of convicts have already been noticed, thought the idea a cure-all leading to affection, religion, cleanliness, order.[20] He based his ideas on an analogy with the sepoys! The Select Committee of the House of Commons on Aborigines (1837) quashed it on the ground that a warrigal suddenly given authority would be sure to land himself in trouble.

After this hopeful outburst of theory, the Port Phillip district came into line with New South Wales and a dilatory policy of reserves, protectors, sponsored missions, and inadequate rationing became the order of the day. Official goodwill, humanitarian instructions from Whitehall, and recurring Select Committees could not save the aborigines. Their numbers diminished steadily. At a rough estimate there were 10,000 in the Port Phillip district at the beginning of white settlement; by 1850 there were only about 3000 left. The comedy had become a tragedy.

In Western Australia, whilst Captain Stirling took it for granted that the aboriginal population would die out, he urged the Home Government to set up a protectorate on humanitarian grounds. Governor Hutt (1795-1880), advanced for his times, believed that the aboriginal problem would solve itself through the assimilation of the dark race into the white one by intermarriage. The disparity of the sexes was very high in Western Australia and that may have coloured his outlook. In the meantime, two protectors were appointed, efforts were made to educate and employ aborigines, land was allotted for reserves, missionaries were encouraged. In a general way the Government looked upon the aborigines as wards, and did the best it could for them according to its lights; missionaries, selfless and well-intentioned, too often looked on all tribal customs as debased and tried to eradicate them and replace them by Christian principles, to the utter confusion of Stone Age man; individuals, too often ignorant and brutal, ill-used and debauched them.

The story in the west was much the same as in the east, good intentions, bad practices, and, in general, until recent times, a complete misunderstanding the problem.

As Mrs Daisy Bates, who spent most of her life with them, said in her book, *The Passing of the Aborigines,* "It was the same story everywhere, a kindness that killed as surely and as swiftly as cruelty would have done." And there was cruelty and incomprehension, too.

III. Blue-print for Welfare

I have spoken continually of the aboriginal problem. It could not fail to be a problem because two races at different stages of development were competing for possession of the same land, with all the advantages on one side. Had there been no humanitarian feeling, no Christian impulse, no myth of the noble savage, there would have been no problem. The aborigines would have been exterminated, directly or indirectly, as the Tasmanians were.

The number of full-blooded aborigines has decreased steadily since the coming of the white man. An accurate census of their numbers is naturally difficult. In New South Wales they were believed to number about 11,800 in 1881, about 3700 in 1901, 2000 in 1911, 1597 in 1921, and 869 in 1936. In Victoria they were completely detribalized by 1850 and the discovery of gold did not help matters. In Western Australia their numbers have steadily diminished. The Trans-Continental Railway spelt tragedy and degradation for many aborigines, according to Daisy Bates. Only in Queensland and the Northern Territory can they really be said to have survived and since 1932 to have maintained their numbers.

With half-castes—and the term covers all shades of colour—the situation is very different. Their rate of increase is high, as it is estimated that they double their numbers every thirty years. They, too, present a problem, but it need not be a serious one because in three or four generations of intermarriage with whites they become indistinguishable from the European population. With the diminution and segregation of full-bloods the half-castes cannot fail to progress steadily towards assimilation. The aboriginal-white cross is, biologically speaking, an eminently successful one. The mixing of bloods and that alone can bridge the gap between the Stone Age and the present.

This is not to say that there is no half-caste problem. A mixed-blood is at a social disadvantage. The process of assimilation cannot be forced, since marriage is a matter of individual and private choice. But since the half-caste, quadroon, and octoroon, given the same advantages and opportunities as a white child, are generally as intelligent and personable, nature in the long run will probably take care of the matter. The operative words here are "the same advantages and opportunities".

Humanitarianism, religion, and patent remedies having failed with the aborigines, anthropology has gradually taken their place as a basis for policy.

It is generally accepted now that the full-blooded aboriginal who has not become detribalized is best served by complete segregation from the white man. He is adjusted to the country, he has a traditional and satisfactory pattern of life, and all that we can do for him is to leave him alone. In the 1954 census it was estimated that there were 20,786 full-blooded aborigines in Australia. For the half-caste, who is inevitably detribalized, the only humane policy is one of progressive acceptance with the community.

Except in the Northern Territory, where they come under the Commonwealth Ministry for the Territories, the care of aborigines is a State matter. Policy is closely allied in all States, though the authorities concerned have different names.

In New South Wales the Aborigines Protection Act (1909-43) set up an Aborigines Welfare Board of eight white and two aboriginal members under the chairmanship of the Superintendent of Aboriginal Welfare. All members are government nominees.

In Victoria an Act of 1860 constituting a Board of Trustees is still on the Statute Book. These two eastern and southern States deal almost exclusively with half-castes. Queensland has a Director of Native Affairs; South Australia a Chief Protector, supported by an Aborigines' Protection Board and responsible to a Cabinet Minister; Western Australia has its Native Administration Act (1905-41) which appoints a Commissioner of Native Affairs.

The Northern Territory has 64,000 square miles of reserves into which no white men, unless they are officials of the Ministry of Territories, or anthropologists granted special permission, may enter. In 1931 the Commonwealth reserved 31,200 square miles in Arnhem Land for about 3000 full-bloods still uncontaminated by civilization. The area is large enough to allow them to lead their normal nomadic life. They are not confined to the area, but it is reserved for their exclusive use.

Western Australia has 167 smaller reserves, covering in all 53,500 acres, and a large North-western Reserve of 34,000 square miles. Queensland has a large reserve on Cape York Peninsula for full-bloods, a number of smaller reserves, four settlements, and nine missions. South Australia has 27,620 square miles allocated to aborigines, but the Commonwealth has taken part of this for the Woomera Rocket Range, pledging itself not to interfere with the aborigines. They might, one feels, find the rocket tests somewhat disturbing.

For half-castes, of whom there were about 28,000 on the mainland of Australia in 1951, mostly half European with about 8 per cent of mixed Asiatic blood in the north, the burning question is citizen rights. Up to 1936 half-castes, with a few exceptions, were treated as aborigines and had no citizen rights. They were segregated and, except as stockmen in the far outback, found it difficult to get employment. In 1937 an interstate Official Congress agreed to unify as far as possible the policies of the different States and to hold more frequent conferences. The Harvard-Adelaide Universities Anthropological Expedition of 1938-9 may have influenced government policy, for in 1939 a policy of assimilation was generally accepted as regards half-castes. This, in theory at least, moved them on to the white side of the blanket. Western Australia in 1944 made a positive move when she passed the Native Citizenship Rights Act. It did not confer citizenship automatically, but made it possible for aborigines to apply for it and, if they were deemed suitable, it was conferred on them. By 1951 only 478 had qualified; the smallness of the number is not surprising as, lacking education and experience, the formality of citizenship would mean little to the majority of the dark people. In 1950 children born of parents who were already citizens automatically received their rights in the same way as a white child.

By 1954 aborigines in New South Wales, Victoria, and South Australia had the franchise, but not in the Northern Territory, Queensland, or Western Australia, where the greatest numbers are. Few were interested in voting and they were not penalized, like white citizens, for failing to take up their privilege.

Participation in social services is much more to the point. In New South Wales, Queensland, South Australia, and Western Australia aborigines receive benefits only when they can produce certificates showing they are exempted from control, that is, when, in the parlance of an earlier day, they are "on their own hands", or not receiving benefits and care in an aboriginal settlement. In Victoria the Director of Social Services may give old-age and other pensions to aborigines if they are detribalized and he is satisfied as to their good character and general responsibility. Half-castes are generally eligible for all benefits. Child endowment is paid to missions for all children in their care.

Education has proved one of the chief difficulties. There are not enough suitable teachers available and the 1938-9 survey of schools attended by aborigines revealed a very low standard. Children could not be compelled to attend and, when the novelty wore off, many drifted away. Language was another difficulty. There are so many Australian dialects that, except in a few instances, as at the Hermannsburg Mission in the Centre, it is impossible to teach children in their own language. They often forget their original tongue without acquiring English properly. The result of this is the use of pidgin, which cuts them off even more effectively from the white community.

In the past it was the practice to segregate half-caste children in their own, grossly inferior, schools. They now have the right to attend State schools and no distinction is made. In the Northern Territory the Commonwealth has opened six schools for full-bloods and has successfully encouraged the attendance of half-castes at its ordinary schools.

After schooling comes the difficulty of employment and of maintaining the half-castes' social standing. During the war, when labour was short, aborigines were employed whenever they were willing. They received award wages and, more often than not, proved themselves very handy with machinery. They entered the Army as volunteers and gave service of great importance and danger as coast watchers in the north. They have always excelled in sport and as early as 1868 an Aboriginal Cricket Team visited England. In competition, it is sad to say that they have not always been accepted with the good sportsmanship on which we, as a nation, have often prided ourselves.

To keep in touch with aboriginal pupils after schooldays, the Aboriginal Welfare Board of New South Wales has published and distributed to them regularly a magazine called *Dawn*. Western Australia does better. The *Westralian Aborigine* is written and produced monthly by aborigines for aborigines.

There is still much to do to ensure them a fair deal. Some individuals have broken through successfully into the white world. Albert Namatjira was free to take his place in it because of his gift as a painter; Harold Blair, the singer, is another. James Noble was ordained as a clergyman in the Church of England. Captain Reginald William Saunders was the first aboriginal to hold a commission in the A.I.F. and he served with distinction in Greece and the Middle East, later volunteering for the Korean campaign. Girls have trained as nurses and teachers. . . . The tally is, I know, pitifully small, but it is a beginning. It is long enough to prove that aborigines are not incapable of learning and progressing.

The dark people today have many and valuable friends who plead their cause, sometimes with more enthusiasm than understanding. Malcolm Muggeridge, after a short stay in Australia, was ready to inveigh against government incompetence and callousness. Dr W. E. H. Stanner was also sweeping in his condemnation: "Australian native policy is a cautious mixture of high intentions and laudable objectives; almost unbelievably mean finance, an obstinate concentration on lines of policy which 150 years of experience have made suspect."[21]

There *are* Australians who discriminate against anyone with a dark skin.

The same people dislike and suspect foreigners, however blond, simply because they are different. There *are* unpleasant incidents, as when some of the white citizens of Nambucca Heads objected to black citizens living in the same street. When something like this happens there is a furore, a healthy sign in itself. There are also, be it remembered, patches of religious intolerance and instances of cruelty to children.

Critics do not always recognize the magnitude of the problem. They think that if the Government spent sufficient money and if every opportunity available to the white man were also open to the dark man, all would be well. It is not as simple as that. A gulf of evolution separates the two peoples. It cannot be bridged by legislation or goodwill or anthropology. It is there. We are what our ancestors and the continuing circumstances of Western civilization have made us. The aboriginal is what aeons of isolation in the last and most difficult of continents have made him. He was nomadic because only so could he find sufficient food all the year round. The habit of walk-about is ingrained and it is unreasonable to expect him to remain at one place even if there is always plenty to eat there. A former necessity has become a present compulsion. Again, for survival, a tribe held all property, and that generally meant food, in common. No personal property sense developed. To call an aboriginal lazy because he follows the ancestral pattern of life, and feckless because he sets no store on money or goods and immediately shares all he has with his relations, is unjust. To give him what we consider a good life, his whole outlook must be changed. The evolutionary pattern cannot be changed in a decade or a generation. To live in a humpy on the river-bank may be an improvement on the gunyah or mia-mia, a surburban villa would probably be torture.

Authority has made many mistakes, some of them ridiculous, most of them with the best of intentions. At last expert advice has been called in and an effort is being made to redress the errors of the past. We owe the aboriginal a debt because we destroyed the immemorial pattern of his life when we took his land from him, by robbing him of his dream world in the endeavour to substitute for it our faith and customs, by spreading amongst the tribes diseases against which they had built no immunity, by confusing him when we broke his taboos and, often unknowingly, desecrated his sacred places and still prospered. We cannot claim to have adjusted ourselves to the land we live in as well as the aboriginal did. We destroyed his adjustment and, confused and beggared, he lost the will to live. In all conscience we owe him a great deal, but it is difficult to pay the debt because our coin is not his. We cannot turn back our destiny and live his life. Gradually we may become one people. The most practical thing that those who criticize native policy could do would be to marry an aboriginal, bring up their half-caste children to marry white again, and so assist nature's remedy of assimilation.

REFERENCE NOTES

[1] *Hist. Rec. Aust.*, ser. I, vol. i, pp. 13-14.

[2] *Ibid.*, p. 29 [3] *Ibid.*, p. 65. [4] *Ibid.*, p. 499.

[5] *Ibid.* [6] *Ibid.*, p. 554. [7] *Ibid.*, p. 689.

[8] *Ibid.*, vol. xi, pp. 512-14. [9] *Ibid.*, vol. xiv, pp. 59-63. [10] *Ibid.*, p. 59.

[11] *Ibid.*, vol. xix, pp. 48-9. [12] *Ibid.*, pp. 253 *et seq.* [13] *Ibid.*, p. 510.

[14] *Ibid.*, vol. xx, p. 450. [15] *Ibid.*, vol. xxi, p. 312. [16] *Ibid.*, vol. xxiii, p. 497.

[17] For a sample of these reports, see *Hist. Rec. Aust.*, ser. I, vol. xxiii, pp. 485-97; vol. xxiv, pp. 258-73.

[18] J. P. Fawkner, "A Short Account of Port Phillip", Port Phillip Papers, pp. 117, 119. (MS. in the possession of the Mitchell Library.)

[19] J. B. Foxcroft, *Australian Native Policy*, p. 39.

[20] *Ibid.*, pp. 50-1.

[21] W. E. H. Stanner in *Some Australians Take Stock* (ed. J. C. G. Kevin), p. 9.

CHAPTER XXIV

ENVOI

LOOKING BACK over the short Australian story, its general outline becomes clear. Accident played a very large part. It was by accident that the continent was first discovered by the Dutch and it was only accidentally that they continued, often unfortunately, to visit the west coast. To call Captain Cook's discovery of the east coast accidental would be perhaps to belittle his fine seamanship. Shall we say he had a blind date with the continent? Chance rather than accident gave the first tentative colony a Governor who had the spiritual tenacity to hold on during the first five critical years of famine and difficulty when most other men would have sailed away to some easier and more fertile Pacific Island, or would perhaps have given up altogether. David Collins, who had a much better equipped expedition than Phillip could ever persuade the Government to give him, abandoned Port Phillip in 1804 as impossible, though the country was more fertile than Port Jackson. A tenuous thread of events brought the Spanish Merino sheep to Australia and their importation found a man who realized their commercial value and took advantage of it, so founding the great wool industry. The Merino not only opened up the country but changed the policy of the Imperial Government to its erstwhile ugly duckling, and attracted to the colony a type of immigrant who would otherwise have shunned it.

That the population was not brindled from the earliest days was the bright side of misfortune. Phillip had explicit instructions to bring in Island women. He disobeyed them because he knew that he could not feed them. For years, whenever a labour shortage threatened prosperity, an agitation for the importation of coolie labour, black or yellow, began anew. Each time it was beaten by public opinion and disallowed by the Home Government.

The next accident that changed the face of Australia was the discovery of gold. From it stemmed not only wealth but a great wave of free and independent immigrants who altered land laws and accelerated the coming of responsible government. The presence of uranium may be just such another "accident" in the atomic age.

By a miracle Australia, with her indefensible coast, has never been invaded, if you discount air-raids on Darwin and Japanese submarines in Sydney Harbour.

Tradition has played a big part in our growth, from the obstinate eating of plum-pudding in the height of summer to the spontaneous and unhesitating participation in England's wars, from a modest contingent sent to the Sudan, through the South African War, to total war in 1914 and 1939.

Tradition is being constantly reinforced by immigration from the United Kingdom, by the two-way stream of visitors, by books, by films, by B.B.C. re-broadcasts, by imports material and immaterial generally. Easy transport and the wool cheque enable many Australians to visit England. The bonds of kinship are strong and proud.

It is good that it should be so, we have a context in the world, we are a small nation in a big Commonwealth of Nations, we have a spiritual point of attachment. There has been an unfortunate aspect of this, and that has been the continual export of brains and special gifts, now to some extent halted. Many Australians have distinguished themselves in many fields outside Australia. Talents are brought to a better market overseas and so we lose, year after year, a high percentage of our ablest and most gifted sons and daughters. This export of brains has kept Australia what she has not so much minded being, a community of the average man. Australians are proud of their ordinariness, of being "one of the blokes", "one of the mob", they distrust brilliance, particularly in the political field. But they reserve the right to be individualists.

There comes the inevitable question: Is there an Australian people? Have we any identity in the world? White history in Australia has been short, but the experience has been intensive, the colonizing material for the most part malleable, distance and isolation have set the new pattern. Isolation made tradition dearer, but it also, in matters of daily life and work, sealed off the new life to breed upon itself. These are matters that can only be touched upon lightly here, food for thought, possible leads, no more.

Most people will agree that there is an Australian people, not just a race of transplanted Englishmen, Scots, and Irish. I am not talking of evolution but of selection; 1788 is still too close for a new people to have evolved. Until the 1930s immigrants were preponderantly of British stock. A new and totally different environment has selected certain traits of character as it has selected certain words. The bush asks other qualities of men than does the English countryside. The pattern of city life in Australia differs, too. It is a matter of climate, of American influence, of greater personal equality, of many things. The squire does not exist in Australia, or if he does he is a curiosity; the ancestral home is as rare. Society is more fluid. The past is negligible, only some six generations Australian-born at the utmost. The origins of population were very mixed, convicts, adventurers in search of gold or of freedom, younger sons, misfits, assisted immigrants, retired army men from India who could not face the northern cold, refugees. ... There is every reason to believe that there has been a reasonable quota of well-born and well-educated men and women among the immigrants, but many of them were torn from their context in life; they began again on their own merits.

Success and money speak more loudly than family. There lingers still from the days of the penal settlement a polite disinclination to probe a fellow-citizen's antecedents, even though it is now generally accepted that convict stock has been largely bred out of the nation or so diluted as to be unimportant. Snobbery exists, but it is often of the inverted type. In a small population there is not the same struggle to preserve identity as there is in a big one. Your Australian is an individualist or, if he is not, he is ashamed.

Of course, Australians have an image of themselves that conforms to the truth as nearly as such conceptions usually do. The typical Australian is from the bush, he is tall and lean, silent, sardonic, and matter-of-factly brave. He is the Anzac, he is the light-horseman of the Wells of Beersheba. Go to the dawn service on Anzac Day and see for yourself. He is also Ned Kelly and one of the boys who lit a bonfire in Trafalgar Square. The ideal includes the picaresque.

The truth is that most Australians live in cities and always have done. Yet it is also true that the average Australian carries the print of great distances on his eyelids and his mind. Even if a window-box is all the earth he owns he is, perhaps sentimentally, aware of the bush, the outback, the back-of-beyond. When he goes abroad he is conscious of his difference and of the size of his country. He has the feeling that in smaller lands he may step over the edge. A certain physical type emerged early. Commissioner Bigge remarked on it in 1819; the nickname for the Australian-born, the "cornstalks", vouches for their superior height.

His speech betrays him. The Australian accent is not a matter of class or of education. It is unscientific to attribute it to climate. It would be truer to attribute it to equality, to the free compulsory education that moulds the majority of children, to the freemasonry of workmates, the lingua franca in particular of a man's world. There is a lot of Cockney in it, a lot of slackness, a widespread desire not to "put on airs". An Australian has as much right to his inflections of speech as a Scot to his. It, too, has a literature.

Vocabulary is a different matter again. There are few words that are of unique Australian origin and even those are usually nicknames, as "billy" for the quart-pot, or "sundowner" for the man who arrives looking for work at knock-off time, knowing that he will get tucker and a shake-down just the same, and be off on the wallaby at sun-up. Vocabulary, when slang is not involved, is a matter of selection rather than of invention. Paddock is as good an English word as field, but it is less lush, a harder, drier word, and so more suitable. We have creeks and waterholes rather than streams and ponds, the countryside is timbered not wooded, a really big estate is a station, from the early days when a hut was the focal point on a vast lease. The words selected are always the tougher ones or those that belittle. "The bush" stands for country as against city. It is a term of rough, secret affection. To use it is not particularly Australian, it is part of the Anglo-Saxon habit of understatement. The general Australian habit of mind and speech is the Anglo-Saxon one emphasized and expressed in a slightly different idiom. Slang is a habit rather than a fashion and, observed closely, it is a compendium of history. It has merited theses and dictionaries. It is part of the pervasive informality and casualness of mind and manner.

An Australian literature is again another matter. There are those who deny its existence, but in doing so they must deny the reality of an Australian nation. It is impossible to transplant either a people or a literature without change. For a hundred years it is safe to say there was no Australian literature, only writing in Australia. Men, however, were gradually beginning to think in terms of their environment. The better their education the more they looked back to the home they had left and the more stubbornly they clung to its traditions of learning and expression. If they were men of small education and many practical problems there was little time for writing and little writing done unless it was in letters home, and even they were difficult and expensive to send in the early days. The eighteenth century was the era of the journal and the diary. Many may have been written, but few were preserved. The "cornstalks", growing up in a rough and ready world, had not much use for such things or much chance, unless their families were successful or well endowed, of schooling. They learnt other things, bushcraft, the handling of horses and sheep, the endless improvisations of a new world. As Sydney acquired a few amenities, men moved farther out into the bush where there were none. Perhaps once a year the bullock-wagons brought out the necessary stores. Brent of Bin Bin, in the novel *Up the Country*, has described this event as if she were an eye-witness. If you are interested, the description is to be found on pages 85-6, but it would be better to read the whole novel. All that could not be brought the laborious miles had to be improvised on the spot with the materials at hand. Children are born creative, but life, by presenting them with so much that is ready-made and ready-thought, robs them of the gift. In Australia adults were forced to be creative or perish. They were eighteenth-century men starting life again almost at its beginning. Not only had the pioneer to work out for himself a way of life to fit the new environment, build his hut or homestead, construct its basic requirements of bunks and tables, but he had to supply his own amusements and satisfy those natural needs that the concert hall, the theatre, broadcasting, and other forms of entertainment, intellectual or otherwise, easily accessible to the city-dweller today, supply so liberally. The campfire or the wayside shanty was the meeting-place where songs were sung and tales told. The tunes had generally come from home, but the words were altered to supplement memory or to meet the circumstances. For instance, the sentimental lyric, "Don't you remember sweet Alice, Ben Bolt?" became:

Oh, don't you remember Black Alice, Sam Holt?
Black Alice, so dusky and dark,
The Warrego gin, with the straw through her nose
And teeth like a Moreton Bay shark. . .[1]

Men were perpetually on the move, overlanding cattle, droving sheep, humping their bluey from job to job, and they carried with them the gossip of the long track. Those that could colour a tale or spin an earthy yarn never lacked an audience. Bushrangers, ghosts, the epic feats of horses and riders, were their subject-matter. Drovers sang, riding round their cattle at night, long-winded droning songs like "The Wild Colonial Boy", to which any number of verses could be added. The cattle were soothed, the drover was kept awake, and the wide dark night was domesticated.

So a folk-lore grew, made up of work songs from the shearing sheds or the drovers' camp (just as sea shanties had so long set the tune of hauling in anchors and other chores of the sea), of stories told when strangers met on the track, works of imagination, feats of the long bow, elaborate and solemn leg-pulls, and now and then genuine reportage, of home-made ballads, impromptu clowning. It was all anonymous and never reached the city, much less print.

All literatures had their origins in folk-lore and they all have followed much the same course: the epic, the *fabulae* (or stories about animals), the ballad, with gossip, more or less creative, as the perpetual camp-follower. This pattern can be traced in Australian folk-lore. An epic is, when it is boiled down, man boasting in the face of overwhelming Nature. A. B. Paterson's "The Man from Snowy River" is an epic in little. Though not in itself original folk-lore, it is a close descendant from it. The bush, with its vastness and its gigantic catastrophes of drought, fire, and flood, is as well calculated to wring from the men pitted against it the epic response as ever were the gods of Greece, but the pioneers were of different stuff, they scaled down their epics and saw through their own boasting with sardonic humour.

In the old world the *fabulae* (Aesop's fables are latter-day examples) often held the idea of animals as totems. To the Australian bushman the dog, the horse, the bullock, were his necessary partners. Of these the bullock had the slave mentality and was productive not so much of stories as of a truly creative line in swearing. Sheep and cattle, the sources of wealth, but not the partners, feature rarely in Australia *fabulae*. For modern *fabulae,* no better examples than Frank Dalby Davison's *Man-Shy* and *Dusty* can be suggested.

A ballad travels more easily than a prose narrative because rhyme is easier to remember, so the yarns took form in verse and travelled the continent, changing and maturing as they went. There is a spirit called aquavit that must travel round the world by sea before it is matured for drinking. So it was with the ballads and stories on the bush tracks.

It was 1888 before any of this treasury of indigenous material found an outlet in print. In that year the *Bulletin* began publication in Sydney. Its policy was revolutionary. It catered, not for polite society, but for readers in the bush, and it opened its columns to them. It tapped a world that had been ignored by the pompous journalism of the day. Men who had never written publicly before were encouraged to send in their verses, their short stories, their comments, their individual clippings from the wonder book of Australia, and they were paid for whatever was accepted. The paper became a club with a wide-flung membership. It travelled the bush tracks and was passed from man to man like the folk-lore whose remnants it was gathering up and giving shape. The ballads and stories published in the *Bulletin* and signed with their authors' names were next of kin to the anonymous folk-lore from which they sprang, the first literary generation of something that had arisen spontaneously from the earth and the new patterns men had drawn on it. The *Bulletin* fostered not only native material, but the vernacular. In its way this was as important a step as when Dante wrote his *Divine Comedy* in Italian instead of Latin. Needless to say the *Bulletin* (traditionally pronounced *Bulleteen*) was not admitted to genteel homes.

Whilst opening doors the *Bulletin* also imposed restrictions, the main one that of brevity. A yarn is by nature long-winded; when it was transformed into a *Bulletin* short story it became brief and compact. In the first twenty years of the journal's existence, with men like Henry Lawson and Ted Dyson writing for it, a continuing tradition was laid down for the short story. A glance at the series of short-story anthologies published under the title of *Coast to Coast* will show that it still holds. The *Bulletin* sponsored a literature of the people which many years later was rediscovered under the uninviting title of proletarian literature.

The novel developed slowly in Australia. It required a more sustained effort. There were difficulties of publication and economic snags. Tom Collins's enormous novel from which *Such is Life* and *Rigby's Romance* were carved and Steele Rudd's *On Our Selection* are of the same vintage and ancestry as the first-generation stories and ballads brought out by the *Bulletin,* but they, particularly Collins, have kept their discursiveness. The trailing discursiveness of the one, the down-to-earth humour of the other, can still be traced in present-day fiction.

It is not necessary to prove that Australia has produced a Shakespeare, a Milton, or a George Bernard Shaw to establish her claim to an individual and truly indigenous literature. It is not a list of names that matters, the significant thing is the literature as a whole, many hands contributing to the expression of a national character and a national way of life.

I have spoken of literature rather than of painting or of any of the other arts, because I know more about it. I know, too, that early paintings of the Australian scene, such as you may see in the Mitchell and Dixson Galleries, swing between a grim brownness and a homesick effort to copy England. It took many years for alien eyes to see and transmit to canvas the secret charm of the Australian landscape. The problem of the Australian artist, Norman Lindsay has said, is the problem of painting light. It is significant that until recently landscape painting has dominated Australian art.

There is an Australian and he has found his tongue. Go to England and you will feel that though you have come "home" you are yet different; your roots have been fed in a different earth and for the first time you will hear your own speech.

For about a hundred and fifty years Australia had the protection of isolation to grow up as she would, to make her own mistakes, to create something that cannot perhaps be labelled either good or bad, but was the civilization she deserved. Space and distance have tempered a small people. Environment and tradition have worked upon them. A new beginning was made in the eighteenth century, the Age of Reason, and a history has been worked out from scratch in the full gaze of the world, had it cared to look. An evolution has been documented; prehistory itself has been caught at work.

History is the study of man in all his activities and man is the product of his history.

REFERENCE NOTES

1 Version in *Old Bush Songs* (ed. A. B. Paterson).

BIBLIOGRAPHY

This bibliography makes no claim to be definitive. It is a list of books, journals and other authorities which will, I hope, extend the scope of this book and lead interested readers to further material, which, in its turn, will open up new vistas.

GENERAL

PRIMARY SOURCES

1. Records

Historical Records of Australia, ed. F. Watson.

Series I, vols i-xxvi (1788-1848). These volumes contain dispatches and their enclosures. Series I is mainly concerned with New South Wales.

Series III, vols i-vi (1803-30). This series covers the history, still in the form of dispatches, of Tasmania, the Northern Territory, and Western Australia in their early days.

Series IV, vol. i (1786-1827). Legal aspects.

There is reason to hope that these series will be continued and Series II compiled.

Historical Records of New South Wales. Various editors.

Vols i-vii (1762-1811). Dispatches and other papers.

2. Parliamentary Papers

Commonwealth Parliamentary Papers 1901-.

New South Wales:

(a) Votes and proceedings of the Legislative Council, 1824-.

(b) Votes and proceedings of the Legislative Assembly, 1856-.

Queensland:

(a) Votes and proceedings of Parliament, 1860-.

(b) Legislative Council journals, 1860-1922.

South Australia:

Proceedings of Parliament, 1854-.

Tasmania:

(a) Votes and proceedings of the Legislative Council, 1849-.

(b) Votes and proceedings of the Legislative Assembly, 1856-.

Victoria:

(a) Votes and proceedings of the Legislative Council, 1851-.

(b) Votes and proceedings of the Legislative Assembly, 1856-.

Western Australia:

Proceedings of Parliament and papers, 1890-.

Parliamentary Debates:

Commonwealth, 1901-.

New South Wales, 1879-.

Queensland, 1864-.

South Australia, 1859-.
Victoria, 1856-.
Western Australia, 1876-.

3. Statutes

The Commonwealth and each State publish annual volumes of Statutes, for example, *Statutes of New South Wales, Public and Private, 1856-.* Compilations, indexes, etc., can be traced through Public Library or Mitchell Library catalogues, for example: Bignold, H. B., *Imperial Statutes in Force in New South Wales* (3 vols); Bignold, H. B., *General Index to the Statutes of New South Wales*, 1926; Horwitz, L., *ed.*, *Victorian Statutes: the Public Acts of Victoria arranged in alphabetical order with notes and indexes.*

4. Government Gazettes

New South Wales, 1882-.
Queensland, 1860-.
South Australia, 1841-.
Tasmania, 1907-.
Victoria, 1851-.
Western Australia, 1836-.

5. Almanacs and Year Books

The Almanac of Australia and Official Record, published by the Australian Mutual Provident Society. 1882.

Official Directory and Almanac of Australia, ed. E. Greville. 1883.

The Official Directory and Year Book of Australia, ed. E. Greville and others. 1884-1917.

Official Year Book of the Commonwealth of Australia. 1908.

Where Year Books of the States are not published or have ceased publication the same material may be found under the sub-heading of "Statistics" in any general reference library.

6. Government Publications

These, far too numerous to list, supply first-hand, specialized information on a great variety of subjects and may easily be tracked down by the intelligent student in the catalogue of any general reference library.

7. Source Books

Australian National University, Research School of Social Sciences, Department of History, *Historical Sources and Techniques.* 1952.

Clark, C. M. H., *Select Documents in Australian History, 1788-1900.* 2 vols. 1950-5.

Clark, C. M. H., *Sources of Australian History.* 1957. ("A collection illustrating political and social history from the earliest discoveries to the Treaty of Versailles.")

Commonwealth Parliament Library Committee, *Beginnings of Government in Australia* (facsimiles).

Ingleton, G. C., *ed.*, *True Patriots All.* 1952. (Reprints and facsimiles of broadsides, etc., with a picaresque slant.)

Swinburne, G. H., *ed.*, *A Source Book of Australian History.* 1919. (Covers the period from Tasman's Voyages to Gallipoli.)

SECONDARY SOURCES

Atkinson, M., *ed., Australia: Economic and Political Studies*. 1920.
Bateson, T., *Short History of Australia*. 1911.
Cambridge History of the British Empire, vol. vii (*Australasia*). 1933.
Crawford, R. M., *Australia*. 1952.
Fitzpatrick, B. C., *The Australian Commonwealth: a Picture of the Community, 1901-1955*. 1956.
Fitzpatrick, B. C., *The Australian People, 1788-1945*. 1946.
Fitzpatrick, B. C., *The British Empire in Australia: an Economic History, 1834-1939*. 1941.
Greenwood, G., *ed., Australia: a Social and Political History*. 1955. (Extensive bibliography.)
Hancock, W. K., *Australia*. 1930.
Shann, E. O. G., *An Economic History of Australia*. 1930.
Shaw, A. G. L., *The Economic Development of Australia*. 1944.
Shaw, A. G. L., *The Story of Australia*. 1955.
Wood, F. L. W., *A Concise History of Australia*. 1935.
Wood, G. L., *ed., Australia: its Resources and Development*. 1947.

BOOKS OF GENERAL INTEREST
(a brief and by no means complete list)

Bartley, N., *Australian Pioneers and Reminiscences*. 1896.
Bean, C. E. W., *The Dreadnought of the Darling*. 1911.
Bedford, R., *Think of Stephen*. 1954. (Sir Alfred Stephen C.J. and family.)
Bennett, M., *Christison of Lammermoor*. 1927.
Blakeley, F., *Hard Liberty*. 1938.
Bonwick, J., *Curious Facts of Old Colonial Days*. 1870.
Boyd, R., *Australia's Home, its Origins, Builders and Occupiers*. 1952.
Forbes, Lady, *Sydney Society in Crown Colony Days*. 1914.
Grattan, C. H., *Introducing Australia*. 1942.
Harris, A., *Settlers and Convicts*. 1847.
Herman, M., *Early Australian Architects and Their Work*. 1954.
Joyce, A., *A Homestead History*. 1942.
Kevin, J. C. G., *ed., Some Australians Take Stock*. 1939.
McCrae, H. R., *ed., Georgina's Journal*. 1934.
McGuire, D. P., *Australian Journey*. 1939.
McGuire, D. P., *Inns of Australia*. 1952.
Moore, W., *The Story of Australian Art*. 2 vols. 1934.
Palmer, V., *National Portraits*. 1940.
Ratcliffe, F., *Flying Fox and Drifting Sand*. 1938.
Ryan, J. T., *Reminiscences of Australia*. 1894.
Scott, G., *Sydney's Highways of History*. 1958.
Taylor, T. G., *Australia: a Study of Warm Environments and their Effect on British Settlement*. Revised ed., 1955.
Taylor, T. G., *Australia in its Physiographic and Economic Aspects*. 1928.
Wilson, W. Hardy, *Cowpasture Road*. 1920.
Wilson, W. Hardy, *Old Colonial Architecture in New South Wales and Tasmania*. 1924.

PERIODICALS

Art in Australia, ed., S. Ure Smith. 1916-42.

Economic Record: the Journal of the Economic Society of Australia and New Zealand, vol. i (1925)-.
Historical Studies, Australia and New Zealand, vol. i (1940)-.
Royal Australian Historical Society, Journal and Proceedings, vol. i (1901)-. (These are published in Sydney. There are bodies similar to the R.A.H.S. in other States whose publications are also invaluable to the student of Australian history.)

BIBLIOGRAPHIES

The Catalogue of the Mitchell Library, Sydney.
Borchardt, D. H., *Checklist of Royal Commissions, Select Committees of Parliament and Boards of Inquiry,* Pt. I, Commonwealth of Australia 1900-1950. 1958.
Ferguson, J. A., *Bibliography of Australia*, vols i-iii (1784-1845).
(Practically all scholarly works on historical subjects carry bibliographies or notes on source material.)

CHRONOLOGIES

Bertie, C. H., *Days of Moment in Australia, 1788-1938*. 1937.
Cramp, K. R., *Calendar of Events in Australian History*. 1933.
Mackaness, G., *ed.*, *Chronology of Momentous Events in Australian History (1788-1846)*. 1952.
Chronologies may also be found in:
Official Year Book of the Commonwealth of Australia.
The Australian Encyclopaedia, 1st edition. 1925.
Coghlan, T. A., and Ewing, T. T., *Progress of Australasia in the 19th Century*. 1903.

ENCYCLOPAEDIAS

The Australian Encyclopaedia, 1st ed., 2 vols, 1925-7; 2nd ed., 10 vols, 1958.

CHAPTER BIBLIOGRAPHIES

These supplement the general bibliography. They do not as a rule include references to articles in periodicals.

CHAPTER I. BACKGROUND

The content of this chapter is general and any necessary references are contained in the text.

CHAPTER II. DISCOVERY

The Hakluyt Society has reprinted the logs and journals of most of the important voyages of discovery in the Pacific.

Banks's Journal. (MS. in the possession of the Mitchell Library.)
Beaglehole, J. C., *Exploration of the Pacific*. 1934.
Besant, W., *Captain Cook*. 1890.
Campbell, G., *Captain James Cook, R.N., F.R.S.* 1936.
Carrington, H., *Life of Captain Cook*. 1939.
Collingridge, G. A., *Discovery of Australia*. 1895.

Cook's Journal and Log. (MSS. in the possession of the Mitchell Library. Extracts from the log may be consulted in *Historical Records of New South Wales*, vol. i, pt. 1.)
Dalrymple, A., *Discoveries Made in the Pacific Previous to 1764.* 3 vols. 1767.
Dalrymple, A., *Historical Collection of the Several Voyages and Discoveries in the South Pacific.* 2 vols. 1770-1.
Dampier, W., *Voyages.* (These can be consulted in a number of editions from 1697 onwards.)
Hawkesworth, J., *An Account of the Voyages Undertaken by order of His Present Majesty for making Discoveries in the Southern Hemisphere and successively performed by Commodore Byron, Captain Wallis, Captain Carteret and Captain Cook. . . .* 1773.
Heeres, J. E., *Part Borne by the Dutch in the Discovery of Australia, 1606-1765.* 1899.
Heeres, J. E., *ed., Abel Janszoon Tasman's Journal of his Discovery of Van Diemen's Land in 1643, with documents relating to his exploration of Australia in 1644. . . .* 1898.
Hicks, Z., *Endeavour's* Journal, commencing 27th May 1768 and ending 19th July 1769. (Photostat in Mitchell Library.)
Kingston, W. H. G., *Captain Cook, his Life, Voyages and Discoveries.* 1904.
Kitson, J., *Captain James Cook.* 1907.
Lloyd, C., *Captain Cook.* 1952.
Mackaness, G., *Sir Joseph Banks.* 1936.
Maiden, J. H., *Sir Joseph Banks, the Father of Australia.* 1909.
Pinkerton, J., *General Collection of the Best and Most Interesting Voyages and Travels. . . .* 17 vols. 1808-14.
Smith, E., *The Life of Sir Joseph Banks.* 1911.
Vandercook, J. W., *Great Sailor.* 1951.
Wilson, Robert, *Voyages of Discoveries Round the World.* 3 vols. 1806.
Wood, G. A., *Discovery of Australia.* 1922.
Wood, G. A., *Voyage of the Endeavour.* 1926.

Chapter iii. BEGINNINGS

Auckland, Lord, *Discourse on Banishment.* 1787.
Bentham, J., *Panopticon.* 3 vols. 1791.
Bentham, J., *Rationale of Punishment.* 1830.
Howard, J., *State of the Prisons in England and Wales.* 4th ed., 1792.
O'Brien, E., *The Foundation of Australia 1786-1800.* 1950. (With an exhaustive bibliography.)
Rutter, O., *ed., The First Fleet: the Record of the Foundation of Australia from its Conception to the Settlement at Sydney Cove. . . .* 1937.
Wood, G. A., "The Plan of a Colony in New South Wales", *J. Roy. Aust. Hist. Soc.,* vol. vi (1920), pp. 36-68.

Chapter iv. VOYAGE AND LANDFALL

Barrington, G., *A Voyage to New South Wales. . . .* 1795.
Bowes, Surgeon, Journal of a Voyage from Portsmouth to New South Wales and China in *Lady Penrhyn.* (MS. in the possession of the Mitchell Library.)
Bradley, W., Journal. (MS. in the possession of the Mitchell Library.)
Clark, R., Journal. (MS. in the possession of the Mitchell Library.)

Easty, J., Diary 1787-93. (MS. in the Dixson Collection, Public Library of N.S.W.)

King, P. G., Journal. (MS. in the possession of the Mitchell Library. Also printed in *Hist. Rec. N.S.W.*, vol. ii, appendix pp. 513-660.)

Scott, J., Remarks on a Voyage to Botany Bay, 1787. . . . (MS. in the Dixson Collection, Public Library of N.S.W.)

Spain, Edward, Journal. (MS. in the possession of the Mitchell Library.)

Tench, W., *Narrative of the Expedition to Botany Bay*. 1789.

Voyage of Governor Phillip to Botany Bay . . . compiled from authentic papers which have been obtained from Several Departments. To which are added the Journals of Lieutenants Shortland, Watts, Ball and Captain Marshall. 1796.

White, H. R., *First Fleet Index*.

White, J., *Journal of a Voyage to New South Wales. . . .* 1790.

Chapter v. TAKING SHAPE

Barrington, G., *The History of New South Wales. . .* 1802. Rev. ed., 1810.

Bond, G., *A Brief Account of the Colony of Port Jackson*. 1803.

Bonwick, J., *First Twenty Years of Australia*. 1882.

Collins, D., *Account of the English Colony in New South Wales, 1798-1802*.

Eldershaw, M. Barnard, *Phillip of Australia*. 1938.

Hunter, J., *Historical Journal of the Transactions at Port Jackson and Norfolk Island. . . .* 1793.

Mackaness, G., *Admiral Arthur Phillip: Founder of New South Wales 1738-1814*. 1937.

Milford, G. D., *Governor Phillip and the Early Settlement of New South Wales*. 1935.

Parker, M. A., *Voyage Round the World in the Gorgon*. 1795.

Chapter vi. THE CORPS AND THE GOVERNORS

Bassett, M., *Governor's Lady: Mrs Philip Gidley King*. 1940.

Evatt, H. V., *Rum Rebellion*. 1938.

Gibbons, P. C., "Administration of Governor Hunter", *J. Roy. Aust. Hist. Soc.*, vol. xxvi (1940), pp. 403-17.

Hill, R. M., "Short History of the New South Wales Corps, 1789-1818", *J. Soc. Army Hist. Res.*, Autumn, 1934, pp. 135-40.

Mackaness, G., *Life of Vice-Admiral Bligh*. 2 vols. 1931.

Piper Papers. 3 vols. (MSS. in the possession of the Mitchell Library.)

Watson, F., "Governor Bligh", *Hist. Rec. Aust.*, ser. I, vol. vi, Introduction.

Watson, F., "Governor Hunter", *Hist. Rec. Aust.*, ser. I, vol. ii, Introduction.

Watson, F., "Governor King", *Hist. Rec. Aust.*, ser. I, vol. iii, Introduction.

Wood, G. A., "Governor Hunter", *J. Roy. Aust. Hist. Soc.*, vol. xiv (1928), pp. 344-62.

Chapter vii. MACQUARIE: "JAIL INTO COLONY"

Abbott, J. H. M., *The Macquarie Book*. 1921.

Antill, H. C., *Early History of New South Wales: Two Old Journals*. 1914.

Barnard, M. F., *Macquarie's World*. 1941.

Bigge, J. T., *Report of the Commissioner of Inquiry into the State of the Colony of New South Wales*. 1823.

Cunningham, P., *Two Years in New South Wales*. 1927.
Eldershaw, M. Barnard, *The Life and Times of Captain John Piper*. Limited Editions Society, 1939.
Lachlan Macquarie, Governor of New South Wales. Journals of his Tours in New South Wales and Van Diemen's Land, 1810-1822. Published by the Trustees of the Public Library of New South Wales.
Macquarie Papers. (MSS. in the possession of the Mitchell Library.)
Mann, D. D., *The Present Picture of New South Wales*. 1811.
O'Hara, J., *The History of New South Wales*. 1817.
Phillips, M., *A Colonial Autocracy: New South Wales under Governor Macquarie, 1810-1821*. 1909.
Slater, J., *A Description of Sydney, Parramatta, Newcastle, etc. . . . in New South Wales with some account of the manners and employment of the convicts*. 1819.
Wentworth, W. C., *A Statistical, Historical and Political Description of the Colony of New South Wales and its dependent settlements in Van Diemen's Land*. 1819.

Chapter viii. THE PASTORAL AGE

Alexander, F., *Moving Frontiers*. 1943.
Bean, C. E. W., *On the Wool Track*. 1910.
Collier, J., *Pastoral Age in Australasia*. 1911.
Harris, A., *Settlers and Convicts*. 1847.
Hobler Papers. (MSS. in the possession of the Mitchell Library.)
Joyce, A., *A Homestead History*. 1942.
Macarthur-Onslow, S., *Some Early Records of the Macarthurs of Camden*. 1914.
Petrie, C. C., *Tom Petrie's Reminiscences*. 1904.
Ranken, G., *The Squatting System of Australia*. 1875.
Roberts, S. H., *The Squatting Age in Australia, 1835-1847*. 1935.
Robertson, W. A. N., "Milestones in the Pastoral Age of Australia", *Aust. & N.Z. Assoc. Adv. Sci.*, Rept 21, 1932.
Satge, O. de, *Pages from the Journal of a Queensland Squatter*. 1901.
Suttor, H. M., *Australian Milestones*. 2 vols. 1925.
Therry, R., *Reminiscences of Thirty Years Residence in New South Wales and Victoria*. 1863.

Chapter ix. VOYAGE IN THE BUSH

Bland, W., *Journey of Discovery to Port Phillip, New South Wales, by Messrs W. H. Hovell and Hamilton Hume*. 1831.
Hovell, W. H., Journal, *J. Roy. Aust. Hist. Soc.*, vol. vii (1921), pp. 307-78.
Hume, Hamilton, *A Brief Statement of Facts in Connection with an Overland Expedition from Lake George to Port Phillip in 1824*. 1st ed., 1853. 2nd ed., 1873.

Chapter x. COLONIZATION, SCIENTIFIC AND OTHERWISE

Mills, R. C., *Colonization of Australia, 1829-1842*. 1915.
Sidney, S., *The Three Colonies of Australia*. 1852.
Wakefield, E. G., *The Art of Colonization*. 1849.

NORFOLK ISLAND

Historical Records of Australia, ser. I.
King, P. G., Journal.
Maconochie, A., *Criminal Statistics and Movement of the Bond Population of Norfolk Island.* 1846.
Spruson, J. J., *Norfolk Island: Outline of its History from 1788-1884.* 1885.

TASMANIA

Barrett, W. R., *History of Tasmania to the Death of Lieutenant-Governor Collins in 1810.* 1936.
Bridges, R., *That Yesterday was Home.* 1948.
Fitzpatrick, K., *Sir John Franklin in Tasmania, 1837-43.* 1949.
Giblin, R. W., *The Early History of Tasmania.* 2 vols. 1928-9.
Hartwell, R. M., *Economic Development of Van Diemen's Land, 1820-1850.* 1954.
Historical Records of Australia, ser. III, vols i-v.
Melville, H., *History of the Island of Van Diemen's Land, 1824-1835.* 1835.
West, J., *The History of Tasmania.* 2 vols. 1852.
Widowson, H., *Present State of Van Diemen's Land.* 1829.

VICTORIA

Bassett, M., *The Hentys, an Australian Colonial Tapestry.* 1954.
Bridges, R., *One Hundred Years.* 1934.
Historical Records of Australia, ser. III, vol. i.
Port Phillip Papers. (MSS. in the possession of the Mitchell Library.)
Turner, H. G., *History of the Colony of Victoria 1797-1900.* 2 vols. 1904.
Ussher, K., *Hail Victoria.* 1934.
Victoria, the First Century: an Historical Survey Compiled by the Historical Sub-committee of the Centenary Celebrations Council. 1934.

QUEENSLAND

Coote, W., *History of the Colony of Queensland.* 1882.
Craig, W. W., *Moreton Bay Settlement: or Queensland Before Separation, 1770-1859.* 1925.
Public Record Office (Great Britain), Index and digest of Record Office documents relative to Moreton Bay for the years 1822 to 1849 inclusive.
Russell, H. S., *The Genesis of Queensland.* 1888.

NORTHERN TERRITORY

Conigrave, C. P., *North Australia.* 1936.
Hill, E., *The Territory.* 1951.
Historical Records of Australia, ser. III, vol. v.
Howard, D., "English Activities on the North Coast of Australia", *Roy. Geog. Soc. Australasia, S. Aust. Br., Proc.,* vol. xxxiii (1931-2).

WESTERN AUSTRALIA

Battye, J. S., *Western Australia: a History from its Discovery to the Inauguration of the Commonwealth* (with chronology). 1924.
Bryan, C. P., *ed., Swan River Booklets,* nos 1-12. 1938-40(?).
Buckton, T. J., *Western Australia.* 1840.
Bunbury, H. W. St. P., *ed., Early days in Western Australia: Letters and Journals of Lieutenant H. W. Bunbury.* 1930.
Calvert, A. F., *Western Australia, its History and Progress.* 1894.

Colebatch, H. P., *Story of a Hundred Years, Western Australia, 1829-1929.* 1929.
Hasluck, A., *Portrait with Background.* 1955.
Irwin, F. C., *The State and Position of Western Australia.* 1835.
Kimberley, W. B., *ed., History of Western Australia.* 1897.
Knight, W. H., *Western Australia.* 1870.
Mennell, P., *Coming Colony.* 1892.
Smart, W. C., *Mandurah and Pinjarrah: History of Thomas Peel and the Peel Estates, 1829-1865.* 1956.
Uren, M. J. L., *Land Looking West.* 1948.

SOUTH AUSTRALIA

Capper, H., *South Australia.* 1837.
Forster, A., *South Australia.* 1866.
Garnett, R., *Edward Gibbon Wakefield.* 1897.
Henderson, G. C., *Sir George Grey.* 1907.
Hodder, E., *History of South Australia.* 2 vols. 1893.
Price, A. G., *The Foundation and Settlement of South Australia, 1829-45.* 1934.
Sinnett, F., *An Account of the Colony of South Australia.* 1862.
Torrens, R., *Colonization of South Australia.* 1835.
Torrens, R., *Systematic Colonization.* 1849.
Trollope, A., *South Australia and Western Australia.* 1875.
Wakefield, E. G., *A Letter from Sydney.* 1829.
Wakefield, E. G., Eleven Letters by P. in the *Spectator*, 1830-1.
Wakefield, E. G., *New British Province of South Australia.* 1834.
Wakefield, E. G., *Outline of a Plan of a Proposed Colony to be Founded on the South Coast of Australia.* 1834.

CHAPTER XI. THE SYSTEM

Admiralty, Copies of instructions to the surgeons, superintendents, and the masters of convict vessels. 1834.
Adventures of Ralph Rashleigh; or, The Life of an Exile, 1825-1844. (Anon.) 1929.
Becke, L., *Old Convict days.* 1899.
Browning, C. A. (Naval Surgeon), *England's Exiles.* 1842.
Gibbings, R., *John Graham, Convict, 1824.* 1956.
Hill, M. D., *Our Convict System, Past and Present. c.* 1861.
House of Commons, Select Committee on Transportation, Report. 1812. (See also Report by Sir W. Molesworth. 1831.)
Maconochie, A., *General Views Regarding the Social System of Convict Management.* 1839.
Maconochie, A., *On the Management of Transported Criminals.* 1843.
Merivale, H., *Lectures on Colonization and Colonies.* 1861.
Reid, W. S. Hill-, *John Grant's Journey: a Convict Story, 1803-1811.* 1957.
Ullathorne, W. B., *The Horrors of Transportation Briefly Unfolded to the People.* 1835.
Ullathorne, W. B., *On the Management of Criminals.* 1866.
"Warung, Price", *Tales of the Convict System.* 1892.

CHAPTER XII. GOLD

Anderson, R. S., *Australian Gold Fields: their Discovery, Progress and Prospects.* 1853. *Ed.* G. Mackaness, 1956.

Bligh, A. C. V., *The Golden Quest: the Roaring days of Western Australia's Gold Rushes. . . .* 1938.
Bonwick, J., *Notes of a Gold Digger.* 1852.
Carboni, Raffaello, *The Eureka Stockade.* (Reprinted in Dolphin Books 1941.)
Hall, W., *Practical Experience at the Diggings of the Gold Fields of Victoria.* 1852.
Sherer, J., *Life and Adventures of a Gold Digger.* 1855.
Uren, M., *Glint of Gold.* 1948.
Wathen, G. H., *The Golden Colony, or, Victoria in 1854.* 1855.

Chapter xiii. LAND

Most of the material for this chapter is to be found in official documents and general works. See also:

Acocks, W. G., *The Settlers' Synopsis of the Land Laws of New South Wales.* 1901.
Chanter, J. M., *The Land Laws of New South Wales: an Address.*
Epps, W., *Land Systems of Australasia.* 1894.
Forster, R. S., *Free Trade in Land not Free Land.* 1882.
George, Henry, *The Land for the People: an Address.* 1889.
George, Henry, *The Land Question, What it Is and How it Can be Settled.* 1881.
Hill, A. F., *The Land and Wealth of New South Wales.* 1894.
Jenks, W., *Land Systems of Australia.* 1894.
Roberts, S. H., *History of Australian Land Settlement, 1788-1920.* 1924. (With bibliography.)
Robertson, Sir J., *The Land Laws: a Speech.* 1867.
Russell, A., *William James Farrer.* 1949.
Spence, J. C., and others, *Land Question.* 1892-6.
United Nations Food and Agriculture Organization, *Bibliography on Land Tenure,* pp. 60-2.
Wadham, S., *The Land and the Nation.* 1943.
Wadham, S., and Wood, G. L., *Land Utilization in Australia.* 1950.

Chapter xiv. THE ROAD TO RESPONSIBILITY

Bland, F. A., *Government in Australia: Selected Readings.* 1944.
Coghlan, T. A., and Ewing, T. T., *Progress of Australasia in the Nineteenth Century.* 1913.
Cramp, K. R., "A Struggle for a Constitution: New South Wales 1848-53", *J. Aust. Hist. Soc.,* vol. iii (1913), pp. 125-30.
Jenks, E., *The Government of Victoria, Australia.* 1891.
Kirwan, Sir J. W., *A Hundred Years of the Legislative Council of Western Australia, 1832-1932.* 1932.
Lang, Rev. J. D., *The Coming Event: or, Freedom and Independence for the Seven United Provinces of Australia.* 1870.
Lowe, Robert, *Life and Letters of the Right Honourable Robert Lowe, Viscount Sherbrooke. . . .* 2 vols. 1893.
Melbourne, A. C. V., *Early Constitutional Development in Australia, 1788-1856.* 1934.
Parkes, Sir H., *Fifty Years in the Making of Australian History.* 1892.
Watson, F., *The Beginnings of Government in Australia.* 1913.

CHAPTER XV. THE LAW AND THE PURSE

The main source of information is in the *Historical Records of Australia*, Series IV. See also:

THE LAW

Buller, C., *Responsible Government for the Colonies*. 1840.
Clark, A. I., *Studies in Australian Constitutional Law*. 1901.
Currey, C. H., *The First Three Chief Justices of the Supreme Court of New South Wales*. 1935.
Evatt, H. V., "The Legal Foundations of New South Wales", *Aust. Law J.*, Feb. 1938.
Forbes, G., *Free Institutions of New South Wales*. 1914.
Townsley, W. A., *The Struggle for Self-Government in Victoria* 2 vols. 1904.

THE PURSE

Arndt, H. W., *Australian Trading Banks*. 1957.
Benton, J. W., *Monetary Problems and Banking*. 1934.
Butlin, S. J., *Foundations of the Australian Monetary System, 1788-1851*. 1953.
Copland, D. B., *What Have the Banks Done?* 1931.
Copland, D. B., and Janes, C. V., *Cross Currents of Australian Finance*. 1936.
Evans, G., *Bank Credit and Profit*. 1935.
Giblin, L. F., *The Growth of a Central Bank*. 1951.
Gifford, J. L. K., and Wood, V., *Australian Banking*. 1947.
Griffiths, N., *A History of the Government Savings Bank of N.S.W.* 1936.
Institute of Public Affairs, New South Wales, *Money and Banking in Australia*. 1945.
MacKay, A., *The Australian Banking and Credit System*. 1931.
Mills, R. C., and Walker, E. R., *Money*. 13th ed., 1952.
Royal Commission on Monetary and Banking Systems in Australia, *Report*. 1937.
Rural Bank of N.S.W., *A Brief History of Australian Banking*. 1936.
Teare, H. E., *Australian Banking, Currency and Exchange*. 1928.
The Financial Returns of the Colony of New South Wales to the Colonial Office may be consulted in manuscript in the Mitchell Library.

TRADE AND COMMERCE

Cusack, D., "Mary Reibey and her Times", *The Peaceful Army, ed.* F. S. P. Eldershaw. 1938.
Dakin, W. J., *Whalemen Adventurers*. 1934.
Forde, J. M., "Genesis of Commerce in Australia", *J. Aust. Hist. Soc.*, vol. in (1917), pp. 559-92.
Heaton, H., *Modern Economic History with Special Reference to Australia*. 1921.
Houison, J. K. S., "Robert Campbell of the Wharf", *J. Roy. Aust. Hist. Soc.*, vol. xxiii (1937), pp. 1-28.
Jose, A. W., *Builders and Pioneers of Australia*. 1928.
Rowland, E. C., "Simeon Lord, a Merchant Prince of Botany Bay", *J. Roy. Aust. Hist. Soc.*, vol. xxx (1944), pp. 157-95.

CHAPTER XVI. THE NINETIES

Atkinson, M., and others, *Trade Unionism in Australia*. 1915.
Bedford, R., *The Story of Mateship*. 1936.
Bellamy, E., *Looking Backward*.

Clark, V. S., *The Labour Movement in Australia.* 1907.
Coghlan, Sir T. A., *Seven Colonies of Australasia.* 11 vols. 1890-1904.
Coghlan, Sir T. A., and Ewing, T. T., *Progress of Australasia in the Nineteenth Century.* 1903.
Collis, E. H., *Lost Years.* 1945.
FitzGerald, J., *The Rise of the Australian Labor Party.* 1915.
Fitzpatrick, B. C., *A Short History of the Australian Labour Movement.* 1940.
Harris, H. L., "Financial Crisis of 1893 in New South Wales", *J. Roy. Aust. Hist. Soc.,* vol. xiii (1927), pp. 305-43.
Haslam, J., *A Glimpse of Australian Life.* 1890.
Hughes, W. M., *Crusts and Crusades.* 1947.
Melbourne Trades Hall Council, Committee of Finance and Control, *The Great Maritime Strike of 1890.* 1891.
Palmer, V., *The Legend of the Nineties.* 1954.
Peel, A. G. V., *Australian Crisis of 1894.* 1894.
Pratt, A., *David Syme: The Father of Protection in Australia.* 1908.
Roberts, R., *The Depression, its Cause and Remedy. . . .* 189-.
Ross, Lloyd, *William Lane and the Australian Labour Movement.* 1937.
Sinclair, W. H., *Economic Recovery of Victoria, 1894-9.* 1956.

Chapter xvii. FEDERATION: "ONE PEOPLE, ONE DESTINY"

Australasian Federal Convention, Official Record of Debates. Sydney, 1897.
Australasian Federal Convention, Record of the Debates. 2 vols. Melbourne, 1898.
Australasian National Convention, Official Report of the Debates. Adelaide, 1897.
Barton, E., Australian Federation, Miscellaneous Papers.
Clark, A. I., *Federal Financial Problem and its Solution.* 1900.
Cockburn, J. A., *Australian Federation.* 1901.
Cramp, K. R., *The State and Federal Constitutions of Australia.* 1913.
Deakin, A., *The Federal Story, 1880-1900.* 1944.
Evatt, H. V., *The King and his Dominion Governors.* 1936.
Evatt, H. V., *Liberalism in Australia: an Historical Sketch of Australian Politics.* 1918.
Griffith, Sir S. W., *Notes on Australian Federation.* 1896.
Hall, H. L., *Victoria's Part in the Australian Federation Movement, 1849-1900.* 1931.
Higgins, H. B., *Essays and Addresses on the Australian Commonwealth Bill.* 1900.
Hunt, E. M., *American Precedents and our Constitutional System.* 1939.
Kerr, D., *Law of the Australian Constitution. . . .* 1925.
Parkes, Sir H., *The Federal Government of Australia: Speeches Delivered on Various Occasions, 1889-May 1890.* 1890.
Sawer, G., *The Commonwealth Government.*
Turner, H. G., *The First Decade of the Australian Commonwealth.* 1911.
Whyte, W. F., *ed., The Australian Parliamentary Handbook.* 1952.
Wynes, W. A., *Legislative, Executive and Judicial Powers in Australia.* 2nd ed., 1958.

Tariffs

Allin, C. D., *Federal Aspects of Preferential Trade in the British Empire.* 1918.
Marcus and Andrew, *Tabulated Tariffs of the Australasian Colonies.* 1893.

DEFENCE

Lang, Rev. J. D., *How to Defend the Colony*. 1860.
Reid, Sir G., *Naval and Military Defence of Australia*. 1908.
Lee, J. E., *Duntroon, the Royal Military College of Australia, 1911-1946*. 1952.
McGuire, D. P., *The Royal Australian Navy*. 1948.

WHITE AUSTRALIA POLICY

Pottinger, E., *Asiatic Problems Affecting Australia*. 1928.
Willard, M., *History of the White Australia Policy*. 1923.

CHAPTER XVIII. WAR

The Anzac Book. 1916.
Bean, C. E. W., *Anzac to Amiens*. 1946.
Bean, C. E. W., *Official History of Australia in the War of 1914-1918*. 12 vols. 1921-38.
Davison, F. D., *Wells of Beersheba*. 1933.
Fitzpatrick, W., *Repatriation of the Soldier. . . .* 1917.
Mann, L., *Flesh in Armour*. 1932. (A novel.)
Masefield, J., *Gallipoli*. 1916.
Turner, C., *Land Settlement for Ex-Service Men in the Overseas Dominions*, pp. 32-62. 1920.

CHAPTER XIX. DEPRESSION AND SOCIAL EXPERIMENT

Bailey, K. H., *Statute of Westminster*. 1931.
Brigden, J. B., and others, *The Australian Tariff*. 1929.
Copland, D. B., *Australia in the World Crisis, 1929-33*. 1934.
Copland, D. B., *The Australian Economy*. 1931.
Copland, D. B., *Facts and Fallacies of Douglas Credit. . . .* 1932.
Copland, D. B., *Inflation and Expansion*. 1951.
Copland, D. B., and Janes, C. V., *ed.*, *The Battle of the Plans and the Australian Price Structure*. 1932.
Duncan, W. G. K., *ed.*, *Marketing Australia's Primary Products*. 1937.
Duncan, W. G. K., *Social Services in Australia*. 1939.
Garnett, A. C., *Freedom and Planning in Australia*. 1949.
Hocking, D. M., and Haddon-Cane, C., *Air Transport in Australia*. 1951.
MacLaurin, W. R., *Economic Planning in Australia, 1929-1936*. 1937.
Shann, E., and Copland, D. B., *The Crisis in Australian Finance, 1929-31*. 1932.
Smith, N. S., *Structure and Working of the Australian Tariff: with Special Reference to Empire Trading*. 1929.
Taylor, P. G., *Call to the Winds*. 1939.
Tew, M., *Work and Welfare in Australia*. 1957.
Walker, E. R., *Australia in the World Depression*. 1933.
Walker, E. R., *Unemployment Policy*. 1936.

CHAPTER XX. WAR AGAIN

Baldwin, H. W., *Great Mistakes of the War*. 1950.
Bartlett, N., *Australia at Arms: an Anthology*. 1955.
Campbell, D. A. S., *ed.*, *Post War Reconstruction in Australia*. 1944.
Cant, G., *The Great Pacific Victory*. 1945.
Chifley, J. B., *Things Worth Fighting For*. 1952.

Foenander, O. de R., *Wartime Labour Developments in Australia*. 1943.
Hall, W. P., *Iron out of Calvary*. 1946.
Hasluck, P., *The Government and the People, 1939-1941*. 1952.
Hetherington, J., *Blamey: the Biography of Field Marshal Sir Thomas Blamey*. 1954.
Hough, F. O., *The Island War*. 1947.
Hughes, W. M., *Australia and War To-Day*. 1935.
Morrison, I., *This War with Japan*. 1943.
Walker, E. R., *Wartime Economics*. 1939.
Walker, E. R., *Australian Economy in War and Reconstruction*. 1947.
A definitive official history of the War in all its aspects touching Australia is in preparation (1958) to be called *Australia in the War of 1939-45*. *The Government and the People*, listed above, is one volume of this history.

CHAPTER XXI. IMMIGRATION: "POPULATE OR PERISH"

Borrie, W. D., Immigration: *Australia's Problems and Prospects*. 1949.
Borrie, W. D., *Population Trends and Policies: a Study in Australian and World Demography*. 1948.
Bushell, N. K., *Australia and the Emigrant*. 1913.
Carrolthers, W. A., *Emigration from the British Isles*. 1929.
Eggleston, F. W., and others, *The Peopling of Australia*. 1933.
Forsyth, W. D., *The Myth of Open Spaces*. 1942.
Gamba, C., *Report on The Italian Fishermen of Fremantle*. 1952.
Holt, H. E., and others, *Australia and the Migrant*. 1953.
Hood, J., *Australia and the East, being a Journal Narrative of the Voyages to New South Wales in an Emigrant Ship*, 1841 and 1842. 1843.
Kiddle, M., *Caroline Chisholm*. 1950.
Madgwick, R. B., *Immigration into Eastern Australia 1788-1851*. 1937.
Munz, H., *Jews in Australia, 1836-1936*. 1936.
Phillips, P. D., and Wood, G. L., *ed.*, *The Peopling of Australia*. 1928.
Price, C. A., *German Settlers in South Australia*. 1945.

CHAPTER XXII. RESULTS IN THE MAKING

Beecroft, E. A., *The Federal Control of State Employees in Australia*. 1935.
Bland, F. A., *Revising the Australian Constitution*. 1930.
Clark, A. I., *Labour Movement in Australasia*. 1907.
Copland, D. B., and Barback, R., *ed.*, *The Conflict of Expansion and Stability, 1945-52*. 1957.
Crisp, L. F., *Parliamentary Government of the Commonwealth of Australia*. 1947.
Garran, Sir R., and others, *Changing the Constitution*. 1950.
Greenwood, G., *The Future of Australian Federation*. 1946.
Isaacs, Sir I., *Australian Democracy and our Constitutional System*. 1939.
Latham, H. V., *Australia and the British Commonwealth*. 1929.
Nicholas, H. S., *The Australian Constitution*. . . . 1952.

STANDARD OF LIVING

Benham, F. C., *Theory of Wages*. . . . 1929.
Burns, E. M., *Wages and the State*. 1926.
Clark, A. I., *Labour Movement in Australia*. 1907.

Foenander, O. de R., *Industrial Regulation in Australia.* 1947.
Foenander, O. de R., *Solving Labour Problems in Australia.* 1941.
Foenander, O. de R., *Towards Industrial Peace in Australia.* 1937.
Giblin, L. F., *Wages and Prices.* 1931.
Palmer, N., *Henry Bournes Higgins.* 1931.
Rankin, M. T., *Arbitration and Conciliation in Australasia.* 1916.

SOCIAL SERVICES

Bland, F. A., *Planning the Modern State.* 1934.
Duncan, W. G., *ed., Social Services in Australia.* 1939.
Fenton, C., *The Flying Doctor.* 1947.
Hill, E., *Flying Doctor Calling.* 1947.
Official Year Book of Australia.

RELIGION, EDUCATION, AND THE PRESS

Arnot, J., *Newspaper Bibliography.* 1944.
Bean, C. E. W., *Here, My Son.* 1950.
Boyd, H. V., *Letters on Education addressed to a Friend in the Bush of Australia.* 1848.
Browne, G. S., *ed., Education in Australia.* 1927.
Chronological Return of all Churches, Chapels and Burial Grounds consecrated . . . from the erection of the See of Australia, 1836 up to December 31, 1850. 1850.
Commonwealth Office of Education, Bull. No. 20, *Public Education in Australia.* 1950. Rev. ed., 1953.
Ferguson, J. A., and others, *The Howes and their Press.* 1936.
Garland, Rev. D. G., "Notes on the Beginning of Education in Australia", *Diocese of Brisbane, College Ann.* 1931.
Giles, R. A., *The Constitutional History of the Australian Church.* 1929.
Law, A., *The Church in Australia.* 1918.
Mackenzie, T. F., *Nationalism and Education in Australia. . . .* 1935.
Rowland, E. C., *A Century of the English Church in New South Wales.* 1948.
Wilcher, L., *Education, Press, Radio.* 1948.

Newspapers:
Age. Melbourne. 1860-.
Australian. 1824-8.
Gleaner. 5th April-29th September, 1827.
Monitor. 1826-41.
Sydney Gazette and New South Wales Advertiser. 1803-42.
Sydney Morning Herald. 1831-.

DEVELOPMENT

Burns, K., *Our Transport.* 1956.
Commonwealth Scientific and Industrial Research Organization (formerly Council for Scientific and Industrial Research, formerly Institute of Science and Industry), Annual Reports.
The Federal Guide: a Handbook on the Organization and Functions of Commonwealth Government Departments. 1933.
Gordon, D. J., *Problems of Transportation and their Relation to Australian Trade and Commerce.* 1914.
Lee, W., *Coaching in Australia.* 1917.

CHAPTER XXIII. THE DARK PEOPLE

Bates, Daisy, *The Passing of the Aborigines: a Lifetime Spent among the Natives of Australia*. 1938.
Elkin, A. P., *The Australian Aborigines: how to understand them*. 1938.
Foxcroft, E. J. B., *Australian Native Policy*. 1941.
Harvard-Adelaide Universities Anthropological Expedition, 1938-9, Results. 1941. (See also University of Adelaide, Collected Papers, Nos. 376, 421, etc.)
Hasluck, P., *Native Welfare in Australia*. 1953.
House of Commons, Select Committee on Aborigines, Report. 1837.
Kaberry, P. M., *Aboriginal Woman, Sacred and Profane*. 1939.
Love, J. B. R., *Stone-Age Bushmen of To-day*. 1936.
Stirling, E. C., *Report of the Horn Scientific Expedition to Central Australia*. 1896.

CHAPTER XXIV. ENVOI

Adams, F., *The Australians*. 1893.
Caiger, G., *The Australian Way of Life*. 1953.
Fullerton, M. E., *Bark House Days*. 1921.
Palmer, V., *Louis Esson and the Australian Theatre*. 1948.
Palmer, V., *A. G. Stephens, his Life and Work*. 1941.
Palmer, V., *Frank Wilmot (Furnley Maurice)*. 1942.
Palmer, V., *Old Australian Bush Ballads*. 1951.
Paterson, A. B., *Old Bush Songs*. 1905.
Phillips, A. A., *The Australian Tradition*. 1958.
Stevens, B., *ed.*, *Bush Ballads*.
Ward, R., *The Australian Legend*. 1958.

Periodicals:

Bulletin. 1888-.
Meanjin. 1947-.
Southerly. 1939-.

INDEX

INDEX